TODAY'S HEALTH INFORMATION MANAGEMENT

AN INTEGRATED APPROACH

by Dana C. McWay, JD, RHIA

DELMAR
CENGAGE Learning

Australia • Brazil • Japan • Korea • Mexico • Singapore • Spain • United Kingdom • United States

DELMAR
CENGAGE Learning

Today's Health Information Management: An Integrated Approach
by Dana C. McWay

Vice President, Health Care Business Unit:
William Brottmiller

Director of Learning Solutions:
Matthew Kane

Senior Acquisitions Editor:
Rhonda Dearborn

Product Manager: **Sarah Prime**

Marketing Director:
Jennifer McAvey

Marketing Coordinator:
Andrea Eobstel

Production Director: **Carolyn Miller**

Senior Art Director: **Jack Pendleton**

Content Project Manager:
Jessica McNavich

Technology Project Manager:
Carolyn Fox
Ben Knapp

For product information and technology assistance, contact us at
Professional & Career Group Customer Support, 1-800-648-7450

For permission to use material from this text or product, submit all requests online at **www.cengage.com/permissions**
Further permissions questions can be emailed to
permissionrequest@cengage.com

ExamView® and ExamView Pro® are registered trademarks of FSCreations, Inc. Windows is a registered trademark of the Microsoft Corporation used herein under license. Macintosh and Power Macintosh are registered trademarks of Apple Computer, Inc. Used herein under license.

Library of Congress Control Number

ISBN-13: 978-1-4180-0143-8

ISBN-10: 1-4180-0143-0

Delmar Cengage Learning
5 Maxwell Drive
Clifton Park, NY 12065-2919
USA

Cengage Learning products are represented in Canada by Nelson Education, Ltd.

For your lifelong learning solutions, visit **delmar.cengage.com**

Visit our corporate website at **www.cengage.com**

Notice to the Reader
Publisher does not warrant or guarantee any of the products described herein or perform any independent analysis in connection with any of the product information contained herein. Publisher does not assume, and expressly disclaims, any obligation to obtain and include information other than that provided to it by the manufacturer. The reader is expressly warned to consider and adopt all safety precautions that might be indicated by the activities described herein and to avoid all potential hazards. By following the instructions contained herein, the reader willingly assumes all risks in connection with such instructions. The publisher makes no representations or warranties of any kind, including but not limited to, the warranties of fitness for particular purpose or merchantability, nor are any such representations implied with respect to the material set forth herein, and the publisher takes no responsibility with respect to such material. The publisher shall not be liable for any special, consequential, or exemplary damages resulting, in whole or part, from the readers' use of, or reliance upon, this material.

Printed in the United States of America
3 4 5 6   14 13 12

Brief Contents

PART 1

INTRODUCTION TO HEALTH INFORMATION MANAGEMENT

1 Health Care Delivery Systems   1
2 The Health Information Management Profession   25
3 Legal Issues   43
4 Ethical Standards   73

PART 2

CLINICAL DATA MANAGEMENT

5 Health Care Data Content and Structures   99
6 Nomenclatures and Classification Systems   123
7 Quality Health Care Management   139
8 Database Management   167
9 Health Statistics   187
10 Research   221

PART 3

MANAGEMENT ISSUES

11 Management Organization   247
12 Human Resource Management   281
13 Information Systems and Technology   311
14 Financial Management   331
15 Reimbursement Methodologies   347

Appendix A   Common HIM Abbreviations   363
Appendix B   Web Resources   371
Appendix C   Sample HIPAA Notices of Privacy Practices   381
Appendix D   Selected Laws Affecting HIM   391
Appendix E   Selected HIPAA Regulations   393
Glossary   445
Index   473

Contents

Preface xv

PART 1
INTRODUCTION TO HEALTH INFORMATION MANAGEMENT

CHAPTER 1

Health Care Delivery Systems   1

Introduction   3
Historical Development   3
  Early History   3
  Health Care in the United States   4
  Public Health   9
  Mental Health   10
  Occupational Health   13
Health Care Delivery Systems   14
  Professional Associations   14
  Voluntary Health Agencies   14
  Philanthropic Foundations   15
  International Health Agencies   15
  Variety of Delivery Systems   15
    Settings   *15*
    Health Care Professionals   *18*
Medical Staff   20
  Medical Staff Organization   20
  Bylaws, Rules, and Regulations   21
  Privileges and Credentialing   21
Conclusion   23
Chapter Summary   23
Case Study   23
Review Questions   23

CHAPTER 2

The Health Information Management Profession   25

Introduction   27
Health Information   27
  Historical Development of the Profession   27
  Educational and Certification Requirements   29
Careers   33
  Traditional Settings   35

v

Nontraditional Settings   37
   Direct Patient Care Settings   37
   Settings Not Involving Direct Patient Care   38
Conclusion   39
Chapter Summary   40
Case Study   40
Review Questions   40
Enrichment Activities   40

CHAPTER **3**

Legal Issues   43

Introduction   45
Overview of External Forces   45
   Roles of Governmental Entities   46
   Roles of Nongovernmental Entities   47
   Role Application   48
Understanding the Court System   49
   The Court System   49
   Administrative Bodies   49
   Legal Procedures   52
Principles of Liability   53
   Intentional Torts   54
   Nonintentional Torts   55
Legal Issues in HIM   55
   HIPAA   56
     Administrative Simplification   56
     Fraud and Abuse   58
   Privacy and Confidentiality   59
   Access to Health Care Data   60
     Ownership and Disclosure   61
     Identity Theft   63
   Informed Consent   64
   Judicial Process   65
Fraud and Abuse   66
   Fraud and Abuse Laws   67
   Resources to Combat Fraud and Abuse   68
Conclusion   70
Chapter Summary   70
Case Study   70
Review Questions   71
Enrichment Activities   71

CHAPTER **4**

Ethical Standards   73

Introduction   75
Ethical Overview   75
   Ethical Models   76
     Ethical Concepts   76
       Autonomy   76
       Beneficence and Nonmaleficence   77
       Best Interest Standard   78
       Fidelity   78
       Justice   78

Rights   79
Veracity   79
Ethical Theories   80
Utilitarianism   80
Deontology   80
Ethical Decision Making   81
Influencing Factors   81
Codes of Ethics   81
Patient Rights   84
Other Factors   85
Decision-Making Process   86
Bioethical Issues   87
Related to the Beginning of Life   87
Family Planning   87
Abortion   88
Perinatal Ethics   89
Eugenics   89
Related to Sustaining or Improving the Quality of Life   90
HIV/AIDS   90
Organ Transplantation   90
Genetic Science   91
Related to Death and Dying   91
Planning for End of Life   92
Euthanasia   92
Withholding/Withdrawing Treatment   92
Ethical Challenges   93
General Challenges   93
Role of Ethics in Supervision   94
Health Care Challenges   95
Health Information Management Challenges   96
Conclusion   97
Chapter Summary   97
Case Study   97
Review Questions   97
Enrichment Activities   98

PART 2 CLINICAL DATA MANAGEMENT

CHAPTER 5

Health Care Data Content and Structures   99

Introduction   101
Types, Users, Uses, and Flow of Data   101
Types of Data   101
Users and Uses of Data   104
Patient Users   106
Data Flow   107
Forms Design and Control   109
Data Storage, Retention, and Destruction   110
Data Storage   110
Data Retention and Destruction   112

Indices and Registries   115
Indices   115
Registries   117
Conclusion   119
Chapter Summary   119
Case Study   119
Review Questions   120
Enrichment Activities   120

CHAPTER **6**

Nomenclatures and Classification Systems   123

Introduction   125
Languages, Vocabularies, and Nomenclatures   125
Nomenclature Development   126
Classification Systems   128
History and Application of Classification Systems   128
Diagnosis-Related Groups   130
HIM Transformation   132
Other Classification Systems   133
Emerging Issues   135
Conclusion   136
Chapter Summary   137
Case Study   137
Review Questions   137
Enrichment Activity   137

CHAPTER **7**

Quality Health Care Management   139

Introduction   141
Data Quality   141
Historical Development   141
Federal Efforts   145
Private Efforts   146
Tools   147
Applications   152
Performance Improvement and Risk Management   156
Performance Improvement   156
Risk Management   158
Utilization Management   159
Utilization Review Process   161
Conclusion   164
Chapter Summary   164
Case Study   165
Review Questions   165
Enrichment Activity   165

CHAPTER **8**

Database Management   167

Introduction   169
Concepts and Functions   169
Database Design   171
Controls   173
Data Standards   173
Retrieval and Analysis Methods   175

Data Sets   176
Data Exchange   181
State and Local Data Exchange Efforts   182
Conclusion   183
Chapter Summary   183
Case Study   184
Review Questions   184
Enrichment Activities   184

CHAPTER **9**   Health Statistics   187

Introduction   189
Overview   189
Statistical Types   190
Statistical Literacy   192
Statistical Basics   192
Measures of Central Tendency   194
Other Mathematical Concepts   194
Data Collection   195
Statistical Formulae   198
Data Presentation   199
Regression Analysis   203
Regression Analysis Models   205
Health Information Management Statistics   209
Productivity   209
Statistical Tools   211
Control Charts   211
Trend Charts   213
Process Capability Analysis   213
Conclusion   214
Chapter Summary   215
Case Studies   215
Review Questions   217
Enrichment Activities   217

CHAPTER **10**   Research   221

Introduction   223
Research Principles   223
Historical Overview   224
Methodology   224
Qualitative and Quantitative Research   225
Study Types   226
Research Study Process   229
Research Design   229
Publication Process   230
Institutional Review Boards   231
Historical Overview   232
Review Process   233
Review of Research on Animals   236
Emerging Trends   237

Epidemiology   238

Historical Overview   240

Epidemiological Basics   240

Disease Progression   241

Types of Epidemiology   242

Descriptive Epidemiology   243

Analytic and Experimental Epidemiology   243

Conclusion   244

Chapter Summary   244

Case Study   245

Review Questions   245

Enrichment Activities   245

PART 3   MANAGEMENT ISSUES

CHAPTER 11   Management Organization   247

Introduction   249

Principles of Management   249

Planning   249

Strategic Planning   249

Management Planning   251

Operational Planning   252

Disaster Planning   252

Planning Tools   254

Organizing   255

Design and Structure   255

Organizing People   256

Organizing the Type of Work   259

Organizing Work Performance   260

Organizing the Work Environment   260

Directing   261

Decision Making   261

Instructing Others   262

Work Simplification   263

Controlling   263

Types of Controls   264

Setting Standards   264

Monitoring Performance   265

Leading   265

Motivating   265

Directing Others   267

Resolving Conflicts   267

Effective Communication   268

Management Theories   268

Historical Overview   268

Specialized Management Theories   270

Change Management   270

Project Management   270

Process Improvement   272

Knowledge Management   275

Effective Meeting Management   276

Conclusion   277
Chapter Summary   277
Case Study   277
Review Questions   278
Enrichment Activities   278

CHAPTER **12**

Human Resource Management   281

Introduction   283
Employment   283
Staffing   284
 Recruitment   284
 Selection   284
 Compensation   286
 Orientation and Training   286
 Retention   290
 Separation   291
Employee Rights   292
 Overview   292
 Employment Law Application   293
  Discrimination   293
   Sex Discrimination   293
   Racial, Religious, and National Origin Discrimination   294
   Age Discrimination   295
   Disability Discrimination   295
  Workplace Protections   297
   Health and Safety   297
   Hours, Pay, and Conditions of Employment   298
Supervision   299
 Performance Evaluations   300
 Problem Behaviors   301
 Discipline and Grievance   302
 Developing Others   303
  Career Development   303
  Coaching   304
  Mentoring   304
 Team Building   304
 Telecommuting   305
Workforce Diversity   307
Conclusion   308
Chapter Summary   308
Case Study   308
Review Questions   309
Enrichment Activities   309

CHAPTER **13**

Information Systems and Technology   311

Introduction   313
Information Systems   313
 Computer Concepts   314
  Hardware   314
  Software   316
  Units of Measure and Standards   317

Information Systems Life Cycle   317
Communication Technologies   319
Security   321
HIPAA Security Rule   322
Informatics   324
Technology Applications and Trends   325
Electronic Health Records   327
Conclusion   329
Chapter Summary   329
Case Study   329
Review Questions   329
Enrichment Activity   330

CHAPTER 14

Financial Management   331

Introduction   333
Overview   333
Accounting   335
Managerial Accounting   335
Financial Accounting   337
Budgets   339
Procurement   342
Request for Proposal   344
Conclusion   345
Chapter Summary   345
Case Study   345
Review Questions   345
Enrichment Activities   346

CHAPTER 15

Reimbursement Methodologies   347

Introduction   349
Third-Party Payers   349
Governmental Payers   350
Nongovernmental Payers   351
Managed Care Organizations   352
Health Maintenance Organizations   354
Preferred and Exclusive Provider Organizations   355
Point-of-Service Plans   355
Integrated Delivery Systems   355
Payment Methodologies   355
Fee For Service   355
Prospective Payment Systems   357
Resource-Based Relative Value Systems   358
Capitation   358
Revenue Cycle Management   359
Conclusion   361
Chapter Summary   361
Case Study   361
Review Questions   362
Enrichment Activities   362

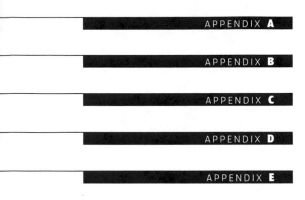

APPENDIX **A**   **Common HIM Abbreviations**   363

APPENDIX **B**   **Web Resources**   371

APPENDIX **C**   **Sample HIPAA Notices of Privacy Practices**   381

APPENDIX **D**   **Selected Laws Affecting HIM**   391

APPENDIX **E**   **Selected HIPAA Regulations**   393

Glossary   445

Index   473

Preface

Over the past quarter century, new developments in technology, law, and organizational management have changed the profession of health information management (HIM). Once seen as the guardian of a paper-based health record, the health information management profession has evolved as health care has evolved, expanding to include the development and implementation of the electronic health record and management of the data contained within it. As the need for health information has grown, so has the need to manage that information. The health information professional plays a more central role in the delivery of health care than ever before.

For those interested in learning about health information management, this text provides a comprehensive discussion of the principles and practices presented in a user-friendly manner. It is designed to serve as a broad text for the health information management discipline and does not presume that the learner is already versed in the subject matter. The text is designed to incorporate the model curriculum of the American Health Information Management Association for both the health information administrator and health information technician programs. Although differences exist in curricula between the programs, it is my belief that the content of this book is applicable to students in both groups because it is written with multiple levels of detail. Instructors may determine the emphasis level of each chapter as it is taught during the semester. This text also serves as a reference point for professionals in the health care field who need to acquire a general understanding of health information management, and as a research tool for other allied health and medical disciplines.

Although this text is intended to be comprehensive, one textbook could not possibly encompass all of the details of the broad discipline of health information management. Long past is the time when one textbook could cover all matters and issues associated with a single discipline—the evolution of the HIM profession is such that other specialized texts are needed to complement this text. Every effort has been made to capture the significant changes and trends that the HIM field and profession have undergone in recent years.

Two things set this text apart from others in the field. First, the book is authored by only one person, allowing for a consistent voice and tone across the chapters. It also means that one chapter will not contradict the contents of another chapter within the same book, and that the difficulty level will not vary from one chapter to the next. Second, the text integrates into each chapter, as applicable, three areas that are significant to health information management: the Health Insurance Portability and Accountability Act (HIPAA), electronic health information management (e-HIM), and informatics. This approach is taken so that while the student is learning the substantive matter, he or she can also understand the interplay between these three areas and the substantive matter. Boxes for each of these three areas are found near the text discussion to highlight this interplay.

Book Structure

This text offers a comprehensive, sequential approach to the study of health information management. Although each chapter is designed to stand alone, it is grouped with related chapters to form units of study. Three major units of study are presented in this text:

Part 1 serves as an introduction to health information management. This unit of study comprises four chapters, beginning with a discussion of health care delivery systems, both historically and in the present day, and the health information management profession, including various career paths. These chapters are followed by a discussion of legal issues, including an overview of the court systems, the principles of liability, HIPAA, and health care fraud and abuse. The last chapter addresses ethical standards, outlining the basis for ethical concepts and theories and their role in decision making, explaining various ethical challenges, and highlighting bioethics issues.

Part 2 serves as an overview of clinical data management. This unit of study consists of six chapters and begins with a discussion of health data content and structures, including types and uses; forms design and control; data storage, retention, and destruction; and indices and registries. Nomenclatures and classification systems make up the next chapter, and a discussion of emerging issues completes the chapter. Quality management, performance improvement, risk management, and utilization management form the basis of the next chapter. A discussion of database management follows, including concepts and functions, data sets, and data exchange efforts. Health statistics is the focus of the next chapter, addressing statistical literacy in general, and regression analysis and HIM statistics in particular. Research issues complete the unit, with sections addressing research principles, the research study process, the role of institutional review boards, and the discipline of epidemiology.

Part 3 serves as an overview of management issues. This unit of study consists of five chapters, beginning with management principles and theories, including change, project, and knowledge management. A discussion of human resource management follows, focusing on staffing, employee rights, supervision, and workforce diversity. Information systems and technology is the subject of the next chapter, including a discussion of various information systems, informatics, and technological applications and trends. The financial management chapter addresses the fundamental concepts that drive financial management, including accounting, budgets, and procurement. The last chapter provides a basis in reimbursement methodologies, including how third-party payers and the revenue cycle function in the health care world.

Wherever the term *health information manager* is used in this text, I refer to both registered health information administrators (RHIA) and registered health information technicians (RHIT). I make this choice consciously, because the experience of the health information management profession during the last two decades has shown that professionals at both levels hold a variety of positions within the discipline. Additionally, care has been exercised to use the terms *health record* and *health information management* in lieu of *medical record* and *medical record management*, because these are the terms in use in the 21st century. Each chapter alternates in the use of the male and female pronouns. Information contained in the text boxes within the chapter provides a quick grasp of concepts that may be new to the learner.

Pedagogical Features

Each chapter contains:

- An integration of HIPAA, e-health information management, and informatics throughout the subject matter

- Learning objectives

- A listing of key concepts that are further explained in the text

- Figures and tables that provide details to illustrate the content of the text

- Case studies to apply concepts learned

- Review questions designed to test comprehension

- Enrichment activities designed to assist critical thinking

- A list of Web sites that relate to the chapter's subject matter for the learner's easy reference

Additionally, appendices contain:

- An extensive glossary of terms

- Web site resources, organized by subject matter and in alphabetical order

- Sample HIPAA privacy notices

- A table of selected federal laws applicable to HIM

- Selected HIPAA regulations

Learning Package

Workbook

The Workbook helps you learn and reinforce the essential concepts presented in the book. Test your knowledge through activities such as abbreviations and key terms review, chapter quiz material, case explorations, and more. The DVD Hookup feature suggests scenes and provides additional questions that relate to *Case Studies for Health Information Management DVD Series.*

ISBN 1-4180-0146-5

Case Studies for Health Information Management DVD Series

This five-program DVD series focuses on applying critical thinking skills to real events and situations that occur in the workplace. Each of the 20 case studies dramatizes a real situation, provides a discussion checkpoint, and follows with an outcome that reflects how the scenario would be resolved in the real world.

ISBN 1-4180-5235-3

Instructor's Manual

The Instructor's Manual provides answer keys for the text and workbook; a curriculum crosswalk for each chapter with links to the AHIMA domains, subdomains, and knowledge clusters; additional enrichment activities; and a mapping guide to the Case Studies in Health Information Management DVD series.

ISBN 1-4180-0144-9

Electronic Classroom Manager

The Electronic Classroom Manager is a CD-ROM loaded with content to provide instructors with complete support in the classroom.

- Use the **electronic Instructor's Manual files** to help prepare for class.

- Deliver effective presentations with chapter **PowerPoint** presentations.

- Create quizzes and tests to monitor student progress with the **Computerized Test Bank,** in ExamView. Each question in the test bank is identified by cognitive level.

ISBN 1-4180-0145-7

Online Companion

The Online Companion provides online access to the instructor support material, including electronic Instructor's Manual files, PowerPoint, and a Computerized Test Bank. It also includes updates to the text, as appropriate. Access the Online Companion through http://www.delmarcengage learning.com/companions. Choose Allied Health from the drop-down menu, and then look for this book's title.

Web Tutor Advantage

Check out the Web Tutor on either Blackboard or WebCT platforms to help manage your course.

- Web Tutor provides a course calendar, chat, e-mail, threaded discussions, Web links, and a whiteboard.

- Web Tutor Advantage is loaded with content related to each chapter, including quizzes, exams, interactive activities, flash cards, and more.

Web Tutor on WebCT ISBN 1-4283-1214-5

Web Tutor on Blackboard ISBN 1-4283-1213-7

Acknowledgments

Many persons have played a role in the creation of this textbook, including family, friends, and colleagues. A special thank you is warranted for my family, who showed patience, understanding, and support for the long hours spent on this, my second textbook. My children, Conor, William, and Ryan, spent many hours at libraries, learning the intricacies of research and authorship. My husband, Patrick, whose patience and encouragement sustained me throughout the development of this text, deserves my unending love. Two HIM professionals, Sharon Farley, RHIA, and Patt Petersen, MA, RHIA, provided valuable assistance in the subjects of quality management and statistics, respectively. My editors for this project, Sarah Prime and Bryan Viggiani, guided me through the creation of this text and encouraged me with every effort. My appreciation is extended to the reviewers of my manuscript. Your comments aided in strengthening this text.

Dana C. McWay, JD, RHIA

Contributors

The author and publisher would like to acknowledge the following health information management educators for their contributions to the content of this text:

Sharon Farley, RHIA
Contributing material to Chapter 7

Patt Peterson, MA, RHIA
Contributing material to Chapter 9

Reviewers

The following health information management educators provided invaluable feedback and suggestions during the development of this text:

Cassie Gentry, MEd, RHIA, CHP
Chair, Department of Health-Related Professions
Program Director, Health Information Technology
Community College of Southern Nevada
Las Vegas, Nevada

Betty Haar, BS, RHIA
Program Director
Kirkwood Community College
Cedar Rapids, Iowa

Diane Howard, MA, RHIA
Instructor
Lake-Sumter Community College
Leesburg, Florida

Karl J. Koob, MMIS, RHIA, CPEHR
Clinical Assistant Professor/Health Information Department
    Chair
University of Kansas
Kansas City, Kansas

About the Author

Dana C. McWay, JD, RHIA, is both a lawyer and a health information management professional. With training and experience in both disciplines, experience as a member of the Institutional Review Board at Washington University Medical School from 1991 to present, and experience in converting a paper-based record management system to an electronic record management system, she brings a wide-ranging perspective to this textbook.

Ms. McWay serves as the Clerk of Court for the U.S. Bankruptcy Court for the Eastern District of Missouri, an executive position responsible for all operational, administrative, financial, and technological matters of the court. In this capacity, she organized the court's conversion to an electronic case filing system, resulting in widespread acceptance by end users. This success led to her appointment as member and, later, chair of the Case Management/Electronic Case Filing (CM/ECF) Working Group, an entity within the federal judiciary responsible for providing guidance and assistance in all phases of the development of bankruptcy CM/ECF software releases. She serves on numerous national committees and working groups within the judiciary, including those involved in identifying the impact of new legislation upon judicial operations and those involved in advising on the education and training needs of court staff. Prior to this position, she worked as the Chief Deputy Clerk of Court for the U.S. Court of Appeals for the Eighth Circuit, responsible for daily operations of the court.

Ms. McWay began her legal career as a judicial law clerk to the Honorable Myron H. Bright of the U.S. Court of Appeals for the Eighth Circuit. She then became an associate with the law firm of Peper, Martin, Jensen, Maichel, & Hetlage, a multi-specialty firm located in St. Louis, Missouri. Ms. McWay's legal practice encompassed a variety of health law topics, including contracts, medical records, and physician practice issues. She is admitted to practice in both Illinois and Missouri.

Prior to her legal career, Ms. McWay worked in health information management as both a director and assistant director of medical records in a large teaching hospital and a for-profit psychiatric and substance abuse facility. She continues to participate in the HIM profession, having served as a project manager for the Missouri Health Information Management Association (MHIMA) and as a member of MHIMA's Legislative Committee. On the national level, she served as faculty for continuing education seminars, a peer reviewer of AHIMA book proposals and texts, a contributing author to AHIMA's HIM Practice Standards, and a member of both the Committee for Professional Development and the Triumph Awards Committee of AHIMA.

Ms. McWay is both an author and an editor. Her textbook, *Legal Aspects of Health Information Management*, is in its second edition. With the Peper Martin law firm, she revised *The Legal Manual to Medical Record Practice in Missouri* in 1991. She has authored numerous other publications and served as coeditor of several online continuing education modules presented by the American Health Information Management Association. She has also presented numerous seminars, serving as faculty and panel presenter. She has served as a guest lecturer at several area colleges and universities, focusing on the intersection of legal issues and health care practices.

Ms. McWay is a magna cum laude graduate of the St. Louis University School of Allied Health Professions, with a degree in medical record administration, and a cum laude graduate of the St. Louis University School of Law. While in law school, Ms. McWay served as the health law editor of the *St. Louis University Law Journal* and as a faculty research fellow. She is a recipient of the Alumni Merit Award from the School of Allied Health Professions and a Triumph Award (the Legacy Award) from the American Health Information Management Association for her textbook, *Legal Aspects of Health Information Management.*

CHAPTER >>

11

Management Organization

Learning Objectives at the beginning of each chapter list the theoretical and practical goals of the chapter. The **Certification Connection** ties the chapter material to the RHIA and RHIT exam outlines.

CERTIFICATION CONNECTION

RHIA

Benchmarking
Best practices
Change management
Communications
Operational planning
Negotiation
Present data
Process engineering
Productivity standards
Project management
Strategic planning
Workflow design

RHIT

Communications
Ergonomics
Labor relations
Policies and procedures
Productivity standards
Strategic planning
Work processes

LEARNING OBJECTIVES

After reading this chapter, the learner should be able to:

1. Understand the general principles of management: planning, organizing, directing, controlling, and leading.

2. Compare and contrast strategic planning with managerial, operational, and disaster planning.

3. Explain the interrelationships between planning, organizing, directing, controlling, and leading.

4. Describe the role that the leading function plays within an organization.

5. Trace the development of management theories over time.

6. Compare and contrast specialized management theories.

CERTIFICATION CONNECTION

RHIA

Benchmarking
Best practices
Change management
Communications
Operational planning
Negotiation
Present data
Process engineering
Productivity standards
Project management
Strategic planning
Workflow design

RHIT

Communications
Ergonomics

Key Concepts

Affinity diagram
Assigning work
Brainstorming
Budget
Cause-and-effect diagram
Change management
Classical management
Communication
Controlling
Critical path
Data

Internal analysis
Job
Job analysis
Job description
Job enrichment
Job evaluation
Job satisfaction
Knowledge
Knowledge management
Knowledge management system
Leading

Organizing
Pareto ch
Participa
mana
Persona
PERT
Physic
Plann
Polic
Posit
Proce
Process imp

Outline

Principles of Management

Planning
Organizing
Directing
Controlling
Leading

Management Theories

Historical Overview
Specialized Management Theories

Important terms, ideas, and acronyms are presented in the **Key Concepts** list, and they are highlighted the first time they appear in the chapter content. The **Outline** lists major headings to provide a roadmap for the chapter content.

ENRICHMENT ACTIVITIES

1. Develop a Gantt chart for one of your class projects.

2. Recall an instance where a decision you reached failed in the implementation stage. Alternatively, recall an instance where a decision reached by an organization failed in the implementation stage. Examine why each implementation failed. If you could reduce such failure in the future, what particular change would you make in the decision-making process?

CASE STUDY

You are part of a research team studying the sa[...] informed consent of potential study enrollees, e[...] available alternatives to using the new medical [...] ticipate in the study but does not wish to read t[...] study and other important information. The pot[...] ethical principles are involved?

Enrichment Activities and *Case Studies* provide opportunities to use critical thinking skills to reflect on the material and relate the concepts to real-life situations.

CHAPTER SUMMARY

The study of ethics has been present for many centuries; ethics a[...] conform to standards of conduct. Multiple approaches to ethical [...] care field. Codes of ethics, patient rights, religious beliefs, and sc[...] cal decision making. The decision-making process is particularly [...] of life and death are present. The number of ethical challenges p[...]

At the end of each chapter, reinforce your understanding of the covered concepts using the *Summary* and *Review Questions.*

REVIEW QUESTIONS

1. How can one distinguish between legal and ethical issues?

2. Compare the steps typically taken in the ethical decision-making process shown in Table 4–2 with the additional steps listed in the last section of the text.

E-HIM

HIM professionals are frequently involved in both the design and implementation stages of an electronic health record.

INFORMATICS

Health care informatics differs from health information management in that informatics focuses primarily on the use of technology to support data whereas HIM focuses primarily on the quality of the data itself.

HIPAA

Regulations implementing HIPAA require covered entities to identify individuals who are responsible for developing and implementing policies and procedures governing privacy and security.

The book highlights the interplay of *informatics, electronic health information (e-HIM),* and the *Health Insurance Portability and Accountability Act (HIPAA)* with the subject matter of each chapter in special boxes.

Software CD-ROM

StudyWARE™

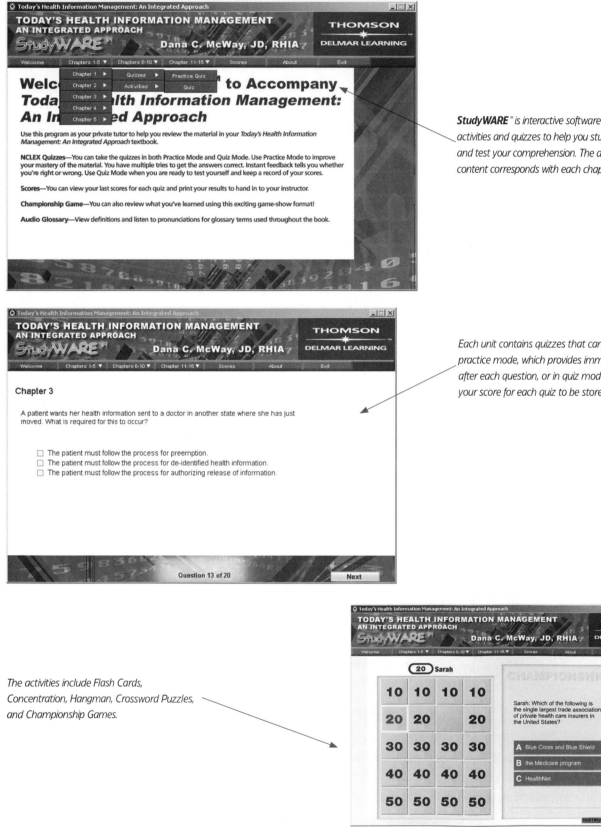

StudyWARE™ is interactive software with learning activities and quizzes to help you study key concepts and test your comprehension. The activity and quiz content corresponds with each chapter of the book.

Each unit contains quizzes that can be taken in practice mode, which provides immediate feedback after each question, or in quiz mode, which allows your score for each quiz to be stored or printed.

The activities include Flash Cards, Concentration, Hangman, Crossword Puzzles, and Championship Games.

Health Care Delivery Systems

CERTIFICATION CONNECTION

RHIA

Accreditation, licensure, and certification

Continuum of health care services

RHIT

Accreditation, licensure, and certification

Provider roles and disciplines

Public health

LEARNING OBJECTIVES

After reading this chapter, the learner should be able to:

1. Trace the historical development of the health care delivery system in early times.

2. Describe the four-stage progression of the health care delivery system in the United States.

3. Describe the increase in stature of hospitals after World War II.

4. Explain the standardization movement of the early 20th century.

5. Define the term *accreditation* and explain its significance to health care organizations.

6. Compare and contrast the federal government's role in health care during stages three and four.

7. Define the concept of managed care and differentiate between the three main types.

8. Trace the historical development of public, mental, and occupational health.

9. Compare and contrast professional associations, voluntary health agencies, philanthropic foundations, and international health agencies.

10. Differentiate between the variety of settings where health care is delivered.

11. Compare and contrast physicians, dentists, chiropractors, podiatrists, optometrists, physician assistants, nurses, and allied health professionals.

12. Understand the organization of a hospital's medical staff, the importance of its bylaws, and the use of the credentialing process in granting clinical privileges.

Outline

Historical Development

Early History
Health Care in the United States
Public Health
Mental Health
Occupational Health

Health Care Delivery Systems

Professional Associations
Voluntary Health Agencies
Philanthropic Foundations
International Health Agencies
Variety of Delivery Systems

Medical Staff

Medical Staff Organization
Bylaws, Rules, and Regulations
Privileges and Credentialing

Key Concepts

Accreditation
Allied health professional
Ambulatory health care
Block grants
Board certified
Bylaws
Capitation
Chiropractor
Clinical privileges
Community mental health care
Continuum of care
Credentialing process
Dentist
Fee for service
Fringe benefits
Generalists
Health savings accounts
HMO
Home health agency

Hospice care
Hospital
IPA
International health agencies
Licensing
Long-term care facility
Managed care
Medicaid
Medicare
Medical staff
Medical staff coordinator
Mental health
Mental illness
Nurse
Occupational health
Optometrist
Outsourcing
Philanthropic foundations

Physician
Physician assistant
Podiatrist
PPO
Primary care
Professional associations
Public health
Quaternary care
Registration
Regulations
Rehabilitation care facility
Rules
Secondary care
Specialists
Surgical assistant
Tertiary care
Tracer methodology
Voluntary health agencies

INTRODUCTION

The health care delivery system of the 21st century is both varied and complex. No one organization or entity is responsible for delivering all health care in the United States. It is important to understand the origins of the health care delivery system in the United States so that the relationships between organizations, entities, and health care professionals becomes clear. This chapter provides that understanding through an overview of the historical development of the health care delivery system, both in the United States and other regions of the world. Some focus is given to specified areas of health care, including public health, mental health, and occupational health. A discussion of the organizations, entities, and professionals who deliver health care services and the settings in which they work follows, allowing the learner to better understand the complexity of health care. A section concerning a hospital's medical staff explains its organization, its governing mechanisms, and the credentialing process. Integrated as appropriate within the entire chapter is a discussion of the influences of technology, financing concerns, and the role of the federal government in the health care delivery system.

Historical Development

The number and quality of professionals, organizations, and entities involved in health care has varied significantly over time. In large measure, this variety is attributable to the knowledge of diseases and their causes possessed by individuals and communities. With the advent of technology and advancements in medicine, an ever-expanding knowledge base has resulted in more, rather than less, complexity in health care.

Early History

To understand the development of health care in the United States, one must first look to the development of health care in earlier times and in other regions of the world. Anthropological studies have helped to trace health care back thousands of years. Table I–I illustrates the early history of health care.

In primitive times, man responded to disease in one of three ways. First, man looked to nature for answers, determining that disease was a result of offended forces of nature such as storms, volcanic eruptions, and earthquakes. Second, man looked to the supernatural for answers, determining that disease may be a way of "possessing" human

beings. Third, man looked to the offended spirits of gods or the dead, concluding that disease was a logical result of any offense incurred. In response to any of these three ways, primitive man treated disease with prayers, offerings, religious ceremonies, diet, or medicinal herbs. Furthermore, man attempted to frighten demons—and, therefore, disease—away with dancing, drumming, and fearful masks. Man employed resources such as amulets, charmed stones, and songs in efforts to banish disease.

As man made the connection between cause and effect, treatments evolved to improve or cure disease. A medicine man or shaman employed methods such as applying warm ashes to induce sweating, applying a tight band around the head to treat a headache, and bandaging the chest to the point of partial immobilization to treat tuberculosis. Man incised wounds to remove foreign bodies such as stones and splinters, doing so by sucking out the foreign body. Fractured bones were splinted with stiffened mud bandages or tree branches. Midwives became recognized figures among primitive peoples.

As civilization emerged, instructions relating to health care were written down. The earliest known written materials—stone tablets, papyri, and inscriptions on monuments and tombs—have been found in Egypt, dating

Table 1–1 | Early History of Health Care

Characteristics	Primitive Times	Early Civilization	Greek Civilization
Health Care Providers	Medicine man or shaman	Physicians/dentists working under authority of gods	Physicians such as Hippocrates
Communication Methods	Drawings	Early writings	Codification of early medical practice
Societal Views of Health Care	Nature/supernatural/offended spirits	Magical/religious approach	Rational/scientific approach

to 2700 B.C. These materials recognize the existence of physicians and dentists working under the authority of gods. As such, physicians were considered priests who received training in temple schools in areas such as diagnosis and treatment. Priests followed the case approach beginning with a preliminary diagnosis, examination of the patient, diagnosis and prognosis, and indication of treatment measures to be employed. An example of such an approach can be found in the famous *Ebers Papyrus* illustrated in Figure 1–1.

Although the above description speaks to a rational approach to medicine, a magical approach to medicine was involved as well. Because of the prevailing belief that disease was caused by demons and evil spirits, curing of disease could only occur through the intervention of the gods. Accordingly, physicians recognized one god over all others as the most important with regard to healing—Imhotep, who they referred to as the god of medicine.

Figure 1–1 | A page of the *Ebers Papyrus*; the lower part is a prescription

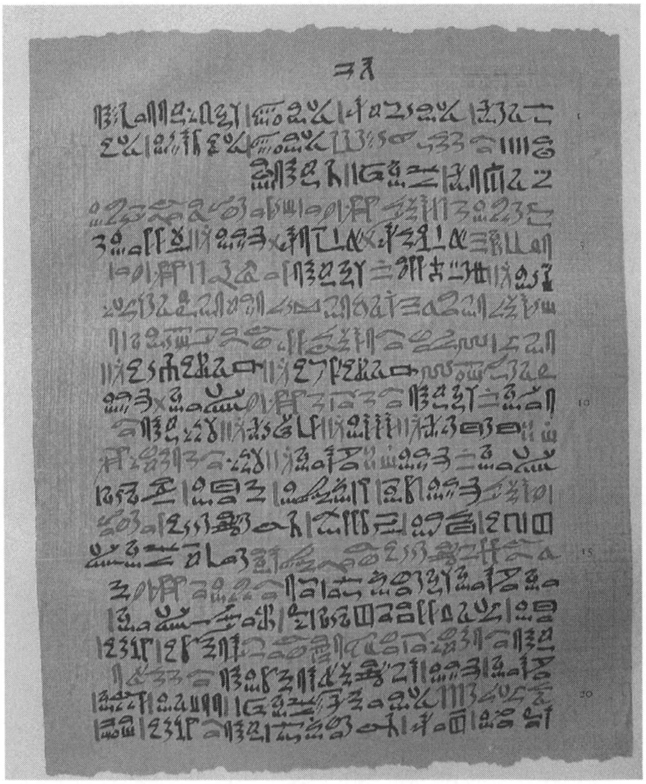

As Egyptian civilization declined, other civilizations adopted and expanded the Egyptians' knowledge of medicine. Arabians refined the concept of pharmacology, and, in another part of the world, the Chinese did the same. The Jewish people became preeminent in the area of public hygiene. The Babylonians codified fees for physician practice and punishments for malpractice in the Hammurabi Code. Eventually, each of these civilizations declined or dispersed.

The next notable civilization to make an impact on medicine was the Greeks, the forerunners of modern Western medicine. The Greeks were the first to reduce and then shed the supernatural view of disease and approach medicine from a rational and scientific point of view. Among the greatest Greek physicians was Hippocrates, from whom the famous oath originates (see Figure 1–2). Hippocrates is famous for codifying medicine through the publication of numerous books, promoting medicine as one of the highest ethical and spiritual endeavors, and establishing the principle that knowledge of disease can be obtained from careful observation and notation of symptoms.

Between the 6th century and the 16th century, little advancement in medicine occurred. Alchemy, magic, and astronomy were prominently identified with medicine. To the extent that medicine existed as we now understand it, the clergy were its practitioners. Religious orders established hospitals to offer hospitality and refuge to old, disabled, and homeless pilgrims. Soon a vast network of hospitals emerged, mainly offering rest and shelter rather than treatment.

Toward the end of the 16th century, a renaissance occurred in many areas of culture, including medicine. Advancements were made in understanding the anatomy of the human body, clinical observations of diseases, and bedside teaching methods. Efforts were made to not only identify disease but to discover specific remedies that could be applied to the patient. The concept of vaccinations was introduced, along with the microscope. Although positive developments were made, medicine still used ineffective methods such as bloodletting, induced vomiting, and the administration of large doses of toxic drugs.

Health Care in the United States

The delivery of health care in the United States has progressed in four stages, as illustrated in Table 1–2. Until 1900, health care delivery was primarily a loose collection of

Figure 1–2 | Hippocratic Oath

I swear by Apollo Physician and Asclepius and Hygieia and Panaceia and all the gods and goddesses, making them my witnesses, that I will fulfill according to my ability and judgment this oath and this covenant:

I will apply dietetic measures for the benefit of the sick, according to my ability and judgment; I will keep them from harm and injustice.

I will neither give a deadly drug to anybody if asked for it, nor will I make a suggestion to this effect. Similarly I will not give to a woman an abortive remedy. In purity and holiness I will guard my life and my art.

I will not use the knife, not even on sufferers from stone, but will withdraw in favor of such men as are engaged in this work.

Whatever houses I may visit, I will come for the benefit of the sick, remaining free of all intentional injuries, of all mischief and in particular of sexual relations with both female and male persons, be they free or slaves.

What I may see or hear in the course of the treatment or even outside of the treatment in regard to the life of men, which on no account one must noise abroad, I will keep to myself holding such things shameful to be spoken about.

If I fulfill this oath and do not violate it, may it be granted to me to enjoy life and art, being honored with fame among all men for all time to come; if I transgress it and swear falsely, may the opposite of all this be my lot.

efforts made by individual physicians who worked independently of one another. These physicians were by and large poorly trained, often obtaining their skills through an apprenticeship with an older physician. Gradually, they began taking courses at medical colleges, which grew in number but varied in quality and sophistication. The majority of a physician's time was spent at patients' homes or in the office, with very limited time spent at hospitals.

During this same time frame, hospitals were established, providing the first visible institutions around which health care services could be organized. Early examples include the Pennsylvania Hospital in Philadelphia, Bellevue General in New York City, Charity Hospital in New Orleans, and Massachusetts General in Boston. These hospitals and others primarily served the sick poor who could not be

cared for at home. They were funded by private beneficiaries, endowments, and donations. For those patients with financial means, the optimum place for treatment was one's home, because hospitals were seen as dirty, crowded, and disease ridden.

During this time, two organizations formed that resulted in long-term improvements in the delivery of health care. The American Medical Association (AMA), created in 1847, began with efforts to improve the poor quality of medical education and examine the questionable ethics of practicing physicians. Although no longer involved in the accreditation of medical schools, the AMA continues to center its efforts on promoting the art and science of medicine, improving public health, influencing and creating health care policy, and serving the professional needs of its members,

Table 1–2 | Stages in the Delivery of Health Care in the United States

Characteristics	1776–1900	1900–WWI	WWII–1980	1980–Present
Health Care Providers	Physicians who worked independently of one another/limited number of hospitals, primarily serving the sick poor	Improved scientific knowledge of physicians; new hospital services; increased hospital use	Development of medical specializations	Rapid growth of allied health professionals
Influence of Technology	Limited	Beginning growth in science and technology	Major advances in science and technology	Use of sophisticated technology in diagnostic and therapeutic procedures
Organizational/Societal Efforts to Improve Health Care	Limited in number and scope	Reform of medical schools/ standardization movements in hospitals	Role of federal government in financing biomedical research and hospital facilities	Role of federal government in containing costs; emergence of managed care industry
Role of Patient	Little factual knowledge	Beginning steps in patient education	Awareness of health care as a political issue; increased use of health insurance	Advent of consumer culture

including continuing medical education. Similarly, the American Hospital Association (AHA) began in 1848 with efforts to improve the public welfare by providing better health care in hospitals. It continues those efforts to this day, representing hospital interests in legal and legislative matters, funding and conducting research and educational programs, and maintaining data on hospital profiles.

In addition to formal organizations, a new movement swept through the country at the end of the 19th century: mental health reform. This movement posited that insanity was a medical or mental disorder that could be managed through the provision of health care services. The mentally ill were no longer housed in poorhouses or prisons but rather in institutions often funded and managed at the state level. Unfortunately, these state-run institutions fell into disrepute as inadequate funding caused overcrowding and deplorable living conditions.

The second stage of medical improvements began in the early 1900s, with exciting changes emerging from research laboratories and medical school reform. Major scientific advances were achieved in the research lab, including the discoveries of insulin, penicillin, and the role vitamins play in disease prevention. Significant advances were achieved in obstetrics and surgery, making these areas of medicine safer for patients.

Reforms of medical schools occurred as the result of the Flexner Report, a study undertaken by Abraham Flexner and funded by the Carnegie Foundation for the Advancement of Teaching in 1910. This report indicated serious deficiencies in medical education and recommended revisions of medical school curricula and affiliation with universities. As a result, numerous proprietary medical schools closed and the remaining schools increased university affiliation. In the remaining medical schools, emphasis was placed on training physicians to be scientists in addition to practitioners.

Licensing of physicians in large numbers also started during this time period. **Licensing** refers to a right conferred by a governmental entity to practice an occupation or provide a service. Licensing controls the number of individuals who are permitted to practice an occupation or provide a service. Licenses are generally granted to individuals who present proof of specified educational requirements and pass an examination administered by an appropriate state board. Those individuals who practice an occupation or provide a service that is subject to licensure but do not possess a license do so at their own risk, as that practice or provision of service is considered illegal. Each state determines which occupation or service is subject to licensure; occupations commonly subject to licensure include medicine, osteopathy, nursing, dentistry, and podiatry, among others.

Although physicians spent a majority of their time with patients in their offices or patients' homes, a trend toward

the use of hospitals emerged in the century's first three decades. Technology began to influence the science of medicine. Because technology was relatively expensive, it became important to concentrate it in hospitals so that a large number of physicians and their patients could gain access to it. As a result, hospitals began to change, offering services unavailable to patients at home or anywhere else.

A movement toward standardization of hospital care soon ensued. This movement was led by the American College of Surgeons (ASC), an organization formed in 1913 to improve patient care. The ASC began its Hospital Standardization Program four years later, resulting in the adoption of the Minimum Standards document in 1919. This document identified the standards deemed essential to proper care and treatment of hospital patients. Among the standards were the requirement of an organized medical staff, the existence of certain diagnostic and therapeutic facilities, and the creation of a written health record for every patient.

The standardization movement also led to expansion of the licensing process beyond individuals to health care facilities. State regulatory bodies developed basic minimum standards for health care facilities to meet. Those health care facilities that met the established standards could obtain a license and provide health care services to the public. As with individuals, health care facilities that provided services to the public without a license did so at their own risk; their actions were illegal.

As World War II began, health care in the United States moved into its third stage. Initially, the focus rested on the need for massive mobilization of health care workers to treat the wounded and solve war-related problems. Soon, wartime developments—such as the treatment of patients with antibiotics, new surgical techniques dealing with burns and trauma, and new approaches to the transportation of the sick and wounded—were adopted by physicians treating the civilian population.

As direct patient care services improved, so did the stature of hospitals. A combination of factors influenced this increase in stature: advances in medicine and technology, the abandonment of the public's view that hospital care was mainly for those too poor to afford home care, the role of the federal government in financing biomedical research and hospital facilities, and the explosion in availability of private health insurance. With this change in stature came a change in expectations. It was no longer merely enough that a hospital emphasized caring for the patient. Rather, the public expected hospitals to integrate advances in medicine and technology made in research laboratories into their daily work so that patients were both cared for and cured. This improvement in stature and increase in expectations resulted in the hospital becoming the central institution of the health care delivery system.

As scientific advances increased rapidly, the knowledge required of health care providers to practice competently exploded. Accordingly, a new trend emerged among physicians: the need for specialty practice. Whereas before World War II, the vast majority of physicians were general practitioners, after World War II the vast majority of physicians specialized in some area of medicine or surgery. Nurses and other health professionals were similarly affected by scientific advances. Training became more oriented to a scientific basis and many training programs were affiliated with universities. For all health care providers, the availability of new technologies resulted in a more complex knowledge base from which to practice.

Significant developments affecting the stature of hospitals merit further discussion. During the 1950s, factors such as the increased specialization of physicians and health professionals, the increased use of technology, advances in medical science, and the sophistication of hospitals impacted the efforts to standardize medical care. In recognition, a new concept emerged: accreditation.

Accreditation is the process by which an external entity reviews an organization or program of study to determine if the organization or program meets certain predetermined standards. In recognition of meeting those standards, the organization or program is said to be accredited. The process used is the survey method, and a wide variety of health care functions considered crucial to patient care are surveyed. Health care organizations and programs have strong incentives to become accredited, because accreditation status is linked with the ability to receive financial reimbursement for services and recognition of the delivery of high quality services.

Two organizations played the largest roles in health care accreditation during this period: the Joint Commission (JC), formerly known as the Joint Commission on Accreditation of Healthcare Organizations (JCAHO), and the American Osteopathic Association's (AOA) Healthcare Facilities Accreditation Program (HFAP). The JC adopted the Hospital Standardization Program of the ACS and played a major role in the improvement of the quality of health care; similarly, the HFAP played a crucial role in accrediting osteopathic hospitals. Additional information concerning the role of accrediting organizations can be found in Chapter 3, "Legal Issues."

Equally important was the rise of the private health insurance industry. Among the most prominent was the development and progression of the Blue Cross Blue Shield (BCBS) insurance companies. These nonprofit, community based health plans insured against hospital costs (Blue Cross) and physician and related services costs (Blue Shield). These plans were offered to employers and industry as fringe benefits, meaning that the benefits were supplemental to the wage and salary offered to the employee. As the BCBS programs increased in popularity, commercial insurance carriers entered the market, and a majority of Americans were soon covered by some form of health insurance.[1] This rise in insurance coverage resulted in a majority of Americans receiving health care services in an economical fashion. It also resulted in the emergence of the health care sector as a significant part of the American economy.

During this same time period, the federal government began to assume major responsibility for combating health problems. It did so through a series of initiatives designed to organize and finance health care.

In 1946, Congress passed the Hospital Survey and Construction Act, commonly known as the Hill-Burton Act, named after the two sponsors of the legislation. The Hill-Burton Act provided funding for construction of hospitals and other health care facilities throughout the United States. It was passed in response to the realization that existing hospitals required substantial modernization and that new hospitals were needed in the rural and suburban communities located outside the urban core areas. Administered through a joint federal-state process, the Hill-Burton Act resulted in a wave of hospital construction and, later, renovation.

The government began to respond to political pressures that charged that the public's health, education, and welfare were the responsibility of the federal government. In 1953, Congress created a cabinet-level department called the Department of Health, Education, and Welfare (DHEW). Congress charged this department with coordinating federal efforts in these three areas and provided it with the authority to promulgate rules and regulations implementing federal legislation.

Prior to the 1960s, those portions of the general population who had health insurance obtained it as a fringe benefit of their employment. Two segments of the general population were excluded from this development: the elderly who were no longer employed, and the poor who were unemployed or employed without fringe benefits such as health insurance. In response, the federal government amended the Social Security Act in 1965 to provide two government-subsidized health care programs: Medicare and Medicaid. Formally known as the Health Insurance Act for the Aged, Medicare is the program designed to provide financing for health care for all persons over the age of 65, regardless of financial need. Formally known as the Medical Assistance Program, Medicaid is the program designed to provide financing for health care for poor or impoverished persons. Medicare and Medicaid markedly changed the face of health care inasmuch as these were the first broad-scale efforts to recognize the receipt of health care as a right of Americans.

As a result of increased access to medical care, the rise and complexity of private health insurance, and the

Medicare and Medicaid programs, an ever-increasing flow of private and public funds moved into the health care arena. As health care costs escalated, it became more difficult to finance the delivery of health care at prior levels. The strain on the American economy was such that changes were needed by the end of the 1970s. Accordingly, the fourth stage in the delivery of health care emerged, one associated with restrictions in growth, resource limitations, and reorganization of the systems used to finance and provide health care.

The first recognized effort to control health care costs came from the federal government, the largest financier of health care in the United States. In 1982 Congress passed the Tax Equity and Fiscal Responsibility Act (TEFRA), which established a mechanism for controlling the costs of the Medicare program. TEFRA revolutionized the financing of health care services by introducing the concept of a prospective payment system (PPS) that set limitations on reimbursement based on the use of diagnosis-related groups (DRGs). State departments of health soon followed, revising the reimbursement program for the Medicaid system and adopting the PPS. Private health insurers soon became convinced that the PPS could assist them in containing costs, and these insurers either adopted or modified the system accordingly. Additional information concerning prospective payment systems can be found in Chapter 15, "Reimbursement Methodologies."

Another significant development was the emergence of the managed care industry in the 1980s and 1990s. The concept of **managed care** is that a defined, enrolled population will receive health care services through either a prepayment or discounted fee-for-services arrangement. The focus of managed care is to approach health care services by facilitating cost containment and control utilization while maintaining a high quality of care.

Three main types of managed care arrangements have proliferated in the United States: health maintenance organizations (HMOs), independent practice associations (IPAs), and preferred provider organizations (PPOs). The main points of each type of arrangement are listed in Table 1–3. An **HMO** is a prepaid, organized system for providing comprehensive health care services within a geographic area to all persons under contract, emphasizing preventive medicine. HMOs almost exclusively use the **capitation** method when

paying physicians, meaning that a fixed amount per person is paid for health care services. An **IPA** is a community-based group of independent practitioners who contract to provide care for prepaid, enrolled individuals. Some IPAs pay participating physicians on a capitated basis, and others on a **fee-for-service** basis, in which payment is made for each service provided. A **PPO** consists of a network of participating hospitals, physicians, medical groups, and other providers who contract with a sponsor, such as an insurance company or employer, to provide services to those enrolled in the PPO. Providers are reimbursed on either a contracted-fee basis using an established fee schedule or a defined, preestablished-discount basis using the provider's usual and customary fees as a starting point for discount. Additional information concerning managed care, including its origins and current trends, can be found in Chapter 15, "Reimbursement Methodologies."

The development of the consumer culture has also influenced health care services. The consumer culture emerged as a result of several circumstances: increased levels of education among the U.S. population, dissatisfaction with the way things were run, and inaction or lax oversight by regulatory agencies. The consumer culture focused on health care and began to demand higher quality. Consumer interests in costs of care, preventive care, sophisticated technology, diagnostic and therapeutic procedures, and patient rights have combined to force a more comprehensive approach to health care.

New developments have arisen in the beginning of the 21st century that influence the delivery of health care. Much discussion has focused on the uninsured and under-insured members of society and how they can receive medical care in a financially prudent manner. Some commentators have suggested using **health savings accounts** (HSA), a means of allowing individuals who buy high-deductible insurance coverage to save money for out-of-pocket costs in tax-free accounts. These insurance plans typically have lower monthly premiums than would be standard in the industry but may require patients to pay large amounts of money before the insurance plan covers any cost. Other commentators advocate the creation of national health insurance, with either a single payer (e.g., the federal government) or a limited number of payers responsible for financing the system. Supporters see

Table 1–3	Managed Care Arrangements		
Title	**Health Maintenance Organization (HMO)**	**Independent Practice Association (IPA)**	**Preferred Provider Organization (PPO)**
Structure	Organized system	Community-based group of independent practitioners	Network of participating hospitals, doctors, medical groups
Payment Means	Capitation method	Capitation method or fee-for-service basis	Contracted fee basis: established fee schedule or defined, preestablished-discount basis

national health insurance as the way to provide access to health care services to underserved populations.

Another focus rests on the changes in accreditation processes. These changes have moved the emphasis from evaluating compliance with regulations to evaluating how actual patient care experiences comply with established standards. Accrediting agencies have begun to visit health care facilities on an unannounced basis partway through the established accreditation cycle, as a means to evaluate operational performance. The JC has announced the use of tracer methodology, a means of tracing the delivery of a patient's care through the health record, interviews with members of the health care team, and often interviews with the patient, as well. This methodology is designed to provide a more meaningful measure of a health care facility's strengths and weaknesses in delivering patient care. Such changes in accreditation processes are thought to spur health care facilities to engage in continuous improvement activities as opposed to only those activities designed to improve the facility when notice of an impending visit is announced.

HIPAA

The Security Rule establishes security safeguards for protected health information (PHI) that a covered entity creates, receives, maintains, or transmits in an electronic format.

A third focus rests on the use of outsourcing in health care. Outsourcing refers to the delegation of non-care operations from internal production of a business to an external entity that specializes in an operation. Some outsourcing is performed offshore (i.e., out of the country), typically overseas. Much of the debate over outsourcing centers on the relationship between the functional area to be outsourced and the quality required of the work performed. Many in the health care field perceive that in-house staff are better at meeting performance and quality standards because of their ownership of the function and their loyalty to the facility as compared to those who are not employed by the facility. Areas that have gained some foothold in outsourcing among health care providers without causing much controversy include pest management services, record destruction services, and software development. Two functional areas that have engendered some criticism include the reading of radiology images remotely and the transcription of physician dictation remotely. Criticism of these forms of outsourcing increased following the discovery that the transmission of images and data were not always performed using encryption or similar technologies to guarantee security, and that sensitive personal identifiers were not redacted before outside contractors

received the data. These discoveries pose implications concerning the Security Rule of the Health Insurance Portability and Accountability Act (HIPAA). The Security Rule imposes standards that specify the use of integrity controls and encryption technology when transmitting protected health information (PHI) electronically. Because failure to comply with these standards can result in penalties, health care facilities that decide to engage in outsourcing of these functions are heavily burdened to establish compliance. Additional information concerning HIPAA is found in Chapter 3, "Legal Issues," while information specific to the Security Rule is found in Chapter 13, "Information Systems and Technology."

One exciting focus of the government sector in the 21st century is the establishment of the Office of the National Coordinator for Health Information Technology (ONCHIT) within the U.S. Department of Health and Human Services. ONCHIT's mission is to lead the development and nationwide implementation of an interoperable health information technology infrastructure as a means to improve the quality and efficiency of health care and the ability of consumers to manage their own care and safety. ONCHIT sponsors numerous initiatives to promote use of information technology in the health care field, including adoption of an interoperable electronic health record (EHR) for every American, developing standards for use with the EHR, assisting in formulation of regulations governing the EHR and e-prescribing, and working with nongovernmental entities on projects. Some of these projects impact both the health care field and the health information management profession in particular. One such project, recently completed by ONCHIT in cooperation with the American Health Information Management Association (AHIMA), focused on combating health care fraud and abuse through the use of automated coding software. More details about the use of this software to combat fraud and abuse can be found in Chapter 3, "Legal Issues."

The combination of changes in financing, the emergence of managed care with its emphasis on both cost control and patient care, the rise of a consumer culture, the changes in the accreditation process, and the use of outsourcing in non-care operations has resulted in a cultural shift in health care delivery. Whereas early U.S. health care delivery emphasized the care of patients in homes or of the poor in charity hospitals, with virtually no use of technology, the current state of health care delivery recognizes the limitations of resources available for patient care and looks to cost containment methods to achieve a more comprehensive approach.

Public Health

Similar to the historical developments described previously, public health has evolved over time. Public health is a health care discipline dealing with the community at large, focused on protecting and improving community health by organized community effort and preventive delivery of medical, social, and sanitary services. Today, the field of public health concentrates on curing communicable and chronic disease, preventing illness, subduing environmental hazards, and providing overall health services to the community.

The concept of public health had its beginnings in the 17th century with the emergence of scientific work focused on biology and medicine. As knowledge of those fields gradually unfolded over the next three centuries, scientists and physicians applied that knowledge to health problems related to the means of achieving better sanitation, the growing of food, and the conditions of work. Scientists and physicians also applied the knowledge to the struggle against communicable diseases, the major cause of death among the U.S. population. Quarantines, sanitariums, and asylums were outgrowths of the application of this knowledge.

From the beginning of the 20th century through 1945, the public health field evolved further. In addition to the work of scientists and physicians, political entities such as local and state health departments came into existence. These health departments provided a mechanism to centralize and coordinate individual efforts in order to maximize the benefit to a given geographic region. Efforts to control communicable diseases became more sophisticated with the addition of systems to report these conditions and awareness campaigns to educate the public of the potential for preventing some diseases. Public health efforts expanded into operating clinics to provide health care for the poor and to detect and treat communicable diseases (e.g., tuberculosis and venereal disease). New surveillance and control techniques improved the handling of food, water, and milk. The concept of recording vital statistics came into its own, providing a wealth of information to track trends in health care.

As rapidly as public health expanded in the first half of the 20th century, it expanded even more rapidly in the latter half. The concept of using political power to combat health problems achieved prominence after World War II. In addition to the increased authority of state and local health departments, the federal government became involved in policy making and funding issues related to public health. At the educational level, the discipline of public health developed into graduate-level degree programs across the nation, focusing attention beyond traditional notions of public health.

This expansion of public health beyond traditional notions was widely embraced. Public health's growing focus included planning and cost issues such as access to health care and health insurance coverage. In addition to communicable diseases, it expanded into the consideration of chronic diseases such as cancer and heart disease, leading causes of death in the late 20th century. Public health began to focus on the social and behavioral aspects of life that affect a person's health—for example, addictive diseases, contemporary stresses, and emotional instability. It even began to explore areas previously overlooked, such as environmental hazards and child abuse.

Significant advancements in public health have emerged from both the public and private sectors. Experimental laboratories and clinical treatment centers have developed vaccines and new medicines to prevent and control diseases. Technology has assisted advances in physiology, virology, and biochemistry. Organ transplants, gene therapies, laser beam surgical techniques, and kidney dialysis are some examples of such technological advancement.

At the federal level, the cause of public health is overseen by the work of the U.S. Department of Health and Human Services (DHHS) and its agencies. For example, the Centers for Disease Control and Prevention (CDC) administer programs for the prevention and control of communicable and vector-borne diseases and other preventable conditions. The Food and Drug Administration (FDA) guards the safety and effectiveness of foods, drugs, medical devices, and cosmetics. The National Institutes of Health (NIH) supports basic and applied research in the cause, treatment, and prevention of disease. The Center for Medicare and Medicaid Services (CMS) administers the Medicare and Medicaid programs, and the Agency for Healthcare Research and Quality (AHRQ) administers programs concerned with the assurance of quality of health care.

Public health remains a strong force at the state and local levels. State health departments not only enforce health laws and regulations, they are concerned with policy, planning, legislation, financial support, research, and evaluation. At the local level, a public health agency provides direct services to the public by operating clinics, administering immunization programs, inspecting and licensing certain public facilities, and monitoring air pollution, among other services.

Finally, the success of the public health movement can be measured by the impact it has had on the number and causes of death in the United States. The death rate per 100,000 people per year decreased significantly between 1900 and 2000. Before the 20th century, epidemics of acute infectious disease were the leading cause of death; by the end of the 20th century, chronic diseases were the predominant cause of death. Table 1–4 contrasts the predominant causes of death of these two periods. As a result of advancements brought on by improvements in prevention and treatment, sanitation, and public awareness of causes of disease, the death rate in the United States has declined.

Mental Health

One of the least understood aspects of medicine is mental health care. **Mental health** refers to "the ability to 'cope with and adjust to the recurrent stresses of living in an

Table 1–4 | Predominant Causes of Death in the United States

1900		2000	
Causes of Death	Crude Death Rate per 100,000 People per Year	Causes of Death	Crude Death Rate per 100,000 People per Year
All causes	1,719.0	All causes	873.1
Pneumonia and influenza	202.2	Disease of the heart	258.2
Tuberculosis	194.4	Malignant neoplasms	200.9
Diarrhea, enteritis, and ulceration of the intestine	142.7	Cerebrovascular diseases	60.9
Diseases of the heart	137.4	Chronic lower respiratory diseases	44.3
Senility, ill defined or unknown	117.5	Accidents (unintentional injuries)	35.6
Intracranial lesions of vascular origin	109.6	Diabetes mellitus	25.2
Nephritis	88.6	Influenza and pneumonia	23.7
All accidents	72.3	Alzheimer's disease	18.0
Cancer and other malignant tumors	64.0	Nephritis, nephritic syndrome, and nephrosis	13.5
Diphtheria	40.3	Septicemia	11.3

Source: Information adapted from U.S. National Center for Health Statistics. (2003). *Vital Statistics of the United States*. Available at www.cdc.gov/nchs/data; Williams, S. J., & Torrens, P. R. (2002). *Introduction to health services* (6th ed.). Albany, NY: Delmar.

acceptable way.'"[2] The inability to cope effectively with the recurrent stresses of living is referred to as mental illness. As with other areas of health care, mental health care has evolved over time from an area of limited understanding to a more complete field. Table 1–5 describes this development.

In primitive times, humans looked for answers to physical and mental diseases by focusing on nature, the supernatural, and offended spirits. Whereas mankind progressed in its discovery of the causes of many physical illnesses and diseases, progress was not as rapid with respect to mental illness. For centuries, societies viewed persons afflicted

Table 1–5 | Historical Development of Mental Health

Primitive Times	• Focus on nature, supernatural, and offended spirits
Middle Ages	• Formation of large institutions to house the mentally ill
	• Brutal physical treatments, practices of exorcising demons, and burning at the stake
19th Century	• Reform movement
	• Mental health hospitals founded
20th Century	• Recognition of psychiatry as a profession
	• Psychotherapy, psychoanalysis, electroshock therapy
21st Century	• Government funding at federal, state, and local levels
	• Focus on multipronged solutions: prevention, care, rehabilitation, training, research, education

with mental illness with fear, allowing those afflicted to remain in society only if they did not cause trouble or disruption. Those who could not comply with society's dictates were often driven away or removed to institutions. In the Middle Ages, large institutions were formed to house the mentally ill, where treatment might include brutal physical treatments, attempts at exorcising demons, and even burning at the stake. Because many viewed mental illness as the result of possession by the devil or as evidence of witchcraft, societal authorities felt justified in treating mental illness in this fashion.

Recognition that mental illness might be the result of a brain disorder occurred during the 16th century. Physicians recorded their observations of behaviors associated with mental illness and classified them into categories such as melancholia. Unfortunately, advances in treatment did not occur in a similar fashion. Those suffering from mental illness received treatments such as bleeding, starving, beating, and purging; nonmedical responses to mental illness included hunting the mentally ill as witches. Mental institutions sometimes used the mentally ill as forms of entertainment, allowing the public to tour institutions for a fee.

Not until the 19th century did medical practitioners begin to question the treatment practices for the mentally ill to an extent that would result in change. One pioneer for change was Benjamin Rush, a medical doctor who wrote the first psychiatric textbook in the United States, *Diseases of the Mind*. In this book, Rush advocated clean living conditions and kind treatment for the mentally ill. In the same century, Dorothea Dix began her crusade for improved treatment after observing deplorable conditions and inhumane treatments. Her efforts resulted in the establishment of mental health hospitals throughout the United States supported by state funds with higher standards of care. Unfortunately, funding never reached adequate levels, resulting in a return to deplorable conditions and overcrowding. Only those fortunate enough to afford private institutions received care that modern society would consider moderately successful.

By the early 20th century, reform movements sweeping many areas of the country addressed the need to improve mental health treatment. Many of the improvements rested on incorporating mental illness into the medical mainstream. The theories and writings of neurophysiologist Sigmund Freud influenced this development, finding their home in the curricula of many medical schools. For generations of physicians, Freud's theories of unconscious thoughts and emotions, along with sexual repression, became accepted as the root of mental illness. Soon, the theories of other physicians such as Alfred Adler and Carl Jung were incorporated into medical curricula, with the terms *psychotherapy* and *psychoanalysis* also introduced into the medical vocabulary.

The military became interested in mental health during the First World War, since some men were considered unable to fight due to mental deficiencies. The federal government, working through the National Committee for Mental Hygiene, developed mechanisms to screen individuals with mental problems and to provide both medical and mental care close to fighting areas. Treatment did not end at the front; the military developed the means to treat soldiers with mental illness in military hospitals and in their homes upon discharge from active service.

New medical therapies were introduced after the war that achieved mixed levels of success. Physicians began employing electroconvulsive therapy (ECT) to improve severe depression and insulin therapy to treat schizophrenia-induced comas. Surgeons performed lobotomies to eliminate violent behaviors. Psychotherapeutic drugs were introduced to alter emotions, perceptions, and consciousness. Combined with the psychotherapies of Freud, Adler, Jung, and others, these activities served to markedly advance mental health care.

Although improvements in mental health care were made during the first half of the century, some setbacks did occur. Many physicians believed in a biological cause for mental illness amenable to prevention and cure, but many other physicians believed that mental illness was the result of hereditary factors. This connection between mental illness and heredity led some physicians to advocate actions such as marriage regulation, immigration restrictions, and involuntary sterilization as the means to inhibit the spread

of mental illness to the remainder of the population. Much of this view became incorporated into the eugenics movement that arose and enjoyed varying levels of support throughout the world. After its application in Nazi Germany, societies around the world rejected the principles of the eugenics movement, particularly as applied to those with mental illness. Additional information concerning eugenics is addressed in Chapter 4, "Ethical Standards."

Substantial improvements in mental health occurred after World War II. A nongovernmental organization developed, the Joint Commission on Mental Illness and Health (JCMIH), as a result of the combined efforts of the American Medical Association and the American Psychiatric Association. The JCMIH issued recommendations for improved public care of the mentally ill, which received mixed acceptance. New psychiatric units were constructed in hospitals throughout the nation and an emphasis on research began in earnest. The National Institute of Mental Health (NIMH) developed, allowing information concerning research and training related to mental illness to be disseminated widely. New federal monies in the form of grants were administered by NIMH to medical schools and other groups nationwide, sparking an increase in the publication of federally funded research.

Among the most significant developments to occur during this time was the introduction of a new delivery system for mental health: **community mental health care**. This new delivery system posited that the least restrictive alternative was the best alternative for the mentally ill patient who could control his behavior and cooperate with treatment plans. Beginning in the 1960s, the concept of community mental health care gained widespread acceptance, as advancements in psychotherapeutic drugs resulted in improved behaviors and compliance with treatment plans. New federal monies supported construction of community mental health centers, and many mentally ill patients who had been institutionalized were returned to the community. Unfortunately, the monies available to treat these newly deinstitutionalized patients were insufficient to address demand.

Numerous legislative solutions were enacted to address this demand, but the skyrocketing costs of delivering this sort of care proved difficult for many politicians to support. Eventually, politicians at the federal level resolved their dilemma by applying the block grant program to the mental health area. **Block grants** provide designated amounts of funding to individual states, which then decide where and how to spend the monies provided. Some states have distributed these block grants equally between mental health care and physical health care, while others have emphasized physical health care over mental health care. Because some states chose not to use this money to support institutional or community mental health centers, many mentally ill patients were left with limited alternatives to receive care. Consequently, some mentally ill patients were discharged to the streets with the hope that charitable organizations would fill the void created by this funding lapse.

Today, the level of mental health care delivered in the United States varies greatly from region to region. Much of that variation is attributable to the availability of financing to support this care and treatment. Most mental health care authorities agree that the monies available for mental health treatment, whether from public or private entities, do not meet the demand for this care. While many industrialized nations worldwide have addressed mental health care and treatment fully, a comprehensive solution for prevention, care, rehabilitation, training, education, research, and financing still awaits development, acceptance, and implementation in the United States.

Occupational Health

One development seen during the 20th century was the emergence of occupational health, sometimes referred to as industrial hygiene. **Occupational health** refers to the sub-specialty of health care focused on anticipating, evaluating, and controlling the environmental factors arising in or from the workplace that result in injury, illness, impairment, or otherwise affect the well-being of the workforce. As it is known today, occupational health concentrates on employee wellness and preventing injury, illness, or impairment by analyzing operations and materials and recommending procedures to protect worker health.

The concept of occupational health began with recognition of a connection between workers' health and what they are exposed to in the workplace. As far back as Hippocrates' time, physicians have been urged to observe the environment when diagnosing the illnesses and injuries of their patients. The first medical treatise addressing this connection, *De Morbis Artificam Diatriba*, was published in 1700 and described multiple diseases associated with various occupations. As jobs and roles changed during the industrial revolution, newer associations between diseases and occupations arose. Acceptance of occupational health as a subspecialty of medicine occurred in the 20th century, with surveys and articles published in scientific and medical journals and lectures included in medical school curricula.

This recognition of a connection between workers' health and what they are exposed to in the workplace continues to the present day. In the United States, the great majority of adults spend half or more of their waking lives at their workplaces. The work they perform and what they are exposed to during that work time may impact their health and the treatment of any health-related problem. For example, scientific studies have connected several respiratory diseases (e.g., asbestosis, byssinosis, sylicosis) to underlying causes related to exposure to substances found in the workplace. While these causes are not present in all instances of respiratory diseases, clinicians may seek details of the patient's occupational history to determine the underlying cause of the disease and treat the patient accordingly.

Occupational health is overseen at the federal level by the Occupational Safety and Health Administration (OSHA), within the U.S. Department of Labor. OSHA's purpose is to assure safe working conditions so that human resources are preserved. OSHA accomplishes this mission in several ways, including: (1) developing and enforcing mandatory job health and safety standards; (2) maintaining a reporting and recordkeeping system to monitor job-related injuries and illnesses; (3) encouraging employers and employees to reduce workplace hazards and implement or improve safety and health programs; (4) providing research on safety and health; (5) establishing training programs; and (6) establishing separate but dependent responsibilities and rights for employers and employees to achieve better safety and health conditions in the workplace.

Occupational health is generally performed in today's organizations according to a comprehensive plan focusing on the diseases that arise from conditions in the workplace. Conditions such as noise and vibration problems, hazardous materials, bloodborne pathogens, radiation, psychological stress, and poorly designed workstations and tools all fall within this focus. Occupational health professionals conduct needs analysis and, using the data collected, prioritize the health needs of the organization. They educate management and staff about health risks and activities, and procedures to follow to prevent injury, illness, or impairment, while also focusing on positive approaches to improve employee health. They may engage in medical surveillance activities, either by targeting categories of workers for examination of occupation-related conditions or by waiting for workers to present themselves with symptoms that may be work related. They also review government regulations and employ approaches that will demonstrate their organization's compliance with governmental requirements. Finally, they may provide direct patient care to the employee himself through physical examinations, emergency care, immunizations, counseling, and education.

In the patient care setting, the focus of occupational health is twofold: improving employee health and reducing exposure to health care facility–acquired infections. Employee health can be improved by employing many of the activities previously described. By providing a healthy work environment, the occupational health professional attempts to reduce absenteeism, employee turnover, and employee illness and injury. Health care facility–acquired infections may occur due to the proximity of ill employees, patients, or visitors; faulty patient-care techniques; mishandling of contaminated material and equipment; poor housekeeping; or inadequate physical facilities or supervision. Many health care facilities operate infection control committees as a means to prevent and reduce these acquired

Table 1–6 | Hospital Infection Control Committee

Purpose	• To prevent and reduce health care facility–acquired infections
Staff	• Multidisciplinary
Activities	• Establish policies and procedures
	• Engage in training
	• Employ awareness techniques
	• Conduct surveys of personal and physical space
	• Track outbreaks of infection

infections. These committees are typically staffed on a multidisciplinary basis with physicians, nurses, and allied health professionals working together to establish policies and procedures addressing this topic. They may also engage in training activities, employ awareness techniques, track outbreaks of infections, and conduct bacteriological surveys of health care facility personnel and the areas where infections have increased in incidence. The purpose, staffing, and activities of a health care facility infection control committee are listed in Table 1–6.

Health Care Delivery Systems

As important as governmental entities and managed care organizations are to health care today, other entities also exert strong influence. Professional associations, voluntary health agencies, philanthropic foundations, and international health agencies all play roles in the health care delivery system. Wide variety also exists in the delivery of health care, both in terms of the settings where health care is delivered and the type and number of professionals delivering care.

Professional Associations
Among the most influential players in the health care field are professional associations. A **professional association** is a body of people with specialized learning who exert mental, rather than manual, labor and organize for a common purpose or object. These groups cover every conceivable health-related profession and institution. The associations are generally national in character, with affiliated organizations at the state and local levels. They serve as sources of information for their membership at every level, often producing a variety of publications such as journals, magazines, and newsletters. These groups hold annual meetings that serve to disseminate information, discuss current issues and research, and provide opportunities for employment exchange.

Originally, these associations served to create standards of professionalism for their membership, focusing primarily on performance improvement. Gradually the associations encouraged additional focus on research and innovation, and discovered the potential for influencing political decision making. Associations take positions and pass resolutions on critical health issues, support political candidates, and testify before legislatures for or against proposed legislation.

Among the most influential professional associations are the American Medical Association (AMA), the American College of Surgeons (ACS), and the American Hospital Association (AHA), all described earlier in this chapter. The American Osteopathic Association (AOA) has greatly influenced the quality of patient care in osteopathic hospitals and organizations, and the American Health Information Management Association (AHIMA) has played a central role in the development of the health information management profession.

Voluntary Health Agencies
Voluntary health agencies are nongovernmental organizations created to perform public work in health care through private means. These agencies are often tax-exempt, providing distinct financial advantages for both the agencies and their financial contributors. Most agencies receive financial support from individuals as well as business and industry. Some possess other sources of income, such as investment earnings, service fees from clients, and membership dues.

Voluntary health agencies came about as a result of several occurrences, including the volunteer movement of the late 19th and early 20th centuries, the developing concern for communicable diseases, the excessive illnesses and deaths of infants and mothers, and the absence of governmental entities playing a role in the delivery of health care. The first voluntary health agency in the United States was the Anti-Tuberculosis Society of Philadelphia, founded in 1892. The National Association for the Study and Prevention of Tuberculosis, now known as the American Lung Association, began in 1904. During the next two decades, national and local movements were formed that focused on cancer control, prevention of blindness, maternal hygiene, deafness, and public health nursing. Later organizations formed to place attention on issues of poliomyelitis, diabetes, heart disease, and acquired immunodeficiency syndrome (AIDS), among others.

One organization that is typically considered a voluntary health agency also possesses a quasi-official status: the American Red Cross exists through the grant of a charter by the U.S. Congress in 1900. The organization originated in the efforts of Clara Barton during the Civil War and moved to an international level of recognition before being formally recognized in the United States. The American Red Cross serves to help people prevent, prepare for, and cope with emergencies and has distinguished itself in disaster relief efforts. Other voluntary health agencies have also distinguished themselves; many are listed in Table 1–7.

Table 1–7	Voluntary Health Agencies
American Cancer Society
American Lung Association
Cystic Fibrosis Association
Easter Seals
Eye Bank Association
Immunization Action Coalition
The Leukemia & Lymphoma Society
Muscular Dystrophy Association
National Kidney Foundation
United Cerebral Palsy Association

Voluntary health agencies can be grouped into three types: (1) those concerned with specific diseases (e.g., cancer or diabetes); (2) those concerned with special organs or structures of the body (e.g., heart or skeletal defects); and (3) those concerned with society as a whole or special groups of people or issues (e.g., mental health or family planning). Some voluntary health agencies provide direct patient care while others concentrate on research and education. Like professional associations, these groups also participate in the political process through lobbying efforts and by testifying before legislative committees.

Philanthropic Foundations

Although not as influential as governmental entities and voluntary health agencies, philanthropic foundations play a substantial role in health care. Philanthropic foundations are organizations designed to distribute donated funds in an effort to better humankind. Numerous such foundations exist in the United States; some, but not all, are dedicated to health care matters. Examples of prominent foundations supporting health care matters are the Robert Wood Johnson Foundation, the Rockefeller Foundation, and the Ford Foundation. Within the health information management field, the Foundation of Research and Education in Health Information Management (FORE) plays a prominent role.

Philanthropic foundations support health care through the awarding of grants of money. These grants support research, training, and demonstration projects. Because they are not bound by the same restrictions as governmental entities who also award grants of money, the amounts of their grant awards may vary with the kind of program they choose to support and the foundation's own size. This flexibility in award amounts has resulted in support and stimulation for researchers that sometimes lead to innovations in the health care field.

International Health Agencies

Because disease does not stop at a national border, the need for international cooperation to improve health care has become imperative. International health agencies are composed of governmental and nongovernmental entities that transcend national borders to perform public work in health care. They provide direct patient care to population groups throughout the world, contribute to the control and prevention of infectious diseases, and support training of health workers.

Efforts to organize international health agencies began in the middle of the 19th century with the creation of a series of International Sanitary Conferences. These conferences concentrated on the topics of communicable diseases, control of epidemics through quarantine, and investigation of the origin of infections. Various organizations came into existence over the next 100 years that expanded beyond the focus of the original conferences to include the standardization of serums, control of drug traffic, training of professional personnel, and provision of limited health services in the field.

After World War II, the United Nations created a specialized agency devoted to health care. The World Health Organization (WHO) has a varied mission, including promoting international standardization of drugs, vaccines; other biologic agents; providing epidemic and statistical service; sponsoring health research; developing international quarantine measures; preparing and distributing publications; and providing technical and program-planning assistance to participating nations.

A second creation of the United Nations, the United Nations Children's Fund (UNICEF), also addresses health issues. Although it was originally created as a temporary, emergency agency to assist children in war-torn countries, UNICEF became a permanent agency of the United Nations in 1953. In addition to its original mandate, UNICEF provides food and supplies to child and maternal welfare programs throughout the world. It also develops and deploys programs for vaccination and control of infectious diseases.

Other international health agencies have made major contributions to improving health care worldwide, including Doctors Without Borders, Global Impact, International Medical Corps, and Project Hope. These organizations provide direct patient care to a variety of population groups in addition to training health workers and controlling infectious diseases. These and other organizations have distinguished themselves in the health care field; many are listed in Table 1–8.

Variety of Delivery Systems

The changes in the health care system since the founding of this country have resulted in a wide variety of places where patients receive care; in addition, the number and type of professionals involved in health care have also greatly expanded.

Settings To understand the variety of settings, one must first understand what is referred to as the continuum of care. The continuum of care is defined as "matching an

Table 1–8 | International Health Agencies

AmeriCares
CARE
Doctors Without Borders
International Federation of Red Cross and Red Crescent Societies
International Medical Corps
Project HOPE
Save the Children
World Vision

individual's ongoing needs with the appropriate level and type of medical, psychological, health, or social care or service within an organization or across multiple organizations."[3] This continuum is seen in the range of services provided to the patient, starting at the least acute and least intensive and moving to the most acute and most intensive. Figure 1–3 illustrates the continuum of care.

The continuum of care can be broken into four types: primary care, secondary care, tertiary care, and quaternary care. **Primary care** refers to the care provided by the health care professional at the initial point of contact and in the coordination of all aspects of the patient's health care. Pri-

mary care typically occurs in an ambulatory setting and encompasses both preventive care and acute care. One example of primary care would be the care offered by a family practitioner in prescribing an antibiotic for a bacterial infection. **Secondary care** is that care provided by a specialist, often at the request of the primary care physician. Examples of secondary care are as varied as there are medical specialists. One example is the radiation therapy provided by the radiologist following breast cancer surgery. **Tertiary care** is the specialized medical and surgical care provided for complex or unusual medical problems. Typically, tertiary care facilities possess advanced technologies and specialized intensive care units. A large medical center containing a trauma center and burn unit is one example of a facility providing tertiary care. **Quaternary care** is the most complex level of medical and surgical care available. One example of quaternary care is the transplantation of baboon marrow to an AIDS patient. Quaternary care facilities are often affiliated with universities and research institutions. Depending on the circumstances of a given medical situation, a patient may receive all four levels of care during the progression of his disease.

Health care is generally delivered in two ways: in ambulatory care settings and in hospitals or other inpatient settings. **Ambulatory health care** is defined as the care given to patients who are not confined to an institutional

Figure 1–3 | Continuum of care

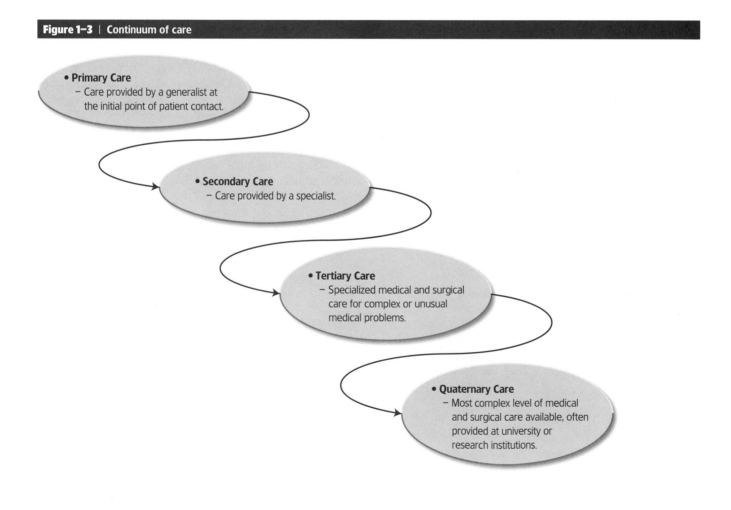

- **Primary Care**
  – Care provided by a generalist at the initial point of patient contact.

- **Secondary Care**
  – Care provided by a specialist.

- **Tertiary Care**
  – Specialized medical and surgical care for complex or unusual medical problems.

- **Quaternary Care**
  – Most complex level of medical and surgical care available, often provided at university or research institutions.

bed as inpatients at the time care is rendered. Accordingly, ambulatory care is referred to as care being provided in an outpatient setting. Ambulatory care can be further subdivided into the care provided by freestanding medical organizations and the care provided in a hospital setting or at hospital direction. Examples of care provided at freestanding medical organizations include physician practices (solo or group), community health centers, neighborhood clinics, and public health departments. Examples of the care provided in a hospital setting or direction include emergency rooms, outpatient departments, hospices, and ambulatory surgery centers. The key to understanding ambulatory care is that the patient travels to and from either the freestanding medical organization or the hospital setting on the same day without being admitted as an inpatient.

By contrast, a home health agency travels to the patient to deliver care. A home health agency is an organization that provides nursing and other professional and technical services to patients at their places of residence. Home health agencies can be community based or hospital based. Home health agencies have grown in popularity because of their ability to be reimbursed for services from government and third-party payers, and consumers' preference to be cared for in their homes.

One area of care frequently addressed by many home health agencies is hospice care. Hospice care refers to the management of symptoms for patients considered terminally ill, with a life expectancy of less than six months if their disease follows its normal course. Symptom management may range from methods to relieve chronic pain and other physical results of the disease process to methods to relieve the emotional and mental stresses of the dying process for both the patient and the family. The majority of hospice care occurs in the patient's home, lending itself to the work of home health agencies.

A hospital is defined as "a health care organization that has a governing body, an organized medical staff and professional staff, and inpatient facilities and provides medical, nursing, and related services for ill and injured patients 24 hours per day, seven days per week."[4] Each state's licensing authority promulgates its own definition of the word "hospital," which can result in some deviation from the above listed definition.

A great variety exists in the types of hospitals operated in the United States. Some vary in ownership, ranging from government owned to nongovernment owned. Among nongovernment-owned hospitals, ownership may vary by those operated for profit and those operated not for profit. Additionally, variety exists as a result of population served (e.g., children's hospitals) and diagnostic and therapeutic services offered (e.g., cancer treatment).

Entire treatises have been devoted to the services offered by hospitals. An attempt is made here to highlight the typical structure of a hospital and the kinds of services typically offered. Hospitals are typically structured as illustrated in Figure 1–4. The governing body of the hospital is a group of individuals who have the authority and responsibility

Figure 1–4 | A hospital organization chart

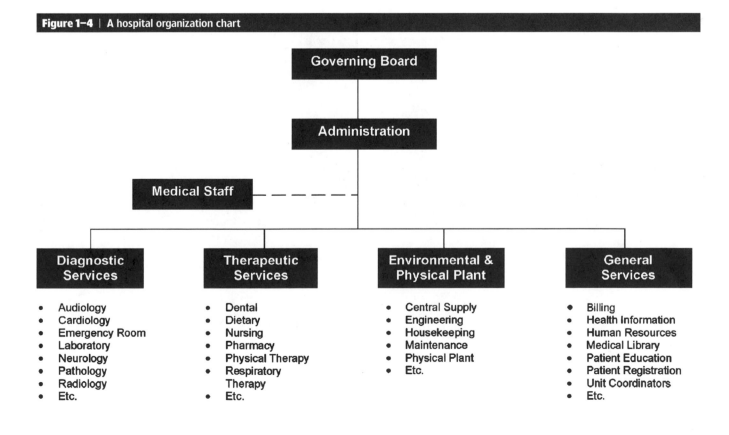

for operation of the hospital. These governing bodies are sometimes referred to as boards of trustees, boards of directors, or boards of governors. They function according to the bylaws established by the board. **Bylaws** are the framework used to identify the roles and responsibilities of the board and its members. Governing boards routinely work through the use of standing committees and special committees.

The administration of the hospital consists of those individuals responsible for its fiscal and general management. They do not provide services directly to patients; rather, they work with management and health care professionals to direct patient care. The chief executive officer (CEO) is the primary administrator of the hospital, answering directly to the governing board for the success of the facility. The CEO is assisted by a chief financial officer (CFO), a chief information officer (CIO), and a chief operating officer (COO). Depending on the size of the hospital and the complexity of the services offered, many other layers of management may assist the CEO.

The types of services offered by a hospital may vary; however, certain services are almost universally offered. These services include nursing care, radiology, pathology, clinical laboratory, pharmacy, and emergency care. A more comprehensive list of services offered in the hospital setting can be found in Table 1–9.

Other inpatient care settings also treat patients who require significant medical resources. A **long-term care facility** is an institution that offers health care to patients who are not in an acute episode of illness but who need continuous nursing service in an inpatient setting. Patients in long-term care facilities are no longer able to care for themselves in their homes, even with the assistance of others, and frequently suffer from incapacitating conditions, permanent cognitive impairment, or chronic respiratory diseases. Long-term care facilities typically address a variety of patient needs, including medical treatment and preventive, rehabilitative, social, spiritual, and emotional care to individuals. Examples of these facilities include nursing homes, rehabilitation hospitals, and skilled nursing facilities.

A **rehabilitation care facility** is an institution that offers health care services to patients who need to restore functional abilities, assume complete activities of daily living (ADLs), or engage in an occupation. Patients in rehabilitation care facilities work with a multidisciplinary team that creates an approach to rehabilitation to suit the patient's needs. Rehabilitation care facilities can be stand-alone institutions or associated with hospitals or long-term care facilities.

Health Care Professionals The number and type of health care professionals in the United States have exploded during the last 100 years. Definitions of the main players in the health care field are provided to assist the learner in understanding the interdisciplinary nature of health care. A list of these professionals is found in Table 1–10.

A **physician** is an individual authorized to practice medicine who graduated from a college of medicine or osteopathy and is licensed by the appropriate board.[5] As

Table 1–9 | Services in a Hospital Setting
Internal Medicine
Neurology
Cardiology
Pediatrics
Obstetrics
Surgery
Psychiatry
Critical Care
Radiology/Radiotherapy
Emergency Care
Clinical Laboratory
Pharmacy
Pathology
Physical Therapy
Nursing Care
Respiratory Therapy

Table 1–10 | Health Care Professionals
Physician
Physician Assistant
Surgical Assistant
Podiatrist
Dentist
Chiropractor
Pharmacist
Optometrist
Lab Technician
Health Information Manager
Dietician
Nutritionist
Medical Social Worker
Respiratory Therapist
Occupational Therapist
Physical Therapist
X-Ray Technician

this definition indicates, two types of physicians practice in the United States: doctors of medicine (MD) and doctors of osteopathy (DO). Both types are devoted to the art and science of diagnosing and treating disease and maintaining health. They each receive four years of medical education, participate in supervised internship/residency programs, and must pass state licensing examinations. Doctors of osteopathy differ from doctors of medicine in that DOs place great emphasis on the role of body mechanics, the interdependence of all body systems, and the use of manipulative methods to correct faulty structure of the musculoskeletal system. Both use generally accepted physical, medicinal, and surgical methods of diagnosis and therapy.

As referenced earlier in this chapter, physicians may be either generalists or specialists. Generalists are those physicians who conduct a wide or unlimited practice, to include comprehensive care of an individual or family. Generalists include family practitioners and general practitioners. Specialists are physicians who limit their practice to a particular branch of medicine and surgery. Medical specialists include oncologists, pediatricians, cardiologists, psychiatrists, and endocrinologists, to name a few. Surgical specialists include orthopedists, urologists, anesthesiologists, neurosurgeons, and cardiothoracic surgeons, to name a few. Specialists are often board certified, meaning that a specialty board of physicians has determined through rigorous examination that the specialist may limit his practice due to advanced training and demonstration of competence.

Closely allied with physicians are physician assistants. Through specialized education and practical training, a physician assistant (PA) provides patient services under the direction and supervision of a physician or surgeon who is responsible for his performance. PAs often diagnose, manage, and treat common illnesses, provide preventive services, and counsel and refer patients as necessary.

Some physician assistants further specialize as surgical assistants. As the name implies, a surgical assistant (SA) helps the surgeon during operative procedures. The SA may also perform physical examinations, patient education and counseling, and monitoring services.

Physician assistants and surgical assistants are considered mid-level practitioners because the medical profession perceives them as extensions of physicians who can perform many of the usual functions completed by physicians. The services of PAs are often viewed by consumers as a lower-cost substitute for physician services and are prevalent in both urban and rural areas.

Other health care professionals also use the title "doctor." These professionals meet educational requirements, possess a specialized body of knowledge, and form professional associations. They tend to specialize in specific areas of the body.

A dentist is an individual with specialized education and training who is concerned with the teeth, oral cavity, and associated structures of the mouth.[6] Dentists graduate from a college of dentistry, receiving either a Doctor of Dental Surgery (DDS) or Doctor of Dental Medicine (DMD) degree, and are licensed by an appropriate state board. Most dentists are generalists. Specialists in the dental field include orthodontists and oral surgeons.

A podiatrist is an individual with specialized education and training who is concerned with diagnosing, treating, and preventing abnormal foot conditions. Podiatrists graduate from podiatric medical schools, receiving the Doctor of Podiatric Medicine (DPM) degree, and are licensed by an appropriate state board. They engage in a wide range of services, including performing surgery, and prescribing and administering pharmaceuticals.

A chiropractor is an individual with specialized education and training who treats the body's structural and neurological systems. Chiropractors graduate from chiropractic schools, receiving the Doctor of Chiropractic (DC) degree, and are licensed by an appropriate state board.

An individual who diagnoses and provides selective eye treatment is referred to as an optometrist. Optometrists graduate from optometry schools, receiving the Doctor of Optometry (OD) degree, and obtain licenses from an appropriate state board. They may perform certain outpatient surgeries and prescribe a limited range of pharmaceuticals.

A nurse is an individual with specialized education and training who provides services essential to the promotion, maintenance, and restoration of health and well-being, and the prevention of illness.[7] Nurses comprise the largest single health care profession in the United States. They are sometimes categorized according to the age of the patients they care for (e.g., pediatric or geriatric), the health problems of the patients they care for (e.g., psychiatric or obstetrical), or the setting in which their services are provided (e.g., school or occupational health).

Nursing education programs vary, ranging from diploma programs that are hospital based to associate-degree programs that are community college based to baccalaureate degree programs associated with universities. Upon graduation from any of these programs, a nurse must pass a state licensing examination administered by an appropriate state board. Furthermore, nurses may become specialists after receiving advanced training and becoming certified. Examples of nursing specialists include nurse anesthetists, nurse midwives, and nurse practitioners.

An allied health professional is an individual—other than a physician, dentist, podiatrist, chiropractor, optometrist, nurse, or physician assistant—who has graduated from an educational program in a science relating to health care and shares the responsibility for the delivery of health care services to the patient with clinicians.[8] The category of allied health professional covers a wide variety of personnel, including pharmacists; dieticians and nutritionists; laboratory technicians; occupational, respiratory, and physical therapists; social workers; home health aides; X-ray technicians; and health information management professionals.

Licensing is not required of all allied health professionals; registration is the predominant method of controlling the number of individuals entering an allied health profession. **Registration** refers to the actions of a nongovernmental entity (such as a professional association) to recognize those individuals who meet specified standards (such as education and experience). This recognition is typically awarded after an individual successfully completes an examination given by the nongovernmental entity. The entity issues a certificate and the individual receives specific credentials. In certain occupations, individuals may seek both licensing and registration.

Over the last century, a virtual explosion in the number and type of allied health professionals has occurred. There are now literally hundreds of occupational titles recognized by the federal government as associated with health care.[9] This rapid growth is attributable to many interrelated factors: (1) innovations in technology; (2) the rise of the hospital as a central institution in the health care delivery system; (3) medical and surgical specialization; and (4) increased health insurance coverage, providing a steady payment mechanism for health care providers. As allied health professionals have grown in number and type, the settings in which they deliver care have grown as well. No longer concentrated in the hospital setting, these professionals are increasingly found in ambulatory care settings and the patient's home.

One of the most rapidly growing allied health professions is health information management. This growth is due in large measure to the increased need for patient data, the correlation between health information and reimbursement, and the regulatory environment of health care in the United States.

Two categories of health information management exist: health information administrator and health information technician. Individuals in both categories work to ensure the quality of health records and health care data. A health information administrator focuses on managing computer-based or paper-based record systems and ensuring compliance with external and internal standards relating to health records and information. A health information technician focuses on completeness, accuracy, and proper entry of data, using computer applications to improve patient care and control health care costs. Health information administrators graduate from a baccalaureate degree program; health information technicians graduate from an associate degree program. Both must pass a national licensing examination. Specializations within the health information management field have emerged; more information concerning the health information management field can be found in Chapter 2, "The Health Information Management Profession."

Medical Staff

Most patients have, at one time or another, sought treatment from physicians at hospitals. Unbeknownst to many patients, physicians treat patients at hospitals only with the permission of the hospital's governing body and pursuant to the restrictions the governing body places upon the physician's practice. This section addresses the organization of a hospital's medical staff; the bylaws, rules, and regulations to which the staff must comply; and the credentialing process.

Medical Staff Organization

Each hospital in the United States is composed of multiple parts, including the governing body, the administrative staff, the medical staff, allied health staff, and other professionals. The **medical staff** consists of those physicians with extensive training in various disciplines who have received permission from a hospital's governing board to provide clinical services at the hospital. The medical staff directs the hospital's patient care efforts and furnishes advice to the hospital's governing body and administrative staff. Medical staff may be categorized by department (e.g., internal medicine, radiology, orthopedics, and family practice) and by the level of permission given to physicians (e.g., active, courtesy, consultative, provisional, and honorary). Medical staff officers are typically elected by members of the full medical staff and include president or chief of staff, vice president or chief of staff-elect, and secretary. These officers are responsible for coordinating and directing the activities of the medical staff.

As an organizational matter, the medical staff functions through a variety of committees arranged in coherent relationships. Among the most significant of these committees is the executive committee. It serves in an oversight role for the activities engaged in by the hospital's medical staff. Many of the responsibilities exercised by this committee are listed in Table I–II. Typically, the executive committee is composed of the chief of staff, department chairpersons, medical staff officers, and the hospital's CEO. It answers to the hospital's governing body—the board of trustees or directors—which has the ultimate authority and responsibility for operation of the hospital.

The medical staff is also organized into additional committees by functional area. For example, one committee may oversee the application process and review of credentials for

Table 1–11 | Responsibility of a Medical Staff Executive Committee

Make Recommendations Concerning:	• Medical staff structure
	• Appointment of medical staff members
	• Delineation of clinical privileges
Create Mechanisms For:	• Medical staff members to participate in hospital-wide activities, including performance improvement work
	• Suspending or terminating medical staff members
	• Appeals procedures, including hearings
Take Action On:	• Reports of medical staff committees
	• Reports of medical staff department chairmen

admission to the hospital's medical staff; another committee may create the bylaws, rules, and regulations under which the medical staff must operate; while still another committee may monitor utilization of hospital services. Other functional areas served by committees include infection control, blood usage, tissue/surgical case review, quality improvement, and pharmaceutical services. Separate committees may be created for each medical staff department, and these committees may conduct business on behalf of the department.

Of particular interest are health information management committees, sometimes referred to as medical records committees. These committees cover a wide area associated with health information management. They may address policy and procedural concerns, such as release, retention, and security of health information, and establish the format for a complete patient health record, whether in electronic or traditional paper-based form. They frequently review patient health records for accuracy, completeness, and timeliness of entries, examining the record to determine whether it reflects the patient's condition, progress of care, and results of all tests and therapeutic interventions that occur during the patient's stay. Where appropriate, these committees may recommend disciplinary action for those medical staff members who fail to meet the standards for health information management set by the institution.

Bylaws, Rules, and Regulations

A significant feature found in each state's administrative code and in the standards of accrediting agencies is the requirement for hospitals to adopt and maintain bylaws, rules, and regulations governing medical practice. **Bylaws**

are the framework used to identify the roles and responsibilities of the board and its members. **Rules** are the principles established by authorities, prescribing or directing certain action or forbearance from action. **Regulations** are the prescribed courses of action that arise from law, principle, or custom. In combination, bylaws, rules, and regulations serve to guide medical practitioners in their interactions with the hospital as an organization, with its staff, and with its patient population. For purposes of this discussion, the term *bylaws* will be referred to as inclusive of bylaws, rules, and regulations.

An important feature contained in bylaws is the manner in which they define how a physician may secure admitting privileges. This is particularly important because the hospital's governing body is responsible for the selection of competent physicians and the delineation of the privileges granted to those physicians. Failure to investigate the qualifications of a physician seeking staff privileges, as required by the hospital's bylaws and state statute, can result in a finding of corporate negligence by the hospital and its governing board.[10]

Bylaws also serve other functions. They identify the standards, qualifications, and requirements that physicians must continue to meet once appointed to the hospital staff. Bylaws also delineate the level of clinical privileges that may be granted to the physician, which include restrictions on activities for each level of privilege. These privilege levels are based on established criteria derived from professional associations and accrediting standards, among other areas. The bylaws also address the peer review process that allows the hospital and its medical staff to evaluate, counsel, and take appropriate action against a physician who may pose unreasonable harm to patients.

Bylaws are considered contracts between the hospital and physician and are subject to enforcement under law. A provision frequently found in bylaws addresses the physician's requirement to agree to and abide by the provisions found in the hospital's bylaws, rules, and regulations. Hospitals may suspend or terminate the clinical privileges granted to physicians if they conclude that the physician violated terms of the bylaws, rules, or regulations. The hospital must comply with the procedural safeguards found in the bylaws, rules, and regulations when taking such action. Aggrieved physicians may appeal the decision, following the procedures outlined in the bylaws, rules, and regulations.

Privileges and Credentialing

The physician's ability to treat patients at any given hospital is governed by the permission granted by the hospital's governing board. The limits set by the governing board are referred to as **clinical privileges**. Clinical privileges are based on criteria generally derived from national standards; are discipline specific; and relate to the type of clinical privileges requested by the physician. To obtain clinical privileges, the physician must participate in the credentialing process. The process of obtaining written proof of qualifications—including diplomas conferred by educational programs, certification, registration by professional groups, and legal licenses conferred by governmental agencies—is referred to as the **credentialing process**.

The privileges and credentialing processes are administered by a **medical staff coordinator**, who coordinates all efforts related to procuring written documentation of a physician's qualifications to provide clinical services. Considered a member of the hospital's administrative staff, the medical staff coordinator verifies primary source material relating to a physician's qualifications and reviews information collected from the National Practitioner Data Bank (Data Bank). This Data Bank contains information, specific by physician, about professional conduct and competency, reportable actions taken by state boards of medical examiners and health care entities, and malpractice payments.[11]

The medical staff coordinator also oversees a complex series of steps related to the privileges and credentialing processes. These steps are seen in Figure 1–5. The processes begin with screening of the physician's application. This application contains information concerning the physician's education, licenses, certification, membership in professional associations, malpractice insurance coverage and history, and written recommendations. After this information is verified, references are checked and the applying physician may undergo a personal interview with a subcommittee of the medical staff. In some institutions, the applying physician may also undergo an evaluation of his physical and mental status. Upon completion of this process, the application, supporting documentation, and other materials are forwarded to the medical staff executive committee for evaluation and recommendation to the governing body. A positive decision by the governing board results in the physician's appointment to the hospital's medical staff and delineation of clinical privileges.

The level of privileges granted by the governing board varies. Full privileges, rights, and responsibilities are granted to *active* members of the medical staff. *Associate* staff privileges are granted to junior physicians or to those who wish to become active medical staff members upon existence of a vacancy. *Courtesy* staff privileges are granted to those physicians who only wish to admit patients on an occasional basis. *Consulting* staff privileges are granted to those physicians who serve primarily as specialty consultants to medical staff members with active privileges. *Temporary* or *provisional* privileges are granted to those physicians whose applications appear initially in conformance with hospital requirements but require further information to be considered complete.

An appeal process exists for instances where an application for medical staff privileges is denied or privileges once granted are suspended or terminated. The first step involves the process detailed in the medical staff bylaws, rules, and regulations. If the appealing physician is dissatisfied with that decision, he may seek relief in the form of a lawsuit. Where the facts demonstrate that the governing body acted unreasonably or capriciously in denying, limiting, suspending, or terminating a physician's staff privileges, courts have found in favor of the physician.

Figure 1–5 | Steps in privileges and credentialing process

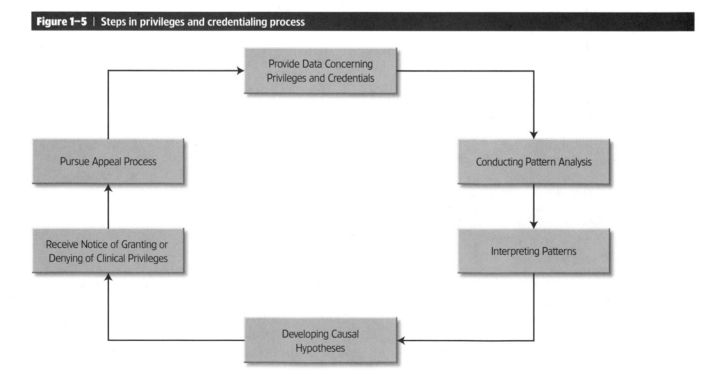

Conclusion

In light of the complex nature of health care in this country in the 21st century, the importance of understanding its historical development cannot be overstated. As this chapter demonstrates, multiple organizations, entities, and professionals have exerted influences that bring us to our present situation. The rise of technology and the power of government in health care seem only to grow. The variety of settings where health care is delivered, along with the variety of health care professionals, further adds to the complexity. Knowing and understanding this complexity will assist the learner in placing the remaining chapters of this book in context.

CHAPTER SUMMARY

The delivery of health care and the practice of medicine can be traced back several thousand years, beginning with the responses of primitive man to the emergence of early physicians and hospitals. Health care in the United States has progressed through four stages, with 21st-century developments such as the use of tracer methodology in the accreditation process, the use of outsourcing, changes in financing, and the rise of a consumer culture resulting in a cultural shift in health care delivery. New areas of concentration have emerged, including public health, mental health, and occupational health. Also emerging are new organizations, entities, and professionals who deliver health care services, and new settings in which they work, adding to the complexity of health care in the United States. One mainstay throughout these changes is the position of physician, who provides care in multiple environments. Where such care has been provided in hospitals, those physicians have been governed by medical staff organizations and their bylaws and rules addressing credentials and privileges.

CASE STUDY

You are employed at a hospital that offers community education on matters relating to both patient care and health care administration. You have been asked to present a lecture to the community addressing the variety of health care delivery systems in the United States, including settings and categories of health care professionals. Discuss how you would structure and present such a lecture to a community audience.

REVIEW QUESTIONS

1. How did primitive man attempt to cure disease?

2. What movement swept the health care delivery system at the end of the 19th century?

3. What is the significance of the Flexner Report?

4. Name and identify the purposes of two organizations formed in the mid-19th century to improve health care.

5. What two organizations played the largest roles in the accreditation process in the 20th century?

6. How did the rise of private health insurance impact health care?

7. What is the difference between the Medicare and Medicaid programs?

8. What is the significance of TEFRA?

9. What agencies oversee public health care at the federal level?

10. Name examples of professional associations, voluntary health agencies, philanthropic foundations, and international health agencies.

11. How do the terms *licensing, registration,* and *accreditation* differ?

12. What is the role of a medical staff coordinator?

WEB SITES

American Academy of Physician Assistants, www.aapa.org

American Association of Medical Assistants, www.aama-ntl.org

American College of Health Care Administrators, www.achaca.org

American College of Healthcare Executives, www.ache.org

American College of Pathologists, www.cap.org

American Dental Association, http://www.ada.org

American Health Information Management Association, http://www.ahima.org

American Hospital Association, http://www.aha.org

American Medical Association, http://www.ama-assn.org

American Medical Informatics Association, http://www.amia.org

American Nurses Association, http://www.ana.org

American Osteopathic Association, www.osteopathic.org

American Pharmaceutical Association, www.aphanet.org

Association of American Medical Colleges, http://www.aamc.org

Healthcare Information and Management Systems Society, http://www.himss.org

Joint Commission, http://www.jointcommission.org

National Association of Medical Staff Services, www.namss.org

National Medical Association, www.nmanet.org

REFERENCES

Ackerknecht, E. H. (1982). *A short history of medicine* (4th ed.). Baltimore: Johns Hopkins Press.

Bender, G. (1961). *Great moments in medicine*. Detroit, MI: Parke, Davis & Co.

Ginzberg, E. (1996). *Tomorrow's hospital*. New Haven, CT: Yale University Press.

Grob, G. N. (1983). *Mental illness and American society, 1875–1940*. Princeton, NJ: Princeton University Press.

Lack, R. W. (Ed.). (1996). *Essentials of safety and health management*. Boca Raton, FL: CRC Press.

Mechanic, D. (1983). *Handbook of health, health care, and the health professions*. New York: Macmillan.

Porter, R. (Ed.). (1996). *The Cambridge illustrated history of medicine*. Cambridge, UK: Cambridge University Press.

Raffel, M. W., & Barsukiewicz, C. K. (2002). *The U.S. health system: Origins and functions* (5th ed.). Albany, NY: Delmar.

Rom, W. N. (Ed.). (1998). *Environmental and occupational medicine* (3rd ed.). Philadelphia: Lippincott-Raven.

Seelig, M. G. (1931). *Medicine: An historical outline*. Baltimore: Williams & Wilkins Co.

Valfre, M. M. (2001). *Foundations of mental health care* (2nd ed.). St. Louis, MO: Mosby.

Williams, S. J., & Torrens, P. R. (2002). *Introduction to health services* (6th ed.). Albany, NY: Delmar.

NOTES

1. It is estimated that less than 20 percent of the American population was covered by health insurance before World War II. By the early 1960s, that figure had increased to more than 70 percent of the population. Williams, S. J., & Torrens, P. R. (2002). *Introduction to health services* (6th ed., p. 12). Albany, NY: Delmar.

2. Valfre, M. M. (2001). *Foundations of mental health care* (2nd ed.). St. Louis, MO: Mosby. (Quoting Anderson, K. N. [1998]. *Mosby's medical, nursing, and allied health dictionary* [5th ed.]. St. Louis, MO: Mosby.)

3. Joint Commission on the Accreditation of Healthcare Organizations. (2003). *Comprehensive accreditation manual for hospitals: The official handbook*. Chicago: Author.

4. Ibid.

5. *Dorland's medical dictionary* (27th ed., p. 1291). (1988). Philadelphia: W.B. Saunders & Co.

6. Ibid., p. 446.

7. Ibid., p. 1161.

8. 42 U.S.C. § 799(5) (2007); The Health Professions Education Extension Amendments of 1992.

9. U.S. Department of Labor (1991). *Dictionary of occupational titles* (4th ed.). Washington, DC: U.S. Government Printing Office.

10. *Johnson v. Misericordia Community Hospital*, 294 N.W.2d 501 (Wis. Ct. App. 1980), aff'd 301 N.W.2d 156 (Wis. 1981).

11. The National Practitioner Data Bank was established pursuant to the Health Care Quality Improvement Act of 1986, 42 U.S.C. §§ 11101-11152 (2007) and is governed by regulations issued by the U.S. Department of Health and Human Services, 45 C.F.R.§§ 60.1-.14 (2007).

2

The Health Information Management Profession

CERTIFICATION CONNECTION

RHIA

Facility-wide HIM

HIM best practices

HIM departmental applications

RHIT

Provide consultation, education, and training to users of health information

Provider roles and disciplines

LEARNING OBJECTIVES

After reading this chapter, the learner should be able to:

1. Define the terms *health record* and *health information*.

2. Trace the development of the American Health Information Management Association and its predecessor organizations.

3. List and describe activities of the American Health Information Management Association in the 20th century.

4. Understand the organizational structure of the American Health Information Management Association.

5. Explain the educational and certification requirements of the health information management profession.

6. Identify the change in career roles of the health information management professional from the last half of the 20th century to present day.

7. List and describe the various roles played by the health information management professional in a traditional setting.

8. Explain the role of the health information management professional in selected nontraditional settings.

Outline

Health Information

**Historical Development
of the Profession
Educational and Certification
Requirements**

Careers

**Traditional Settings
Nontraditional Settings**

Key Concepts

Admissions coordinators

American Health
Information
Management
Association

Charge description
master coordinators

Claims examiners

Clinical research
associates

Communities of practice

Component state
associations

Data analysts

Document and
repository manager

Electronic health record

Health care informatics

Health information

Health information
administrator

Health information
department

Health information
department director

Health information
management

Health information
technician

Health insurance
specialists

Health record

Health services
managers

Managed care

Medical library science

Medical office managers

Medical staff
coordinators

Medical transcription

Outsourcing

Privacy Officer

Quality assurance

Quality assurance
coordinators

Risk managers

Security Officer

Tumor registrar

Utilization review

Utilization review
coordinators

Value-added concept

INTRODUCTION

Contemporaneous with each and every health care encounter, the health care professional records what she observed and how she treated the patient. This act of recording detailed information about the patient and her treatment results in the creation of a health record. The body of knowledge required and the practice of managing that record and the data contained within it—all in compliance with regulatory, accrediting, quality, legal, and ethical standards, and with the goal to facilitate health care delivery and decision making for multiple purposes across diverse organizations, settings, and disciplines—constitute health information management (HIM). This chapter introduces the health information management profession and traces its historical development, including establishment of its primary professional association in the United States, the American Health Information Management Association (AHIMA). Attention is focused on the educational requirements and certifications of the profession, its changing nature as evidenced by the explosion of career choices seen in the last few decades, and the opportunities offered to health information managers working in nontraditional settings.

Health Information

The health information management profession is centered around two concepts: the patient's health record and health information. A **health record** is an ordered set of documents, in the paper context, or a collection of data, in an electronic context, that contains a complete and accurate description of a patient's history, condition, diagnostic and therapeutic treatment, and the results of treatment. Other descriptors have been used for the health record, including hospital chart, medical record, outpatient record, clinical record, electronic health record, and computerized patient record. By contrast, **health information** refers to the meaningful data relating to the health of an individual that is created or received in any form or medium by a health care provider, health plan, public health authority, employer, life insurer, school or university, or health care clearinghouse. [1] Health information may be physically housed in or derived from the data found in the health record. A simple way to differentiate between the two concepts is to consider health information to be the content (oral or recorded data) and the health record to be the package, form, medium, or collection of that data. Both concepts have been the focus of the health information management profession since its inception.

Historical Development of the Profession

Patient health records, of one sort or another, have existed for thousands of years, having been found in written materials, papyri, and stone tablets in ancient Egypt. In the early years of the United States, the importance of recording patient clinical data in the form of health records was recognized in such facilities as the Pennsylvania Hospital in Philadelphia, New York Hospital, Charity Hospital in New Orleans, and Massachusetts General in Boston. To the extent that patient clinical data was recorded, it generally could be found in a ledger-style format, with a leather-bound volume used to record whatever data was deemed important. At the beginning of the 20th century, many hospitals determined that minimal ledger entries were insufficient and created individual health records for each patient. Unfortunately, standards for creating and maintaining these records failed to develop at the same time, resulting in wildly inconsistent recordkeeping requirements among hospitals. This inconsistency made the comparison of data found in health records in the earliest years of the 20th century virtually impossible.

Efforts to standardize the patient health record began soon thereafter, resulting in the development of professional groups. In 1912, a group of five women serving as record clerks at leading Boston hospitals formed the Club of Record Clerks to study and evaluate standards for clinical records, with the concept that better documentation would result in enhanced patient care. Groups with similar missions also formed in other parts of the country. Formation of the Association of Record Librarians shortly thereafter constituted the first effort at an association beyond the local level. This association was not truly national in character but rather a nucleus with which smaller groups could associate.

The movement for standardization of hospital care also influenced the standardization of the patient health record and the organization of the health information management profession. The Minimum Standards document issued by the American College of Surgeons (ACS) in 1919 included requirements for the creation of a written health record for every patient. Prominent ACS physicians, including Dr. Franklin Martin and Dr. Malcolm MacEachern, encouraged inclusion of subjects pertaining to the health record at annual hospital standardization conferences and encouraged workers in the health record field to organize. By 1928, sufficient interest existed to organize a meeting devoted to issues relating to health record content, availability, and presentation. From this meeting, a new group emerged at the national level called the Association of Record Librarians of North America (ARLNA), with Grace Whiting Myers elected as president. ARLNA's main objectives were to elevate the standards of clinical records, serve as a means of communication among health record practitioners, encourage training among practitioners, and help those with the least experience in the profession.

ARLNA moved rapidly to meet those objectives in several ways. The Bulletin of the Association of Record Librarians of North America debuted as a method to provide education and communication among members. ARLNA members wrote a certification exam resulting in the granting of the Registered Record Librarian (RRL) credential. ARLNA required hospitals that provided training to submit course curricula to ensure that the training corresponded with ARLNA's educational goals. ARLNA continued to hold annual meetings on topics of interest to its members,

focusing on learning new methods and advances in medical science. By 1938 ARLNA had changed its name to the American Association of Medical Record Librarians (AAMRL) and began formal affiliations with state and local organizations.

During the next few decades, AAMRL focused its efforts on improving educational programs. It developed uniform standards for the curriculum of medical record librarians and collaborated with the American Medical Association (AMA) to accredit educational programs in the field. In recognition of a shortage of graduates to meet the needs of hospitals, AAMRL approved the development of a second level of personnel in the field, called the medical record technician, and granted the Accredited Record Technician (ART) credential to students who wrote a successful examination. Additionally, AAMRL changed its name in 1970 to the American Medical Record Association (AMRA) and dropped the title medical record librarian in favor of the title medical record administrator and the credential Registered Record Administrator (RRA).

During the next few decades, multiple changes occurred in the health care industry relating to the reimbursement of health care costs, the emergence of the managed care industry, and the introduction of new technologies. In particular, the emergence of the accreditation movement and increased governmental regulation resulted in standardization of health record content. These same changes also altered the role of the medical record administrator, moving from one of recordkeeping to one of managing the data contained within the record. In recognition of this change, AMRA changed its name to the **American Health Information Management Association** (AHIMA) in 1991. The evolution of this name change is illustrated in Figure 2–1. AHIMA eventually changed the credentials it awarded to Registered Health Information Administrator (RHIA) and Registered Health Information Technician (RHIT) and collaborated with several health-related organizations to create a new accrediting body titled the Council on Accreditation of Allied Health Education Programs (CAAHEP). AHIMA later changed to a new accrediting body, the Commission on Accreditation for Health Informatics and Information Management Education (CAHIIM).

Figure 2–1 | Evolution of AHIMA

1928	1938	1970	1991
Association of Record Librarians of North America (ARLNA) organized	American Association of Medical Record Librarians (AAMRL)	American Medical Record Association (AMRA)	American Health Information Management Association (AHIMA)

During the same time period, the profession experienced rapid growth. In the 21st century, AHIMA has over 50,000 members and issues several credentials beyond those of RHIA and RHIT. Credentials recognize specialties in coding, security, and privacy. In each instance, these credentials may be held in addition to the RHIA or RHIT credential.

AHIMA continues the tradition of accrediting educational programs and promulgating new curriculum standards. AHIMA also provides opportunities for lifelong learning through workshops and other offerings to meet continuing education requirements. With its Foundation of Research and Education (FORE), AHIMA works to foster and recognize innovations, advancements, and excellence in the field through research, education, and public awareness initiatives.

AHIMA's public awareness efforts also take another form, that of advocacy in support of defined causes. AHIMA engages in advocacy through a number of means, including testifying before governmental entities, commenting on pending regulatory matters, and issuing position statements on a broad range of public policy issues. Through advocacy, AHIMA attempts to influence the legislative branch in creation of statutes and the executive branch in development of implementing regulations to those statutes. The nation's health care system is affected on a regular basis by new legislation and regulations promulgated by various governmental bodies. These laws and regulations are often created in a vacuum, since many of those in government service do not have personal experience working in a health care facility. As such, some laws and regulations are less effective than they otherwise would be. AHIMA responds to this by lobbying— an obligation to play a role in the future of the profession.

AHIMA has initiated strategic alliances with organizations possessing similar interests, with the goals of building relationships and sharing information. For example, AHIMA has worked actively with a prominent medical technology organization, the Healthcare Information and Management Systems Society (HIMSS) and a prominent medical informatics organization, the American Medical Informatics Association (AMIA), to educate professionals and the public regarding the use of health information. AHIMA has also established relationships with organizations such as the Canadian Health Information Management Association (CHIMA) and the International Federation of Health Records Organizations (IFHRO), both of which are committed to improving the quality of health care through excellence in health information management.

AHIMA also offers support to its membership through two networking processes. The first, **Component state associations** (CSAs), are health information management associations located in every state, Washington, D.C., and Puerto Rico. CSAs provide leadership, networking, and professional education opportunities at the state level for

Table 2–1	Educational Programs and Certification Levels in HIM	
Education	**Credential**
High school diploma and job experience	CCA, CCS, CCS-P
Associate's degree	RHIT
Bachelor's degree	RHIA
Master's degree	FAHIMA

AHIMA members. The CSAs and AHIMA have a symbiotic relationship, communicating and sharing information on matters of importance at both the state and national levels. AHIMA also manages a Web-based program that provides a virtual network for members who share common interests. Called the **communities of practice** (CoP), this network allows members with similar interests and backgrounds to contact one another to share best practices, offer support and advice, and problem solve.

AHIMA accomplishes all of these many activities through an organizational structure that includes both volunteer leaders and managerial staff. The volunteer leadership consists of members who serve on the board of directors, the Councils on Certification and Accreditation, and committees with targeted focuses such as professional development, coding policy and strategy, and bylaws. A House of Delegates serves as the legislative body of AHIMA. Among its many duties, the House of Delegates approves resolutions and professional standards and advises the board of directors. The managerial staff includes an executive director responsible for the management of day-to-day operations, along with managers and staff assigned to separate divisions and departments such as certification, accreditation and education, and professional practice.

Educational and Certification Requirements

The changes that took place in the professional association also reflected changes in the profession of health information management. The increased needs for patient data, the correlation between health information and reimbursement, and the regulatory environment of health care in the United States have resulted in rapid growth of the profession. This rapid growth led to a refinement of educational programs and the development of a preprofessional program in health information management. The educational programs and the certification levels that are tied to them are illustrated in Table 2–1.

Health information management focuses on health data, whether in the form of paper-based records or the form of computer applications such as electronic clinical data repositories and electronic health record systems. The focus on health data addresses both the systems and processes for collecting, validating, and disseminating this data. Concerns over core principles such as the quality, privacy, and security of this data, its compilation and analysis, and its use in clinical quality assessment and improvement are of paramount importance. Those who work in this field must be knowledgeable about health data content, structure and standards, work-flow management, clinical classification systems, statistics, information technology, medical sciences, reimbursement systems, legal requirements, ethical standards, and organization and management. The functional aspects of this knowledge are illustrated in Figure 2–2. This combination of knowledge separates health information management from other fields.

E-HIM

The focus of E-HIM is electronic health data and the manner in which it is collected, validated, stored, and disseminated.

The educational and certification requirements of the discipline vary according to the complexity of the work performed. At the preprofessional level, a high school diploma combined with different levels of coding experience or formal training qualifies an applicant for any of three different coding credentials. In addition to performing the work processes specific to their credential, those who hold a preprofessional certification must comply with established data quality principles, legal and regulatory standards, and preprofessional best practice guidelines.

The credential designed for entry-level coding individuals who have coding training but lack significant job experience is the Certified Coding Associate (CCA). Six months of on-the-job experience, or completion of an AHIMA-approved coding program or other formal training, is required to take the examination and receive this credential. Those who hold the CCA credential should be able to perform basic coding, billing, and abstracting functions in a health care facility. Job titles held by persons with this credential include coding associate, coder, medical record analyst, and health data analyst.

By contrast, three years of on-the-job experience and formal coding education are recommended to take the Certified Coding Specialist examination and receive the CCS credential. This credential is designed for those individuals who hold a broader and deeper coding knowledge than the CCA and work in hospital inpatient and outpatient settings. Those who hold the CCS credential should be able to review patient records and assign numeric codes for each diagnosis and procedure, and serve in their organizations' compliance and training efforts. Job titles held by persons with this credential include health record coding analyst, medical coding specialist, health data analyst, and coding compliance specialist.

A third preprofessional credential is the Certified Coding Specialist-Physician Based (CCS-P). Although it has similar requirements to those for the CCS credential, it differs in that the individuals holding the CCS-P credential possess and demonstrate through an examination expertise in physician-based

Figure 2–2 | HIM functional knowledge

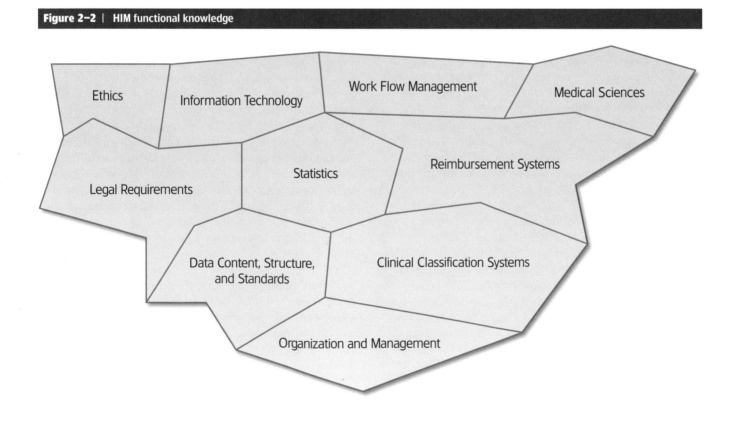

Ethics

Information Technology

Work Flow Management

Medical Sciences

Legal Requirements

Statistics

Reimbursement Systems

Data Content, Structure, and Standards

Clinical Classification Systems

Organization and Management

settings, particularly as that expertise relates to the CPT and HCPCS classification systems. Similar job duties and titles are held, with emphasis on the documentation, data integrity, quality, and reimbursement of physician services.

At the professional level, two categories of health information management exist: health information administrator and health information technician. Individuals in both categories manage individual and aggregate patient and health care data and information resources in all types of health care organizations and settings. As a general matter, a health information administrator focuses on managing computer-based or paper-based record systems and ensuring compliance with external and internal standards relating to health records and information. Health information administrators are responsible for collecting, interpreting, and analyzing patient health data in settings across the continuum of care. A health information technician focuses on completeness, accuracy, and proper entry of data, using computer applications to improve patient care and control health care costs. Health information technicians can also be found in settings across the continuum of care. Health information administrators graduate from a baccalaureate degree program; health information managers graduate from an associate degree program. Both must pass a national registry examination before receiving their respective credentials, Registered Health Information Administrator (RHIA) or Registered Health Information Technician (RHIT). The role competencies for both categories, as established by AHIMA, are listed in Table 2–2 and Table 2–3.

Although the progression stated here would indicate that these credentials are not shared by a single individual, that is not always the case. Those who have earned their RHIA and RHIT credentials are knowledgeable about coding and other competencies. They may also choose to earn the CCS or CCS-P credential to demonstrate a mastery level of coding skills.

HIPAA

New requirements mandated by HIPAA influenced AHIMA to create new credentials to address expertise in health care privacy and security.

Several other credentials are also available to health information professionals. With the introduction of standards for transactions, privacy, and security issued pursuant to the Health Insurance Portability and Accountability Act (HIPAA) and their effect upon the health information management profession, AHIMA created new credentials, including Certified in Healthcare Privacy (CHP), Certified in Healthcare Security (CHS), and Certified in Healthcare Privacy and Security (CHPS). These credentials denote a mastery level of competency in health care privacy and security management. One must meet certain eligibility requirements and complete an examination to attain any of these credentials.

Educational opportunities also exist at the graduate level in health information management. Those who complete a master's-level degree in health information management often

Table 2–2 | Role Competencies and Domains of Registered Health Information Administrators	
Health Data Management	• Health data structure, content, and standards
	• Health care information requirement and standards
	• Clinical classification systems
	• Reimbursement methodologies
Health Services Organization and Delivery	• Health care delivery systems
	• Health care privacy, confidentiality, legal, and ethical issues
Information Technology and Systems	• Information and communication technologies
	• Data, information, and file structure
	• Data storage and retrieval
	• Data security
	• Health care information systems
Organization and Management	• Human resources management
	• Financial and resource management
	• Strategic planning and organizational development
	• Project and operations management
Health Statistics, Biomedical Research, and Quality Management	• Health care statistics and research
	• Quality management and performance improvement

Source: Information adapted from American Health Information Management Association. (2006). *Role competencies for bachelor degrees and associate degrees.* **Available at http://www.ahima.org.**

Table 2–3 | Role Competencies and Domains of Registered Health Information Technicians

Health Data Management	• Health data structure, content, and standards
	• Health information requirements and standards
	• Clinical classification systems
	• Reimbursement methodologies
Health Statistics, Biomedical Research, and Quality Management	• Health care statistics and research
	• Quality assessment and performance improvement
Health Services Organization and Delivery	• Health care delivery systems
	• Health care compliance, confidentiality, ethical, legal, and privacy issues
Information Technology and Systems	• Information and communication technologies
	• Data, information, and file structures
	• Data, storage, and retrieval
	• Data security
	• Health care information systems
Organizational Resource	• Human resources
	• Financial and physical resources

Source: Information adapted from American Health Information Management Association. (2006). *Role competencies for bachelor degrees and associate degrees.* Available at http://www.ahima.org.

work in executive-level positions engaging in administrative, research, and education or in consulting activities dealing with data and information resources. Graduate education is not confined to health information management; one may pursue graduate degrees in such related areas as business administration, health/hospital administration, management and decision sciences, public health, social work, health care informatics, medical library science, and law. Those professionals who possess at minimum a graduate degree, 10 years of full-time professional experience, 10 years of continuous membership, and evidence of sustained and substantial professional achievement are eligible to apply for the credential, Fellow of the American Health Information Management Association (FAHIMA).

While the levels of education may vary, one element common to many of the programs is the professional practice experience. Sometimes referred to as practicums or externships, these opportunities provide a student with nonpaid, on-the-job experience prior to graduation. Placement is made with health care organizations and facilities, and work assignments are designed to build upon theory learned in the formal education process. Students are evaluated by those within the health care organization or facility assigned to supervise them, and feedback is provided to the educational institution the student attends. Many times the professional practice experience will assist the student in defining the direction of her future career and obtaining employment immediately following graduation.

As stated previously, the health information management field possesses a uniqueness that distinguishes it from

other disciplines, including the discipline of medical library science. In **medical library science**, the focus is on published data and how it is catalogued, abstracted, and retrieved by groups and individuals. In essence, medical library science concentrates on information-seeking behavior. By contrast, health information management concentrates on the privacy and security of patient-derived data, with disclosure of that data strictly regulated.

INFORMATICS

Health care informatics differs from health information management in that informatics focuses primarily on the use of technology to support data whereas HIM focuses primarily on the quality of the data itself.

Though it is closely related, health information management also differs from the discipline of health care informatics. The focus on health care data in HIM differentiates it from **health care informatics**, which focuses on studying both the structure and general properties of information and the design and implementation of technology to use and communicate that information. As such, health care informatics focuses on how to use technology to facilitate acquiring, processing, interpreting, using, and communicating health care data. By contrast, health information management concentrates on managing the quality of the data itself, with the technology used to store and retrieve the data seen as an aid. Over the last decade, these two fields have reached some level of commonality as the emphasis in health information management has moved to address more strongly the data analytics, content, structure, and standards as a result of implementation of the electronic health record. As such, some commentators have begun to refer to health information management professionals as applied clinical informatics specialists and the field of health information management to health informatics.

Careers

As discussed in further detail in Chapter 1, "Health Care Delivery Systems," changes in science have significantly impacted the health care field during the last century. Advances in public health areas such as sanitation and vaccinations, coupled with developments of new medicines and treatment modalities, have increased life expectancy and improved the overall health of the United States' population. Enormous technological changes have taken place as well, as seen by the proliferation of the use of electronic mail (e-mail) in patient care, the development of databases and networked systems, the delivery of information through the Internet, and the introduction of telemedicine. These changes and others have significantly impacted health care professionals.

Health information management professionals are no exception, finding that the roles traditionally assumed by them are also undergoing transition. Professionals involved with health information traditionally worked in an acute care setting, literally in a hospital's record room. The focus was on such roles as department manager, transcription supervisor, coder, statistics collector, and tumor registrar, among others. These roles emphasized practices related to the physical aspect of the health record (i.e., maintaining complete and accurate content of the record in an orderly manner) and, to a lesser extent, upon the data contained within reports and notes in the record (i.e., compiling cross-indices of diseases, operations, and physicians). Work did not generally extend beyond the confines of the department, and when it did, it focused mainly on the physical aspect—for example, record tracking and transportation to different parts of the hospital or off-campus offices.

During the 1970s, requirements were developed under the Medicare reimbursement rules and the Professional Standards Review Organizations (PSRO) to include quality assurance and utilization review activities in health care facilities. **Quality assurance** refers to those actions taken to establish, protect, promote, and improve the quality of health care. **Utilization review** refers to the process of comparing preestablished criteria against the health care provided to the patient to determine whether that care is necessary. Both functions involve collection and review of patient-specific data ordinarily contained within the health record. HIM professionals quickly expanded into both of these areas. Overall, the practice focus still rested on tasks

associated with record control, such as quantitative analysis, forms control, and record tracking, retrieval, and storage.

During the 1980s, the business aspect of health care gained emphasis. In 1983, the federal government introduced the Prospective Payment System (PPS) for reimbursement of inpatient hospital services for Medicare patients. As a result of this development, HIM professionals were increasingly focused on the connection between the coding of health data and financial reimbursement. Accordingly, health information professionals increased their regular interaction with other health care and business professionals, leading to roles such as diagnosis-related group (DRG) coordinator and to a higher professional profile.

This increased interaction led many in health care to apply the value-added concept to the work of the health information management professional. The **value-added concept** states that the unique contribution of an activity is measured by the difference between the original component materials and the finished work product. In this context, the work performed by the health information management professional to analyze data and code it appropriately for reimbursement purposes results in an added value to the health care organization.

Even more rapid change in health care occurred in the 1990s with the emergence of the managed care industry. **Managed care** refers to health plans that integrate fully the financial and delivery aspects of health care. Begun as an alternative delivery system designed to contain costs, managed care has emerged as a significant force within the health care industry. Because of the increasing emphasis on cost containment, new roles such as reimbursement specialist emerged for health information management professionals.

The early years of the 21st century also portend changes for the profession. The ramifications of changes brought about by the implementation of the Health Insurance Portability and Accountability Act (HIPAA) are extensive, as traditional areas of health information management, such as privacy and security, have received heightened consideration. Efforts to combat health care fraud and abuse have focused attention on the health information manager's role in documentation and reimbursement. Developments in technology and computer applications will expand the ability to manipulate data even more than can be manipulated today. In response to these developments, new roles such as Privacy Officer, Security Officer, and Compliance Officer are being created and filled by health information management professionals.

Today's environment requires new skills for new roles. The focus has changed from records management to include data manipulation and information management. The introduction of technology, including the transition to the electronic health record, has prompted health information management professionals to develop skills in maintaining data dictionaries, creating data models, analyzing data using sophisticated electronic tools, and ensuring data security and quality. These developments and more have brought about changes in existing roles and the emergence of new roles.

In an effort to assist its membership to prepare for changing and emerging roles, AHIMA developed a strategy it called Vision 2006. This effort capitalized on the information revolution that was evolving in the health care community and resulted in the identification of new roles. Those roles are listed in Figure 2–3.

Developments that have occurred since the creation of Vision 2006 in 1996 have proven the accuracy of this strategic blueprint, with most of the roles envisioned coming about. For example, the role of information security manager identified in Vision 2006 can be viewed in relation to the Security Officer position created pursuant to HIPAA. Both positions deal with protecting and securing *electronic* patient information. Furthermore, the Privacy Officer position required under HIPAA relates to the information security manager position in that supervision

of *all* protected health information, whether or not it is created and maintained in electronic form, is the purview of the Privacy Officer.

Rapid changes, particularly as they relate to technology, have prompted AHIMA to engage in further strategic analysis, resulting in the electronic health information management (e-HIM) initiative. This initiative articulates a vision of the future state of health information management, identifies roles that health information management professionals will play, and creates a strategic plan to bridge existing HIM functions into an e-HIM future. Specifically, it serves to: (1) promote the transition from a paper-based to an electronic health information infrastructure; (2) reinvent the manner in which institutional and personal health information is managed; and (3) deliver measurable cost and quality results from improved information management.[2] It recognizes the need to advance health information management practices so that standards-based technology may be fully utilized. In doing so, the profession of health information management may itself be advanced and transformed. The future roles envisioned in this initiative are listed in Table 2–4.

Figure 2–3 | Interrelationship of vision 2006 roles

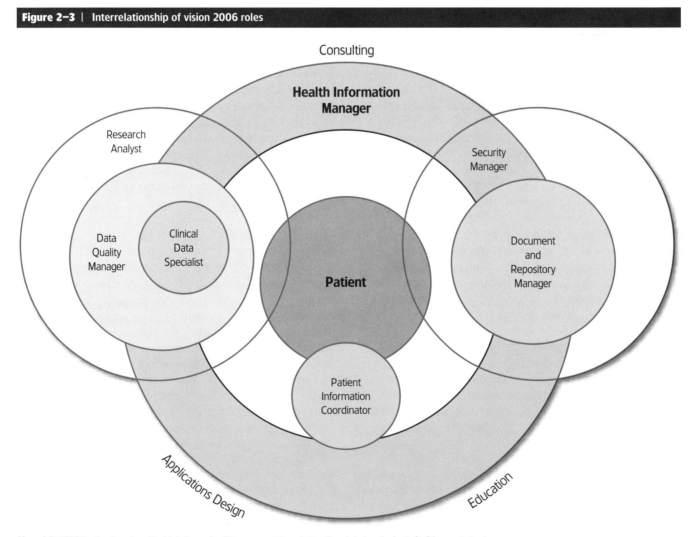

Table 2–4	Future HIM Roles
Business process engineer
Clinical research protocol designer and manager
Clinical trials manager
Clinical vocabulary manager
Consumer advocate
Data analyst
Data facilitator
Data/information broker
Data/information presenter
Data sets, nomenclature, and classification standards developer
Data miner
Data navigator
Data quality and integrity monitor
Data resource manager
Data security, privacy, and confidentiality manager
Data translator
Information system designer
Work and data flow analyst

Source: Information compiled from the E-HIM Task Force. (2003). *A vision of the e-HIM future: A report from the AHIMA e-HIM task force.* Chicago: American Health Information Management Association.

As a result of the changes brought by efforts to implement the electronic health record, AHIMA joined with AMIA, academicians, government officers, and the vendor community to address the need to create a workforce that could support this change. This group published a document entitled *Building the Work Force for Health Information Transformation,* which described the need to educate two existing populations in the health care workforce: those who work as specialists in health information and those who use information technology to support the delivery of patient care. The group formalized an action agenda designed to address the needs of both populations, raise awareness of the need for new members of the workforce, and improve health care educational programs to include information technology. Such undertakings complemented AHIMA's activities concerning the electronic health record.

Traditional Settings

Health information managers who work in traditional settings often are members of a **health information department**. This department is responsible for managing appropriate use of and access to patient-specific health information. This management may involve several services, including record documentation assembly and analysis; release of information functions; coding and reimbursement functions; statistical compilation and presentation; transcription; image processing; and record retention and destruction functions. Other services often located within or closely aligned to the department include quality assurance, performance improvement, cancer/tumor registry, medical staff coordination, and admissions.

The administrative functions of health information departments are directed by a **health information department director**, who may be a Registered Health Information Administrator (RHIA) or a Registered Health Information Technician (RHIT). This director is responsible for the traditional managerial functions associated with running a department, such as planning, organizing, directing, controlling, and leading, along with addressing the human resources, budgeting, and information technology concerns of the department. The focus of these functions is the health information itself, whether it exists in patient-specific form or in the aggregate. The director is responsible for developing, monitoring, and improving systems, policies, and procedures related to this information. The director participates in the organization's accreditation process and its various committees, including the health records, quality improvement, and utilization review committees. The director monitors trends in health care delivery to determine which trends should be incorporated into practice and monitors changes in legislation and accrediting standards so that compliance can be achieved. By engaging in these activities, the department director furthers the organization's aim to enhance the delivery of patient care.

Within the department, a number of roles exist for health information management professionals. Some serve as **data analysts**, responsible for analyzing records and data quantitatively and qualitatively. Some act as the **document and repository manager**, responsible for ensuring long-term data integrity and access through the development of retention policies and procedures, determination of appropriate media for data and record storage, and maintenance of data control inventories. Some possess responsibility for statistical functions, using their skills at statistical analysis to further the organization's mission and support research design, survey design, and epidemiology. Some are responsible for the coding function, applying principles of classification systems to such health data as diagnoses, procedures, and services. This often ties into responsibility for the reimbursement function, because coded data are used to support reimbursement (e.g., assignment of DRGs). Some are responsible for the release of information function, processing external requests for information, including subpoenas and court orders, and acting as the organization's representative at depositions and in court. Still others are responsible for records processing activities or assisting physicians with patient record completion.

A significant area of responsibility for many health information management professionals is medical transcription. **Medical transcription** refers to the act of transcribing prerecorded dictation to create medical reports, correspondence, and other administrative material. These medical reports vary by type, and may include histories and physicals, radiology reports, discharge summaries, and operative reports, among others. These reports become part of the patient's health record upon authentication (review, correction if needed, and signature) by the individual whose dictation is transcribed. The HIM professional in this context implements and maintains a transcription system designed to achieve optimal quality and quantity standards, applies digital dictation techniques, and supervises staff dedicated to this function.

HIPAA

The use of outsourcing to complete medical transcription implicates the standards of HIPAA's Security Rule.

In some instances, the staff dedicated to this function performs its work offshore, typically overseas; this is the result of a trend that focuses on employing outsourcing practices in health care. **Outsourcing** refers to the delegation of non-core operations from internal production of a business to an external entity that specializes in an operation. Wide variance exists across the United States in the use of outsourcing as a means to transcribe physician dictation remotely. Where it is used, the HIM professional faces challenges to not only supervise these workers but also ensure compliance with the standards imposed by the Security Rule promulgated pursuant to HIPAA. This Rule imposes standards that specify use of integrity controls and encryption technology when transmitting protected health information (PHI) electronically. Because physician dictation by definition includes PHI, it is incumbent upon the HIM professional, and the health care organization itself, to ensure that contracting documents specify and actual implementation employs these controls and technology.

HIPAA

Regulations implementing HIPAA require covered entities to identify individuals who are responsible for developing and implementing policies and procedures governing privacy and security.

With the enactment of HIPAA and the promulgation of implementing regulations, two new roles have emerged: the Privacy Officer and the Security Officer. A **Privacy Officer** develops and implements policies and procedures relating to the HIPAA Privacy Rule and serves as the covered entity's point of contact to receive complaints, while also disseminating information about the entity's privacy practices. A **Security Officer** serves in a similar role, developing and implementing policies and procedures relating to the HIPAA

Security Rule and held accountable for a covered entity's security procedures. The unique combination of knowledge gained through education and derived from professional experience positions the HIM professional particularly well to serve in either or both roles.

Tumor registry often plays a prominent role in health information management, whether as part of the HIM department or as a closely aligned area within the organization. A **tumor registrar** identifies, collects, and maintains information about tumors (neoplasms), including cancer, diagnosed or treated by an organization. The tumor registrar utilizes computer databases and generates statistics and graphs as part of her work. The tumor registrar also disseminates this information to federal, state, and local governmental entities and accrediting organizations according to applicable laws, regulations, and guidelines. Tumor registrars often participate in research studies that track longitudinal data and utilize the tumor registry data system. Many tumor registrars obtain the credential of Certified Tumor Registrar (CTR) after receiving a combination of formal education and experience in the tumor registry profession. The CTR credential is administered by the National Cancer Registrars Association (NCRA). The role of the tumor registrar has seen considerable growth since passage of the Cancer Registries Amendment Act of 1992.[3] This act authorized the Centers for Disease Control and Prevention (CDC) to fund cancer registries at the state and territorial levels; set standards for data completeness, timeliness, and quality; and establish a computer-based reporting and data processing system.

E-HIM

HIM professionals are frequently involved in both the design and implementation stages of an electronic health record.

Among the most significant responsibilities of a health information management professional is the transition to and operation of an electronic health record. An **electronic health record** (EHR) is a record that resides in an electronic system specifically designed to support users by providing accessibility to complete and accurate data, alerts, reminders, clinical decision support systems, links to medical knowledge, and other aids. HIM professionals who are involved in the early stages of an EHR may work under different position titles but are frequently responsible for developing, implementing, and evaluating health record areas; related data collection/storage systems that compose an EHR; and the training aids, instructional guides, and policies and procedures to support the EHR. Once an EHR is implemented, HIM professionals work to plan and manage system-wide changes and innovations, ensure operational standards are met, and adjust operating programs, instructional guides, training aids, policies, and procedures as needed.

A number of other roles exist that closely align with the knowledge, skills, and abilities possessed by health information management professionals. **Utilization review coordinators** compare preestablished criteria against the health care provided to the patient to determine whether that care is necessary and communicate those results through narrative and graphical reports. **Quality assurance coordinators** measure and assess the quality of clinical and patient-care services and offer recommendations for improvement. **Admissions coordinators** direct the patient registration functions, setting guidelines for preregistration and registration of patients and managing the computerized registration process. **Medical staff coordinators** direct the credentialing process of physicians and allied health staff of an organization. **Risk managers** act to reduce medical, financial, and legal risk to an organization through investigation, analysis, and recommendations for corrective action. **Clinical research associates** assist in the design, implementation, and monitoring of clinical research studies, including the design of data collection instruments and preparation of reports concerning study findings. **Health insurance specialists**, sometimes referred to as **claims examiners**, review health care claims for medical necessity and reasonableness of costs. **Charge description master** (CDM) **coordinators** oversee the coding and claims processing functions associated with revenue cycle management. **Health services managers** coordinate the delivery of health care, whether on a departmental or organization-wide basis. **Medical office managers** coordinate the activities of a health care provider's office, including the health information, personnel, finance, insurance, and risk management functions.

Nontraditional Settings

Opportunities for health information managers exist in multiple settings, as illustrated by Table 2–5. Changes occurring in the health care industry indicate the profession's need to look beyond traditional settings to broader horizons. To that end, a select number of nontraditional settings are discussed here, including those settings that involve direct patient care and those that do not. Emphasis is placed on the role played by the health information manager in these nontraditional settings.

Direct Patient Care Settings Nontraditional settings involving direct patient care vary considerably, whether that variation is measured by the requirements of regulatory bodies, the influence of governmental entities, the role of third-party payers, or the manner in which care is delivered. In all of these settings, however, the delivery of patient care generates patient-specific health information that must be managed, implicating directly the profession of health information management. The following nontraditional settings offer opportunities for the health information management professional to strike a balance between a traditional role and a more expansive role.

In a correctional facility, health care is delivered to inmates either by medical staff who are employed by the

Table 2–5 | HIM Employment Settings

Accreditation agencies
Consulting firms
Correctional facilities
Data standards organizations
Durable medical equipment companies
Educational organizations
Governmental agencies
Governmental contractors involved with reimbursement
Hospital inpatient/acute care settings
Hospital outpatient/ambulatory care settings
Home health agencies
Hospice organizations
Information system companies
Insurance companies
Laboratories
Law firms
Managed care organizations
Medical billing companies
Mental retardation/developmentally disabled agencies and mental health agencies
Peer review organizations
Pharmaceutical companies
Physician practices
Professional associations
Rehabilitation hospitals
Research organizations
Skilled nursing facilities
Software/technology vendors

governmental agency operating the facility or by private firms under contract to the agency. Typically, mental health, dental, and clinical services are provided to inmates. The roles and responsibilities of a health information manager in a correctional health care setting are similar to those faced by the professional in a traditional setting. Many traditional functions, such as record management, retention, and destruction, along with data collection, storage, and management, are involved. Data are converted into statistical information for routine reporting to a variety of organizations and governmental agencies interested in the welfare and management of an inmate population. In addition, clinical research studies sometimes involve inmate populations, providing the health information manager with the opportunity to ensure proper techniques for collection and use of data. One significant difference is that the HIM professional's involvement with the judicial process is higher here than in a traditional setting, because the level of litigation found in a correctional setting is quite extensive and usually requires the HIM professional to respond to numerous subpoenas and court orders. A second difference is the reduced influence of third-party payers; health care delivered in a correctional setting is often taxpayer supported and not subject to reimbursement by third parties.

In a veterinary setting, health care is delivered to animals, both domestic and wild, by caregivers with specialized training such as veterinarians, veterinary technicians, and veterinary technologists. Typically, clinical, dental, and surgical services are provided. The roles and responsibilities of a health information manager in this setting are similar to those settings involving human health records, with the exception of fewer layers of governmental regulations and third-party payer requirements. The health information manager must be aware of documentation requirements established under state law and accrediting agency standards along with three specialized classification systems: the Standard Nomenclature of Veterinary Disease and Operations (SNVDO), the Systematized Nomenclature of Medicine, Clinical Terms (SNOMED-CT), and the Systematized Nomenclature of Human and Veterinary Medicine (SNOMED International). Furthermore, it is important for those individuals working in veterinary teaching hospitals to be aware of the data sets used to satisfy the reporting requirements of the Veterinary Medical Database (VMDB), a database designed to collect data on various forms of cancer in animals. Finally, the HIM professional should be aware of the distinction between the patient and the client in terms of ownership of health information. In a veterinary setting, the patient is the animal who receives health care and the client is the animal's owner. It is the client, not the patient, who possesses an ownership interest in the patient's health information in a veterinary setting. Accordingly, it is the client who possesses rights and obligations concerning informed consent, release of information, and judicial process. A professional organization dedicated to supporting HIM professionals in a veterinary setting is the American Veterinary Health Information Management Association (AVHIMA).

In a home health setting, health care is delivered to a recovering, disabled, or chronically ill person in the home environment by caregivers as diverse as nurses, physical therapists, speech therapists, respiratory therapists, occupational therapists, medical social workers, and nutritionists. Typical services may be either medical or nonmedical. The roles and responsibilities of the health information manager in this setting are similar to those in an acute care environment, since home health settings are subject to government regulation, accrediting standards, and third-party payer requirements. Because of the mobility involved in the delivery of care, many home health agencies are moving toward the use of technologies such as

laptop computers and personal digital assistants (PDAs). This movement toward fuller use of technology focuses the health information manager's attention to a large degree on issues such as security, privacy, and confidentiality of patient data. The HIM professional's attention is also focused on reimbursement, particularly as it relates to Medicare's Home Health Prospective Payment System and the use of Home Health Resource Groups (HHRGs). Furthermore, management of health information in a home health setting requires knowledge of the data elements of the Outcome and Assessment Information Set (OASIS) used for Medicare reporting.

Consulting is a nontraditional role that may involve health care settings where direct patient care is involved and settings where it is not. Consulting plays a role in the full spectrum of health care settings, from acute care hospitals to ambulatory care centers to medical offices to nursing homes. Consulting may also be performed for the corporate offices of health care organizations, third-party billing companies, governmental agencies, and technology vendors. The expertise a health information management professional brings to consulting is the broad knowledge base of biomedical science, computerized databases, records management, and legal/accrediting/regulatory requirements governing health information. The roles and responsibilities vary according to the client's needs and assignment of work. For example, an HIM consultant may assist an acute care hospital with developing and implementing its HIPAA compliance plan; assessing coding and billing practices; auditing documentation to determine performance measures; planning and implementing an electronic health record system; leading process improvement activities; or ensuring sound practices are employed by the medical staff coordinator in the medical staff credentialing process. Similar activities dealing with reimbursement and compliance may be performed in other patient care settings, such as nursing homes, rehabilitation centers, and ambulatory care centers.

Settings Not Involving Direct Patient Care   Similar to non-traditional settings that involve patient care, nontraditional settings that do *not* involve direct patient care vary considerably. These settings offer health information management professionals the opportunity to expand their horizons, utilize their areas of expertise, and develop new skills.

In a software development company, health care is not delivered to patients directly. Rather, the company works to develop products for use by health care providers and organizations that deliver patient care. Products familiar to the health information manager may include document imaging systems and an electronic health record system. The roles and responsibilities of the health information manager in this setting work to ensure that the direction taken in product development aligns with the solution needed in the health care market. For example, the health information manager may develop functional requirements for the software product, test the product for defects prior to release, market the product to end users, or provide ongoing support following implementation.

Similar to software development, pharmaceutical sales does not involve direct patient contact. Rather, the pharmaceutical salesperson interacts with health care providers and organizations that use pharmaceutical products to improve patient health. The roles and responsibilities of the health information manager are to contact health care professionals, present a patient profile for applicability of individual prescription drugs, and influence the health care provider's choice of those prescription drugs. The actions associated with these roles and responsibilities call on the health information manager's knowledge of medical science, business structure, statistical analysis, and professionalism skills to be successful.

While attention is often given to pharmaceutical sales, other sales opportunities abound. Vendor products respond to a variety of needs within the health care arena, and each of these products requires salespersons who understand the underlying business in order to be successful. The roles and responsibilities may vary, with career ladders advancing to marketing managers, customer managers, and corporate account managers.

A relatively new area of involvement for HIM professionals is employment in regional health information organizations (RHIO). Because HIM professionals understand health care data content and structure and are versed in both database management and the legal implications of sharing data, a natural progression in career development is association with a health data exchange network, commonly referred to as a RHIO. The operational understanding many HIM professionals possess of the variety of health care facilities and providers who participate in these networks gives them advantages in the design and implementation of the RHIO. Because RHIOs are a relatively new development in health care, opportunities abound for participation by HIM professionals. Additional information concerning RHIOs can be found in Chapter 8, "Database Management."

Another relatively new area involves clinical data representation, an area that allows the health information management professional to employ knowledge of classification systems and vocabularies in the mapping process. Clinical data representation differs from coding in that it is not based on a clinical encounter; mapping is the process of linking terminology between two different schemes (e.g., SNOMED-CT to ICD-9-CM). HIM professionals who have engaged in this activity are in great demand, because the electronic storage and mining of data require a thorough understanding of not only classification systems and vocabularies but data standards and information infrastructure activities. Each of these requirements falls within the educational competencies AHIMA has prescribed for health information management professionals.

One area that is similar to health information management is court administration. Just as in health care, where every patient encounter results in the creation of a record, each lawsuit requires the creation of a court record. Similarly, the data and information contained in that record require management. Two important differences exist, however. In court administration, the record is presumed public with very little, if any, information held confidential; the exact opposite presumption applies in the health care context. Furthermore, knowledge of legal processes and terms is required for court administration, rather than biomedical sciences. The roles and responsibilities of court administration mirror much of health information management, since many of the same principles governing record and information management apply in this context. Furthermore, many court systems have moved to electronic court record systems, making skills with data and information management more valuable.

As each of these examples indicates, today's health information management professional can find employment opportunities in a wide variety of settings. With advancements in technology, even more nontraditional settings will become available to the health information management professional who possesses the knowledge and skill to manage data and its flow within and among these settings.

Conclusion

Just as health care has changed over time, so has the health information management profession. Beginning with a focus on records management in acute care settings, the profession moved to embrace organization-wide functions and numerous types of health care organizations. In this century, the profession has advanced its focus to information and data management, with the promise of further developments occurring with the establishment of regional health information organizations and possible linking at the federal level. New careers and professional credentials have accompanied these changes. Those professionals who continue to gain new knowledge and skills will be well suited to handle the roles and responsibilities emerging in the health information management field.

CHAPTER SUMMARY

This chapter addresses the health information management profession, from its origins to the current day. The health record has changed over time to become standardized in content and more inclusive of the entire patient encounter. The need to manage this changing record and the data contained within it resulted in recognition of the requirement for health information management professionals. Beginning with traditional roles in the acute care environment, these professionals have expanded into nontraditional roles that go well beyond the delivery of patient care. Health information management professionals formed the leading professional association, now known as the American Health Information Management Association (AHIMA). AHIMA accredits educational programs and offers multiple levels of certification to its members. It operates through an organizational structure that includes both volunteer leaders and managerial staff, advocating policy positions that affect both its members and the delivery of health care in the United States. With the implementation of the electronic health record, new opportunities for the profession have grown, and AHIMA has responded by assisting its membership in preparing for these opportunities.

CASE STUDY

You are the director of health information management at Anywhere Hospital. Staff members at Anywhere Hospital are often called upon to speak at career days held at local high schools. For each speaking engagement, the staff member is required to provide a handout describing the career for students to review. You will be scheduled to speak at one of these career days next month. What would you include in the brochure that addresses educational requirements and career opportunities of a health information management professional?

REVIEW QUESTIONS

1. How can one differentiate between the terms *health record* and *health information*?

2. Name and compare the credentials offered at the preprofessional level of health information management.

3. How may one qualify to become a Fellow of the American Health Information Management Association?

4. Give an example of a role identified in Vision 2006 that has since come about.

5. What is the e-HIM initiative?

6. Why is the level of involvement with the judicial process higher for an HIM professional in the setting of a correctional facility?

7. Name some examples of an HIM consultant under contract with an acute care hospital.

ENRICHMENT ACTIVITIES

1. Visit the Web site of the American Health Information Management Association, http://www.ahima.org, to search for information about position statements or practice briefs that they have issued. Write a short summary of one position statement or practice brief for your instructor. Alternatively, research student membership opportunities—including benefits and rates—using the same Web site. If you are already a student member of AHIMA, join the student member community of practice offered on the same Web site and explore its offerings, including the student newsletter.

2. Review the job listings in the health care section of your local newspaper or an online job service, such as http://www.monster.com, http://www.careerbuilder.com, or http://www.nationjob.com. Identify which of these listings fall within the traditional roles of the health information management professional and which lie outside the traditional roles. Decide which of these listings meet your ambitions for a position following completion of your studies.

WEB SITES

American Health Information Management Association, http://www.ahima.org

American Medical Informatics Association, http://www.amia.org

American Veterinary Medical Association, http://www.avma.org

Canadian Health Information Management Association, http://www.chra.ca.org

Commission on Accreditation for Health Informatics and Information Management Education, http://www.cahim.org

Healthcare Information and Management Systems Society, http://www.hims.org

International Federation of Health Records Organizations, http://www.ifhro.org

National Alliance for Health Information Technology, http://www.hospitalconnect.com

National Cancer Registrars Association, www.ncra-usa.org

National Commission on Correctional Health Care, www.corrections.com/ncchc

REFERENCES

American Health Information Management Association. (2000). *A blueprint for the 21st century* [Brochure]. Chicago: Author.

American Health Information Management Association & American Medical Informatics Association. (2006). *Building the work force for health information transformation* (Report). Chicago: Author.

Anderson, S., & Smith, K. J. (1998). *Delmar's handbook for health information careers.* Albany, NY: Delmar.

E-HIM Task Force. (2003). *A vision of the e-HIM future: A report from the AHIMA e-HIM task force.* Chicago: American Health Information Management Association.

Englebardt, S., & Nelson, R. (2002). *Health care informatics.* St. Louis, MO: Mosby.

Peden, A. (2005). *Comparative records for health information management* (2nd ed.). Albany, NY: Delmar.

Treloar, R. W., Smith, P., & Mahoney, M. E. (2003). A nontraditional day in the life. *Journal of AHIMA, 74*(9), 27–33.

Van Bemmel, J. H., & Musen, M. A. (Eds.). (1997). *Handbook of medical informatics.* Netherlands: Springer-Verlag.

NOTES

1. Health Insurance Portability and Accountability Act, 45 C.F.R. §160.103 (2007).

2. E-HIM Task Force. (2003). *A vision of the e-HIM future: A report from the AHIMA e-HIM task force.* Chicago: American Health Information Management Association.

3. Cancer Registries Amendment Act of 1992, 42 U.S.C § 280e (2007).

Legal Issues

CERTIFICATION CONNECTION

RHIA

Access, disclosure, and use of PHI
Confidentiality policies and procedures
Data security
Investigate/mitigate privacy issues/problems
Privacy and confidentiality
Privacy training

RHIT

Access and disclosure of PHI
Compliance issues
Confidentiality of PHI
Legal and regulatory requirements
Legal standards of practice
Privacy issues/problems
Security of PHI

LEARNING OBJECTIVES

After reading this chapter, the learner should be able to:

1. Differentiate between laws, regulations, rules, requirements, and standards.

2. Compare and contrast the roles of governmental entities in health care.

3. Explain the roles of nongovernmental entities in health care.

4. Compare and contrast the court system with administrative bodies.

5. List and describe the principles of liability.

6. Understand the goals of administrative simplification and combating fraud and abuse under the Health Insurance Portability and Accountability Act.

7. Explain the interrelationship between confidentiality and privacy.

8. Discuss the principles of ownership and disclosure of health information.

9. Define the informed consent doctrine and discuss its relationship to advance directives.

10. Compare and contrast a court order authorizing disclosure of health information with a subpoena.

11. Understand the concept of fraud and abuse, the underlying statutory mechanisms supporting the concept, and the resources available to combat it.

Outline

Overview of External Forces

Roles of Governmental Entities
Roles of Nongovernmental Entities
Role Application

Understanding the Court System

The Court System
Administrative Bodies
Legal Procedures

Principles of Liability

Intentional Torts
Nonintentional Torts

Legal Issues in HIM

HIPAA
Privacy and Confidentiality
Access to Health Care Data
Informed Consent
Judicial Process

Fraud and Abuse

Fraud and Abuse Laws
Resources to Combat Fraud and Abuse

Key Concepts

Abuse
Administrative bodies
Administrative law
Advance directives
Appeal
Assault
Battery
Breach of contract
Business associates
Civil law
Common law
Complaint
Completeness
Compliance program
Confidentiality
Constitutional law
Corporate integrity
  agreement
Corporate negligence
Court order
Court system
Covered entities
Criminal law
Deeming authority
Defamation
Defendant
De-identified health
  information
Discovery

Durable power of
  attorney for health
  care
E-discovery
Executive orders
Failure to warn
False imprisonment
Fraud
Health record content
Identity theft
Informed consent
Intentional torts
Invasion of privacy
Involuntary
  commitments
Jurisdiction
Law
Living will
Malpractice
Medical abandonment
Metadata
Minimum necessary
  standard
Negligence
Nonintentional torts
Ordinances
PHI
Plaintiff
Preemption

Pretrial conference
Privacy
Privacy Officer
Privacy Rule
Private law
Public law
Record retention
  policies
Regulations
Release of information
Requirements
Res ipsa loquitur
Respondeat superior
Rules
Security Officer
Security Rule
Separation of powers
Standards
Statutory law
Subpoena
Subpoena *duces tecum*
Trial
Unbundling
Upcoding
Waste
Whistle-blowers

INTRODUCTION

The health information contained in a paper-based health record, a computerized health record, an abstract of patient-specific information, or some other format plays a primary role in the delivery of health care. In addition to its role in direct patient care, health information maintained in these formats serves as the health care provider's legal record of patient care. As such, health information is subject to stringent oversight, including laws, regulations, rules, requirements, and standards.

To comply with the oversight governing health information, one must understand the many sources from which the laws, regulations, requirements, and standards arise. Beyond understanding these external forces, it is necessary to understand how they affect the management of health information.

This chapter addresses the interplay between health information and law. The roles of governmental and non-governmental entities are examined and applied to the issues of health record content, completeness, and retention. A description of the court system is provided and principles of liability are explored. Legal issues affecting health information management (HIM), including the Health Insurance Portability and Accountability Act (HIPAA), confidentiality and privacy, access to health care data, informed consent, and judicial process are discussed. An exploration of fraud and abuse principles completes the chapter.

Overview of External Forces

Similar to many complex disciplines, one cannot look to a single source for definitive guidance on all matters relating to the management of health information. One main reason for the discipline's complexity is the influence of external forces on health information management. For example, governmental entities, accreditation organizations, professional associations, and health care organizations themselves all play a role in the collection and use of health data. Furthermore, laws, regulations, rules, standards, and requirements all influence the management of health information. Combined, these external forces subject the collection and management of health information to stringent oversight.

To understand the oversight provided by these external forces, one must first work from a common set of definitions. **Law** is a body of rules of action or conduct prescribed by a controlling authority that has binding legal force. In the United States, laws issued by legislatures are in the form of statutes. Law can also be found in constitutions and court decisions. **Regulations** are the prescribed courses of action that arise from law, principle, or custom; in other words, regulations are a method of implementing a law, principle, or custom. Regulations have the force of law if issued by a governmental entity. **Rules** are principles established by authorities, prescribing or directing certain action or forbearance from action. **Requirements** are those things considered necessary, obligatory, or demanded as a condition. For example, medical schools establish requirements for student entrance. **Standards** are criteria established as a basis for comparing matters such as quantity, quality, value, or weight. For example, clinicians establish standards of care to determine if a patient has received a sufficient level of care. Requirements and standards by themselves do not constitute law; coupled with statutes, constitutional provisions, or court decisions, they can have the force of law.

The different types of law are also crucial to an understanding of the legal system. **Private law** refers to conflicts

Figure 3–1 | The differences between public law and private law

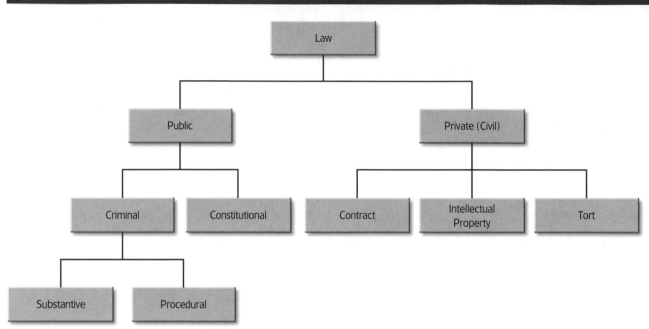

between private parties, whereas **public law** refers to conflicts between the government and private parties or between two or more branches of government. The distinction between public and private law is illustrated in Figure 3–1. **Criminal law** refers to that conduct the government has declared injurious to the public order, with specific punishments identified for violations. **Civil law** is generally defined as that part of the law that does not include criminal law. Although it frequently focuses on private rights and remedies, civil law can include governmental entities. A listing of the different types of civil law is found in Table 3–1. Public law can encompass both civil and criminal law; private law encompasses only civil law. For example, an assault and battery violates both public and private law.

In addition to understanding these definitions, an understanding of the sources of law is needed. The U.S. Constitution serves as the primary source of law in the United States; it not only outlines the roles and responsibilities of each branch of government but it also contains provisions of law. Provisions found in the Constitution are called **constitutional law** and are considered superior or

supreme above laws arising from other sources. Laws may also be created by the legislative branches of federal and state governments; these are referred to as **statutory law**. Laws that arise from the actions of municipal bodies such as boards of aldermen and city councils are referred to as **ordinances**. **Administrative law** refers to the decisions and regulations issued by government agencies that are charged with interpreting statutory law. Rules and regulations are examples of administrative law. **Executive orders** are issued by the chief executive at either the federal or state level and are used to interpret or implement a provision of a constitution or law. Finally, judicial decisions can serve as a source of law. Often referred to as **common law**, judicial decisions interpret relevant constitutional provisions, federal or state statutes, regulations, and previous court decisions.

The roles of both governmental and nongovernmental entities can be examined by applying these definitions and their sources, once they are understood.

Roles of Governmental Entities

Governmental entities play roles in health care through all three branches of government and at all three levels: federal, state, and local. The legislative branch functions to enact laws, determining the need for new laws and for changes in existing laws. The executive branch functions to enforce and administer the laws. The executive branch is organized on a departmental basis, with each department assigned a particular responsibility. The departments are subdivided into administrative agencies, each with defined powers to administer and implement particular legislation. The judicial branch functions to interpret the law through the adjudication and resolution of disputes.

Table 3–1	Different Types of Civil Law
Contract law
Tort law
Intellectual property law
Administrative law
Bankruptcy law
Constitutional law

The separation of powers doctrine works to enforce the differences between the branches of government. **Separation of powers** refers to the division of power between the branches of government and the system of checks and balances that supports that division. By exercising only those powers given to its branch and refraining from exercising those powers belonging to other branches, no one branch of government will dominate the other two. For example, the president can veto a bill that he believes demonstrates that the Congress has over-reached its authority. Similarly, the Supreme Court may declare invalid or unconstitutional a bill passed by Congress that is believed to violate the Constitution. Finally, the Congress may pass constitutionally sound legislation that replaces a law declared unconstitutional by the Supreme Court.

HIPAA

All three branches of government play a role in HIPAA: the Congress created the statute, the executive branch enforces it, and the judicial branch resolves litigation relating to it.

Although all three branches of government are distinct, they do not work in isolation. For example, the United States Congress passed HIPAA in part to battle perceived health care fraud and abuse.[1] HIPAA established or strengthened five programs to assist with fraud enforcement, all to be administered by the executive branch. The judicial branch of government in turn works to resolve the litigation brought by law enforcement agencies of the executive branch concerning HIPAA. These resolutions may result in injunctions, fines, and jail time.

A further example from HIPAA demonstrates the interplay between laws, rules, and standards. Among its many provisions, HIPAA required the Congress to take action to establish privacy standards for health information within a prescribed time frame of passing the law; if it did not take such action, the U.S. Department of Health and Human Services (DHHS) would be charged with establishing these privacy standards. After Congress failed to act within the requisite time period, DHHS published a proposed privacy rule in the Federal Register concerning privacy standards and received widespread commentary. After determining what comments to incorporate, DHHS issued the revised rule in the Federal Register. This rule would have become effective in the ordinary course with its publication in the Code of Federal Regulations (CFR), but because a new presidential administration was taking office, the effective date of the rule was delayed by several months to allow additional commentary. Eventually, the further revised privacy rule was incorporated into the CFR, meaning that it received the force of law.

Executive branch agencies possess the greatest day-to-day influence in health care, because they are the govern-mental bodies charged by legislatures with administering and implementing particular legislation. Executive branch agencies discharge this duty by promulgating rules, adopting regulations, and deciding how statutes, rules, and regulations apply to particular situations.

At the federal level, the Centers for Medicare and Medicaid Services (CMS), the Indian Health Service (IHS), the Department of Veterans Affairs (VA), and the Food and Drug Administration (FDA), among others, are the most prolific in promulgating rules, adopting regulations, and applying statutes, rules, and regulations to particular health care situations. At the state level, departments of public health and like entities have far-reaching influence through the licensing activities of health care professionals and institutions and the requirements to report public health threats such as communicable diseases. At the county and local government level, public hospitals and clinics operate under standards and requirements issued pursuant to municipal health codes.

Roles of Nongovernmental Entities

Although nongovernmental entities by definition are not cloaked by the force of law, the requirements and standards they set are considered quasi-legal requirements. For example, requirements and standards of nongovernmental entities may be used to establish the standard of care in a medical malpractice lawsuit or licensing hearing. In addition, these organizations greatly influence the running of health care organizations. The most prominent nongovernmental entities are accrediting organizations and professional associations.

Accrediting organizations set requirements and standards for a wide variety of health care organizations, including hospitals, nursing homes, and clinical laboratories. A more complete listing of health care organizations evaluated by accrediting bodies is found in Table 3–2. Using the survey method, the accrediting bodies evaluate the compliance of health care organizations against those requirements and standards. Health care organizations that meet the standards and requirements are generally recognized as high-quality institutions.

Two widely recognized voluntary accrediting bodies are the Joint Commission (JC), formerly known as the Joint Commission on Accreditation of Healthcare Organizations (JCAHO), and the American Osteopathic Association's (AOA) Healthcare Facilities Accreditation Program (HFAP). Both bodies have been granted deeming authority by CMS to conduct accreditation surveys. **Deeming authority** means that compliance with the requirements and standards of both accrediting organizations may substitute for compliance with the federal government's *Medicare Conditions of Participation for Hospitals* as published by CMS.[2]

The JC is the most widely known accrediting body in health care; accreditation by this organization often enhances

Table 3–2 | Health Care Organizations Subject to Accreditation Review

General, psychiatric, children's, and rehabilitation hospitals
Healthcare networks, including health maintenance organizations (HMOs), preferred provider organizations (PPOs), managed behavioral health organizations, and integrated delivery networks (IDNs)
Home care organizations, including those providing home health services, personal care services, home infusion and other pharmacy services, and durable medical equipment services
Ambulatory care/surgery services
Clinical laboratories
Nursing homes and other long-term care facilities
Assisted living facilities
Behavioral health organizations, including mental health and substance abuse facilities

a health care facility's public image, competitiveness, and ability to borrow money or float bond issues. Several levels of accreditation are offered, the highest being accreditation with commendation. Accreditation focuses on the health care facility's compliance with established standards falling into three categories: patient-focused functions, organization-focused functions, and structures with functions.

Additional accrediting bodies exist, often covering specialized areas of health care. For example, the National Committee for Quality Assurance (NCQA) accredits managed care organizations. The Commission on Accreditation of Rehabilitation Facilities (CARF) accredits programs and services in medical rehabilitation, assisted living, behavioral health, adult day care, and employment and community services. The Community Health Accreditation Program (CHAP) accredits home care organizations. The College of American Pathologists (ACP) accredits clinical laboratories. The Accreditation Association for Ambulatory Healthcare (AAAHC) accredits ambulatory care centers. The National Commission on Correctional Health Care (NCCHC) and the American Correctional Association (ACA) accredit correctional institutions. A listing of additional accrediting bodies is found in Table 3–3.

Professional associations also set standards and requirements and issue recommendations. In addition, they may serve as accrediting bodies. The American Medical Association (AMA) sets standards for medical ethics, practice, and education; it also serves a dual purpose by accrediting medical

Table 3–3 | Professional Associations in Health Care Providing Educational, Certification, and Accreditation Services

American Nurses Association
American College of Healthcare Executives
American Dietetic Association
American Association of Nurse Anesthetists
American College of Surgeons
American Society of Clinical Pathologists

schools and residency programs. The American Health Information Management Association (AHIMA) has developed general documentation guidelines for the content and structure of health records; it also serves to accredit college programs in health information management. The American Dental Association (ADA) has developed general standards for dental hygiene; it also serves to accredit college programs in dentistry.

In response to state licensing requirements, accrediting standards, and recommendations of professional associations, health care organizations frequently develop their own policies, procedures, and medical staff bylaws. Although not laws in themselves, these policies, procedures, and bylaws have legal consequences if the health care organization fails to abide by them.

Role Application

The management of health information is most profoundly affected by laws, the regulations promulgated by executive agencies at the federal and state levels, and the standards issued by accrediting organizations. These laws, regulations, and accrediting standards are wide ranging; this discussion focuses on their effect upon the content, completeness, and retention of the health record.

Laws, regulations, and accrediting standards define the content of the patient's health record.[3] By definition, **health record content** refers to the characteristics essential to constitute an adequate health record. These characteristics typically include sufficient information to identify the patient clearly, to justify the diagnosis and treatment, and to document the results accurately. Certain general categories of data are often present, including patient needs assessments, plans of care, reports of treatment and clinical findings, and final diagnosis and prognosis.

The categories of data need to be not only present but complete. **Completeness** means to be entire, or lacking in nothing; it is measured against the laws, regulations, and standards defining health record content.[4] As it is sometimes phrased: "If it wasn't charted, it didn't happen" or "not documented, not done." If an event or aspect of patient care is not recorded in the health record, it is appropriate to conclude that it did not occur. Without a complete health record, the health care provider's ability to present a defense in a lawsuit is called into question. In addition, the health care provider's ability to render patient care and conduct research and education is impaired.

The same rationale used to encourage completeness of the health record also supports issues of record retention. Record retention policies are the general principles determining the length of time that health records must be maintained by the health care provider. Statutes on the state level and regulations on both the state and federal levels address retention requirements. Additionally, accrediting bodies establish retention standards. These statutes, regulations, and standards establish specific time frames for which to retain the health record and may differ if the patient is an adult or a minor or has a mental disability.[5]

Understanding the Court System

Perhaps the least understood branch of government is the judiciary branch. Whether attributable to inadequate instruction, limited contact, or other reasons, the general public does not possess a thorough understanding of the court structure in the United States. Furthermore, the public does not understand that administrative bodies are vested with limited legal authority to sanction individuals and entities that do not comply with administrative rules and regulations. This section addresses this lack of understanding by focusing on court systems, administrative bodies, and legal procedures.

The Court System

The phrase court system refers to the judicial branch of government. This branch is vested with the authority to adjudicate and resolve disputes among parties who cannot resolve their disputes themselves. Courts do not actively seek out these parties; disputes are resolved when the parties seek a court's help. The parties seek court assistance by filing a lawsuit.

Lawsuits are filed in the court that has jurisdiction over the matter in question. Jurisdiction refers to the authority of a court and its judicial officers to hear and decide a case. This jurisdiction may be conferred by constitutional or statutory provision and provides authority over the subject matter in question and the parties involved. The type of jurisdiction varies between courts, with federal courts possessing limited jurisdiction and state courts possessing general jurisdiction. Some courts possess jurisdiction based on certain legal areas, such as taxes, traffic, or small claims matters, while other courts do not have limits on their jurisdiction. In certain instances, the parties have a choice of which court to bring their lawsuit in, since jurisdiction may be concurrent between federal and state courts.

The court system also refers to court structure. Courts in the United States operate within a multi-tier structure as illustrated in Figure 3–2. Trial courts conduct trials in civil and criminal matters and supervise the discovery process that occurs before a trial. A trial is a hearing or determination by a court of the issues existing between the parties to a lawsuit. In a trial, judges and juries listen to the testimony of witnesses and view exhibits in order to reach a verdict. Trial courts may have various names, depending on whether they are part of the federal, state, or local court systems. Regardless of their proper names, trial courts are charged with determining the credibility of witnesses and the reliability of evidence.

Inevitably, one side is unhappy with the verdict, in whole or in part, and decides to pursue the case further by filing an appeal. An appeal asks a higher court, whether an intermediate court or a supreme court, to review the activities in the trial court to determine if an error occurred. Upon finding such an error, the appellate court must decide whether the error is significant enough to warrant reversal or modification of the result reached at trial. Appeals from that decision can be made to the court of last resort, the Supreme Court. The United States Supreme Court hears appeals brought from both the state and federal appellate courts.

Administrative Bodies

In addition to having contact with the judicial branch, health information managers, health care providers, and many others interact with administrative bodies on a regular basis. These administrative bodies are found on the federal, state, and local levels. While their roles vary, administrative bodies generally operate to interpret law, and to promulgate and enforce rules and regulations for the substantive area within their jurisdiction. Whereas administrative bodies differ substantially from court systems, some groups have confused the two because of the enforcement capacity possessed by administrative bodies.

Numerous administrative bodies exist at the federal level that address health care matters. Most fall within the authority of the U.S. Department of Health and Human Services, a cabinet-level agency charged with the administrative tasks associated with national health and human services policy objectives. An organizational chart listing these bodies can be found in Figure 3–3.

HIPAA

The Centers for Medicare and Medicaid Services (CMS), located within the U.S. Department of Health and Human Services, is charged with administering the federal government's efforts concerning HIPAA.

Figure 3–2 | Structure of court systems

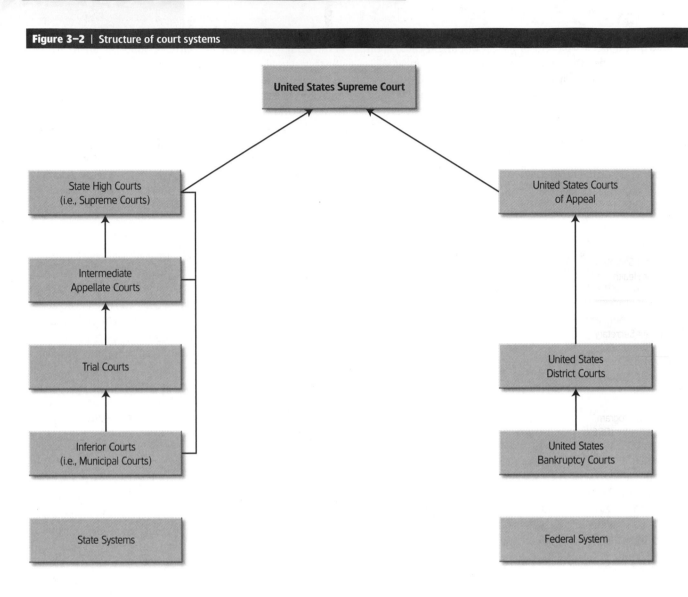

Although each agency within DHHS may address health concerns, four agencies are of particular importance to health information management professionals. The Centers for Disease Control and Prevention (CDC) administer programs for the prevention and control of communicable and vector-borne diseases and other preventable conditions. In addition to receiving guidance and education from CDC, health information management professionals interact with CDC through the mandatory reporting requirements for communicable and vector-borne diseases. The CMS administers the Medicare and Medicaid programs, both of which are designed to fund the health care needs of the elderly and financially needy, respectively. The payment mechanisms that CMS employs, particularly the prospective payment systems, have influenced the demand for the health care data traditionally managed and maintained by HIM professionals. CMS also administers the federal government's efforts concerning HIPAA. The standards set by CMS in furtherance of HIPAA's goals also affect the health care data traditionally managed and maintained by HIM professionals. The National Institutes of Health (NIH) is the federal government's principal biomed-

ical research agency. In addition to providing grant support, it promulgates numerous rules and regulations concerning the protections of human subjects used in research studies. HIM professionals participate actively in design and review of research protocols in many institutions. The Agency for Healthcare Research and Quality (AHRQ) provides information to the public about its research concerning health care outcomes, quality, cost, use, and access. Much of the work performed by HIM professionals concerning quality management is guided by this agency.

Other administrative bodies at the federal level may address health care concerns as part of their overall mission. The Department of Labor houses the Occupational Safety and Health Administration (OSHA), whose purpose is to assure safe working conditions so that human resources are preserved. Within the health care context, OSHA focuses on health standards and education programs, research in employee health matters, and monitoring trends associated with job-related injuries and illnesses. The National Labor Relations Board (NLRB) is responsible for

Figure 3–3 | **Department of Health and Human Services organizational chart**

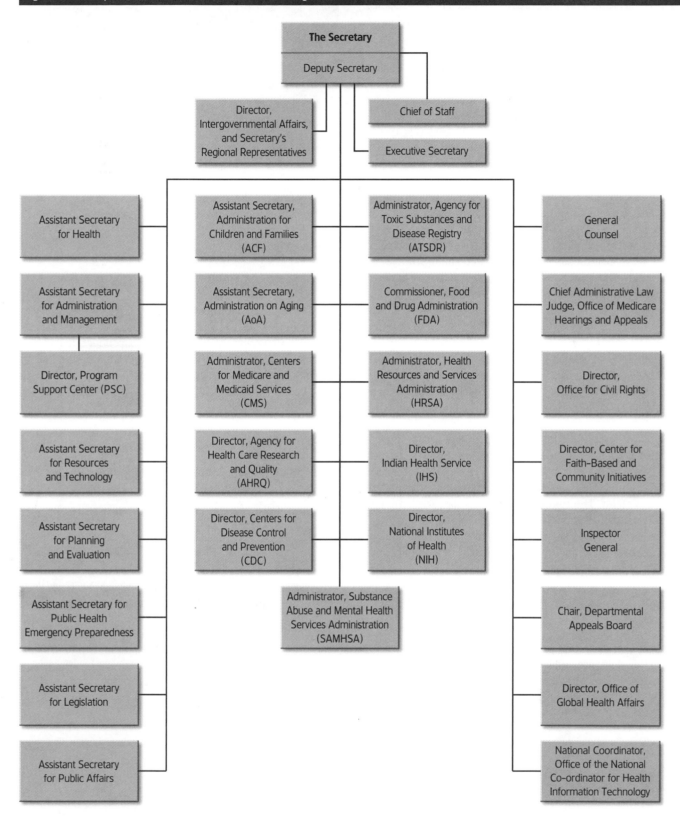

preventing and remedying unfair labor practices in the workplace. As the health care industry has become more unionized, the NLRB has played a more prominent role in the delivery of health care services. The Department of Jus-

tice (DOJ) prosecutes civil and criminal law violations and, through its Antitrust Division, oversees the mergers of health care entities. DOJ has increased its emphasis on prosecuting health care fraud and abuse.

Administrative bodies at the state and local levels address many of the same matters addressed by administrative bodies at the federal level. The main difference is that state and local bodies focus their attention on the residents of their state or municipality and possess no authority beyond their geographic area. These bodies may include state boards of health, licensing boards, coroners, medical examiners, and public health agencies, among others. These bodies also include state attorneys general and county prosecutors who address civil and criminal law violations at the state and local levels.

Whether at the federal, state, or local levels, administrative bodies are authorized by law to act in furtherance of their missions. Their actions are not limited to promulgating rules and regulations, but may extend to investigation and enforcement. Where authorized by statute, administrative bodies possess subpoena power and may levy fines and other sanctions against those who have violated administrative rules and regulations. In many instances, health care providers and HIM professionals interact with administrative bodies on a more regular basis than they do with the court system.

Legal Procedures

Although they are sometimes referred to by different names, certain legal procedures are present in every lawsuit. These procedures follow a particular pattern, referred to as the steps in a lawsuit. For illustration purposes, the steps in a civil lawsuit are shown in Figure 3–4. Two parties are present in every lawsuit, the plaintiff and the defendant. The **plaintiff** initiates the lawsuit; the **defendant** is the person sued by the plaintiff.

The initial step in each lawsuit is the filing of the plaintiff's complaint. The **complaint** describes the jurisdiction of the court in which the lawsuit is filed, the grounds for the lawsuit, and the type of relief the plaintiff demands (e.g., damages). Each complaint must be filed with the court and

Table 3–4 | Methods of Discovery

Method	Defined
Deposition	Testimony given under oath outside the courtroom pursuant to a subpoena
Interrogatories	Written questions presented to a party or witness designed to gather information
Production of documents and things	Inspection or copying of documents or other physical evidence upon written request
Requests for admission	Written questions presented to a party designed to obtain admission of a certain fact

served upon the defendant and any other party named in the lawsuit. Upon receipt of the complaint, the defendant must file a response, either admitting or denying the contents of the plaintiff's complaint.

As part of trial preparation, the discovery process is undertaken. **Discovery** refers to the devices or tools used by one side to obtain facts and information about the case from the other side. Several types of discovery exist, including depositions, written interrogatories, productions of documents or things, physical and mental examinations, and requests for admission. These discovery methods are described in Table 3–4.

Health information stored electronically stands on an equal footing with, and is subject to the same rules of discovery as, health information stored in paper form.

Figure 3–4 | Steps in a civil lawsuit

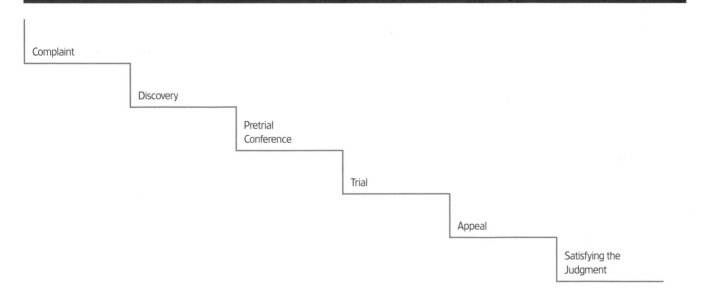

Complaint

Discovery

Pretrial Conference

Trial

Appeal

Satisfying the Judgment

When discovery seeks information stored electronically in any medium, including business records such as the patient health record, it is referred to as **e-discovery**. The Federal Rules of Civil Procedure govern all forms of discovery conducted in proceedings filed in federal court. These rules were revised in 2006 to recognize the existence of information stored electronically and to address how that information may be produced in response to discovery requests.[6] Under these rules, a responding party should produce information stored electronically that is relevant, not privileged, and reasonably accessible, subject to any limitations ordinarily present in discovery. State and local courts also promulgate rules covering discovery, and many of these courts adopt e-discovery rules modeled upon the Federal Rules. Two important concepts are included in the Federal Rules governing e-discovery: undue burden and metadata.

The undue burden concept allows the individual or organization from whom the information is sought (the responding party) to indicate that complying with the discovery request will constitute an undue burden or cost because the information is stored in sources that are not reasonably accessible. Although it is generally true that electronic storage systems make it easier to locate and retrieve information, the volume of information to be searched, the age of the technology in which the information is stored, and the need to review all the information produced to determine if it is subject to privilege may cause the responding party to incur substantial burdens or costs. For example, information stored in a legacy system that can be used only by superseded systems may require the responding party to convert the information into a more usable form at considerable effort and expense. Merely responding that the information sought will not be produced because of unreasonable burden or cost is not sufficient; rather, the responding party must show that the burdens and costs to search for, retrieve, and produce the responsive information that is found cannot be justified in the circumstances of the case. The requesting party may reply that its need for discovery outweighs the burdens and costs of locating, retrieving, and producing the electronically stored information. At this point, the parties may either negotiate between themselves to share the cost or otherwise seek a mutually acceptable solution, or they may ask the judge assigned to the case to determine what amount or type of electronically stored information must be produced in response to the e-discovery request.

The second important concept concerning e-discovery is metadata. **Metadata** refers to unseen information in common text files, which can indicate when a document was created or revised and can contain edits, notes, or other private data. For example, word processing files may retain electronically a number of editorial comments, draft language, or deleted matter that are not otherwise apparent to the reader of the word processing document produced in hard copy or as a screen image. This information describing the history, tracking, or management of an electronic file can pose substantial risks to the responding party if the party is not aware of its presence when producing electronically stored data pursuant to an e-discovery request. For this reason, it is incumbent upon health care organizations and those who manage information and data to establish and maintain policies and procedures that govern production of discovery materials, whether in paper or electronic form.

In many jurisdictions, the parties must engage in a pretrial conference before a trial begins. A **pretrial conference** refers to a meeting between the parties and the trial judge to discuss the status and issues of the case. This conference typically occurs before a trial date is set. At the pretrial conference, the judge may resolve discovery disputes, narrow or define the issues, and assist the parties in discussing a settlement in lieu of going to trial.

The parties follow an established pattern and practice during the trial. After jury selection, each party may make opening statements summarizing its view of the case and the evidence it plans to present. The plaintiff then begins with a presentation of witnesses and evidence, followed by a presentation of witnesses and evidence by the defendant. Each side may cross-examine the witnesses of the other and object to the evidence presented. Once both sides have completed this process, they each make closing statements to the jury. These closing statements summarize the evidence presented and highlight the weaknesses of the other side's case. Upon instruction from the trial judge, the jury applies the law to the facts of the case and reaches a verdict.

The remaining two steps include appeal and satisfying the judgment. An appeal may affirm, modify, or reverse the decision of the trial court. The decision reached is issued in a written opinion that explains the appellate court's reasoning. If a money award has been made, the party entitled to the money will move to satisfy the judgment. This process typically involves a writ of execution, allowing the sheriff to seize property of the losing party and sell it, or an order of garnishment, directing a third party to whom the losing party is indebted to pay money directly to the winning party. In either instance, the winning party receives the amount of money specified in the trial court's verdict.

Principles of Liability

A pressing concern among many health care providers is the fear of liability for injury. This fear does not arise because injury is especially prevalent in health care; rather, the fear arises from the fact that many Americans choose to resolve disputes through litigation instead of by other means. Because the threat of litigation, whether real or imagined, is felt by many health care providers, an understanding of the principles of liability is in order.

Health care providers incur liability for their actions because of the special relationships they hold with patients. Without a relationship, no duty exists about which a party may complain. This relationship exists whether the health care provider is an individual, such as a doctor or nurse, or an institutional entity, such as a hospital or nursing home. The relationship begins when the patient requests treatment and the health care provider agrees to render that treatment. This relationship is considered under the law as being in the nature of contract, where an offer (by the patient requesting treatment) has been accepted (by the health care provider to render treatment). This contractual relationship is centered on direct patient care and continues until it has been properly terminated or the patient no longer requires treatment.

Variations on this relationship exist. For example, health care providers may have relationships with one another that do not involve the delivery of direct patient care. These contractual relationships can involve the granting of clinical privileges from a hospital to physicians, a business relationship involving the rental of office space, direct employment relationships between hospitals and physicians, or ownership interests in ancillary businesses, among other relationships. Whatever form these relationships take, a breach in the agreement reached between the parties can result in liability for one or both sides.

Once a relationship is established, duties arise between the parties. It is the breach of these duties that forms the basis for theories of liability. These theories can be grouped under the headings of breach of contract, intentional torts, and nonintentional torts. A **breach of contract** involves the failure of the parties to a contract to perform according to the contract's terms. **Intentional torts** refers to civil wrongs committed by persons with the intent to do something wrong. **Nonintentional torts** refers to civil wrongs committed by persons who lack the intent to do something wrong. Because most litigation in the health care context involves either intentional or nonintentional torts, those theories are presented here in detail and are listed in Table 3–5.

Intentional Torts

Several intentional torts arise within the health care context, including assault and battery, defamation, invasion of privacy, medical abandonment, and false imprisonment. The

commonality of these torts is that the wrongdoer must have possessed the intent to do something wrong. A body of law has developed around each tort, making an understanding of each important.

Although they are often used together, the terms assault and battery refer to two separate concepts. **Assault** refers to a threat that does not involve physical contact. By contrast, **battery** refers to physical contact involving injury or offense. Under both concepts, the victim does not give permission or authority to the wrongdoer to act. Assaults are generally not seen within the health care context; however, batteries do occur on occasion. These instances may involve the health care provider acting beyond the permission of the patient, such as when a patient consents to exploratory surgery but receives a mastectomy instead. These instances may also involve a mistake by the health care provider, such as when the patient consents to surgery in one site but surgery is performed at another site.

Defamation refers to the wrongful injuring of another person's reputation. Defamation that occurs in print is referred to as libel; defamation that occurs by oral expression or transitory gestures is referred to as slander. To be considered either libel or slander, the defamatory statement or gesture must be published in the sense that a third party becomes aware of the statement or gesture. Truth is an absolute defense to an allegation of defamation, and statements made in good faith, without malice, under a reasonable belief to be true, and by someone with an interest or legal duty to disclose may be protected by qualified privilege. For example, a wrongful release of protected health information will not be brought pursuant to a defamation theory because the contents of a medical record are generally considered true.

Invasion of privacy involves the dissemination of information about another person's private, personal matters. Claims of invasion of privacy may be brought when a patient's protected health information is improperly disclosed; this is a wrongful intrusion upon the patient's private concerns and activities. Similarly, using a patient's likeness for commercial purposes without the patient's consent may constitute an invasion of privacy.

Medical abandonment refers to the unilateral severing, by the physician, of the physician-patient relationship without giving the patient reasonable notice at a time when there is a necessity for continuing care. Medical abandonment claims are among the oldest intentional tort claims in the health care context. Examples of this theory include a physician leaving a patient alone at a critical time, failing to be available to the patient because of the needs of other patients, vacation, and a physician's erroneous belief that the patient had recovered and did not require additional treatment.

False imprisonment refers to the unlawful restraint of an individual's personal liberty or the unlawful

Table 3–5	Tort Theories	
Intentional Torts	**Nonintentional Torts**
Assault	Negligence
Battery	Malpractice
Defamation	*Res ipsa loquitur*
Invasion of privacy	*Respondeat superior*
Medical abandonment	Corporate negligence
False imprisonment	Failure to warn

restraining or confining of an individual. To make a claim of false imprisonment, an intent to confine must exist, the individual must be aware of confinement, and confinement must occur against the individual's will. Claims of false imprisonment within the health care context generally concern involuntarily committed mental patients or the use of protective devices or restraints. **Involuntary commitments** are admissions that occur against a patient's will. Involuntary commitments follow the standards set in the individual states but generally occur upon proof that a person is dangerous to himself or others or cannot function in a reasonable manner. Commitments vary in length and range from emergency to temporary to indefinite. Protective devices or restraints are used with physically violent persons when it is necessary to prevent immediate injury to those persons or others.

Nonintentional Torts

Several nonintentional torts arise within the health care context, including negligence, *res ipsa loquitur, respondeat superior,* corporate negligence, and failure to warn. The commonality of these torts is that the wrongdoer lacks the intent to do something wrong.

Negligence refers to the failure to do something that a reasonably prudent person would do in a similar situation, or to do something that a reasonably prudent person would not do in a similar situation. Although negligence can be a form of malpractice, the term *malpractice* encompasses a wider area of conduct. **Malpractice** refers to professional misconduct and can include both intentional and nonintentional torts. The patient must be able to prove four elements to succeed with a negligence claim: (1) a duty of care is owed to the patient; (2) a breach of this duty of care occurred; (3) a causal connection between the breach of duty and the patient's injury; and (4) damages. Each element requires presentation of evidence to support the plaintiff's theory.

Among the more difficult elements to prove are breach of the duty of care and the causal connection. A breach of the duty of care refers to the health care provider's failure to maintain a certain standard of care. A reasonable person standard is applied to the standard of care, and deviations from the appropriate standard of care will support a claim of negligence. The causal connection, often referred to as causation, can be difficult to prove because all or part of an injury may not be the result of the health care provider's negligence, but instead, the indirect result of an intervening force. In such an instance, causation will be proven by applying the foreseeability test: If a prudent health care provider could have anticipated that the intervening force would occur, then the injury was foreseeable and the health care provider is liable.

Res ipsa loquitur is Latin for the phrase "the thing speaks for itself" and applies in situations where the

defendant had exclusive control over the thing that caused harm to the patient and the harm itself could only have occurred through negligence. Because the patient possesses no control over the situation, this doctrine shifts the burden of proof to the health care provider to rebut the presumption of wrongdoing. To succeed with this type of claim, the patient must not have contributed to the injury.

Respondeat superior, sometimes referred to as vicarious liability, refers the liability of a superior for the acts of a subordinate or servant acting within the scope of his authority. This doctrine is often used to impose liability upon an employer for the acts of the employee. For example, the negligent actions of a nurse employed by a hospital could also result in liability against the hospital under this theory.

Corporate negligence refers to the failure of a hospital, entrusted with the task of providing accommodations necessary to carry out its purpose, to follow the established standard of conduct to which it should conform. This doctrine differs from *respondeat superior* because it involves a direct duty to the patient with regard to care and treatment. Corporate negligence can also be applied to the hospital's duty to adhere to its own bylaws and the applicable state statute governing the credentialing process.

Failure to warn, sometimes referred to as failure to protect, refers to a psychotherapist's failure to take steps to protect an innocent third party from a dangerous patient. The failure-to-warn theory recognizes a duty on the part of the psychotherapist, both legal and ethical in nature, to protect others if the psychotherapist determines, or should have reasonably determined, that his patient poses a serious danger of violence. This duty overrides the psychotherapist's general duty of confidentiality to his patient.

Legal Issues in HIM

As mentioned earlier in this chapter, health information contained in the health record serves a variety of purposes, including that of the legal document recording a particular episode of a patient's care. This legal document serves as the backbone of virtually every professional liability action and is used to establish whether the applicable standard of care was met. It may be used in criminal actions to establish the cause of the victim's death, an insanity defense, or a party's physical condition (e.g., blood alcohol content). Furthermore, credentialing and disciplinary proceedings of physicians and other health care professionals require the admission of the health record as evidence. These legal uses are illustrated in Table 3–6.

Extensive literature exists concerning the legal issues associated with health information management. Focus is placed on the most central legal issues relating to health information management: HIPAA, privacy and

Table 3–6 | Some Legal Uses for the Health Record

To establish the applicable standard of care
As evidence in civil cases
As evidence involving the credentialing process
For disciplinary proceedings of health care professionals
To establish the cause of death
To determine blood alcohol content
To support an insanity defense
As proof of a party's physical condition

confidentiality, access to health care data, informed consent, and judicial process. The focus is placed on HIPAA at the beginning of this section because of its impact upon the other areas of the discussion.

HIPAA

The Act's main impact on health information management involves administrative simplification and combating waste, fraud, and abuse.

HIPAA

HIPAA is one of the most significant pieces of legislation to affect the health information management profession. Passed in 1996, HIPAA was designed with several goals in mind: (1) provide insurance portability; (2) promote the use of medical savings accounts; (3) decrease the costs of health care administration by simplifying insurance processes; and (4) combat waste, fraud, and abuse. The statute itself is divided into five titles, as seen in Table 3–7. The U.S. Department of Health and Human Services is charged with administering HIPAA and has promulgated rules and regulations to implement the statute's goals. Literature concerning the statute's first two goals may be found outside this text; this text focuses on the goals of administrative simplification and combating waste, fraud, and abuse. The implementing rules and regulations designed to achieve these goals are integrated as appropriate.

Table 3–7 | Health Insurance Portability and Accountability Act

Title I	Health Care Access, Portability, and Renewability
Title II	Preventing Health Care Fraud and Abuse; Administrative Simplification; Medical Liability Reform
Title III	Tax-Related Health Provisions
Title IV	Application and Enforcement of Group Health Plan Requirements
Title V	Revenue Offsets

Administrative Simplification The main focus of HIPAA's administrative simplification effort is to increase the use of electronic patient information. The governing assumption of this approach is that by replacing a paper-intensive method for transferring patient information between health care providers and third-party payers with an electronic method, overall costs will decrease. This decrease in costs has not yet been seen; however, his is largely attributable to the increase in costs associated with preparing for the transition to HIPAA. It is anticipated that cost decreases will be seen after the transition period is completed.

HIPAA provides DHHS with several layers of authority. First, DHHS possesses the authority to mandate use of standards for the electronic exchange of health care data. This authority allows DHHS to specify the medical and administrative code sets to be used in the electronic exchange standards. This authority is commonly referred to as the Electronic Transactions and Code Sets Rule. Second, DHHS is empowered to require use of national identification systems for health care patients, providers, payers, plans, employers, and sponsors. This authority is commonly referred to as the Unique Identifier Rules. Information concerning these rules is addressed in Chapter 5, "Health Data Content and Structures," and Chapter 15, "Reimbursement Methodologies." Third, DHHS may specify the types of measures required to protect the security and privacy of personally identifiable health information.

HIPAA

The requirements to protect the security and privacy of personally identifiable health information are written into information security and privacy safeguards, commonly referred to as the Privacy and Security Rules.

In support of the third level of authority, DHHS has developed health information privacy and security standards. These are commonly referred to as the Privacy and Security Rules. These rules apply to **covered entities**, a term that includes health plans, health care clearinghouses (e.g., claims data processors or billing services), and health care providers who transmit standard transactions in electronic formats. The Privacy Rule also applies to **business associates**, who are defined as those individuals or organizations doing business with covered entities that are involved in the use or disclosure of protected health information (PHI). While it is conceivable that some very small minority of health care providers may not engage in electronic transmission of these standard transactions, for practical purposes, the comprehensive nature of the list of standard transactions ensures that virtually every health plan, health care clearinghouse, and health care provider in the United States are governed by these rules.

The **Privacy Rule** establishes the concept of protected health information. **PHI** refers to individually identifiable health information that has been electronically maintained or transmitted by a covered entity as well as such information when it takes any other form. PHI includes individual health information that is spoken, written, or stored in hard copy or electronic form. The rule protects oral or recorded health information created or received by a covered entity or employer relating to: (1) the past, present, or future physical or mental health of an individual; (2) the provision of health care to an individual; or (3) the payment for provision of health care to an individual. By grouping the concept of physical and mental health with the activities of providing and paying for health care, the Privacy Rule works to protect virtually all forms of patient-specific health information.

The **Security Rule** establishes the concept of protecting the confidentiality, integrity, and availability of electronically formatted PHI created, received, maintained, or transmitted by a covered entity. The rule accomplishes this by delineating the administrative, physical, and technical safeguards that should be used by covered entities to protect identifiable PHI in electronic formats. These safeguards are categorized into required and addressable standards. The term *required standards* means what it says: covered entities have no choice but to implement the standard and cannot apply a reasonableness test to their actions in complying with the standard. Addressable standards, however, offer some flexibility to the covered entity in implementation. This flexibility takes the form of a reasonableness test. The covered entity must review the addressable standard and decide whether the standard is a reasonable and appropriate security measure for its organization. Should the covered entity determine that a given standard is not reasonable for its organization, the covered entity is excused from compliance if it can document the conclusion fully. This documentation must include the reasons supporting the reasonableness conclusion and the reasonable steps the covered entity has undertaken on an alternative basis to safeguard the referenced PHI. Additional information concerning the administrative, physical, and technical safeguards is discussed in Chapter 13, "Information Systems and Technology."

Both the Privacy and Security Rules require covered entities to identify an individual who will be responsible for developing and implementing requisite policies and procedures. With regard to the Privacy Rule, that person is referred to as the **Privacy Officer**. In addition to policy and procedure development and implementation, the Privacy Officer serves as the contact person to receive complaints and disseminate information about the entity's privacy practices. With regard to the Security Rule, that person is referred to as the **Security Officer**. The Security Officer is accountable for the covered entity's security procedures. The same individual may serve as both the Privacy and

Table 3–8	Patient Rights under HIPAA
To access, inspect, and maintain a copy of their protected health information
To be notified of the information privacy practices a health care entity follows
To limit the use or disclosure of protected health information, including for marketing purposes
To request that the health care provider take reasonable steps to ensure that communications with the patient are confidential
To request an accounting of all disclosure of protected health information
To file a formal complaint concerning the privacy practices of the health care entity

Security Officer; the decision to combine or separate the two positions is made by the covered entity.

An important focus of the HIPAA provisions is the granting of rights to patients concerning their protected health information. A listing of those rights is found in Table 3–8. Several states, including Hawaii, Montana, and Washington, have enacted statutes granting similar rights to patients, following either the HIPAA language or the language contained in the Uniform Health-Care Information Act.[7] For a fuller understanding of the concept of patient rights, see Chapter 4, "Ethical Standards."

HIPAA

Enforcement responsibilities rest with the Office of Civil Rights of DHHS and the Centers for Medicare and Medicaid Services of DHHS.

Of significant interest to covered entities are the HIPAA provisions addressing compliance and enforcement. As of 2007, the dates for compliance with the Privacy and Security Rules have largely passed, with only minimal exceptions applicable to covered entities. Accordingly, these rules are no longer prospective in nature but are in application throughout the United States. Now that the compliance window has passed, the enforcement and penalty provisions come into play. Enforcement responsibilities are placed with the Office of Civil Rights of DHHS for the Privacy Rule and with the Centers for Medicare and Medicaid of DHHS for the Security and Electronic Transactions and Code Sets Rules. These two groups process complaints against covered entities that are alleged to be in noncompliance with the rules. If, upon investigation or compliance review, either group determines that the covered entity has violated one of the rules, the covered entity is notified in writing. An informal resolution process follows. If no informal resolution can be reached, a formal noncompliance report is

Figure 3–5 | HIPAA complaint process

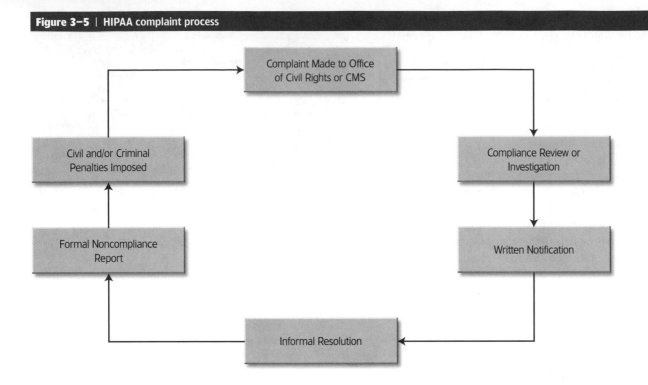

issued to both the complainant and the covered entity. At this point, the provisions for civil and criminal penalties are imposed. This process is illustrated in Figure 3–5.

HIPAA

HIPAA establishes a "floor" of protections for PHI and permits states and local governmental bodies to impose more stringent protections.

All of the rules promulgated as part of the administrative simplification effort do not serve to replace existing federal, state, and local laws, rules, and regulations but serve to add complexity. Covered entities must remain aware of the provisions issued under these rules as well as any other federal, state, or local laws if they are to conform to legal requirements. In some instances, the provisions of the HIPAA rules differ from the obligations imposed on covered entities by other federal, state, or local laws, raising the issue of preemption. **Preemption** refers to a legal doctrine that states that certain matters are of such a national—as opposed to local—nature that federal laws preempt, or take precedence over, state and local laws. As a general rule, preemption only applies in the HIPAA context if a provision of state or local law is contrary to HIPAA standards. State or local laws are considered contrary to HIPAA if compliance with state law would prevent compliance with HIPAA requirements or would pose an obstacle to accomplishing

and executing the full purposes of HIPAA. If no obstacle or compliance problem exists and there is merely a difference between HIPAA requirements and other federal, state, or local laws, the preemption doctrine does not apply. In practice, the covered entity is required to reconcile the difference. For example, if an HIPAA provision merely allows but does not mandate an activity (e.g., specific disclosure) but a state law prohibits that same activity, the covered entity can reconcile this difference by choosing not to disclose the information sought. In summary, the protections afforded by the HIPAA administrative simplification provisions establish a floor of protections, allowing states and localities the ability to enact more stringent protections.

HIPAA

Five programs are created or strengthened by HIPAA: the Healthcare Fraud and Abuse Control Program, the Medicare Integrity Program, the Beneficiary Incentive Program, the Medicaid Fraud and Abuse National Initiative, and the Healthcare Fraud and Abuse Data Collection Program.

Fraud and Abuse The main focus of HIPAA's effort to combat fraud and abuse is the creation or strengthening of programs and the provision of new criminal and civil enforcement tools. Administered by different departments of the executive branch, these programs serve as a means to coordinate federal efforts to combat fraud and abuse.

The Healthcare Fraud and Abuse Control Program operates jointly between the Department of Justice and the Office of Inspector General (OIG) of DHHS. The aim of this program is to control health care fraud and abuse and to conduct investigations relating to the delivery of health care services. To accomplish this goal, the program coordinates efforts at the federal, state, and local levels involving law enforcement agencies, private entities, and the public, and provides guidance to the health care industry regarding fraudulent practices.

The Medicare Integrity Program, housed within DHHS, is designed to reduce payment errors and to protect and strengthen the Medicare Trust Fund. The program partners with health care providers, beneficiaries, contractors, and other federal and state agencies to carry out its work. The program's central activities include cost report audits, medical reviews, antifraud activities, and Medicare secondary payer activities. These activities are conducted by contractors, some of whom are also employed by DHHS to process Medicare claims.

The Beneficiary Incentive Program encourages Medicare beneficiaries and others, including health care professionals, to report suspected cases of fraud and abuse. Complaints are often resolved by communication and education or by collecting an overpayment, without a referral to a law enforcement agency ever occurring. Besides the incentive of reducing fraud to the Medicare system overall, this program offers two forms of reward to members of the public. The first offers a portion of the amount collected by the government as a reward if the complainant's allegations are sustained after further review. The second offers a reward to an individual who submits a suggestion that, after adoption, results in savings to the program.

The Medicaid Fraud and Abuse National Initiative addresses fraud and abuse in the Medicaid program. To accomplish this, the initiative utilizes a partnership with the various state Medicaid agencies and their respective attorneys general offices. Within the state Medicaid agencies, a Surveillance and Utilization Review System (SURS) unit exists that possesses responsibility for analyzing post-payment data from the Medicaid Management Information System. Using the data contained in the system, the SURS units can create profiles identifying suspected fraudulent patterns. Where appropriate, the SURS units may refer instances of suspected fraud for investigation and possible prosecution.

The Healthcare Fraud and Abuse Data Collection Program was designed to create a national health care fraud and abuse database in coordination with the National Practitioner Data Bank. This fraud and abuse database is referred to as the Healthcare Integrity and Protection Data Bank (HIPDB) and contains reports of final adverse actions taken against health care providers, suppliers, or practitioners when liability is admitted or found. The information to be reported includes the name and tax identification number of the provider, supplier, or practitioner who is subject to the adverse action; the name of any health care entity with which the provider, supplier, or practitioner is associated; the nature of the adverse action and whether such action is on appeal; and a description of the acts, omissions, or injuries that form the basis for the adverse action. Examples of adverse actions include improper payments, medically unnecessary services, delays in diagnosis or treatment, and adverse patient outcomes. Access to the HIPDB is limited to federal and state governmental agencies and health plans that are required to report adverse actions and to individual providers, suppliers, and practitioners who query about themselves.

Privacy and Confidentiality

Privacy and confidentiality are sometimes regarded loosely as having the same meaning. In reality, they are two separate but related concepts. As a general matter, the underpinning to legal protections for patient-specific health information is the patient's right to privacy. This right to privacy is frequently defined as the right to be left alone; it is also defined as the right to control personal information. The choice of definition varies based on the source of law on which the right is based. Constitutional provisions, statutory provisions, and common law provisions form the foundation for rights to privacy, as illustrated in Figure 3–6.

In the health care setting, confidentiality refers to the obligation of the health care provider to maintain patient information in a manner that will not permit dissemination beyond the health care provider. The concept of confidentiality of patient information arose from the Hippocratic Oath, which states in part:

> "What I may see or hear in the course of the treatment or even outside the treatment in regard to the life of men, which on no account one must noise abroad, I will keep to myself holding such things shameful to be spoken about."[8]

This oath still serves as the foundation for the current medical profession's guidelines on the confidentiality of health information.

The requirements of confidentiality apply only to certain patient-specific information. For example, information

Figure 3–6 | Foundation for the rights to privacy

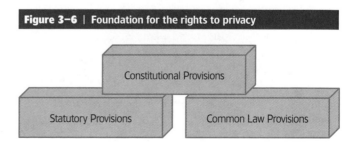

is considered confidential when the information is made available by the patient to the health care provider during the course of their confidential relationship (e.g., clinical or medical data). By contrast, information is nonconfidential when it is considered common knowledge, with no restrictions requested by the patient (e.g., demographic data). It is the sensitive nature of this confidential information that has been targeted under the law as requiring special protection.

To assist matters, the HIPAA Privacy Rule defines confidential health information as protected health information. The health information considered protected under HIPAA contains identifiers by which an individual can be recognized. These identifiers are listed in Table 3–9. Numerous restrictions are placed on individually identifiable health information under HIPAA. By contrast, the information that is stripped of all the identifiers listed in Table 3–9, plus any other information that could be used to identify an individual, is referred to as **de-identified health information**. De-identified information can be used and disclosed by covered entities without consent or authorization.

Confidentiality serves to protect patient-specific health information from disclosure. That protection applies whether health information concerns a living person or a deceased individual.[9] Not only must those persons involved with direct patient care act to protect health information, but health information managers must assume responsibil-

ity for protecting confidential patient-specific health information. Actions by both groups to maintain confidentiality have become increasingly difficult as demands for patient-specific information increase.

In response to these increasing demands, the HIPAA Privacy Rule now requires health care providers to issue a Notice of Privacy Practices to each patient. This notice informs the patient of the health care provider's duties concerning PHI, including how the provider may use and disclose PHI, with whom PHI will be shared, and the safeguards in place for the PHI. The notice also informs the patient of his rights under HIPAA, among them the right to an accounting of any disclosures of his PHI and the right to complain if he feels his privacy rights have been violated, along with the name and phone number of a contact person with whom he can lodge a complaint. Furthermore, the Privacy Rule requires the health care provider to inform the patient that disclosures, other than for treatment, payment, or operations, will only be made with the patient's consent. The Privacy Rule also requires the provider to make a good faith effort to obtain the patient's acknowledgment that the notice has been received. Finally, the Privacy Rule requires the covered entity to post a complete copy of the notice in a clear and prominent location of its facility. An example of a Notice of Privacy Practices is included in the Appendix section of this textbook.

HIPAA requirements and the implementation of the electronic health record have influenced health information managers to expand their responsibilities for confidentiality and privacy in recent years. Instead of viewing the protection of health information as it relates to a set of paper-based patient records, health information managers now view privacy protection from an enterprise-wide perspective. Health information found in the electronic health record and other related databases requires the use of computer data security programs to address confidentiality and privacy concerns. These changes will continue to widen both the influence and responsibilities of health information managers for years to come.

Access to Health Care Data

Questions of access to and disclosure of health care data frequently arise within the health care context. Patients, fellow health care providers, third-party payers, and governmental entities all have increased the demand for access to health care data. This growing demand has resulted in more regulation and an increased need to educate those who deal with the demand.

Table 3–9 │ Individual Identifiers under HIPAA
Name
All address information
Dates, including birth, death, admission, discharge, and any data indicating age
Telephone numbers
Fax numbers
E-mail addresses
Social Security number
Medical record number
Health plan beneficiary number
Account numbers
Certificate/license numbers
Vehicle identifiers
Device identifiers
URLs
IP addresses
Biometric identifiers
Facial photographs
Any other unique identifying number, characteristic, or code

Source: 45 C.F.R. section 164.514 (2007).

HIPAA

The Privacy Rule establishes a patient's right of access to his own health information.

Ownership and Disclosure To understand the access and disclosure issues associated with health care data, one must understand principles of ownership and disclosure of health information. Under traditional rules, the ownership of health care information centered on who owned the medium in which the information was stored (i.e., the health record). Decisions about whether to allow access to the medium in which the information was stored fell within the sole province of the health care provider. Over time, the concept developed that the patient had a limited right of access to his own information contained in the medical record. This ill-defined right of access later became codified in the HIPAA Privacy Rule as a clear statement which recognizes that the patient possesses a right of access to his own information.[10] Some commentators see this right evolving even further, to a position where health information is held in trust by the health care provider for the benefit of the patient. Figure 3–7 illustrates this continuum of views.

Because ownership was the determining factor for access to health information, the law was developed to place duties and restrictions upon the owner of the information (i.e., the health care provider) concerning disclosure of infor-

mation. For example, the recent HIPAA Privacy Rule places duties upon the health care provider to allow the patient to consent, reject, or request restriction of patient-specific information for many of the uses the medical record serves, including treatment, payment, and health care operations. This duty is carried out through a form typically referred to as "Consent to the Use and Disclosure of Health Information for Treatment, Payment, or Health Care Operations."

The HIPAA Privacy Rule recognizes that patients may wish to restrict the uses and disclosures of their PHI and allows them to do so at the time of receipt of the "Consent to the Use and Disclosure" document. Covered entities are not required to honor the patient's request and may even condition treatment (in the case of a health care provider) or enrollment (in the case of a health plan) upon obtaining the patient's consent to use and disclose PHI.

In addition to the consent form, the HIPAA Privacy Rule further requires the health care provider to obtain written authorization (permission) from the patient for specific disclosures not otherwise authorized by law.

Figure 3–7 | Continuum of patient rights of access to health information

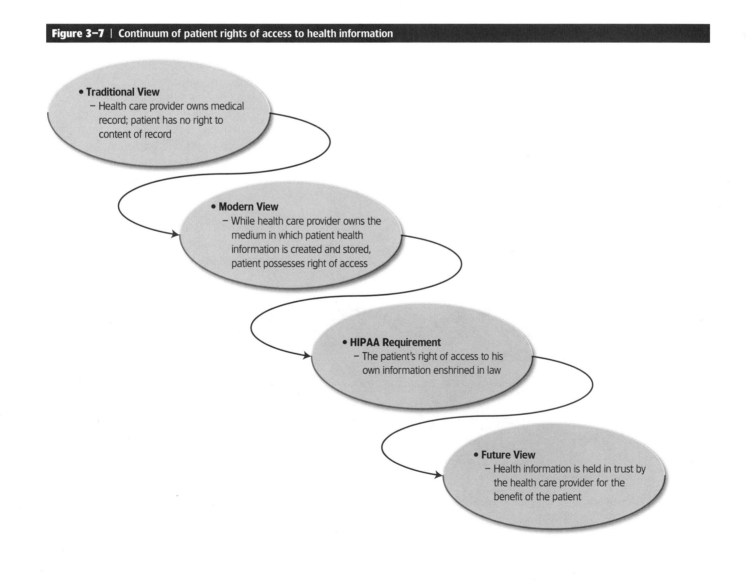

- **Traditional View**
  - Health care provider owns medical record; patient has no right to content of record

- **Modern View**
  - While health care provider owns the medium in which patient health information is created and stored, patient possesses right of access

- **HIPAA Requirement**
  - The patient's right of access to his own information enshrined in law

- **Future View**
  - Health information is held in trust by the health care provider for the benefit of the patient

Table 3–10 | **HIPAA Mandatory Disclosures**

Circumstances under which PHI may be disclosed without first obtaining the patient's authorization include, but are not limited to:
Emergencies concerning public health or safety
Quality assurance reviews by authorized authorities
Instances concerning victims of abuse, neglect, or domestic violence
Reporting of adverse events, tracking of products, recalls of products, and postmarketing surveillance to entities subject to FDA regulation regarding FDA-regulated products or activities
Law enforcement authorities for use in identifying or apprehending an escapee or violent criminal

Although this is a new federal requirement, express authorization by the patient has been a long-standing requirement of many state laws. Some disclosures are mandated by law, negating the need to obtain the patient's authorization before releasing information. Examples of those mandated disclosures are found in Table 3–10.

Commonly referred to as the process for authorizing **release of information**, a valid release of information form provides health care providers and institutions with the authority to disclose patient-specific health information to persons not otherwise authorized by law. Such releases of information must be in writing or, where state law permits, via computer. Certain core elements are necessary to constitute a valid release of information form and are identified in Table 3–11.

HIPAA

The Privacy Rule establishes the principle of the minimum necessary standard for release of protected health information.

What information may be released is the subject of federal law. Introduced as part of the HIPAA Privacy Rule, the principle of the **minimum necessary standard** governs the release of patient-specific health information. This principle requires the health care provider to make reasonable efforts to limit the patient-specific health information disclosed to the least amount necessary to accomplish the intended purpose of the use, disclosure, or request. To accomplish this within the organization, the health care provider must identify those who need access to the information to carry out their duties, what category of access is needed, and what conditions, if any, are appropriate to such access. Where release is not routine or recurring, as in the case of those outside the organization, the health care provider is expected to develop criteria designed to reasonably limit the items of patient-specific health information disclosed such that the purpose for which disclosure is sought is accomplished and to review requests for disclosure on an individual basis in accordance with the criteria established.

With regard to those persons outside the organizations requesting information, the health care provider must look to two things: (1) the person who may grant authority to release information and (2) the identity of the third party seeking access.

Who may grant authority to release health information is a matter governed by state law and regulation. Generally, the authority to release information rests with: (1) the

Table 3–11 | **Core Elements of a Valid Release of Information Form**

The individual's name and identifying information
A specific and meaningful description of the information to be used or disclosed
The name or other specific identification of the person or class of persons authorized to make the requested use or disclosure
The name or other specific identification of the person or class of persons to whom the disclosure is to be made
An expiration date or expiration event that relates to the individual or purpose of the use or disclosure
A statement of the individual's right to revoke the authorization, the exceptions to the right to revoke, and a description of the individual who may revoke the authorization
A statement that the information used or disclosed is subject to redisclosure and may lose its protected status
The signature of the individual and date
If the authorization is signed by the individual's personal representative, a description of the representative's authority to act for the individual

patient, if the patient is a competent adult or emancipated minor; (2) a legal guardian or parent on behalf of a minor child; or (3) the executor or administrator of an estate if the patient is deceased. For purposes of this discussion, we will limit future references to the patient's authorization.

The extent of access and the need for patient authorization is defined by the identity of the third party seeking access. For example, if the party seeking access is the patient's attorney or insurance company, the health care provider may disclose patient-specific health information only with the patient's authorization. Similarly, patient authorization is generally necessary before disclosure may be made to a federal, state, or local government agency. Patient authorization may also be required in certain instances for access by the researcher and the health care provider's business associate. By contrast, patient authorization is not generally needed when the health care provider reports public health threats to a state's department of health or similar agency. In each of these instances, the HIPAA Privacy Rule requires the health care provider to verify the identity and authority of the person who is requesting PHI before releasing this information.

The extent to which the health care provider permits access to this information by third parties is subject to regulation. A patient's friends and family may have access to a patient's PHI under the HIPAA Privacy Rule if the patient agrees, or is given an opportunity to object but does not do so, or if the health care provider can reasonably infer from the circumstances that the patient would not object to disclosure. When the patient is an unemancipated minor, the parent, legal guardian, or person acting with parental rights may have access to PHI, unless the minor could lawfully obtain the health care without parental consent. In those instances where the unemancipated minor could lawfully obtain health care without parental consent (e.g., health care involving female reproductive rights), the covered entity must follow state law concerning disclosures. A covered entity may place a patient's name in its facility directory if the patient has not exercised his option to opt out of the directory. Covered entities must treat a patient's personal representative as the patient for access purposes, absent an indication that the personal representative lacks authority to act on behalf of the patient. Finally, the HIPAA Privacy Rule requires that, upon request of the patient, health care providers must prepare an account of disclosures made. In response to the patient's request, the health care provider must review disclosure records for a six-year period, measured from the date of the patient's request; the health care provider must act upon the request within sixty days. Should the health care provider be unable to do so, he is obliged to notify the requesting patient in writing and is given thirty additional days to respond.

Finally, wrongful disclosure of individually identifiable health information is also the subject of HIPAA protection.

This protection resides in HIPAA's statutory provisions rather than the Privacy Rule and specifies that knowing disclosure of individually identifiable health information to another person in violation of the HIPAA provision is a federal offense.[11] This offense is subject to punishment of fines, imprisonment, or both, and the level of fine or imprisonment gradually increases if the offense was committed under false pretenses or with the intent to steal, transfer, or use the information for commercial advantage, personal gain, or malicious harm.

Identity Theft An assumption central to the discussion so far is that the demand for access to protected health information is made to the HIM professional, who in turn can decide how to address the request. Unfortunately, not all demands for access are legitimate but may be made pursuant to a crime. In criminal circumstances, the wrongdoer seeks access to health care data surreptitiously, either by concealing the true purpose of a request or not making a request at all. Accordingly, the health information management professional is unaware of the improper attempt at access and is not in the position to refuse the request for data. This position raises new issues for the HIM professional to resolve.

One such crime that has increased in the last decade is identity theft. **Identity theft** involves the knowing transfer or use, without lawful authority, of the identity of another person with the intent to commit, aid, or abet any unlawful activity that constitutes a violation of federal, state, or local law.[12] Identity theft knows no geographic, racial, gender, or age boundaries and is illegal on both federal and state law levels.[13] Personal data sought by identity thieves include names, addresses, Social Security numbers, bank or credit card numbers, and identities of minor children. Armed with this data, thieves may attempt to obtain money from bank accounts, charge to existing or open new credit card accounts, submit false insurance claims, obtain health care benefits, or damage another's credit rating by falsely filing for bankruptcy protection. Those who are victims of identity theft face an enormous challenge in clearing their name and recovering full possession of their identity.

Health information management professionals can address the potential for identity theft by employing preventive measures. Such measures can include employing the technology available to safeguard electronic PHI, including passwords, access controls, encryption, firewalls, and electronic audits. Nontechnological safeguards—such as background checks for employees and business associates, redaction of portions of Social Security numbers or credit card account numbers, and restricted access to paper-based medical records—may all be employed. Policies and procedures that address record retention, destruction, disposal, or reuse all should include provisions to restrict access to PHI to only those with a need to know. Review of these safeguards, policies, and procedures should occur on a routine basis, along with training for health care staff members.

Even with preventive measures in place, identity theft may still occur. It is incumbent upon HIM professionals to develop a strategy to respond to and address the occurrence once it is reported. This strategy should include the level of response deemed appropriate by the health care provider, the mechanism to investigate the report, and how notification to law enforcement or governmental agencies and the victim will occur. This notification step involves reconciling the HIPAA provision that allows release of evidence of criminal conduct to law enforcement authorities with state or local law that may require such release only upon patient authorization or court order.[14] The strategy should also address the extent to which the health care provider may assist the identity theft victim with health-care-related matters such as billing or inaccurate entries in the medical record or non-health-care-related matters such as filing a police report or a fraud alert to a credit reporting agency. By having such a strategy in place, the HIM professional is well positioned to assist the identity theft victim.

Informed Consent

Demands for patient-specific health information arise not only from third-party payers and governmental entities, but also from patients themselves when deciding to consent to or forgo treatment. This demand for information has initiated a significant development in the relationship between law and medicine: the doctrine of informed consent.

Informed consent is defined as the communication of definite knowledge of an event or fact to the patient so that he may voluntarily agree to or forgo treatment. Informed consent applies in multiple situations, from simple testing to participation in complex clinical research trials. Informed consent may be implied—such as when the health care provider takes the patient's pulse or temperature—or express—such as when the health care provider asks the patient's permission to perform invasive surgery.

The scope of the informed consent doctrine can be measured in several ways: who may consent to treatment, how much information the health care provider must disclose to the patient, and what situations require informed consent. The scope of the informed consent doctrine is illustrated in Figure 3–8.

As a general rule, it is the patient and the patient alone who decides whether to consent to or forgo treatment. This general rule assumes two things: that an emergency situation is not present and that the patient is competent under the law to consent to treatment. An emergency situation is considered present when the patient is unable to give consent, another person authorized to give consent is unavailable, and a delay in treatment would likely result in death or serious bodily harm to the patient. Adult patients are presumed competent absent an adjudication of incompetency by a court of law or where legal competency is clearly an issue (e.g., a comatose patient). For those patients who are considered legally incompetent, advance directives may be used to address the issues associated with informed consent.

Advance directives are written instructions that describe the kind of health care the patient wishes to have or not have in the event that he becomes incapacitated. These advance directives inform the health care provider of the patient's preferences *before* the need for medical treatment arises. Advance directives take the form of either durable powers of attorney for health care or living wills. A durable power of attorney for health care is a written document in which the patient names someone else (the *proxy*) to make health care decisions on the patient's behalf if he is later

Figure 3–8 | Scope of informed consent doctrine

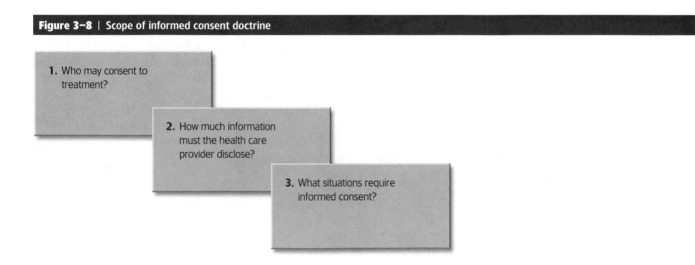

1. Who may consent to treatment?

2. How much information must the health care provider disclose?

3. What situations require informed consent?

unable to do so. A **living will** is a written document that provides direction as to medical care in the event that the patient becomes incapacitated or unable to make personal decisions. Unlike a durable power of attorney for health care, a living will does not involve a third party and may include a list of treatments and procedures that the patient wishes to undertake or forgo in the event that they apply to the future situation. They are similar in the sense that both documents are created when the patient is competent and are used when the patient is incompetent or otherwise unable to make personal decisions. Many patients elect to employ both durable powers of attorney for health care and living wills, reasoning that the living will provides specificity to their wishes as to treatments and procedures, and the durable power of attorney provides a means for decision making in areas not covered by the terms of the living will.

Advance directives are matters governed by both state and federal law. State law defines the patient's substantive legal rights and the manner in which certain health care actions can be taken, such as the criteria to be used when seeking authority to remove life-sustaining treatment to a terminally ill individual. A large variation exists between the states concerning patients' substantive legal rights, what actions can be taken legally, and the manner in which those actions may proceed. Federal law interplays with state law in the context of how health care facilities use advance directives. The Patient Self-Determination Act of 1990 (PSDA) requires health care facilities to inform their patients of the status of state law governing the patient's right to make an advance directive. The PSDA also requires health care facilities to place a copy of the patient's advance directive in the medical record and inform the patient of the facility's policies concerning implementation of advance directives. What is significant about the interplay between federal and state law in the context of advance directives is that state law addresses the patient's substantive legal rights whereas federal law addresses the procedures by which those rights must be exercised when the patient receives treatment from a health care facility. To further complicate the situation, advance directives are also subject to regulation by administrative bodies and standards set by accrediting bodies.

The amount of information a health care provider discloses to the patient is governed by state law, and, as such, some variation exists across the United States. Informed consent is also governed by federal regulations, such as those issued pursuant to the Medicare program, and the standards of accrediting agencies, such as the Joint Commission (JC). At minimum, the health care provider is required to disclose the nature of the patient's diagnosis, the reason for the proposed course of treatment or procedures, the risks involved therein, any available treatment alternatives, the likelihood of success, and the benefits that may be expected. With regard to identifying risks, the law requires the health care provider to disclose any known and existing dangers associated with the proposed course of treatment or procedures, including the risks associated if the patient

forgoes treatment. The health care provider's failure to disclose the dangers associated with a proposed course of treatment or procedure can result in the patient's revocation of consent plus potential liability for the health care provider.

In addition to being a legal doctrine, informed consent is also a process. This process entails not only the discussion between health care provider and patient, but physical evidence that this discussion took place and the results of that discussion (i.e., consenting to or forgoing treatment). Using a paper-based medical record, this evidence consists of a paper form labeled as "Informed Consent." Using an electronic health record, this evidence can be shown through a digitized image of such a paper form or through an entry in the electronic health record that contains the essential elements of informed consent along with evidence of the patient's decision to consent to or forgo treatment or procedure.

Judicial Process

The health information manager, serving as custodian of the record, encounters the judicial process when responding to subpoenas and court orders. A **subpoena** is a command issued by a court or other authorized official to appear or present certain documents and other items. The subpoena authorizes disclosure consistent with statute and regulation. A subcategory of subpoena is a **subpoena** *duces tecum*, which is a command to produce books, documents, and other physical things. A **court order** is a judge's ruling that authorizes disclosure that would otherwise be prohibited by statute and regulation.

When faced with a subpoena or court order, the health information manager is placed in the difficult position of deciding how to respond. Should he release the requested records, refuse to release the requested records, or excise those portions of the records that he determines are protected and release the remainder? If the health information manager fails to respond to the subpoena, he exposes the health care provider to negative consequences such as potential contempt of court charges. If the health information manager improperly releases the records, he may subject the health care provider to liability for breach of confidentiality. Only upon a determination that a valid subpoena or court order has been presented and that a valid legal defense against disclosure does not exist should the health information manager release the requested records.

HIPAA

The Privacy Rule impacts the manner in which disclosures are made pursuant to subpoenas and court orders.

As a practical matter, the health information manager should be guided by the policies and procedures of the manager's organization when deciding how to respond to the presentation of either a subpoena or a court order. These policies and procedures should address the provisions of the HIPAA Privacy Rule, which limits disclosures pursuant to either of these documents. With regard to subpoenas, the covered entity may only disclose PHI when the subpoena is accompanied by a valid release of information. With regard to court orders, the covered entity may only disclose that PHI expressly authorized by the court. The organization's policies and procedures should be developed with the advice of the health care organization's legal counsel long before subpoenas or court orders are tendered to the health information manager for response.

These policies and procedures should also address how the health information manager should respond to requests for PHI that may be in the public interest. Such requests may be made by law enforcement officials, medical examiners, coroners, funeral directors, and public health bodies and may or may not be accompanied by a subpoena or court order. The Privacy Rule also addresses these situations, providing guidance to covered entities on how to limit disclosure to only that PHI necessary for those groups to carry out their duties or to prevent a serious threat to the health or safety of the public. The Privacy Rule also addresses disclosures to appropriate governmental entities concerning victims of abuse, neglect, or domestic violence. The rule allows such disclosure if authorized by the patient, if the disclosure is required by law, or if the disclosure is authorized by statute.[15]

The health information manager should not automatically assume that every subpoena presented requires the release of the information requested. In some jurisdictions, a patient's valid written consent is required along with the subpoena before release of information is considered proper. In some instances, a valid legal defense such as physician-patient privilege may exist that protects certain information from release. Finally, strict confidentiality restrictions protect certain specialized health information such as substance abuse, mental health, and acquired immunodeficiency syndrome (AIDS). These restrictions may require special handling of subpoenas before health information is released.

At no time, however, should the health information manager ignore a subpoena or court order. Substantial penalties exist for failing to obey a subpoena or court order, including fines and contempt of court proceedings. Consultation with the health care organization's counsel is warranted whenever the health information manager questions the validity of the subpoena or court order.

Fraud and Abuse

One of the areas with the highest profile in health care today concerns fraud and abuse. Newspaper and journal articles are often filled with allegations on this topic, and continuing education programs that provide updates on this topic are well attended. The heightened emphasis this topic receives is appropriate since the effects of fraud and abuse of the health care system are widespread, impacting both the nation's economy and individual patient care. One report estimates that 3 percent of the nation's annual health care expenses are attributable to fraudulent activities.[16] In fact, the efforts of the U.S. Departments of Justice and Health and Human Services to combat fraud and abuse resulted in $1.8 billion in judgments, settlements, and administrative impositions during fiscal year 2003, the last year for which figures are available. For that same time period, some 3,275 individuals and entities were excluded from participation in Medicare, Medicaid, and other federally sponsored health care programs.[17]

Activities to combat fraud and abuse are not exclusive to the federal level. State legislatures have granted various public agencies new powers to issue regulations, conduct investigations, and take actions against those who commit fraud and abuse in their states. Third-party payers, such as private insurance companies, have recognized cases of fraud and abuse and have escalated their efforts to expose fraudulent claims. Even some consumer watch groups have taken action to educate the general public on how to recognize and report fraud and abuse in health care.

For all of the attention the phrase "fraud and abuse" has engendered, it is important to understand what it actually means. Fraud and abuse encompasses the actions of fraud, abuse, and waste in the health care system. **Fraud** refers to the intentional deception of another person to that person's detriment. **Abuse** refers to a pattern of practices or customs that are unsound or inconsistent with ethical business, fiscal, or health care practices or customs. **Waste** refers to the squandering of resources or the use of resources without gain or advantage. Any of these three actions, standing alone or in combination with one another, may fall within the definition of fraud and abuse.

Within the health care context, fraud and abuse can vary according to who commits the actions and the type of actions committed. Convictions and settlements have involved hospitals, nursing homes, home health agencies, pharmaceutical companies, durable medical equipment suppliers, Internet pharmacy services, physicians, physical therapists, ambulance services, and Medicare contractors, among others. Actions include misrepresentations in the marketing of pharmaceuticals, conspiracies to fraudulently bill Medicare and Medicaid, filing false cost reports to Medicare, unlawful patient referrals between health care entities for financial gain, payment of bribes, and failure to submit medical device reports to the Food and Drug Administration documenting a serious injury or death.

Of particular importance to the health information management profession are instances of fraudulent documentation, coding, and billing, since these are areas over which HIM professionals frequently have responsibility. For example, one hospital convicted of Medicare fraud manipulated documentation to inflate the amount of reimbursable nursing time spent on Medicare patients. Upon investigation, the hospital compounded its problems by creating false documents to support its prior actions, all of which were verified during the investigation.[18] Others have engaged in unethical coding practices referred to as upcoding and unbundling. **Upcoding** refers to submitting a billing code for a higher level of reimbursement than the billing code that actually applies to the services rendered to the patient. For example, submitting diagnosis codes that reflect the patient's diagnosis at the time of admission instead of at the time of discharge, in order to receive higher reimbursement, would fall within the definition of upcoding. **Unbundling** refers to the practice of submitting separate bills in a piecemeal or fragmented fashion as a way to maximize reimbursement for various tests or procedures. For example, submitting separate bills for each component of a laboratory test instead of for the entire laboratory test falls within the definition of unbundling. Examples of fraudulent billing include billing for services not rendered, double-billing for services rendered, billing for services considered medically unnecessary, and billing for a covered service when in fact the service provided was not covered.

Fraud and Abuse Laws

Health care providers, whether individuals or organizations, must be well versed in the various laws governing fraud and abuse if they are to comply with these laws and minimize their exposure to liability. Health information management professionals should be aware of these laws so that they may influence and ensure organizational compliance. A list of the major laws addressing fraud and abuse can be found in Table 3–12.

The False Claims Act (FCA) is a Civil War-era statute created as a means to address corruption by military contractors. Though the FCA did not sit dormant, attorneys for the federal government did not utilize the FCA to address health care concerns until the end of the 20th century, when concerns over fraud and abuse became more vocalized. The FCA prohibits the submission of false claims to the government for payment or the knowing concealment or avoidance

of records or statements that would reduce an obligation to pay money or property to the government. FCA lawsuits are often brought by private plaintiffs known as "relators." These relators, or **whistle-blowers** as they are commonly termed, typically are current or former employees of a health care provider or organization who have learned of fraud and abuse and wish to expose the activity. The lawsuit they bring is called a *qui tam* action, meaning that a private plaintiff stands in the place of the government to correct a wrong perpetrated against the government. Whistle-blowers who bring successful *qui tam* actions share in a percentage of the recovery that will be paid to the federal government.

A second effective law to combat fraud and abuse is the federal anti-kickback statute. This statute makes it a criminal offense for a person to knowingly and willfully offer, pay, solicit, or receive any remuneration, including kickbacks and rebates, in exchange for referrals of federally payable health care services. Although the statute is expansive in scope, it is commonly used to address improper patient referrals where one purpose of the referral is to receive a payment in return. Several exceptions to the statute apply—called "safe harbors"—so that those activities listed in the exceptions will be considered legitimate practices. Those health care providers who question whether any individual transaction falls within a safe harbor may seek an advisory opinion from the Office of Inspector General of the U.S. Department of Health and Human Services.

Another form of referral addressed by law involves physician self-referral. Referred to as the "Stark laws" after the congressman who sponsored the original law, these prohibitions operate to ban a physician from referring a patient to a designated health services entity in which the physician or immediate family member possesses a financial interest. Designated health services have been interpreted broadly, and include durable medical equipment, clinical laboratories, occupational therapy, orthotics and prosthetics, radiology, physical therapy, hospital services, parenteral and enteral nutrition services and supplies, home health services, and outpatient prescription drugs. Very limited ownership and compensation exceptions are available, and the criteria to qualify under them are very specific. Requests for an advisory opinion concerning these exceptions are directed to the CMS.

Several other statutes sometimes form the basis of fraud and abuse lawsuits or serve as an adjunct to a claim filed under one of the statutes previously addressed. Mail and wire fraud charges may be included, because it is routine practice for a health care provider to use the mail system or wire services as part of his modern business. If use of the mail system or wire services facilitated the wrongdoing, a charge of mail or wire fraud may be brought. Other charges may include false statements made pursuant to obtaining a

Table 3–12 | Major Laws Addressing Fraud and Abuse

False Claims Act
Qui tam actions
Anti-kickback statutes
Self-referral prohibitions (Stark I & II)
Mail and wire fraud
Health Insurance Portability and Accountability Act
Deficit Reduction Act of 2005

benefit or payment under the Social Security Act, conspiracy to defraud, money laundering, or Racketeer Influenced and Corrupt Organizations (RICO). State laws may also apply, allowing state attorneys general to charge wrongdoers with claims of kickbacks, self-referrals, improper fee-splitting, bribery, and deceptive trade practices.

Fraud and abuse laws that address the remedies available to the federal government include the civil money penalty law and the ability to exclude practitioners from participation in Medicare, Medicaid, and other federally sponsored programs. The civil money penalty law permits the government to recover damages for false or fraudulent claims up to $10,000 and an assessment of three times the amount of damages. The exclusion provisions apply to practitioner violations of both criminal and civil law.

HIPAA

Increased penalties and new enforcement mechanisms are part of HIPAA's focus on fraud and abuse.

HIPAA modified the civil money penalty law to increase penalties and provide new enforcement mechanisms. These modifications address specific fraudulent actions, such as upcoding, unbundling, and seeking reimbursement for services rendered after being excluded from participation in Medicare or Medicaid. Additionally, HIPAA created or strengthened several programs to combat fraud and abuse; these programs were addressed earlier in this chapter.

Finally, the Deficit Reduction Act of 2005 provides additional strength to combating fraud and abuse in the Medicaid program. This law changes the nature of compliance programs for some institutions from voluntary to mandatory, requires employers to educate staff concerning administrative remedies to violations of the False Claims Act, adds more resources at the federal level for combating fraud and abuse, and provides a financial incentive to states to adopt laws similar to the federal False Claims Act. Furthermore, the language of this Act allows states to make their laws even more stringent or broad than the federal False Claims Act.

Resources to Combat Fraud and Abuse

Combating fraud and abuse is a varied and complex process. The resources available to combat fraud and abuse are subject to the whims of funding and political will. At the present time, fiscal constraints at the federal, state, and local levels have caused extensive examination of publicly funded programs to determine whether taxpayer monies are well spent. Part of this examination has led to the conclusion that fraud and abuse not only exist but must be combated with vigor and zeal. Similar examinations have occurred in the private sector, with comparable conclusions reached.

Among the most effective means to combat fraud and abuse are law enforcement agencies. A list of the law enforcement agencies that share responsibility to investigate and prosecute fraud and abuse is found in Table 3–13. One prominent law enforcement agency is the Office of Inspector General (OIG), located within the U.S. Department of Health and Human Services. Created in 1976 to identify and eliminate fraud, abuse, and waste in DHHS programs, it also works to promote efficiency and economy in departmental operations. OIG accomplishes its work through audits, investigations, inspections, and initiatives.

OIG has experienced considerable success during the last decade by launching several initiatives aimed at recovering alleged overpayments made in connection with specific types of improper claims. The Physicians at Teaching Hospitals (PATH) initiative focused on the billing of services rendered by residents and teaching physicians, differentiating between services already paid under Medicare Part A's graduate medical education and indirect medical education programs from those services that could be billed properly under Medicare Part B. The "72-Hour Rule" Project focused on the payments made to hospitals for services provided to patients within a 72-hour window of the patient's admission, collecting overpayments made due to double billing. The Hospital Outpatient Laboratory Project focused on unbundling practices for claims dealing with hematology and automated blood chemistry tests. The PPS Patient Transfer Project focused on payments made through the prospective payment system (PPS) that did not follow the practice of paying the transferring hospital according to the applicable diagnosis-related group (DRG) code and the transferee hospital according to the per diem allowances and applicable DRG code. Finally, a project focusing on pneumonia upcoding has indicated that some

Table 3–13 Law Enforcement Agencies Responsible for Fraud and Abuse Investigations	
Office of Inspector General (OIG) of DHHS	Investigates civil, criminal, and administrative fraud in the federal Medicare and Medicaid programs. Provides guidance on compliance efforts.
Postal Inspection Service	Investigates fraud schemes involving the U.S. mail system.
Federal Bureau of Investigation (FBI)	Investigates fraud schemes across governmental programs, including whistle-blower claims.
Defense Criminal Investigative Service (DCIS)	Investigates fraud schemes committed against the military's health insurance programs.

hospitals have improperly assigned DRG codes as a means to increase reimbursement.

Although each of these initiatives has resulted in recoupment of funds to the government, OIG's strong emphasis on this approach has not been without criticism. Some have claimed that the subjects of these initiatives committed honest mistakes or, at most, negligence, and should not have been prosecuted but educated as to the proper manner in which to submit claims for payment. DHHS has responded by instituting and emphasizing preventive programs to be operated by the CMS. Examples include the Correct Coding Initiative (CCI), designed to promote national correct coding methodologies, and the Payment Error and Prevention Program (PEPP), designed to reduce the Medicare payment error rate. CMS also coordinates with OIG to publish numerous guidance materials, available on the CMS Web site, to explain and clarify its regulations. These materials identify risk areas and offer suggestions on proper billing practices and internal controls.

While much of the effort to combat fraud and abuse occurs at a governmental or third-party payer level, efforts are also in place within health care entities. Many of these actions fall under the broad heading of corporate compliance programs. A **compliance program** is a program that ensures the use of effective internal controls that promote adherence to applicable local, state, and federal laws and regulations and the program requirements of federal, state, and private health plans. Health care entities operate compliance programs for two reasons: (1) as a means to reduce their exposure to civil damages and penalties, criminal sanctions, and administrative remedies; and (2) a way to assess and improve the efficiency, effectiveness, and quality of patient services. Corporate compliance programs have become so prevalent in the health care industry that entities that do not operate such programs risk being perceived as operating below the standard of care.

The federal government has recognized the value of corporate compliance programs and, for years, has taken action to encourage their use. Such actions include publishing compliance program guidelines for the health care areas listed in Table 3-14. These program guidelines offer suggestions, not mandates, for health care entities to incorporate when developing a compliance program to fit their own culture, structure, and processes. Furthermore, the government has reduced sanctions against those entities accused of fraud and abuse that operate compliance programs. With the passage of the Deficit Reduction Act of 2005, those entities who receive $5 million or more in annual Medicaid reimbursement must educate their employees using handbooks and written policies about the administrative remedies available for violations of the False Claims Act and any corresponding state laws. This

Table 3-14 | Voluntary Compliance Guideline Areas

Ambulance industry, including suppliers
Clinical laboratories
Durable medical equipment industry
Home health agencies
Hospices
Hospital industry
Individual and small-group practices
Nursing facilities
Medicare+Choice organizations
Pharmaceutical manufacturers
Third-party medical billing companies

Source: Adapted from Green, M., & Bowie, M. (2005). *Essentials of health information management: Principles and practices.* Albany, NY: Delmar.

requirement alone changes the practice of corporate compliance from one of a voluntary nature to one of a mandatory nature. It is unknown how soon this requirement may be applied to entities receiving lesser amounts of Medicaid reimbursement.

Whereas compliance programs can assist the health care entity in preventing and detecting improper conduct, they cannot serve as a shield from liability. Health care entities who violate the law are subject to sanctions, including fines; exclusion from participation in Medicare, Medicaid, and state health programs; and incarceration. Not all prosecutions proceed to trial; some may be settled beforehand. Settlements between the government and health care entities may be memorialized into corporate integrity agreements. A **corporate integrity agreement** (CIA) is a written agreement that specifies the rules of conduct to be followed to remedy the fraud and abuse found, plus any monitoring and reporting requirements. It differs from a corporate compliance program in that the compliance program is an internal, not external, document that is adopted by the health care entity voluntarily as opposed to under direction of the government. Further, a CIA can be more stringent and expensive to implement than a compliance program. For these reasons, many health care entities place great emphasis on their corporate compliance programs, since the risk of being subject to a CIA outweighs the risks associated with adopting and operating a compliance program.

Whether part of a compliance program or operating outside the program, some health care entities have employed technology as a means to combat fraud. Most of this technology exists in two forms: advanced analytics software for use in the national health information infrastructure, and automated coding software. The advanced analytics software allows multiple parties who operate within the infrastructure (an interoperable electronic exchange between health care providers, government, and third-party payers) to examine data to detect fraud. For example, a third-party payer may be able to review electronically stored clinical encounter data to validate a claim submitted by the health care provider for payment. By validating the clinical encounter before making payment, the third-party payer reduces the opportunity for financial loss in the first place, as opposed to discovering the invalidity of the claim after payment has been made. Automated coding software assigns the correct code based on official guidelines and reporting rules programmed into the software. These codes are assigned after evaluation of the patient's clinical data that is stored electronically. A coding professional or clinician reviews the automated assignments and edits as necessary, with more editing needed in instances where the clinical encounter is complex or the coding software is not highly sophisticated. By validating or editing the automated assignments, the health care provider is in a position to prevent submission of fraudulent codes to a third-party payer. Some coding software programs allow a review of all codes assigned over a period of time, allowing the health care provider to detect patterns that may indicate instances of manipulation of the computer program or other forms of fraud. As technology develops further, both advanced analytics software and automated coding software should grow more sophisticated in preventing, detecting, and prosecuting fraud.

Conclusion

As this chapter indicates, health information is subject to stringent oversight, including laws, regulations, rules, requirements, standards, and guidance considerations. The interplay between this stringent oversight and health information is extensive and influences the day-to-day operations of health care providers. Health information managers must review and understand the areas of law so that they may apply those areas properly to their particular situations. Failure to consider these many factors when reaching a decision exposes both the health information management professional and the health care entity to risk of liability.

CHAPTER SUMMARY

Legal issues in health information management arise from a variety of sources, including laws, regulations, rules, requirements, and standards. All three branches of government greatly influence how legal issues are addressed in health care, with nongovernmental entities such as accrediting bodies and professional associations also playing a role. The court system and the legal procedures that flow from it are tied to principles of liability that, within the health care context, center on intentional and nonintentional torts. Legal issues central to health information management focus on both traditional issues—such as privacy and confidentiality, access to health care data, informed consent, and judicial process—and newer developments—such as HIPAA and health care fraud and abuse. Both HIPAA and fraud and abuse have changed the landscape of the health care system in the United States, and the health information management profession in particular, causing both to develop responses that offer promise of greater patient protection and wiser use of fiscal resources.

CASE STUDY

You are the director of health information management at Anywhere Hospital. Because of the increased awareness of instances of identity theft in your local community, you have resolved to minimize the potential for identity theft occurring in your facility. Identify the measures you can employ to prevent identity theft and discuss how you would respond to a reported occurrence of identity theft.

REVIEW QUESTIONS

1. Do the three branches of government work in isolation? How so, or how do they not?

2. What branch of government possesses the greatest day-to-day influence in health care?

3. What are the most prominent nongovernmental entities in health care? How do they influence health care?

4. How do the issues of health record content, completeness, and record retention policies interplay with laws, regulations, and standards?

5. What are the many legal uses served by the health record?

6. What is the minimum necessary standard and how is it applied?

7. How are living wills and durable powers of attorney similar, and how are they different?

8. Should the health information manager assume that each subpoena presented requires the release of the information requested? Why or why not?

9. What matters are of particular importance to health information management professionals concerning health care fraud and abuse?

10. How does a corporate compliance program differ from a corporate integrity agreement?

ENRICHMENT ACTIVITIES

1. Using the Internet, research recent news articles that address the use of advance directives. Compare the way these articles explain the concepts of advance directives with the descriptions contained in this chapter. Do these articles differentiate between durable powers of attorney for health care and living wills? Do they describe the use of these documents accurately?

2. Visit the Web site of the Centers for Medicare and Medicaid Services, at http://www.cms.hhs.gov, and search for information

concerning the Health Insurance Portability and Accountability Act. Identify the many ways in which HIPAA affects the work of CMS. Alternatively, review the Web site for guidance materials concerning fraud and abuse. Identify which sets of material either help clarify the agency's underlying regulations or offer guidance on how to avoid errors.

WEB SITES

Agency for Healthcare Research and Quality, http://www.ahrq.gov

American Correctional Association, http://www.corrections.com/aca

Centers for Disease Control and Prevention, http://www.cdc.gov

Centers for Medicare and Medicaid Services, http://www.cms.hhs.gov

Commission on Accreditation of Rehabilitation Facilities, http://www.carf.org

Community Health Accreditation Program, Inc., http://www.chapinc.org

Federal Register, http://www.gpoaccess.gov

Joint Commission, http://www.jointcommission.org

National Commission on Correctional Health Care, http://www.corrections.com/ncchc

National Committee for Quality Assurance, http://www.ncqa.org

National Health Law Program, http://www.healthlaw.org

National Institutes of Health, http://www.nih.gov

REFERENCES

Baumann, L. A. (Ed.). (2002). *Health care fraud and abuse: Practical perspectives.* Washington, DC: American Bar Association.

Beaver, K., & Herold, R. (2004). *The practical guide to HIPAA privacy and security compliance.* Boca Raton, FL: Auerbach.

Carp, R. A., Stidham, R., & Manning, K. (2004). *Judicial process in America* (6th ed.). Washington, DC: CQ Press.

Loucks, M. K., & Lam, C. C. (2001). *Prosecuting and defending health care fraud cases.* Washington, DC: Bureau of National Affairs, Inc.

McWay, D. C. (2003). *Legal aspects of health information management* (2nd ed.). Clifton Park, NY: Delmar.

Practice Brief. (2004). Identity theft and fraud—The impact on HIM operations. *Journal of AHIMA, 74*(4), 64A–64D.

NOTES

1. 42 U.S.C. § 1320d (2007).

2. 42 C.F.R. § 488.5 (2007).

3. Laws include: 42 U.S.C. § 1395x(e) (2) (2003); ARIZ. STAT. ANN. § 12-2291 (2000); TENN. CODE ANN. § 68-11-302 (2000). Regulations include: 42 C.F.R. § 405.1722 (b) (2003); MASS. REGS. CODE tit. 105, § 130.200 (1987); MONT. ADMIN R. 16.32.320 (1990). Standards include: Joint Commission, Comprehensive Accreditation Manual For Hospitals, Management of Information, IM 7.2 (2001).

4. See, e.g., 42 C.F.R. § 405.1722 (c) (2003) (Medicare Conditions of Participation); Joint Commission, Comprehensive Accreditation Manual For Hospitals, Management of Information, IM 7.1-.10 (2001).

5. See, e.g., ALASKA STAT. § 18.20.085 (2000) (7 years); HAW. REV. STAT. § 622-58 (2000) (7 years); MISS. CODE ANN. § 41-9-69 (1999) (retain for a period of minority plus 7 years, not to exceed 28 years); TENN. CODE ANN. § 68-11-305 (2000) (10 years); American Accreditation Healthcare Commission/Urac, Health Network Accreditation Manual, Standard 7 (1999).

6. Federal Rules of Civil Procedure 16 (pretrial conferences), 26 (duty of disclosure), 33 (interrogatories), 34 (production of documents, including business records), 37 (failure to disclose/sanctions), 45 (subpoena), and form 35 (report of planned meeting) (2006).

7. 19 HAW. REV. STAT. §§ 323C-1 to -54 (2007); MONT. CODE ANN. §§ 50-16-501 to -542 (2007); WASH. REV. CODE ANN. §§ 70.02.005 to 904 (2007).

8. Edelstein, L. (1943). *The Hippocratic Oath: Text, translation, and interpretation* (p. 3). Chicago Ridge, IL: Ares Publishers.

9. 45 C.F.R. § 164.502 (2007).

10. 45 C.F.R. § 164.524 (2007). Some exceptions to individual access to PHI include (1) psychotherapy notes; (2) information that is, or could be used for, a civil, criminal, or administrative action or legal proceeding; (3) that PHI which is subject to access prohibitions found in the Clinical Laboratory Improvements Amendments (CLIA) of 1988; and (4) PHI held by certain research laboratories.

11. 42 U.S.C. § 1320d-6 (2007).

12. The Identity Theft and Assumption Deterrence Act of 1998, 18 U.S.C. § 1028 (2007). Some states with provisions addressing identity theft include IA STAT. ANN.§ 554D.122 (2007); MINN. STAT. ANN. § 609.527 (2007); MO. REV. STAT. § 570.223.1 (2007); S.D. STAT. ANN. § 22.30A (2007).

13. Ibid. See also ARK. CODE ANN. § 5-37-226 (2007); IA. STAT. ANN. § 554d.122 (2007); MN. STAT. ANN. § 609.527 (2007); MO. STAT. ANN. § 570.223.1 (2007); SD STAT. ANN. § 22.30A (2007).

14. 45 C.F.R. § 164.512(1) (5) (2007).

15. 45 C.F.R. §§ 164.512(f) (2007) (law enforcement officials), .512(c)(1) (victims of abuse), .512(g) (medical examiners, coroners, and funeral directors), and .512(j) (public health agencies to avert a serious threat to health and safety).

16. National Health Care Anti-Fraud Association. (2005). *Healthcare fraud: A serious and costly reality for all Americans.* Retrieved December 17, 2006 from http://www.nhcaa.org

17. U.S. Department of Health and Human Services & Department of Justice. (2004). *Health care fraud and abuse control program annual report for FY 2003.* Retrieved May 28, 2005 from http://www.usdoj.gov/dag/pubdoc/hcfacreport2003.htm

18. St. Luke's Subacute Hospital and Nursing Center Inc., 2004 WL 2905237 (N.D.Cal.), Med & Med GD (CCH) P 301, 576.

CHAPTER 4

Ethical Standards

CERTIFICATION CONNECTION

RHIA
Coding compliance/reporting
Ethical issues
Investigate/mitigate privacy issues/problems

RHIT
Coding guidelines
Ethical standards of practice
Privacy issues/problems

LEARNING OBJECTIVES

After reading this chapter, the learner should be able to:

1. Differentiate between ethics, morals, values, etiquette, and law.

2. Compare and contrast ethical concepts and theories.

3. Understand the ethical decision-making process.

4. Define codes of ethics and discuss their importance.

5. Restate the dilemmas posed by bioethical issues.

6. Identify ethical challenges in general and their application to the role of supervision, the field of health care, and the specialized area of health information management.

Outline

Ethical Overview

Ethical Models

Ethical Decision Making

Influencing Factors
Decision-Making Process

Bioethical Issues

Related to the Beginning of Life
Related to Sustaining or Improving the Quality of Life
Related to Death and Dying

Ethical Challenges

General Challenges
Role of Ethics in Supervision
Health Care Challenges
Health Information Management Challenges

Key Concepts

Abortion	Ethical acts	Nonmaleficence
Active euthanasia	Ethical challenges	Organ transplantation
Advance directives	Ethical concepts	Passive euthanasia
Allografts	Ethical theories	Paternalism
Artificial insemination	Ethics	Patient rights
Autografts	Ethics committees	Perinatal ethics
Autonomy	Etiquette	Placebos
Beneficence	Eugenics	Prenatal surgery
Best interest standard	Euthanasia	Prenatal testing
Bioethics	Family planning	Privacy
Categorical imperative	Fidelity	Rights
Codes of ethics	Gene therapy	Stem cell research
Comparative justice	Genetic screening	Sterilization
Confidentiality	Heterografts	Surrogate mother
Conflict of interest	Homografts	Utilitarianism
Contraception	Human Genome Project	Values
Cost/benefit analysis	Impaired colleagues	Veracity
Deontology	In vitro fertilization	Withdrawing treatment
Disparagement	Justice	Withholding treatment
Distributive justice	Law	Xenografts
Double effect principle	Living will	
Durable power of attorney for health care	Morals	

INTRODUCTION

Although at times it may seem that laws, regulations, and accrediting standards and requirements govern every aspect of the health care field, this is simply not the case. It is not possible for every health care issue to be addressed by laws, regulations, and standards. In the absence of laws, regulations, and standards, health care professionals can look to ethical principles to provide a framework for decision making.

This chapter addresses ethics in general, in the workplace, and in the context of health care from both conceptual and practical perspectives. A discussion of the many approaches to ethical reasoning is followed by discussion of the ethical decision-making process. Identification of bioethical issues that have occurred in the last half-century follows thereafter. Ethical challenges are presented to demonstrate the application of ethical reasoning and decision making on a personal level and as a health information manager. The purpose of these discussions is to frame ethical issues so that the learner recognizes them in her personal and professional lives and also understands them when they are discussed in society at large. Armed with this knowledge, the learner is better positioned to apply critical thinking to situations at work and in everyday life.

Ethical Overview

To understand ethical issues, one must start from a common set of definitions. **Ethics** is the formal study of moral choices that conform to standards of conduct. Ethics is often thought of as listening to one's conscience. Ethics is derived from the Greek word *ethos*, which means customs, habitual usage, conduct, and character. It involves examining reasoning, personal responsibility, emotions, and constitutional issues of freedom. Actions that can be judged as proper or acceptable behavior based on some standard of right and wrong are referred to as **ethical acts**. In essence, ethics involves making judgments between right and wrong.

Ethics differs from morals in that **morals** are recognized as the principles or fundamental standards of "right" conduct that an individual internalizes. The term *morals* is derived from the Latin word *mores*, which means custom or habit. Right moral conduct is based on traditional religious teachings and personal moral choices. By contrast, ethics is a branch of philosophy, which is the formal study of beliefs and assumptions. The two terms are related in that ethics puts personal moral principles and standards into practice in the manner of making judgments with clarity and consistency.

Ethics differs from etiquette in that **etiquette** is concerned with how human beings relate to one another under certain circumstances. In other words, etiquette is a social code of customs and rituals. Examples of etiquette include courtesy, politeness, and proper dress. In addition to being a part of everyday life, etiquette is often associated with ceremonial behavior, such as the president's inauguration ceremony or a wedding ceremony. In some areas, etiquette is highly developed, as in the etiquette expressed through customs and rituals that each branch of the armed forces observes.

Law, by contrast, is a body of rules of action or conduct prescribed by controlling authority that has binding legal force. Laws are created as a means to control behavior and protect the public from danger. Law and ethics are closely related. Many times, law only expresses the minimum level of one's expectations of right and wrong, leaving ethics to fill the void. In these instances, behavior that would be considered legally correct may not be considered ethically correct. Consider the situation of a person who could save a drowning man but fails to make an attempt. Failing to make an attempt

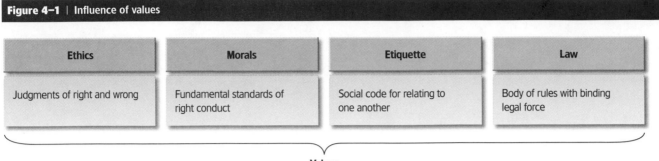

Figure 4-1 | Influence of values

Ethics	Morals	Etiquette	Law
Judgments of right and wrong	Fundamental standards of right conduct	Social code for relating to one another	Body of rules with binding legal force

Values
Concepts that give life meaning

to save the drowning man may be legally correct if the law does not require a person to make such an attempt but may be ethically incorrect, and the person may be considered personally irresponsible for failing to make such an attempt.

Distinguishing between legal and ethical issues has been problematic for many. Ordinarily, one looks to ethics: (1) when there is no obvious right or wrong; (2) when the enforcement of law does not appear to bring about justice; (3) when right behavior appears to bring about a wrong effect; or (4) when personal sacrifice is the consequence of following ideals. One can also distinguish between legal and ethical issues by looking to consequences. Breaking the law results in penalties enforced by the law; breaking ethical codes results in the disapproval of at least one segment of society, such as professionals in an organization. Finally, one can distinguish between law and ethics by looking at whether the focus of a choice is external or internal. Because law by definition involves some form of controlling authority (e.g., legislature or city council), the focus of the choice is external. Because ethics involves listening to one's conscience, the focus of the choice is internal.

All four concepts—ethics, morals, etiquette, and law—are based on values. Values are the concepts that give meaning to an individual's life and serve as the framework for decision making. Hard work, honesty, sincerity, genuineness, and cleanliness are all examples of values. Values are based on societal norms, religion, and family orientation, and they assist in the decision-making processes of everyday life. The influence of values is illustrated in Figure 4–I.

Often, values are so interwoven into everyday life that people do not think of them until a conflict arises. This conflict may arise when something goes wrong, when a difficult decision must be made, or from contact with other persons who do not share the same values. For example, the societies of two different countries may place different values on the role of women in the workplace or in the political setting. These different values would result in a values conflict. Once the conflict is identified, one engages in the values clarification process. This process requires a person to become more conscious of what she considers worthy and to name those

Table 4-1 | Ethical Concepts and Theories

Ethical Concepts	Ethical Theories
Autonomy	Utilitarianism
Beneficence/nonmaleficence	Deontology
Best interests standard	
Fidelity	
Justice	
Rights	
Veracity	

values. By becoming more aware and understanding of values, the person is better equipped to make choices.

Ethical Models

Philosophers and ethicists have suggested multiple approaches to ethical reasoning for thousands of years. These ethical approaches are articulated as concepts and theories designed to assist a person in assessing right from wrong in a particular situation, and are listed in Table 4–I. Generally, individuals find comfort in one or more of the approaches addressed in the following section, applying the appropriate approach to an ethical dilemma.

Ethical Concepts Ethical concepts refer to abstract ideas or thoughts that deal with ethics. It is significant that these ideas and thoughts exist in the abstract form, helping to serve as part of the values that undergird the decision-making process. Numerous ethical concepts exist, including autonomy, beneficence/nonmaleficence, best interest standard, fidelity, justice, rights, and veracity. Although this section addresses these concepts in alphabetical order, no hierarchy of importance should be associated with any one concept.

Autonomy One of the most readily understood ethical concepts is autonomy. Autonomy refers to independence, self-determination, or freedom. The word autonomy is derived from the Greek words *autos*, meaning self, and *nomos*, meaning governance. In the ethical sense, autonomy operates as respect for the individual and an expectation that she will participate in and make her own decisions in accordance with a plan of her own choosing. Autonomy is often associated with the concepts of dignity, self-reliance, and individualism.

Autonomy consists of three main elements; the first is the ability to decide. This ability requires the receipt of adequate information and the possession of the intellectual capacity to understand this information. Second, the individual must possess the power to actualize or implement the decisions she makes. This is especially important because decisions can be viewed as hollow if no implementation follows. The third element is a respect for the individual autonomy of others. This respect requires that persons be treated as unique and yet equal to all other individuals. This respect fosters professional behavior, since it recognizes the danger of exploiting others and the potential for becoming overly involved with others, particularly patients.

Within the health care field, autonomy is embedded in the concept of informed consent. The concept requires health care providers to disclose to patients adequate information in a manner the patient can understand. Armed with this information, the competent patient determines whether and what actions to take or forgo in relation to her medical care. This type of decision making—often in the form of granting permission to the health care provider to take action that will benefit the patient—is voluntary, demonstrating that the power rests with the patient and not with the health care provider.

Although autonomy encompasses individualism, the concept does not mean that the individual can do whatever she pleases, as her autonomy may interfere with another person's rights, health, or well-being. Restrictions on autonomy have been recognized as a means to maintain order in society. The ethical dilemma arises from the extent to which autonomy is curbed. For example, the smoking debate pits the individual's freedom to smoke against the dangers secondhand smoke

poses to the rest of society. Solutions to dilemmas such as this are not arrived at easily and require careful weighing of individual freedoms against the common good of the community.

Beneficence and Nonmaleficence Two concepts central to ethics are beneficence and nonmaleficence. **Beneficence** refers to the qualities of kindness, mercy, and charity. Beneficence operates in the ethical sense through the obligation to do good in all circumstances. **Nonmaleficence** refers to the prohibition against doing harm and operates in the ethical sense through the obligation to prevent evil or harm. The two concepts differ in that beneficence addresses action from a positive perspective (e.g., promote good) whereas nonmaleficence addresses action from a negative perspective (e.g., refrain from inflicting harm).

A prime example that illustrates both concepts is the Hippocratic Oath, shown in Figure 4–2. This oath contains multiple examples of beneficence, stating in part that the physician will apply "measures to benefit the sick," creating an obligation to promote the health and welfare of the patient above other considerations. The oath contains multiple examples of nonmaleficence as well, stating in part that the physician will keep the patient "from harm and injustice" and will refrain from "all intentional injustice." In essence, the oath stresses the physician's obligation to maximize the good for the patient (beneficence) and minimize the harm to the patient (nonmaleficence).

Beneficence and nonmaleficence are viewed as part of one's professional duty in the health care field. The expectation is that the health care services rendered will not make the patient worse but will serve to improve the patient's health. At times, the patient's health may actually worsen unintentionally due to receipt of these services—nosocomial infections, adverse drug reactions, and side effects of cancer treatments and other serious

Figure 4–2 | Hippocratic Oath

I swear by Apollo Physician and Asclepius and Hygieia and Panaceia and all the gods and goddesses, making them my witnesses, that I will fulfill according to my ability and judgment this oath and this covenant:

I will apply dietetic measures for the benefit of the sick, according to my ability and judgment; I will keep them from harm and injustice.

I will neither give a deadly drug to anybody if asked for it, nor will I make a suggestion to this effect. Similarly I will not give to a woman an abortive remedy. In purity and holiness I will guard my life and my art.

I will not use the knife, not even on sufferers from stone, but will withdraw in favor of such men as are engaged in this work.

Whatever houses I may visit, I will come for the benefit of the sick, remaining free of all intentional injuries, of all mischief and in particular of sexual relations with both female and male persons, be they free or slaves.

What I may see or hear in the course of the treatment or even outside of the treatment in regard to the life of men, which on no account one must noise abroad, I will keep to myself holding such things shameful to be spoken about.

If I fulfill this oath and do not violate it, may it be granted to me to enjoy life and art, being honored with fame among all men for all time to come; if I transgress it and swear falsely, may the opposite of all this be my lot.

diseases can result in harm to the patient. These unfortunate events can be reconciled with beneficence and nonmaleficence concepts using the principle of double effect. The double effect principle recognizes that ethical choices may result in untoward outcomes. If the untoward outcome is not the intended outcome but a secondary outcome, and it is outweighed by the intended positive or neutral outcome (good vs. harm analysis), one may still be considered ethical if she proceeds with a choice that results in a double effect. Because health care practitioners are not intentionally inflicting harm in the cases of nosocomial infections and adverse drug reactions, and the patient has consented to the treatment resulting in side effects after gaining a thorough understanding of the associated risks and benefits, the health care practitioner is still considered to be acting ethically.

Best Interest Standard The best interest standard refers to the process of determining what is in the best interest of an individual when the individual cannot make such a decision herself. The inability to make a decision is generally determined by competency. For example, severely mentally retarded individuals are generally considered persons who cannot meet the criteria of competence as a matter of law. Additionally, the best interest standard often applies to persons who once met the competency standard but are now considered incompetent due to illness or injury. When using this standard, the decision maker considers whether and how the individual will benefit or be harmed, examining mental, physical, and fiscal risks and whether the individual ever expressed an opinion on the subject at issue. The focus rests more on concepts such as beneficence and nonmaleficence than autonomy.

Within the health care field, the best interest standard is most often seen when a decision must be made about the direction of a patient's health care treatment and the patient is unable to provide informed consent. In such instances, health care providers look to past evidence of the patient's expressed wishes—such as a living will or power of attorney for health care—for guidance. Absent such documents, health care providers may look to family members and guardians for guidance. If these steps do not determine the direction of treatment, the health care provider may turn to the judicial system.

Many famous cases involving the health care treatment of incompetent patients have emerged in the last half-century, such as those involving Karen Ann Quinlan, Nancy Cruzan, and Terry Schiavo. Some of these cases arose because of the application of technology to health care, resulting in prolonged life for the patient. Because questions of life and death are so often at stake in these cases, they are fraught with emotion. While judges frequently apply the best interest standard in these cases, many persons have disputed the results. It appears unlikely that these cases will dwindle in the near future, since medical technology continues to make new advances not previously anticipated.

Fidelity Another readily understood concept in the health care field is fidelity. Fidelity refers to faithfulness, loyalty, and devotion to one's obligations or duties. Fidelity is most often seen in the context of agreements and commitments between individuals. This concept undergirds much of the discussion on accountability, because accountability is often measured by the level to which a person adheres to her responsibilities and obligations.

Fidelity is sometimes addressed in the health care field in terms of the role each health care professional plays. In the modern health care world, multiple professionals attend to a patient's care. Each professional operates within the constraints of acceptable practice, some of which are imposed by law and some of which are imposed by custom. Working within these constraints requires the health care professional to exercise fidelity to her role in treating the patient. For example, delivering and explaining a diagnosis to a patient for the first time is generally seen as the responsibility of the physician and not of the allied health professional.

Justice Justice refers to the obligation to be fair to all people. Justice encompasses several ideas, including fairness, honesty, and impartiality. Although justice requires that no person is favored over another, it does not require that all persons are treated the same. Opinions vary considerably over the concept of justice—what one person considers to be fair may conflict with the opinion of others. This same disagreement exists, to a lesser extent, over the ideas of impartiality and entitlement.

The concept of justice can be subdivided into two parts: comparative justice and distributive justice. Comparative justice refers to balancing the competing interests of individuals and groups against one another, with no independent standard used to make this comparison. This concept posits that because the needs or interests of some individuals or groups are greater than the needs or interests of other individuals or groups, it is acceptable for the individual or group with the greater need or interest to receive more resources than those with the lesser need or interest. For example, an individual who is close to death and in need of an organ transplant would be considered more needy than a person diagnosed with the same disease but who is not close to death and in need of an organ transplant. Distributive justice refers to the fair distribution of burdens and benefits using an independent standard. This concept posits that all persons have an equal opportunity to resources and requires that those in a position of authority provide the service that is due to others. For example, distributive justice applied in the legal sense is exemplified by the rule that all are innocent until proven guilty.

Within the health care context, distributive justice often applies to questions raised about access to scarce resources, requiring health care providers and health plans to provide an individual recipient with the care and service she is due. The concept encompasses six criteria to define just distribution where resources are limited: need, equity, contribution, ability to pay, effort, and merit. Need refers to required, not elective, procedures. Equity refers to the effort to distribute equally to all in need. Contribution refers to what a person might be expected to contribute to society at a future date. Ability refers to the power to pay and is considered part of distributive justice in the sense that needed services may be rendered to one who cannot afford to pay for those services. Effort refers to the willingness to comply or not comply with instruction (medical advice). Merit refers to the potential for benefit after the initial investment of limited resources. Considering all six criteria together can assist in solving problems associated with providing fair distribution of benefits and burdens to all patients.

Distributive justice is sometimes considered as an issue related to the financial controls imposed by prospective payment systems and health maintenance organizations (HMOs). Prospective payment systems establish limits on the amount a health care provider may be reimbursed for rendering care, and HMOs establish gatekeeping procedures that may limit access to specialty care. Both systems reward health care providers monetarily for maintaining lower costs and penalize those providers who do not keep costs within preestablished limits. With regard to ethics, placing such monetary rewards and penalties before health care providers may impact both the quantity and quality of patient care.

Rights **Rights** refer to a just claim or entitlement, whether based on law, ethics, or morality, that others are obliged to respect. The concept of rights derives from the concept of justice in the sense that both involve obligations; however, rights do not always encompass the values of fairness, honesty, and impartiality. The rights concept also relates to autonomy in that both encompass the idea of self-determination. The rights concept considers actions as they relate to affirming or violating basic human rights.

Rights can vary according to the moral values of a given culture. What may be considered a right in one culture may not be considered a right in another culture. For example, societal norms in the Western tradition view circumcision of female children as a form of mutilation, thereby recognizing a woman's right to be free from circumcision. Some non-Western cultures view this in an exactly opposite light, seeing the lack of female circumcision as an insult to womanhood, thereby making the right to female circumcision a right to be upheld and enforced. Because the values underpinning societal norms in cultures vary greatly across the globe, it is difficult to argue that all rights must be applied to all cultures. This difficulty is one impediment to international organizations—they must clearly identify and agree upon the rights and values they cherish before they can identify the aims they seek to accomplish.

Within the health care context, rights are often addressed in terms of confidentiality and privacy. **Confidentiality** refers to the obligation of the health care provider to maintain patient information in a manner that will not permit dissemination beyond the health care provider. **Privacy** refers to the right to be left alone or the right to control personal information. Both of these rights have legal and ethical bases; they can be enforced using both penalties (law) and disapproval by one's peers (ethics). Both confidentiality and privacy are referred to in many ethics codes. In practice, these rights grant patients control over how sensitive information is shared and place restrictions on health care providers over what to do with the information they have learned during the course of treatment.

Veracity **Veracity** refers to habitual truthfulness and honesty; it is the opposite of intentional deceiving or misleading. While the concept seems straightforward, in practice the concept is less clear because situations arise where not telling the truth can potentially be justified to protect another person. For example, some argue that not disclosing all relevant information is acceptable if the recipient of this information is not strong enough to handle the truth, if more time is needed to prepare the recipient to handle unpleasant facts or information, or if doing so would make the recipient less anxious and afraid. It is very difficult to justify such an approach, however, because no clear lines exist to guide one in this practice and it could easily lead to a slippery slope from which it would be difficult to escape.

Veracity occurs in the health care field in the special relationship between the patient and the health care provider. It is important to the patient's care that she inform the health care provider of all relevant information pertaining to her health; failure to do so may result in misdiagnosis or improper treatment. Similarly, veracity requires the health care provider to disclose factual information to the patient so that she can exercise her autonomy and determine the course of her care. Failure to do so can lead to a lack of trust between not only the patient and her health care provider but between the health care provider and others (e.g., family members and other health care staff), who would then view the health care provider as unreliable at best and deceitful at worst.

Veracity also plays a role in medical research; the research subject must be informed of all information pertaining to the research and its potential effect upon her health. Some medical research involves the use of **placebos**, medically inert substances that are used as a control in testing the effectiveness of another, medicated substance. In essence, the placebo is a form of deception, since the research subject does not know whether she has received the real medication or the placebo when she participates in the research trial. Researchers justify the use of placebos by seeking informed consent from the research subject. The consent process requires informing the research subject that placebos will be used but that the patient will not know whether she is receiving the placebo or the real medication during the course of her participation. Only upon receipt of this informed consent may the researcher ethically proceed with the medical research. Additional information concerning the use of placebos in medical research can be found in Chapter 10, "Research."

Ethical Theories Ethical theories refer to systematic statements or plans of principles used to deal with ethical dilemmas. These theories exist so that individuals, organizations, and groups can act consistently and coherently when making ethical decisions. Ethical theories contrast with ethical concepts, which do not achieve the level of a systematic statement or plan. Two main ethical theories exist: utilitarianism and deontology. Similar to ethical concepts, no hierarchy of importance is attached to these theories; each theory has its own strengths and weaknesses.

Utilitarianism Utilitarianism, sometimes referred to as consequentialism, proposes that everyone, including persons, organizations, and society in general, should make choices that promote the greatest balance of good over harm for everyone else. Under this theory, society promotes conditions that would allow an individual to seek the greatest amount of happiness or benefits. Developed by Jeremy Bentham and John Stuart Mill, utilitarianism posits that an act is right when it is useful in bringing about a desirable or good end. Utilitarianism encourages consideration of the effects of actions on everyone involved in a situation, not merely the effects upon one individual. This theory fits well into Western society's values regarding work ethic and the behavioristic approach to education, philosophy, and life.

In application, utilitarianism is often used when preparing cost/benefit analyses. In a cost/benefit analysis, all possible options are considered, the utility or value of each option is determined, and the option that poses the highest total utility is chosen. Net benefits are compared against costs to reach a decision. The option that offers society the best benefits at the least cost or offers businesses the greatest return for the lowest costs is seen as the logical choice.

Utilitarianism has been used to justify the capitation approach of managed care organizations in the health care field. Using the capitation approach, a fixed amount per member per month is paid to a contracted provider for health care services, regardless of the quantity or nature of the services rendered by the contracted provider. Under such an arrangement, the managed care organization asserts that it has provided the greatest good for the greatest number of members, a central tenet of utilitarianism.

Weaknesses are present with utilitarianism. Some have interpreted this theory to support the principle of the end justifying the means. Using this interpretation, even immoral acts can be justified if substantial benefits will be afforded to a majority of persons, even though the minority may face unbearable costs. As such, a decision that results in violating others' rights or creates an injustice is exonerated. Another weakness is the difficulty present in identifying and

measuring all of the possible benefits that may result from a decision, since this involves looking to the future and making, at best, informed predictions.

Deontology Deontology, sometimes referred to as formalism or duty orientation, asserts that ethical decision making is based on moral rules and unchanging principles that are derived from reason and can be applied universally. These universal rules and principles must be considered separately from the consequences or facts of a particular situation. By looking to the intrinsic nature of an act to determine its basic rightness or wrongness, the consequences of the act are considered irrelevant. Although a positive result is always helpful, the deontologist would not consider advancing the public good an adequate basis for ethics—what is considered the public good is ever evolving and is not considered an unchanging principle.

Developed by philosopher Immanuel Kant, the fundamental principle of deontology is called the categorical imperative, which is a command derived from a principle that does not allow exceptions. The categorical imperative requires application of unconditional commands in a similar manner in all situations, without exception. For example, the deontologist who considers life to be sacred could never justify killing, no matter what factual circumstance might have led to a killing, such as self-defense. The duty to protect life remains the universal command.

In application, deontology requires one to compare possible solutions to an ethical dilemma against universal rules and principles to determine which solution should be chosen. Where the possible solutions both comply and conflict with the universal rules and principles, those that pose a conflict are discarded from consideration as unacceptable and the remaining compliant solutions are ranked according to their acceptability with universal rules and principles. That compliant solution that ranks highest in acceptability is the logical choice.

Deontology has been used in the health care field in the context of research involving human subjects. All research projects involving human subjects are subject to both ethical and legal restrictions, including making sure that the subject fully understands the study's purposes and what is expected of the subject, resulting in informed consent. From an ethical perspective, the subject must be treated as one who possesses freedom of choice and not as a means to the end of implementing a research protocol. From the viewpoint of deontology, no subject could be coerced or tricked into participating in the research project because the value placed on freedom of choice is an unchanging principle.

Similar to other ethical theories, deontology poses some weaknesses. Because it does not consider the variety of real-life situations that create ethical dilemmas and brooks no exceptions, it is often considered overly rigid. Additionally, the disregard for consequences derived from actions may lead to absurd results, such as when one obeys the letter of the law to such an extent that it conflicts with the spirit of the law. Furthermore, some disagree that People's motivation are derived from universal values, but argue that they actually derive from changing values instead.

Ethical Decision Making

Each person will face many ethical dilemmas throughout her life and will be forced to reach a decision about these dilemmas. Some of these decisions will be made on an individual level, affecting her professional or personal life, while other decisions will be made on an organizational or group level, affecting many others. The quality of the ethical decision reached may vary greatly, depending in large measure on the factors that influence her and the process she chooses to follow. No one universal "right" answer exists that can be applied to every situation. The decisions reached at one stage in life may be challenged later in life by new problems and realities that confront the decision maker. Accordingly, the decision maker must examine what factors influence her decision making and what process she will follow if she is to be well equipped for future decision making.

Influencing Factors

Numerous factors influence the ethical decision-making process. Whereas one person may rely on a particular ethical concept or theory to reach a decision, another person may rely on her religious beliefs. Still others may rely on personal experiences or may look to a professional code of ethics to guide them. Whether an individual relies on one factor or a combination of factors, it is important to recognize that she does not operate in a vacuum when reaching a decision. Many factors influence the decision-making process, including those discussed here.

Codes of Ethics One of the most significant features of professional associations are their codes of ethics. Codes of ethics are written lists of a profession's values and standards of conduct. Codes of ethics are important because they identify for the broader community what the professional association defines as the basic ethical and moral standards to which its members must adhere. These ethical and moral standards are to be used by the profession's membership as the guiding principles governing their conduct.

Codes of ethics embody many concepts. One is that the members of the profession are differentiating themselves from the broader group of occupations and technical careers that exist in the working world. These ethics codes also show that the professional is an autonomous, responsible decision maker, not someone who just follows orders. A related concept is that the professional possesses a loyalty to both the client/patient and fellow members of the profession. Within this concept is an implied promise that the practitioner who is governed by

an ethical code will not pursue her own interests at the expense of a client or patient. Balanced with this promise is the professional's loyalty to fellow members of the profession, which manifests in both positive ways (prohibitions on disparagement of colleagues) and negative ways (reporting professional misconduct). When the professional must choose between her loyalty to a client or patient and her loyalty to other members of her profession, codes of ethics elevate the client or patient above the interests of fellow professionals.

Codes of ethics are living documents in the sense that they are open to change over time. Initially, some ethics codes operated more as statements that limited competition, promoted a profession's particular image, or imposed restrictions on members rather than as statements of ethical and moral standards. While the restrictions element persists in some ethics codes (e.g., restrictions on advertising), these codes have evolved over time as professions have developed. Ethics codes are now seen as statements of ethical and moral principles that govern the conduct of a given profession's members.

Virtually every professional association has promulgated an ethics code, as have many firms, businesses, and organizations. A prominent example is the ethics code of the American Osteopathic Association, illustrated in Figure 4–3. The principles articulated in this document address many salient points of a physician's everyday life, such as the obligations to provide competent medical service, safeguard patient confidences, and to study and advance scientific knowledge through research. These principles also address the balance the physician must make as a professional. For example, the physician is obliged to recognize the patient's right to "complete freedom to choose his/her physician" while not refusing "to accept patients because of the patient's race, creed, color, sex, national origin or handicap."[1]

Similar to other professions, ethics has been a cornerstone of the health information management profession since its beginning. The most recently revised Code of Ethics promulgated by the American Health Information Management Association (AHIMA) can be seen in Figure 4–4. This code not only guides the health information professional in her obligations to herself but also guides the professional in her obligation to the patient, other members of the health care team, her employer, her peers, her professional association, and the public. Examples of the ethics codes from other professions can be found at the Web site addresses listed at the end of this chapter.

The effectiveness of ethics codes is diminished when the codes are not widely communicated. It is insufficient to merely publish a code of ethics; the profession, firm, business, or organization that adheres to a code of ethics should communicate it widely to its members, staff, and customers. One of the most effective means of communicating an ethics

Code of Ethics

The American Osteopathic Association has formulated this Code to guide its member physicians in their professional lives. The standards presented are designed to address the osteopathic physician's ethical and professional responsibilities to patients, to society, to the AOA, to others involved in healthcare and to self.

Further, the American Osteopathic Association has adopted the position that physicians should play a major role in the development and instruction of medical ethics.

Section 1. The physician shall keep in confidence whatever she/he may learn about a patient in the discharge of professional duties. The physician shall divulge information only when required by law or when authorized by the patient.

Section 2. The physician shall give a candid account of the patient's condition to the patient or to those responsible for the patient's care.

Section 3. A physician-patient relationship must be founded on mutual trust, cooperation, and respect. The patient, therefore, must have complete freedom to choose her/his physician. The physician must have complete freedom to choose patients whom she/he will serve. However, the physician should not refuse to accept patients because of the patient's race, creed, color, sex, national origin or handicap. In emergencies, a physician should make her/his services available.

Section 4. A physician is never justified in abandoning a patient. The physician shall give due notice to a patient or to those responsible for the patient's care when she/he withdraws from the case so that another physician may be engaged.

Section 5. A physician shall practice in accordance with the body of systematized and scientific knowledge related to the healing arts. A physician shall maintain competence in such systematized and scientific knowledge through study and clinical applications.

Section 6. The osteopathic medical profession has an obligation to society to maintain its high standards and, therefore, to continuously regulate itself. A substantial part of such regulation is due to the efforts and influence of the recognized local, state and national associations representing the osteopathic medical profession. A physician should maintain membership in and actively support such associations and abide by their rules and regulations.

Section 7. Under the law a physician may advertise, but no physician shall advertise or solicit patients directly or indirectly through the use of matters or activities, which are false or misleading.

Section 8. A physician shall not hold forth or indicate possession of any degree recognized as the basis for licensure to practice the healing arts unless he is actually licensed on the basis of that degree in the state in which she/he practices. A physician shall designate her/his osteopathic school of practice in all professional uses of her/his name. Indications of specialty practice, membership in professional societies, and related matters shall be governed by rules promulgated by the American Osteopathic Association.

Section 9. A physician should not hesitate to seek consultation whenever she/he believes it advisable for the care of the patient.

Section 10. In any dispute between or among physicians involving ethical or organizational matters, the matter in controversy should first be referred to the appropriate arbitrating bodies of the profession.

Section 11. In any dispute between or among physicians regarding the diagnosis and treatment of a patient, the attending physician has the responsibility for final decisions, consistent with any applicable osteopathic hospital rules or regulations.

Section 12. Any fee charged by a physician shall compensate the physician for services actually rendered. There shall be no division of professional fees for referrals of patients.

Section 13. A physician shall respect the law. When necessary a physician shall attempt to help to formulate the law by all proper means in order to improve patient care and public health.

Section 14. In addition to adhering to the foregoing ethical standards, a physician shall recognize a responsibility to participate in community activities and services.

Section 15. It is considered sexual misconduct for a physician to have sexual contact with any current patient whom the physician has interviewed and/or upon whom a medical or surgical procedure has been performed.

Section 16. Sexual harassment by a physician is considered unethical. Sexual harassment is defined as physical or verbal intimation of a sexual nature involving a colleague or subordinate in the workplace or academic setting, when such conduct creates an unreasonable, intimidating, hostile or offensive workplace or academic setting.

Figure 4-3 | *(continued)*

Section 17. From time to time, industry may provide some AOA members with gifts as an inducement to use their products or services. Members who use these products and services as a result of these gifts, rather than simply for the betterment of their patients and the improvement of the care rendered in their practices, shall be considered to have acted in an unethical manner. (Approved July 2003)

Section 18. A physician shall not intentionally misrepresent himself/herself or his/her research work in any way.

Section 19. When participating in research, a physician shall follow the current laws, regulations and standards of the United States or, if the research is conducted outside the United States, the laws, regulations and standards applicable to research in the nation where the research is conducted. This standard shall apply for physician involvement in research at any level and degree of responsibility, including, but not limited to, research, design, funding, participation either as examining and/or treating provider, supervision of other staff in their research, analysis of data and publication of results in any form for any purpose.

Figure 4-4 | AHIMA Code of Ethics

Preamble

The ethical obligations of the health information management (HIM) professional include the protection of patient privacy and confidential information; disclosure of information; development, use, and maintenance of health information systems and health records; and the quality of information. Both handwritten and computerized medical records contain many sacred stories—stories that must be protected on behalf of the individual and the aggregate community of persons served in the healthcare system. Healthcare consumers are increasingly concerned about the loss of privacy and the inability to control the dissemination of their protected information. Core health information issues include what information should be collected; how the information should be handled, who should have access to the information, and under what conditions the information should be disclosed. Ethical obligations are central to the professional's responsibility, regardless of the employment site or the method of collection, storage, and security of health information. Sensitive information (genetic, adoption, drug, alcohol, sexual, and behavioral information) requires special attention to prevent misuse. Entrepreneurial roles require expertise in the protection of the information in the world of business and interactions with consumers.

Ethical Principles

The following ethical principles are based on the core values of the American Health Information Management Association and apply to all health information management professionals. Health information management professionals:

  I. Advocate, uphold and defend the individual's right to privacy and the doctrine of confidentiality in the use and disclosure of information.

 II. Put service and the health and welfare of persons before self-interest and conduct themselves in the practice of the profession so as to bring honor to themselves, their peers, and to the health information management profession.

III. Preserve, protect, and secure personal health information in any form or medium and hold in the highest regard the contents of the records and other information of a confidential nature, taking into account the applicable statutes and regulations.

 IV. Refuse to participate in or conceal unethical practices or procedures.

  V. Advance health information management knowledge and practice through continuing education, research, publications, and presentations.

 VI. Recruit and mentor students, peers and colleagues to develop and strengthen professional workforce.

VII. Represent the profession accurately to the public.

VIII. Perform honorably health information management association responsibilities, either appointed or elected, and preserve the confidentiality of any privileged information made known in any official capacity.

 IX. State truthfully and accurately their credentials, professional education, and experiences.

  X. Facilitate interdisciplinary collaboration in situations supporting health information practice.

 XI. Respect the inherent dignity and worth of every person.

Revised and adopted by AHIMA House of Delegates—June 2004.

code is by professional education. This may be accomplished through staff training involving both discussion of the applicable ethics codes and their application to the workplace. In some organizations, this training is more focused on making staff aware of ethical aspects of their business lives and the consequences of unethical behavior than on the wording of the ethics code itself. Still other training programs use a case-by-case analysis approach with active discussion and interaction by participants. Both of these approaches stress the need for each participant to think for herself rather than merely repeat the themes of the organization's ethics code.

Codes of ethics—like all forms of communication—are more effective if they are enforced than if they are merely statements posted on a wall. One of the most effective means to enforce an ethics code is to use an ethics committee. **Ethics committees** are groups formed within an organization to establish new and evaluate existing ethics codes and corporate policies and to address ethical issues that arise in the workplace. The functions of ethics committees may vary among organizations, with some committees focusing on communicating information while others focus on classifying and interpreting ethical issues, and still others focus on compliance with the organization's ethics code. Regardless of the extent of their function, ethics committees contribute to the discussion and debate of ethical issues within their organizations.

Within the health care setting, ethics committees often perform philosophical and practical functions. One of these functions is to establish institutional policy concerning bioethical issues, including the removal of life support systems, the treatment of seriously ill newborns, and procedures governing organ procurement. These committees may also establish policies that deal with the intersection of financial and health care matters. These include questions associated with treating the uninsured or medically indigent or the premature discharge of patients under diagnosis-related group (DRG) regulations. The ethics committee may also serve a consultative function, addressing questions related to the ethical use of new treatments or medical devices or other emerging ethics areas.

Patient Rights One of the most significant developments of the last half-century has been the recognition that patients are not merely passive participants in the delivery of health care but play an integral role in their own treatment. Whereas this concept may seem elementary to many who read this book, recognition of this concept has not been the hallmark of medical care until recently.

The extent to which the patient has played a role in her own health care and treatment has varied over time. Patients have always played some role in their treatment, initially with the decision to seek care and later with the decision to comply with the advice of a treating physician. This participation has been limited to some extent by the way in which the health care delivery system in the United States operates. In many respects, the patient cannot enter a health care institution for treatment without the express approval of a physician, save for emergency medical care. Although the patient could for many years control who became her health care provider, some patients have seen this control limited by the advent of HMOs and preferred provider organizations (PPOs) that require the patient to select a health care provider from a pre-approved list.

Payment for health care services also may limit the patient's participation, since third-party payers generally control funding, not the patient. This control over who gets paid, how much they will be paid, and when payments will be made often influences the level of service a patient may receive. For example, the patient may forgo elective surgery that could result in a positive outcome if the third-party payer determines that it will not cover the costs of the surgery. For a more detailed discussion of the concept of insurance coverage, see Chapter 15, "Reimbursement Methodologies."

Though the patient's role in health care has varied, a general recognition that a patient possesses certain health care rights emerged simultaneously with two developments: the rise of the consumer culture and a movement away from paternalism in health care. These two developments derived from several circumstances, including increased levels of education among the U.S. population, dissatisfaction with the way things were run, and inaction or lax oversight by regulatory agencies. Consumers began to focus on health care, demanding higher quality care and a larger say in its delivery. They rejected the prevailing principle of paternalism that had been a part of the ethical model followed by health care professionals for centuries. Under **paternalism**, the health care professional acted in the role of a father to his children, deciding what was best for the patient's welfare without first being required to consult with the patient. Utilizing this principle, the physician alone would determine the treatment for a patient with a certain disease, presenting only the preferred treatment to the patient and omitting disclosure of any other possible treatment alternatives. Paternalism served to limit the patient's autonomy intentionally. As consumers—and, to some extent, health care professionals—became more dissatisfied with this approach, they began to demand consultation before the professional took action. All of these demands in combination directly affected the patient's health care role, developing into the concept of patient rights.

Patient rights are essentially the recognition that a patient is entitled to determine for herself the extent to which she will receive or forgo care and treatment. One aspect of this recognition began to occur in the form of provisions found in the ethics codes of professional associations during the 1950s. Wider recognition did not occur until the 1970s, with the advent of the American Hospital Association's publication of the "Patient's Bill of Rights." This document initially served to express to the patient the existence of such rights as privacy, confidentiality, and informed consent. In later revisions, provisions were added concerning the health care provider's responsibilities to the patient, such as the expectation that a hospital will reasonably respond to the patient's request for appropriate and medically indicated care and services. In its current iteration, this document is referred to as the "Patient Care Partnership," emphasizing the collaborative nature of health care in the 21st century. This document, continuing to emphasize patient rights, also explains what a patient may expect during her hospital stay and how she can express any concerns over her care. A full printing of the "Patient Care Partnership" can be found in the Appendix section of this text.

Although patient rights have generally been viewed from an ethical context, they also can be viewed from a legal context. Some states have formalized the concept of patient rights into statutory provisions. Furthermore, the U.S. Congress has repeatedly attempted to pass a statute incorporating the full concept of patient rights into federal law. Those rights are enumerated in Chapter 3, "Legal Issues." By taking such action, these legislative bodies attempt to change the consequences for failing to honor patient rights from one of an ethical breach with limited opportunities for redress to one of a legal breach that can result in penalties enforced by law.

One of the most successful efforts in moving the concept of patient rights from an ethical basis to a legal basis is the federal Patient Self-Determination Act (PSDA). Congress's goal in passing the PSDA is "to ensure that a patient's rights to self-determination in health-care decisions be communicated and protected."[2] The PSDA obligates health care providers who are Medicare or Medicaid certified to inform their patients of the status of state law governing a patient's rights to make advance directives for accepting or refusing health care services, and the health care provider's written policies concerning implementation of the patient's rights. By placing this obligation on health care providers, the law recognizes that it is the patient's right to determine the extent of the health care services she will receive, not the exclusive right of the health care provider. Additional information concerning the PSDA can be found in Chapter 3, "Legal Issues."

HIPAA

New rights are granted to patients pursuant to this act.

A second example of granting patient rights at the federal level is the Privacy Rule issued pursuant to the Health Insurance Portability and Accountability Act (HIPAA) of 1996. In addition to offering confidentiality protections to patient information, this rule enumerates several rights to patients pertinent to their health information. These rights include, but are not limited to, the right to be informed of the uses and disclosures of this information, the right to restrict uses or disclosures of this information, the right to amend this information, and the right to inspect and copy this information. A full list of these rights can be found in Chapter 3, "Legal Issues."

In summary, the concept of patient rights influences ethical decision making in the sense that health care providers must consider the patient's rights as one element in the decision-making process. By recognizing these rights, the health care provider sees the patient as a stakeholder whose values are important. Accordingly, the patient's interests must be weighed heavily in each and every decision.

Other Factors Whereas codes of ethics and the concept of patient rights are significant factors in the decision-making process, a variety of other factors also play a role. The extent to which an individual considers these factors depends heavily upon the value the decision maker places on them.

For generations, religious beliefs and philosophical views have served as the centerpiece for the values cherished by many. Some ethical dilemmas are seen through these frameworks. While some individuals adhere firmly to their religious beliefs and philosophical views when facing ethical dilemmas, others rely on their religious beliefs and philosophical views less strictly, using them as one of many bases from which to reach a decision. Decisions reached through these frameworks can be based on both moral belief and ethical reasoning.

Advances in science and technology also play a role in ethical decision making. New medical devices, surgical techniques, treatment modalities, and pharmaceutical creations have not only enhanced the quality and length of life, they have created some new ethical dilemmas. Examples include determining who should receive these new technologies when they are scarce in number, whether embryonic stem cells should be used for research, and whether animal tissues should be used for transplantation purposes in lieu of human tissues. These and other ethical dilemmas will continue to challenge health care providers into the near future.

Legal factors also influence ethical decision making. As explained in the beginning of this chapter, legal and ethical issues are often closely related. Ethical questions may spur subsequent legal action. For example, the civil rights movement in the 1960s progressed mainly as a challenge to values and beliefs that were seen as unethical in modern society. Some of the solutions identified by this movement were later transformed into legal protections. Even when the law addresses an ethical concern, it may not do so fully but will merely serve as a bare minimum, leaving ethics to fill the void. For example, abortion is legal in the United States but many persons strongly oppose it, including some health care providers. For those health care providers, the ethical issue is whether to participate in the procedure in any respect. What these examples illustrate is that the law will not serve

Figure 4–5 | Different aspects of ethical problems

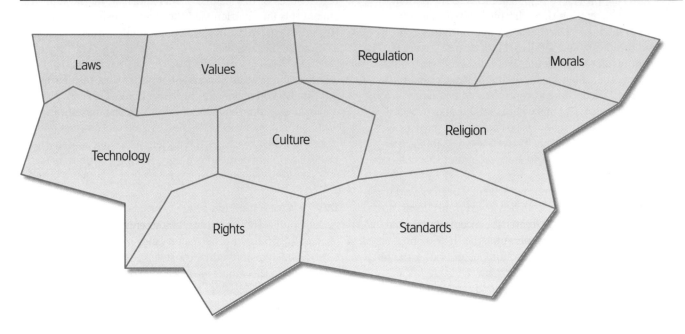

as a deciding factor in all instances; rather, it will serve as one of the factors on which to base an ethical decision.

Decision-Making Process

Just as ethical challenges come in many forms, solving these ethical challenges may take many forms as well. Decisions may be reached individually or as a group, or may be the result of consensus building or negotiation. These decisions do not stand alone, since decisions made in one aspect of an ethical situation may affect other aspects of the same problem. Figure 4–5 provides an example of the relationships between different aspects of a fictional ethical problem.

Though the literature addressing ethics identifies several approaches to problem solving, in essence, these approaches can all be addressed as part of a multistep process. The steps in this process are listed in Table 4–2. Included in the initial steps are defining the ethical issue clearly and determining the facts. The defining step involves identifying and clarifying the problem presented and examining what values are in conflict. Determining the facts can be accomplished by gathering data. Data gathering can occur by speaking with others who may have information about the situation or by reviewing relevant records. Once the problem is clearly defined and data are gathered, one must determine who has a stake in making the decision. At times, the person faced with making the ethical decision is not the same person or party who is the victim of the problem. There might be more parties with interests who should be taken into consideration than may be immediately obvious, warranting a wider approach to identifying stakeholders. Additionally, the relationships between stakeholders should be explored, as should potential biases or other motivations.

The information gleaned at each of these prior steps leads to a determination of the options available to the decision maker. These options should be examined thoroughly, looking at both the short-term and long-term outcomes each option will reach and their impact upon each person or group involved. Each option can be compared against an ethical theory for guidance in decision making. For example, which option presents the greatest good for the greatest number (utilitarianism), which option supports doing one's duty (deontology), and which option promotes the rights and dignity of all persons (social equality and justice)? By linking an ethical theory with each option, the decision maker clarifies the basis supporting each one.

Table 4–2 | Steps in Ethical Decision Making

1. Clearly define the issue.
2. Determine the facts of the situation.
3. Determine who the stakeholders are, the values at stake, and the obligations and interests of each stakeholder.
4. Determine what options are available and evaluate them.
5. Decide what should be done.
6. Justify the decision made by identifying reasons that support the decision.
7. Implement the decision.
8. Evaluate the outcome of the decision.
9. Examine how to prevent the issue from recurring.

Source: Information adapted from Harman, L. (2001). Ethical challenges in the management of health information. *Journal of AHIMA, 72*(3), 27–30; Navron, F. (2001). Crossing the spectrum: Steps for making ethical decisions. *Journal of AHIMA, 72*(3), 31–36.

Table 4-3 | Guidance Questions for Ethical Decision Making

Analogous situations	Do analogous situations exist?
	How similar or different are they from the present situation?
	What course of action was chosen?
	What was the outcome?
Legal implications	Does any option violate the law, a clear moral rule, or a provision of an ethics code?
	Are there legal consequences to any option, such as arrest, conviction, or other punishment?
Sensibility	Which option makes the most sense?
	Can you justify it as sensible to others whom you admire and respect?
	Will the chosen option stand up to media scrutiny?
Feelings	Can you sleep at night without guilt when choosing this option?
	Are you comfortable enough with the chosen option in the event that friends, relatives, coworkers, supervisors, and the community become aware of it?
	How would you feel if the Golden Rule applied and you were the subject or victim of the ethical problem at issue?
	Does the decision reflect accurately the type of person or organization you are or want to be?

After weighing each option, the decision maker must reach a decision and act upon it. Choosing the course of action is not always easy and sometimes is fraught with difficulty. Some guidance for choosing the course of action is provided in the list of questions found in Table 4–3. Once a decision is implemented, the decision maker must evaluate the outcome, comparing the actual outcome against the predicted outcome. When the actual outcome is unforeseen, the decision maker can evaluate what she may have missed in the data-gathering and option-generation stages and learn from this for future reference. If steps can be taken to prevent the ethical problem from recurring, the decision maker should engage in these actions. The decision maker may wish to record the entire situation for use in the future as part of an educational program or dissemination to a wider audience.

In summary, the complexity of the ethical decision-making process shown in this section demonstrates the difficulties with which individuals and organizations are faced. Some of the approaches addressed may resonate with the learner's personal experiences or may be entirely new. By examining the factors that influence decision making and understanding the steps of the process, the decision maker is better positioned to reach decisions she knows are ethically sound.

Bioethical Issues

It is virtually impossible for an individual to function in the modern health care world unaware of bioethical issues. Without such knowledge, the health care provider cannot protect both patients and providers adequately. Bioethics is the study of ethical issues that result from technologic and scientific advances, especially in biology and medicine. As science and technology advance, the number and complexity of bioethical issues seems to grow larger. At times, science and technology

have progressed at such a fast pace that society in general and governmental entities in particular have not been prepared to address the public policy questions that accompany the ethical dilemmas created. Many of the bioethical dilemmas that society has faced during the last half-century are discussed in this section and are listed in Table 4–4.

Related to the Beginning of Life

A multitude of ethical issues surround the beginning of life: family planning, abortion, perinatal ethics, and eugenics. Many of these issues elicit strong emotional reactions because they ask us to question our fundamental beliefs and values about reproduction and the relationships associated with it. This questioning is not only performed on a personal level but on a societal level, resulting in extensive debate and efforts toward political and social control.

Family Planning Family planning refers to the behavior associated with controlling the size of one's family or spacing the births within that family. Family planning can encompass

Table 4-4 | Current Bioethical Issues

Relating to the Beginning of Life	Family planning
	Abortion
	Perinatal ethics
	Eugenics
Relating to Sustaining and Improving Quality of Life	HIV/AIDS
	Organ transplantation
	Genetic Science
Relating to Death and Dying	Planning for the end of life
	Euthanasia
	Withholding/withdrawing life support

a wide range of behaviors, including controlling family size through methods of contraception and increasing family size through adoption or infertility treatment.

The term most commonly associated with the phrase "family planning" is *contraception.* Contraception, sometimes referred to as birth control, refers to efforts to prevent or interfere with conception or impregnation through voluntary or artificial means. The ethical issues surrounding contraception are legion and are often closely tied to the moral beliefs and values held by various religious groups. Some view contraception as evil because it interferes with the purpose of sexual activity, which they consider a means to create life. Some view contraception as wrong only when it requires the use of artificial birth-control methods. Others are strong advocates of contraception, citing the need to control population growth because of its impact upon physical resources. Still others advocate the use of contraception methods as a means to provide a woman with the ability to control both her own body and the course of her life.

Among the most problematic ethical areas dealing with contraception is the question of minors. Whereas much discussion focuses on those adults who employ contraception methods, the ethical question regarding whether minors can consent to employing these same contraception methods has created considerable anxiety. In instances of medical care not related to reproduction, consent must be obtained from the parent or legal guardian before care is rendered to a minor. This consent is required because both the law and society in general recognize that the concept of the best interest standard and the principle of paternalism apply to these situations. Where reproductive issues are involved, the best interest standard and paternalism are not recognized as strongly because a different concept comes into play: the concept that a minor possesses a "right" to control her reproduction. This rights concept conflicts directly with the best interest standard and paternalism. In most states, the legislatures have solved this conflict by granting minors who are mature and able to give informed consent the legal right to obtain contraceptive care and treatment without the consent of a parent or legal guardian. Often this legal right extends to care and treatment of other areas surrounding reproduction, such as pregnancy care and treatment for sexually transmitted diseases. Although the questions surrounding these matters may be addressed by law, they still remain ethical questions that cause considerable debate.

Increasing family size through adoption or infertility treatment raises serious ethical questions that are also emotionally charged. Ethical questions relating to adoption include the extent to which identity and genetic information about the birth parents should be disclosed. If an adoption does not succeed, can the adoptive parents return the child, and, if so, what criteria should be applied to allow the adoptive parents to do so? Several ethical questions were initially raised during the development of infertility treat-

ment, such as whether scientific procedures should be employed to separate reproduction from the act of sexual intercourse. Although the question of whether to use scientific procedures is no longer as prominent, related questions remain, such as what scientific procedures can be employed that will be considered responsible ethical conduct? Does responsible conduct include artificial insemination, the planting of sperm into a woman's body to facilitate conception? Does responsible ethical conduct include fertilization of human gametes outside the human body in a test tube or other artificial environment, called in vitro fertilization? Should those gametes be implanted in only the donor or can another woman act as a surrogate to bring a baby to term? Can a surrogate mother, defined as one who agrees to bear a child conceived through artificial means and relinquish it upon its birth to others for rearing, change her mind and retain the baby? What should happen to embryos if they are no longer wanted by the donors or the donors are no longer living? What genetic information should be provided about the donors to any adoptive parent? For each of these questions, concepts of autonomy, beneficence/nonmaleficence, justice, and rights must be considered.

Abortion   Although abortion is sometimes considered a form of family planning because it acts to reduce family size, it is addressed separately here because of the unparalleled attention it has received. Abortion refers to the termination of pregnancy before the viability of the fetus. Several forms of abortion exist, including those due to natural causes (referred to as spontaneous abortion or miscarriage), those performed for medical reasons (therapeutic abortion), and those performed for personal reasons (elective abortion). Those abortions that are classified as therapeutic and elective are the focus of ethical concerns.

Stripped to its essentials, the abortion debate revolves around the definition of human life and when a fertilized egg should be considered a human being worthy of protection. Ideas about the definition of human life and related questions have been hotly contested for generations. On one side, some view human life as beginning at the moment of conception, making the fetus a human being worthy of protection. These views rest on the moral beliefs and values held by various religious groups. Seen from this viewpoint, abortion amounts to murder and therefore should be stopped. Others believe that human life does not begin at conception and that the fetus is not considered a human being until its birth, or until the age of viability, the earliest age a baby can survive outside the womb. These views not only rest on the moral beliefs and values held by various religious groups, but also on the concepts of autonomy and the right to personal liberty inherent in an individual's control over her own body and course of life. In between these two views lie several variations. Some believe that abortion constitutes murder but feel that the value placed on personal liberty is such that only the individual facing the crisis may decide whether to proceed with an abortion. Some view abortion as wrong but find that other considerations, such as a rape leading to conception, out-weigh the wrongness, justifying an abortion to proceed. Others do not view abortion itself as wrong but believe it is misused and treated as merely another form of birth control.

These ethical views have spilled over into both the political and legal arenas. The U.S. Supreme Court, in the case of *Roe* v. *Wade*,[3] decided the abortion question from a rights perspective by recognizing that state laws restricting abortion could impair a woman's personal liberty and her right to privacy. The court addressed the protection question by splitting pregnancy into three trimesters, allowing abortion to proceed freely in the first trimester, allowing states to issue some restrictions related to maternal health in the second trimester, and allowing states to severely restrict or ban abortion outright in the third trimester. Numerous battles have been fought in subsequent years over how to interpret, expand, or restrict the rights articulated in this case, on both a political and legal basis.

The abortion issue has been further complicated by additional issues. What is the male's role with regard to abortion? How should informed consent be handled, particularly where minors are concerned? Should fetal tissue from an abortion be used for stem cell research or some therapeutic purpose? What role should politicians play in this debate of an intensely personal subject? These and other questions indicate that the abortion debate will continue for some time.

Perinatal Ethics Some of the same concerns voiced over abortion are also present in the discussion regarding perinatal ethics, the ethical questions involved in or occurring during the period closely surrounding birth. These ethical questions center on prenatal testing, genetic screening, and prenatal surgery.

Prenatal testing refers to those tests performed after conception but before birth that are designed to detect fetal abnormalities. These tests include amniocentesis, chronic villus sampling (CVS),and sonograms or other technological forms of viewing the fetus in utero. Each of these tests poses risks, and the first two are not generally employed without an indication or suspicion of a medical disorder. Some question whether or how often the tests should be employed, since the results may force the patient into a difficult ethical decision over whether to proceed with the pregnancy or with an abortion. Some see this as an issue of autonomy and personal liberty, similar to what is articulated concerning abortion, since many of these tests are performed in the early stages of pregnancy when the right to an abortion is protected by law. Others view this type of testing as unreliable because false positives can be reported, requiring retesting for confirmation and causing stress and anxiety for those involved.

Prenatal testing is interrelated to the practice of genetic screening. In genetic screening, a person's genetic makeup is tested to reveal a predisposition to certain diseases or other abnormalities. These predispositions or abnormalities may affect the subject of these tests or a child borne of that subject. Viewpoints differ concerning the ethics of genetic screening, ranging from the autonomy/personal liberty view to concerns that genetic screening promotes abortion. In between these views exist concerns for the guilt that may be placed on the person carrying the defective gene and the stress that the results may place on a marriage bond.

Fetal abnormalities can be corrected in some instances through prenatal surgery. Prenatal surgery refers to surgery conducted upon the fetus prior to birth. The level of risk associated with these surgeries varies, with some performed so rarely that they are considered experimental in nature. Some see the risk level as too high to condone prenatal surgery, arguing that life with an abnormality is just as valuable as a life without an abnormality. Others weigh the risks and determine that the opportunity to correct an abnormality will result in an enhanced life for the fetus, thereby justifying the surgery. Still others view prenatal surgery not as a scientific advancement but as a chance for a human being to play God. As these views illustrate, the ethics issues surrounding prenatal surgery are fraught with both reason and emotion.

Eugenics Eugenics refers to the effort to improve the human species through control of hereditary factors in mating. Essentially, eugenics is a breeding practice aimed at producing superior offspring. Although it was not given the name "eugenics" until more recent history, the idea of eugenics has been advocated since the days of ancient Greece.[4] Eugenics has been advocated by some scientists during different time periods, worldwide, but its most famous application was in Nazi Germany in 20th-century Europe.

Eugenics has been applied in modern history using two methods: encouragement of reproduction by those groups deemed desirable and sterilization of those persons who some authority group has decided should not reproduce. The first method is not really one of science but one of persuasive rhetoric. Those persons deemed superior by some controlling authority were persuaded or pressured to reproduce, and those deemed inferior were pressured or persuaded to refrain from reproducing. The second method, however, requires the use of science. Sterilization refers to the actions taken to make an individual incapable of reproducing, whether by removing the reproductive organs or by preventing them from functioning effectively. Utilizing eugenics principles, if those persons who should not reproduce did not voluntarily agree to sterilization, forced sterilization should occur.

The ethical issues related to eugenics are many. The idea that some forms of human life are inferior to others, whether judged by race, sex, creed, or some other criteria, affronts the concept of justice in which no person is favored over another. The concept of autonomy becomes involved, since decisions to reproduce are considered highly personal and not to be decided by others. Nonmaleficence is also an issue, because the individual undergoing a forced sterilization views the procedure as harm done to him or her and nonmalificence tries to do no harm. Finally, the concept of rights comes into play, since individuals frequently view reproduction as one of their basic rights. These objections, combined with the repugnance engendered by Nazi Germany's application of eugenics, have led eugenics into disrepute.

Related to Sustaining or Improving the Quality of Life

Ethical issues related to sustaining or improving the quality of life are fraught with great emotion, because they challenge the belief systems and values held dear by many. What is considered an improvement to the quality of life may differ based on the perspectives brought to the discussion.

HIV/AIDS Human immunodeficiency virus (HIV) and acquired immunodeficiency syndrome (AIDS) are among the most significant health threats worldwide. In some areas of the world, these health threats have spread so rapidly and become so prevalent as to constitute an epidemic. Known causes of HIV and AIDS include intravenous drug use and the sharing of contaminated needles, tainted blood supply used for transfusion purposes, sexual intercourse, and direct mucous-to-mucous contact. Because no vaccine or cure has been discovered, most medical efforts have focused on containing the spread of infection.

Several methods to contain the spread of infection have been employed, including clean needle exchange programs for IV drug users, extensive screening of blood supplies, sexual abstinence programs, and the use of condoms during sexual intercourse. All of these methods have raised ethical issues, because they implicate the concepts of autonomy, justice, and rights.

Entangled with any discussion of HIV/AIDS are questions related to confidentiality. As one would expect, those who are afflicted with the disease view confidentiality as extremely important; many have suffered from stigmatization or outright discrimination as a result of unauthorized disclosure. Balanced against this are the legitimate policy concerns of health authorities that need to know the extent of the disease's existence in their community and the health care resources needed to combat it. Many health authorities have resolved their policy concerns by implementing testing policies (voluntary, mandatory, confidential, and anonymous) and requiring health care providers to report test results on a mandatory basis without revealing the subject's identity.

The confidentiality question relates to both the patient who suffers from HIV/AIDS and to the health care provider who is afflicted. Without a legal reporting requirement, health care providers may not disclose a patient's HIV/AIDS status to third persons without consent. This prohibition against disclosure may even continue after the patient's death, as identified in the ethical guidelines of the American Medical Association.[5] Furthermore, ethical guidelines frequently require the HIV/AIDS-infected health care provider to disclose her status to those patients upon whom she per-

forms invasive procedures so that they are aware of the risks she poses.[6] These ethical precautions rest on the concepts of beneficence and nonmaleficence, as well as the patient's autonomy as the ultimate decision maker in her own care.

Although confidentiality is a central concern for HIV/AIDS patients, a separate issue also exists: the health care provider's duty to treat the afflicted patient. It is difficult for some health care providers to separate the patient suffering from HIV/AIDS from the high-risk behavior that may have caused the disease. As a result of the disapproval of these high-risk behaviors and the statistically small, but real, risk of contracting the disease from the patient, these health care providers are reluctant to treat patients suffering from HIV/AIDS. Professional associations have responded to this concern by incorporating provisions into their ethics codes that identify a duty to provide care commensurate with the scope of practice. They have also published universal precautions guidelines for use in creating a barrier to infection, thereby reducing risk to the health care provider.

Organ Transplantation One of the most effective developments in improving the quality of life in the 20th century has been organ transplantation. Organ transplantation is a form of surgery wherein one body part (tissue or organ) is transferred from one site to another or from one individual to another. Transplants using one's own body parts are called autografts. Transplants using a donor's body part are called allografts or homografts. Transplants involving animal tissue, cells, or organs into human bodies are called xenografts or heterografts. By receiving a transplant, the patient's quality of life can improve, since the healthy tissue or organ substitutes for the diseased or failing tissue or organ.

The number of tissue/organs available has never met or exceeded the demand. Government entities and professional associations have engaged in various efforts to increase the number of organs available, including instituting publicity campaigns, making tissue/organ donor cards readily available, and providing space on driver's licenses where individuals can authorize permission for organ donation. Although these efforts are laudable, demand still outstrips supply, creating competition for the limited number of tissue/organs available.

How to address the scarcity of these tissue/organs and how to allocate those that are available are difficult ethical questions. Society, worldwide, generally abhors the concept of dealing in human organs for profit, and many nations have codified this concept into law. They instead rely upon educational efforts to persuade individuals to donate tissue/organs. Some nations, such as the United States, support this effort by promulgating regulations that require hospitals that receive federal government funds to ensure they have in place policies requesting permission from the next of kin for the removal of organs after death. Other efforts include publicity campaigns and outreach efforts at the community level designed to decrease barriers to donations.

Once the tissue/organ becomes available, allocating it among the many who are in need becomes very difficult. To assist with this dilemma, the federal government funds an organization called the United Network for Organ Sharing, which serves as a clearinghouse for organ procurement and matching. Using the criteria of medical acceptability, the organization looks for compatibility in the tissue and blood type between the donor and the recipient.

One answer to the overall scarcity is the use of nonhuman tissue and organs. These nonhuman tissue and organs may be created artificially in a medical laboratory or they could come from animals. Neither artificially created nor animal tissue and organs have proved to be effective for long-term use, but they have provided humans with additional time to locate a suitable donation of human tissue or organ. Some of the work and research involved in these efforts has led to the development of artificial joints, valves, and other prostheses, which have proved to be successful for long-term use.

Genetic Science Much of the progress in medicine during the past century has been due to scientific advancements and the application of technology to the health care setting. Future progress in medicine appears to focus on genetic science and its application in the health care setting. Several efforts in genetics are in progress, including the Human Genome Project, gene therapy, and stem cell research.

The Human Genome Project (HGP) is an enterprise designed to map the genes found in human DNA and determine the sequences of the chemical base pairs that make up human DNA. These genes comprise the 46 human chromosomes, which considered together are called the human genome. By obtaining knowledge of the genome, scientists hope to discover new ways to diagnose, treat, and someday prevent diseases and disorders affecting humankind. Some find this effort to obtain such knowledge laudable; others view it with reluctance because of concerns over application of this knowledge; and still others view it as immoral because they think it indicates hubris and an attempt to equate oneself with God. Of particular ethical concern is the application of this knowledge, because issues of justice, fairness, privacy, and confidentiality of genetic information are all present. Ethicists are also concerned over philosophical implications such as the role of free will versus genetic determination in human development. Many of these issues have yet to be fully explored and will remain with us for some time.

One application currently being explored is gene therapy. Gene therapy, sometimes referred to as genetic engineering, involves genetically altering organisms for various purposes. For example, one purpose may be to supply the missing portion of a length of DNA that is the cause of a disorder like sickle cell anemia or cystic fibrosis. Today's exploration involves experimentation on mice or other animals, not human beings. Many of these experiments have not been successful; science is still trying to better understand gene functionality and determine a mechanism for inserting the altered gene into the animal's body. Although these therapies show some promise, ethical questions surround them. Will altered genes help or harm humans or other living beings? Can scientists be trusted to act responsibly in these experiments? Will veracity be sacrificed for the sake of medical progress? These and other concerns will need to be addressed fully for society to accept gene therapy efforts.

Another area engendering considerable debate is stem cell research. Stem cell research is the careful, systematic study and investigation of a special kind of cell not committed to conduct a specific function that has the capability to renew itself and differentiate into specialized cells. These cells are not committed to differentiating into specialized cells until they receive a signal to do so. Because of the wide variety of specialized cells that can be generated and used for replacement, scientists view stem cell research as a promising area for medical advancement. Stem cells may be derived from adult stem cells or early human embryos. Adult stem cells may replicate and differentiate into specialized cells, but they are considered rare and difficult to identify. Early human embryos also replicate and differentiate, but are less rare and much easier to identify. Because of this, the scientific community generally utilizes embryonic stems cells in research.

This reliance on embryonic stem cells has fueled national debates in the United States and elsewhere. Some of the debates are similar to those conducted over the subject of abortion. For those who view human life as beginning at conception, these embryonic stem cells are human life and cannot be the subject of research and experimentation under any circumstances. They argue that research should continue only with adult stem cells or with existing stem cells drawn from embryos previously destroyed. Others view these same embryonic stem cells as devoid of human life, thereby justifying research and experimentation. Some view embryonic stem cells as potentially human but not yet human, thereby justifying research because of its potential to reap life-saving benefits. Others are concerned with the financing of this research, arguing that public funds cannot be used to support such a divisive area of research. Individuals and groups on all sides of this issue have spent a considerable amount of time and money lobbying politicians to achieve their respective goals, and the debate does not appear to be ending anytime soon.

Related to Death and Dying
Whereas each of the bioethical issues previously addressed engenders heated debate, ethical issues related to death and dying are especially problematic because death and dying are not abstract concepts but real events with which virtually all persons are familiar. Accordingly, strong emotions accompany the issues of planning for the end of life, euthanasia, and withholding or withdrawing life support.

Planning for End of Life Issues of death and dying have always been present in society, but the increase in educational levels and advancements in medical science and technology have caused more individuals to contemplate the meaning of the term *quality of life* as it applies to the ends of their own lives. Employing the ethical concept of autonomy, some plan in advance what level of medical care they wish to receive or forgo at the end of life.

Facilitating these planning efforts are various documents that can provide guidance to family members and health care providers in the event that the patient is unable to communicate her wishes at the time a decision must be reached. Combined together under the term **advance directives**, these written instructions describe the kind of health care the patient wishes to have or not have if she becomes incapacitated. Advance directives are based on the substantive legal rights found in state law but are also recognized on the federal level through the Patient Self-Determination Act described earlier in this chapter.

Two types of advance directives are used in the health care setting: living wills and powers of attorney for health care. A **living will** is a document, executed while a patient is competent, that provides direction as to medical care the patient should receive in the event she is incapacitated or unable to make personal decisions. Living wills are analogous to blueprints or maps of the patient's wishes. The value of a living will is that it specifies the patient's wishes, thereby lessening the decision-making burden on family members and health care providers concerning what actions they should or should not take with regard to the patient's care. A living will provides a measure of assurance to family members and health care providers that if they follow the terms specified in the living will, they will act in compliance with the patient's wishes.

A second form of advance directive is a **durable power of attorney for health care**. This document allows a competent individual to name someone else to exercise health-related decisions on her behalf in the event that she becomes incapacitated or unable to make decisions. Under a durable power of attorney for health care, the person empowered to act by proxy may or may not know the patient's wishes; the document may merely name the person empowered to act by proxy or it may include details of the patient's wishes. The level of detail contained in a durable power of attorney for health care depends upon the patient's preference.

Euthanasia The term **euthanasia** refers to the act or practice of causing death painlessly, with the aim to end suffering. Euthanasia derives from the Greek words *eu*, meaning good, and *thanatos*, meaning death. Euthanasia practices are divided into two categories: passive and active.

Passive euthanasia, also called negative euthanasia, involves the practice in which no heroic measures are taken to preserve life. Passive euthanasia is recognized in the health care setting with the use of Do Not Resuscitate (DNR) or "no-code" orders. These orders essentially instruct the health care provider not to engage in extraordinary measures or otherwise attempt to revive those persons whose vital processes have ceased to function on their own. Several difficulties arise with this concept. As part of their training, health care providers learn how to save or improve patient lives. Asking them to forgo action at the end of a patient's life seems contradictory to this training. Definitions of extraordinary measures also differ between health care professionals, causing confusion during application to a specific situation. Additionally, the patient's decision regarding end of life may not have taken into consideration when the DNR or no-code orders should be implemented.

Active euthanasia, also called positive euthanasia, involves the practice of actions that speed the process of dying. Within the health care setting, active euthanasia occurs in situations where the provider prescribes, supplies, or administers an agent that results in death. Such a situation occurs most frequently when the patient has suffered excruciating pain from a terminal illness or from a disease for which no cure or hope for improvement exists. Active euthanasia may not be limited to health care providers, as recent high-profile situations involving close family members who facilitated the death of a loved one have been publicized. These so-called "mercy killings" by close family members have been received by the public with varying degrees of sentiment, ranging from acceptance to outrage. The variation in sentiment generally correlates with the facts of the particular situation.

The practice of euthanasia raises a variety of ethical issues. Some view euthanasia from a deontological approach, seeing it as an outgrowth of patient autonomy in those situations where the patient has made her wishes known. Some view the idea of mercy killings with a utilitarian approach, seeing it as a compassionate and concerned answer for those who are painfully or terminally ill. Some employ the double-effect principle, citing instances where the administration of strong narcotics to a terminally ill patient to relieve pain (the intended outcome) can be justified, even if such administration hastens death (the untoward outcome). Religious beliefs also play a role, with the sanctity of life principle operating to either support or condemn euthanasia. Some consider Judeo-Christian principles to tolerate passive euthanasia because the absence of actions permits death, whereas those same principles are employed to condemn active euthanasia because overt acts cause the patient's death. Some reject euthanasia principles entirely, applying the slippery slope argument that allowing passive euthanasia will lead to active euthanasia in the future. Regardless of the ethical approach that is used, the public debate over euthanasia does not appear to be over.

Withholding/Withdrawing Treatment Closely related to passive euthanasia is the concept of withholding or refusing treatment. **Withholding treatment** refers to the decision of the patient, her family, or legal guardian to refrain from giving permission for treatment or care. Both euthanasia and withholding treatment may result in the death of the patient but they differ in the sense that withholding treatment does not always include activities that would be considered heroic measures. Activities that may be withheld or refused may serve to improve the quality of a patient's life but not hasten or result in her death.

Withdrawing treatment refers to the decision of the patient, her family, or legal guardian to discontinue activities or remove forms of patient care. Decisions to withdraw treatment frequently, but not always, result in the patient's death. Used in the context of discontinuing treatment that results in death, this concept is sometimes referred to as the "right to die." Arguments supporting the right to die address many fears, including the patient's fear of loss of control over her life, fear of degradation or lack of dignity in death, and fear of a prolonged death due to medical interventions.

Withholding or withdrawing treatment is based upon the concepts of autonomy and the right to personal liberty. Many people support these concepts as a general rule but differ with regard to their application, particularly as the application relates to vulnerable persons such as children or the mentally impaired. When dealing with those populations, health care providers may look to the ethical guidelines of their professional associations or to the judicial system for guidance in how to proceed with the patient's care. This last approach particularly applies to questions of withdrawal of treatment for incapacitated patients when family members disagree over whether or what support measures may be withdrawn.

Ethical Challenges

Ethical challenges are situations in which no clear-cut "right" answer exists, and an individual is required to make a choice between two or more equally unfavorable alternatives or between a neutral alternative and a tempting but unfavorable alternative. The choice may center on a conflict between the individual rights of two separate people, on a conflict between the obligations of one person and the rights of another, or on some combination of the above. Honest differences of opinion between sincere and virtuous persons may lead to frustration over how to make the right choice. Perfect solutions may not exist for every ethical dilemma, and the person who has made a choice may have to defend her decision to others.

Ethical challenges primarily center upon the relationship an individual has with another, whether the other is a person, a firm or an organization, a specific community, or society as a whole. When a person engages in activities beyond herself and establishes relationships with a larger group, she accepts broader obligations to that group. When these relationships and obligations clash, ethical challenges often result.

General Challenges

Although some ethical challenges also present legal implications, the focus of this discussion rests solely on the ethical aspect of a problem. Ethical challenges may arise in home or work environments, with a seemingly endless variety of challenges emerging on a regular basis. This discussion focuses on the work environment, since employees who practice ethical behaviors in their home environment may be influenced by those in their organization who are unethical, by the values of the organization itself, by the so-called "corporate culture," or by opportunities to take advantage of others for personal gain—and therefore face ethical challenges. This discussion illustrates challenges as they relate to the work environment, but one can apply many of the areas addressed in this section to the home environment.

One of the most significant ethical challenges that may be encountered in any endeavor is the conflict of interest. A conflict of interest is the clash between an individual's selfish interests and her obligation to an organization or group. Such conflicts exist when the individual uses her position in or with an organization or group to promote her own interests or those with whom she is closely aligned at the expense of the best interests of the organization or group. Conflicts of interest are sometimes addressed as company policy, such as a prohibition on secondary employment with a competitor.

Conflicts of interest may be either potential or actual. Potential conflicts are those conflicts that give the appearance of harm or impropriety without resulting in the harm or impropriety itself. Actual conflicts are those conflicts that go beyond appearance and actually involve the impropriety and harm. For example, a strong-minded purchasing agent who maintains independent judgment but accepts favors from a vendor may still act in the best interests of the organization if she makes purchasing decisions based on the merits of the bids received. Although she has not actually harmed the organization, she has placed herself in a position of being perceived as not acting in the best interests of the organization and, therefore, has a potential conflict of interest. If that same purchasing agent allowed the favors to influence her decision making and chose not on merit but based on receipt of favors, she would be engaged in an actual conflict of interest.

A second ethical concern is the issue of substance abuse in the workplace. Those colleagues who can no longer function appropriately in the workplace due to substance abuse such as alcohol or drugs are often referred to as impaired colleagues. Impaired colleagues may impede business performance, pose safety risks to both their organization and fellow workers, and engage in unethical and illegal conduct such as embezzling to support a drug habit. No easy answers exist for how to deal with such a situation. One perspective is to adopt a no-tolerance policy that advocates employment termination for those found guilty of substance abuse. A second perspective is to view the substance abuse as a disease, warranting an opportunity to attend a rehabilitation program and, upon successful completion, reinstatement of a job. Both opposing perspectives are supported by different values, and neither perspective is necessarily right or wrong.

A third ethical challenge involves disparagement, which is the belittling or criticizing of the skills, knowledge, or qualifications of another professional. The concept of disparagement is included in the codes of ethics of some professions; engaging in disparagement is considered by many a form of professional misconduct. This concept does not mean that a professional cannot attempt to affect positive change through the presentation and discussion of problems. What it does mean, however, is that the nature of a presentation or discussion should not be tainted with personal attacks upon other professionals but should focus on the merits of an issue instead. By exercising such care, the professional increases the possibility of persuading others of the correctness of her position.

Whereas each of the conflicts addressed above may not occur with frequency, other ethical challenges seem to arise on an almost daily basis. It seems that questions concerning truth telling abound in the workplace, with some instances that are more severe than others. For example, personal memos and daily conversations with coworkers may involve shading of the truth or lack of full disclosure. Some advertising messages may cross the boundary of puffery into outright deceptive communications. Some businesses may not meet their obligations to disclose to government entities all of the information required by statute, reasoning that the less information given the better, in light of competitive pressures. Some government entities may not disclose all of the information requested by reporters or members of the public, citing concerns of national defense or security. Some employees may copy another employee's work, such as a planning document, add a quick change of name, and submit it as their own. Whether these practices are seen as lying, lack of full disclosure, or plagiarism, they lead to the erosion of trust in the workplace, a matter of vital importance to organizations that rely on honesty and dependability to conduct ordinary business exchanges.

Role of Ethics in Supervision

Any manager must recognize that ethical issues extend beyond concerns for her own personal conduct and into supervision. The supervisor plays three direct ethical roles in an organization: serving as a role model, encouraging ethical behavior, and monitoring employee conduct. Figure 4–6 illustrates the relationships of these three roles. These three roles require increased accountability from supervisors, causing them to be more alert to ethical issues than they otherwise might be.

Serving as a role model requires the supervisor to engage in ethical behaviors that can be emulated by others. One such behavior is setting a good example. For example, the supervisor who can confront problems in a constructive and ethical manner signals to employees that their future

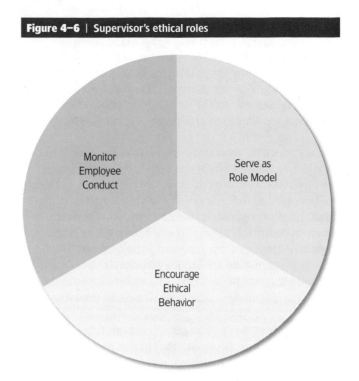

Figure 4–6 | Supervisor's ethical roles

Monitor Employee Conduct

Serve as Role Model

Encourage Ethical Behavior

problems will be handled that way. The supervisor who refrains from actions that could be construed as conflicts of interest or unethical conduct influences others to follow this example when making ethical decisions.

Another role-model behavior is accepting responsibility for mistakes. This requires the supervisor to admit that a mistake has occurred and to assume responsibility for the predicament. This action communicates to others that the supervisor is ethical and honest and seeks some form of resolution to a problem. It also may reduce anxiety within the organization because others might view this action to mean that, by admitting her own limitations, the supervisor is signaling to staff that she may also be accepting of other's mistakes.

Though role modeling can be an effective means of influencing staff behavior, supervisors also play a separate ethical role in organizations: encouraging staff to engage in ethical behavior through supervisory actions. These two roles differ in that role modeling does not require the supervisor to interact with staff and is therefore a more passive behavior, whereas encouragement involves interaction between supervisor and staff, making this an active behavior. These encouragement actions can take several forms. First and foremost are the organization's ethical standards or codes of ethics. Communicating these policies and procedures clearly and frequently, and enforcing them fairly, can lead to improved ethical behavior throughout the organization. Second, ethical content can be inserted into policies and procedures used every day by staff. By not limiting ethical content to the organization's standards or codes of ethics, the organization and it supervisors send the message that ethical behavior is part of every department and function.

In addition to encouraging ethical behavior through policies and procedures, supervisors may influence such behavior using rewards and punishment. Rewards in this context refer to both providing respect and praise for those acting ethically and making certain that unethical behavior is not inadvertently encouraged by the organization through approval and increased status. Specifying the boundaries for and ensuring punishment of unethical behavior may influence those who are supervised and reduce the opportunity for such behaviors to occur in the future.

Although role modeling and encouragement may influence staff to behave in an ethical manner, staff may not consistently do so. For that reason, a third supervisory function exists: monitoring employee conduct. This monitoring function is analogous to the monitoring function the supervisor engages in to determine whether an employee meets productivity and performance standards, only this function involves ethics. The supervisor may monitor employee conduct in multiple ways, including a review of compliance with organizational policies and procedures. Policies that address an employee's outside interests, such as prohibitions on a second job, may require the supervisor to address the matter before it becomes a problem and also to address it in the event a problem is presented to the supervisor for resolution. For example, the supervisor may follow a procedure to address the organization's second-job prohibition policy during the new employee's entrance interview or at regularly scheduled staff meetings as a means to prevent a future problem. If a problem emerges, the supervisor should engage in an extensive examination of the facts before taking action. If the second job poses a potential conflict of interest with the employee's position in the organization, the supervisor has a responsibility to address the matter with the employee and to enforce the organization's policy.

When the management hierarchy in some organizations involves multiple levels of supervision, the behaviors of both the line supervisor and the employee are monitored by a higher-level supervisor. For example, many organizations have promulgated policies that consider it inappropriate for supervisors to receive expensive gifts from an employee on a birthday or holiday. Because most people can understand the inappropriateness of giving expensive gifts to supervisors, it is easy for higher-level supervisors to monitor and enforce this type of ethical policy.

Another way to monitor employee conduct is to make the matter of ethics an explicit part of an employee's performance evaluation. Whether it falls under the category of judgment or business ethics, a portion of the evaluation can address whether and how the employee applies ethical standards in the workplace. Elements of ethics that can be evaluated include whether the employee treats others with respect, keeps commitments, inspires the trust of others, works with integrity, models ethical behavior, and upholds the values of the organization. Each of these elements can be rated and explained to the employee as part of the performance evaluation. Specific deviations from the organization's ethical expectations can be addressed, with goals set for future performance.

Other methods can be used to monitor the ethical behavior of employees as well. These include employing a well-developed structure that provides a system of checks and balances. These checks and balances serve as both a means to detect noncompliance with the organization's ethical standards and a way to limit the opportunities for an employee to act unethically.

In summary, the three direct ethical roles require a supervisor to engage in behaviors that focus beyond herself. These behaviors vary in the amount of interaction required with others and the level of complexity. Some supervisory issues require little more than common sense to address, whereas other issues require extensive examination and counseling. Because of the wide range of ethical issues that may occur in the work environment, it is necessary for supervisors to be aware of the roles they play and their influence upon others in the workplace.

Health Care Challenges

Ethical challenges can be found in numerous places and in differing situations within the general health care field. The ethical challenges addressed in this section illustrate areas that are of importance and that have been the subject of considerable discussion during the last 20 years.

Conflicts of interest exist in the health care field, just as they do in the business arena. For example, physicians who engage in joint venturing or self-referral practices raise the question of a conflict of interest. Under these scenarios, the physician invests financially in a health care facility but does not provide direct medical service at that facility. The health care facility might offer a broad range of activities or services, such as physical therapy, diagnostic imaging, ambulatory surgery care, and durable medical equipment. The physician then refers her patient to the health care facility in which she has the financial interest and the insurance company or government payer is billed for the activities or services rendered at the facility. Such referrals have drawn considerable criticism as—at minimum—ethically suspect and have resulted in professional groups such as the American Medical Association adopting policies against these practices.[7]

Conflicts of interest are also present if the health care practitioner engages in sexual relations with a patient. The nature of the practitioner-patient relationship is one of inequality; the practitioner is in a position of advantage over the patient in terms of knowledge, power, and status. At the same time, the patient may be vulnerable, especially when she has experienced intense pressures or traumatic life events. In view of this inequality, true consent cannot be forthcoming from the patient and the sexual relationship will be viewed at best as ethically inappropriate.

Substance abuse issues are also present in the health care context and are particularly troubling because of the increased risk to patient safety. Under the ethical concept of nonmaleficence, health care workers must consider how, not whether, to address situations involving substance abuse. Whether addressing the situation requires informing management personnel, confronting an impaired colleague directly, or intervening by group, it is important that fellow health care workers understand the obligations, policies, and practices articulated by their professional associations and their employers before taking action. Within many health care contexts, the impaired colleague will be treated like a patient who needs effective assistance and guidance to a treatment program. Such a humane approach may permit the impaired colleague to salvage her practice.

Another organizational policy may prohibit an employee from using nonpublic health information for private financial gain. Again, the supervisor may need to conduct an extensive examination of the facts of the situation before reaching a conclusion that the policy has been violated.

The finance of health care influences ethics. For example, third-party payers may affect the clinical decisions of some physicians by authorizing inpatient stays for a shorter time frame than the physician thinks is medically prudent, thereby exposing the patient to the potential of discharge from the hospital in a seriously ill condition. The ethical dilemma is whether the physician should place the well-being of the patient first by only discharging the patient when she is clinically ready, thereby forcing the hospital or patient to bear the expense of prolonged treatment, or discharge the patient earlier than desired in order to financially benefit the hospital and not jeopardize the physician's place on the hospital staff. Ethical challenges also exist in areas such as research involving human subjects, the allocation of organs for transplant, withholding or withdrawing life support, and employee health and safety on the job.

Health Information Management Challenges

As the health information management field has evolved, new ethical challenges have emerged. These challenges have generally arisen from: (1) changes in the health care environment, such as the development of managed care; (2) requirements for documentation and access to and release of information; (3) developments in technology, including the ease of sharing information electronically; and (4) changes in reimbursement systems and their attendant coding systems.

In the specialized area of health information management, ethical challenges also arise. The most frequent ethical challenges center on the coding-reimbursement connection, quality review, information security, data resource management, and the protection of sensitive information, including genetic, drug and alcohol abuse, mental health, and sexual abuse information. Of these, the most substantial number of recent ethical challenges has focused on the coding-reimbursement connection and protection of sensitive information.

Those health information professionals assigning diagnostic and procedural codes have seen an increased focus on third-party payer reimbursement as the means for a health care facility to remain financially viable. Most, if not all, reimbursement mechanisms tie the coded diagnosis and procedure to the amount reimbursed to the health care facility. Along with the growing complexity of coding and reimbursement guidelines, some coders face the dilemma of whether to focus on the accuracy of coding or on coding to obtain a better reimbursement for the health care facility. When assigning codes for reimbursement, the individual coder may be pressured by a health care institution into relying on inaccurate, incomplete, or misleading information, or information without a sound clinical basis or documentation, in order to obtain the maximum reimbursement for the facility. AHIMA provides Standards for Ethical Coding to guide coding professionals in ethical gray areas such as this.[8]

As a result of the increased demand for patient information, health information professionals have faced a growing challenge for access to sensitive patient information. It has long been a core ethical obligation of a health information management professional to protect patient privacy and confidential communication. Consider the instance of admission of a celebrity patient to an acute care hospital. Inquiries from the press or hospital staff for detailed health status information about the celebrity patient are inappropriate, since neither group has an inherent right to this information without the patient's consent. With the advent of computers, the temptation is present to satisfy curiosity by gaining access to the celebrity's health information in a seemingly anonymous fashion. Such temptations should be tempered by the existence of audit trails, which allow the hospital the ability to determine how frequently the celebrity patient's health information is accessed and by whom. If inappropriate access is found, the hospital can take appropriate disciplinary action.

Other ethical examples in the health information field may include pressure by a health care facility to obtain fully accredited status from an accrediting organization by "fudging" statistics that would indicate that the health information management department meets the required percentage of completed charts. Or a physician may complete progress notes long after seeing a patient and ask that the health information manager indicate that she completed those notes in a contemporaneous fashion. Other examples include failure to disclose conflicts of interest and incorrectly representing one's professional credentials.

In addition to ethical challenges internal to the health care organization, health information managers may face ethical challenges from third parties. Some third parties seek inappropriate access to genetic, adoption, or behavioral health information. Others, such as commercial vendors, may seek to be paid for work not performed. For example, the health information manager may audit invoices submitted by an outside vendor providing transcription services and discover that the vendor has submitted an inaccurate invoice where a discrepancy exists between billed and actual line counts. If the manager determines that the discrepancy is not an error but an inflated line count, the manager may consider revising the transcription contract to require greater invoice detail and include penalty clauses for any future discrepancies.

In working through the decision-making process of situations such as these, the health information manager should use the steps listed earlier in Table 4–2. Additional steps include turning to colleagues for a so-called "reality check" to determine if the ethical dilemma is legitimate or based on misperception. Assuming that a colleague confirms that the dilemma is legitimate, the manager should document the situation, including underlying facts and times, dates, and places of conversation about the matter. Where possible, the manager should address the issue through the organizational hierarchy and, if necessary, through the organization's ethics committee. If it remains unresolved, the manager can seek expert advice from a local health information management chapter or AHIMA. In the end, the manager must determine a personal course of action.

Conclusion

The awareness gained from this chapter should assist the decision maker in identifying the ethical concepts and theories she relies upon to reach a decision. By understanding the various problems associated with bioethics issues, the learner is better positioned to address both personal and public policy questions that may arise during her lifetime. She is also armed with the knowledge needed to address the ethical challenges that confront her.

CHAPTER SUMMARY

The study of ethics has been present for many centuries; ethics assists individuals in reaching moral choices that conform to standards of conduct. Multiple approaches to ethical reasoning exist, each of which applies to the health care field. Codes of ethics, patient rights, religious beliefs, and scientific advances all play a role in influencing ethical decision making. The decision-making process is particularly important in bioethical issues, because concerns of life and death are present. The number of ethical challenges present in the workplace, particularly relating to supervision and health information management, is almost limitless. Personnel matters, conflicts of interest, the pressure on health care providers to remain fiscally solvent, the connection between coding and reimbursement, and the protection of sensitive information all pose ethical issues for the health information management professional to resolve.

CASE STUDY

You are a health information manager in a financially troubled acute care hospital, responsible for coding functions. The hospital's administration has retained an independent consultant who has promised to increase the hospital's financial reimbursement under Medicare. The consultant recommends that your staff be more aggressive in applying diagnostic codes in order to elevate reimbursement. Furthermore, the consultant shares with you methods that can be used to avoid detection of the aggressive coding scheme. You believe this more aggressive approach is, at minimum, inappropriate—and at worst, illegal. You have further learned that the consultant's fee is based in large measure on a percentage of the hospital's increased reimbursement under Medicare. Identify the ethical challenge and discuss how you would handle this situation.

REVIEW QUESTIONS

1. How can one distinguish between legal and ethical issues?

2. Compare the steps typically taken in the ethical decision-making process shown in Table 4–2 with the additional steps listed in the last section of the text.

3. Why should health care providers be aware of bioethical issues?

4. Name the three direct ethical roles that supervisors play in organizations.

5. What are the most frequent ethical challenges in health information management?

6. How can health information managers experience ethical challenges from third parties?

ENRICHMENT ACTIVITIES

1. Review each of the ethical concepts and theories addressed in this chapter. Decide which concept or theory best fits with your personal point of view. Examine how you have used that concept or theory in the past, and decide how you will use it in the future.

2. Consider an ethical decision that you have made within the last three years. Examine how you reached this decision, and compare that process against the ethical decision-making model discussed in this chapter. In light of the materials addressed in this chapter and your personal experiences since the decision was made, determine whether you would make the same decision today. If not, examine how and why your decision would be different.

3. Identify one bioethics issue in your lifetime that engendered sufficient media attention to warrant political involvement. Discuss with a small group the parameters of that bioethics issue and what role politics played in shaping the issue's outcome.

WEB SITES

Codes of Ethics

American Association of Medical Assistants, http://www.aama-ntl.org

American Association for Medical Transcription, http://www.aamt.org

American Dental Hygienists' Association, http://www.adha.org

American Health Information Management Association, http://www.ahima.org

American Medical Association, http://www.ama-assn.org

American Nurses Association, http://www.nursingworld.org

American Occupational Therapy Association, http://www.aota.org

American Osteopathic Association, http://www.osteopathic.org

American Pharmaceutical Association, http://www.aphanet.org

American Physical Therapy Association, http://www.apta.org

American Society of Radiologic Technologists, http://www.asrt.org

Bioethics

Johns Hopkins Bioethics Institute, http://www.med.jhu.edu/bioethics_institute

Human Genome Project, http://www.ornl.gov/hgmis

Midwest Bioethics Center, http://www.midbio.org

National Catholic Bioethics Center, http://www.ncbcenter.org

National Reference Center for Bioethics Literature, http://www.georgetown.edu/research/nrcbl

United Network for Organ Sharing, http://www.unos.org

REFERENCES

Beauchamp, T. L., & Childress, J. F. (2001). *Principles of biomedical ethics* (5th ed.). New York: Oxford University Press.

Edge, R. S., & Groves, J. R. (1994). *The ethics of health care*. Albany, NY: Delmar.

Farrell, O. C., & Gardiner, G. (1991). *In pursuit of ethics*. Springfield, IL: Smith Collins.

Gillon, R. (Ed.). (1994). *Principles of health care ethics*. Chichester, UK: John Wiley & Sons.

Harman, L. B. (2001). *Ethical challenges in the management of health information*. Gaithersburg, MD: Aspen.

Levine, R. J. (1986). *Ethics and regulation of clinical research* (2nd ed.). New Haven, CT: Yale University Press.

Shannon, T. A. (1987). *An introduction to bioethics*. New York: Paulist Press.

NOTES

1. American Osteopathic Association. (2007). *American Osteopathic Association code of ethics*. Chicago: Author.

2. 42 U.S.C. § 1396a(w)(1)(A)(i) (2007).

3. 410 U.S. 113 (1973).

4. Plato referred to the practice of infanticide for the disabled or diseased newborn in his work *The Republic*, Book V, 460C (380 B.C.), as cited in Edge, R. S., & Groves, J. R. (1994). *The ethics of health care*. Albany, NY: Delmar.

5. American Medical Association Council on Ethical and Judicial Affairs. (1992). *Confidentiality of human immunodeficiency virus status on autopsy reports*. Chicago: Author.

6. Centers for Disease Control. (1991, July 12). *Recommendations for preventing transmission of human immunodeficiency virus and hepatitis B virus to patients during exposure-prone invasive procedures*. Retrieved February 9, 2007, from http://www.cdc.gov/mmwR/preview/mmwrhtml/00014845.htm.

7. American Medical Association. See also American Association of Respiratory Care prohibition on referral arrangements involving home care providers.

8. AHIMA Standards of Ethical Coding, http://www.ahima.org. See also: Fighting Fraud and Abuse: Medicare Integrity Program, http://www.hcfa.gov/medicare/fraud; Health Care Compliance Association, http://www.hcca-info.org.

5

Health Care Data Content and Structures

CERTIFICATION CONNECTION

RHIA

Abbreviation usage
Accuracy and integrity of health data
Apply laws, accreditation, licensure, and certification standards to health information
Data/record storage
Documentation guidelines
Organizational survey readiness
Retention and reporting

RHIT

Abbreviation usage
Abstracting
Accuracy and appropriateness
Archival/retrieval systems
Audit trails
Completeness/timeliness
Compliance with regulations/standards
Documentation guidelines
Enterprise MPI
Filing/retrieval systems
Forms design
Indices
Master patient index
Organizational survey readiness
Patient numbering/filing systems
Personal health record
Qualitative analysis
Quantitative analysis
Registries
Timeliness and completeness

LEARNING OBJECTIVES

After reading this chapter, the learner should be able to:

1. Describe the categories of data collected and maintained by health care providers.

2. Summarize the uses and users of health care data.

3. Trace the development of the concept of the personal health record.

4. Explain the concept of data flow and describe three data flow approaches.

5. Compare and contrast the concepts of forms design and forms control, and explain their application to paper-based and electronic health records.

6. Define the terms *data storage, data retention,* and *data destruction,* and explain their relationship to a records management system.

7. Distinguish between the concepts of indices and registries, and identify multiple examples of each.

Outline

Types, Users, Uses, and Flow of Data

Types of Data
Users and Uses of Data
Data Flow

Forms Design and Control

Data Storage, Retention, and Destruction

Data Storage
Data Retention and Destruction

Indices and Registries

Indices
Registries

Key Concepts

Abstracting

Administrative data

Admission register

Authentication

Authorship

Bidirectional data flow

Birth register

Cancer registry

Certificate of destruction

Clinical data

Completeness

Data

Data flow

Death register

De-identified patient data

Digital imaging system

Discharge register

Disease index

Electronic health record

Emergency room register

Enterprise master patient index

Forms control

Forms design

Health record

Incident report

Index

Master patient index

Multidirectional data flow

Number index

Operating room register

Personal health record

Physician index

Primary data

Procedure index

Qualitative analysis

Quantitative analysis

Record retention policies

Record retention schedules

Records management system

Registry

Secondary data

Serial numbering system

Serial-unit numbering system

Statute of limitations

Timeliness

Unidirectional data flow

Unit numbering system

INTRODUCTION

Data and the manner in which it is managed are driving forces in health care today. Virtually every process in the health care environment is measured, from the quality and outcome of care to the cost of that care. To provide a quantitative assessment of these processes, one must possess data. These data can be combined, compared, and interpreted to reach conclusions about a health care provider's or organization's performance.

Central to the success of a health information management professional is an understanding of the role of data in the health care environment. One must first possess a solid knowledge of both the content and structure of health care data to reach this understanding. This chapter provides that understanding, beginning with a discussion of the types, users, uses, and flow of data in the health care environment. A discussion of forms design and control, and the storage, retention, and destruction of data, follows. Secondary databases such as indices and registries complete the chapter.

Types, Users, Uses, and Flow of Data

To understand the types, users, uses, and flow of data, one must first understand the term data. Data refers to raw facts and figures. These facts and figures have not yet been interpreted or processed into useful information. Within the health care context, data are stored in a patient health record. This structure can be found in either a paper-based form or an electronic form. A health record is generally defined as an ordered set of documents, in the paper context, or as a collection of data, in an electronic context, that contains a complete and accurate description of a patient's history, condition, diagnostic and therapeutic treatment, and results of treatment. The health record also contains detailed personal, financial, and social data about the patient. Although it is sometimes described as a medical record, hospital chart, outpatient record, or clinical record, the term *health record* is used in this text for uniformity purposes. The data stored in the patient's health record are used in numerous ways for numerous purposes.

Types of Data
The data collected and maintained by health care providers and organizations concerning their patients generally fall into one of two categories: administrative data or clinical data. Figure 5–1 illustrates these categories. Administrative data are the basic identification and financial data routinely collected from every patient. These data are frequently collected at the preadmission or admission processing stages and include socioeconomic data such as patient name, address, date of birth, next of kin, occupation, and name of employer. Such socioeconomic data serve to positively identify the patient and differentiate his from other patients who are being treated by the same health care provider or organization. Administrative data are not limited to socio-economic information, however; the health care provider is frequently required by law or regulation to maintain other data or forms related to patient care. This may include forms involving consents for treatment, authorization for use and release of information, and advance directives such as powers of attorney for health care and living wills. Financial data, which are particularly important for reimbursement purposes, are also collected for each patient.

By contrast, clinical data refers to the collected and maintained data that relate to the patient's health and course of treatment and care. Clinical data can include such information as the patient's past health history, the data contained in orders and progress notes, and the patient's final diagnosis, to name only a few examples. Examples of clinical data typically found in an acute care health record

Figure 5–1 | Data categories

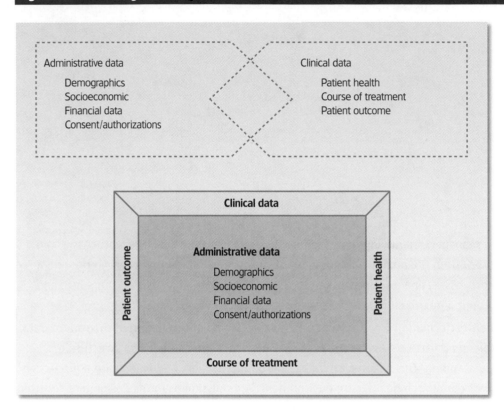

are listed in Table 5–1. Clinical data can be subdivided between permanent medical data (e.g., blood group, gender, and allergies) and variable medical data (e.g., patient history, physical exam, drug prescriptions, lab results, images [X-rays], and biological signals recorded by electrocardiograms [ECGs]). Clinical data are recorded—whether in manual or electronic form—by a variety of individuals, including physicians, nurses, and allied health professionals.

Requirements for collecting and maintaining clinical data are highly regulated. Statutory provisions, administrative regulations, accrediting standards, institutional standards, and professional guidelines all influence what administrative and clinical data are collected and maintained. Among the most significant of these requirements are the Conditions of Participation in the Medicare program, which are promulgated by the U.S. Department of Health and Human Services, and the accrediting standards of the Joint Commission (JC), formerly known as

the Joint Commission on Accreditation of Healthcare Organizations (JCAHO). These requirements contain specific, detailed provisions concerning the content of the health record and serve as a minimum standard for health care organizations to follow in defining the content of the health record within their respective organizations. Health care organizations are free to supplement these requirements with additional provisions designed to meet their specific needs.

Three main groups share responsibility for the health care organizations' compliance with the requirements for collecting and maintaining clinical data: the health care provider, the health information management (HIM) professional, and the organization's health record committee. It is the responsibility of the health care provider authorized by the organization to provide patient care to document the care rendered in an accurate, complete, and clinically pertinent manner. It is the responsibility of the HIM professional

Table 5–1	Clinical Data Typically Found in an Acute Care Health Record	
History and Physical	A report of the patient's current and past history, and findings of a physical examination
Clinical Observations and Progress	Reports and summaries by health care providers of the patient's illness and treatment, including a needs assessment and a plan of care
Reports of Treatment and Procedures	Descriptions of treatments rendered and procedures performed, including findings and results
Consultation Reports	Reports of the patient's condition provided by a health care provider other than the attending physician
Discharge Summary	A summary of the patient's stay in the acute care facility, including final diagnoses and prognosis

to assist the health care provider in documenting patient care by administering policies uniformly and developing procedures to facilitate completion of incomplete records and compliance with external and internal standards. It is the responsibility of the health record committee to set the organization's standards for quality of the health record, including the terminology and abbreviations that will be used. Working in concert, the three groups operate to ensure that proof of high-quality patient care is rendered and that the standards and requirements imposed externally and developed internally are met.

Four concepts directly relate to content of the health record: authorship, authentication, timeliness, and completeness. Authorship refers to the method of identifying the health care provider who made an entry in the record. Authorship can be identified via an entry by writing or dictation, in the case of a paper-based record, or via an entry by keyboard or keyless data entry, in the case of an electronic health record. Authentication refers to the act or process of ensuring the entry in the record for both accuracy and authorship. Authentication can be shown by a written signature or initials, in the case of a paper-based record, or by a computer-generated signature cord, in the case of an electronic health record. Timeliness refers to the entry of data in the health record within a suitable time period—contemporaneously or as soon as possible after care is rendered. Completeness refers to possessing all parts or elements necessary to be considered whole or entire. All four concepts contribute to the integrity of the health record; if documented properly, the health record shows who created an entry, that the entry is confirmed as recorded and accomplished in a timely fashion, and that the entry contains all requisite parts to reflect the care rendered to the patient.

Before data collection begins, consideration must be given to how the data will be organized or displayed once collected. Before the advent of electronic health records or databases, data were arranged on paper. In many parts of the country and in many types of health care practice, the paper form is still predominantly used. Using the paper form, any of three formats may be seen: the source-oriented health record, the problem-oriented health record, and the integrated health record.

The source-oriented health record is organized according to the "source" or department that provided the data. For example, all forms related to laboratory results are separated from those related to physical therapy progress notes. The data and forms are arranged in reverse chronological order by source or department, so that the most current entries are located at the beginning of the record. The strength of a source-oriented medical record is that all data and forms related to the specific source or department are readily available for review. This allows the reviewer to evaluate the assessments, treatments, and observations of the specific source as they relate to the patient's care. The drawback is that organizing data by source makes it more time consuming and difficult to determine the overall picture of a patient's health and treatment, because the reviewer must review multiple areas to reach a determination.

The problem-oriented health record, developed and popularized by Dr. Lawrence Weed, organizes data according to the patient's problems, frequently in order of importance. Grouped with each problem are plans for the patient's treatment, progress notes detailing each visit, and identification of which problems have been solved and what new ones have emerged. The strengths of a problem-oriented health record are many, including the ease of placing all of a patient's problems in context with one another, clearly identifying the goals and methods of treatment, following the logic employed by the health care team during the patient's care, and identifying the interrelationship of the health care team with the patient. The drawback is that the documentation requirements are time consuming for the health care provider; even simple cases with multiple problems require extensive documentation. Because the problem-oriented record has not been widely adopted among health care organizations and training programs, it requires additional training and commitment when it is used. To the extent that concepts of the problem-oriented record have been adopted, it is mainly seen in organizing progress notes according to the SOAP (Subjective, Objective, Assessment, Plan) approach, as illustrated in Table 5–2.

The integrated health record follows a strict chronological order for organization. Frequently placed in reverse chronological order, all forms and data from various sources are intermingled according to date order. This may mean that a progress note will be followed by an operating report, then a pathology report, then laboratory results, then a history and physical, and so forth. The integration stops by episode of patient care, meaning that each episode of care is separated into a different section of the record. The strength of the integrated health record is that all information relating to a specific episode of care may be found together, allowing the reviewer to receive a clear picture of the patient's treatment. The drawback is that the arrangement of materials makes it difficult to compare similar information over time, such as laboratory results.

Table 5–2	SOAP Progress Notes	
S	Subjective
O	Objective
A	Assessment
P	Plan

E-HIM

Electronic health records offer many advantages over paper-based records, including the ability to store vast amounts of data in a small space.

In some parts of the country and in varying forms of health care practice, electronic health records have emerged as the data-storage medium of choice. An **electronic health record** (EHR) refers to a record that resides in an electronic system specifically designed to support users by providing accessibility to complete and accurate data, alerts, reminders, clinical decision support systems, links to medical knowledge, and other aids. An EHR is essentially a database that contains multiple data elements relating to a patient and his care. An EHR contrasts with a paper-based health record in that a paper record is static whereas a database is not; a paper record can be in only one place at a time, but a database may be accessed from multiple locations; a paper record has a fixed order for organizing the data, but a database can retrieve data in different sorting orders and be selective based on user criteria; and a paper record makes the reviewer browse multiple pages searching for data, but a database allows almost instant access to the latest available and valid data.

Regardless of what format is followed, the integrity of the health record is of paramount concern. The integrity of the health record is supported by the activities of quantitative and qualitative analysis. Quantitative and qualitative analysis refers to the activities involved in reviewing the health record for completeness, adequacy, and accuracy. Quantitative analysis concentrates on what forms or data should be present in, but are missing from, the health record. In essence, quantitative analysis involves assembling and analyzing a record for accuracy and completeness. Qualitative analysis of the health record concentrates on the quality of the *record content* and not the quality of the *medical care* rendered to the patient. This analysis is performed by health information management personnel, either concurrently or retrospectively, with the focus on ensuring that the requirements of statutory provisions, administrative regulations, accrediting standards, professional guidelines, and institutional standards are met. If the analysis indicates that those requirements are not met or that inconsistencies or inaccuracies are present, specific omissions or deficiencies are noted and a mechanism is established so that the omissions or deficiencies can be cured while memories of the patient's care are fresh and have not been forgotten. For example, a qualitative review could include deciding whether sufficient documentation exists in the record to support billing a third-party insurer for the diagnoses reached or the procedures performed, or whether all test results are reported in the record to support a particular diagnosis. Those omissions or deficiencies

found in the qualitative analysis are noted for completion or correction.

HIM professionals traditionally performed quantitative and qualitative analysis retrospectively, after the patient's discharge or encounter with the health care provider. Although this retrospective approach offered the advantage of reviewing the record at one time, as a whole, its negative impact upon a health care organization's financial well-being could be significant. The nature of certain deficiencies could delay the coding and sequencing of diagnoses and procedures, in turn delaying the billing process and the subsequent payment of those bills by patients and insurers. For this and other reasons, many HIM professionals have moved to performing quantitative and qualitative analysis on a concurrent basis. This concurrent review occurs on the nursing unit while the patient is still hospitalized, with deficiencies and omissions identified so that they may be addressed by the health care provider before the patient is discharged. Other developments in quantitative and qualitative analysis include focusing the review on select items or forms as opposed to a review of each item or form, and streamlining the authorship/authentication process by using electronic signatures.

Similarly, the integrity of the health record is impacted by the quality of the data contained within it. A number of characteristics are central to data quality and are listed in Table 5-3. These characteristics not only support the health record but serve as the basis for applying and analyzing data. More information about data quality can be found in Chapter 7, "Quality Healthcare Management."

Users and Uses of Data

The data collected and maintained by health care providers and organizations serve a variety of interests and form the basis for addressing a variety of issues, including patient

Table 5-3	Characteristics of Data Quality
Accuracy	Values are correct and valid.
Accessibility	Data are collected easily and legally.
Comprehensiveness	Required data items are all collected.
Consistency	Data values do not vary across applications.
Currency	Data are up-to-date at time of collection.
Definition	Each data element has a clear meaning.
Granularity	Each data element is defined to the necessary level of detail.
Precision	Data values fall within acceptable ranges.
Relevancy	Each data element correlates in meaning to the collection purpose.
Timeliness	Data are collected when necessary.

Source: Adapted from Practice Brief. (1998). *Data quality management model*. Chicago: American Health Information Management Association.

Table 5–4 | Uses Served by Health Care Data

Deliver patient care.
Act as evidence of patient care.
Support compliance efforts.
Assist planning efforts of governmental entities.
Support educational efforts.
Support research.
Indicate quality of care.
Support reimbursement.
Support public health efforts.
Assist media in informing public of health issues.
Support employment decisions.
Verify disabilities.

care, cost, and quality. The users of health care data seem to grow exponentially each decade, as do the uses to which these users put the data. These uses may be both clinical and nonclinical in nature and are listed in Table 5–4.

Within a health care organization, the data found in and extracted from the health record assist caregivers who make clinical decisions in response to the patient's situation. These caregivers may include doctors, nurses, and allied health professionals, all of whom may need to communicate with one another during a particular episode of care. The data found in the medical record serve this purpose. The data used to provide direct patient care facilitate the continuity of care, whether it is provided in the same setting or between health care providers across settings. Furthermore, these data can be supplied to caregivers involved in a patient's subsequent episode of care. The data found in the medical record also assist the health care organization in a multitude of internal functions such as utilization management, planning, credentialing, statistical analysis, and complying with regulatory and accrediting requirements.

Public health officials use the data in the health record in their efforts to control disease and monitor the overall health status of a population. By identifying specific incidences of disease, public health officials can make projections or track trends in diseases. These data are also valuable to their efforts to cure communicable and chronic diseases, prevent illness, subdue environmental hazards, and provide overall health services to the community.

The data in the health record serve as documentary evidence of the course of a patient's illness and treatment during each episode of care and are frequently used for legal purposes. These data serve as the legal record of what did or did not occur in a particular case and can be used to establish whether the applicable standard of care was met.

The data serve as the basis of evidence in adjudication of criminal and civil cases to reconstruct an episode of patient care.

Third-party payers in both the public and private sectors rely on the data found in the health record to document the course of the patient's illness and treatment, making the use of these data an effective means to verify that the patient received treatment or care. These data routinely serve as the basis for claims processing, which is essential to the financing of health care in this country. At a higher level, these data are used by many to manage the costs of care, including managed care entities who make appropriate pricing and cost estimates and health care organizations that contract with managed care entities.

The data in the health record also serve as an indicator of the quality of patient care. Various accrediting and regulatory bodies require health care providers to engage in some function that focuses on the quality of patient care.[1] Data recorded at the time patient care is rendered can serve as the basis for the review of quality patient care. These data can assist the health care organization in quality improvement activities because they serve as the source from which to evaluate the adequacy and appropriateness of patient care and to define opportunities for and methods of improvement.

Educational purposes are also served by the data in the health record. On a regular basis, many individuals in the health care field are engaged in training opportunities designed to correlate theory into practice. Physicians, nurses, dentists, and allied health personnel are constantly learning and improving their skills. These data serve particularly well as the basis of educational programs and presentations focusing on patient outcomes, because the data correlate medical facts to disease, treatment, care, and results. The data in the health record can also serve to educate the patient himself, who needs to understand enough to actively participate in maintaining or improving his own health. Patients need to know and understand data so as to direct their own care and make informed choices. Active participation by patients with chronic diseases and conditions may particularly affect their quality of life. Education of the patient using health data serves these purposes.

Additionally, the data found in the health record can provide support for numerous studies within the research context. National research bodies, drug companies, genetic engineering firms, academic institutions, and individual researchers are all involved in biomedical research. Through concurrent and retrospective analysis, these data are relied upon as a primary source of research materials.

The data found in the health record also support the planning efforts of governmental entities at the local, state, and federal levels. These entities look to the data to determine the appropriate use of taxpayer dollars. Regardless of budget levels, those associated with governmental planning must balance competing demands for funds to support schools, health care facilities, and educational institutions, to name only a few entities. Data found in the medical record, particularly where transformed into statistical form, support those arguments in favor of funding for health care purposes.

The data found in the health record also support compliance efforts. Health care providers and organizations are subject to numerous regulatory and accrediting requirements. Furthermore, efforts to enforce laws concerning fraud and abuse continue to grow at an ever-increasing pace. Governmental and accrediting entities utilize the data supplied to them by health care providers and organizations to assess compliance with laws, regulations, and accrediting standards.

The data found in the health record are sometimes used in the employment context. These data are used to evaluate and assess job-related conditions and injuries, evaluate occupational hazards that may impede performance in the workplace, and determine the extent of employee disabilities and the ability to provide reasonable accommodation.

Though it is not a traditional use, the data found in the health record can serve to assist the media. The media is particularly effective in informing the public about health hazards, incidents and effects of bioterrorism, diseases that affect the public health, and new developments in research. Careful dissemination of data to the media, particularly in statistical form, can assist the media in its communication role.

Patient Users Conspicuously absent from many discussions of health data users are patients themselves. For generations, health care providers and organizations failed to recognize the significance of the patient's need for data about his own health conditions and the care and treatment he received from those providers and organizations. Health care providers and organizations shared a paternalistic viewpoint, believing that because they possessed a high level of scientific and technical knowledge, they knew what was best for the patient and protected the patient's interests accordingly. This viewpoint rejected the possibility that the patient was the user and owner of his own health data and that the health care provider or organization only held the data provided by the patient in a trust capacity for the patient's benefit. To the extent that providers and organizers recognized the need of the patient as a user, they generally employed the need as part of an education program or the face-to-face contact between patient and provider, wherein patients and their families provided information to the health care provider or organization and were given the opportunity to ask questions as circumstances permitted. Failure to recognize the patient as a user of health care data

was so commonplace that providers and organizations looked with apprehension upon those patients who asked for copies of their own patient health records, concerned that the patient's possession of that data may lead to misunderstanding at best or lawsuits and liability at worst.

HIPAA

The Privacy Rule establishes a patient's right of access to his own health information, subject to limited exceptions.

As a result of the rise of the consumer culture, patients began to demand greater access to their own health data. Because technology developments resulted in ready access to health data, objections based on technical impediments were no longer viable. Viewpoints began to change, resulting in a wider acceptance of the concept of a patient possessing a right to his own health data. This viewpoint eventually became codified as part of the implementing regulations to the Health Insurance Portability and Accountability Act (HIPAA) of 1996. These HIPAA regulations specifically recognize that the patient possesses a right of access to his own health information.[2] Many states have followed suit, recognizing the same right through legislation or regulation and sometimes expanding that right.

With the right of access now recognized under federal law, many patients have begun to obtain their own health data. This presents a dilemma for some patients, since the amount of data received can be voluminous and hard to organize or understand. As a result, many patients have begun to develop their own personal health records. A **personal health record** (PHR) is a collection of a patient's important health information that is actively maintained and updated in paper or electronic form, providing the patient with a lifelong resource for making health decisions.[3] Patients may keep their own personal health records, or they may keep a personal health record for another person, such as a child or parent for whom the person has responsibility.

The data that are collected, maintained, and updated may vary, but a personal health record generally includes certain attributes; these attributes are listed in Table 5–5. Once collected, the data may be stored in a paper file or binder or stored electronically. The data may be organized by the subject matter of a given illness (e.g., treatment for diabetes or high blood pressure) or by year. Over time, data can be added to the personal health record, offering the patient the ability to see a longitudinal record of his health and the care he has received. This longitudinal record presents advantages not only to the patient, who is more

Table 5–5 | Features of a Personal Health Record

Administrative Data	Clinical Data
Personal identifiers such as name, date of birth, and Social Security number	Personal and family history
Contact information in case of an emergency	Recent physical examination results
Billing and insurance information, including receipts	Immunization and allergy records
Contact information for health care providers	Test results
Living wills and advance directives	Eye and dental records
Authorization for organ donation	Medication, exercise, and counseling records
Correspondence between patient and health care provider	Opinions of specialists
Consent to treat, release of information, and notice of privacy practices forms	

educated about trends in his own health, but can be shared with health care providers who now have a readily accessible tool containing information about the patient in one place, as opposed to information scattered across numerous provider and organization sites. Where readily available, the personal health record can assist health care providers in a medical emergency by alerting them to serious medical conditions and the treatment the patient has received to date. Last, the personal health record offers the patient the opportunity to participate in his own healthcare actively by making pertinent health data readily accessible to him and to those with whom he wishes to share the data.

Although personal health records show great promise for patients and their health care providers, several issues remain unsettled. Should the health care provider attempt to exercise any control over the personal health record by retaining an identical copy at the provider's office? Should any content of the PHR be created by the patient, or should the content be restricted only to materials obtained from the health care provider? If content is created by the patient, does the health care provider possess any responsibility to review, and correct if necessary, any of that content? Although each of these questions alone does not stand as an impediment to creation of a PHR, together they serve to create uncertainty with regard to the successful acceptance of the PHR by health care providers.

Data Flow

Though much of the data collected and displayed in the health record results from identifying the needs of the many health care providers involved in patient care and the many external forces that influence health care in the 21st century, how those data are made available and disseminated to those who need them is a matter deserving serious consideration. The movement of data through a system and to those in need of them is referred to as **data flow**. A data flow diagram displays how data movement is tracked. Figure 5–2 depicts the basic symbols of a data flow diagram. The emphasis is on data as opposed to the manner in which the data are maintained (e.g., paper or electronic form).

This requires an examination of how data are created, stored, and manipulated.

Data flow can be unidirectional, bidirectional, or multidirectional. In **unidirectional data flow**, data move in a linear arrangement, crossing from one person to another without interruption. An example is the data entered into the health record by a clinician, processed by the HIM professional, and later stored according to established standards and requirements. Unilateral data flow was the method used by many in the health information management profession during the first half of the 20th century. This type of data flow began to change with the rise of the insurance industry and the need of third-party payers for data to support billing charges, leading HIM professionals to view data flow from a bidirectional approach. **Bidirectional data flow** begins by moving data in a linear arrangement but rearranges the data so that they return to the sender at some point and then continue on the original linear path. For example, concurrent review of the health record may result in identifying deficiencies for the clinician's correction during the course of the patient's care; upon correction of the deficiency, new data are entered in the health record that support the remainder of the patient's treatment. As a result of the introduction of sophisticated computer systems and the implementation of other technology devices, the HIM profession's view of data changed once again, this time to a multidirectional approach. **Multidirectional data flow** may begin as bidirectional but then rearranges data to send them to multiple locations, or it may begin by sending the data to multiple locations before the course of the data flow ends. Figures 5–3, 5–4, and 5–5 depict these data flow approaches.

The typical flow of information in a health care facility today is multidirectional, involving collection of data at multiple sites, with numerous persons gaining access to those data and subsequently modifying them through interaction with the patient and other health care providers. Data collection typically begins at the time of patient registration or admitting, when personal and financial information is obtained from the patient. This information may be shared with the health care treatment team and third-party

Figure 5–2 | Data flow symbols

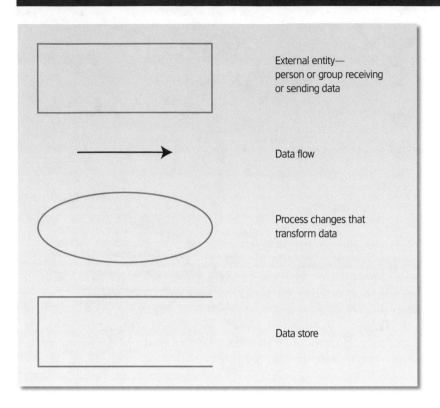

External entity—
person or group receiving
or sending data

Data flow

Process changes that
transform data

Data store

payers, some of whom may require advance notice before authorizing payment for treating the patient. Additional data are collected and recorded by the health care provider during treatment. As treatment continues, more data are added, sometimes modifying the data that was previously collected. This data may be shared with third-party payers again, as a means to authorize payment for continued treatment. Throughout the course of care and thereafter, these data are managed by a health information management professional to ensure that it is accurate, complete, and protected from unauthorized disclosure.

The challenges posed to the flow of health care data are complicated by the demands of the many users and the various uses to which health information is put. For example, the HIM professional may simultaneously be the recipient of patient health information from health care providers while complying with the requests of non-health-care providers such as third-party payers and life insurers for the same information. Alternatively, health care providers themselves may simultaneously need to lessen the flow of health information as a means to ensure the confidentiality of patient data while also reporting that same data to state

Figure 5–3 | Unidirectional data flow

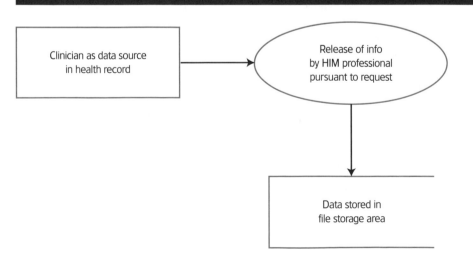

Clinician as data source
in health record

Release of info
by HIM professional
pursuant to request

Data stored in
file storage area

Figure 5–4 | Bidirectional data flow

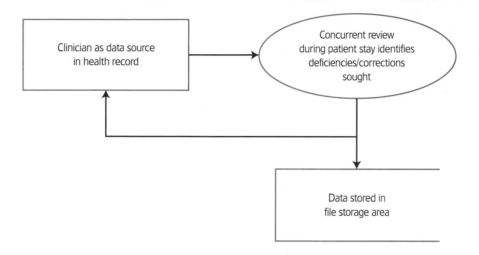

Figure 5–5 | Multidirectional data flow

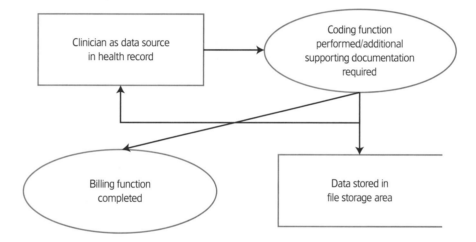

disease registries or county/state health departments as required by law. Although the data flow may be complicated, the standards of accuracy, completion, and protection from unauthorized disclosure serve to guide all who deal with health care data in their many activities.

Forms Design and Control

Accompanying any discussion of the formats used to organize data are the issues of forms design and control. **Forms design** focuses on determining the purpose, use, and users of a form. These determinations dictate the data elements to be contained in the form. For example, the data elements contained in narrative forms, such as patient history and nurses' notes, differ from the data elements contained in summary forms, such as laboratory findings. Once the data elements are decided upon, the design process focuses on arranging the data elements in such a manner as to facili-

tate ease in data entry, thereby reducing the chance for error. **Forms control** focuses on the management of the forms already designed, including how those forms will be amended or changed over time. Forms control functions by establishing: (1) a numbering and tracking system to ensure that duplicate forms are not created for the same function; (2) a process for continued revision of forms already created; (3) a mechanism for testing and evaluating new forms; and (4) a system for storing, inventorying, and distributing forms. Together, good forms design and control contribute to communicating pertinent data readily to those who provide patient care and to those who subsequently review all patient care provided.

Forms design and control invariably involve the contributions of health information management (HIM) professionals, because they possess primary responsibility over the patient health record. HIM department managers frequently work with members of a forms committee in designing and managing forms, ensuring that the requirements for delivery of patient care and of regulatory, accrediting, and reimbursement organizations are met. Additional issues are considered, such as eliminating duplication; ensuring uniformity in size, content, and appearance; and enhancing the quality of the data entered in the patient record. HIM professionals and forms committee members often design forms to comply with a standard format that specifies the location and sequence of information common to every form (e.g., patient identification data).

Forms design of paper-based records often focuses on uniformity and simplicity, which contribute to the flexibility and ease of use of the form. Uniformity may be illustrated by the standardization of the size of the form, the legibility of the font size used, the presence of the name of the health care organization, or the use of bold print in select spots for emphasis purposes. Simplicity may be illustrated by ensuring that the form is user friendly and contributes to the ease and timeliness in completing the form with the requisite data. The formatting of any form should follow a logical sequence so that relationships between the data being recorded make sense and accomplish the function for which the form is designed. In turn, each item on the form should only be present if it serves a purpose or need; any superfluous items can be deleted. Forms control often focuses on creating and maintaining a catalog of forms that provides a list of approved, numbered forms, their titles and a brief statement of the purpose and principle uses of each form, and the dates of approval.

E-HIM

Forms design and control are important in both the electronic and paper context; the focus, however, differs between each context.

Similar issues exist in the EHR context; however, the focus of forms design and control is more expansive. For example, forms design may address the format of a computer screen, using methods to simplify collection of data such as the use of drop-down menus and radio buttons to select or enter text. Similarly, forms design may consider how a paper printout of the data displayed on a computer screen will look. Forms control may entail the field testing of forms using data validation techniques such as data completeness, format, and range checks. Concerns over compliance with standards for data entry may also considered, since an EHR facilitates the electronic interchange of data between and among various groups within and beyond the health care organization. Although they are more expansive in the electronic context, basic forms design and control principles apply to the development of screens used in computer applications.

Numerous forms are found within the patient record, whether in paper-based or electronic format. Within an acute care setting, these forms include the admissions face sheet; history and physical; physician orders; treatment and procedure results; summaries of operations and consultations; progress notes of physicians, nurses, and allied health care providers; discharge summary; therapy notes; and discharge instructions. Other settings may include many or some of these same documents, depending on the type of health care rendered to the patient. These other settings may include additional forms specific to the setting and the particular care rendered (e.g., cardiac intensive care unit or psychiatric care unit).

One form not found within the patient record is an incident report. An **incident report** refers to the documentation of an adverse incident, describing the time, date, and place of occurrence; the incident itself; the condition of the subject of the incident; statements or observations of witnesses; and any responsive action taken by the health care provider or organization. Adverse incidents may include accidents or medical errors that result in personal injury or loss of property. Because incident reports are created for purposes inconsistent with the purposes of a health record, they are maintained separately from the patient health record.

Data Storage, Retention, and Destruction

Data storage, retention, and destruction are the three components of a **records management system**. Such systems operate to control data, and the records housing that data, from the time of creation, collection, or receipt until destruction. Storage concerns address how data, once collected and displayed, must be maintained and made available to those users with a legitimate reason for access. Retention concerns center upon the need for data to be available over time to assist a health care organization to achieve its mission, comply with governmental regulations, and defend itself against legal actions. Destruction concerns address how the data—once it has been determined that is no longer needed—can be destroyed according to the protocols developed by health care organizations in accordance with applicable laws, regulations, and standards.

Data Storage

Because so many purposes are served by health data, it is essential that data be available in a timely and ready manner to those in need of using them. In both the paper-based and electronic health record contexts, data are maintained in patient files and organized according to a record identification system. Such record identification systems may be based on alphabetic or numeric characters, allowing a systematized method for retrieval and storage. Furthermore, these record identifications systems are integrated into a health care organization's master patient index—a concept addressed later in this chapter.

Alphabetical systems are used with paper-based health record systems and rely on the use of a patient's surname, first name, middle initial, and suffix to differentiate the storage of one patient's data from another patient's data. A phonetic indexing system emerged as a result of the confusion engendered by surnames that sound alike but are spelled differently; this system is referred to by the trade name Soundex. Soundex provides a mechanism for a surname to be located even though it may be filed under various spellings. As a general rule, alphabetical systems arrange patient files in alphabetical order, with the surname first, the first name second, the middle initial third, and the suffix last. Files from multiple episodes of care can be grouped together, allowing for a longitudinal approach to record-keeping. Strict alphabetical systems work best with small groups of health records; groups of health records of 1,000 or more make the use of alphabetical systems problematic.

A more frequently used system involves the use of numeric characters. These numeric characters are organized in preassigned order, with each patient designated one of the ordered number arrangements according to a specified system. Some numbering systems assign patients using chronological order as the patient is admitted or readmitted to the same health care facility, creating the potential for the same patient to receive two or more numbers depending on the frequency of admissions to that facility. This method is referred to as the **serial numbering system**. Another numbering system assigns patients using chronological order as the patient is registered or admitted but does not assign the same patient any additional numbers. Rather, the patient is reassigned the original number that was assigned when the patient was initially registered or admitted to the health care facility. This method is referred to as the **unit numbering system**. This system is compatible with the unique identifier system advocated by some accrediting agencies, including the JC. Still other organizations use a modified system, referred to as the **serial-unit numbering system**. This system assigns a new number to the same patient regardless of the number of times the patient is admitted or registered at the same health care facility, but the number that was assigned at the prior admission or registration is updated to reflect the most recently assigned number.

Space considerations frequently influence the organization of physical storage facilities for paper-based records, allowing for either a centralized or decentralized filing approach. Using a centralized filing approach, all records created by the health care provider are stored in a single location. Using a decentralized filing approach, records or parts of records created by the health care provider may be

Figure 5–6 | Paper-based record storage space formula

$$\frac{\text{No. of filing inches currently required} + \text{no. to be filed in future period}}{\text{Total no. of filing inches available in the chosen filing storage unit}}$$

stored in separate locations; for example, active records may be stored separately from inactive records. Record-tracking mechanisms are employed so that users of data may gain access to the data efficiently and with minimal delay. Other considerations for paper-based filing systems include the number of records to be filed, the length of time those records will be stored, the type and cost of filing equipment, and the need for ready access to case records. Some filing equipment choices include lateral filing units, vertical file cabinets, and open-shelf files that may be stationary, mobile, or compact.

Determining the amount of storage space required for a paper-based records system is generally achieved by applying a formula, as depicted in Figure 5–6. The most common formula determines filing inches by adding the amount of filing inches currently required to store patient records with the amount of patient records expected to be filed in a set future period (e.g., 5 or 10 years) and then dividing that sum by the number of filing inches available in the chosen filing storage unit. That calculation indicates the number of filing storage units required, including how many will need to be purchased to accommodate the additional records over time.

With regard to electronic health records, data can also be maintained in patient files organized according to a record identification system. In this context, the record identification system is based on numeric characters. Serial or unit numbering systems can be employed; unit numbering systems rely upon a linking system between records for the same patient. Space considerations are influenced by the capacity of the EHR system. Active records may be stored in the health care provider's live database, and inactive records may be stored in an archive database. To the extent that record tracking mechanisms exist, they help to allow users access to different databases containing the data at issue.

A storage choice that serves as a bridge between a paper-based health record and an electronic health record is a digital imaging system. A **digital imaging system** operates by scanning paper documents on devices that work similar to a photocopier, allowing the image to be saved to an optical disc, a compact disc (CD), or magnetic tape. Once the image is electronically indexed, it can be viewed through a server or Web browser and documents can be retrieved readily. Digital imaging systems offer several advantages, particularly for those organizations not ready to commit fully to an electronic health record, because these systems can reduce the need for physical storage space, offer ready accessibility to document images, increase department work flow, and introduce the concept of storage in electronic media—an essential component of an electronic health record. More information about digital imaging systems can be found in Chapter 13, "Information Systems and Technology."

Records should not only be stored in the ordinary course pursuant to a record storage policy, they must be protected from a business interruption such as a fire, flood, or other disaster. This protection may involve storing paper records or backup tapes at another location of the organization, at an off-site location managed by a vendor, or at an on-site location using a fire-rated vault, safe, or file-cabinet system. These options are not mutually exclusive; a health care organization may choose to employ various combinations as they see fit. By considering this issue, the health care provider ensures that records are not lost and will be available for use in the future.

HIPAA

Security requirements under HIPAA impose burdens upon health care providers to secure patient data from unauthorized access and use.

Whereas it is essential that those with a legitimate need of access to patient data may retrieve those data readily, it is incumbent upon those who store patient data to employ all necessary security precautions. The need for these security precautions arises both from legal requirements and common sense, since the patient will be less willing to disclose needed information to the health care provider if the patient believes the information will not be protected. The most significant recent development in the area of data security is the Health Insurance Portability and Accountability Act, mentioned earlier in this chapter. HIPAA's Security Rule, applicable to protected health information that a covered entity creates, receives, maintains, or transmits in an electronic format, is designed to enhance the security of this data. Using a series of standards and specifications, the Security Rule focuses on data integrity and access controls, specifying administrative, physical, and technical safeguards that a covered entity must or should employ. Further information about the Security Rule and other security-related issues can be found in Chapter 13, "Information Systems and Technology."

Data Retention and Destruction

Similar to data security, the retention and destruction of data are governed and influenced by numerous requirements. These requirements are designed to meet the needs of continuing patient care, education, research, and defense of liability actions. They may arise from legal sources, such

Table 5–6	Record Retention Guidelines from AHIMA	
Health Information	**Recommended Retention Period**
Diagnostic images (such as X-ray film)	5 years
Disease index	10 years
Fetal heart monitor records	10 years after the infant reaches the age of majority
Mastic patient/person index	Permanently
Operative index	10 years
Patient health/medical records (adults)	10 years after the most recent encounter
Patient health/medical records (minors)	Age of majority plus statute of limitations
Physician index	10 years
Register of births	Permanently
Register of deaths	Permanently
Register of surgical procedures	Permanently

as statutes and regulations, or from nonlegal sources, such as accrediting standards, professional guidelines, institutional needs, or the capabilities offered by new technology. An example of retention guidelines issued by the American Health Information Management Association (AHIMA) can be found in Table 5–6.

Essential to any discussion of data retention are record retention policies. **Record retention policies** are the general principles determining the length of time that health data, and the medical records in which those data are housed, must be maintained by the health care provider. These policies are developed using the minimum standards set by statute, regulation, or accrediting standard—whichever is greater—and enlarged by measuring institutional need (e.g., education and research) against storage capabilities. These policies are also affected by a given state's **statute of limitations**, the period of time in which a person can bring a legal action for an injury or breach of contract. These policies result in the establishment of a **record retention schedule**, a document that details what data will be retained, the retention period, and the manner in which the data will be stored. Data storage choices include paper files, microfilm/microfiche, magnetic tape, optical discs, and electronic systems, including archiving systems.

An additional area that deserves attention is the retention of health care business records. These business records may include books of accounts, vouchers, canceled checks, personnel and payroll documents, sales records, compliance documents, and correspondence, to name only some of the many business records in existence in health care organizations today. Retention requirements for these types of records are based on statutes and regulations at both the federal and state levels. As with health data, business record retention policies must encompass all forms of media in which the business record is created or stored, including paper and electronic records.

HIPAA

Although it is typically thought of as addressing individually identifiable patient data, HIPAA also addresses business records, specifying retention periods for those records.

One of the regulations that health care organizations must consider when developing a business record retention policy deals with the HIPAA requirement that covered entities must retain records showing HIPAA compliance for a period of six years.[4] Such records include those documents that demonstrate the integrity and effectiveness of the compliance program, and may include audit and monitoring results, internal investigations, hotline reports, documentation of employee training, the original details of the compliance program plus any modifications, and self-disclosures.

E-HIM

Data and information stored electronically require the creation of policies that govern retention and destruction of this electronic material.

A further consideration is the retention of data and records created and stored in an electronic medium. As a result of the introduction of electronic health record systems, some or all patient information may be available only in electronic form. Because vast amounts of data and information can be stored in this fashion, the importance of creating a record retention policy that addresses electronic storage systems takes on added importance. Guidelines that address creating, identifying, retaining, retrieving, and destroying electronic data are listed in Figure 5-7.

At some point the requirements of the record retention schedule will be met or exceeded, resulting in the need to consider data destruction. Data destruction is another area governed by statute, regulation, accrediting standards, professional guidelines, institutional needs, and the capabilities offered by technology. Similar to data retention, data destruction involves policies and schedules that provide guidance to health care organizations on how to proceed. These policies and schedules indicate what data should be destroyed in the ordinary course and what data should be destroyed because of an organization's closure.

An organization's closure poses many challenges relating to the destruction of data. For example, the closure date may not coincide with the requisite retention period, forcing the health care provider to determine that he cannot destroy data but must make arrangements for the data to be stored by another organization until the retention period is met. A state licensing agency may assume storage responsibilities in such instances or may direct how such storage will be handled. When data addressing alcohol or drug abuse services exist, data destruction is governed by federal regulations that may require contact with the patient or his representative before any action is taken. When data destruction is considered pursuant to a health care provider filing for bankruptcy protection, new federal laws and implementing rules provide guidance on how to handle the situation. The Bankruptcy Abuse Prevention and Consumer Protection Act of 2005 and Federal Rule of Bankruptcy Procedure inform the case trustee, a person appointed by the court to make administrative decisions on behalf of the bankrupt health care provider, what actions to take and how to reconcile those actions with other federal and state laws and regulations. These and other situations present complexities for the health care provider and the health information manager to address when considering data destruction due to closure.

HIPAA

The Security Rule's requirement for effective information security policies encompasses the concept of handling data destruction.

The HIPAA Security Rule also plays a role in data destruction: the rule establishes a requirement for effective information security policies. Because information security policies provide answers to the "who, what, where, when, why, and how" questions of information security, they of necessity cover the issue of destruction of protected health information. As a general rule, data are only destroyed after the retention period has expired, using only those methods specified in an information security policy. With regard to data stored in paper-based records, such methods may include dissolving the records in acid or burning, pulverizing, or shredding the records. With regard to data stored in electronic media, such methods may include magnetic degaussing, overwriting of data, and destruction of backup tapes or other backup media.

Whatever destruction method is chosen, it is important that the health care organization document the actions taken to destroy the data and records. Such documentation shows that the organization has complied with its destruction policies and schedules, thereby blunting later criticism or claims of suspicious destruction activity. Typically, this documentation takes the form of a **certificate of destruction** (COD),

Figure 5-7 | The Sedona Guidelines for Managing Information and Records in the Electronic Age

1. **An organization should have reasonable policies and procedures for managing its information and records.**
   a. Information and records management is important in the electronic age.
   b. The hallmark of an organization's information and records management policies should be reasonableness.
   c. Defensible policies need not mandate the retention of all information and documents.

2. **An organization's information and records management policies and procedures should be realistic, practical and tailored to the circumstances of the organization.**
   a. No single standard or model can fully meet an organization's unique needs.
   b. Information and records management requires practical, flexible and scalable solutions that address the differences in an organization's business needs, operations, IT infrastructure and regulatory and legal responsibilities.
   c. An organization must assess its legal requirements for retention and destruction in developing an information and records management policy.
   d. An organization should assess the operational and strategic value of its information and records in developing an information and records management program.
   e. A business continuation or disaster recovery plan has different purposes from those of an information and records management program.

3. **An organization need not retain all electronic information ever generated or received.**
   a. Destruction is an acceptable stage in the information life cycle; an organization may destroy or delete electronic information when there is no continuing value or need to retain it.
   b. Systematic deletion of electronic information is not synonymous with evidence spoliation.
   c. Absent a legal requirement to the contrary, organizations may adopt programs that routinely delete certain recorded communications, such as electronic mail, instant messaging, text messaging and voice-mail.
   d. Absent a legal requirement to the contrary, organizations may recycle or destroy hardware or media that contain data retained for business continuation or disaster recovery purposes.
   e. Absent a legal requirement to the contrary, organizations may systematically delete or destroy residual, shadowed or deleted data.
   f. Absent a legal requirement to the contrary, organizations are not required to preserve metadata.

4. **An organization adopting an information and records management policy should also develop procedures that address the creation, identification, retention, retrieval and ultimate disposition or destruction of information and records.**
   a. Information and records management policies must be put into practice.
   b. Information and records management policies and practices should be documented.
   c. An organization should define roles and responsibilities for program direction and administration within its information and records management policies.
   d. An organization should guide employees regarding how to identify and maintain information that has a business purpose or is required to be maintained by law or regulation.
   e. An organization may choose to define separately the roles and responsibilities of content and technology custodians for electronic records management.
   f. An organization should consider the impact of technology (including potential benefits) on the creation, retention and destruction of information and records.
   g. An organization should recognize the importance of employee education concerning its information and records management program, policies and procedures.
   h. An organization should consider conducting periodic compliance reviews of its information and records management policies and procedures, and responding to the findings of those reviews as appropriate.
   i. Policies and procedures regarding electronic management and retention should be coordinated and/or integrated with the organization's policies regarding the use of property and information, including applicable privacy rights or obligations.
   j. Policies and procedures should be revised as necessary in response to changes in workforce or organizational structure, business practices, legal or regulatory requirements and technology.

5. **An organization's policies and procedures must mandate the suspension of ordinary destruction practices and procedures as necessary to comply with preservation obligations related to actual or reasonably anticipated litigation, government investigation or audit.**
   a. An organization must recognize that suspending the normal disposition of electronic information and records may be necessary in certain circumstances.

Figure 5-7 | *(continued)*

> b. An organization's information and records management program should anticipate circumstances that will trigger the suspension of normal destruction procedures.
>
> c. An organization should indentify persons with authority to suspend normal destruction procedures and impose a legal hold.
>
> d. An organization's information and records management procedures should recognize and may describe the process for suspending normal records and information destruction and indentify the individuals responsible for implementing a legal hold.
>
> e. Legal holds and procedures should be appropriately tailored to the circumstances.
>
> f. Effectively communicating notice of a legal hold should be an essential component of an organization's information and records management program.
>
> g. Documenting the steps taken to implement a legal hold may be beneficial.
>
> h. If an organization takes reasonable steps to implement a legal hold, it should not be held responsible for the acts of an individual acting outside the scope of authority and/or in a manner inconsistent with the legal hold notice.
>
> i. Legal holds are exceptions to ordinary retention practices and when the exigency underlying the hold no longer exists (*i.e.,* there is no continuing duty to preserve the information), organizations are free to lift the legal hold.

Reprinted with the permission of The Sedona Conference® (www.thesedonaconference.org).

a document that shows what data and records were destroyed, who destroyed those data and records, and the method used for that destruction. Such certificates are particularly important if the destruction is performed by a third party pursuant to an outsourcing contract, because the health care organization possesses a duty to ensure that the contracting agent follows the instructions outlined in the contract's terms for handling and processing data and records for destruction.

Indices and Registries

One of the most important functions of health information management is to maintain and retrieve data. Indices and registries help facilitate this function by organizing data according to specific criteria. An **index** serves as a pointer, indicator, or guide to facilitate reference.[5] An index is not an official document, but rather a tool useful for finding specific information. By contrast, a **registry** is a collection of records in which regular entry is made of particulars or details of a kind that are considered important enough to be exactly and formally recorded.[6] Registries are always formal collections and are often official collections as well; many states require by law or regulation the collection and reporting of certain health care data.

Indices and registries are considered secondary databases. **Secondary data** are those data derived from primary data. **Primary data** are those data obtained from an original data source, such as a patient record or a daily census report. The patient record is often considered the best source of primary data in the health care environment because it contains patient-specific information documented by those health care professionals who provided care to the patient. Secondary databases include those centered within a particular health care facility, such as disease, operative, and physician indices, and those centered beyond a particular health care

facility, such as organ sharing and medical device registries. Because so much information is now available in an electronic format, the number of secondary databases has proliferated. In addition to facilitating direct patient care, secondary databases serve as valuable resources to researchers, health care policy makers, and educators.

Indices

Many types of indices are used by health care facilities. A **master patient index** (MPI) is among the most important; it is a listing or database of all the patients treated by a health care facility, indexed according to an identification process. Using a traditional manual system, the indexing is often performed according to an alphabetical identification process. Using an electronic system, the indexing is often performed according to a numerical identification process. An MPI is a tool used to locate a patient medical record, whether stored electronically or in a traditional paper format. An MPI serves as a permanent record that identifies who has been treated at a health care facility or in a provider practice setting. An MPI can facilitate access to longitudinal patient records and, in electronic format, can be linked to clinical data repositories, pharmacies, and outside laboratories. The MPI is maintained by the health care facility or provider even after the statute of limitations period has expired for retaining an individual patient medical record.

The content of a master patient index is fairly standard across health care practice settings. Demographic data elements such as full name, date of birth, address, identifying patient number, and sex are almost always included; some data elements such as race, ethnicity, or mother's maiden name may also be included to aid in differentiating between entries in the MPI. Limited additional data elements concerning patient care may be included, such as dates of treatment and physician names. Some facilities go even further, designating additional data elements for collection purposes, such as advance directive status, organ donor

Table 5-7 | Contents of a Master Patient Index

Internal patient identification
Person's name
Date of birth
Date-of-birth qualifier
Gender
Race
Ethnicity
Address
Alias/previous name
Social Security number
Facility identification
Universal patient identifier (if established)
Account number
Admission or encounter date
Discharge or departure date
Encounter/service type
Patient disposition

Source: Practice Brief. (1997). *Merging Master Patient (Person) Indexes (MPI)*. Chicago: American Health Information Management Association.

status, and allergies or reactions. Recommended content of an MPI is listed in Table 5-7. If multiple health care facilities share the same MPI, it is referred to as an **enterprise master patient index**. The content of an enterprise MPI would also include facility identification.

One of the most difficult challenges of an MPI is maintaining data integrity, often with regard to the existence of duplicate records. Duplicate MPI records exist because the number of persons interacting with an MPI has steadily increased over time, even if the MPI is automated. Because more people are involved, the opportunity for human error increases. Other data integrity issues include the improper assignment of one patient in an MPI to another patient's record, and the entry of erroneous, invalid, or default data in a computerized MPI in lieu of patient data.

Solutions to these data integrity challenges include improving data input and search accuracy and cleaning the MPI database. Strict policies and procedures for data input can be publicized internally and enforced through periodic audits so that errors can be prevented and corrected in a timely manner. In some computerized MPI systems, the patient can improve the input process by accessing his MPI data through an online portal. Typically, the patient can correct inaccurate personal identifiers—a major reason duplicate records are created in the first instance. Search accuracy can be improved through the use of software that mathematically models human similarity algorithms. Finally, an MPI can be cleaned using analysis and determination of

which duplicate record should be eliminated or how incorrect or invalid data can be corrected. This process can be performed by internal staff or by outside vendors under contract. Either way, this cleaning improves both the operation of the health care organization and patient care.

HIPAA

Provisions of HIPAA originally envisioned assignment of unique identifiers to individual patients; implementation of such provisions has been postponed indefinitely.

Recent new developments in the law have affected the maintenance of master patient indices. HIPAA contained provisions for the introduction of a National Health Identifier for Individuals (Personal Identifier), which would have assigned a unique identifier to each consumer of the health care delivery system. The concept of a Personal Identifier engendered extensive criticism as an invasion of privacy and was seen by many commentators to be in direct contradiction to the already established Privacy Rule, which protects personally identifiable patient health information. In light of this criticism, the U.S. Department of Health and Human Services has postponed implementation of this identifier standard indefinitely.

A **number index** is a listing of all the identification numbers assigned to patients at a health care facility or provider practice setting, indexed with the accompanying patient name. The numbers are assigned at the time of patient admission or initial treatment. Each number in the number index is also located in the master patient index, making the number index particularly useful as a quality check of the master patient index. The two indices differ in that the master patient index contains more identifying information than the number index, and one is indexed according to number (number index) but the other is indexed according to patient name (MPI).

Two particularly important indices are disease and procedure indices. A **disease index** lists diseases and conditions according to the classification system used by the health care facility or private provider. A **procedure index** lists operations and procedures according to the classification system used by the health care facility or private provider. Both indices contain similar content, including the patient's age, sex, race, ethnicity, dates of treatment, patient outcome, and associated diseases and procedures. This information is abstracted from a primary data source such as the patient record. **Abstracting** is the process of collecting, tabulating, aggregating, and summarizing selected data elements. These indices are important because they allow researchers to compare data on diseases and procedures and to gain insight into the incidences of complications. The indices also assist in quality care review, supply data for accrediting review, qualify a facility for accredited internship and residency programs, and serve as educational material for staff and students.

A physician index is a listing of all the patients a given physician has treated at a health care facility, indexed by physician name or code number. The content of the physician index includes the patient's name and identifying number and whether the physician served as the attending, consulting, or operating physician. Additional data such as length of stay, numbers of admissions, and charges are sometimes included. Physician indices serve a number of purposes, including as a means to track trends and changes in individual and group physician practices, to identify requirements for additional physician specialists, and to make appointments to various committees.

Registries

Similar to indices, multiple registries exist within the health care context, varying by purpose, design, and size. These registries generally relate to a single topic and usually contain de-identified patient data, meaning that the data in the registry cannot be traced to a particular patient. Some registries, such as organ donor registries, do contain patient-identifiable data because the nature of the data means it cannot be made completely anonymous without sacrificing efficiency and effectiveness. Examples of single-topic registries include cancer, trauma, cardiac, diabetes, and medical device registries. These and other single-topic registries are listed in Table 5–8.

Some registries are kept at the level of the local health care facility. An admission register lists the patients admitted to a particular health care facility, arranged in chronological order by date and time of admission. A discharge register lists the patients discharged from a particular health care facility, arranged in chronological order by date of discharge. An operating room register lists the patients who have undergone operations at a particular health care facility. An emergency room register lists those patients treated at a particular health care facility's emergency room, arranged in chronological order by date of treatment. A birth register lists those patients born at a particular health care facility, arranged in chronological order by date of birth. A death register lists all patients who died at a particular health care facility, arranged in chronological order by date of death and sometimes differentiated by age (e.g., fetal death registries). All of these registries contain similar content, including patient name, identifying number, and physician, but differ with regard to what data they record.

One common registry found in health care facilities is the cancer registry. In the most simplistic sense, a cancer registry lists all patients who have been diagnosed with or received treatment for a form of cancer and certain benign conditions. A cancer registry extends beyond a mere listing of patients; it also addresses topography, morphology, and other information relevant to the disease. Furthermore, many cancer registries contain data on the patient's follow-up treatment and length of survival. This interconnection of information qualifies a cancer registry as a relational database. Cancer registries have evolved to a status separate and distinct from other registries maintained by health care facilities due to the use that epidemiologists and other researchers have made of the data contained in the registries for cancer-related studies and research. Additional distinction is warranted because the data maintained in these registries are subject to reporting standards of such organizations as the Centers for Disease Control and Prevention's National Program of Cancer Registries; the North American Association of Central Cancer Registries; the National Cancer Institute's Surveillance, Epidemiology, and End Results (SEER) Program; and the American College of Surgeons' Commission on Cancer.

Many states maintain registries for the reporting and tracking of certain diseases and public health threats. For example, most of the states require the reporting of cancer information to a central registry maintained by the state's department of public health or a similar agency.[7] Similar reporting requirements exist for head and spinal cord injuries,[8] birth defects,[9] communicable diseases (e.g., venereal diseases and acquired immunodeficiency syndrome [AIDS]),[10] and child abuse.[11]

Some registries restrict access to only researchers, providing them with specific information and locations for individual entities. For example, the Chemical Abstracts Service Registry allows researchers access to an online database containing chemical structure and dictionary information on unique substances. Similarly, the National Cancer Institute's Cooperative Breast Cancer Tissue Registry allows researchers to search an online database to gain information and location of tissue specimens to be used in approved research protocols.

Some registries exist on an international level, such as the United Network for Organ Sharing and the International Implant Registry. These registries are integrated health information networks that cross national borders. They arose for both practical and fiscal reasons—many countries benefit from the sharing of data concerning organ donors and implants allowed on the relevant market. Secure access is of paramount concern in these registries, because they often contain sensitive genetic and immunological data. For example, the registry maintained by the United Network for Organ Sharing contains patient-identifiable information that indicates rankings on disease severity scales.

Table 5–8 | List of Registers and Registries in the United States

Register/Registry	Sponsor	Description
Adoption Information Registries	State agencies	Helps adoptees obtain available nonidentifying information about birth parents. Enables the reunion of registered adoptees with birth parents and biological siblings. Provides a place for birth parents to file medical information updates that may be shared with registered adoptees.
Alzheimer Registries	State agencies	Collects data to evaluate prevalence of Alzheimer's disease and related disorders. Provides nonidentifying information and data for policy planning purposes and to support research.
Birth Defects Registries	State agencies	Maintains statewide surveillance for collecting information on birth defect incidence. Monitors annual trends in birth defect occurrence and mortality. Conducts research studies to identify genetic and environmental risk factors for birth defects. Promotes educational activities for the prevention of birth defects.
Birth Defects Registries or Congenital Anomaly Register or Congenital Malformations Registries	Health care facilities and state agencies	Repository for case reports on children diagnosed before age two who have suspected or confirmed congenital anomalies, which are structural, functional, or biochemical abnormalities determined genetically or induced during gestation and are not due to birthing events. Facilities and state agencies identify ICD codes to use for case reporting.
Cancer Registries	Health care facilities, groups of health care facilities, state and federal agencies	Collects information about all cancers diagnosed. Develops strategies and policies for cancer prevention, treatment, and control. Allows researchers to analyze geographic, ethnic, occupational, and other differences to identify cancer risk factors.
Cardiac Registries	Health care facilities	Captures cardiac surgery information as a research tool for assessing cardiac patient outcomes and pinpointing how patient care can improve.
Immunization Registries	Federal and state agencies	Computerized systems that consolidate vaccination histories as provided by individual health care providers.
Implant Registries	Various organizations, depending on type of implant	Tracks successful implants and assesses failures through retrieval analysis. Improves patient care through improvements of implants. Monitors device performance inside the body to permit early corrective therapy.
Inpatient Discharge Database	State and federal agencies	Contains hospital inpatient discharge data. Collected to study patterns and trends in the availability, use, and charges for inpatient services. Consists of core data elements, as defined by state and federal agencies.
Insulin-Dependent Diabetes Mellitus (IDDM) Registries	National Institutes of Health	Determines incidence of IDDM in defined populations. Identifies persons for subsequent enrollment in case–control studies and other research projects.
National Exposure Registry	Centers for Disease Control and Prevention Agency for Toxic Substances and Disease Registries	Identifies, enrolls, and monitors persons who may have been exposed to a hazardous environmental substance.
National Registry of Cardiopulmonary Resuscitation	Sponsored by the American Hospital Association; managed by Tri-Analytics, Inc.	Collects and analyzes in-hospital resuscitation data. Allows health care facilities to evaluate equipment, resources, and training, and to improve practices.
National Registry of Myocardial Infarction	Sponsored by Genetech, Inc.	Examines trends in treatment, length of hospital stay, mortality, and variations among specific patient populations.

Table 5–8 | *(continued)*

Register/Registry	Sponsor	Description
National Trauma Data Bank	American College of Surgeons	Improves quality of patient care. Provides established information system for evaluation of injury care and preparedness. Develops injury scoring and outcome measures. Provides data for clinical benchmarking, process improvement, and patient safety.
Organ Donor Registry	Organizations, state agencies	Computerized database that documents an individual's plan to be an organ donor.
Rare Disease Registries	National Organization for Rare Disorders	Collects clinical and genetic data. Provides referrals to genetic counseling and other services. Conducts ongoing research.
Surveillance, Epidemiology, and End Results Program	National Cancer Institute	Collects cancer data on a routine basis from designated population–based cancer registries in nine areas of the United States.
United States Eye Injury Registry	Helen Keller Eye Research Foundation	Provides prospective, population–based, epidemiologic data to improve the prevention and control of eye injuries.
Vital Records	Health care facilities, county and state agencies	Records births, deaths, fetal deaths, induced abortions, teen pregnancies, and teen suicides. Files certificates for births, deaths, divorces, and marriages. Collects mortality, fetal death, and natality data, and prepares reports. Distributes certificates to eligible persons.

Source: Adapted from Green, M. (2005). *Essentials of health information management.* Clifton Park, NY: Delmar.

Conclusion

Every health information management professional working today, whether in a traditional or nontraditional setting, deals with data of some type. To be effective in a health information management role, one must understand the concept of data and the applications to which data are made. Understanding health data content and structure provides the framework the health information manager needs to assist in the viability and well-being of both the patient and the health care organization.

CHAPTER SUMMARY

This chapter focuses on the role of data in the health care field. The different types of data, the uses to which these data are put, and the number of data users seem to grow every passing year. Accompanying this growth has been a gradual movement away from a paper-based system for collecting and maintaining data to one that relies upon electronics. This movement has influenced the design and control of forms and how data are stored, retained, and destroyed. Maintaining and retrieving data is an important role of the health information management professional and is accomplished through the use of indices and registries. As a result of the implementation of electronic health records and storage devices, the importance of the master patient index has grown.

CASE STUDY

You are a health information management professional who has been asked to make a presentation to a community group on the topic of personal health records. Prepare a presentation that addresses how the concept of a personal health record developed, why a patient would want to create and maintain a personal health record, and what that record should contain.

REVIEW QUESTIONS

1. What are the three formats commonly used for a paper-based health record?

2. How can the data in a health record assist the media?

3. What are the features typically found in a personal health record?

4. What forms design issues exist with regard to the electronic health record context?

5. What is an incident report? Is it filed with the health record? Why or why not?

6. Name some examples of a numeric record identification system.

7. What advantages are offered by a digital imaging system?

8. What is a certificate of destruction and why is it important?

9. What are the similarities and differences between a master patient index and a number index?

10. How does a cancer registry differ from other registries?

ENRICHMENT ACTIVITIES

1. Visit any of the following Web sites to view the features of chart filing or tracking systems: http://www.adldata.com, http://www.filingtoday.com, http://www.hale-systems.com, or http://www.bibberosystems.com. Compare the considerations of record storage addressed in this chapter against the features identified on these Web sites. Discuss your comparisons with your instructor and classmates.

2. Visit any of the following Web sites to view the features of paper-based and electronic personal health records: http://www.healthframe.com, http://www.checkupsoftware.com, http://www.medicalert.org, or one of your choosing. Compare and contrast the solutions offered to patients with regard to creating a PHR, including such factors as ease of use and cost. Discuss your findings with your instructor and classmates.

WEB SITES

American Health Information Management Association, http://www.ahima.org

American Records Management Association, http://www.arma.org

HIPAA Privacy and Security Regulations, http://www.hhs.gov/ocr

Joint Commission, http://www.jointcommission.org

Medical Records Institute, http://www.medrecinst.com

President's Information Technology Advisory Committee, http://www.nitrd.gov/pitac

REFERENCES

Green, M., & Bowie, M. J. (2005). *Essentials of health information management: Principles and practices.* Clifton Park, NY: Delmar.

Huffman, E. (1994). *Health information management* (10th ed.). Berwyn, IL: Physicians' Record Company.

Hurst, J. W. (1971) Ten reasons why Lawrence Weed is right. *New England Journal of Medicine, 284,* 51.

Hurst, J. W., & Walker, H. K. (Eds.). (1972). *The problem-oriented system.* New York: Medcom Press.

Johns, M. (1997). *Information management for health professionals.* Clifton Park, NY: Delmar.

Moczygemba, J., & Biedermann, S. (2000). MPIs in healthcare: Current trends and practices. *Journal of AHIMA, 4,* 55–60.

Practice Brief. (1997). *Merging Master Patient (Person) Indexes (MPI).* Chicago: American Health Information Management Association. Available at http://www.ahima.org.

Practice Brief. (1998). *Data quality management model.* Chicago: American Health Information Management Association. Available at http://www.ahima.org.

Skurka, M. A. (Ed.). (2003). *Health information management: Principles and organization for health information services.* San Francisco: Jossey-Bass.

Tomes, J. P. (2002). Retaining healthcare business records [Practice brief]. *Journal of AHIMA, 73*(3), 56A–56G.

Van Bemmel, J. H., & Musen, M.A. (1997). *Handbook of medical informatics.* Netherlands: Springer-Verlag.

NOTES

1. See, e.g., *2003 Comprehensive Accreditation Manual for Hospitals: The Official Handbook* (Joint Commission on the Accreditation of Healthcare Organizations), Performance Improvement Measures, PI.1—PI.5, and Performance Measurement and the ORYX Initiative.

2. 45 C.F.R. § 164.524 (2007). Some exceptions to individual access to PHI include (1) psychotherapy notes; (2) information that is, or could be used for, a civil, criminal, or administrative action or legal proceeding; (3) that PHI which is subject to access prohibitions found in the Clinical Laboratory Improvements Amendments (CLIA) of 1988; and (4) PHI held by certain research laboratories.

3. American Health Information Management Association e-HIM Personal Health Record Work Group. (2005). The role of the personal health record in the EHR. *Journal of AHIMA, 76*(7), 64A–64D.

4. 45 C.F.R. § 164.540 (j) (1) (2007).

5. *Webster's new world college dictionary* (4th ed.). (2001). Springfield, MA: Merriam-Webster.

6. Ibid.; Bemmel, J. H. van, & Musen, M. A. (Eds.). (1997). *Handbook of medical informatics* (p. 369). Netherlands: Springer-Verlag.

7. See, e.g., ALA. CODE §22-13-31 (2007); 7 ALASKA STAT. § 18.15.370 (Michie 2007); ARK. STAT. ANN.§ 20-15-201 (2007); CAL. HEALTH & SAFETY CODE § 103885 (2007); COLO. REV. STAT. § 25-1.5-101 (2007); 16 DEL. CODE ANN. § 3204 (2007); FLA. STAT. § 385.202 (2007); HAW. REV. STAT.§ 321-43 (2007); IDAHO CODE § 57-1702 (2007); 20 ILL. COMP. STAT. 2310-365 (2007); IND. CODE ANN § 16-38-2-1 (West 2007); KENTUCKY REV. STAT. § 214.556 (2007); LA. REV. STAT. §40:1299.42 (2007); ME. REV. STAT. ANN. tit. 22, § 1404 (West 2007); MD. CODE ANN., HEALTH-GEN. § 18,204 (2007); MASS. GENL. LAWS ANN. 111 § 111 B (2007); MICH. COMP. LAWS ANN. § 333.2619 (West 2007); MINN. REV. STAT. § 144.672 (2007); MISS. CODE ANN. § 41-91-5 (2007); MO. REV. STAT. § 192.650 (2007); NEB. REV. STAT. § 81-644 (2007); NEV. REV. STAT. ANN.§457.240 (2007); N.H. REV. STAT. ANN. § 141-B:7 (2007);N.J. STAT. §26:2-105(2007); N.Y. PUB. HEALTH § 2401 (Consol. 2007); OHIO REV. CODE ANN. §3701.261 (2007); OR. REV. STAT. § 432.510 (2007); 35 PENN. STAT. §5636 (2007); S.D. CODIFIED LAWS ANN. §1-43-11 (2007); TENN. CODE ANN. § 68-1-1006 (2007); TEX. HEALTH & SAFETY CODE § 82.008 (2007); UTAH ADMIN. CODE R 386-702-2 (2007); VA. CODE ANN. § 32.1-70 (2007); WASH. ANN. CODE § 70.54.240 (2007); W. VA. CODE §16-5A-2a (2007); WIS. STAT. §255.04 (2007). See also The Cancer Registries Amendment Act.

8. See, e.g., ALA. CODE 22-11 C-7 (2007); MO. REV. STAT. § 192.737 (2007).

9. See, e.g., MISS. CODE ANN. § 41-21-205 (2007); 63 OKLA. STAT. §1-550.2 (2007); TEX. HEALTH & SAFETY CODE § 87.022 (2007).

10. See, e.g., IDAHO CODE § 39-609 (2007); KAN. STAT. ANN. §65-6002 (2007); MO. REV. STAT. § 191.653 (2007); S.D. ADMIN. R. 44:20:01:04 (2007).

11. See, e.g., HAW. REV. STAT. § 350-1.1 (2007); MO. REV. STAT. § 210.110 (2007); R.I. GEN. LAWS §40-11-3.1 (2007); S.D. CODIFIED LAWS ANN. §26-8A-6 (2007).

6

Nomenclatures and Classification Systems

CERTIFICATION CONNECTION

RHIA

Clinical classifications
Clinical vocabularies
Coding
Coding accuracy
Coding compliance/reporting
Electronic applications
Terminologies

RHIT

Clinical classifications
Clinical vocabularies
Coding accuracy/discrepancy reconciliation
Coding guidelines
Diagnosis/procedure codes
Diagnostic/procedural groupings
Terminologies

LEARNING OBJECTIVES

After reading this chapter, the learner should be able to:

1. Differentiate between the terms *medical language, vocabulary,* and *nomenclature*.

2. List nomenclatures that are prominent in the health information management field.

3. Understand the goal of the Unified Medical Language System.

4. List and explain the three Knowledge Sources of the Unified Medical Language System.

5. Identify the major classification systems currently in use.

6. Understand how the introduction of the prospective payment system and diagnosis-related groups affected the health information management field.

7. Describe the concept of case mix management.

8. Identify the impact of technology upon the coding function.

Outline

Languages, Vocabularies, and Nomenclatures

Nomenclature Development

Classification Systems

History and Application of Classification Systems
HIM Transformation
Other Classification Systems

Emerging Issues

Key Concepts

ABC codes

Case mix

Case mix management

CDT

Classification systems

Clinical data representation

Clinical terminology

Clinical vocabulary

Coding

Coding compliance program

Compliance

CPT

Data mapping

Diagnosis-related group

DSM–IV

Encoders

Eponyms

Evaluation

Groupers

HCPCS

Health care fraud and abuse

ICD

ICD–O–3

ICD–9–CM

ICD–10

ICF

ICIDH

Lexicon

Major diagnostic category

Management

Medical language

Metathesaurus

Natural language processing encoding systems

NDC

Nomenclature

Nosologists

Optimizing programs

Prospective payment system

RBRVS

Semantic Network

SNDO

SNOMED

SNOP

Taxonomies

Terminology

Unified Medical Language System

Upcoding

Vocabulary

INTRODUCTION

In the course of any given day, clinicians and administrators use vocabularies, clinical terminologies, and classification systems to deliver patient care and comply with the requirements of regulatory and accrediting agencies. For example, one clinician may communicate with another clinician regarding the type of care to be rendered to the patient through the use of a common vocabulary. A manager in a health care facility may utilize clinical terminologies while supervising the educational experience of a student. A health care facility may use a classification system to report incidences of communicable diseases to governmental authorities charged with monitoring public health threats. These are but three examples of the multitude of ways in which vocabularies, clinical terminologies, and classification systems are used in the health care field.

Because of the complex use of data in today's health care system, the need for a common understanding of medical language and uniform standards of classifying data cannot be overstated. Medical vocabularies, clinical terminologies, and classification systems were created to describe the medical care process in a standard manner, thereby easing communication between individuals, groups, and organizations and helping to organize health care data for easy retrieval by many groups. Those standards that deal with uniform nomenclature and classification systems are addressed in this chapter; standards that deal with the transmission of data and communication between databases are addressed in Chapter 8, "Database Management."

Semester-long courses are sometimes devoted to the teaching of medical vocabularies, clinical terminologies, and classification systems. The level of information necessary to give the reader an extensive understanding of these topics is beyond the scope of this book. Nonetheless, it is possible to gain an awareness and understanding of these topics from the material presented here. Accordingly, this chapter employs an overview approach, beginning with a discussion of languages and a description of nomenclature development. Classification systems are explored, with a focus on issues related to the introduction of the prospective payment system and its effect upon the health information management field. Emerging issues and trends in these areas complete the chapter.

Languages, Vocabularies, and Nomenclatures

Languages have long played a role in distinguishing countries, communities, and organizations from one another. Languages play the same role in the professions, distinguishing one profession from another—for example, law from medicine. The language of medicine forms the basis for the understanding and management of health information. Accordingly, one must become knowledgeable of the medical language to be a successful health information manager.

Medical language refers to the words, their pronunciation, and the methods of combining them that have been established by long periods of usage and are understood by the medical profession. Medical language, like any other language, has a long history of development. Some medical language terms, such as *femur* and *hemorrhage*, are based on Greek and Latin word parts. Other terms used in medical language are eponyms, which are words that are based on the personal names of people, such as Addison's disease or Parkinson's disease. Still other terms used in medical language come from modern language; the word *laser*, for example, is an acronym meaning light amplification by

Figure 6-1 | Interrelationship of vocabularies and nomenclatures

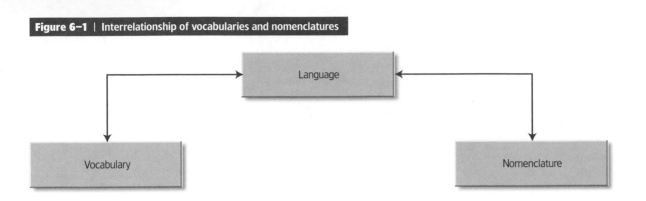

stimulated emission of radiation. Over time, some terms are discarded, some are added, and some change their meaning.

Within the concept of language is a subset of concepts referred to as vocabularies and nomenclatures. A **vocabulary** is a list of words or phrases and their associated meanings that have been accepted by a discipline, group, or organization to express, organize, and index concepts and phenomena of interest. In other words, a vocabulary is a chosen set of words, usually arranged in alphabetical order, that are understood and accepted by a community. A **clinical vocabulary** is a vocabulary that specializes in words or phrases of a clinical or medical nature. Vocabularies that function mainly to assign names to unique concepts are sometimes referred to as nomenclatures. A **nomenclature**, also referred to as **terminology**, is a systematic listing of proper names for concepts, items, actions, and other aspects of a *particular* area of interest or knowledge. Within the broad concept of nomenclature is the concept of **clinical terminology**, a recognized system of preferred clinical or medical terminology. Without a nomenclature, studies that compare diseases are difficult to understand at best and impossible to understand at worst. Figure 6-1 illustrates how these concepts relate to one another.

Many nomenclatures exist within the medical community, each arising from the needs of a separate community. Several nomenclatures prominent in the health information management (HIM) field are discussed here, including the Standard Classified Nomenclature of Disease (SNDO), the Systematized Nomenclature of Pathology (SNOP), the Systematized Nomenclature of Medicine (SNOMED), and Current Procedural Terminology (CPT). Although some of these nomenclatures are no longer in use, it important to be aware of them because data have been indexed to these systems for many decades and they may be needed for access when conducting longitudinal research. A broader listing of both historical and currently used nomenclatures is found in Table 6-1.

Nomenclature Development

In the late 19th and early 20th centuries, numerous attempts were made to accurately describe and identify all of the disease entities known to mankind. One early effort, the *Basic Nomina Anatomica*, developed from the work of the Anatomical Society. Early efforts in American hospitals, such as

Massachusetts General Hospital in Boston and Bellevue Hospital in New York City, resulted in nomenclatures and classification systems that were specific to certain hospitals; these systems made it difficult to compare data across hospitals. In an effort to remedy the situation, the American Medical Association published the Standard Classified Nomenclature of Disease (**SNDO**) in 1933. SNDO classified diagnostic terminology in order of localization (site) and etiology (cause). SNDO was used through 1961, when it was deemed too simplistic to apply to increasingly sophisticated medical knowledge.

The Systematized Nomenclature of Pathology (**SNOP**) is a nomenclature published by the American College of Pathologists that is useful in classifying pathological specimens. Although commonly used by pathology departments in hospitals from 1965 onward, SNOP gradually lost favor when focus was placed by accrediting agencies on standardized nomenclatures that could cross fields of specialization.

One such standardized nomenclature that crosses fields of specialization is the Systematized Nomenclature of Medicine, or **SNOMED**. SNOMED is a comprehensive nomenclature that was first published by the American College of

Table 6-1 | Listing of Historical and Currently Used Nomenclatures

Complete Complementary Alternative Medicine Billing and Coding Reference
Current Medical Information and Terminology (CMIT)
Current Procedural Terminology (CPT)
International Nomenclature of Diseases (IND)
Nursing Intervention Lexicon and Toxonomy (NILT)
Standard Nomenclature of Athletic Injuries
Standard Nomenclature of Disease and Operations (SNDO)
Standard Nomenclature of Veterinary Diseases and Operations (SNVDO)
Systematized Nomenclature of Medicine (SNOMED)
Systematized Nomenclature of Medical Reference Terminology (SNOMED-RT)
Systematized Nomenclature of Pathology (SNOP)
Systematized Nomenclature in Veterinary Medicine (SNOVET)

Pathologists in 1977 as an expansion of SNOP. SNOMED is similar to SNDO in the sense that it classifies terminology in order of localization and etiology. It differs, however, in that it also classifies terminology in other ways, such as by morphology, function, disease, and procedures. SNOMED is associated with a universal standard medical vocabulary for identifying laboratory and clinical observations called the Logical Observation Identifiers Names and Codes (LOINC). SNOMED is among the first nomenclatures designed for automated encoding of medical text, allowing for its use in the current computerized world.

A second nomenclature that lends itself to automated use is Current Procedural Terminology (CPT). Published by the American Medical Association, CPT is a comprehensive listing of medical terms and codes used to designate diagnostic and therapeutic procedures. Currently in its fourth edition, CPT-4 is commonly used in physician offices and serves as a means to report physician services for reimbursement purposes.

Although computerization is sometimes considered during the development of nomenclatures, the variety and differences of these nomenclatures in the medical profession have posed numerous obstacles to the computerization of health care data. The meaning of a word in one vocabulary or nomenclature may be slightly different from the same word used in a separate vocabulary or nomenclature. Whereas this variation may be addressed and explained in further detail in a verbal conversation, it is extremely difficult to communicate electronically that variances in meaning exist. There must be some standardization for electronic communication to be effective. In recognition of the dilemma posed by the variety of and differences among vocabularies and nomenclatures, the National Library of Medicine embarked on an ambitious research and development project to link various biomedical vocabularies and nomenclatures together. This project is entitled the Unified Medical Language System (UMLS). The goal is to enable computer systems to understand medical meaning, thereby allowing health professionals and researchers to retrieve and integrate electronic biomedical information from various sources, including electronic health records, bibliographic databases, factual databases, and expert systems. Such databases include the National Library of Medicine's

bibliographic citation database, MEDLINE, and the reference database MEDLARS. The index to the journals contained in these databases is referred to as the Medical Subject Headings (MeSH), a controlled-vocabulary thesaurus.

E-HIM

Standardization of vocabularies and nomenclatures is essential to the development and implementation of an electronic health record.

The Unified Medical Language System project has resulted in a set of three Knowledge Sources: the UMLS Metathesaurus, the SPECIALIST Lexicon, and the UMLS Semantic Network. These three sources are illustrated in Figure 6-2 and are freely accessible on the Internet using the URLs found at the end of this chapter. The Metathesaurus provides a uniform, integrated distribution format for more than 100 biomedical vocabularies and classifications, linking many different names for the same concepts. The Lexicon contains syntactic information for many terms, component words, and English words—including verbs—that do not appear in the Metathesaurus. The Semantic Network contains information about the types or categories to which all Metathesaurus concepts have been assigned and the permissible relationships among these types. For example, one type or category may be "virus" and a second type or category may be "disease or syndrome." The relationship between these types or categories is that a virus may cause a disease or a syndrome. All three Knowledge Sources are updated regularly and distributed to the public at no cost on CD-ROMs and over the Internet, subject only to an obligation to sign and submit a license agreement for the products selected.

E-HIM

The Metathesaurus portion of the Unified Medical Language System project presents a wide range of applications, including the development of the electronic health record.

Figure 6-2 | Unified Medical Language System Knowledge Sources

UMLS Metathesaurus	SPECIALIST Lexicon	UMLS Semantic Network
Uniform, Integrated Distribution Format for Vocabularies and Classifications	Syntactic Information for Terms and Words Not Appearing in the Metathesaurus	Types or Categories to Which All Concepts Are Assigned and Their Interrelationships

Knowledge Sources

Table 6-2 | Sample Listing of Sources for the UMLS Metathesaurus

Systematized Nomenclature of Medicine (SNOMED International)
International Classification of Diseases-Clinical Modification (ICD-9-CM)
Classification of Nursing Diagnosis (NANDA)
Physician's Current Procedural Terminology (CPT)
Diagnostic and Statistical Manual of Mental Disorders (DSM-IV)
Thesaurus of Psychological Index Terms
Medical Subject Headings (MeSH)
WHO Adverse Drug Reaction Terminology
Universal Medical Devise Nomenclature System
Home Health Care Classification of Nursing Diagnoses and Interventions
Read Thesaurus

Of the three Knowledge Sources, the Metathesaurus is of the most interest to health information managers because it has greatly influenced the progress of the electronic health record. In essence, the Metathesaurus is a large database designed to link together biomedical vocabularies—such as clinical terminologies, drug sources, and vocabularies in different languages—from disparate sources. Its scope is determined by the vocabularies linked within it. Examples of some of the sources used are found in Table 6-2. The Metathesaurus supplies information that computer programs can use to interpret user inquiries, interact with users to refine their questions, identify which databases contain information relevant to particular inquiries, and convert the users' terms into the vocabulary used by relevant information sources. The Metathesaurus is used for a wide range of applications, including information retrieval from databases with humanly assigned subject index terms and from free-text information sources; linking patient records to related information in bibliographic, full-text, or factual databases; natural language processing and automated indexing research; and structured data entry.

Classification Systems

Whereas vocabularies serve to differentiate professions from one another, classification systems relate similar items. Classification systems, sometimes referred to as taxonomies, are groupings of similar items—such as diseases and procedures—that have one or more common denominators serving as a way to organize related entities for easy retrieval. Classification systems differ from nomenclatures in that they include all of the terms that could fall within a classification, not just those names deemed proper for inclusion in the nomenclature. Coding takes the classification system one step further. Coding is the process by which a numeric or alphanumeric code listed in a classification system is assigned to data found in the health record (e.g., diagnoses

and procedures). This translation of diagnoses, procedures, services, and supplies into numeric or alphanumeric codes results in a clear picture of the reason for the patient's encounter with the health care provider. These codes are abbreviations that represent clinical concepts.

A wide variety of groups use classification systems for many different purposes. Clinicians collect, process, and retrieve data. These data support clinical research, disease prevention, and direct patient care. For example, a classification system can be used to furnish quantitative data on the incidence of certain diseases, procedures, and causes of death. Health care facilities, professional organizations, and governmental entities find the data useful to support administrative, statistical, and reimbursement functions. For example, classification systems such as ICD-9-CM are used by insurance companies to determine reimbursement. Governmental entities use classification systems such as ICD-9-CM to ensure compliance with health care laws.

History and Application of Classification Systems

The variety of users and uses for classification systems can be traced through history. The London Bills of Mortality, published in 1629, was the first attempt at registration of causes of death. A second attempt at a classification system occurred in the mid-1700s, when Francois Bossier de Lacroix developed the *Nosologia Methodica*. A century and a half later, Jacques Bertillon presented the first International List of Causes of Death, which became a widely used classification system. This initial attempt at classifying mortality was so well received that demand then grew for the classification of morbidity. The World Health Organization responded by developing the International List of Diseases and Causes of Death, which later became the International Classification of Diseases (ICD). New iterations of ICD are issued approximately every 10 years.

ICD began to be used in American hospitals during the 1940s and 1950s, with some modifications required due to the prevalence of chronic diseases. The modification most prominently used in the United States is referred to as ICD-9-CM, referring to the ninth iteration of ICD, Clinically Modified. Changes occur on an annual basis, requiring review and incorporation of revisions into business practices on a routine basis. The newest iteration, ICD-10, is currently in use in parts of Europe and is subject to adoption in the United States in the near future. ICD-10 incorporates standard definitions, which should enhance the accuracy and consistency of coded data.

In the United States, four groups share responsibility for updating the ICD series. The National Center for Health Statistics (NCHS) maintains and updates the diagnosis portion of ICD-9-CM (Volumes 1 and 2), and the Centers for Medicare and Medicaid Services (CMS)—the government agency responsible for administering Medicare—maintains and updates the procedure portion of ICD-9-CM (Volume 3). The American Hospital Association maintains the Central Office on ICD, for the purpose of answering questions from coders, and produces the official guidelines for usage, the Coding Clinic for ICD-9-CM. The American Health Information Management Association provides training and certification for coding professionals.[1]

To apply these classification systems to data, the individual in question (the coder) must possess the requisite knowledge. Central to a coder's success are knowledge and understanding of biomedical sciences, information technology, health care data content and structure, health care delivery systems, and reimbursement methodologies. Biomedical sciences such as anatomy and physiology, medical terminology, pathophysiology, and pharmacology/pharmacotherapy serve to provide the coder with the foundation from which to base coding selection, understand the management of patient care, and enhance communication between medical professionals. Information technology knowledge and understanding are essential because automation is an integral component of most health care organizations, especially those that employ software tools to aid the coder in his work. Knowledge and understanding of health care data content and structure are indispensable; the content and documentation contained in the health record serve as the underpinning to the selection of codes that reflect the patient's care. Comprehensive knowledge and understanding of health care delivery systems provide context for how coding corresponds to both the needs of the health care organization and the legal, ethical, fiscal, and regulatory constraints under which health care organizations operate. Knowledge and understanding of reimbursement methodologies allow the coder to use coded data and health information to support reimbursement and payment systems in an ethical and fiscally responsible manner.

Although knowledge and understanding are essential, it is also important for the coder to possess skills with regard to the coding schemes employed most commonly in the United States today. The two most commonly employed schemes are ICD-9-CM and Current Procedural Terminology (CPT). Considerable study and practice will enable the coder to become conversant with both schemes; the following discussion provides an overview of working with each classification scheme to assign codes.

The ICD-9-CM system is composed of three volumes. Volume 1 contains a tabular numerical listing of diagnosis codes. Chapter titles to this tabular listing are found in Table 6–3. Volume 2 includes the alphabetical listing of diagnoses. Volume 3 includes both the tabular and alphabetical listings of procedures that are primarily used in a hospital setting. Chapter titles to this tabular listing are found in Table 6–4. Operating from the data contained in the patient health record, the coder identifies the main terms to be coded. To code the diagnoses, the coder uses

Table 6–3	Chapter Titles to Tabular Listing in ICD-9-CM, Volume 1
1.	Infectious and Parasitic Diseases
2.	Neoplasms
3.	Endocrine, Nutritional, and Metabolic Diseases and Immunity Disorders
4.	Diseases of the Blood and Blood-Forming Organs
5.	Mental Disorders
6.	Diseases of the Nervous System and Sense Organs
7.	Diseases of the Circulatory System
8.	Diseases of the Respiratory System
9.	Diseases of the Digestive System
10.	Diseases of the Genitourinary System
11.	Complications of Pregnancy, Childbirth, and the Puerperium
12.	Diseases of the Skin and Subcutaneous Tissue
13.	Diseases of the Musculoskeletal System and Connective Tissue
14.	Congenital Anomalies
15.	Certain Conditions Originating in the Perinatal Period
16.	Symptoms, Signs, and Ill-Defined Conditions
17.	Injury and Poisoning

Volumes 1 and 2 in conjunction, locating in the alphabetic index of Volume 2 the main diagnostic term to be coded. Because the alphabetic index is extensive, the coder may need to search any subterms indented under the main term to identify the code to be used. The coder then turns to the tabular listing in Volume 1 to verify the code, checking all

Table 6–4	Chapter Titles to Tabular Listing in ICD-9-CM, Volume 3
1.	Operations on the Nervous System
2.	Operations on the Endocrine System
3.	Operations on the Eye
4.	Operations on the Ear
5.	Operations on the Nose, Mouth, and Pharynx
6.	Operations on the Respiratory System
7.	Operations on the Cardiovascular System
8.	Operations on the Hemic and Lymphatic System
9.	Operations on the Digestive System
10.	Operations on the Urinary System
11.	Operations on the Male Genital Organs
12.	Operations on the Female Genital Organs
13.	Obstetrical Procedures
14.	Operations on the Musculoskeletal System
15.	Operations on the Integumentary System
16.	Miscellaneous Diagnostic and Therapeutic Procedures

of the instructional terms in the tabular list so that the assigned code has the highest degree of specificity. This activity continues until all diagnostic terms have been coded. A similar process is followed to assign codes to procedural terms, with the exception that Volume 3 contains both the tabular and alphabetical listings. Although it is described simplistically here, coding under ICD-9-CM is complex; diagnoses are not always available, making the coding of signs and symptoms a requirement, and some codes may only be used as additional codes rather than as primary or principal codes. These secondary codes, referred to as E-codes to describe external causes of injury or V-codes to describe further information about a patient's condition, are used sparingly and according to a health care organization's policy.

The focus of the CPT system is to address what a practitioner does when providing or performing medical services. The scope is broad and includes evaluation and management, anesthesia, surgery, pathology and laboratory, radiology, and medicine. Medical services and procedures are represented by a five-digit code. For purposes of illustration, the evaluation and management code section will be used. Evaluation refers to the assessment of information to reach a specific conclusion, such the process of obtaining a medical history and examination. Management in this context refers to the process of working within a framework to achieve a goal, such as when a diagnosis is reached and a treatment plan is formed. In determining the code to assign, the coder reviews the level of exam performed: problem-focused, expanded problem-focused, detailed, or comprehensive. Three key components are evaluated: history, examination, and medical decision making. Depending on the clinical setting in which the examination occurs (e.g., office or outpatient services), the coder uses an appropriate number category (e.g., 99201–99215 for office and other outpatient services). The coder then reviews the data contained in the patient health record to determine the level of examination performed and what services were rendered or procedures performed, assigning the code with the highest degree of specificity. Although it is described simplistically here, coding under CPT can be complex because clinical settings vary; contributory components must be considered, such as counseling, coordination of care, and the presenting problem; and code modifiers may apply.

Finally, the individual's knowledge and understanding of the coding process is aided somewhat by previously established standards. First, the coder may rely upon the coding standards set by professional organizations and the policies and procedures of individual health care organizations. The coder should also rely upon the elements of quality coding: reliability, validity, completeness, and timeliness. These elements can be monitored routinely by internal review audit practices. Furthermore, the coder can follow the steps of the coding process meticulously, relying upon the documentation found in the health record to verify the diagnosis and procedure codes assigned.

Diagnosis-Related Groups The previously discussed classification systems were used in the past primarily by health care facilities to generate internal statistics and to organize indices and registries. Change came about in 1983, with the introduction of the prospective payment system and the diagnosis-related groups classification system. As a strategy to reduce costs, the United States Congress passed the Tax Equity and Fiscal Responsibility Act (TEFRA) of 1982, which mandated limits upon Medicare payments to hospitals. CMS introduced the prospective payment system (PPS) for inpatient hospital services the following year. To make PPS work, Medicare adopted the diagnosis-related group (DRG) model developed by Yale University. This model is a classification system that groups patients who are medically related by diagnosis, treatment, length of stay, age, and sex, using the ICD-9-CM codes. DRGs are designed to be both statistically consistent, meaning that the patients grouped in a given DRG consume similar amounts of resources as measured by length of stay and cost, and medically meaningful, meaning that the patients grouped in a given DRG possess similar clinical conditions or treatment. In essence, DRGs classify hospital stays in terms of what was wrong with the patient (major diagnosis) and what was done for the patient (resources used).

Diagnosis-related groups are formed using a logical decision tree model. This decision tree model is illustrated in Figure 6–3. The first level of the tree is the major diagnostic category (MDC), a grouping based on the organ or system involved. The MDCs cluster patients according to medical and surgical categories. Those patients in the medical category are subdivided by principal diagnosis. Those patients in the surgical category are subdivided based on the surgical procedure performed. Patients who undergo multiple procedures are assigned to the surgical DRG that ranks highest in the hierarchy of the MDC. Complications, comorbidities, and the presence or absence of malignancies are factored into the model in both categories. Twenty-three major diagnostic categories were originally formed, from which 467 diagnosis-related groups were created. Over time, more than 500 diagnosis-related groups have been created, all falling within 25 mutually exclusive major diagnostic categories.

Health care facilities are reimbursed pursuant to these DRGs on a flat-rate basis. A predetermined rate is established for each DRG, and Medicare pays the hospital according to that rate.[2] Adjustments are made to the PPS rates on an annual basis. Further adjustments are made for cost outliers, patient transfers, capital costs, and medical education. This form of reimbursement is termed prospective because both the payer and the health care provider know the flat rate that will be paid before the care is provided to a patient.

Figure 6–3 | A typical DRG structure for a major diagnostic category

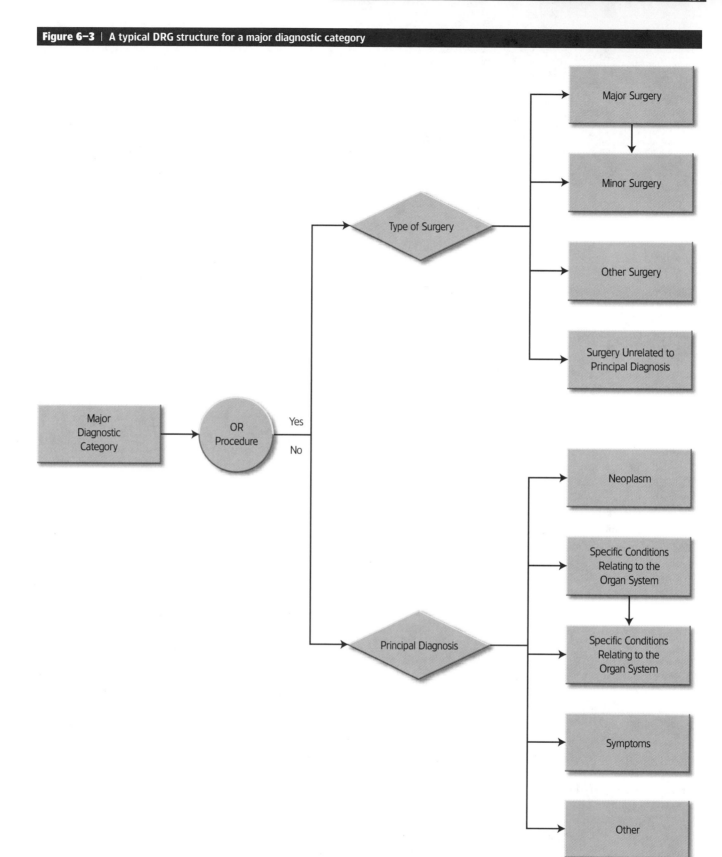

In addition to calculating reimbursement, DRGs serve two additional purposes. First, they play a role in evaluating the quality of care that is rendered to a patient. Using DRGs as a clinical framework, one can perform outcome analysis and benchmarking of patient care. Furthermore, DRGs provide the framework with which to assess coding practices and record documentation. Second, DRGs play a role in evaluating the utilization of services. Each DRG

Table 6-5 | Application of PPS to Care Settings

PPS	Care Setting
Acute Care Facilities (PPS)	Diagnosis–Related Groups (DRG)
Skilled Nursing Facilities (SNF PPS)	Resource Utilization Groups, Version III (RUG-III)
Outpatient Settings (OPPS)	Ambulatory Payment Classification Groups (APC)
Home Health Settings (HH PPS)	Case Mix Groups (CMG)
Inpatient Rehabilitation Facilities (IRF PPS)	Home Health Resource Groups (HHRG)

Table 6-6 | HIM Response to Increased Complexity

Employ automated approaches	Groupers
	Optimizing programs
	Encoders
	Natural language processing encoding systems
Employ coding guidelines	Published by professional organizations
	Published by governmental entities
	Internal to health care institutions
Focus on ethics and compliance	Adhere to ethical standards
	Create compliance program
	Foster compliance culture

represents the average resources needed to treat patients within that DRG. One can correlate the average resources expended in a single health care facility against the national average of resources to treat all Medicare patients. This correlation to the norm can assist a facility in determining whether they are expending too few or too many resources for a given DRG.

Despite criticism that DRGs did not sufficiently address the severity of a patient's illness and the resulting effect upon the amount of resources consumed, Medicare considered PPS such a success in the inpatient hospital setting that it expanded its application to other settings. Currently, PPS applies to skilled nursing facilities (SNF PPS) using resource utilization groups, version III (RUG-III); outpatient settings (OPPS) using ambulatory payment classification groups (APC); home health settings (HH PPS) using home health resource groups (HHRG); and inpatient rehabilitation facilities (IRF PPS) using case mix groups (CMG). The application of PPS to different care settings can be found in Table 6-5. In addition to government payers, an increasing number of private payers, such as insurance companies, rely on DRGs as a means to pay for health care services. For further information concerning the financial state of the health care field leading up to the introduction of PPS, see Chapter 15, "Reimbursement Methodologies."

HIM Transformation

The introduction of PPS and DRGs in the 1980s transformed the field of health information management because it highlighted the connection between classification systems (a traditional health information management function) and reimbursement (a traditional accounting function). The financial viability of a health care facility had traditionally been dependent on the amounts reimbursed by third-party payers in a fee-for-service arrangement. Using PPS and DRGs, reimbursement mechanisms tied the coded diagnosis and procedure to the amount reimbursed to the health care facility. In turn, reimbursement became interwoven with how accurately, consistently, and quickly the health information professional could assign diagnostic and procedural codes.

As a result of this change in circumstances, the responsibilities of health information managers became more complex. Existing coding issues, such as the difficulty in reconciling the language found in the clinical record with the language found in the classification system, took on new urgency. New issues, such as concerns over the potential for fraudulent billing practices, emerged. New positions and titles arose, including **nosologists**—persons who are responsible for the development, maintenance, and management of vocabularies and classification systems. Health information management professionals have responded to this increased complexity in a variety of ways, as listed in Table 6-6 and in the following discussion.

Over time, virtually all health information managers worked to manage this complexity by employing automated approaches. One approach is the use of **encoders**, software tools that incorporate the text and logic of coding systems into an automated form. These programs operate by browsing the classification system to match the language contained in the patient health record. Additionally, many health information managers employ **groupers**, software programs that use branching logic to arrive at the most accurate DRG. Furthermore, **optimizing programs** are sometimes employed. These automated programs seek the highest-paying DRG based on the codes assigned and in compliance with prevailing regulations. With the use of **natural language processing encoding systems**, software programs can read and interpret digital text from online documents and automatically assign appropriate codes.

Another approach to handling the added complexity is the use of new resources in the form of coding guidelines. These guidelines are educational materials published by organizations to serve as resources for the individual who assigns the diagnostic and procedural codes. Examples include the ICD-9-CM Coding Handbook, the Coding Clinic for ICD-9-CM, and the Coding Clinic for HCPCS. All of these guidelines arose as an outgrowth of cooperative efforts between such diverse parties as the American

Hospital Association, the Centers for Medicare and Medicaid Services, the National Center for Health Statistics, and the American Health Information Management Association, and they are still in use today.

In addition to these guidelines, some health care institutions developed or strengthened their own internal coding policies to provide guidance to coders. For example, a health care facility that does not perform elective abortions because of religious reasons may decide that its policy is to specify use of only those codes addressing spontaneous abortion in the event of a miscarriage diagnosis. Furthermore, the facility may specify that it will not assign codes to many diagnostic and nonsurgical procedures, such as X-rays, if the codes are not required for reporting purposes to outside agencies.

A third approach is to focus on the ethical aspect of coding. Pressure exists in some health care facilities to maximize reimbursement at the expense of accurate coding. Instances of upcoding, the practice of selecting a code and submitting a bill for a higher level of reimbursement than actually rendered in order to receive a higher reimbursement, have been reported across care settings. The American Health Information Management Association (AHIMA) has responded to this situation by providing Standards for Ethical Coding to guide coding professionals through ethical gray areas. The Standards for Ethical Coding may be found in Figure 6–4. Other entities, such as the Health Care Compliance Association and the federal government (CMS), also provide guidance to coders on ethical issues.[3]

A fourth approach, related to coding guidelines and ethics, is to develop a coding compliance program. Compliance refers to efforts made to establish a culture that promotes prevention, detection, and resolution of instances of conduct that do not conform to applicable local, state, and federal laws and regulations. A coding compliance program ensures the establishment of effective internal controls that detect, correct, and prevent coding errors and promote adherence to the applicable local, state, and federal laws and regulations and the program requirements of federal, state, and private health plans. A coding compliance program operates to prevent health care fraud and abuse, the false misrepresentation or intentional deception of fact that is a departure from reasonable use that could result in unauthorized payment. In addition to using coding guidelines and applying ethical standards, a coding compliance program involves other activities such as designating a compliance officer, using editing and auditing functions, deploying training sessions, and tracking a facility's case mix index for any deviations from the established baseline. In some health care facilities, a coding compliance program also includes the monitoring of accounts receivable on a daily basis to determine which health records are most important to code based on their effect on the facility's cash flow.

HIPAA

Many of the fraud and abuse investigations initiated pursuant to HIPAA focus on a health care provider's documentation, coding, and billing.

Such compliance programs are especially important in light of statutory and regulatory initiatives to combat fraud and abuse. These initiatives, including those found in the Health Insurance Portability and Accountability Act (HIPAA), focus on instances of fraudulent documentation, coding, and billing, areas over which health information management professionals exercise considerable responsibility. The goal is to recoup any overpayments made pursuant to this fraud, punish any wrongdoer engaged in this activity, and send a warning to others to conform with established rules, regulations, and guidance. Health care providers operate coding compliance programs as a means to reduce their exposure to civil damages and penalties, criminal sanctions, and administrative remedies. More information concerning corporate compliance programs and their interrelationship with health care fraud and abuse can be found in Chapter 3, "Legal Issues."

Other Classification Systems

Although they are prominently discussed in this chapter, ICD and DRGs are not the only classification systems in current use. SNOMED, a nomenclature developed and published by the American College of Pathologists, serves a dual purpose as a classification system. Based on a preceding system called SNOP, Systematized Nomenclature of Pathology, SNOMED codifies all activities involved in the patient's care, including medical diagnoses and procedures, nursing diagnoses and procedures, patient signs and symptoms, occupational history, and the etiologies of diseases. Variations on SNOMED exist, including SNOMED-RT (Reference Terminology) and SNOMED-CT, which combines SNOMED-RT with the United Kingdom's National Health Service's Clinical Terms 3, also known as the Read Codes, allowing for application across international boundaries.

Current Procedural Terminology (CPT), a nomenclature used in ambulatory care settings, also serves a dual purpose as a classification system. Health care facilities use CPT for outpatient surgery and ancillary department reporting. Physician offices use CPT for reporting thousands of types of medical and surgical procedures and services. Three categories comprise CPT: Category I includes the general code set; Category II includes tracking codes for performance measurement; and Category III includes temporary codes for reporting emerging technology, services, or procedures that have not yet met the qualifications required for inclusion in Category I.

Figure 6–4 | AHIMA's Standards of Ethical Coding (revised 12/99)

In this era of payment based on diagnostic and procedural coding, the professional ethics of health information coding professionals continue to be challenged. A conscientious goal for coding and maintaining a quality database is accurate clinical and statistical data. The following standards of ethical coding, developed by AHIMA's Coding Policy and Strategy Committee and approved by AHIMA's Board of Directors, are offered to guide coding professionals in this process.

1. Coding professionals are expected to support the importance of accurate, complete, and consistent coding practices for the production of quality healthcare data.

2. Coding professionals in all healthcare settings should adhere to the ICD-9-CM (International Classification of Diseases, 9th revision, Clinical Modification) coding conventions, official coding guidelines approved by the Cooperating Parties, (AHIMA, AHA, CMS, and NCHS) the CPT (Current Procedural Terminology) rules established by the American Medical Association, and any other official coding rules and guidelines established for use with mandated standard code sets. Selection and sequencing of diagnoses and procedures must meet the definitions of required data sets for applicable healthcare settings.

3. Coding professionals should use their skills, their knowledge of currently mandated coding and classification systems, and official resources to select the appropriate diagnostic and procedural codes.

4. Coding professionals should only assign and report codes that are clearly and consistently supported by physician documentation in the health record.

5. Coding professionals should consult physicians for clarification and additional documentation prior to code assignment when there is conflicting or ambiguous data in the health record.

6. Coding professionals should not change codes or the narratives of codes on the billing abstract so that meanings are misrepresented. Diagnoses or procedures should not be inappropriately included or excluded because payment or insurance policy coverage requirements will be affected. When individual payer policies conflict with official coding rules and guidelines, these policies should be obtained in writing whenever possible. Reasonable efforts should be made to educate the payer on proper coding practices in order to influence a change in the payer's policy.

7. Coding professionals, as members of the healthcare team, should assist and educate physicians and other clinicians by advocating proper documentation practices, further specificity, and resequencing or inclusion of diagnoses or procedures when needed to more accurately reflect the acuity, severity, and the occurrence of events.

8. Coding professionals should participate in the development of institutional coding policies and should ensure that coding policies complement, not conflict with, official coding rules and guidelines.

9. Coding professionals should maintain and continually enhance their coding skills, as they have a professional responsibility to stay abreast of changes in codes, coding guidelines, and regulations.

10. Coding professionals should strive for optimal payment to which the facility is legally entitled, remembering that it is unethical and illegal to maximize payment by means that contradict regulatory guidelines.

CPT also forms the basis for a separate classification system called the Healthcare Common Procedure Coding System (**HCPCS**, pronounced "Hicpics"). This expanded version of CPT includes codes for nonphysician services, including caregivers such as nurse practitioners, clinical social workers, nurse midwives, and physician assistants. HCPCS serves as the basis for a reimbursement system for physician services under Medicare similar to the way that DRGs have served as a basis for a reimbursement system for inpatient hospital services. This DRG-type system for reimbursement of physician services is called the Resource-Based Relative Value Scale (**RBRVS**). Additional information concerning RBRVS can be found in Chapter 15, "Reimbursement Methodologies."

Although ICD and CPT address many aspects of medical care, neither contains a sufficient structure to address mental health issues. Accordingly, a separate classification system was developed—the Diagnostic and Statistical Manual of Mental Disorders. Published by the American Psychiatric Association, the manual is in its fourth edition and is referred to as **DSM-IV**. It is used by psychiatric institutions and psychiatric units within health care facilities. DSM-IV provides both a glossary and categories for classification. It is also useful in collecting data for research, education, and administrative information on mental health issues. DSM-IV is not entirely compatible with ICD-9-CM, the classification system used by CMS for reimbursement purposes. For that reason, health information managers who work in psychiatric institutions and health care facilities with psychiatric units must be aware of both classification systems.

Similarly, health information managers who work in facilities for the mentally retarded or the developmentally disabled must be aware of two additional classification systems. The first, the Manual on Terminology and Classification in Mental Retardation, 1983 edition, is used both as a source of definitions in mental retardation and as a classification system. Published by the American Association on Mental Retardation (AAMR), it contains both behavioral and medical classifications and, in some respects, follows the ICD-9-CM and DSM classification systems. The second system, Mental Retardation: Definition, Classification, and Systems of Supports, ninth edition, was published by AAMR in 1992 to replace the first manual. This system describes the etiology of mental retardation through the use of a table that can also serve as a coding system. Although one system was designed to replace the other, many facilities for the mentally retarded or developmentally disabled choose between both systems.

Although they are not widely used for reimbursement purposes, classification systems have been developed in the nursing profession under the leadership of the American Nurses Association. Examples include the Nursing Intervention Classification (NIC), the Nursing Outcome Classification (NOC), the Omaha System, and the Home Health Care Classification. These classification systems are used to describe the nursing process, document nursing care, and facilitate aggregation of data for comparison purposes. Unlike ICD and CPT, which are often assigned at the end of a patient's care or after the patient's release from care, the nursing classification systems are assigned by the nurse during the course of patient care. Nursing classification systems have not yet been found compatible with the currently envisioned electronic health record.[4]

Several other classification systems are in current use or were in use recently enough that health information management professionals who perform longitudinal studies must be aware of them. The International Classification of Diseases for Oncology, third edition (ICD-O-3), is a classification system that used a 10-digit code to describe a tumor's primary site topology, histology, behavior, and aggression. The International Classification of Injuries, Disabilities, and Handicaps (ICIDH), now known as the International Classification of Functioning, Disability, and Health (ICF), classifies health and health-related domains that describe body functions and structures, activities, and participation. Current Dental Terminology (CDT), published by the American Dental Association, classifies dental procedures and services. National Drug Codes (NDC), published by a variety of vendors and managed by the U.S. Food and Drug Administration, serves as a universal product identifier for prescription drugs and select over-the-counter

Table 6-7	Listing of Classification Systems
Alternative Billing Codes (ABC Codes)
American Association of Mental Deficiency (AAMD)
American Spinal Injury Association Classification System (ASIACS)
Current Dental Terminology (CDT)
Current Procedural Terminology (CPT)
Diagnostic and Statistical Manual of Mental Disorders (DSM)
Healthcare Common Procedure Coding System (HCPCS)
Home Health Care Classification
Index for Roentgen Diagnosis (IRD)
International Classification of Disease (ICD)
International Classification of Disease-Oncology (ICD-O)
International Classification of Functioning, Disability, and Health (ICF)
International Classification of Health Problems in Primary Care (ICHPPC)
International Classification of Injuries, Disabilities, and Handicaps (ICIDH)
Manual of Terminology and Classification in Mental Retardation
Mental Retardation: Definition, Classification, and Systems of Support
National Drug Codes
Nursing Intervention Classification (NIC)
Nursing Outcome Classification (NOC)
Omaha System
Read Codes
Reason for Encounter Classification (RFEC)
Reason for Visit Classification System (RVS)
Systematized Nomenclature of Medicine (SNOMED)
Systematized Nomenclature of Pathology (SNOP)

products. Alternative Billing Codes (ABC codes) are used to classify services, supplies, or therapies provided in outpatient settings and not ordinarily found in CPT. In addition to the classification systems already explained, other systems exist to address multiple specialties. Examples of these systems can be found in Table 6-7.

Emerging Issues

Classification systems and coding practices have existed and evolved over decades, but the 21st century brings with it a renewed emphasis on existing issues such as case mix management and a focus on new issues such as the application of technology to the coding function and the emergence of clinical data representation.

During the last 20 years, new awareness of the importance of a health care organization's case mix has emerged. Case mix refers to the type and volume of patients a health care organization treats. In other words, case mix refers to the clientele the health care facility serves. Using **case mix management**, an organization analyzes the patient case mix as it relates to reimbursement and the organization's financial health. Case mix management is fraught with complexity; key areas contributing to this complexity include severity of illness, prognosis, treatment difficulty, need for intervention, and resource intensity. These key areas are not factored into the reimbursement provided under a given DRG, making it important for a health care provider to analyze its case mix on a routine basis.

Case mix analysis can be performed in several ways. Cost and utilization of services are among the most significant areas of review. Facilities can identify high-volume conditions and services and perform trend analyses. Depending on the outcome of the analysis, the organization takes steps from a financial perspective to improve or stabilize its case mix. DRGs, APCs, and RBRVS can all be used as methods to relate the type and volume of patients that a hospital, ambulatory care center, or physician practice treats (case mix) to the costs incurred by the hospital, ambulatory care center, or physician. These methods of providing a relationship between case mix and costs allow hospitals, ambulatory care centers, and physician practices to reach strategic decisions concerning the types of services they will continue to offer to their patient populations and how to staff those services in the future.

Analyzing case mix depends upon a variety of factors. First, the classification systems employed by the organization must yield quality data with which to perform analysis. Second, reports must be developed that provide detailed information. For example, a report could include material on the number of patients per DRG or APC, the amount reimbursed per DRG or APC, and the charges billed per DRG or APC. All of these data can be related back to physician practice, permitting the DRG or APC systems to also serve as a means for profiling physician practice. These data can also be used to facilitate such functions as quality improvement and operational planning.

Case mix management requires the merging of financial and clinical data through the use of sophisticated software programs; similar strides in automation have affected how coding staff are utilized. Many health care organizations have begun utilizing digital imaging software to make patient health records available off-site, permitting these organizations to consider outsourcing the coding function if sufficient security protocols are in place. Similarly, some health care organizations support home-based coders through the use of digital imaging and computerized coding applications such as encoders. This approach has been reported to increase productivity, lower costs, and improve the quality of coders' work lives by eliminating long commutes and related hassles.[5]

Automation also holds the potential to change the role of coders in health care organizations. As a result of the adoption of the electronic health record, the possibility exists to correlate digitized data with classifications systems such as ICD-10 and CPT. Natural language processing and auto-coding technologies are being developed that can extract diagnoses and procedure codes directly from dictated reports or allow physicians the ability to assign codes at the point of care. Instead of searching for information to support the codes they wish to assign, coders will verify the accuracy of the codes assigned by the physician or computerized system. They will examine whether the automated systems optimize reimbursement in compliance with health care regulations. In essence, the changes brought on by technology will influence the future role of coders, moving them from the technical area of assigning codes to roles in oversight and quality assurance.

These new technologies have brought focus to the use of classification systems, vocabularies, and terminologies in new ways—namely, clinical data representation. **Clinical data representation** refers to the manner in which clinical data are presented using classification systems, clinical vocabularies, other forms of data, and standards. One of the major functions of clinical data representation is data mapping. **Data mapping** is the process of linking terminology between two different schemes, a target and a source, for a given purpose. For example, the terminology used in the ICD-9-CM classification system may be mapped to the terminology used in the SNOMED-CT classification system for the purpose of supporting the reimbursement function. This contrasts with the coding function, which bases the use of classification systems on a patient's clinical encounter. The development of clinical data representation as a function has presented new employment possibilities to health information management professionals.

Conclusion

As this chapter demonstrates, vocabularies, clinical terminologies, and classification grouping systems have long played a role in the health care field. Health information managers need to possess clearly understood and applied vocabularies, clinical terminologies, and classification systems to facilitate patient care and comply with the requirements of regulatory and accrediting agencies. The multitude of users, the changes in uses, and the emergence of the role of technology in these areas will continue to influence the health information field. Those health information managers who understand this convergence of forces will be well positioned to create new opportunities for themselves and their field.

CHAPTER SUMMARY

Vocabularies, clinical terminologies, and classification systems were created to describe the medical care process in a standard manner and date back several centuries. Vocabularies list words or phrases and their associated meanings; terminologies indicate the proper names for concepts, items, actions, and other aspects of a *particular* area of interest or knowledge. The medical community relies upon both on a daily basis to ease communication between individuals, groups, and organizations. Classification systems group similar items, such as diseases and procedures, that have one or more common denominators. Classification systems such as ICD-9-CM and CPT work to organize health care data for easy retrieval by many groups, and they serve as the basis for reimbursement and case mix management. One future trend involves clinical data representation and linking terminologies and classification systems for various purposes, including reimbursement.

CASE STUDY

You are the director of health information services at Anywhere Hospital. As part of its new employee orientation, the hospital asks each department director to describe to the new employees the services offered by that department and the responsibilities of managers and staff. You have been asked to include as part of your description an explanation of diagnosis-related groups. Describe what you would include in your explanation.

REVIEW QUESTIONS

1. Why did SNOP fall out of favor with the health care field?

2. Explain the role of the Metathesaurus in the Unified Medical Language System.

3. How do vocabularies and nomenclatures differ from classification systems?

4. What is meant by saying that DRGs are both statistically consistent and medically meaningful?

5. What are the three purposes served by DRGs?

6. Name four approaches taken by health information management professionals to address the complexities brought on by the introduction of PPS and DRGs.

ENRICHMENT ACTIVITY

1. Review copies of coding guidelines obtained either over the Internet, from your instructor, or through the health information department of a local health care facility. Compare these guidelines against AHIMA's Standards for Ethical Coding found in Figure 6–4. Compare the similarities and contrast the differences between these documents.

WEB SITES

American Health Information Management Association, http://www.ahima.org

American Spinal Injury Association, http://www.asia-spinalinjury.org

Centers for Medicare and Medicaid Services, http://www.cms.hhs.gov

Medline Retrieval Service PubMed, http://www.pubmed.gov

National Center for Health Statistics, http://www.cdc.gov/nchs

National Library of Medicine's Internet Grateful Med, http://www.nlm.nih.gov

National Library of Medicine's Unified Medical Language System, http://www.nlm.nih.gov/research/umlsmain.html

Office of Inspector General Compliance Guidelines and Annual Work Plan, http://oig.hhs.gov/publications/workplan.html

REFERENCES

Current Procedural Terminology: CPT 2002. (2001). Chicago: American Medical Association.

DRG Desk Reference. (2004). Eden Prairie, MN: Ingenix, Inc.

Englebardt, S. P., & Nelson, R. (2002). *Health care informatics.* St. Louis, MO: Mosby.

Johns, M. (2005). A crystal ball for coding. *Journal of AHIMA,* 71(1), 26–33.

Johnson, S. L. (2000). *Understanding medical coding: A comprehensive guide.* Albany, NY: Delmar.

Peden, A. (2005). *Comparative records for health information management.* Albany, NY: Delmar.

Prince, T. R. (1998). *Strategic management for health care entities.* Chicago: American Hospital Publishing, Inc.

Practice Brief. (2001). *Developing a coding compliance policy document.* Chicago: American Health Information Management Association. Available at http:// www.ahima.org/xpedio/groups/ public/documents/ahima.

Schnitzer, G., & Stanfill, M. (2001). Coding notes: Outwit, outlast, outcode. Surviving in the autocoding era. *Journal of AHIMA,* 72(9).

Skurka, M. A. (Ed.). (2003). *Health information management* (5th ed.). San Francisco: Jossey-Bass.

Van Bemmel, J. H., & Musen, M. A. (Eds.). (1997). *Handbook of medical informatics.* The Netherlands: Springer-Verlag.

NOTES

1. Johnson, S. L. (2000). *Understanding medical coding* (p. 6). Albany, NY: Delmar.

2. Several types of hospitals are excluded from the Medicare PPS and are paid according to the usual, customary, and reasonable costs. These hospitals include: children's hospitals, cancer hospitals, psychiatric and rehabilitation hospitals and units within larger medical facilities, and long-term care hospitals, defined as hospitals with an average length of stay of 25 days or longer.

3. AHIMA Standards of Ethical Coding, http://www.ahima.org. See also Fighting Fraud and Abuse: Medicare Integrity Program, http://www.hcfa.gov/medicare/fraud; Health Care Compliance Association, http://www.hcca-info.org.

4. Warren, J. J. (2002). Update on standardized nursing data sets and terminologies. *Journal of AHIMA,* 73(7), 78–83.

5. Hoaglang, M. (2002). Revolution in progress: How technology is reshaping the coding world. *Journal of AHIMA,* 73(7), 32–35.

Quality Health Care Management

CERTIFICATION CONNECTION

RHIA

Benchmarking

Best practices

Data for decision making

Data integrity

Patient care related studies

Performance improvement

Present data

Quality management

Risk management

Utilization management

RHIT

Data integrity

Performance improvement

Present data

Quality assessment

Quality improvement

Quality management

Quality standards

LEARNING OBJECTIVES

After reading this chapter, the learner should be able to:

1. Trace the historical developments of data quality management, performance improvement, risk management, and utilization management.

2. Differentiate between the various approaches to quality in the health care context.

3. Explain the relationship between quality and health care.

4. Use quality analysis tools to display and interpret data effectively.

5. Understand the role of government and private initiatives to promote and utilize data to support quality initiatives.

6. Understand the concept of performance improvement, including benchmarking, the ORYX Initiative, and CATCH.

7. Define the terms *risk* and *risk management*.

8. Describe the utilization review process.

Outline

Data Quality

Historical Development
Tools

Performance Improvement and Risk Management

Performance Improvement
Risk Management

Utilization Management

Utilization Review Process

Key Concepts

Admission review

Affinity diagram

Bar graph

Benchmarking

Brainstorming

Case management

Case manager

CATCH

Cause-and-effect diagram

Concurrent review

Continuous quality improvement

Control chart

Core measurements

Criteria

Data quality

Discharge planning

Discharge status

Enterprise risk management

Gantt chart

Histogram

Line graph

Nominal group technique

ORYX Initiative

Outcomes

Pareto chart

Performance improvement

Personal health record

PERT

Pie chart

Preadmission review

Process improvement

Professional Standards Review Organizations

Quality assurance

Quality improvement

Quality management

Risk

Risk management

Root-cause analysis

Scatter diagram

Sentinel event

Total quality management

Utilization coordinators

Utilization management

Utilization review

INTRODUCTION

Quality health care "means doing the right thing at the right time, in the right way, for the right person and getting the best possible results."[1] The term *quality*, by definition, can mean excellence, status, or grade; thus, it can be measured and quantified. The patient, and perhaps the patient's family, may interpret quality health care differently than health care providers interpret it. Therefore, it is important to determine—if possible—what is "right" and what is "wrong" with regard to quality health care. The study and analysis of health care are important to maintain a level of quality that is satisfactory to all parties involved. As a result of the current focus on patient safety, and in an attempt to reduce deaths and complications, providing the best quality health care while maintaining cost controls has become a challenge to all involved. Current quality initiatives are multifaceted and include government-directed, private sector-supported, and consumer-driven projects.

This chapter explores the historical development of health care quality including a review of the important pioneers and the tools they developed. Their work has been studied, refined, and widely used in a variety of applications related to performance-improvement activities. Risk management is discussed, with emphasis on the importance of coordination with quality activities. The evolution of utilization management is also reviewed, with a focus on its relationship to quality management.

In addition, this chapter explores current trends in data collection and storage, and their application to improvements in quality care and patient safety. Current events are identified that influence and provide direction to legislative support and funding. This chapter also provides multiple tips and tools for both personal and institutional use.

Data Quality

Data quality refers to the high grade, superiority, or excellence of data. Data quality is intertwined with the concept of quality patient care; it refers to data that can demonstrate and represent in an objective sense the delivery of quality patient care. When the data collected are reflective of the care provided, one can reach conclusions about the quality of care the patient received.

Historical Development

The concept of studying the quality of patient care has been a part of the health care field for almost 100 years. Individual surgeons, such as A. E. Codman, pioneered the practice of monitoring surgical outcomes in patients and documenting physician errors concerning specific patients. These physicians began the practice of conducting morbidity and mortality conferences as a means to improve patient care. Building on the prior work of individual surgeons, the American College of Surgeons (ACS) created the Hospital Standardization Program in 1918. This program served as the genesis for the accreditation movement of the 20th century, which included the concept of quality patient care and the formation of the Joint Commission on Accreditation of Hospitals (JCAH) in 1951. The ACS transferred the Hospital Standardization Program to the JCAH in 1953.

Efforts to improve the quality of patient care have varied during the 20th century, beginning with the establishment of formalized mechanisms to measure patient care against established criteria. A timeline illustrating these efforts is shown in Figure 7–1. These mechanisms focused on an organization's reaction to individual events and the

Figure 7–1 | Quality management timeline

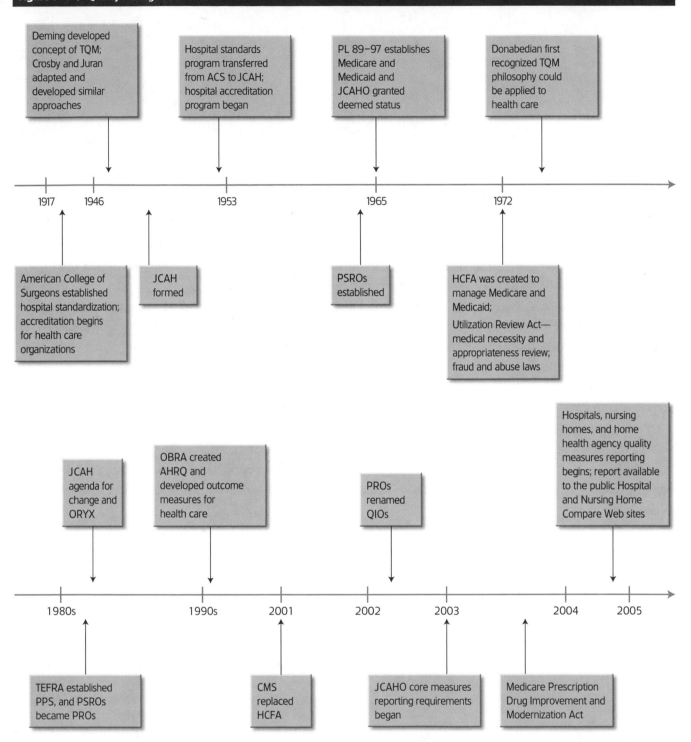

mistakes of individual health care providers. A variety of quality efforts followed, including ones developed in other industries that were adapted to the health care environment. The concepts of total quality management, defined as the organization-wide approach to quality improvement, and continuous quality improvement, defined as the systematic, team-based approach to process and performance improvement, introduced the team-based approach to quality health care. These newer efforts moved the focus from

individual events and health care providers to an organization's systems and their potential for improvement.

Accompanying the change in focus were new terms such as quality management, quality assurance, process improvement, and performance improvement. Quality management generally means that every aspect of health care quality may be subject to managerial oversight. Quality assurance refers to those actions taken to establish, protect, promote, and improve the quality of health care. **Process improvement** refers to the improvement of processes involved in the delivery of health care. **Performance improvement** refers to the improvement of performance as it relates to patient care. Regardless of the names applied and their respective approaches, most health care organizations in the 21st century are bound by the requirements of various accrediting and regulatory bodies to engage in some function that focuses on the quality of patient care.[2]

In order to measure patient care for quality purposes, one must first possess data. The data crucial to supporting any quality initiative are the data found in the patient health record. These data must be reliable with respect to quality. Data errors can be made during many stages, such as when data are entered into the record (the documentation process), when data are retrieved from the record (the abstracting process), when data are manipulated (the coding process), when data are processed (the indexing and registry processes), and when data are used (the interpreting process). At each stage, the data must be both consistent and accurate. Furthermore, good quality data are the result of coordinated efforts to ensure integrity at each stage. A recent focus on the legibility of handwritten data, the appropriate use of abbreviations, and their relationship to medication errors has increased pressure from accrediting agencies to improve the quality of data as a means to improve patient safety.

Quality health care management is the result of the dedication of a variety of professionals working in all levels of employment and in all aspects of health care. These professionals are supported by governmental offices at the federal, state, and local levels that define what data they require to be reported to them. When data definitions are not specified by the agency or organization requiring a report, the responsibility to define the data falls to the team or group that is responsible for collecting and disseminating the data. Fundamental to the collection and dissemination of data is the application of the appropriate collection format and reporting tools. However, before data collection can begin, there must be consensus on the perimeters of the data to be collected. The team or group should also select an assessment model, such as quality circles, PDSA, or FOCUS PDCA. Quality circles are small groups of workers who perform similar work that meet regularly to analyze and solve work-related problems and to recommend solutions to management. These groups are also known as *Kaizen teams*, a Japanese term meaning to generate or implement employee ideas.[3] PDSA (*Plan, Do, Study, Act*), also known as PDCA (*Plan-Do-Check-Act*),[4] is illustrated in Figure 7-2. FOCUS PDCA[5] involves finding a process to improve, organizing a team that knows the process, clarifying the current knowledge of the process, understanding the causes of special variation, and selecting the process improvement. Figure 7-3 illustrates the FOCUS PDCA approach.

Figure 7-2 | Plan, do, study (or check), and act assessment model

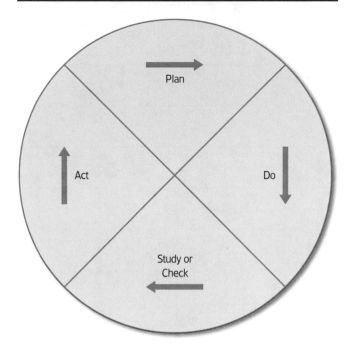

Essentially, these assessment models provide groups with guidance about how to organize the process. These models were developed largely as a result of the manufacturing industry quality movement of the 1950s and 1960s led by W. Edwards Deming, J. M. Juran, and Philip Crosby. In the 1960s, these models were applied to the health care sector by Avedis Donabedian, who separated the quality of health care measures into three distinct categories: structure, process, and outcomes.[6] In the 1970s, when the Joint Commission on Accreditation of Healthcare Organizations, now known as the Joint Commission, and the Health Care Financing Administration (HCFA), now known as Centers for Medicare and Medicaid Services (CMS), began to mandate quality initiatives, health care looked to the successes of the manufacturing industry for direction and ideas.

The quest for quality, and the tools necessary to achieve it, eventually led to the development of the Malcolm Baldridge National Quality Award. The U.S. Congress created this award in 1987,[7] which led to the creation of a new public-private partnership. Principal support for the award comes from the Foundation for the Malcolm Baldridge National Quality Award. The U.S. president announces the award annually. The award initially recognized the manufacturing and service sectors, including both large and small businesses, but it was expanded in 1999 to include the education and health care sectors; several health care organizations have applied for and received this award since then. In 2006, the program expanded even further to consider non-profit and governmental organizations in the application process. The seven categories in which participants are judged for the Malcolm Baldridge Award are listed in

Figure 7–3 | FOCUS assessment model

	Problem-Solving Step	Key Points
F	Find the Problem	
O	Organize to Solve	
C	Clarify the Problem/Process	
U	Understand Sources of Variation	
S	Solutions	

P	Plan/Do	
D	Plan or Project	
S or C	Study Results or Check	
A	Act	

Table 7–I. The focus of the evaluation centers on total quality management with emphasis on sustaining results.

Early pioneers who applied the Malcolm Baldridge concepts found it difficult at times to achieve effective implementation and/or sustain improvement. In an effort to achieve the greatest possible savings from the improvement projects, the Juran Institute, working with Motorola, developed a methodology called Six Sigma.[8] Six Sigma is defined as the measurement of quality to a level of near perfection or without defects. GE and Allied Signal (now Honeywell) also contributed to the development and popularity of the methodology. Part of its success is attributed to the organization of training and leadership. High-level executives are trained and appointed as "champions" to drive the program, and employees receive training and support to become certified internal experts. The amount of training one receives results in different belt levels: black belts are technical personnel who are trained to apply the statistically based methodology. Master black belts coach black belts and coordinate projects. The project team members are referred to as green belts and also receive basic process-improvement training.

The Six Sigma Improvement Methodology is similar to that of PDCA and FOCUS PDSA, but it utilizes six steps known as (D)MAIC: Define, Measure, Analyze, Improve, and Control. Many components of the health care industry have applied the Six Sigma improvement methodology toward the elimination of errors rather than the correction of defects (as it has been applied in industry). The approach is similar and both ultimately strive for perfection. In light of the fact that one error can be of catastrophic consequence if it involves a sentinel event or even death, the concept of near perfection in the Six Sigma standards is important for all applications of health care delivery.

Table 7–1 | Categories in the Malcolm Baldridge Award

Leadership
Strategic planning
Customer and market focus
Information and analysis
Human resource focus
Process management
Business results

Source: Maldolm Baldridge National Quality Award, http://www.quality.nist.gov

Federal Efforts Whereas the quest for quality led to the development of the Baldridge Award and Six Sigma, efforts at the federal level resulted in the formation of the Agency for Health Care Policy and Research (AHCPR) in 1989. Later changed to the Agency for Healthcare Research and Quality (AHRQ) as part of the Healthcare Research and Quality Act of 1999, this body is a scientific research agency located within the Public Health Service (PHS) of the U.S. Department of Health and Human Services. AHRQ focuses on quality of care research and acts as a "science partner" between the public and private sectors to improve the quality and safety of patient care. Over time, the agency has changed its focus from developing and supporting clinical practice guidelines to developing evidence-based guidelines. AHRQ's mission is to develop scientific evidence that enables health care decision makers to reach more informed health care choices. The agency assumes the responsibility to conduct, support, and disseminate scientific research designed to improve the outcomes, quality, and safety of health care. The agency is also committed to supporting efforts to reduce health care costs, broaden access to services, and improve the efficiency and effectiveness of the ways health care services are organized, delivered, and financed.

AHRQ has achieved numerous accomplishments since its inception. These accomplishments range in focus from the Medical Expenditure Panel Survey (MEPS), the Healthcare Cost and Utilization Project (HCUP), and the Consumer Assessment of Healthcare Plans Survey (CAHPS), to the grant component of AHRQ's Translation of Research into Practice (TRIP) activity and the Quality/Safety of Patient Care program. The latter program encompasses both the Patient Safety Health Care Information program and the Health Care Information Technology program. Each of the programs listed here provides valuable information to the agency. For example, the Medical Expenditure Panel Survey (MEPS) serves as the only national source for annual data on how Americans use and pay for medical care. The survey collects detailed information from families on access, use, expense, insurance coverage, and quality. This information provides public and private sector decision makers with important data to analyze changes in behavior and the market. The Healthcare Cost and Utilization Project (HCUP) also provides information regarding the cost and use of health care resources but focuses on how health care is used by the consumer. HCUP is a family of databases containing routinely collected information that is translated into a uniform format to facilitate comparison. The Consumer Assessment of Health Plans (CAHP) uses surveys to collect data from beneficiaries about their health care plans. The grant component, Translation of Research into Practice (TRIP), provides the financial support to initiate or improve programs where identified. Patient safety research is also an important element of these activities and includes a significant effort directed toward promoting information technology, particularly in small and rural communities where health information technology has been limited due to cost and availability. Other research efforts for

patient safety are focused on reducing medical errors and improving pharmaceutical outcomes through the Centers of Excellence for Research and Therapeutics (CERT) program.

E-HIM

AHRQ has provided grants to increase the use of health information technology, including electronic health records.

As a result of the growing concern for the increased use of health information technology (HIT) to improve the quality of health care and control costs, AHRQ awarded $139 million in contracts and grants in 2004 to promote the use of health information technology. The goals of the AHRQ projects are listed in Table 7–2. Grants were awarded to providers, hospitals, and health care systems, including rural health care settings, critical access hospitals, hospitals and programs for children, as well as university hospitals in urban areas. The locations were spread throughout the country from coast to coast, border to border, and included Alaska and Hawaii. Many grant recipients sought to develop HIT infrastructure and data-sharing capacity among clinical provider organizations. Other grant recipients sought to improve existing systems that were considered outdated, or to install technology where it had not previously existed, such as pharmacy dispensing systems, bar coding, patient scheduling, and decision-support systems. Some grants went toward the construction of a fully integrated electronic health record (EHR), such as one effort by the Tulare District Hospital Rural Health Consortium. Some universities received grants to employ technology for disease-specific projects, such as the Trial of Decision Support to Improve Diabetes Outcomes at Case Western Reserve University; others sought to develop cancer care management programs, such as the Technology Exchange for Cancer Health Network (TECH-Net) established by the University of Tennessee; and others worked to automate tracking of adverse events, such as the Automated Adverse Drug Events Detection and Intervention System established by Duke University. Still other grants focused on promoting statewide and regional networks for health information exchange, sometimes referred to as regional health information organizations (RHIOs). The goal of these projects is to develop a health information exchange that connects the systems of various

Table 7–2	Goals of the AHRQ Projects
Improve patient safety by reducing medical errors
Increase health information sharing between providers, labs, pharmacies, and patients
Help patients transition between health care settings
Reduce duplicative and unnecessary testing
Increase our knowledge and understanding of the clinical, safety, quality, financial, and organizational values and benefits of HIT

Table 7-3 | Aims for Health Care Improvement

Safe	Avoiding injuries that result from care that is intended to help
Effective	Based on scientific knowledge to all who could benefit
Patient-Centered	Respectful of and responsive to individual patient preferences, needs, and values
Timely	Reducing waits and harmful delays for those who receive and give care
Efficient	Avoiding waste, including waste of equipment, supplies, ideas, and energy
Equitable	Care that does not vary in quality because of personal characteristics such as gender, ethnicity, geographic location, and socioeconomic status

local health care providers so they can better coordinate care and enable clinicians to obtain patient information at the point of care.[9] More information concerning the work of RHIOs is found in Chapter 8, "Database Management."

E-HIM

The U.S. president connects the use of electronic health records with improvement in quality patient care.

One of the most significant efforts to focus attention on the importance of advancing health information technology as a means to improve the quality of patient care has been made by U.S. President George W. Bush. In his State of the Union Address on January 20, 2004, he stated, "By computerizing health records, we can avoid dangerous medical mistakes, reduce costs, and improve care."[10] He acted on this statement shortly thereafter, establishing a national coordinator for health information technology within the U.S. Department of Health and Human Services. This coordinator announced that a 10-year plan would be developed to outline the steps necessary to transform the delivery of health care by adopting

health information technology in both the public and private sectors. Included in these steps are the EHR and a national health information infrastructure (NHII), topics that are addressed in further detail in Chapter 8, "Database Management," and Chapter 13, "Information Systems and Technology."

Private Efforts Concern for improving the quality of health care also moved others to action. The Institute of Medicine, a private nonprofit organization that provides health policy advice under a congressional charter granted to the National Academy of Sciences, conducted an in-depth analysis of the U.S. health care system and issued a report in 2001. This report, *Crossing the Quality Chasm: A New Health System for the 21st Century*,[11] identified a significant number of changes that had affected the delivery of health care services, specifically the shift from care of acute illnesses to care of chronic illnesses. The report recognized that current health care systems are more devoted to dealing with acute, episodic conditions, and are poorly organized to meet the challenges of continuity of care. The report challenged all health care constituencies— health professionals, federal and state policy makers, purchasers of health care, regulators, organization managers and governing boards, and consumers—to commit to a national statement of purpose and adopt a shared vision of six specific aims for improvement. These aims are listed in Table 7-3.

Table 7-4 | Ten Steps for Redesign

1. Care is based on continuous healing relationships. Care should be available whenever the patient needs it and in many forms, not just face-to-face. Other means of communication, such as telephone and the Internet, are encouraged.
2. Care is customized according to patient needs and values. Care should be able to meet common types of needs, but also individual patient choices and preferences.
3. The patient is the source of control. Encourage shared decision making.
4. Knowledge is shared and information flows freely. Patients should have access to their own medical information and to clinical knowledge.
5. Decision making is evidence based. Care should be based on the best available scientific knowledge and should not vary illogically from clinician to clinician or from place to place.
6. Safety is a system property, reduction of errors.
7. Transparency is necessary. Information should be made available to patients and families that enables them to make informed decisions.
8. Needs are anticipated rather than reactionary to events.
9. Waste is continuously decreased; reduce waste of resources and/or patient time.
10. Cooperation among clinicians is a priority. Ensure appropriate exchange of information and coordination of care.

Source: Crossing the quality chasm: A new health system for the 21st century. Institute of Medicine (2001).

The report did not include a specific "blueprint" or standard for the future because it encouraged imagination and innovation to drive the effort. Specific recommendations included a set of guiding principles known as the Ten Steps for Redesign (see Table 7–4), the establishment of the Health Care Quality Innovation Fund to initiate the process of change, and development of care processes for common health conditions—most of them chronic—that afflict great numbers of people. This report served as a driving force behind the funding of grants through AHRQ and the other programs that have already been identified.

The National Committee for Quality Assurance (NCQA) is another organization involved in improving health care quality. Established in 1990, this organization focuses on the managed care industry. It began accrediting these organizations in 1991 in an effort to provide standardized information about them. Its Managed Care Organization (MCO) program is voluntary, and approximately 50 percent of the current HMOs in this country have undergone review by NCQA. Earning the accreditation status is important to many HMOs, because some large employers refuse to conduct business with health plans that have not been accredited by NCQA. In addition, more than 30 states recognize the accreditation for regulatory requirements and do not conduct separate reviews.

In 1992, NCQA assumed responsibility for management of the Health Plan Employer Data and Information Set (HEDIS), a tool used by many health plans to measure performance of care and service. Purchasers and consumers use the data to compare the performances of managed health care plans. Because more than 60 measures are present in the data set, containing a high degree of specificity, performance comparisons are considered very reliable and comprehensive. The NCQA has designed an audit process that utilizes certified auditors to assure data integrity and validity. HEDIS data are frequently the source of health plan "report cards" that are published in magazines and newspapers. Included in HEDIS is the CAHPS 3.0H survey that measures members' satisfaction with their care in areas such as claims processing, customer service, and receiving needed care quickly. The data are also used by the plans to help identify opportunities for improvement. A sample of HEDIS measures is shown in Table 7–5.

Table 7–5 | Sample HEDIS Measures, Addressing a Broad Range of Important Topics

Asthma medication use

Controlling high blood pressure

Antidepressant medication management

Smoking cessation programs

Beta–blocker treatment after a heart attack

Source: Information compiled from the National Association for Healthcare Quality (NAHQ), http://www.nahq.org.

The NCQA also operates recognition programs for individual physicians and medical groups. These programs are voluntary, and physicians may apply through NCQA. Doctors who qualify must meet widely accepted evidence-based standards of care. One program includes a Diabetes Physician Recognition Program that was developed in conjunction with the American Diabetes Association. This program recognizes physicians who keep their patients' blood sugar and blood pressure at acceptable levels and routinely perform eye and foot examination. The Heart/Stroke Recognition Program (HSRP) is a partnership with the American Heart Association/American Stroke Association and recognizes doctors and practices that control their patients' blood pressure and cholesterol levels, prescribe antithrombotics such as aspirin, and provide advice for smokers looking to quit.

The organization that brings all of the professionals involved in quality health care management together is the National Association for Healthcare Quality (NAHQ). This organization is based on the idea that quality health care professionals drive the delivery of vital data for effective decision making in health care systems. Organized in 1975 as the National Association for Quality Assurance Professionals (NAQAP) to represent these health care workers, the organization provides educational, research, and certification programs to its membership. Members include a wide range of professionals who focus on quality management, quality improvement, case/care/disease/utilization management, and risk management. The membership is composed of all levels of employment from all types of health care settings. Members achieve certification through examination and earn the credential of Certified Professional in Healthcare Quality (CPHQ); the examination recognizes professional and academic achievement. The organization also promotes networking and mentoring through educational meetings and publications. Membership includes physicians, nurses, health information management professionals, health care management professionals, information systems management professionals, social workers, and physical and occupational therapists, all with a common focus on improving the outcomes of health care.

Tools

Equally important as selecting a methodology is using assessment tools effectively. Several tools are often employed, including idea generation, data gathering and organizing techniques, cause analysis, and data display methods. While each tool is applicable in many environments, they apply especially well in the context of data quality because they assist in identifying progress, relationships, and the presence or absence of trends. This process of identification leads to a determination of the presence, absence, or level of quality. One useful resource for quality assessment tools is the Web site of the American Society for Quality (http:// www.asq. com), where instructions and samples are available.

When new ideas are needed to address an issue or problem, brainstorming and benchmarking are often employed. **Brainstorming** refers to an idea-generating tool in which ideas are offered on a particular topic, in an unrestrained manner, by all members of a group within a short period of time. Brainstorming can be structured or unstructured, and it generally employs guidelines to assure that ideas are not criticized and that all ideas are accepted during the process. **Benchmarking** refers to the structured process of comparing outcomes or work practices generated by one group or organization against those of an acknowledged superior performer as a means of improving performance.

Once ideas are generated, the challenge lies in organizing them into a fashion in which they can be processed or analyzed. Organizational tools frequently used include affinity diagrams, nominal group techniques, Gantt charts, and PERT. An **affinity diagram** refers to a diagram that organizes information into a visual pattern to show the relationship between factors in a problem. This diagram is developed following a brainstorming session by grouping ideas into categories. **Nominal group technique** is an organizational tool wherein a list of ideas is labeled alphabetically and then prioritized by determining which ideas have the highest degree of importance or should be considered first. **Gantt charts** are graphic representations that show the time relationships in a project; these are often used to track the progress of a project and the completion of milestones and

goals. Within the health care context, they are often used in process improvement activities to depict clinical guidelines or critical paths of treatment. **PERT** stands for Program Evaluation and Review Technique and is a tool used to track activities according to a time sequence, thereby showing the interdependence of activities. Concurrent activities are called parallel activities and follow arrows to document their paths. PERT is often used by health care teams as a means to complete process improvement activities on time and in the proper order.

When the root of a problem or situation is particularly difficult to understand, analysis tools such as cause-and-effect diagrams and Pareto charts may be used. A **cause-and-effect diagram**, sometimes referred to as a fishbone or Ishikawa diagram, identifies major categories of factors that influence an effect and the subfactors within each of those categories. The diagram begins with broad causes and works toward specifics, often examining the categories of the 4 Ms (methods/manpower/materials/machinery) or the 4 Ps (policies/procedures/people/plant). See Figure 7–4 for a sample cause-and-effect diagram. Within the health care context, this diagram is often used to conduct root-cause analysis of sentinel events as required by the Joint Commission. A **Pareto chart** is a bar graph used to identify and separate major and minor problems. It is based on the Pareto Principle, which posits that, for many events, 20 percent of problems pose 80 percent

Figure 7–4 | A sample cause-and-effect diagram

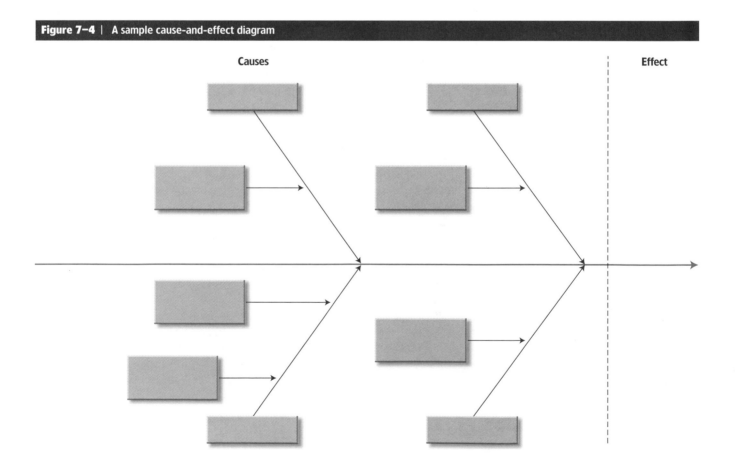

of the impact. This chart orders categories according to frequency in descending order from left to right and is used to determine priorities in problem solving.

In addition to tools that generate ideas, tools are available to gather data in both time- and labor-efficient fashions. Data gathering can be accomplished using forms, check sheets, surveys, questionnaires, written inventories, or computer screens with database or spreadsheet applications. Data can be gathered concurrently (i.e., at the same time the activity occurs) or retrospectively (i.e., looking backward at activity), with a time limit set for the period in which data are collected. The decision about which tool to employ rests on issues of whether a given project is time sensitive, cost sensitive, or both.

Once data are gathered, one must determine how to display it. Frequently used methods include bar graphs, histograms, pie charts, line graphs, control charts, and scatter diagrams. A **bar graph** demonstrates the frequency of data through the use of horizontal and vertical axes. Typically, the horizontal axis, or x-axis, shows discrete categories; the vertical axis, or y-axis, shows the number or frequency, as seen in Figure 7–5. A **histogram** is similar to a bar graph, containing both the x- and y-axes, with the exception that it can display data proportionally. This proportionality is

shown through the use of continuous intervals for categories on the vertical axis, as seen in Figure 7–6. Histograms are chosen over bar graphs when trying to identify problems or changes in a system or process, or where large amounts of continuous data are difficult to interpret in lists or other nongraphic forms. A **pie chart** is a graph used to show relationships to the whole, or how each part contributes to the total product or process. The frequency of data is shown through the use of a circle drawn and divided into sections that correspond to the frequency in each category. The 360 degrees of the circle, or pie, represent the total, or 100 percent. The "slices" of the pie are the proportions to each component's percentage of the whole. A pie chart is seen in Figure 7–7. A **line graph** uses lines to represent data in numerical form, as seen in Figure 7–8. These graphs can show a process or progress over time, with several sets of data displayed concurrently in a graph to show relationships. A **control chart** is a graph with statistically generated upper and lower control limits used to measure key processes over time. Control charts focus attention on a variation in the process and help a team determine whether a variation is normal or the result of special circumstances. An example of a control chart is shown in Figure 7–9. A **scatter diagram** is a graph that shows the relationship between two variables and is often used as the first step in regression analysis. The graph pairs numerical data, with

Figure 7–5 | Bar graph

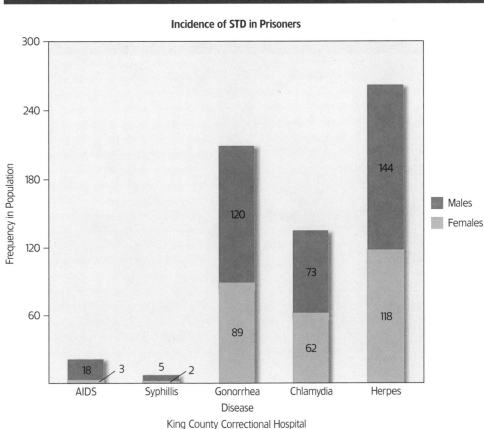

Incidence of STD in Prisoners

King County Correctional Hospital

Figure 7–6 | Histogram

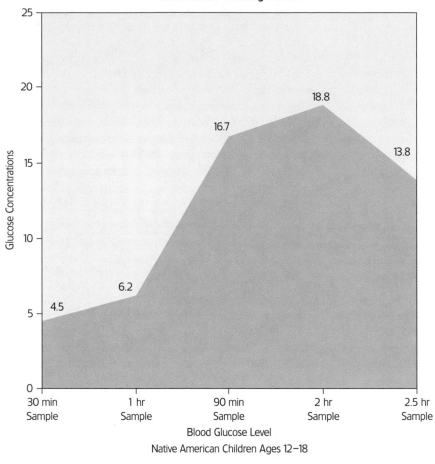

Blood Glucose Challenge Levels

Native American Children Ages 12–18

Figure 7–7 | Pie chart

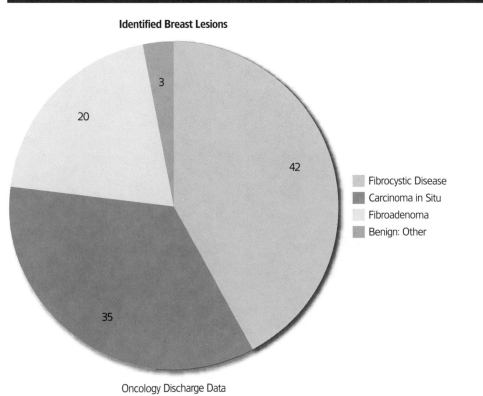

Identified Breast Lesions

Fibrocystic Disease
Carcinoma in Situ
Fibroadenoma
Benign: Other

Oncology Discharge Data

Figure 7–8 | Line graph

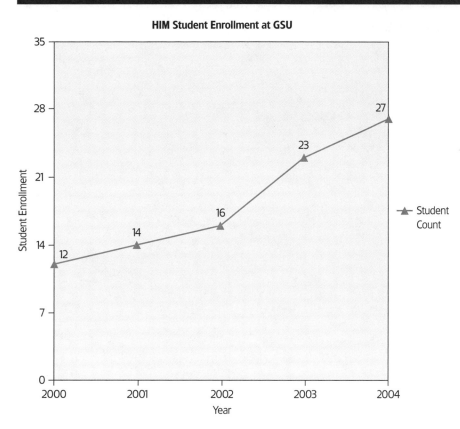

HIM Student Enrollment at GSU

Figure 7–9 | Control chart

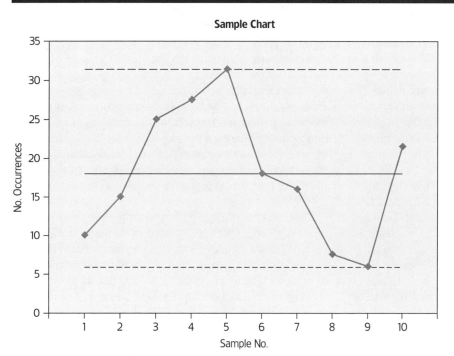

one variable in each axis, to help identify a relationship. An example is shown in Figure 7–10.

Deciding which tool to employ is often driven by determining the purpose behind an assignment, question, or project (e.g., is it to analyze, compare, or plan?) and how best to display the data. By becoming familiar with the tools and learning what they are used for, the learner is better able to reach these decisions. The tools, for the most part, can be useful for both planning and organizing, whether drawn by hand or using automated means via a computer or template. For example, in the study stage of a

Figure 7–10 | Scatter diagram

Scatter (Plot) Diagram Displaying Alpha and Beta

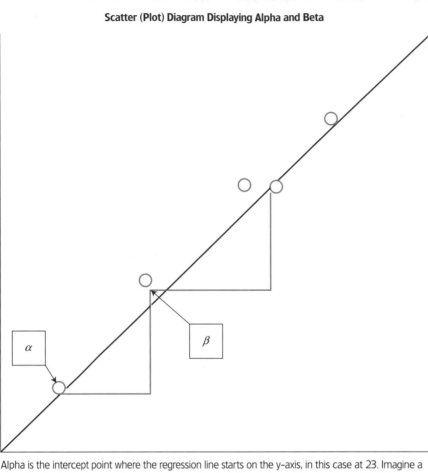

Alpha is the intercept point where the regression line starts on the y-axis, in this case at 23. Imagine a stair-step line being drawn between each value. The beta is the slope of the line formed. In this case, the beta demonstrates that with every unit increase in the predictor there is a beta change in the slope—as beta increases upward (exam scores), I.Q. increases.

project, one may choose to employ a cause-and-effect diagram to help sort the information into categories. Whereas textbooks display neatly drawn diagrams with examples of completed projects, it is sometimes beneficial to use the tools oneself as a means to understand how to better choose from among them. Drawing diagrams, graphs, or charts by hand after generating ideas is a common way to organize thoughts. These diagrams, graphs, or charts can be changed repeatedly as the process progresses and formalized by automated means.

Applications Data quality refers to more than just the "correctness" of data. Inherent in the concept of quality data is that data must be comprehensive, current, relevant, accurate, complete, legible, timely, and appropriate. To accomplish this, data must be viewed from prospective, concurrent, and retrospective approaches. Utilizing the prospective approach, appropriate protocols and procedures for capturing required data must be established before a patient is even treated. For example, protocols regarding what data should be captured during preregistration and at the time of patient admission,

who is responsible for capturing the data, and what procedures must be employed should all be coordinated in advance. Such protocols often involve the use of minimum data sets, a concept discussed in detail in Chapter 8, "Database Management." The concurrent approach to data viewing allows for the ability to clarify, verify, and edit data while the patient receives treatment. The concurrent approach is most practical when the patient receives treatment over time, as in an inpatient setting or during a nursing-home stay. The retrospective approach to data viewing applies to a review of all data after the fact, allowing for editing where necessary and the completion of the coding and billing processes.

Just as important as putting the processes and procedures in place is determining what to do with the data that have been captured. Originally, the focus rested on internal examination of data, such as a hospital tracking the number of patients who had a certain diagnosis during a certain window of time. Reporting requirements to public health agencies and accrediting bodies gradually emerged, along with the needs of third-party payers to verify the provision

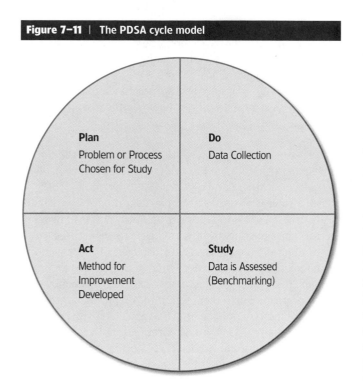

Figure 7–11 | The PDSA cycle model

Plan
Problem or Process
Chosen for Study

Do
Data Collection

Act
Method for
Improvement
Developed

Study
Data is Assessed
(Benchmarking)

of services for reimbursement purposes. Researchers began to demand quality data for studies, as did health care administrators and policy makers who compare costs associated with specific diseases. As a result of these demands for quality, the scope and amount of data required for comparison and study have also increased.

During the most recent decade, the discussion of data quality has focused on how to use data to improve patient care and safety. One way to improve care and safety is through careful and constant observation. This observation activity involves the use of the quality monitoring cycle PDSA, the steps of which are described in Figure 7–11. The quality monitoring cycle uses data to recognize patterns and trends. This recognition serves as the connection between raw data and real-life circumstances, thereby turning data into meaningful information.

A second way to improve patient care and safety using observation is through benchmarking. Benchmarking is the process of comparing outcomes with those of an acknowledged superior performer. Utilizing this definition, outcomes refers to the changes or end results, whether positive or negative, that can be attributed to the task at hand (i.e., the delivery of health care). For example, outcomes could include changes in health status, knowledge, behavior, or satisfaction. The usefulness of benchmarking, however, extends beyond the mere comparison of outcomes. Rather, it helps people and organizations to learn how the superior performer achieved its goals and to determine how to incorporate those methods into operational practice. Within the data quality context, benchmarking has most recently involved the collection of core measurements—standardized

sets of valid, reliable, and evidence-based measures. These measures are used in benchmarking as a way to determine whether a health care institution meets the standards of superior performance. For example, a surgical prevention measure may require administration of prophylactic antibiotics one hour prior to surgery as a means to reduce postoperative infections. A health care institution may examine its own records to determine the number of times it meets this standard compared to the number of surgeries performed.

Benchmarking has often been used in conjunction with the quality improvement model in the health care context. Using the quality improvement model, a problem or process is chosen for study, data are collected to measure the problem or process, data are assessed, and a method for improvement is developed. It is at the data assessment level that benchmarking comes into play. Once the state of the problem or process is assessed using the appropriate data, the health care provider compares itself to the benchmarked competitor and decides the "what and how" of incorporating the competitor's methods into its own operational practice. Within the patient safety context, common areas of focus for error reduction have included medication prescribing, dispensing, administering, and monitoring; exposures to communicable diseases and bodily fluids; and patient injuries.

A third way to improve patient care and safety is by the pressure exerted from the issuance of quality indicator (QI) reports. QI reports originally developed as an outgrowth of reporting requirements to public health agencies. For example, nursing homes have submitted a tremendous volume of data to CMS since 1996 through the use of the Minimum Data Set (MDS). CMS in turn has used this data to develop both public and nonpublic reports on the quality of care in nursing homes.

The public report, entitled Nursing Home Compare, currently focuses on 15 quality measures.[12] Because virtually every nursing home in the United States accepts patients whose care is funded by CMS, each nursing home receives a Nursing Home Compare report from CMS indicating its performance in relation to the quality measures. The Nursing Home Compare report also compares the data from an individual nursing home against national and state averages. Of the 15 measures, 12 are considered long-term measures and 3 are short-stay measures. The observation (or "look back") time varies for each measure, lasting 7, 14, or 30 days. Regulations currently require that an MDS assessment be performed during admission, quarterly, annually, and whenever a resident experiences a change in status. Using this report, the nursing home is able to gauge its performance with regard to the 15 quality measures. More significantly, the Nursing Home Compare reports are available to the public over the Internet. This enables consumers to make more informed comparisons when choosing a nursing home. It also permits public scrutiny of nursing homes, which may result in improved patient care. The reports to the public are updated quarterly.

Other information that is made available to the public at the Nursing Home Compare Web site is compiled from the CMS Online Survey, Certification, and Reporting (OSCAR) database. This very comprehensive report includes nursing home characteristics, citations issued during the three most recent state inspections, and recent complaint investigations. The information is a combination of that reported by the nursing home through the survey and that of the state survey agencies compiled during on-site evaluations. The OSCAR data are updated on a monthly basis but may not reflect the most recent survey results.

The nonpublic report provides data on 24 performance measures to state public health agencies. These agencies use the data to specify deficiencies that require investigation during on-site inspections. Comparisons are made during the on-site inspection, and quality indicator reports are developed. State agencies issue these QI reports to the nursing homes in their respective states. The facilities then have the ability to gauge their performance against state averages and, where appropriate, introduce measures to improve the quality of patient care. In some states, the QI reports issued to nursing homes are also made available to the public over the Internet.

The concept of using quality indicator reports has followed a slow process to fruition. Because the reports are only as accurate as the data collected, some reports have been criticized as not reflecting the actual quality of care delivered in a given institution. This perceived lack of correlation has highlighted the need to assure the recording and transmission of quality data, because those data may serve as a representation to the public of the quality of care at a given institution. The use of QI reports does not appear to abate, though; CMS now issues similar QI reports for the hospital and home health industries.

The Hospital Compare report currently reports on four core measures: heart attack (acute myocardial infarction, or AMI), heart failure, pneumonia, and surgical infection pre-

vention. Measures exist for each condition that represent the best practices for treatment. The performance rate for a particular facility is reported, along with comparisons to state and national averages. There is also a checklist for the consumer to use to gather and document comparative information. This information is available on the Hospital Compare Web site.[13]

The requirement for reporting data is one of the components of the Medicare Prescription Drug Improvement and Modernization Act of 2003 (MMA), Section 501(b),[14] which established the incentive payment program for eligible acute care hospitals to report on an initial set of 10 quality performance measures, known at the "starter set," and to agree to have their data publicly displayed. This new requirement became effective with patient discharges beginning in 2004. These are the same measures collected by the JC for participation in their accreditation programs as well as the voluntary reporting effort established by the Hospital Quality Alliance (HQA), a collaboration that includes CMS, the American Hospital Association, the Federation of American Hospitals, and the Association of American Medical Colleges. This collaboration received the support of numerous public and private organizations, including the Agency for Healthcare Research and Quality, the Joint Commission, the National Quality Forum, the American Medical Association, the American Nurses Association, the National Association of Children's Hospitals and Related Institutions, the Consumer-Purchaser Disclosure Project, the AFL-CIO, the AARP, and the U.S. Chamber of Commerce.

Additional measures exist for which hospitals may submit data and elect the option of displaying this data to the public on the Hospital Compare Web site. Some of these additional measures are listed in Table 7–6. Four core measures have been identified as the leading causes of hospitalization or for extending the length of stay. Heart attack and heart failure are common causes of admission for patients aged 65 or older, and these present high rates for morbidity

Table 7–6	Additional HQA Measures
Heart Attack (Acute Myocardial Infarction)	• Thrombolytic agent received within 30 minutes of hospital arrival
	• Percutaneous Coronary Intervention (PCI) received within 120 minutes of hospital arrival (previously Percutaneous Transluminal Coronary Angioplasty)
	• Adult smoking cessation advice/counseling
Heart Failure	• Discharge instructions
	• Adult smoking cessation advice/counseling
Pneumonia	• Blood culture performed prior to first antibiotic received in hospital
	• Adult smoking cessation advice/counseling
	• Appropriate initial antibiotic selection
Surgical Infection Prevention	• Prophylactic antibiotic received within one hour prior to surgical incision
	• Prophylactic antibiotic discontinued within 24 hours after surgery end time

Source: Information adapted from Hospital Compare, http://www.hospitalcompare.hhs.gov.

Table 7–7	Selected Surgeries
Colon surgery
Hip and knee arthroplasty
Abdominal and vaginal hysterectomy
Cardiac surgery (including coronary artery bypass grafts [CABG] and vascular surgery)

and mortality. The measures are evidence based and represent best practices for treatment. One of the AMI measures is the documentation of the administration of aspirin within 24 hours of the patient's arrival at the hospital. Another measure relating to AMI is the documentation of the prescription of aspirin at discharge. For both sets of core measures with patients who have a history of smoking, there is the additional requirement that they be given smoking cessation advice or counseling. The core measure for pneumonia also includes a requirement for smoking cessation advice or counseling and includes other measures related to the appropriate selection and timing of the administration of antibiotics. Another measure requires the documentation of patient screenings for pneumococcal vaccine status and the administration of the vaccine prior to discharge, if appropriate.

The core measures for surgical infection prevention represent the best practices for the prevention of infection after selected surgeries, as listed in Table 7–7. The evidence-based measures indicate that the best practices for the prevention of infections after these procedures are related to the timing of the administration of antibiotics and the avoidance of prolonged administration of prophylaxis with antibiotics. One core measure requires the documentation of the prophylactic antibiotic within one hour of surgery, with another measure requiring documentation that the prophylactic antibiotic be discontinued within 24 hours after surgery.

Home health data went public with the Home Health Quality Initiative (HHQI), which started publishing data in the spring of 2003. The Home Health Compare report examines 10 quality measures related to outcomes of an episode or service (see Table 7–8). Three of the measures are related to improvement in mobility; four measures are related to meeting the patient's activities of daily living, such as improvement in bladder control and the ability to take medicines correctly; two measures are related to patient medical emergencies, such as the percentage of patients who had to be admitted to the hospital and needed urgent, unplanned medical care; and one measure indicates the percentage of patients who remain at home after the episode of home health care ends. The information collected is called the Home Health Outcome and Assessment Information Set (OASIS). The public information is updated monthly, but there is a two- to three-month data lag time.

Quality indicator reports have begun to take a foothold at the state level, perhaps forecasting a trend toward wider use. For example, Pennsylvania, Missouri, and Illinois each require hospitals to report data concerning hospital-acquired or nosocomial infections to the state health department.[15] This reporting allows not only for the tracking of trends related to antibiotic-resistant microbes but also for the development of quality indicators related to infection rates that are disseminated to the public via the Internet. Public demand for this information has increased, so that patients may make informed choices when selecting health care facilities; additionally, this information has been somewhat instrumental in passing legislation for public reporting of statistical and study results.

Pennsylvania was the first state to release reports to the public, beginning with information about four types of hospital-acquired infections in 2004. The hospitals were required to submit data to the Pennsylvania Health Care Cost Containment Council (PHC4). The reporting includes four types of hospital-acquired infections, three surgical site infection categories, Foley catheter-associated urinary tract infections, ventilator-associated pneumonia, and central-line

Table 7–8	Home Health Outcome and Assessment Information Set	
Measures related to improvement in getting around	• Patients who get better at walking and moving around
	• Patients who get better at getting in and out of bed
	• Patients who have less pain when moving around
Measures related to meeting the patient's activities of daily living	• Patients whose bladder control improves
	• Patients who get better at bathing
	• Patients who get better at taking their medicines correctly (by mouth)
	• Patients who are short of breath less often
Measures related to patient medical emergencies	• Patients who have to be admitted to the hospital
	• Patients who need urgent, unplanned medical care
Measures related to living at home after an episode of home health care ends	• Patients who stay at home after an episode of home health care ends

Source: Information adapted from Home Health Compare, http://www.homehealthcompare.hhs.gov.

associated bloodstream infections. In 2006, the PHC4 began requiring hospitals to submit data on all hospital-acquired infections. The intent is to encourage health care facilities to take appropriate actions to decrease the risks of infection. Making information available to the public encourages facilities to direct resources toward improving or maintaining their statistical reports on infections.

One of the driving forces behind the passage of the legislation in Missouri was a father whose adolescent son developed an infection following a sledding accident and resultant fractured arm. The infection led to osteomyelitis and required six subsequent surgical procedures and five months of drug treatment, forcing the young man to miss school, a season of sports, and a summer lifeguarding job. The purpose of the legislation was not to be punitive but to spur hospitals to reduce the incidence of infection. The Missouri Nosocomial Infection Control Act of 2004 includes hospitals, ambulatory surgery centers, and other facilities that have procedures for monitoring compliance with infection-control regulations and standards. Physician offices are exempt. This information will also be available for the licensing of hospitals and ambulatory surgical centers in Missouri at a future date.

Mandatory reporting of infections is a part of the Illinois Hospital Report Card Act. Like Missouri, Illinois requires reporting of nosocomial infections related to Class I surgical site infections, central-line-related bloodstream infections, and ventilator-associated pneumonia. Other states, including Florida, New York, and Virginia, have since joined this trend to require hospitals to disclose or report information about infection rates to federal or state authorities.[16] These requirements center upon nosocomial infections and may include tracking and reporting data concerning surgical site infections, infections associated with catheters, and pneumonia in patients on ventilators.

Reports are also available to the public that rate hospitals, physicians, and nursing homes. Some use Medicare Provider Analysis and Review (MEDPAR) data, which are composed of data from the Medicare population that are reported from claims data submitted by health care facilities. One organization, HealthGrades.com, uses MEDPAR data to form parts of comparison reports that are made available to the public. Another organization, the Leapfroggroup.org, uses data that are submitted voluntarily by health care organizations. One advantage offered by these data is that they are derived from a wide variety of organizations and include multiple categories of third-party payers, as opposed to data collected from only Medicare claims. Still other reports are issued as rankings by benchmarking organizations to which hospitals and other health care delivery systems may subscribe. One quality rating system for health care that uses surveys is available from the Consumer Checkbook, a nonprofit consumer information and service resource. The results of physician surveys that rank facilities by "desirability" ratings, risk-adjusted mortality figures, and adverse outcomes for several surgical procedures is available on a subscription basis for consumers; however, the rankings are a matter of physician opinion. Still other reports—such as those generated by WebMD (part of WebMD Health), a leading provider of health information services to consumers, physicians, and health care professionals—are only available to members who participate.

One newer application related to improving patient care and reducing errors, particularly with regard to medication, is the development of the personal health record (PHR). As patients and consumers become better informed of the expected outcomes of illnesses, the modalities of treatment, and the interactions of medications, they are taking more responsibility for keeping their own records. Through the promotion and use of patient PHRs, health care providers are offered the opportunity to compare their records against those of their patients, thereby leading to the possibility of improved consistency of data between both parties. This, in turn, can lead to a decrease in the risk of errors and complications from current treatments and medications; health care providers are able to assist patients in recalling all historical information accurately when they provide information to providers at various facilities.

Performance Improvement and Risk Management

Two areas that relate to data quality and quality patient care are performance improvement and risk management. Similar to statistics and research, both performance improvement and risk management rely upon data that are collected, stored, and retrieved by automated methods. Some data collection, however, may still be abstracted from open or closed health care records, either in paper or electronic versions. Performance improvement and risk management are not limited to acute care facilities but are integral parts of the quality management programs within all types of health care systems, such as skilled nursing facilities (SNFs); home health agencies; and ambulatory, long-term, and rehabilitation facilities.

Performance Improvement

Performance improvement is a clinical function that focuses on how to improve patient care. It is related to database management in that the trend is toward the use of automated data to measure the performance of a health care provider or institution. The HIM professional may be involved in collecting data and compiling reports, as well as provide trending reports. Strong coding and analytical skills, along with database management skills, are essential to provide the appropriate data for effective performance activities.

Fundamental to the concept of performance improvement is the review of a given process, including a determination of how well that process should function. During the review activity, it is important to understand who is affected by the process (e.g., patients and staff), what product is produced by the process (e.g., quality health care), and what is not working with regard to the current process. Some of this understanding can be gained through the extraction of data from clinical data repositories, data warehouses, and data marts.

It is often helpful to use a benchmarking methodology for performance improvement. Benchmarking, as previously discussed, is the process of comparing outcomes with those of an acknowledged superior performer as a means to improve performance. Data for benchmarking are available from many agencies, as described earlier in this chapter.

To compare its performance with those of other organizations, the health care organization can utilize the data found in external databases. As stated in Chapter 9, "Health Statistics," health care data are reported to local, state, and federal government agencies pursuant to legal requirements. In addition, some health care organizations voluntarily report data to nongovernmental institutions pursuant to access/participation agreements. These data are collected and maintained under recognized standards and guidelines that govern form and content.

Within the context of accreditation, the most influential performance improvement method of recent years has been the ORYX Initiative of the Joint Commission. The goal of the ORYX Initiative is to "provide a continuous, data-driven accreditation process that focuses on the actual results of care (performance measurement) and is more comprehensive and valuable to all stakeholders."[17] Under the ORYX Initiative, performance data are defined, collected, analyzed, transmitted, reported, and used to examine a health care organization's internal performance over time and to compare a health care organization's performance with others. Those data serve as part of the information used by the Joint Commission to determine the accreditation status of health care organizations.

To assess its internal performance under ORYX, a health care organization would collect and aggregate its own data to measure patient outcomes. For example, an organization could aggregate data collected from similar patients and analyze them to determine whether certain treatment options are more effective than others. This analysis could further indicate if the effectiveness of the treatment options has varied over time. From this analysis, the organization could determine the need for additional improvement. Data used for comparisons concerning the ORYX initiative are available to the public through the JC Web site (under "Quality Check"). Reports are available for hospitals, nursing homes, home care agencies, mental health facilities, HMOs, and outpatient services that are accredited by the Joint Commission.

Core measures under ORYX support the integration of outcome data and other performance measurements into the accreditation process. The Joint Commission has developed specific core performance measures that can be applied across health care accreditation programs. These core performance measures are developed using precisely defined data elements, calculation algorithms, and standardized data collection protocols based on uniform medical language. These measures have been communicated to health care organizations for embedding in their respective databases, and data about these measures are to be reported to the Joint Commission on a quarterly basis.[18] At this time, three core measures must be reported to the Joint Commission, with additional core measures scheduled for reporting over the next few years.[19]

Performance improvement as a continuous process has been a part of the Joint Commission reviews since the early 1990s. Prior to then, requirements for quality assessment focused on outcomes and processes; some of these reviews of clinical processes must still be conducted. Documentation review is one type of peer review that has changed its requirements, moving from a review of a designated number of elements—in a specified number of records in monthly and quarterly cycles—to a focused review based on periodic sampling. This review is essential to ensure that the health care record accurately reflects the care provided to the patient and also for safety and quality of care, as well as reimbursement and compliance issues. Health information management professionals usually conduct these documentation reviews, compile the data, and report the results to the appropriate committee or department responsible for initiating corrective action or improvement. Study results are reported to the medical staff as defined in the medical staff bylaws and a hospital's performance improvement plan. Deficiencies in documentation that become discipline issues are also included in the physician's record for re-credentialing considerations. Although the format for review and criteria may have changed, the responsibility still remains with the medical staff. The involvement and leadership of the medical staff in these activities is crucial to the success of the performance improvement program.

Physician involvement in other performance activities, such as surgical case review, medication usage review, blood and blood component review, mortality review, and infection control, are often accomplished by committees composed of medical staff, with assistance in data collection and abstraction provided by members of the Health Information Management and Quality Assurance staff. The Joint Commission specifies that these activities be consistent, timely, defensible, balanced, useful, and ongoing. The processes need to be defined clearly, with the participants and their roles, design methods, and criteria all identified. Criteria are the standards upon which judgments can be made or the expected level(s) of achievement. Criteria are described by the JC as the specifications against which performance or quality may be compared.

Within the public health context, the most respected performance improvement initiative is the Comprehensive Assessment for Tracking Community Health (CATCH).[20] Developed by the University of South Florida and supported by multiple public and private entities, CATCH collects, organizes, analyzes, prioritizes, and reports data on over 250 health and social indicators on a local community level. These data are gathered from hospitals; local, state, and federal government agencies; and national health care groups. Data are also gathered from door-to-door and mail-in surveys. These data are stored in a data warehouse, then mined and disseminated to Florida communities in the form of indicators of community health. This information brings greater awareness to communities and allows them to focus on initiatives, such as training and education, to improve the public's health.

Risk Management

Risk management is a nonclinical function that focuses on how to reduce medical, financial, and legal risk to an organization. This reduction is tied to the definition of risk: the estimate of probability of loss from a given event upon the operational or financial performance of an organization. Understanding the universe of probable events, the strategies employed to mitigate and minimize the effects of each of these events, and how to contain negative consequences is central to managing risk.

Traditionally, risk management dealt with assessing patient outcomes and events, writing incident reports, and reviewing past events to determine the need for changes in policy and procedure. Traditional statistical methods were employed to measure risk, and these statistics were reported to higher management levels and boards of directors. Risk management still uses these processes but now includes more focus on database management, primarily in two areas: using data in an automated fashion to measure a health care institution's risk, and identifying the risk inherent with databases that contain enormous amounts of sensitive data.

Automated databases can be powerful tools in risk management. Because a database is a structured collection of data on multiple entities and their relationships, often arranged for ease and speed of retrieval, it is an ideal method for storing risk management data. The traditional approach of storing paper-based incident reports in a file cabinet did not provide a mechanism for sophisticated information searches, which can be performed in a database format with ease. Using a common and controlled database approach, data can be added and modified over time, thereby providing end users the data needed to perform their jobs as efficiently as possible. With the advent of sophisticated software applications and techniques such as data mining, databases can be searched for risk patterns

that may be difficult to detect using traditional statistical methods. Once discovered, these data can be analyzed to predict the probability of future occurrences and to determine how to proceed with action, including mitigation efforts. This effort can lead to more effective loss prevention and reduction programs.

The incident report is still an integral component of any loss prevention program. This report can be prepared and submitted electronically in many facilities, although the paper version is usually still available. The data from the paper report may then be abstracted to facilitate data storage and documentation requirements. A trend has emerged toward developing specialized reports, such as medication and surgical occurrence reports. Other occurrences that organizations often require to be reported to the risk manager are falls, lost property, IV complications, mislabeled lab specimens, and against medical advice discharges. Management of these types of occurrences is integral to an effective loss prevention program. In addition, risk managers are involved in investigations coordinated with clinical engineering to comply with the federal Safe Medical Devices Act, safety inspections mandated by the Joint Commission, and COBRA investigations.

Risk management also involves claims management; risk managers often act as liaison to a health care organization's attorneys. This may include conducting record reviews, arranging depositions, and providing the necessary documentation for claims investigations. The risk manager may also participate in interviews with professional and other staff related to adverse occurrences.

HIPAA

The Security Rule requires a risk analysis of electronically protected health information.

Risk management and database management also intersect with regard to the clinical data stored in automated systems, such as an electronic health record. The security management process standards (Security Rule) issued pursuant to the Health Insurance Portability and Accountability Act (HIPAA) require a covered entity to perform a risk analysis to determine security risks and implement standards to reduce risks and vulnerabilities to electronic protected health information.[21] Such security risks may include breaches to the confidentiality, integrity, and availability of the electronic protected health information. The standards of the Security Rule do not specify the approach for this analysis nor do they specify what security measures should be implemented, allowing for flexibility by the covered entity. The standards do require, however, that the covered entity document its efforts, maintain this documentation for six years, and provide review and modification of the efforts on a regular basis.[22]

Installing security measures such as access and integrity controls are just the beginning of risk management efforts relating to an EHR; nontechnological risks also pose threats. For example, access and security controls installed at the technological level can help prevent unauthorized access to sensitive patient information, and, on a nontechnological level, in-service education programs can raise employee awareness about handling the same information. Similarly, complete and accurate information in the EHR can support the claims management function, serve as the basis of a defense in a lawsuit, and assist in promoting safety education programs—all areas that are central to a successful risk management program. With the use of data mining techniques, the EHR can be searched to assist in analyzing different areas of a health care delivery system, such as obstetrics, psychiatry, anesthesia, and surgery, to determine if they carry higher levels of risk. Finally, the EHR has been helpful in the risk management context through analyzing the occurrence of medication errors, inconsistent data entries, and contradictions in data.

Another part of an effective risk management program is Sentinel Event Review, a requirement of the Joint Commission since 1998. A **sentinel event** is an unexpected occurrence involving death or serious physical or psychological injury, or other risks thereof; serious injury includes loss of limb or limb function. The standards that relate specifically to the management of sentinel events are found in the Improving Organization Performance section of the JC accreditation manual. Organizations are required to establish mechanisms to identify, report, and manage these events. Organizations are also required to conduct a **root-cause analysis** to identify the cause of the event and should include a clinical as well as an administrative review. Examples of sentinel events that must be reviewed include significant medication errors, significant adverse drug reactions, confirmed transfusion reactions, and surgery on the wrong patient or wrong body part. Infant abduction or the discharge of an infant to the wrong family are also considered sentinel events.

Facilities are encouraged but not required to report sentinel events to the JC within 45 days of the event. If a facility chooses not to report the event and a family member makes the JC aware, or the JCAHO becomes aware by other means, the JC will communicate to the facility the requirement to submit the findings of the root-cause analysis and action plans. Failure to do so within the specified time frame could result in placing the organization on Accreditation Watch status until the response is received

and the protocol approved. An on-site review will not occur unless the JC deems it necessary due to a potential threat to patient health or safety or if there appears to be significant noncompliance with the Joint Commission standards.

Although risk management has already moved from a traditional focus to one that includes database management, it is evolving even further in the new century. In view of the many external factors that influence health care organizations, particularly those beyond the organization's control, a new concept has been applied to risk management: enterprise risk management. **Enterprise risk management** (ERM) refers to the function of analyzing and evaluating all of the risks that confront an organization, not just the legal, financial, and medical risks that are traditionally considered. These additional risks include the threat of terrorism and its impact on professionals, patients, and the community; the heightened emphasis on corporate governance and compliance with statutes, regulations, and ethical standards; the increased presence of oversight authorities over business practices; the expanded awareness of patients and the public in general to medical and medication errors; the shortage of qualified staff in certain health care professions or in certain geographic regions; and the effect of the economy in general and in specific local regions upon the demand for unreimbursed health care. ERM considers these risks, and others not listed here, in combination and determines how they affect the health care organization's strategic plan and overall health. ERM also considers risks in the context of the opportunities they may present, with the goal of exploring how those risks may be exploited to gain a competitive advantage.

A feature central to ERM is the focus on interrelationships and interdependencies. Instead of viewing risks in isolation and organizational departments as separate entities, ERM examines risks together across departmental lines. ERM also examines risks across activities and functions, factoring in how they interplay. Furthermore, ERM examines the health care organization's relationship with external entities, sometimes resulting in a collaborative regional effort to mitigate and control loss. Such an approach is particularly applicable to emergency preparedness planning, because it permits the risk manager to examine the organization's infrastructure and estimate how it will be affected by a catastrophic event. Such a proactive approach may well reduce costs to the health care organization, in both financial terms and how well the organization accomplishes its mission. As ERM increases in acceptance, its use in the health care industry should also increase.

Utilization Management

Utilization management refers to a combination of planned functions directed to patients in a health care facility or setting that includes prudent use of resources, appropriate treatment management, and early comprehensive discharge planning for continuation of care. The process uses established criteria as specified in the organization's utilization review plan. **Utilization review** is the clinical review of the appropriateness of admission and planned use of resources, that can be and often is initiated prior to admission and conducted at specific time frames as defined in an organization's utilization review plan. This review involves the process of comparing preestablished criteria against the health care services to be provided to the patient to determine whether the care is necessary.

Efforts at utilization management began in the 1950s and were employed at facilities that had frequent bed shortages as a way to allocate space to patients who demonstrated the greatest need. Utilization management first became mandatory in 1965 with the passage of the federal law establishing the Medicare program. The focus of the legislation at that time was on reducing the patient's length of stay (LOS) in an effort to control the rising costs of health care. Medical evaluation studies were also part of the review process that focused on improving the quality of patient care. Physician involvement was central to the process and continues to this day, although many changes in the procedures employed have taken place through the years.

During the 1970s, utilization management became a required component of JC accreditation standards as well as a requirement for participation in the Medicaid reimbursement program. Further legislation in 1972 led to the formation of **Professional Standards Review Organizations** (PSROs), groups tasked with monitoring the appropriateness and quality of outcomes. In 1977, new legislation known as the Utilization Review Act defined the review process by requiring hospitals to conduct continued-stay reviews for medical necessity and the appropriateness of Medicare and Medicaid inpatient hospitalizations. The Health Care Financing Administration (HCFA), now called Centers for Medicare and Medicaid Services, began operation, charged with managing the Medicare and Medicaid programs that had previously been the responsibility of the Social Security Administration. Simultaneously, Congress passed fraud and abuse legislation to enable enforcement of the provisions of the act.

With enactment of the Tax Equity and Fiscal Responsibility Act (TEFRA) in 1982, the titles of these PSROs changed to Peer Review Organizations (PROs). TEFRA also established the first Medicare prospective payment system (PPS), which was implemented the following year. Using PPS, reimbursement was no longer based on a per diem rate, but on a predetermined rate based on the discharge diagnosis in relation to diagnosis-related groups (DRGs). More information concerning DRGs can be found in Chapter 6, "Nomenclatures and Classification Systems," and Chapter 15, "Reimbursement Methodologies." TEFRA's changes placed additional focus on managing the length of stay

through early and effective discharge planning. While these changes in the reporting and scope of utilization management occurred, the focus continued to be directed toward managing the cost of health care and assuring the best level of quality health care possible. CMS recently changed the PRO designation to Quality Improvement Organization (QIO) as a part of the "7th Scope of Work" (SOW), a document that updates the direction and focus of the organization.[23]

By the 1990s, the process of determining medical necessity expanded beyond the beneficiaries of Medicare and Medicaid to include the efforts of many managed care and group health insurance plans. Precertification for hospital admissions and surgical procedures became requirements of many of these private entities. In addition, some plans required authorization from primary care physicians before treatment in emergency care centers in nonemergency circumstances would be reimbursed as well as preauthorization for diagnostic radiological procedures.

Utilization review has evolved in the 21st century to incorporate evidence-based guidelines as part of the screening process. Several private companies, such as Milliman and McKesson (InterQual), have published evidence-based guidelines that are widely used in the health care field. The guidelines may be used at the time of preadmission, admission, and continued stay or concurrent review, as well as during discharge planning. Some are based on the level of illness and the patient services required, whereas others focus on ambulatory care, observation status, inpatient and surgical care, general recovery, home care, and chronic care.

Complying with the changing aspects of utilization review has been a challenge for many health care professionals. **Case management** refers to the ongoing review of patient care in various health care settings related to assuring the medical necessity of the encounter and the appropriateness of the clinical services provided. **Case managers,** also known as **utilization coordinators,** are frequently nurses or health information managers with responsibility for managing the review process and coordinating the patient's care with physicians, nurses, and other allied health professionals. In many settings, the case management function is organized into a department and may also include social workers and clerical assistants to help with communication and coordination of the review activities. Utilization management continues to be a physician-centered function, though it is coordinated by case managers. In large facilities, case managers may specialize in specific areas, such as cardiology, orthopedics, or pediatrics; in smaller facilities, case managers must be trained to facilitate the variety of cases that the organization treats. Long-term care facilities and home health services are also required to have an established utilization management plan, although their requirements differ. In all settings, the focus rests on medical necessity and appropriate management of health care resources.

Figure 7–12 | Steps in the utilization review process

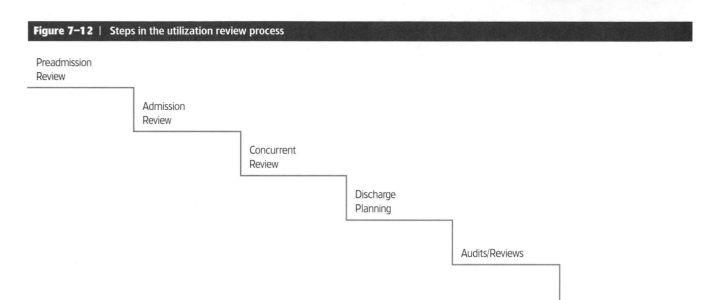

Utilization Review Process

The utilization review process consists of several steps or levels of review; these are listed in Figure 7–12. The process may begin with **preadmission review,** an element often required by managed care organizations. Preadmission review is performed prior to admission to the facility and operates to determine if the admission or procedure/treatment plan is medically necessary and appropriate for the setting. The case manager uses criteria and screening software, and in some cases may contact the patient's third-party payer, to confirm that the admission is approved. If approval is deemed inappropriate, the patient is directed to the appropriate level of care.

If preadmission review is not conducted, **admission review** is performed at the time of admission or as soon as possible thereafter to determine the medical necessity of the admission and the appropriateness of the plan of treatment. Criteria are also used here, as well as consultation with the patient's third-party payer for authorization. An estimate of the length of stay may be established during this step. If some services can't be performed at the facility, plans are initiated for the appropriate transfer. If any services are not deemed appropriate, the patient is notified that responsibility for payment rests with the patient and not with the third-party payer. The notification process is defined by the patient's third-party payer and varies according to the types of notifications that must be made to the patient.

Concurrent review, or continued-stay review, is similar to preadmission and admission review. This review must assure the continued medical necessity and appropriateness of care being delivered to the patient. The review continues at specific intervals that may be tied to the diagnosis or procedure, or determined by the patient's third-party payer. Case managers and health information management professionals are also responsible for assuring that appropriate

documentation exists to support the decisions made regarding appropriateness of admission and the continued necessity and appropriateness of care. Facilities must have a Corporate Compliance Policy and Plan that addresses the documentation of appropriateness of admission and continued stay, and observation versus inpatient documentation requirements.

Discharge planning is the process of coordinating the activities employed to facilitate the patient's release from the hospital when inpatient services are no longer needed. Discharge planning can be initiated at any stage of the utilization review process and evolves with the determination of the patient's needs following discharge from the facility. When discharge planning is initiated at preadmission, there may be coordination with outside agencies, such as a home health agency for continuation of care and delivery of durable medical equipment to the patient's home. Other arrangements may include transfer to another type of facility for continuation of care. Social workers and other health care professionals may become involved in the stages of discharge planning as well. Changes in the patient's recovery can alter these plans and the participation of the various agencies involved. Case managers may coordinate this process; alternatively, separate discharge planners might possess primary responsibility for this function. Good communication and coordination are essential to efficient discharge planning.

An important aspect of the discharge planning process is the appropriate and clear documentation of the discharge status of the patient in the patient's health record. CMS established this requirement in 1998 as part of its post-acute transfer policy (PACT). The **discharge status** is the description of the facility or service—such as a skilled nursing facility, rehabilitation care facility, or home health service—to which the patient will be transferred upon discharge. This documentation is essential to establish the appropriate

Figure 7–13 | The UB-04 claim form

1

2

3a PAT. CNTL #

b. MED. REC. #

4 TYPE OF BILL

5 FED. TAX NO.

6 STATEMENT COVERS PERIOD FROM THROUGH

7

8 PATIENT NAME a

b

9 PATIENT ADDRESS a

b c d e

10 BIRTHDATE | 11 SEX | ADMISSION 12 DATE 13 HR 14 TYPE 15 SRC | 16 DHR | 17 STAT | CONDITION CODES 18 19 20 21 22 23 24 25 26 27 28 | 29 ACDT STATE | 30

31 OCCURRENCE CODE DATE | 32 OCCURRENCE CODE DATE | 33 OCCURRENCE CODE DATE | 34 OCCURRENCE CODE DATE | 35 OCCURRENCE SPAN CODE FROM THROUGH | 36 OCCURRENCE SPAN CODE FROM THROUGH | 37

a

b

38

39 VALUE CODES CODE AMOUNT | 40 VALUE CODES CODE AMOUNT | 41 VALUE CODES CODE AMOUNT

a

b

c

d

	42 REV. CD.	43 DESCRIPTION	44 HCPCS / RATE / HIPPS CODE	45 SERV. DATE	46 SERV. UNITS	47 TOTAL CHARGES	48 NON-COVERED CHARGES	49	
1									1
2									2
3									3
4									4
5									5
6									6
7									7
8									8
9									9
10									10
11									11
12									12
13									13
14									14
15									15
16									16
17									17
18									18
19									19
20									20
21									21
22									22
23		PAGE ____ OF ____	CREATION DATE		TOTALS				23

	50 PAYER NAME	51 HEALTH PLAN ID	52 REL. INFO	53 ASG. BEN.	54 PRIOR PAYMENTS	55 EST. AMOUNT DUE	56 NPI		
A							57		A
B							OTHER		B
C							PRV ID		C

	58 INSURED'S NAME	59 P. REL	60 INSURED'S UNIQUE ID	61 GROUP NAME	62 INSURANCE GROUP NO.	
A						A
B						B
C						C

	63 TREATMENT AUTHORIZATION CODES	64 DOCUMENT CONTROL NUMBER	65 EMPLOYER NAME	
A				A
B				B
C				C

66 DX | 67 A B C D E F G H | 68

I J K L M N O P Q

69 ADMIT DX | 70 PATIENT REASON DX a b c | 71 PPS CODE | 72 ECI a b c | 73

74 PRINCIPAL PROCEDURE CODE DATE | a. OTHER PROCEDURE CODE DATE | b. OTHER PROCEDURE CODE DATE | 75

c. OTHER PROCEDURE CODE DATE | d. OTHER PROCEDURE CODE DATE | e. OTHER PROCEDURE CODE DATE

76 ATTENDING NPI QUAL
LAST FIRST

77 OPERATING NPI QUAL
LAST FIRST

78 OTHER NPI QUAL
LAST FIRST

79 OTHER NPI QUAL
LAST FIRST

80 REMARKS

81CC a b c d

UB-04 CMS-1450 APPROVED OMB NO.

NUBC National Uniform Billing Committee LIC9213257

THE CERTIFICATIONS ON THE REVERSE APPLY TO THIS BILL AND ARE MADE A PART HEREOF.

patient status code that identifies where the patient will be sent at the conclusion of a health facility encounter or at the end of a billing cycle.

Often referred to as the Special 10 Transfer DRGs, the initial PACT policy specified calculation for reimbursement for all cases assigned to one of the 10 DRGs if the patient was discharged to certain facilities that were considered to be continuation of the episode of care. Patients discharged to home or custodial care, such as residential care or assisted living facilities, were not included in the calculation. In 2004, CMS expanded the list of DRGs for which the transfer rule applies from 10 to 29. The next year, CMS again expanded the list to include 182 DRGs.

The patient status code is a two-digit code that is entered on the UB-04 claim form, formerly known as the UB-92 claim form, an example of which is seen in Figure 7–13. Examples of patient discharge status codes are listed in Table 7–9. Omitting the status code or submitting a claim with the incorrect status code is a claim billing error and could result in rejection of the claim and loss of revenue. The Office of the Inspector General (OIG) has focused attention on those facilities that have high error rates and may assess fines for failure to achieve compliance with the requirement to document accurately. CMS performs edits to assure compliance, comparing the patient status code at discharge against the code used by the post-acute care facility in its billing process. For example, if a patient is transferred from an acute care facility to a skilled nursing facility, the discharge code on the UB-04 should correlate with the billing code from the SNF. This editing underscores the importance of documentation in the record that clearly supports the appropriate transfer status code. Facilities often conduct random audits as a part of their Corporate Compliance Policy and Plan, seeking to assure compliance and initiate corrective measures as well as reduce the potential for revenue loss and fines.

Case managers work closely with health information managers to conduct various audits and reviews. The activities may include audits for compliance with regard to

Table 7–9	Patient Discharge Status Codes	
Code	**Description**	**Includes**
01	Home or self-care	Home, assisted living, home IV without home care, retirement home, foster care, home with home O2, homeless shelter, residential care facility, jail or prison. Also includes transfer to OP services such as catheter labs, or for radiology purposes.
02	Short-term hospital for acute inpatient care	All acute hospitals except children's hospitals, VA hospitals, psychiatric hospitals, and rehabilitation facilities.
03	Skilled nursing facility (SNF)	SNF with Medicare certification. Does not include SNF with Medicaid only.
04	Intermediate care facility (ICF)	Facilities without Medicare or Medicaid certification. Includes patients returning to Medicare facilities for custodial care.
05	Another type of facility for inpatient care	Does not include SNFs, rehabilitation, or long-term hospitals with specific status codes. Children's, cancer, or chemical dependency hospitals are examples.
06	Home care	Home care services for skilled services. Does not include durable medical equipment (DME) supplier, or home IV service only.
07	AMA	Left against medical advice or discontinued care.
20	Expired	Expired.
30	Still a patient	Partial billing or interim bill.
43	Federal hospital	Any inpatient care at a VA facility (acute, psychiatric, rehabilitation, or SNF).
50	Hospice	Hospice at home.
51	Hospice—medical facility	Hospice service in a hospital, SNF or ICF.
61	Swing bed	SNF care in a swing bed arrangement.
62	IRF	Inpatient rehabilitation facility.
63	LTAC	Long-term acute care hospital.
64	Medicaid-only nursing facility	Nursing facility certified under Medicaid only, not Medicare.
65	Psychiatric hospital	Psychiatric hospital or distinct part or unit of a hospital.
66	Critical access hospitals	Hospitals with designation as critical access hospitals.

Source: Information from *UB-92 Handbook for Hospital Billing*, 2006 edition; American Medical Association and Patient Status Code FAQs; National Uniform Billing Committee, http://www.nubc.org.

observation versus inpatient stays, premature discharges and subsequent readmissions, and inpatient procedures performed in outpatient settings. Familiarity with the current OIG Work Plan assists case managers in designing the annual compliance activities accordingly. The Work Plan is not limited to acute care facilities but includes review of every facet of health care that receives reimbursement from the Medicare and Medicaid programs.

Although this discussion of the steps in the utilization review process has focused on the acute care setting, utilization review may vary in other settings. For example, utilization review in home care and skilled nursing facilities is similar to the acute care setting in design and process, but it uses criteria that are more specific to the scope of the facility. Medical necessity and appropriateness of the plan of care are central to utilization review. Coordinators who work with the discharge planners or case managers at acute care facilities usually conduct preadmission reviews before

the patient receives this new form of treatment. The type and amount of service provided are determined using specific criteria or in consultation with the patient's third-party payer.

Utilization management remains central to the delivery of patient care in the 21st century. Both accrediting and licensing standards contain elements of utilization management with which health care organizations must comply. For example, the current JC standards specify that the provisions of ongoing care are based on patient needs even when denial of payment has been determined. The standard also includes provisions for the patient's family to be involved in the decision-making process. Similar requirements are present in the Condition for Participation in the Medicare and Medicaid reimbursement programs.[24] Utilization management will continue to evolve as health care in the United States adapts to new changes.

Conclusion

As this chapter illustrates, quality health care management is important to the entire health care system, affecting patients, health care providers, governmental entities, accrediting bodies, and third-party payers. Whether used to study clinical outcomes, support performance improvement and risk management efforts, or facilitate the utilization review process, the ready availability and quality of data are essential. Quality management is an equally integral part of health information management. The data that are collected, abstracted, coded, stored, and reported by health information management professionals must be accurate and timely to meet the demands of the health care professionals who use them for patient care delivery, as well as the needs of others for billing, payment, and health care research. Furthermore, the growing use of data to improve patient safety, reduce risks, and improve the allocation of health care dollars signals exciting developments for the future of health care.

CHAPTER SUMMARY

Because of its ability to provide objectivity, data are an essential element used to measure the quality of patient care. Data have been used to study the quality of patient care for over a century, leading in part to the formation of accrediting organizations that focus on improving patient care. Data collected from the patient's health record are a crucial part of any quality initiative in the health care field, including those at the federal level. Private efforts to improve patient care have measured the performance of care and service through data collected at the health care provider level, with the HEDIS data set serving as a model for managed care plans. The use of quality monitoring cycles, benchmarking processes, and quality indicator reports has expanded greatly in the last few decades, helping those within the health care field to improve the delivery of patient care and those outside the field to evaluate care given. Two areas that rely greatly upon data quality are performance improvement and risk management, with performance improvement focusing on the review of clinical processes as a way to improve the quality of patient care and risk management focusing on the review of nonclinical processes as a way to reduce medical, financial, and legal risk to an organization. Both areas have received considerable attention because of their potential to affect both the administration and delivery of patient care. By contrast, utilization management focuses on the appropriateness and planned use of resources as an effort to control health care costs. This focus has become central to the delivery of patient care, as both accrediting and licensing standards require health care organizations to comply with utilization management requirements.

CASE STUDY

You are a quality analyst in a health information management department appointed to lead a project team. Your team must assess the problem with the documentation of the patient's discharge disposition status in the health record. An increasing number of errors have been reported and frustration among the coders has risen. These coders claim that conflicting information is often present in the record, requiring them to spend an inordinate amount of time trying to obtain verification. Coding productivity has been affected. How would you assess the problem? Give examples of tools to use in a meeting, some ideas that may develop, and a study mechanism.

REVIEW QUESTIONS

1. Name the stages in which data quality errors found in a health record most commonly occur.

2. What are the steps in the quality improvement model, and how is benchmarking involved?

3. What agency is focused on developing the scientific evidence used in decision making?

4. When should a histogram be used to display data?

5. How do performance improvement and risk management relate to database management?

6. Identify the tools that could be used when a group needs to develop new ideas or organize the performance improvement project.

7. How would an organization examine its internal performance under ORYX?

8. How is information collected in the Compare reports for hospitals, nursing homes, and home health agencies?

9. During what stage of the utilization review process is the appropriateness of the admission assessed?

10. Why is it important to have accurate and clear documentation of the patient's discharge status?

ENRICHMENT ACTIVITY

Using Medicare's Web site, http://www.medicare.com, search for "Nursing Home Compare" and compare reports for nursing homes located in your geographic area. Compare the data from at least three individual nursing homes against the national and state averages. Report to your instructor the conclusions of your comparison. As an alternative, three hospitals or three home health agencies can be researched by searching on the Medicare home page for "Hospital Compare" or "Home Health Compare." Use the different comparison tools of your choice to display the data.

WEB SITES

Academy of Certified Case Managers, http://www.academyccm.org

Agency for Health Care Research and Quality, http://www.ahrq.gov

American Health Information Management Association, http://www.ahima.org

American Society for Quality, http://www.asq.com

Case Management Society of America, http://www.cmsa.org

Commission for Case Manager Certification, http://www.ccmcertification.org

Consumer Checkbook, http://www.checkbook.org

HealthGrades, http://www.healthgrades.com

Home Health Compare reports, http://www.medicare.gov/hhcompare/home.asp

Hospital Compare reports, http://www.hospitalcompare.hhs.gov/hospital/home.asp

Institute of Medicine, http://www.iom.edu

Joint Commission, http://www.jointcommission.org

Juran Institute, http://www.juran.com

Leap Frog Group, http://www.leapfroggroup.org

Malcolm Baldridge National Quality Program, http://www.quality.nist.gov

National Association for Healthcare Quality, http://www.nahq.org

National Committee for Quality Assurance, http://www.ncqa.org

NCQA's Health Plan Report Card, www.hprc.ncqa.org

Nursing Home Compare reports, http://www.medicare.gov/nhcompare/home.asp

Pennsylvania Health Care Cost Containment Council, http://www.phc4.org

Select Quality Care, http://www.selectqualitycare.com

Six Sigma, http://www.isixsigma.com

The W. Edwards Deming Institute, http://www.deming.org

WebMD, http://www.WebMD.com

REFERENCES

Carroll, R. (Ed.). (2004). *Risk management handbook for health care organizations* (4th ed.). San Francisco: Jossey-Bass.

Donabedian, A. (2003). *An introduction to quality assurance in health care.* Oxford, UK: Oxford University Press.

Green, M. A., & Bowie, M. J. (2005). *Essentials of health information management.* Clifton Park, NY: Delmar.

Institute of Medicine. (2001). *Crossing the quality chasm: A new health system for the 21st century.* Rockville, MD: Author.

Kavaler, F., & Spiegel, A. (2003). *Risk management in health care institutions: A strategic approach* (2nd ed.). Sudbury, MA: Jones and Bartlett.

LaTour, K., & Eichenwald, S. (2002). *Health information management concepts, principles, and practice.* Chicago: American Health Information Management Association.

Shaw, P., Elliott, C., Isaacson, P., & Murphy, E. (2003). *Quality and performance improvement in healthcare.* Chicago: American Health Information Management Association.

NOTES

1. Centers for Medicare and Medicaid Services (CMS) Resources, Glossary of Definitions, http://www.hospitalcompare.hhs.gov/.

2. See, e.g., *2003 Comprehensive Accreditation Manual for Hospitals: The Official Handbook,* Performance Improvement Measures PI.1–PI.5, Performance Measurement, and the ORYX Initiative.

3. http://www.tutor2u.net/business/production/quality_circles_kaisen.htm (last accessed May 20, 2006).

4. http://www.isixsigma.com/dictionary/Deming_cycle_PDCA-650.htm (last accessed May 20, 2006).

5. http://www.isixsigma.com/dictionary/FOCUS-_-PDCA-823.htm.

6. Donabedian A. (1966). *Evaluating the quality of medical care.* Retrieved March 5, 2007, from http://qshc.bmjjournals.com/cji/content/full/13/6/472

7. Public Law 100 107, signed into law on August 20, 1987, created the Malcolm Baldridge National Quality Award. See http://www.quality.nist.gov.

8. Six Sigma is a federally registered trademark of Motorola Corporation. See http://www.isixsigma.com.

9. Listings of other grants are available on the Agency for Healthcare Research and Quality Web site at http://www.ahrq.gov.

10. January 26, 2004. Wkly. Compilation Presidential Documents 94, 2004 WLNR 11425351.

11. Institute of Medicine. (2001). *Crossing the quality chasm: A new health system for the 21st century.* See http://www.iom.edu.

12. Nursing Home Compare reports available at http://www.medicare.gov/nhcompare/home.asp (last accessed 5/20/06).

13. Hospital Compare reports available at http://www.hospitalcompare.hhs.gov.

14. Medicare Prescription Drug Improvement and Modernization Act (MMA), 42 U.S.C. § 1395w (2007).

15. Hospital Report Card Act, 210 ILL. COMP. STAT. 86/1-99 (West 2007); Missouri Nosocomial Infection Control Act of 2004, MO. REV. STAT. § 192.667 (2007); Healthcare Cost Containment Act, PA. STAT. ANN. tit. 35, § 449.1-.19 (West 2007).

16. FLA. STAT. ANN. § 408.05 (1–3) (2007) (hospitals to report infection rates); N.Y. PUB. HEALTH LAW § 2819 (McKinney 2007) (hospitals to report nosocomial infections); VA. CODE ANN. § 32.1-35.1 (Michie 2007) (hospitals to report infections to federal and state authorities).

17. Joint Commission. (2003). *Comprehensive accreditation manual for hospitals: The official handbook, performance measurement, and the ORYX initiative* (IM.8, IM.10). Chicago: Author.

18. Ibid.

19. Ibid. Current core measures include: acute myocardial infarction (AMI), heart failure (HF), community acquired pneumonia (CAP), and pregnancy-related conditions (PR).

20. Information on CATCH may be found on the USF Center for Health Outcomes Research Web site at http://www.chor.hsc.usf.edu.

21. 45 C.F.R. § 164.306 (2007).

22. 45 C.F.R. § 164.306(e) (2007).

23. The 7th Scope of Work (SOW), Title XI of the Social Security Act, Part B, as amended by the Peer Review Act of 1982. Details of the workplan are available at http://www.cms.hhs.gov/QualityImprovementOrgs/04_sow.asp (last accessed 5/20/06).

24. 42 CFR, Part 456. Utilization Control, Subparts B and C (2007).

CHAPTER 8

Database Management

CERTIFICATION CONNECTION

RHIA

Data bases
Data dictionary sets
Data elements
Data integrity
Data mining
Data modeling
Data queries
Data sets
Data warehousing
Manage databases
Routine/custom reports

RHIT

Data integrity
Data sets
Data bases
Query/generate reports

LEARNING OBJECTIVES

After reading this chapter, the learner should be able to:

1. Define the terms *database* and *database management*.

2. Describe database design and its role in the information systems life cycle.

3. Trace the historical development of database management programs.

4. Explain the nature of data standards, particularly Health Level Seven as a messaging standard for hospital information systems.

5. Distinguish between the terms *clinical data repository, data warehouse, data mart,* and *data mining*.

6. Differentiate between the terms *data set, data element,* and *minimum data set*.

7. Identify the data sets most commonly used in health care institutions in the United States.

8. Trace the development of data exchange networks and identify efforts at the federal, state, and local levels to implement them.

Outline

Concepts and Functions

Database Design
Controls
Data Standards
Retrieval and Analysis Methods

Data Sets

Data Exchange

State and Local Data Exchange Efforts

Key Concepts

Access control

ASC X12

Clinical data repository

Concurrency control

Data

Database

Database design

Database design specification

Database management

Data dictionary

Data element

Data mapping

Data mart

Data mining

Data model

Data set

Data standards

Data warehouses

Electronic data interchange

Graphical user interface

Health Level Seven

Information

Information system

Integrity control

Interface

Interoperability

Limited data set

Minimum data set

National Health Information Infrastructure

Object query language

Online analytical processing

ORYX Initiative

Regional health information organization

Structured query language

Traceability

INTRODUCTION

A generation ago, communications among health care providers and patients, third-party payers, government agencies, consumer groups, and the public were limited in number, straightforward in nature, and allowed enough time for health care providers to feel that they had formed adequate responses to the inquiries received. As time has passed, communications have become more complex and demands have increased for complete and accurate information upon which to base decisions in a myriad of contexts. Health care providers have felt pressure as a result of having insufficient time to respond to the information demands made upon them in this modern age. One response to these circumstances has been the automation of the collection and storage of data and the retrieval of information. The manner in which collection, storage, and retrieval operate constitutes database management.

Database management is central to the practice of health information management (HIM) in many respects. The health information management professional is responsible for the management of information found in the patient's health record. The health record provides a wealth of data concerning patient encounters with health care providers. These individualized patient data, combined with the massive amounts of data generated by health care providers, are captured using automated systems. The value of these data depends upon the uses to which they are put. Through sophisticated programming, these data can be retrieved, analyzed, and presented to serve a variety of functions, including strategic planning, policy formation, patient education, and operational support.

Database management is also central to other areas related to health care and health information management. Two areas of particular significance are statistics and research. In the modern age, both areas are intimately connected with database management because data are now collected, stored, and retrieved using automated methods. The proper management of databases can assist in ensuring statistical validity and the correct design of research studies.

To properly manage and safeguard data, it is important that the health information professional possess a fundamental knowledge of database management. This chapter provides an understanding of the development and management of database systems, beginning with a discussion of concepts and functions. The concept of data sets is then explored to illustrate the broad uses of data by both external and internal users. A discussion of data exchange efforts across geographic regions completes the chapter.

Concepts and Functions

To understand the concept of database management, one must first understand the definitions supporting the phrase. Data generally refers to raw facts and figures. Considered by themselves, these raw facts and figures are meaningless and pose little value to individuals and organizations. By contrast, information refers to knowledge that results from the processing of data, or so-called "meaningful data." Data that are processed and organized in such a way that they become meaningful provide value to individuals and organizations. It is this information that serves as the basis for decision making at the clinical, operational, and administrative levels. A database is the structured storage or collection of data on multiple entities and their relationships, often arranged for ease and speed of retrieval. In other words, it is a large collection of related data stored in a computer. A database serves as a tool to process and organize large amounts of data into information. Data are added to a database and modified using a common and controlled approach. A **data dictionary** contains the standardized definitions of each data element in a database. **Data mapping** refers to the process of linking terminology between two different schemes—a target and a source—for a given purpose. **Database management** refers to the ability to manage a database so as to create, modify, delete, and view given data as necessary. The goal of database management is to provide end users with the meaningful data they need to perform their jobs as efficiently as possible.

Databases are a relatively new concept that emerged with the advent of computers. Table 8–1 outlines the development of database management during the past century. Using early computer systems, data were stored in files of records that were managed by an unsophisticated file system. These file systems would allow a user to create and delete files, insert new data into records, and update and retrieve data. Utilizing such a system, an application software program had to be written to define, maintain, and use the database. Any time a change occurred in the type of data entered or the way the database was used, the application program required modification. This traditional form of file processing worked because the data were embedded in the application program. As a result of this inherent inflexibility, traditional file processing proved limited in its usefulness to the work environment.

Beginning in the 1960s, database management programs were developed that could operate on any set of stored data found in a system catalog. This differed from the traditional file processing approach because the data were no longer embedded in the application program and therefore only workable in a specific database; these newer programs were independent of the programs that used them. Database management programs also had the ability to control redundant data and allow access to multiple users at the same time. This ability to share data proved particularly useful because it allowed one person access to a database in read mode (i.e., to obtain specific information stored in the database) and another person access to the same database in write mode (i.e., to update the database) all at the same time. These database management programs revolutionized the practical nature of computers in the work environment because all ranges of data could be accessed and all ranges of users could be served, from the naive end user to the sophisticated database administrator.

Database management programs continued to develop in the decades that followed. In the late 1960s, the hierarchical model emerged, which structures data in a certain order. The relational model emerged in the early 1970s, wherein data are stored in one or more relations or tables containing attributes. The relations and attributes are then displayed in two-dimensional arrays, similar to a spreadsheet. For example, personnel data may be stored in a relational database to connect employee names with employee numbers, departments, or salaries. Relational databases store data such as currency, real numbers, integers, and strings (characters of data). The development of relational databases spurred private companies in the 1980s to develop commercial products for installation in the work environment. Examples of these products include Oracle, Informix, Sybase, and Access.

As these commercial products became widely used, limitations to the relational database approach emerged, generally with regard to the challenges posed by nonstandard or sophisticated applications. Accordingly, a new object-oriented model emerged in the 1990s. As the name indicates, object-oriented databases store objects (discrete or abstract things) and advanced data types such as graphics, movies, and audio. The 21st century has seen the combination of the relational and object-oriented models, called the object-relational model. Such a model incorporates both traditional data—such as currency, integers, and real numbers—and advanced data types—such as graphics, movies, and audio.

Table 8–1 | Stages in the Development of Database Management

1940s	1960s	1970s–1980s	1990s	Present
Computers and databases	Data-sharing and hierarchical model	Relational model	Object-oriented model	Object-relational model
Direct integration of database and database application	Application no longer embedded in database	Data stored in one or more relations or tables	Storage of objects and advanced data types	Integration of traditional data with objects and advanced data
Limited in usefulness in work environment	Practical for use in work environment	Development of commercial products for use in work environment	Helpful for nonstandard or sophisticated applications	Useful for even more sophisticated applications

Table 8–2 | Database Design Specification

General Information	A summary of the purpose and general functions of the software application
	The organization, technical, and operational environments
Description	Identification of the functional name of the database, the conventions used, any special instructions, and the support software
Logical Characteristics	An overview of the design, including rationale, data model, structure diagram, and file/table descriptions
Physical Characteristics	The online and off-line storage required, including access methods and system-dependent limitations

End users interact with a database through graphical user interfaces or query languages. A **graphical user interface** (GUI) is a method of displaying text and graphics on a computer screen. Using GUI, picture icons are displayed on a computer screen to help the end user develop a mental model of the operation of the computer. Virtually every personal computer in use today utilizes GUIs. **Structured query language** (SQL) is a language used by nonprogrammers to retrieve information contained in relational databases. **Object query language** (OQL) is an extension of SQL that can be used with object-oriented databases. A detailed explanation of how to use these query languages is beyond the scope of this book; however, either query language can be used to query and retrieve data and to generate reports from their respective databases.

Today, databases proliferate at all levels of American culture. Databases store data on practically any topic imaginable. As a result of increases in the power of computer storage, databases continue to grow in storage capacity. Not only are more data captured, new types of data are now being added to databases. The total number of databases is unknown because new databases can be created at any time. As individuals and organizations gain more understanding of the power data can offer them, additional efforts will be made to organize those data into databases that allow even faster, more efficient retrieval of information.

Database Design

Whenever a new database is required or an existing database needs revision, the practice of database design is employed. **Database design** refers to a description of the logical and physical characteristics of an operational database. The logical characteristics address the structuring of the database into one or more files, the composition of data elements within those files, the relationships among those files, and file indexing. The physical characteristics address storage devices, access methods, and physical constraints. These characteristics are defined and described in a document commonly referred to as a database design specification.

A **database design specification** defines and describes where the data created, retrieved, updated, or deleted by a software application resides, both logically and physically, and specifies the format the data possesses. Additionally,

the specification provides the rationale for the decisions made during database design and relates them to the system or application requirements previously decided. The specification serves the purpose of **traceability**—the mechanism employed to track computer data elements, records, and files back to their antecedent user requirements. This traceability functions as an audit trail, ensuring that changes to the database are maintained. Many specifications also include the application data dictionary as an appendix to the document. An outline of a typical database design specification is found in Table 8–2.

Database design is a function of the information systems life cycle and typically occurs toward the beginning of the cycle. The design specification arises from the documentation produced at the time an application's requirements are defined and from the alternatives analysis indicating that an application should be developed. More information concerning the information systems life cycle may be found in Chapter 13, "Information Systems and Technology."

Database design requires the involvement of many people. If database design occurs as part of project management, the project manager possesses responsibility over the project direction and execution. Someone in a management capacity—a project manager, product administrator, or another manager—must ensure that all appropriate technical reviews take place that check for completeness and accuracy. Computer programmers and analysts must write the programming code and supporting documentation. End users of the application often participate in a review of the design specification, correcting or concurring as warranted. If the project or system is particularly large, a system librarian may be engaged to control and maintain documentation in an electronic or physical form. By identifying and defining the responsibilities of each person involved in database design, the probability of a successful design increases.

An essential component of database design is data modeling. A **data model** is a representation of exactly what a database should exemplify to the end user, specifying the structures to be used, the operations that will validate and manipulate the structures, what types of records will be held, what fields each will contain, and the types of relationships among the various data items stored in the database. Data modeling systems generally fall within two categories: the entity-relationship model and the semantic object model.

Figure 8–1 | Simple entity-relationship model

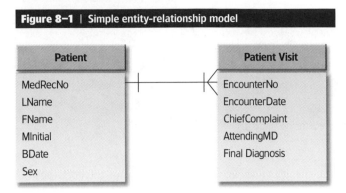

The entity-relationship (E-R) model is the more frequently used data model and applies to the relational database concept. Four elements comprise the E-R model: entities, attributes, identifiers, and relationships. An entity is something that the end user wishes to identify and track, such as a person, place, thing, or concept. Entity classes are groupings of entities, such as all of the items that relate to a patient. An attribute is a fact or piece of information about an entity that would be of interest to the end user. Using the patient example, attributes

may include name, date of birth, address, and so forth. An identifier is a combination of attributes used to uniquely identify an entity; a Social Security number is a unique identifier of a U.S. resident. A relationship is an association between entities. Relationships may vary by degrees; some relationships exist between just two entity classes, whereas other relationships exist among multiple entity classes. An entity is represented by a rectangle, with attributes either listed below the entity title or shown as ovals and relationships shown as diamonds or arrows. Figure 8–I illustrates a simplified entity relationship, listing the attributes under the entity title and showing arrows instead of diamonds.

The semantic object model (SOM) focuses on semantic objects, which are collections of attributes and identifiers that sufficiently describe a distinct entity. The difference offered by the SOM approach is that objects contain not only attributes and identifiers but also the operations or processes that the objects can perform. Like entities, these semantic objects can be grouped into classes. Figure 8–2 illustrates a semantic object model.

Figure 8–2 | Semantic object model

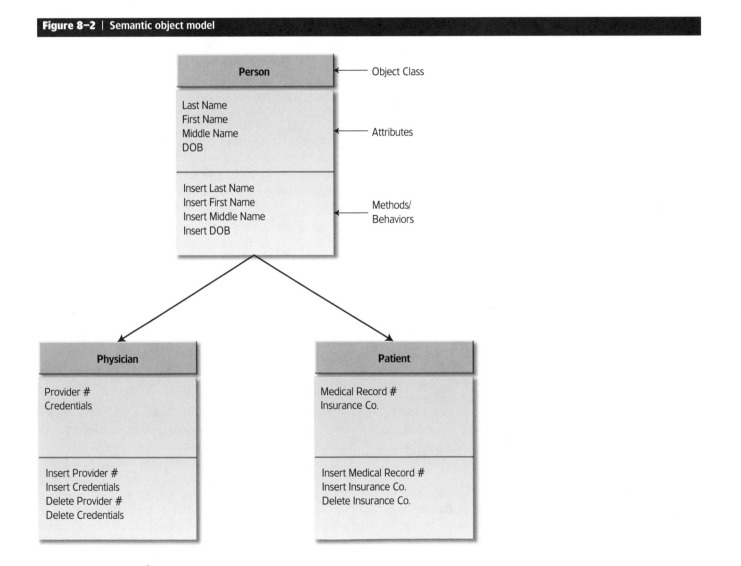

If health information management professionals are to participate in database design, they must possess the knowledge, skills, and abilities required to succeed. These include an understanding of how databases function, the purposes they serve for the end user, and the models used; fluency in structured query language; knowledge of database programs; the ability to perform data retrieval and reporting functions; and the ability to normalize data. These knowledge, skills, and abilities—combined with such skills as the ability to communicate effectively, solve problems creatively, and interact with a wide variety of people—will assist the HIM professional in both developing and managing databases.

Controls

Certain controls are necessary for a database to function properly. Concurrency control refers to the ability of a database to resolve a conflict between two simultaneous uses of the same portion of the same database. For example, two hospital employees may independently access the database at the same time to schedule two different patients for an appointment for the same diagnostic test during the same desired time slot. Using concurrency control, the database would limit access to only one of these two hospital employees and effectively lock out or block the other hospital employee's access. The end result is that only one patient is scheduled for an appointment for the diagnostic test during the desired time slot, instead of two patients scheduled for the same time. This should not be confused with the concurrency that is allowed when different functions are involved. The hospital employee can still schedule the patient if another hospital employee accesses the database for a different function (e.g., to retrieve data on the number of patients with scheduled appointments on a certain date).

A second control function is access control. Access control involves the level of permission granted to a particular user. Utilizing passwords that are tied to permission levels, a database management system may restrict access to portions of the database. This type of access control operates within many organizations, granting certain permission levels to clinicians so they can access data for those patients under their care but blocking other clinicians from accessing the same data if they do not care for the same patients. Similarly, access levels can be differentiated by operating department, allowing members of one department access to portions of data but allowing members of another department access to a wider portion of the same data. For example, members of a radiology department may have access to a database that allows them to see not only what radiology tests were conducted but the results of those tests. By contrast, members of the finance department may have access to that portion of the database that lists the radiology tests that generate a charge to the patient, but they will have no access to the results of the tests.

A third control function is integrity control. Integrity control refers to the ability of the database management system to check all entered data against specified constraints or rules and to determine whether there is an inconsistency. Integrity controls prevent an authorized user from entering certain data incorrectly. For example, a user who tries to enter scheduling data for an appointment on a day when a department or clinic is closed would be caught through integrity control.

Data Standards

As the number of databases used in the health care setting increases, so does the risk for redundant information systems. Furthermore, information systems that cannot communicate in a meaningful way severely limit the use of information, both within and outside an organization. This limitation decreases market opportunities and increases the cost of equipment and services to users. The need to develop a common approach to representing and exchanging health data became apparent in the 1980s as the number of databases increased and it became nearly impossible to link data from one site to another—hence, the development of data standards. Data standards are uniform uses of common terms and methods for sharing data. For example, the data standard commonly used to display a patient's date of birth is "yyyymmdd." Data standards are often grouped into the categories of messaging, vocabulary, networking, security, and authentication. Data standards that deal with uniform nomenclature and classification systems are addressed in Chapter 6, "Nomenclatures and Classification Systems"; data standards that deal with communication among databases are addressed in this chapter.

Data standards benefit many people within the health care community: those who collect data from outside sources; those who enter it into the computer system; those who analyze it; those who verify its findings; those who communicate the information for use in patient care, financial matters, and administrative planning; and those who use it to compare data across health care sites. Because so many individuals and organizations benefit from the use of data standards, many voluntary organizations have become involved in standards development. The two main U.S. entities that are responsible for coordinating the efforts of standards development organizations (SDOs) are the American National Standards Institute (ANSI) and the Workgroup for Electronic Data Interchange (WEDI).

ANSI is a voluntary organization that serves to accredit and coordinate the work of qualified groups that develop national standards within the private sector. ANSI is the sole U.S. member of the International Standards Organization (ISO). ANSI works by facilitating an open forum to identify, plan, and agree upon standards. Once consensus is developed, ANSI promotes the agreed-upon standards within the United States and internationally.

Within the health care arena, ANSI works through its Health Care Informatics Standards Board (HISB) to coordinate the work of SDOs. For example, ANSI-HISB has developed standard data submission forms to be used with electronic billing systems, obviating the need to use proprietary forms. Other standards areas addressed by ANSI-HISB are the electronic health record, coding, terminology, international data exchanges, and patient privacy.

WEDI is a formal organization commissioned by the U.S. Department of Health and Human Services to identify ways of increasing the use of electronic billing to reduce administrative costs. WEDI has developed an action plan to promote electronic data interchange standards, architectures, confidentiality, identifiers, and health cards, among other areas.

To understand data standards, one must first understand the concepts of information systems and interfaces. An **information system** is a set of connecting and communicating computers, devices, and software that support the delivery of patient care and the day-to-day business of health care. For example, a laboratory may have its own information system composed of separate computers, each with its own purpose and format for communicating (e.g., one for blood testing, another for serum chemistry, and a third for specimen tracking). In this example, a laboratory information system is composed of all three computers with their associated devices and software. An **interface** is the hardware or software necessary to connect the components of an information system together or to connect one information system to another. In the laboratory information system example, the interface makes it possible for one person to access the lab data from all three computers at a single computer terminal.

To make an interface successful, it is necessary to look beyond the physical connection between systems; one must also apply a logical approach to the communication of the data itself. Among the most successful, cost-effective, and dynamic methods of sharing data is the use of electronic data interchange. **Electronic data interchange** (EDI), sometimes referred to as electronic messaging, is a method of electronic mail messaging that is conveyed among computers without manual intervention. A successful mail messaging system requires the use of standards to convey the syntax and semantics of a message. In other words, standards are rules for the description, storage, and transmission of messages or the composition of a program statement. Such rules or messaging standards are needed to sequence data elements in a stream of data, to define how a data element is recognized, and to format individual items. Within the health care context, messaging standards delineate how clinical information is sent among users (e.g., who sent the information, who received it, and the name of the patient who is the subject of the information exchange).

The two major messaging standards development organizations for health information are Health Level Seven (HL7) and Accredited Standards Committee (ASC) X12. **Health Level Seven** is an ANSI-accredited SDO that develops specifications that allow different health care software applications within an organization to communicate with one another. As a generality, these specifications apply within the health care environment to clinical decision support systems.

The most widely used HL7 specification is the Application Protocol for Electronic Data Exchange in Healthcare Environments. This application allows for the immediate electronic transmission of data among systems once data are originally entered. For example, the application would allow the finance department of a hospital to create, without manual intervention, an electronic account for a patient immediately after a hospital employee enters data about the patient into a software application at the time of admission, discharge, or transfer. The opportunity for mistakes in data entry is reduced by creating the finance account electronically, as is the need to purchase or develop customized software programs to allow for an exchange of data.

Similar to HL7, **ASC X12** is an ANSI-accredited SDO that develops specifications for communication among software applications. It differs from HL7, however, in that the focus is on developing a national standard for exchanging business information so as to facilitate business-to-business operations. Such business transactions include ordering, shipping, and invoicing products. The most widely used specification, referred to as X12N, deals with standards related to insurance and reimbursement by private third-party payers and government health care programs such as Medicare and Medicaid. Many other messaging SDOs exist that establish specifications for certain areas of health care. A listing of these SDOs is found in Table 8–3.

HIPAA

The Administrative Simplification provisions establish data standards for data exchange performed electronically.

Both of these data standards are very important to the data exchange initiatives developed as a result of the Administrative Simplification Provisions of the Health Insurance Portability and Accountability Act (HIPAA). HIPAA has established that health care providers must supply certain data through electronic means to facilitate claims processing. These data may be both financial and clinical in nature, because both may be needed to determine the appropriateness of a specific claim. As noted above, the secretary of Health and Human Services (HHS) has chosen X12N for claims processing of financial data and HL7 as the standard for communicating clinical content. In practical terms, the provider transports both sets of data to Medicare in a "wrapped" fashion, with the header and footer of the message in X12N and the content of the message in HL7. By doing so, the provider can transmit information that involves two data standards in just one transaction.

Table 8–3 | Standards Development Organizations That Establish Messaging Standards

HL7	Health Level Seven	Clinically focused
ASCX12	Accredited Standards Committee	Business focused
DICOM	Digital Imaging and Communication in Medicine	Radiology focused
ASTM Communication Standards	American Society for Testing and Materials	Broadly focused to include clinical laboratory, emergency care, and health records
ASTM International	American Society for Testing and Materials	Focused on products, materials, systems, and services across more than 130 industries
IEEE Medical Information Bus	Institute of Electrical and Electronic Engineers	Medical device communications focused
Publish Health Data Standards Consortium	Part of the National Center for Health Statistics	Public health focused
NCPDP	National Council on Prescription Drug Programs	Pharmacy prescription focused

HL7 is of particular importance to the health information management profession because it has been selected by the National Committee on Vital and Health Statistics (NCVHS) as the standard for electronic exchange of core patient health record information. As such, it will influence the development of the electronic health record for years to come.

HL7 is also central to the National Electronic Disease Surveillance System (NEDSS), a recently released automated technology application sponsored by the Centers for Disease Control and Prevention (CDC). NEDSS standardizes those data elements fundamental to creating a public health database that allows for epidemiological analysis. Some suggest that NEDSS may assist in the development of a national public health database that can be used in the bioterrorism context, including early detection and monitoring.[1]

All of these standards provide support for the effort to create a National Health Information Infrastructure (NHII), also referred to as a National Health Information Network (NHIN). Sponsored by the National Committee on Vital and Health Statistics (NCVHS), a public advisory body to the U.S. Secretary of Health and Human Services, the NHII is an attempt to create a knowledge-based system capable of delivering information to consumers, patients, and health care professionals when and where they need it to make informed health care decisions. The NHII includes technologies, standards, applications, systems, values, and laws that support all facets of individual health, health care, and public health. It also includes tools such as clinical practice guidelines, educational resources for health professionals and the public, geographic information systems, health statistics at all levels of government, and many forms of communication among users.[2]

This joint public and private effort focuses on many areas of health care. The focus on defining the recommended archi-

tecture under NHII describes where patient data will be stored, how data will be moved and retrieved, and how patients will be identified. A central focus of NHII is the further development of patient health record information (PMRI) standards, which will allow individual health record data to be collected, stored, and retrieved in the chosen architecture according to common standards for data exchange and content. For example, standards specifications can assist the health care facility in exercising their duty to promptly report vital statistics and diseases to public health authorities. Further foci include creating consistency with the health data mandates stemming from HIPAA; enhancing public health preparedness, especially as it relates to bioterrorism or chemical threat; ensuring confidentiality of electronically transmitted information; ensuring appropriate exchange and use of data for research and population health purposes; and improving patient safety and the quality of care.

Retrieval and Analysis Methods

As the demands for health care information to be used in decision making have increased, the need for more complex retrieval and analysis methods has also grown. Three responses to these demands based on database management systems are clinical data repositories, data warehousing, and data mining. A clinical data repository is the electronic storage of data and information from individual patient medical records. This single database captures information from numerous systems, including digital images, and aggregates and reorganizes the data over time. Uses of a clinical data repository include real-time analysis of a patient's health status and development of reports. State data systems that require information from health care facilities and provider organizations are examples of a clinical data repository.

Data warehouses are very large databases that store both historical and current information from a variety of sources and are optimized for fast query answering. Typically, multiple databases exist within a large health care setting such as a hospital; patient data may be stored in one database, laboratory result data may be stored in a second database, and pharmacy data may be stored in a third database. In this scenario, selected data from each of these separate databases are extracted and housed in a data warehouse. As a result of this extraction process, the data in the warehouse are accurate up to the point in time at which they were extracted—a "snapshot," so to speak. At the time of extraction, the data are scrubbed to remove duplicate records and inconsistent coding, and to standardize name and address formats. The data are stored in the warehouse according to design techniques that utilize data tables, and relationships between the tables. Utilizing these tables and the relationships among them, an end user can access data housed in the data warehouse and combine the results into a single question-and-reporting interface. End users accomplish this through data analysis programs called **online analytical processing** (OLAP) applications. A data warehouse works retrospectively to report trends, offer comparisons, and provide strategic analyses. Examples of uses of a data warehouse in the health care setting are found in Table 8–4.

A subset of a data warehouse is a **data mart**. A data mart is restricted to a single business process/function or a group of related business processes/functions targeted toward a particular business group. This stands in contrast to the data warehouse, which can store data for an entire organization. Some organizations use data marts as alternatives to data warehouses because they are less complex, easier to maintain, and less costly overall. Although data marts do not contain a wide scope of data, they can be efficient and effective for specific departments or business units within an organization.

Data mining refers to the process of finding unknown dependencies in large data sets using automated means. Data mining uses automated pattern recognition to uncover patterns in data that may be difficult to detect with traditional statistical methods. Once discovered, these data can be analyzed to predict future trends and determine how to proceed with action. Specialized software techniques are required to conduct data mining. Examples include decision trees, genetic algorithms, neural networks, predictive modeling, rule induction, and fuzzy logic. Data warehouses and data mining are related, in that data warehouses are a good source of data to be mined. Similarly, the value of data warehouses is optimized through the use of data mining.

To illustrate the concepts of data warehousing and data mining, it is instructive to think of making purchases at a grocery store. Many grocery stores use sophisticated databases to accumulate data about the purchasing habits of their customers. By using online analytical processing applications, the grocery store management can obtain information about purchasing trends, compare sales of different products within a given category, and even create associations between customers' past behavior and what they may purchase in the future. This latter feature can assist the grocery store management in creating a personalized experience for the customer by presenting to the customers data that interest them (e.g., by issuing coupons for products based on the purchases made at the time of checkout). This ability to spot trends, offer comparisons, and create associations places the grocery store in a more competitive position than their rivals in the same industry.

Although data warehousing and data mining techniques have been used in commercial industry for some time, they are still new to the health care industry. In this context, it is instructive to think of data warehousing and data mining with regard to a master patient index (MPI). By definition, an MPI is a database that receives data from multiple sources, contains both historical and current information, and is used for fast query answering. As such, MPIs are sometimes viewed as data warehouses. The challenge to maintain clean data is present when using an MPI, just as it is when using other databases. The main challenge of an MPI is the presence of duplicate records for the same patient. Numerous types of algorithms are employed to compare a user's query with the data previously entered in the MPI, resulting in a list of those data contained within the MPI that best match the user's query. Data in the MPI can be mined to detect patterns, such as where the facility's patient population resides and how it has changed over time, the variations in length of stay over different time periods, and the ages and genders of the patient population. Based on the data that are mined, health care facilities can run predictive models for use in strategic planning and other purposes.

Data Sets

Health care data sets came about as a result of the need to compare hospital discharge data between institutions. A **data set** is a list of recommended data elements with uniform definitions. A **data element** is a single fact or measurement. A **minimum data set** is an agreed-upon and accepted set of terms and uniform definitions that constitute a core of data; in other words, it is a collection of related data items for each patient. Minimum data sets allow for comparisons among the nation's health care facilities because they provide a uniform system with which to collect and report data, all using a standard definition. Minimum data sets also serve the purposes of verifying the provision of services for reimbursement purposes, satisfying reporting

Table 8–4	Uses of a Data Warehouse
Determining the impact of funding changes through patient activity costing
Extracting utilization reports and statistics
Extracting billing patterns
Providing access to data from incompatible, previously isolated systems

Source: Adapted from Handbook of Medical Informatics J.H. van Bemmel & M.A. Musen, Springer-Verlag (1997).

requirements of external accreditation, and supplying data for statistical and research studies.

Data sets categorize patients according to personal characteristics, services received, facilities used, and sources of payment. Data sets can be separated into those that are mandated for reporting purposes to government agencies, those that are recommended for reporting purposes to government agencies, and those that are used for reporting purposes to private entities. Data sets most commonly used by health care institutions in the United States include the Uniform Hospital Discharge Data Set, the Minimum Data Set for Long-Term Care, the Outcome and Assessment Information Set, the National Practitioner Data Bank, the Uniform Ambulatory Care Data Set, the Data Elements for Emergency Department Systems, the Health Plan Employer Data and Information Set, and the ORYX Initiative. These data sets and others are listed in Table 8–5.

The Uniform Hospital Discharge Data Set (UHDDS) is a minimum data set used for reporting by short-term general hospitals in the United States. In effect since its adoption in 1974 by the U.S. Department of Health and Human Services' predecessor agency, the UHDDS has applied to all short-term general hospitals treating patients enrolled in the Medicare and Medicaid programs. The department, through its subordinate agency, the National Committee on Vital and Health Statistics (NCVHS), has revised the UHDDS several times. Furthermore, the department has incorporated the UHDDS into its rules and regulations governing the use of diagnosis-related groups (DRGs), making it a required data set for reporting purposes. Since 1986 the UHDDS has been applicable to all federal programs. Because virtually all short-term general hospitals treat Medicare and Medicaid patients, the UHDDS has become a standard for reporting across all patient categories to both the state and private sectors. The federal and state governments compare health

care facility discharge data reported through UHDDS. Table 8–6 illustrates the current UHDDS data elements that are required to be reported.

The Minimum Data Set for Long-Term Care (MDS) is a minimum data set applicable to long-term care settings. Long-term care patients are persons who cannot live independently because of chronic illness or disability and therefore live in residential facilities to receive health care services. Originally adopted by the U.S. Department of Health and Human Services in 1980 and updated several times since, the MDS addresses both patient background and health problems. Similar to the UHDDS, the MDS has been incorporated into the rules and regulations governing long-term care facilities treating patients enrolled in the Medicare and Medicaid programs, making it a required data set for reporting purposes. A fuller listing of these data categories may be found in Table 8–7. The MDS operates in conjunction with Resident Assessment Protocols, which require assessment of the patient within 14 days of admission and at least annually, or more frequently if a significant change in the patient's condition occurs. Each time the patient is assessed, the elements of the MDS are collected and the resident's care plan is revised as needed.

The Outcome Assessment and Information Set (OASIS) is a minimum data set applicable to home health settings. Regulations issued in 1999 by the U.S. Department of Health and Human Services pursuant to the Omnibus Budget Reconciliation Act (OBRA) of 1987 address the collection of OASIS data for Medicare beneficiaries. The core data elements collected include clinical record items, patient demographics and history, living arrangements, and patient health status. A fuller listing of these data categories can be found in Table 8–8.

Unlike the data sets discussed previously, the National Practitioner Data Bank is not by itself a minimum data set

Table 8–5	Common Health Care Data Sets	
Mandatory Reporting to Governmental Agencies	
Uniform Hospital Discharge Data Set (UHDDS)	Applicable to short-term general hospitals
Minimum Data Set for Long-Term Care (MDS)	Applicable to long-term care facilities
Outcome Assessment Information Set (OASIS)	Applicable to home health settings
National Practitioner Data Bank (NPDB)	Applicable to malpractice payments and other adverse actions taken against physicians
Healthcare Integrity and Protection Data Bank (HIPDB)	Applicable to final adverse actions involving fraud and abuse
Medical Provider Analysis and Review Files (MEDPAR)	Applicable to Medicare claims data
Recommended Reporting to Governmental Agencies	
Uniform Ambulatory Care Data Set (UACDS)	Applicable to ambulatory care settings
Data Elements for Emergency Department Systems (DEEDS)	Applicable to emergency and trauma care settings
Recommended Reporting to Private Entities	
Health Plan Employer Data and Information Set (HEDIS)	Applicable to managed care plans
ORYX Initiative	Applicable to the accreditation process

Table 8-6 | UHDDS Data Elements

Data Element	Notes
Patient Identification	Unique number differentiating patient from all other patients treated by the institution
Date of Birth	Month, day, and year
Sex	
Race and Ethnicity	
Residence	Full address and, if available, nine-digit ZIP code or code of foreign residence
Hospital Identification Number	Medicare provider number recommended
Admission Date	Month, day, and year
Type of Admission	Scheduled or unscheduled
Discharge Date	Month, day, and year
Attending Physician Identification	Unique personal identification number (UPIN)
Operating Physician Identification	Unique personal identification number (UPIN)
Principal Diagnosis	
Other Diagnosis	All conditions that coexist at the time of admission, or that develop subsequently, that affect the treatment received or the length of stay
Qualifier for Other Diagnosis	Indicating whether the onset of the diagnosis preceded or followed admission to the health care facility
External Cause of Injury Code	Indicating whether there has been a diagnosis of an injury, poisoning, or adverse effect
Birth Weight of Neonate	
Procedures and Dates	
Disposition of Patient	
Patient's Expected Source of Payment	
Total Charges	

Source: The U.S. Department of Health and Human Services, http://www.aspe.hhs.gov/datacncl.

but is the repository of a series of minimum data sets, all dealing with the professional competence and conduct of physicians, dentists, and other health care professionals. The data sets used for the National Practitioner Data Bank concern malpractice payments, licensure actions, and adverse actions such as the loss of staff privileges of physicians and dentists. The data must be reported to the Data Bank by hospitals, medical societies, licensing boards, prepaid medical practices, and other health care entities. In addition, these same entities are required to query the Data Bank whenever they receive an application for a position on the medical staff, and on a routine basis thereafter. A fuller listing of these data categories can be found in Table 8-9.

Table 8-7 | Minimum Data Set Long-Term Care Data Elements

Resident Background
Cognitive Abilities
Behavioral Patterns
Ability to Perform the Activities of Daily Living
Health Problems
Specific Body Systems Review
Physical Functioning
Psychological Status

Source: U.S. Department of Health and Human Services, http://www.aspe.hhs.gov/datacncl.

Table 8-8 | OASIS Data Elements

Clinical Record Items
Patient Demographics and History
Living Arrangements
Supportive Assistance
Activities of Daily Living
Equipment Management
Medications
Therapy Need
Emergent Care
Inpatient Facility Admission/Agency Discharge
Patient Health Status (Sensory Status, Integumentary Status, Respiratory Status, Elimination Status, Neuro/Emotional/Behavioral Status)

Source: U.S. Department of Health and Human Services, 2007, http://www.cms.hhs.gov/OASIS; Center for Health Services and Policy Research, Denver, CO.

Table 8–9 | Data Sets Used for the National Practitioner Data Bank

The physician's, dentist's, or licensed health care practitioner's name, date of birth, work address, and, if known, home address and Social Security number
The name of each professional school attended and the year of graduation
For each professional license, the physician's, dentist's, or licensed health care practitioner's license number, the field of licensure, and the name of the state or territory in which the license is held
The physician's, dentist's, or licensed health care practitioner's Drug Enforcement Administration registration number, if known
A description of the acts, omissions, or other reasons for the claim, sanction, or adverse action taken
If involving a malpractice allegation, the payment amount, date of payment, and whether the payment is for a judgment or settlement
A description of the board's or entity's action, the date the action was taken, and its effective date
Classification of the action in accordance with a reporting code adopted by the Secretary of Health and Human Services

Source: U.S. Department of Health and Human Services, http://www.aspe.hhs.gov/datacncl.

The Uniform Ambulatory Care Data Set (UACDS) is a minimum data set applicable to ambulatory care settings. Adopted in 1989 by the National Committee on Vital and Health Statistics, it is recommended for use with all ambulatory care patients—those patients who return to their homes the same day they receive care. Unlike the UHDDS, the UACDS is not a required data set for reporting purposes because it has not been incorporated into federal rules and regulations. Accordingly, it is a recommended data set. Three major areas are addressed in the data set: patient data, provider data, and encounter data. A fuller listing of these data categories may be found in Table 8–10.

The Data Elements for Emergency Department Systems (DEEDS) is a minimum data set applicable to hospital-based emergency rooms. DEEDS originated through the collaborative efforts of the American College of Emergency Physicians, the Emergency Nurses Association, and the American Health Information Management Association. The U.S.

Department of Health and Human Services, through its subordinate agency the Centers for Disease Control and Prevention, recommends the use of DEEDS to collect data involving emergency and trauma care services. DEEDS address patient data, provider data, and encounter data. A fuller listing of these data element categories can be found in Table 8–11.

The Health Plan Employer Data and Information Set (HEDIS) is a minimum data set applicable to managed health care plans. Unlike the previously listed data sets, HEDIS did not originate or proliferate because of the efforts of the federal government. Rather, HEDIS originated as a result of the efforts of the National Committee for Quality Assurance (NCQA), as a means to collect administrative and claims data along with health care data for patients participating in managed care plans. The data collected are used primarily to assess the outcomes of treatment, measure the effectiveness of a managed care plan's efforts to improve the functional status of its enrolled patients, and compare managed care plans against one another. On a secondary level, HEDIS data are used toward performance improvement efforts and developing physician profiles. HEDIS includes more than 60 measures, including patient outcome and treatment process. A fuller listing of the domains in which these measures fall can be found in Table 8–12.

Table 8–10 | Uniform Ambulatory Care Data Set Data Elements

Patient Data	Personal identification
	Residence
	Date of Birth (month, day, and year)
	Sex
	Race and ethnicity
	Living arrangement and marital status (optional)
Provider Data	Provider identification (name and UPIN)
	Location or address
	Profession (M.D., D.O., D.D.S., etc.)
Encounter Data	Date, place or site, and address of encounter
	Patient's reason for encounter (optional)
	Services (diagnostic, therapeutic, or preventative)
	Disposition (to follow-up or follow-up planned)
	Patient's expected source of payment
	Total charges

Table 8–11 | Data Elements for Emergency Department Systems

Patient Identification Data	
Facility and Practitioner Identification Data	
Encounter Data	Arrival and First Encounter Data
	History and Physical Examination Data
	Procedure and Result Data
	Medication Data
	Disposition and Diagnosis Data

Source: Centers for Disease Control and Prevention, 2007, http://www.cdc.gov.

Table 8–12 | HEDIS Domains

Effectiveness of Care, Access/Availability of Care
Health Plan Stability
Health Plan Descriptive Information
Satisfaction with the Experience of Care
Use of Services
Cost of Care
Source: HEDIS 2007, National Committee for Quality Assurance, http://www.ncqa.org.

The ORYX Initiative is a minimum data set applicable to the accreditation process. Similar to HEDIS, the ORYX Initiative originated as a private sector endeavor. The Joint Commission (JC), formerly known as the Joint Commission on Accreditation of Healthcare Organizations (JCAHO), developed and introduced the ORYX Initiative in an effort to integrate the results of patient care into the accreditation process. The ORYX Initiative establishes data sets for core measures, allowing for standardization of the data collection process across health care facilities. This standardization is useful in examining both a health care organization's performance over time and how it compares to other health care organizations. Such examinations and comparisons are used to determine accreditation status. A listing of the current core measures required by the JC can be found in Table 8–13.

HIPAA

Data set requirements are governed by the Electronic Transactions and Code Sets Rule.

Of recent note are the data set requirements put forth by HIPAA, which address what sets of data are required for purposes of electronic transmission. The data sets referred to by HIPAA are governed by the Electronic Transactions and Code Sets Rule. The rule's intent is to make claims processing more efficient, reduce costs, and improve service for covered entities and patients. Although not all health care providers are required to use the rule for service billing, they are encouraged to do so. All health plans, however, are required to comply with this rule when accepting claims submitted by health care providers who use the standard electronic form.

Table 8–13 | ORYX Initiative Core Measures

Acute Myocardial Infarction
Heart Failure
Pneumonia
Pregnancy and Related Conditions
Surgical Care Improvement Project
Source: Joint Commission, 2006, http://www.jointcommission.org.

HIPAA

Unique identifiers for employers and health care providers are currently in place, with identifiers for health plans to follow.

Additional HIPPA requirements include unique identifiers for employers, health care providers, health plans, and patients. The National Employer Identifier (NEI) is a nine-digit number—the same number as the Federal Employer Identification Number (EIN) that is used for tax purposes. The National Provider Identifier (NPI) is an 8-digit alphanumeric character, or a 10-digit number with a check digit, that is used by hospitals, doctors, nursing homes, and other health care providers when filing claims electronically. An NPI assigned to an individual health care provider remains with that person indefinitely, no matter where they practice in the country or whether their specialties change. Both the NEI and NPI are currently in use. The National Health Plan Identifier (PlanID), currently under development, would create a unique identifier for health plans. Such an identifier would assist health care providers who conduct business with multiple health plans. The National Health Identifier for Individuals (Personal Identifier) would assign a unique identifier to each consumer of the health care delivery system. The concept of a Personal Identifier has engendered extensive criticism as an invasion of privacy and is considered by many to be a direct contradiction of the HIPAA Privacy Rule, which established the concept of protected health information. In light of this criticism, DHHS has postponed this identifier standard indefinitely.

HIPAA regulations extend beyond the issues associated with electronic transmission of data and into the use of data sets in the research context. These regulations allow researchers to use limited data sets. According to HIPAA, a limited data set refers to a form of data in which direct patient identifiers have been removed, but other data such as city, state, zip code, dates of service, birth, or death remain. To employ limited data sets, researchers are required under HIPAA to enter into data use agreements with the covered entity that provides the data set.

The HIPAA Privacy Rule exists to protect health information that identifies a patient. One unintended result of this rule is general confusion over what data may be considered protected health information with regard to disseminating the data to public health authorities. Pursuant to regulatory authority, public health agencies collect numerous types of health data and specify the data sets to be used by health care providers and organizations when reporting those data. For example, public health authorities may require the submission of data that measure patient safety, quality management, and vital statistics. For each of these areas, the appropriate public health authority specifies the data sets to be used. Public health authorities have received inconsistent data due to conflicting interpretations of the Privacy Rule by health care providers and organizations. To add further confusion, some public health authorities possess different levels of understanding with regard to whether the Privacy Rule prevents them from using and disclosing health information in certain contexts.

As a result of the disparities that currently exist among health care providers and public health authorities, several organizations are working to reduce and eliminate confusion through the issuance of white papers and other documents that provide guidance on these issues. With this guidance, the flow of health data to and among public health authorities should improve.

Data Exchange

Health care providers and organizations frequently employ sophisticated databases to manage tremendous amounts of data in the 21st century. At the same time, regulatory agencies, third-party payers, and researchers all demand access to these data to support their missions. Calls for improvements to the quality, safety, and efficiency of the health care system are voiced by many, and such improvements depend upon reliable data to succeed. Combined, these factors have resulted in recognition of the need to exchange health information using information technology. This recognition has coalesced into the development of regional health information organizations to exchange needed data.

A **regional health information organization** (RHIO) is a network of individuals, businesses, groups, and associations working to establish the means to share patient information in an electronic fashion within a region or a community. Sometimes referred to as regional health information exchanges, community health information networks, and local health information infrastructures, RHIOs are collaborative efforts designed to achieve interoperability, the ability of software and hardware on machines belonging to different vendors to communicate with one another, thus facilitating data exchange. By being able to exchange this data electronically, RHIOs hope to bring data to those who need them most in a secure, private, and timely fashion.

The members of RHIOs are as varied as health care itself. Most RHIOs are composed of health care providers, such as physicians and hospitals, third-party payers, public agencies, employers, patients, and consumer groups. Some may also include health care purchasers, pharmacies, laboratories, quality improvement organizations, health care information technology suppliers, and researchers based at universities and corporations. Variances further exist concerning whether

public agencies at federal, state, and local levels are involved. Some RHIOs are supported by private funds while others function through a combination of public and private funds.

The impetus for the creation of RHIOs began with the recognition that comprehensive data are necessary to gauge both an individual's and a community's health. Because the health care system in the United States takes a decentralized, free-market approach, patient data are stored in a variety of formats and locations, many of which are incompatible with one another. For example, some patient data may be found in paper-based health records located in file cabinets, whereas other patient data may be located in electronic health records, and still other patient data may be partially kept in electronic form and partially kept in paper form. The inability to access these data readily frustrates the clinician at the point of care and those responsible for improving public health who are charged with measuring progress and facilitating improvement.

At the federal government level, an awareness of this frustration played a role in the formalization of RHIOs by the Office of the National Coordinator for Health Information Technology (ONCHIT) in the U.S. Department of Health and Human Services. As part of its mission, the ONCHIT is charged with directing

> the implementation of a strategic plan to guide the nationwide implementation of interoperable health information technology in both the public and private health care sectors that will reduce medical errors, improve quality, and produce greater value for health care expenditures.[3]

This effort has taken many forms, including the creation of a 17-member advisory commission on health information technology called the American Health Information Community (AHIC); the issuance of reports and vision statements; and requests for proposals that would address privacy, security, standards, certification, and standards issues.

One outgrowth of the strategic plan is an effort to interconnect care across communities. For example, the competition between health care providers and systems for market share reduces the probability that these providers will share data in the ordinary course of their businesses. An RHIO permits health care providers within a region to access clinical information by identifying and linking health records to one another using a decentralized technology environment. This linkage is possible because of legal agreements that allow the sharing of data for clinical—and not business—purposes. By formally recognizing the need for RHIOs, the federal government communicates to regional and local leaders that they should collaborate and develop consensus to establish RHIOs in their areas.

Like any new technological development, RHIOs are not without criticism. For health care providers to achieve access

Table 8-14 | Definitions for Functionalities to Support Patient Care

Clinical Documentation	The ability to record, and make available others, documentation from a clinician about a clinical encounter, either through direct entry by the healthcare provider or through transcription from dictation or other means by a third party.
Repository	The capacity to maintain information on a patient that may come from multiple sources so that it may be accessed by other information systems when needed. The information in a repository may or may not be standardized, but is probably centrally secured, backed up, and made available 24/7 to authorized requestors.
Enrollment or Eligibility Checking	The ability to contact the payer before the patient is seen and get a response that indicates whether or not the services to be rendered will be covered by the payer.
Reminders	The ability to remind clinicians to consider certain actions at a particular point in time, such as prompts to ask the patient appropriate preventive medicine questions, notifications that ordered tests have not produced results when expected, and suggestions for certain therapeutic actions, such as giving a tetanus shot if one has not been given one for 10 years.
Consultation or Referral	The ability to generate and/or receive summaries of relevant clinical information on a patient that are typically transferred between healthcare providers when a patient is referred to a specialist or admitted or discharged from a hospital.
Results Delivery	The ability to accept messages from other data sources, such as clinical laboratories, radiology sources, pathology reports, etc, and integrate the data for presentation to a clinician.
Alerts to Providers	The ability to interpret the clinical data that is entered about a patient using a set of rules or algorithms which will generate warnings or alerts at various levels of severity to a clinician. These are intended to make the clinician aware of potentially harmful events, such as drug interactions, patient allergies, and abnormal results, that may affect how a patient is treated, with the intention of speeding the clinical decision process while reducing medical errors.

Source: eHealth Initiative, August 2005 (permission to reprint granted by the eHealth Initiative).

to data when rendering care to patients, those data must be identifiable by patient. The ability to identify the patient directly raises concerns over the loss of privacy and confidentiality of protected health information. It also leads to concerns that, once accessed, the data will not be controlled properly. If data are not properly controlled by the RHIO, some fear that patients will withhold information from their health care providers as a means to exercise that control themselves. Potential withholding of information could reduce the effectiveness of the RHIO. Responses to these concerns generally include: the recognition of the central role that privacy and confidentiality must play in data exchange; the need for health care professionals to act as patient advocates to ensure patient privacy; and the real risk that RHIOs may not reach their full potential if privacy and confidentiality are not maintained. Many of those involved in the development of RHIOs acknowledge these concerns and call for the use of strict security mechanisms, such as sophisticated access controls, as the means to answer these concerns.

State and Local Data Exchange Efforts

As efforts progress at the federal level, considerable work is being performed at the state and local levels to create regional networks for exchanging patient data. One recent study counted 109 initiatives across 45 states and the District of Columbia, each varying in its level of operation from the organizational phase through full operation.[4] Many of these initiatives perceive the need to increase efficiencies among providers and the desire to contain costs as the main reasons behind their efforts. These initiatives employ different functionalities to accomplish these purposes; Table 8-14 lists several functionalities employed by RHIOs to support patient care. Although multiple efforts are ongoing, the following section highlights several of these efforts in particular to illustrate the variety of activities occurring in the United States.

One of the earliest efforts to exchange data was the creation of the Massachusetts Health Data Consortium (MHDC) in 1978. Among its many endeavors, the MHDC operates the MA-SHARE program, a data exchange network designed to provide patient data at point-of-care in a cost-effective manner. MA-SHARE focuses on improving connectivity within the clinical community, with plans to foster adoption of electronic health records, electronic prescribing protocols, and bioterrorism surveillance techniques in the future. Similar efforts to enhance connectivity within the clinical community are the focus of the Indiana Health Information Exchange and the Volunteer eHealth Initiative of Tennessee.

Another early effort involved the North Carolina Healthcare Information and Communications Alliance (NCHICA). Begun in 1994 when the concept of a regional health information organization was in its infancy, NCHICA began as a method to encourage accelerated adoption of information technology as a means to improve health care. Two areas already implemented for data exchange include an immunization registry and an emergency room database. Other areas of future focus include medication management and patient safety.

Because of its large population, the effort to build a statewide information exchange in California is an ambitious project. The California Regional Health Information Organization (CalRHIO) serves as an independent umbrella organization that defines the infrastructure necessary to foster data exchange, helps those involved in local and regional data exchange efforts in California to work toward common goals, and ensures that statewide efforts are consistent with national technology platforms and networks. CalRHIO's operational focus is multifold and includes linking hospital emergency departments to one another, supporting enhanced safety in medication management, improving administrative functions, and providing consumers access to their patient information through use of a personal health record.

One effort being made in New York focuses on community-based physicians. Called the Taconic Health Information Network and Community (THINC), this program works to foster adoption of electronic health records and transmission of prescription and performance measurement data using a Web-based data exchange portal. THINC offers access to test results, radiology reports, admissions/discharge/transfer data, and dictated physician notes. One of THINC's goals is to gain the participation of health insurers, who in turn could offer financial incentives to community-based physicians to install information technology in their offices, including electronic health record systems.

Although the efforts previously discussed in this section all employ a central repository to store data exchanged between members, one organization has chosen a different approach. The Colorado Health Information Exchange (COHIE) relies on messaging between health care entities and does not collect the messages and store them in a central repository. For this reason, COHIE's focus is on designing and implementing infrastructure that facilitates the exchange of point-of-care patient data.

HIPAA

Many consider RHIOs to be health care clearinghouses subject to the Privacy and Security Rules.

One issue that all of these efforts share is the challenge to apply the HIPAA Security and Privacy Rules to their networks. These rules establish safeguards for protected health information that a covered entity creates, receives, maintains, or transmits in an electronic format. Although some RHIOs do not consider themselves to be health care clearinghouses subject to these rules, many RHIOs think otherwise; as such, they must consider privacy, security, and access safeguards when designing and implementing their programs.

A second challenge centers on the involvement of health information management professionals in each of these efforts. Because HIM professionals understand health care data content and structure and are well versed in both database management and the legal implications of sharing data, a natural progression in HIM career development is association with a health data exchange network. The operational understanding that many HIM professionals possess in the variety of health care facilities and providers who participate in these networks gives them advantages in the design and implementation of the network.

Conclusion

The marked increase in the demand for data seen over the last decade in the health care field has spurred the development of database management systems. These systems are used by multiple entities to serve a variety of functions. The success of database management has affected many traditional health care areas such as statistics, research, performance improvement, and risk management.

The future of database management is bright, and it continues to evolve with the advent of the electronic health record and regional health information organizations. The requirements of the Health Insurance Portability and Accountability Act, and the need to improve public health surveillance, bring further attention to database management. Health information management professionals who understand the underlying concepts of database management and stay abreast of its changes will be well served in their professional careers.

CHAPTER SUMMARY

This chapter introduces the concepts and functions behind databases and their management. As a result of the increased application of electronics, databases have become more sophisticated; they require the user to have knowledge of database design, controls, and standards in order to operate them. This sophistication has led to new analysis and retrieval methods, including data warehousing and data mining. The variety of data sets that exist and continue to be developed have influenced the daily operations of health care providers and have increased the complexity of databases used in the health care field. Because of the capabilities offered by databases and advancements in interoperability, new developments have emerged, including regional health information organizations that permit data exchange between networks of interconnected groups.

CASE STUDY

You are a health information management student who has been asked to summarize and explain the concept of database management to your class. Your presentation should last no more than 20 minutes and must include discussion of significant areas within this topic. What areas would you include? What areas would you emphasize?

REVIEW QUESTIONS

1. How does an end user interact with a database?

2. How did the development of database management programs in the 1960s revolutionize the practical nature of computers in the work environment?

3. What is a data design specification, and what purpose does it serve?

4. What are the two types of data modeling systems currently in use?

5. What are the three control functions used in databases?

6. Why do some organizations consider data marts an alternative to data warehouses?

7. What is the difference in focus between HL7 and X12?

8. What are the purposes served by minimum data sets?

9. What does the term *interoperability* mean?

ENRICHMENT ACTIVITIES

1. Your instructor has asked you to make a presentation, not to exceed five minutes in length, on data standards. Develop a handout that provides an overview of data standards, particularly addressing the definition and benefits of data standards in health care and the concept of electronic data interchange. Identify in the handout the two major messaging standards development organizations for health information. Make your presentation to your class.

2. Visit any of the following Web sites to view features of health data exchange networks: http://www.calrhio.org, http://www.ihie.com, http://www.nchica.org, and http://www.volunteer-ehealth.org. Compare and contrast these sites, particularly as they relate to purposes, goals, governance structure, and financing sources. Discuss your findings with your instructor and classmates.

WEB SITES

Administrative Simplification Provisions of the Health Insurance Portability and Accountability Act, http://www.aspe.hhs.gov/admnsimp

American National Standards Institute, http://www.ansi.org

American Society for Testing and Materials, http://www.astm.org

Association for Public Health Laboratories, http://www.aphl.org

California Regional Health Information Organization, http://www.calrhio.org.

Centers for Disease Control and Prevention, http://www.cdc.gov

Colorado Health Information Exchange, http://www.ccbh.ehealthinitiative.org/profiles

Community Health Information Technology Alliance, http://www.chita.org

Data Interchange Standards Association, http://www.disa.org/x12/x12n

Foundation for eHealth Initiative, http://www.ehealthinitiative.org

Health Level Seven, http://www.hl7.org

Indiana Health Information Exchange, http://www.ihie.com

Joint Commission, http://www.jointcommission.org

National Committee on Vital and Health Statistics, http://www.ncvhs.hhs.gov

North Carolina Healthcare Information and Communications Alliance, Inc., http://www.nchica.org

Office for Civil Rights, U.S. Department of Health and Human Services, http://www.hhs.gov/ocr

Office of the National Coordinator for Health Information Technology, http://www.hhs.gov/healthit

Taconic Health Information Network and Community, http://www.ccbh.ehealthinitiative.org

Volunteer eHealth Initiative of Tennessee, http://www.volunteer-ehealth.org

Workgroup for Electronic Data Interchange, http://www.wedi.org

REFERENCES

Beaver, K., & Herold, R. (2004). *The practical guide to HIPAA privacy and security compliance*. Boca Raton, FL: Auerbach.

Brandt, M. D. (2000, April). Health informatics standards: A user's guide. *Journal of AHIMA, 71*, 39–43. Available at http://www.ahima.org/journal/features/feature.0004.1.html.

Carter, J. (Ed.). (2001). *Electronic medical records: A guide for clinicians and administrators*. Philadelphia: American College of Physicians.

Foundation for eHealth. (2005). *Second annual survey of state, regional, and community-based health information exchange initiatives and organizations: Emerging trends and issues in health information exchange*. Retrieved September 21, 2005, from http://www.ehealthinitiative.org

Johns, M. L. (2002). *Information management for health professions* (2nd ed.). Albany, NY: Delmar.

Jordan, T. (2002). *Understanding medical information: A user's guide to informatics and decision making*. New York: McGraw-Hill.

Lumpkin, J. (National Committee on Vital and Health Statistics). (2002, February 27). *Letter to the Hon. Tommy G. Thompson, Secretary of U.S. Department of Health and Human Services*. Retrieved February 28, 2006, from http://www.ncvhs.hhs.gov

Mon, D. T. (2003, June). Relational database management: What you need to know. *Journal of AHIMA, 74*(6), 40–45. Available at http://www.library.ahima.org.

Norris, T. E. Fuller, S., Goldberg, H., & Tarczy-Hornoch, P. (2002). *Informatics in primary care*. New York: Springer-Verlag.

Rojas, R. (Ed.). (2001). *Encyclopedia of computers and computer history* (Vols. 1–2). London: Fitzroy Dearborn Publishers.

Tracy, W., & Dougherty, M. (2002, August). HL7 standard shapes content, exchange of patient information. *Journal of AHIMA, 73*(8), 49–51. Available at http://www.library.ahima.org/intradoc-cgi.

Van Bemmel, J. H., & Musen, M. A. (Eds.). (1997). *Handbook of medical informatics*. The Netherlands: Springer-Verlag.

NOTES

1. Dixon Lee, C. (2003, January). A shot in the arm for public health: Weak systems require reinforcement at all levels. *Journal of AHIMA, 73*(1), 36–42. Available at http://www.library.ahima.org/intradoc-cgi.

2. National Committee on Vital and Health Statistics. (2001, November 15). *Information for health: A strategy for building the national health information infrastructure*. Retrieved February 28, 2006, from http://www.ncvhs.hhs.gov/nhiilayo.pdf.

3. Office of the National Coordinator for Health Information Technology (ONCHIT). *Mission statement*. Retrieved May 31, 2006, from http://www.hhs.gov/healthit/mission.

4. Foundation for eHealth. (2005). *Second annual survey of state, regional, and community-based health information exchange initiatives and organizations: Emerging trends and issues in health information exchange*. Retrieved September 21, 2005, from http://www.ehealthinitiative.org.

9

Health Statistics

CERTIFICATION CONNECTION

RHIA

Data validity
Present data
Patient care-related studies
Routine/custom reports

RHIT

Data collection
Present data

LEARNING OBJECTIVES

After reading this chapter, the learner should be able to:

1. Identify the representative types of statistics found in health care.

2. Understand the concepts involved in statistical literacy.

3. Distinguish between the measures of central tendency: mean, median, and mode.

4. Determine the appropriateness of a statistical instrument.

5. Recognize the different types of data and the sources from which data can be obtained.

6. Describe the typical formulae applied in health care settings.

7. Become familiar with the rate formula applied in health information management settings.

8. List the presentation methods used to communicate data in numerical form.

9. Outline the rules of construction that govern the creation of graphs.

10. Discern whether a graph is complete or incomplete.

11. Explain the value of productivity analysis and identify two methods.

Outline

Overview

Statistical Types

Statistical Literacy

Statistical Basics
Data Presentation
Regression Analysis

Health Information Management Statistics

Productivity

Key Concepts

80/20 Rule

Aggregate data collection

ANOVA test

Applied statistics

Autopsy rate

Bar graph

Bivariate regression

Case fatality rates

Case mix

Categorical data

Census

Chi-square

Cold feed

Concurrent data collection

Consultation rate

Continuous data

Control chart

Correlation

C-section rate

Daily inpatient census

Demographic statistics

Descriptive statistics

Discrete data

Distribution

Epidemiology

Fraction

Frequency polygon

Histogram

Incidence rates

Inferential statistics

Inpatient service day

Interval data

Labor analytics

Length of stay

Line graph

Mathematical statistics

Mean

Median

Mode

Morbidity

Morbidity rates

Mortality

Mortality rates

Multivariate regression

Natality

Nominal data

Nosocomial infection rate

Null hypothesis

Occupancy rate

Ordinal data

Pareto principle

Pearson product–moment correlation

Percentage

Pie chart

Population

Prevalence rates

Process capability analysis

Process capability ratio diagram

Productivity

Public health surveillance statistics

Rate

Rate formulae

Ratio

Regression analysis

Retrospective data collection

Rounding

Sample

Simple regression

Standard deviation

Statistical literacy

Statistically significant

Statistics

Trend chart

T-test

Type I error

Type II error

Univariate regression

Vital statistics

INTRODUCTION

Health care uses a special language called medical terminology to describe the actions that are taken on behalf of a patient. When students enter the health care field, they learn the concepts of this new language, acquire an understanding of how terms are formed, and memorize root words, prefixes, and suffixes. Similarly, a special language exists to express the outcomes of mathematical calculations; this special language is known as statistics. It too requires students to learn new concepts, acquire an understanding of new terms, and memorize formulae. This special language is the focus of this chapter.

Statistics are used to "tell the story" of health care delivery and patient outcomes in the United States. In the course of any given day, statistics are employed in the health care field in a variety of ways. They may be used to support the delivery of patient care, justify the building of new facilities, or comply with regulatory requirements. Alternatively, they may be used to support productivity and labor analyses, to complement planning activities, or to judge the effectiveness of an organization. Because of the variety and complexity surrounding the use of statistics, the need for a common understanding of the term takes on a great importance.

To understand statistics, one must first build a statistical vocabulary. An explanation of different statistical types begins this chapter, followed by a discussion of statistical literacy. Basic statistical concepts, methods of data presentation, and regression analysis join these topics. A discussion of statistics as it is applied to health information management completes the chapter.

Overview

Health care organizations, like many other organizations, collect enormous amounts of data on a daily basis. Although most data collection efforts support direct patient care, health care organizations are required to report data to state and local health agencies that, in turn, report selected data to the federal government. Examples of collectors of health data at the federal level are listed in Table 9–I. At all levels, these data are transformed into information for statistical dissemination. Health care data, combined with census data and immigration and emigration data, support multiple objectives, including planning for current and future health care services, analyzing birth rates, projecting school needs, and making population projections. At the individual health care facility level, statistics are used for multiple purposes, including to justify the opening or closing of clinical units in a hospital, the purchase of new equipment, and the hiring of additional staff.

For collected data to be considered meaningful, statistical methods and formulae must be applied. **Statistics** is defined as the mathematics of the collection, organization, and interpretation of numerical data, especially the analysis of population characteristics by inference from

Table 9–1	Collectors of Health Data at the Federal Level
Centers for Disease Control and Prevention
Centers for Medicare and Medicaid Services
National Association for Public Health Statistics
National Center for Health Statistics
National Committee on Vital and Health Statistics
U.S. Department of Labor, Bureau of Labor Statistics

sampling. Statistics involves both the numbers and the techniques and procedures used in collecting, organizing, analyzing, interpreting, and presenting information in a numerical form.

Numbers and mathematical concepts have played important roles in society for thousands of years. The activities involved in census taking, the official counting of a population, illustrate this premise. Although these concepts and actions have existed over a long period, recognition of the field of statistics is relatively new. This field began in the 1700s, when governments and centralized administrative bodies began to seek data about the work they did. At that time, the purpose of statistics was to describe data about the government. Over the last few centuries, the purpose of statistics has broadened to include describing data about individuals and organizations. Numerous disciplines, governmental bodies, individuals, and organizations now use statistics to conduct their work. As a result, advances have occurred in statistical practices, including the creation of new research tools such as automated software programs. These advances have greatly aided the explanation of facts, situations, and other conditions that exist within the medical community and in society as a whole.

Statistical Types

Numerous types of statistics are found in health care today. Descriptive statistics are the statistics used to characterize or summarize a given population (e.g., the breakdowns provided by census data). Descriptive statistics can have a narrow focus, such as coding exam results, or a very wide focus that represents millions of encounters. For example, the national census report that occurs every 10 years is an example of descriptive statistics. Such tabulation organizes the U.S. population into distinct categories by age, occupation, income, and so forth. A population is an entire group that has a common observable characteristic. For example, all patients suffering from a certain disease or undergoing a specific form of treatment can be considered a population. More commonly, a sample of the population is used. A sample refers to a subset or small part of a population. For example, it would be difficult to identify every patient with diabetes because some people may be unaware that they have diabetes and others would decline to participate in the study. Therefore, research on diabetes is performed using a sample of patients with diabetes.

Generalizations about an entire population (e.g., all those with diabetes) can be made through statistics by studying a sample of that population. Because only part of the population is studied, a special type of statistic is employed so that assumptions made from the review will be valid. Inferential statistics refers to reaching conclusions based upon data from a sample, where the patterns in the data are modeled so that randomness and uncertainty in observations are addressed. A common example of inferential statistics are the conclusions reached from opinion polls.

Often used in research, inferential statistics are used to judge the reliability and validity of the research instruments.

Both descriptive and inferential statistics are considered forms of applied statistics, a term that refers to the use of statistics and statistical theory in real-life situations. By contrast, mathematical statistics refers to the theoretical basis of statistics. Within the health information management (HIM) context, descriptive statistics dominate; morbidity, mortality, and natality rates are examples of descriptive statistics. Inferential statistics are more commonly used in the research context of health care, where statistical significance is measured and the probabilities of an occurrence in a sample population are applied to an entire population to draw a conclusion.

Many who work in health care are familiar with vital statistics. Vital statistics refers to data on human events, such as the statistics related to births, deaths, fetal deaths, marriages, divorces, and induced terminations of pregnancy (abortions). The primary focus of vital statistics at the small-scale level is the individual human being and the major events in his life. The primary focus of vital statistics at the large-scale level is the aggregation of data to be used for a multitude of purposes, including prediction of future trends and needs in the larger community.

Vital statistics are generated from data collected at the local level and later reported to the federal government by individual states. For example, health care providers, coroners, and funeral homes all report data on deaths (mortality) on a routine basis to the state level by completing death certificates specified by the respective governing authority. The death certificate captures demographic data about the dead person's age, place of residence, and cause of death. These certificates are captured electronically and transmitted to a state entity. The state entity creates a statewide database that can be used to report death counts by city, age at death, and the causes of death in a state. In turn, each state provides mortality data to the National Center for Health Statistics (NCHS), the federal government's principal health statistics agency housed within the Centers for Disease Control and Prevention (CDC). The NCHS maintains these data as part of its National Vital Statistics System (NVSS). These statistical tabulations about death rates and causes are then made available for a variety of reporting purposes. For example, data about death and disease incidents are disseminated to the public by the U.S. Public Health Service in its Morbidity and Mortality Weekly Report.

Similar data are collected on the other areas that comprise vital statistics. For example, data on births (natality) are collected from birth certificates generated at the facilities where births occur. These data are reported on a routine basis to the state level. In turn, each of the states provides birth data to NCHS at the federal level. Other programs related to the NVSS include the Linked Birth and

Table 9-2	Vital Statistics Reporting and Registration Systems	
Vital Events Collected	• Births
	• Deaths
	• Fetal deaths
	• Marriages
	• Divorces
Vital Registration Systems Operated at Various Levels	• Municipalities, including Washington, D.C.
	• All 50 states plus 5 territories (Guam, Virgin Islands, Puerto Rico, American Samoa, and Northern Mariana Islands)
	• U.S. government, through numerous departments and agencies, including the CDC's National Center for Health Statistics
Additional Programs	• Linked Birth and Infant Death Data Set
	• National Survey of Family Growth
	• Matched Multiple Birth Data Set
	• National Death Index
	• National Maternal and Infant Health Survey
	• National Mortality Followback Survey

Source: National Vital Statistics Systems, http://www.cdc.gov/nchs/nvss.html.

Infant Death Data Set, the National Maternal and Infant Survey, the National Mortality Followback Survey, and the National Death Index.

The responsibility to collect these data rests with state governments. To discharge this responsibility, state governments operate registration systems and cooperate with NCHS to develop standard forms for the collection of data and model procedures for the uniform registration of events. The costs to operate these systems and develop forms and procedures are shared between each state and NCHS. Underpinning these registration systems are state laws that mandate the reporting of events constituting vital statistics.[1] Each state's law details its reporting requirements, including the time frames within which to report the required data.

Similar in concept to vital statistics, **public health surveillance statistics** focus on illnesses, conditions, and diseases of human beings (**morbidity**). These statistics commonly cover communicable diseases (e.g., AIDS and venereal diseases), child abuse, injuries caused by deadly weapons, and cancer. Most recently, these statistics have been used to track bioterrorism events. The field of **epidemiology**, the study of the cause and distribution of diseases, utilizes these statistics to develop prevention and treatment programs. Epidemiology is not limited to these data; statistics are also collected concerning incidence rates and prevalence rates, patient outcomes, and the occurrence of diseases. As with vital statistics, reporting is performed in a three-tier level, beginning at the local level, progressing to state level, and moving to the national level. Examples of the statistics kept and the agencies who keep them can be found in Table 9-2.

The issue of process control (how data are collected) and the reliability of results are central to determining the rates of epidemiological statistics. Of special importance is the timeliness of reporting certain diseases from the local level to the federal level. Rapid notification to the CDC is critical in light of the threat of bioterrorism in the United States today. The need to identify a possible attack, such as anthrax poisoning, and alert the CDC quickly revolves around the notification process. Notification can take the form of phone, fax, or electronic mail transmissions. At the local level, the HIM practitioner is a crucial member of the early response team and should be involved in creating and maintaining a speedy notification process. The key elements to consider in the notification process are listed in Table 9-3. More information concerning epidemiology can be found in Chapter 10, "Research."

Demographic statistics focus on the study of human populations, looking to the size of the populations and how they change over time. Demographic statistics incorporate factors such as age, sex, ethnicity, income, and health status. These statistics are used in disease prevention and control and in planning community health care programs.

Table 9-3	Key Elements in the Notification Process
1.	Establish a predetermined policy of ownership (i.e., who is accountable for each step of the process).
2.	Establish how many steps will be involved.
3.	Establish a reasonable time range within which notification should occur.

HIM practitioners may find themselves in roles that expose them to any and all of the statistics described in this chapter. They might also find themselves in roles that require advanced statistical preparations. The emerging fields of clinical and applied informatics use advanced statistics to resolve questions of clinical importance (e.g., does smoking cause cancer?).These statistics are also used to engage health care leaders in creating business models to address health care questions (e.g., does race affect a person's access to quality health care?). The nature of the statistics used in informatics research reflects a need for more refined tools. A common approach is to select an area of study and to apply the most appropriate statistical applications to achieve the best results.

Statistical Literacy

Miles per gallon. Miles per hour. Mortality rates. Morbidity rates. Test scores. Return on investment. As a society, we use these and other statistics to measure ourselves and others and to draw conclusions relating to the success, failure, quality, and quantity of what we do and produce. This use of measurement is widespread in the health care field, as well. Statistical literacy, the ability to determine if a conclusion or study is credible based on the results of statistical findings, is essential if measurements are to be used properly. The special language of statistics adds meaning to these measurements. As with other languages, it is important to learn and understand the terms and concepts before applying them. The following section introduces new statistical terms and provides a brief refresher of basic math concepts. Application of these concepts through statistical formulae and an explanation of regression analysis follow this discussion.

Statistical Basics

Any survey of math concepts used in statistics includes a discussion of percentages, rounding up, ratios, rates, and fractions. These concepts are so frequently used that a failure to understand them can lead to confusion regarding the matter the concepts are used to support. For example, not understanding the percentage concept would pose great confusion to a learner who is tasked with self-grading a test, calculating it as a percent, and reporting a score. Accordingly, each concept is explained and illustrated in this section to aid the learner's understanding.

Percentage refers to a specified amount in every hundred. People use percentages to understand changes in a value over time. To create a percentage, the old value is subtracted from the new value. That amount is then divided by the old value, and the resulting amount is multiplied by 100 and assigned a percent sign (%). An example illustrates this concept:

Anywhere Health Services, Inc., treated 85 patients on January 12 and 93 patients on January 18. Using the formula just described, the old value (85) is subtracted from the new value (93) for a total of 8. This number is divided by 85, and the result equals 0.09411764705. At this point, the rounding concept comes into play. Rounding refers to the process of reducing the total of significant digits in a number; this results in a shorter number with fewer digits. The most common method for rounding a number is to: (1) decide which is the last digit to keep; (2) increase by 1 if the next digit is 5 or more (round up); and (3) leave the same if the next digit is 4 or less (round down). In the present example, the last digit to keep is the third digit after the decimal point (the number 4). The next digit is 1, which means that the last digit will remain 4 (round down). This brings the number to 0.094. At this point, the number 0.094 is multiplied by 100, and the result is 9.4. The percentage difference in the number of patients seen between the two dates is 9.4%.

One point of clarification is required when rounding numbers to new positions, and that involves understanding the most commonly encountered rounding phrases. Examples of the most commonly used rounding phrases are listed in Table 9–4. This is particularly important when an analyst

Table 9–4	Most Commonly Used Rounding Phrases		
Phrase	**Meaning**	**Example**
Hundred	Correct to the nearest whole number	3256 = 3300
Tenth	Correct to one decimal place	5.781 = 5.8
Hundredth	Correct to two decimal places	46.7385 = 46.74
Thousandth	Correct to three decimal places	.0045 = .005
Million	Correct to the nearest whole number	3,893,369 = 4,000,000
Ten	Correct to the nearest second number to the left of the decimal	2184.72 = 2180
Thousand	Correct to the nearest third number to the left of the decimal	45,679.99 = 46,000

begins working on a series of statistical reports and finds that some answers are expressed to differing degrees of accuracy. By understanding the different rounding phrases, the analyst is able to translate statistics of differing degrees.

Two common math concepts are ratios and rates. A **ratio** is a quantity that signifies the amount of one quantity relative to another. A ratio is written as two numbers separated by a colon (:), which is interpreted to mean "to." For example, a ratio of 3:5 indicates that the whole is composed of 3 parts of one thing and 5 parts of another thing, making the whole 8 parts in all. For example, if a container holds 3 red balls and 5 blue balls, the ratio of red balls to blue balls would be 3 to 5.

Ratios address questions related to quantities of the same kind. In the example above, the same kind means balls. A **rate** is a special type of ratio in which the two quantities being compared are of different units or kinds. A rate is expressed as the quantity of first kind separated by the word "per" from the quantity of the second kind. Examples used in everyday activity include miles per hour or miles per gallon.

The final concept addresses fractions. A **fraction** is a part of an entire whole. Fractions allow us to understand the whole of something by studying its parts. Fractions were invented long before decimal numbers and were useful for showing portions less than one. They apply to everyday activities, such as cooking and sewing, and to specialty uses, such as building and health care. For that reason, it is important to understand fractions. Fractions are most commonly understood when presented visually, as in the pie chart in Figure 9–1. Mathematically, a fraction is expressed in terms of a numerator and a denominator. The denominator, located on the bottom of the fraction, describes how many parts the whole is divided into. The numerator, located on top of the fraction, describes how many of those parts one is dealing with. For example, the fraction "two-thirds" is expressed as 2/3, with the number 2 serving as the numerator and the number 3 serving as the denominator. An easy memory aid to use to remember the difference between numerator and denominator is: *D is for Denominator and D is for Down.*

Three additional features of fractions require understanding. First is the quotient, or a fraction that is divided. The top number (the numerator) is divided by the bottom number (the denominator). An example of a quotient is 600/25, which is expressed mathematically either as $600 \div 25 = 24$ or $25\sqrt{600} = 24$. In this case, 600 is divided by 25, and the answer is 24. The second feature occurs when the answer is less than a whole number, meaning that the answer is less than one. For example, in the quotient 3/8, the expression is $3 \div 8 = .0375$ or $8\sqrt{3} = .0375$. In this case, the numerator is smaller than the denominator, so the resulting answer is less than a whole number. The third feature is conversions, in which a fraction can be converted to a decimal. When working with decimals, the placement of the decimal point (.) is key. If the answer is less than one, a placeholder "0" will be used to make it clear that this number is less than one. For example, when converting the fraction 64/100 to a decimal representation, 0.004, notice how a zero is placed to the left of the decimal to indicate that the number is less than one. Also note the two zeros to the right of the decimal point. The larger the denominator, the more zeros there will be present in the answer.

A simple math problem illustrates the value of fractions. At Anywhere Hospital, on the first day of the calendar year, 99 patients were treated. Of those, 33 were female and 66 were male. To determine what fraction of the 99 patients were male, the numerator would be 66 (the total number of male patients) and the denominator would be 99 (the total number of patients as a whole). The fraction of patients who are male would be expressed as 66/99. At this point, it would aid understanding to reduce or simplify the fraction to its lowest terms. This is done by finding an equivalent number in which the numerator and denominator are as small as possible. When a fraction is as small as possible, no number, except the number 1, can be divided evenly into both the numerator and the denominator. In this example, both the numerator and denominator would be divided by their most common factor, the number 33. Dividing 33 into the numerator equals 2; dividing 33 into the denominator equals 3. This results in a reduced or simplified fraction of 2/3, which means that two-thirds of the patients seen at Anywhere Hospital on the first day of the calendar year were male. This same number can also be expressed as the ratio 2:3; for every two female patients there are three male patients.

The result of this math problem can lead to multiple questions for the health care facility, and a series of business

Figure 9–1 | Pie chart divided into thirds

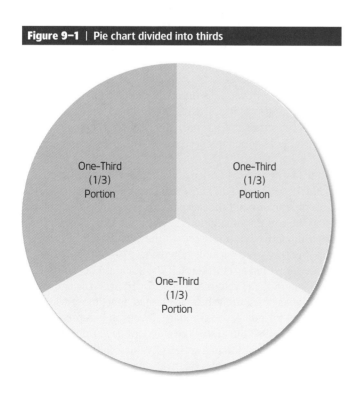

One-Third (1/3) Portion

One-Third (1/3) Portion

One-Third (1/3) Portion

decisions may then be reached. For example, should Anywhere Hospital try to increase the percentage of female patients it treats? Should Anywhere Hospital retain the current percentage and allocate its resources accordingly? Should changes in the hospital's physical plant be planned to address the targeted or current patient population? Should medical staffing changes be made to increase or retain the number of patients treated under a medical specialty that is specific to gender? These questions illustrate only a few examples, but the questions that could be generated are virtually endless. Depending upon the answers to these questions, business decisions may be reached and changes within Anywhere Hospital can begin to take place.

Measures of Central Tendency In order to capture information about a population or a series of random variables and then to discuss that information in terms of a single quantity, measurements of central tendency are often used. Measurements of central tendency are typical or representative of a set of data. They tend to lie near the center of a distribution when data are arranged according to magnitude. They are often helpful abstractions that are used to characterize a quantified activity and to compare one quantified activity to another. Common measures include mean, median, and mode. A mean is an arithmetical average; it is reached by adding together all of the scores in a distribution and dividing that total sum by the number of scores in the distribution. For example, assume that 7 students are present in class, and their ages are 23, 28, 29, 29, 30, 38, and 43. Added together, the total amount of the ages of these students is 220. The total number of students is 7. By dividing 7 into 220, the average age (or mean) of those 7 students is discovered to be 31.

A second example illustrates the mean concept but raises questions about what is meant by the word "average." Nine employees of Anywhere Health Services, Inc., are paid the following amounts: 1 staff physician: $100,000; 1 clinical supervisor: $40,000; 1 nurse: $35,000; 1 administrative manager: $30,000; 2 medical assistants at $25,000 each; and 3 clerical staff at $20,000 each. Adding together the salaries of the 9 employees equals $315,000. Dividing 9 into $315,000 equals a total of $35,000. Thus, the average employee salary (or mean) is $35,000. Closer examination reveals, however, that only 3 of the 9 employees actually earn $35,000 or more, with more than half of the employees not even reaching the average salary. For this reason, a more accurate way to gauge what amount the "average" employee earns at Anywhere Health Services, Inc., is to examine the median.

The median is the middle score in a distribution when the scores are arranged in order of magnitude (e.g., high to low). In other words, it is the value in the middle when all of the values are lined up in order of largest to smallest. Using the first example, the median age of the 7 students

is 29. Using the second example, the salaries would be arranged as follows: $100,000; $40,000; $35,000; $30,000; $25,000; $25,000; $20,000; $20,000; $20,000. The median salary would be $25,000 (the middle number of the 9 numbers). The median provides an understanding of what the middle of something looks like. In the second example, it is far more revealing to use the median ($25,000) to describe the "average" salary of an employee at Anywhere Hospital than it is to use the mean amount of $35,000.

A mode is a score or number that occurs with the greatest frequency. Using the students in the classroom example, the mode age is 29—it is present twice in the distribution. In the salary example, the mode salary is $20,000, because 3 of the 9 employees earn this amount. Modes are not always present in a given distribution; conversely, more than one mode may be present in a given distribution. The mode indicates the "most" (greatest frequency) within a series of numbers.

By learning the meaning of measures of central tendency, students are better able to analyze how statistics are reported, whether in research studies, press releases, or even routine journalism pieces. The choice regarding whether to report mean, median, or mode in a document can greatly influence the perceptions taken from the document. Using the salary example, the mean is $35,000, the median is $25,000, and the mode is $20,000. As a result of these differences, a learner may determine that a press release citing a mean of $35,000 to describe the average salary of employees at Anywhere Health Services, Inc., is mathematically accurate, but that it does not tell the whole story. By focusing on the median, the learner may conclude that the middle salary is $25,000. By focusing on the mode, the learner is able to conclude that "most" of the employees earn the lower salary of $20,000; this leads to the further conclusion of a wide salary gap between the highest-paid employee ($100,000) and the lowest-paid employee ($20,000). These same concepts are shown in Figure 9–2. This example illustrates not only how the choice of whether mean, median, or mode is reported can lead to different conclusions, it provides the reader with the ability to look beyond the surface of a report to understand how data might otherwise be interpreted.

Other Mathematical Concepts Though the mean, median, and mode are helpful in many situations, other mathematical concepts can also aid the learner. It is particularly helpful to know the concept of standard deviation in the research context. Standard deviation refers to the square root of a variance. In other words, it tells how widely spread apart the values are within a set of data. If the standard deviation is small, many of the values are close together; if the standard deviation is large, the values are spread apart more widely. In statistical formulae, the standard deviation is represented by (s). Figure 9–3 illustrates the standard deviation concept by showing the variation in a series of values. In this example, 10 noncredentialed coders take a coding accuracy test with a

Figure 9-2 | Measures of central tendency

Anywhere Health Services, Inc., Payroll:

One Physician	$100,000
One Clinical Supervisor	$40,000
One Nurse	$35,000
One Administrative Manager	$30,000
Two Medical Assistants	$25,000
Three Clerical Assistants	$20,000

Three Ways to Measure Salary:

Mean Salary	$35,000
Median Salary	$25,000
Mode Salary	$20,000

highest possible score of 80 points. Standard deviation reveals an (*s*) of 9 points. This means that the majority of score results fell within a 9-point spread. Without discussing individual results, the coding manager can report to his supervisor that the (*s*) of 9 points varies from the established policy standard of 8 points and suggest that additional training be offered to the noncredentialed coders.

Figure 9-3 | Mean, variance, and standard deviation

Results of Coding Exam for South Haven Community Hospital for: Noncredentialed Coding Staff

Noncredentialed:

X	$\bar{X}$		D	D²
36	− 43	=	−7	49
42	− 43	=	−1	1
36	− 43	=	−7	49
34	− 43	=	−9	81
29	− 43	=	−14	196
53	− 43	=	10	100
44	− 43	=	1	1
46	− 43	=	3	9
51	− 43	=	8	64
59	− 43	=	16	256
430			0	806

$\bar{x} = 430/10 = 43$ (MEAN)

$S^2 = 806/10 = 80.6$ (VARIANCE)

$S = \sqrt{80.6} = 9$ (STANDARD DEVIATION)

The standard deviation is meaningful, but is it significant? A result is **statistically significant** if it is unlikely to have occurred by chance and the test condition being examined has no effect. With regard to the coder example just provided how can we determine what the difference in scores would be between noncredentialed and credentialed coders? To answer this question, the coding manager would need to test the credentialed coders and separate these test results from those of the noncredentialed coders. The two sets of test results (samples) would be compared to determine the statistical significance—a two-sample *t*-test is performed. A *t*-test is used when one variable is categorical (e.g., credentialed/noncredentialed) and one variable is nominal (i.e., a number that one can add, subtract, multiply, and divide—for example, scores on the exam). The results of the coder exam reveal interesting differences, as seen in Figure 9-4.

A *t*-test is a measurement of the observed beta [$T = \beta - b\hat{} / s$] where the observed data (*T*) equals beta (β) minus the null hypothesis (b^), divided by the standard deviation (*s*). The **null hypothesis** means that there is no difference in the variables—it will always be zero. In the example shown in Figure 9-4, the *t*-test had a finding of 5.65, which means that the calculation is 5.65 standard deviations from the null hypothesis (0). In other words, the finding is *highly predictive* that coders who have coding certifications will score higher on tests of coding knowledge. The difference between the two samples represents a real difference, so the additional training that the coding credential represents is an important aspect to consider when hiring new coding staff.

Most research done today uses a variety of computer applications to perform the actual calculations. The SPSS is a popular analytical software application that is used to run an assortment of statistical tests. Any HIM analyst must be familiar with what each test measures in order to select the best test for the variables being analyzed. Automated statistical applications (like SPSS) will perform mathematical operations on any data and produce results, but the results may make no sense if the wrong test is selected. It is the responsibility of the analyst to consider the findings, confirm that correct measurements were performed, read the results, and determine whether a finding is significant and valid. Questions an analyst may ask when deciding among tests are listed in Table 9-5.

Data Collection Determining how effectively an organization conducts its business requires the skilled use of data and statistics. It is not enough merely to identify the representative types of statistics; one must also understand what data are collected. Some of the collected data are reported to local and state health agencies at an identifiable level (e.g., a reviewer knows that a particular disease is associated with an identified patient). For example, all patients identified as having an active tuberculosis infection must be reported to the local health agency so that measures can be taken to avoid an epidemic. The majority of the collected data, however,

Figure 9–4 | Two-sample *t*-test

Results of Coding Exam for South Haven Community Hospital for:
Noncredentialed Coding Staff & Credentialed Coding Staff

Noncredentialed: Credentialed:

X		$\bar{X}$		D	D^2
$\overline{36}$	–	$\overline{43}$	=	$\overline{-7}$	49
42	–	43	=	–1	1
36	–	43	=	–7	49
34	–	43	=	–9	81
29	–	43	=	–14	196
53	–	43	=	10	100
44	–	43	=	1	1
46	–	43	=	3	9
51	–	43	=	8	64
59	–	43	=	16	256
430				0	806

76	–	64	=	12	144
50	–	64	=	–14	196
73	–	64	=	9	81
64	–	64	=	0	0
55	–	64	=	–9	81
64	–	64	=	0	0
60	–	64	=	–4	16
66	–	64	=	2	4
71	–	64	=	7	49
61	–	64	=	–3	9
640				0	580

$\bar{x}1 = 430/10 = 43$ (MEAN) $\bar{x}2 = 640/10 = 64$ (MEAN)

$S^2 = 806/10 = 80.6$ (VARIANCE) $s^2 = 580/10 = 58$ (VARIANCE)

$S = \sqrt{80.6} = 9$ (STANDARD DEVIATION) $s = \sqrt{58} = 7.6$ (STANDARD DEVIATION)

$t = \bar{x}1 - \bar{x}2 = 43 - 64 = \underline{-21}$

$$\sqrt{\frac{s1 + s2}{N1 \; N2}} = \sqrt{\frac{80.6 + 58}{10 \quad 10}} = 3.72 = 5.65$$

are shared using a process in which the individual patient's identity is shielded.

Data begin at the patient level, and include identifiable information about the patient's demographic profile and disease and procedure processes. This is known as the collection of personal health information (PHI) data collection. As the data are analyzed, they are transformed into aggregate data. In **aggregate data collection**, specific data are combined into larger groupings that can be used to describe a bigger concept. For example, disease rates (e.g., tuberculosis) in small areas may be grouped together for a particular location (e.g., a state), but individual patients with the disease will not be identifiable. The majority of data sharing that occurs between direct care providers (such as hospitals) and the agencies that possess health care oversight responsibilities fall within the category of aggregate data.

Table 9–5 | Questions for Test Selection

Reliability	How is the measurement consistent? Statistical measurements exist that will calculate the reliability of the results. For example, an instrument (such as a multiple-choice survey) purports to measure patient satisfaction. The problem that a high reliability score presents in this situation is that a survey tool could be consistent (reliable) but could also be consistently measuring the wrong thing.
Validity	Does the instrument measure what it should measure accurately and in an unbiased fashion (in this case, patient satisfaction)? Validity cannot exist without reliability, but reliability can exist without validity.
Conceptualization	Has the researcher defined the variables as clearly and precisely as possible? For example, are the variables related or is there a direct relationship? Are the independent and dependent variables identified? An example of a related variable is that people who are obese will have different sleep patterns than people who are not. An example of a direct relationship is that people who are obese will have disturbed sleep cycles. The independent variable is obesity, and the dependent variable is disturbed sleep.
Operationalization	How will the study measure the variables? Will it be a quantitative study (measuring the differences in the amounts of variables) or a qualitative study (measuring the differences in the types of variables)?

Historically, the HIM staff would perform retrospective data collection, meaning that the process of converting the paper record into a computerized abstract of the same would be performed after a patient was discharged. This occurred primarily because the health record used by those who provide direct patient care (e.g., physicians, nurses, and other allied health professionals), is needed to enter orders and view test results while care is delivered. Following patient discharge, the record would be collected from the nurses' station and delivered to the HIM department, and the process of manually entering data items into a special HIM database (data abstraction) would begin.

Today, most HIM departments either already support an electronic HIM (e-HIM) environment or are moving toward doing so. In this scenario, data abstraction duties are transferred from data clerks to automated data collection systems. At this point concurrent data collection can occur, meaning that data can be gathered at the time they are entered through the use of modern interface and transmission standards. The process of having one computer application (e.g., Admission, Discharge, and Transfer, or ADT system) directly deposit data elements into a specialized data collection system is referred to as a cold feed process. In this process, interface rules are set up to capture certain data elements from all complementary computer systems and deposit them into a receiving data bank. The HIM analyst's main focus in this arrangement is on report generation rather than traditional data abstraction.

Health care facilities typically collect seven broad categories of patient data: dates, counts, test results, diagnoses, procedures, treatment outcomes, and assessments. These seven categories can be applied to many populations, including inpatients, outpatients, emergency room patients, and employees. Dates and counts are specifications that include dates of admission or discharge, dates of delivery, counts of the number of patients treated at a health clinic, and counts of the number of tests performed, among others. Formulae that support the collection and reporting of these statistics include the Average Daily Census, the Average Length of Stay, and the Percentage of Occupancy. Test results cover a broad range, including hematology workups, urinalysis, bone marrow tests, blood typing, and toxicology. Test counts are reviewed from both nonclinician and clinician perspectives. Nonclinicians look to test counts as simple counts used to evaluate workloads and turnaround times. Clinicians view test results to gain insight into how to improve patient outcomes. For example, an oncologist would review test results to correlate the incidence of acceptable bone marrow matches compared to the degree of familial relationships (e.g., donor = parent, donor = sibling, donor = no familial relationship).

Diagnosis and procedure codes are important data categories. Diagnosis codes are assigned to patients at different stages of care (e.g., admitting and discharge), and they permit a disease index or database to be generated. These codes can be used for nonclinical purposes also, such as the creation of productivity count statistics per coder (number of charts coded per hour) and the incidence count by diagnosis, which will be used by the hospital's administrative staff for planning purposes (e.g., an increase in births could signal a need for a new mothers' unit). Procedure codes are assigned after surgical or diagnostic procedures are performed on patients, permitting a procedures index or database to be generated. Procedural codes offer nonclinical value as well, particularly when they are used to track resource utilization. Unlike diagnosis codes that may not be directly tied to reimbursement (e.g., a patient could have a chronic condition that is not treated), the procedure code is linked to the delivery of services with each procedure having a corresponding financial value for the institution. For example, an ultrasound has a current procedural terminology (CPT) code that has a charge associated with it. This linking of procedures to charges is tracked using a computerized program known as a Charge Description Master (CDM). An institution can determine detailed usage statistics on procedures by monitoring the CDM activity.

Indices are created once the diagnoses and procedures are translated into codes and stored in an index (a directory of similar values). HIM departments may maintain numerous indices, but, at a minimum, they will maintain a diagnosis index and a procedure index. These indices are used as source documents in statistical reporting for clinical needs. For example, surgical residents must perform a certain number of surgeries during their surgical rotation tour. The procedure index kept by the HIM department provides residents with reports that identify the types of procedures they have performed, the dates of the procedures, and, if desired, the patient discharge status (home, transfer to another facility, deceased, etc.).

The outcomes of a patient's treatment can be measured and assessed with comparisons. Outcomes typically track incidence rates of care provided by service. The patient information collected includes the type of patient, the patient's service, the length of stay, the service transfer rates, and the patient's discharge status. For example, the HIM department may need to create a report of all outpatients (type) with a fracture (ICD-9 diagnosis) assigned to Surgery (service) who had a cast applied (ICD-9 procedure) and were discharged home (status) within 24 hours or less (date/times).

Assessments use the personal health information data to support effective clinical studies. Assessments tend to be either qualitative or quantitative in nature. In a qualitative study, the data are categorized by a quality or characteristic, such as scoring of patient satisfaction surveys. In a quantitative study, the data are identified by the differences in amount, frequency, or degree that exists (e.g., the incidence of nosocomial infections for a particular operative unit).

Figure 9-5 | Inpatient service day

The total number of inpatients at census-taking time

+ admissions

− discharges

+ transfers-in

− transfers-out

+ those admitted and discharged the same day

= Inpatient Service Day

Table 9-6 | Abbreviations Used in HIM Formulae and Rates

A&D	Admission & Discharge; inpatients admitted and discharged on the same day (includes deaths)
A&C	Adults & Children; any inpatient other than a newborn
ALOS	Average Length of Stay
CTT	Census-Taking Time; number of inpatients (only) at time of count
DC or DIS	Discharge
DD	Discharge Days
DIPC	Daily Inpatient Census; number of inpatients at CCT and A&D
DIPC+ IPSD	Total Inpatient Service Days; the sum of all IPSD for each of the days in consideration
DOA	Dead on Arrival
IP	Inpatient
IPSD	Inpatient Service Days
LOS	Length of Stay
NB	Newborn; the count of live births that occur in the hospital
OB	Obstetrical
OP	Outpatient
TRF-in TRF-out	Transfer in and Transfer out; the count of patients transferred from one service to another

Statistical Formulae   Once the data are collected, formulae are applied. The results are compiled into a form that possesses significance and can be used for decision-making purposes. Multiple formulae exist within the health care context—more than 50 formulae apply to the HIM profession alone. A limited number are discussed here to illustrate typical formulae applied in a hospital context. The **daily inpatient census** describes the number of patients who were present at the official census-taking time each day plus the number of patients who were admitted and discharged that same day. Accordingly, the inpatient census reflects the total number of patients treated at the hospital within a 24-hour period. The **inpatient service day** describes the services received by one patient during one 24-hour period. This 24-hour period occurs in the 24-hour window between census-taking times. Both of these daily figures are totals for one specific day. **Length of stay** describes the number of calendar days between the day of patient admission and the day of discharge. Formulae illustrating the daily inpatient census and average length of stay are found in Figures 9-5 and 9-6.

Rate formulae are also utilized in hospitals and other health care settings and can be explained as the number of times something happens divided by the number of times it *could* have happened. This general pattern can be applied to multiple situations and areas, including occupancy, morbidity, mortality, natality, autopsy, cesarean sections, complications, and nosocomial infections. Although not every possible rate is discussed in this chapter, a fair number are discussed as a way to illustrate how the general pattern applies in different situations and areas. Furthermore, these rates commonly use abbreviations as a way to condense instructions. A listing of abbreviations used in HIM formulae and rates can be found in Table 9-6.

Before applying a rate formula to the health care setting, it is instructive to apply the general pattern to the context of everyday life. Doing so provides a basic understanding of how the formula works so that its application in the health care setting makes sense. Say a commuter takes the same route to work every day for 50 days. On 35 of those days, the commuter stops at the red light at one particular intersection. Using the general pattern, the number 50 would be divided into 35 to reach a total of 0.70. Viewed as a rate, one could state that the commuter stopped at the red light 35/50 times. Viewed as a percentage, the number .70 would be multiplied by 100 to equal 70%. This same pattern can be used for virtually any example where quantities are to be compared. Within the health care setting, rates are used to study the types of events and diseases that occur in a given period, as well as to examine the quality of care provided during that same period.

Two measures are frequently used to determine **morbidity rates**, the ratio of sick to well persons in the community: prevalence and incidence. **Prevalence rates** are the proportion of known cases of a disease for a particular time period divided by the total population for the same period; this is shown mathematically in Figure 9-7. For example, the number of deaths that result from the disease of whooping cough in infants aged 0-12 months in year one divided by

Figure 9-6 | Average length of stay

Total length of stay (discharge days)

Total discharges (includes deaths)

Figure 9-7 | Prevalence rate

$$\frac{\text{Number of known cases of a disease (for a period of time)}}{\text{Population count for the period}}$$

the number of live births in year one would show the prevalence of this disease in the infant population. If 504 cases of whooping cough are reported, and the number of recorded live births is 4,500,000, the formula would be: $504 \div 4,500,000 \times 100,000 = 11.2$. This is then presented as a ratio: the ratio of whooping cough is 11.2 cases per 100,000 births. Incidence rates are the proportion of newly reported cases of a disease for a particular time period divided by the total population at risk during the same period. This rate is shown mathematically in Figure 9-8. Incidence rates are particularly important when new diseases emerge, such as when incidences of the hantavirus in the American Southwest were reported during the 1990s. One rate that can be associated with prevalence and incidence rates is the case fatality rate. Case fatality rates are the measurement of how deadly a disease is within a given population; this rate is shown mathematically in Figure 9-9.

When determining mortality rates, the rate of death in a given population or community, it is important to understand that many factors can influence the occurrence of death. For example, a patient's severity of illness, age, sex, and race may all play a role in death. Many types of mortality rates are commonly calculated, including anesthesia death rate, postoperative death rate, maternal death rate, fetal death rate, and infant death rate. The formulae for these mortality rates are illustrated in Figure 9-10.

Although rates are not calculated as percentages, in a technical sense, some rates are referred to so commonly in percentage form that this has become the standard reference. For example, occupancy rates, nosocomial infection rates, C-section rates, consultation rates, and autopsy rates are all commonly referred to using the percentage form. An occupancy rate refers to the percentage of use of available beds or bassinets on a specific day or for a specific time period. A nosocomial infection rate refers to the number of hospital-based infections divided by the total number of discharges (including deaths). A C-section rate refers to the percentage of deliveries performed by Cesarean section as compared to all deliveries. A consultation rate refers to the number of patients who receive a consultation by a physician whose expertise is different from the patient's attend-

Figure 9-8 | Incidence rate

$$\frac{\text{Newly reported cases of a disease (for a period of time)}}{\text{Population count at the mid-period}}$$

Figure 9-9 | Case fatality rate

$$\frac{\text{Number of deaths for a given disease}}{\text{Number of cases of the disease reported}}$$

ing physician, divided by the total number of patients discharged. An autopsy rate refers to the total number of autopsies (postmortem) performed on inpatient deaths for a specific time period divided by the total number of inpatient deaths (including newborns, children, and adults). Each of these rates follows the same general pattern outlined earlier in this section, allowing for ease in understanding; these rates are shown mathematically in Figure 9-11.

Calculations of daily census and length of stay are widely performed by HIM professionals. The census is "the number of inpatients present in a healthcare facility at any time."[2] A variety of census formulae exist that reflect different types of census calculations, including the Adult and Children Average Daily Inpatient Census, the Newborn Inpatient Census, and the Average Daily Census for a Clinical Unit. The Average Daily Census describes the number of patients present at the official census-taking time each day and includes patients who were admitted and discharged the same day. The following conditions are of particular concern when calculating census: Adult & Children and Newborn data are to be collected separately; the number of days in the month must be considered (not every month has 30 days); and leap years must be accounted for when calculating annual totals. Figure 9-12 shows the average daily census calculation. Like the census, length of stay also includes a variety of formulae, including Length of Stay (LOS) for Inpatient; Total LOS for all Inpatients; and Average LOS. This last formula describes the average length of hospital stays of a group of inpatients for a given time period. A special concern when calculating length of stay is not to include the day of discharge.

Data Presentation

As important as it is to collect data and apply formulae, communication of the data in numerical form is required to aid understanding. To accomplish this, one must understand the different types of data, scales of measurement, and how data can be presented.

Multiple types or classifications of data are recognized and used in statistics. Several main types exist, with many variations existing within each type. Discrete data refers to data in which the specific values are distinct and separate, and points between these values are not considered valid. Two typical examples of discrete data are the grades assigned to a course (A+, A, A−, B+, B, B−, etc.) and blood groups (O, A, B, AB). Only the grades that are assigned to the course are valid—for example, a grade of B+++ would be considered invalid. Similarly, only the categories of blood groups

Figure 9–10 | Mortality rate formulae

Anesthesia death rate	$\dfrac{\text{Total no. of anesthesia deaths for period} \times 100}{\text{Total no. of anesthesia administered for same period}}$
Postoperative death rate	$\dfrac{\text{Total no. of deaths (within 10 days of surgery)} \times 100}{\text{Total no. of patients who received surgery for the same period}}$
Maternal death rate	$\dfrac{\text{Total no. of deaths of obstetric patients} \times 100}{\text{Total no. of discharges (including deaths) of obstetric patients for same period}}$
Fetal death rate	$\dfrac{\text{By category total no. of fetal deaths that occurred} \times 100}{\text{Total no. of births (including fetal deaths) for same period}}$

1. Early fetal death < 20 weeks gestation or 500 grams or less

2. Intermediate fetal death > 20 weeks gestation or 501-1000 grams

3. Late fetal death > 28 weeks gestation or over 1001 grams

Infant death rate (from moment of birth to first year of life)	$\dfrac{\text{Total no. of deaths of infants born in hosp. for period} \times 100}{\text{Total no. of infants discharged (including infant deaths) for same period}}$

are valid—a blood group of Z would be considered invalid. **Continuous data** refers to the values that lie within a certain range. Examples include height, weight, temperature, length, and the time required to run a mile. In some instances, continuous data cannot be measured to infinite precision; a level of discreteness is applied in those instances. For example, a person's height is generally measured in feet and inches as opposed to only to the nearest foot or at levels smaller than the nearest inch. **Categorical data** refers to a set of data in which the values belonging to the set can be sorted according to logical categories wherein each category does not overlap another category. An example of categorical data is sorting towels according to color (red, blue, brown, green, etc.).

Some categories of data can also serve as scales of measurement. **Nominal data** is a data set that classifies values but does not require a logical ordering of those values. "Male" and "female" are typical examples of nominal data. It does not matter if male is placed before female in a set of data, or if female or male is greater or less than the other.

Figure 9–11 | Various rate formulae

Occupancy rate	$\dfrac{\text{Total no. of beds/bassinets in use for time period}}{\text{Total no. of available beds or bassinets for same period}}$	$\times 100$
Nosocomial infection rate	$\dfrac{\text{Total no. of hospital-based infections}}{\text{Total no. of patients discharged (including deaths) for the same period}}$	$\times 100$
Cesarean-section rate	$\dfrac{\text{Total no. of deliveries performed by C-section}}{\text{Total no. of deliveries (vaginal and C-section) for same period}}$	$\times 100$
Consultation rate	$\dfrac{\text{Total no. of patients receiving consultations}}{\text{Total no. of patients discharged for same period}}$	$\times 100$
Autopsy rate (including newborns, children, and adults)	$\dfrac{\text{Total no. of autopsies performed for period}}{\text{Total no. of inpatient deaths for same period}}$	$\times 100$

Figure 9–12 | Average daily census

Total service days for the unit for the period
Total number of days in the period

What matters is that some classification of males and females is made according to the values in the data set. The example used in the fraction problem earlier in the chapter showed nominal data of 33 females and 66 males; yet another example of nominal data is "married" and "single." **Ordinal data** refers to a data set that is ordered, though the differences between the values are not important. This allows data to be ranked even though the differences between two ordinal values cannot be quantified. For example, a survey that ranks answers on a Likert scale (i.e., 1 = Strongly agree; 2 = Agree; 3 = Neutral; 4 = Disagree; 5 = Strongly disagree) shows a scale of ordinal values. Although a difference exists between "Agree" and "Strongly agree," this difference cannot be quantified. Ordinal values are used in other contexts as well, including restaurant ratings and political party determinations (e.g., the Green party lies to the left of the Democratic party on the political spectrum). **Interval data** refers to a data set that is both ordered and constant but contains no natural zero as a point of reference. For example, the time that elapses between the start of the year 2005 and the year 2006 is constant: 365 days. There is no significance or meaning to the zero point of 1 A.D. because it is arbitrary in this context. Temperature scales are another example of interval data. A physical meaning can be interpreted from the difference between the interval values of 10°F and 20°F. Because 0°F is arbitrary in this context, to say that 20°F is twice as hot as 10°F makes no sense.

Once the type of data and the scale to which it can be measured have been determined, the next step is to present the data in visual form, typically in graphs. Graphs that are clear, concise, and correct are invaluable and can serve to "tell the story" in a manner that extensive written materials cannot. This is particularly true for topics that consist mostly of numbers, which some readers may find boring or intimidating. Presenting the same information with a visual image (a graph) instead may make it easier for the reader to understand the results.

Several graphing rules apply to most situations. First and foremost, a graph should be self-explanatory: a title, labeled axes, and all information necessary to understand the graph should be included. Abbreviations should be avoided. If a pie chart is used, wedges should be displayed clockwise in descending order, from largest to smallest, and the label for each wedge should indicate the data it references. As a result, the reader should know exactly what information is being presented. Second, the scale should be easily readable—the values should not be crowded into one corner or spread apart too thinly. In essence, there should be proportion of scale on both

Table 9–7 | Managing Graphs: An Accuracy Check

Title reflects the content of the graph; synonyms are avoided.

Color is used to help identify categories.

Bars *within* a category are limited for multiple bar charts.

Each pie slice is labeled with its percentage (and, if possible, category label).

Date of data collection appears in the legend.

The x-axis and the y-axis are properly labeled.

Legends include all information needed to interpret the graph.

Bar chart categories reflect a logical flow (alphabetical or numerical order).

Pie slices are displayed in order, from largest to smallest.

The y-axis begins at 0 to preserve the scale.

A single graph is not overloaded; if necessary, more than one graph is used, with each image focused on a key aspect.

the x-axis and the y-axis. Third, if more than one curve or line is displayed on a single graph for comparison purposes, the curves or lines should be differentiated from one another. This may be conveyed through the use of dotted, broken, or colored lines, or by using different symbols. Fourth, the starting point of the graph should be clearly marked. Although many graphs begin with the two axes intersecting at the number zero, this is not always appropriate. The graph should clearly indicate the starting point, whatever it may be. Finally, the independent and dependent variables should be plotted on the proper axes—the independent variable on the x-axis and the dependent variable on the y-axis. An accuracy check should be conducted for each graph created. Table 9–7 lists some of the elements in an accuracy check.

The easiest way to understand presentation methods are bar graphs, line graphs, pie charts, and histograms. A **bar graph** is used to present the frequency of categorical data through the use of horizontal and vertical axes. Discrete categories of data are displayed on the horizontal axis. The vertical axis shows the frequency, using a scale beginning at zero so as to correlate the height of the bars with the frequency measured. The bars do not touch and are of uniform width, with only the height of the bars differing. A bar graph is illustrated in Figure 9–13.

A **line graph** resembles a bar graph except that it uses lines instead of bars to represent data in numerical form. A line graph is frequently used to display time trends, with a line showing a connection of single points. The classic example of a line graph is a sales graph that shows how sales have gone up or down over a period of time. A line graph is illustrated in Figure 9–14.

A **pie chart** represents the frequency of data through the use of a circle divided into sections that correspond to the frequency of each category. A good rule of thumb is that

Figure 9–13 | Bar graph

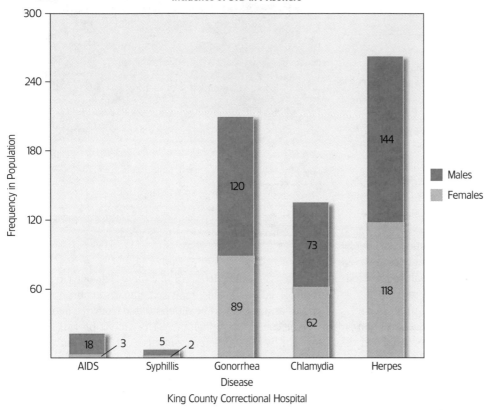

Incidence of STD in Prisoners

King County Correctional Hospital

Figure 9–14 | Line graph

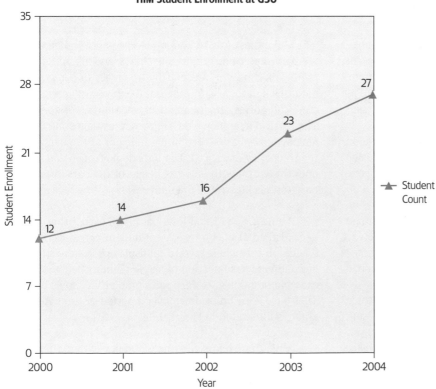

HIM Student Enrollment at GSU

Figure 9–15 | Pie chart

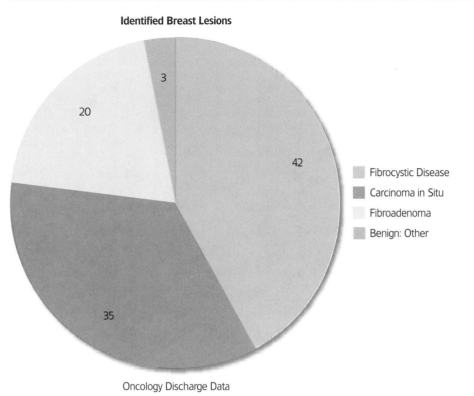

Identified Breast Lesions

- Fibrocystic Disease
- Carcinoma in Situ
- Fibroadenoma
- Benign: Other

Oncology Discharge Data

a pie chart should not have more items than the number of days in a week (seven). If more than seven categories need to be displayed, a pie chart should be avoided and another graph should be chosen instead. The use of color can assist the reader in tracking the changes from one category to the next. A pie chart is illustrated in Figure 9–15.

A **histogram** is similar to a bar graph in its use of horizontal and vertical axes but differs in that the vertical axis contains continuous intervals for categories. A histogram is used to convey how a single variable is used continuously through a set of data, as well as the "magnitude" of the relationship between variables. The y-axis (vertical) in a histogram shows frequency using the calculated width and height of the bars. A wide bar reflects more frequency; a thin bar reflects less frequency. Histograms are often reserved for advanced statistical presentations because a special statistical program application may be required to calculate the height and area of the bar. A histogram is illustrated in Figure 9–16.

A **frequency polygon** resembles a histogram except that it takes a line form rather than a bar form. This type of graph is very well suited to superimposing the data within one graph (e.g., male and female results), thus making comparisons easy for the reader. The frequency polygon should only be used to display numerical values (e.g., amounts, weights, scores, etc.). Points are plotted on a graph and con-

nected by a straight line from one point to the next. A frequency polygon is shown in Figure 9–17.

Not every display option includes a graph; some information may be easily presented in table form. For example, assume that three transcribing vendors are competing to win a contract to provide transcription services to Anywhere Hospital. The HIM manager has viewed three sales demonstrations and reviewed the vendors' sealed bids. The manager summarizes the findings for submission to the decision maker, using a desktop application such as a word processing program. Table 9–8 shows how the HIM manager's table may look.

Regression Analysis

While statistics are often used to "tell the story," some stories are more difficult to tell because the data comprising the statistics are hard to understand or do not clearly show a pattern. This is where regression analysis comes into play. **Regression analysis** is a statistical tool that is used to investigate relationships between variables by modeling these relationships and determining their magnitude. In other words, regression analysis uses statistical techniques to identify correlations between variables that were not otherwise obvious. Regression analysis seeks to determine the correlation between at least one variable and another. **Correlation** refers to a mutual relation or interdependence between two or more things. To illustrate, think of things from everyday life

Figure 9–16 | Histogram

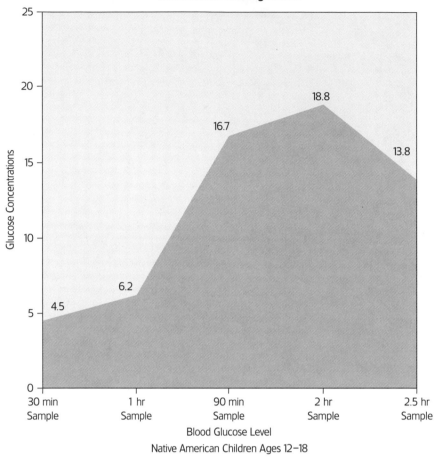

Blood Glucose Challenge Levels

Native American Children Ages 12–18

that may have relationships with one another. For example, snow and rain do not typically occur at the same time that a bright sun appears in the sky; this is an example of negative correlation. If the sky is cloudy and the weather is cold, it may snow or rain; this is an example of positive correlation.

The strength of regression analysis is that it can establish correlations; the weakness of regression analysis is that it can't always prove causation. For example, one can establish through regression analysis that a relationship exists between *A* and *B*, but it may be possible that *A* causes *B*, that *B* causes *A*, or that *A* and *B* are caused by something entirely different, *C*. For that reason, regression analysis often attempts to look at multiple variables, isolate two for purposes of focus, and establish controls for the other variables. This requires gathering data on underlying variables and employing a regression model to estimate the quantitative effect of the variables upon the variable being influenced. The end result of these estimated relationships is then analyzed for statistical significance to determine that a degree of confidence exists between the true relationship and the estimated relationship.

Regression analysis concerns itself with predictive power. Why should we be concerned with predictive power? A simple example illustrates the reason. Imagine a hospital

that is down to its last 200 units of antibiotics. Once this supply is exhausted, there will be no more. A regression analysis on existing data (how many patients received antibiotics previously) can be used to solve the problem and predict the future outcome—in this case, how many days are left before the hospital runs out of antibiotics.

Regression analysis is particularly useful when only one variable can be explained—in other words, when data are known about the predictor data, but data on the outcome variable are unknown or unavailable. Because only one variable will provide the answer, this is referred to as **simple regression** or **univariate regression**. For example, a univariate study could involve a review of body temperatures in patients experiencing acute appendicitis, in which the body temperature is the single variable. If two variables will provide the answer, the term **bivariate regression** is employed. Using the same example, the study may track the temperatures of appendicitis patients following the administration of antibiotics. If numerous variables are used to provide the answer, the term **multivariate regression** is employed. Studies that use multivariate regression analysis are common in medical research because of the nature of the disease process. Medical research often defines these variables as anything that will affect the course of a disease in a particular patient (i.e.,

Figure 9–17 | Frequency polygon

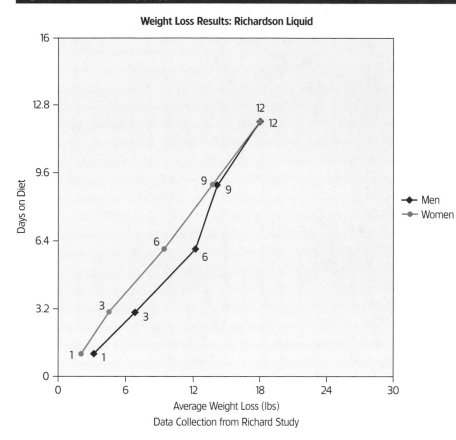

Weight Loss Results: Richardson Liquid

Average Weight Loss (lbs)

Data Collection from Richard Study

complications and comorbidities). For example, a study using multivariate regression analysis could examine the patient's age, weight, presence of chronic illnesses, and whether the patient uses tobacco, alcohol, or recreational drugs.

Although many people think that regression analysis belongs primarily to the disciplines of mathematics and economics, its application is quite widespread. It has become particularly prominent in the legal field during the last few decades; in particular, it has been used to prove racial discrimination in death penalty litigation and to prove damages in antitrust litigation and contract actions. Within the health care field, regression analysis has been used to support the policy, planning, and operational components of health care organizations, to add validity and reliability to research studies, and to serve as a key element in the development of diagnosis-related groups and their use in prospective payment systems. Several models of regression analysis exist and are discussed in this section.

Regression Analysis Models The statistic generated in regression analysis is R^2, which is a score that lies somewhere between 0 and 1. The closer the score is to 1, the stronger the predicted outcome and the larger the degree of confidence between the true relationship and the estimated relationship.

Pearson product-moment correlation (r) is a regression analysis formula used to determine whether a relationship exists between two variables when both variables are numbers (either interval or ratio data). It is important to note that the intent of Pearson is to measure the relationship between variables, not differences between variables. For example, to determine if a relationship exists between an intelligence quotient (IQ) and how students perform on an exam, one could sample students taking the test and plot the results using a Pearson product-moment correlation. A Pearson correlation can be a negative number or a positive number between −1 and 1. The closer the value is to 0, the

Table 9–8 | Table of Transcription Bids

Vendor:	On the Spot, Inc.	Every Word, Inc.	4Word, Inc.
24 month quote:	$85,400	$52,000	$120,000
References:	6+, 1−	1+, 10−	New, no references
HIM Dept. Recommendation:	Midrange quote with strong history of meeting customer promises	Difficult to find a satisfied customer, seems to win business on aggressive bids but fails to deliver timely reports	Most expensive of the vendors, no installed sites; recommend reevaluation in two years

Figure 9–18 | Pearson product-moment correlation

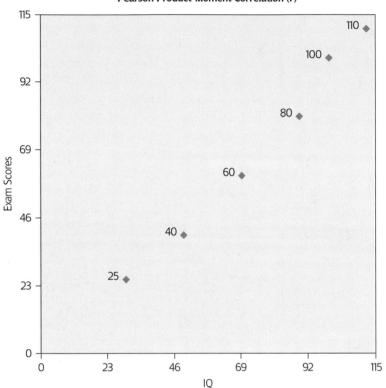

Pearson Product-Moment Correlation (r)

weaker the relationship. The closer the value is to $+1$ or -1, the stronger the relationship. A value of .6 to 1 is considered a strong relationship.

In this example, the IQ and exam scores of six students are put into a formula. A Pearson product-moment correlation formula is then applied to the scores. Once the scores are summed, they are plotted on a basic x/y graph with IQ scores on the x-axis and exam scores on the y-axis (Figure 9–18). The points are then examined to see if a pattern of syncing exists. If the values are moving in sync, this indicates a positive number relationship. If the values are moving opposite of one another, this indicates a negative number relationship. If no syncing occurs, there is no relationship. In this example, a low IQ reveals a low exam score, and a high IQ reveals a high exam score for a correlation of .69. This indicates a positive relationship between IQ and the ability to score well on exams.

Though we know that a positive relationship exists, does a relationship also exist between the *degree of intelligence* and the exam score? Can one predict that someone with an IQ of 135 would score 100 on the exam? A bivariate regression formula is used to determine this. Like the Pearson correlation, a mathematical formula is used to calculate the regression; however, the focus is not on interpreting the formula but on understanding why bivariate regression is the proper tool to use.

To begin, the data from the original Pearson correlation is plotted onto a scatter plot (or diagram), with alpha (α) and beta (β) measurements appearing on the graph. Alpha is the intercept point on this graph, or the first point to appear on the y-axis (the lowest exam score). Beta is the line drawn to connect the points, with consideration given to the slope of the line on the plotted graph. Beta shows how an increase in IQ affects the exam score, as seen in Figure 9–19.

The scatter diagram in Figure 9–20 has been enhanced with a line drawing that resembles the rise and rung of stairs, wherein the rungs are the horizontal surface on the graph and the rise is the vertical surface. The point where the two meet is the beta. Beta measures the rung and rise of each point. In this example, each plot value (rung) represents one point of the IQ, and the rise (exam score) goes up a half a point ($\beta = .49$). By drawing a line to connect the tops of the stairs, we see the regression line appear. In this example, beta proves that with each point increase in IQ (from 100 to 101), the exam score goes up half a point (e.g., from 82 to 82.5). Accordingly, a relationship exists between IQ and exam scores: smarter students do better on the exam (this is proven with the Pearson correlation). The bivariate regression (the beta) also shows a half-point improvement in exam scores for every point increase in IQ.

One question worth asking is: how likely are these results to be the consequence of pure chance or coincidence

Figure 9–19 | Bivariate regression using data from Pearson correlation

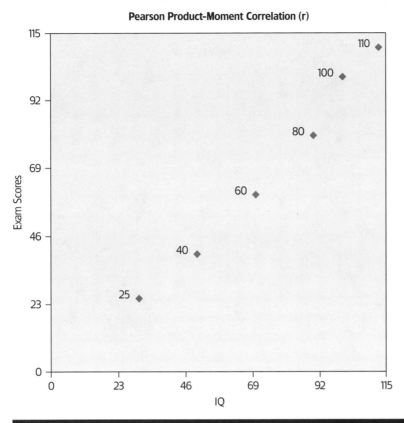

Pearson Product-Moment Correlation (r)

Figure 9–20 | Scatter (plot) diagram displaying alpha and beta

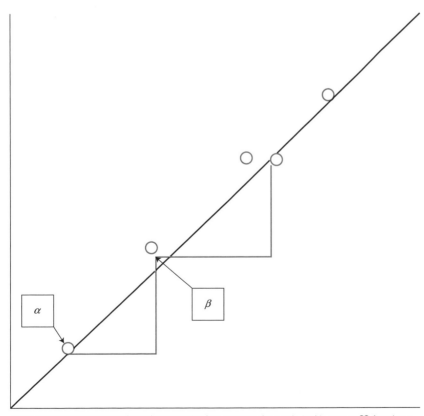

Alpha is the intercept point where the regression line starts on the y-axis, in this case at 23. Imagine a stairstep line being drawn between each value. The beta is the slope of the line formed. In this case, the beta demonstrates that with every unit increase in predictor there is a beta change in the slope—as beta increases upward (exam scores), I.Q. increases.

Figure 9–21 | Bell shape distribution

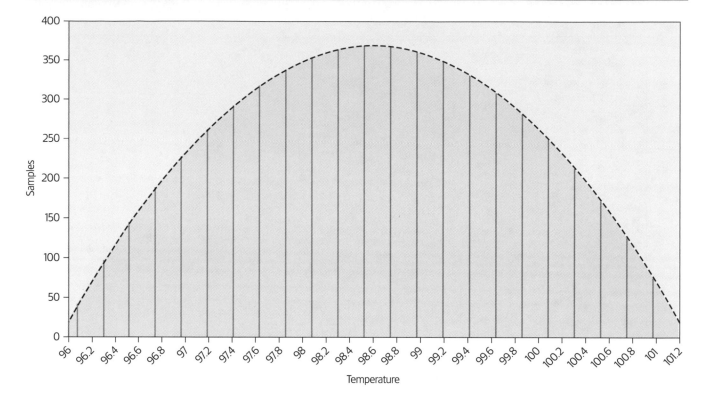

rather than the result of the variable under study (in this case, the student's IQ)? Regression analysis determines this significance (R^2), which measures how much of the variance in one variable is attributable to the other variable under study. According to most published papers, a research study that is measuring human nature will accept a significance value of .05 as a valid result. This means that if one were to test a large group of students for IQ and HIM exam scores, 5% or less would have a higher exam score as a result of pure chance. In other words, a 95% or greater likelihood exists that the results are because of the student's natural IQ. With regard to human-based performance studies, a confidence level of .05 is acceptable. However, when the research study examines pharmacology results or clinical outcomes for a special treatment, it is not unusual to see the study held to a standard of .01. This means that the researcher is confident that the results are because of pure chance only 1% of the time or less.

When a research study is conducted, the variable is measured and these measurements are evaluated for range (highs and lows) and frequency (how often a measurement repeats). With enough measurements, the researcher will see a pattern emerge in the collected samples. For example, body temperature is the variable in an appendicitis study. If the study is tracking 100 patients, a wide variety of temperatures will be recorded, depending upon how sick the patients are. Nonetheless, an upper limit and a lower limit will exist—for example, no temperature of 200° will be seen, and a clustering of scores around a middle

measurement will occur. This pattern is referred to as the **distribution** of the variable. Most distributions will reveal a bell-shaped curve with some extremely high temperatures at one end, some extremely low temperatures at the other end, and most temperatures clustering in the middle (the 98.6° to 103° range), thus creating the bell-shaped distribution. Figure 9–21 illustrates this example.

Some studies are quite complex; for that reason, a different regression model may be needed. Similar to a t-test is the **ANOVA test** or F-test. This test is performed when a need exists to compare more than two groups. The ANOVA correlation (sometimes referred to as analysis of variance) test has limitations; one should think of it as an early warning system to test a hypothesis—sort of a "go"/"no go" type of test to see if the researcher is on the right track. If the significance level is below .05, the null hypothesis is rejected. The researcher's next step would likely be to perform multiple t-test analyses to obtain a better idea of what is causing the differences in the variables. If the significance level is above .05—for example, a p value of .241—the hypothesis is rejected because of the significance in the difference between the variables.

As discussed earlier in the chapter, the Pearson product-moment correlation (r) is a formula used to determine whether a relationship exists between two variables when both variables are numbers (either interval or ratio data). Another type of predictive statistic is the **chi-square** (X^2). If a study is attempting to measure the relationship between two variables that are categorical (placing subjects into categories), the chi-square test is used. Chi-square is often used in qualitative studies, wherein one is attempting to determine the degree of association among qualitative variables.

A real-life example can be used to illustrate the chi-square test. Assume that an HIM director has experienced a high turnover in staff and chooses to use a chi-square test to determine the cause. The director's hypothesis is that employees with certification are more likely to stay on the job than staff hired without certification. Chi-square looks at two data sets: the observed data (what is seen) and the predicted data (what is expected). The predicted data are derived from the observed data. In this example, nine certified staff members stay one year (75%) and four noncertified staff members stay one year (28%). The chi-square is computed to determine the likelihood of this outcome (predicting the expected stay rates) to be that six certified staff will stay one year and seven noncertified staff will stay one year. As a result, the director has rejected the null hypothesis (no association between length of employment and certification) with a p of .017. This means that the director's hypothesis is proven: an association exists between certification and staying on the job.

Regression analysis is a fundamental element of grouper programs. A variety of grouper programs are used in the health care field—diagnosis-related groups (DRGs), all patient refined-diagnosis related groups (APR-DRGs), and ambulatory payment classification groups (APCs) are only a few. These groupers are methods used to place patients into similar disease or procedure categories so that predictive values are available to anticipate resource utilization (how much) and length of stay (how long) with regard to patient stays.

Within the HIM department, a case mix analysis (a type of DRG) report is run every day. This report helps guide a variety of departments to plan their workload and assist patients in making the transition to home. **Case mix** refers to the types and volume of patients treated by a health care facility. Groups of diagnostically related patients are clustered under general headings; being aware of the types, volume, and nature of patients being treated helps a health care facility anticipate need in the near future.

A DRG assignment is derived from a computer algorithm that considers a mix of variables: patient's age, gender, length of stay, discharge status, diagnoses, and procedures. Millions of possible outcomes exist based on these variables. Regression analysis is performed on millions of patient records (MEDPAR files) in order to derive a high confidence level that the DRG is measuring what it purports to measure. The DRG can predict an expected length of stay (how many days are needed to treat the patient) and the expected amount of dollars need to treat the patient (resource usage). Statistical analysis is performed annually on the diagnostic-related groups, and refinements are made to the individual DRG assignment in light of changes to treatment protocols, new medications, and new surgical tools that can affect the two key measurements of DRGs (length of stay and resource utilization).

Health Information Management Statistics

Most of the statistics collected in health information management departments are of the descriptive type. Results are presented as actual counts or percentiles and are created by using standardized formula sets. The most commonly used statistical formulas in HIM include: inpatient service days, occupancy ratios, mortality rates, length of stay, and discharge days; frequency statistics are traditionally captured in acute care environments. The results of these statistics are shared with a wide range of other hospital departments because they represent the level of activity in the hospital. Other uses include justification for opening new services, closing existing services, purchasing new medical equipment, and determining whether to increase or decrease staff. For example, a hospital experiencing a rapid increase in growth in their community could determine by looking at usage rates in the trauma center that it is time to add additional doctors and nurses to handle the increased workload. Conversely, if a community suffers the loss of a large employer, the neighborhood hospital may be forced to reduce existing services to reflect the new lower census rate. Often, these types of decisions can only be made via the use of statistics that show trends over time.

The burden placed on HIM staff to collect data has been largely eliminated with the introduction of the computerized cold feed of data. As a result, other activities have filled the void. In this case, the HIM department has seen a sharp increase in the amount of statistical reports needed by others, including administration and medical staff. The role of the HIM analyst is to determine whether existing data feeds are adequate or if requests are received for which data are unattainable. The analyst will track such things as what reports are needed routinely, what reports are needed by new federal or state regulations, and whether a novel approach can be employed to present results that can help clinicians make better health care decisions (e.g., the automated collection of clinical errors).

Productivity

Every organization requires feedback to operate effectively. Is work evenly distributed? Are productivity and timeliness standards being met? Are resources being allocated effectively and appropriately? What will the workload be next month? Next year? These and similar queries are asked continuously, and the accuracy and timeliness of the responses to these queries determine how effectively an organization conducts its business. These responses often require the use of statistics.

Determining how effectively an organization conducts its business requires the skilled use of data and statistics. A wide array of statistics is tracked by HIM professionals at the business level, particularly related to issues of **productivity**, or the ability to produce work outcomes in a timely manner. Although the following discussion focuses on productivity statistics in an acute care environment, the principles discussed are applicable in all health care settings. At a hospital department level, it is important to monitor staff productivity because this is directly related to the needs of an operating budget. This monitoring is often accomplished by tracking the daily work flow output of each member in the department. This type of statistical analysis is known as labor analytics, or the study of productivity.

Labor analytics refers to the activity and business of determining whether a work area has enough staff, too many staff, or is working with a staffing shortage. The HIM department routinely gathers statistical data to measure labor analytics; however, since staffing levels are fairly well set, these measurements are taken on a monthly or quarterly basis. At the end of the review period, a statistical report is created and studied to determine whether the workload managed by the department for that period reflects a need to make staffing adjustments. If the department sees an increase in workload (e.g., charts to code, reports to transcribe, release of information data to ship), the manager will use the statistics as an objective basis to form his request to hire a new staff person. Conversely, if the department sees a continued drop in workload, the statistics may be used by the organization's senior management team to force a staff reduction.

Some hospital departments are very sensitive to changes in labor needs. Their workload is directly affected by the census; as the hospital bed count increases, the need for additional nurses, nursing assistants, housekeeping staff, and lab technicians increases as well. These departments usually have flexible staffing levels, meaning that as the census rises, additional staff members are called in to handle the higher workload. If the census drops, the additional staff members are sent home. Within these flexible staffing areas, labor analytics are run either on a daily basis or on a shift-by-shift basis.

Being able to read labor analytic reports and respond quickly to labor excesses or shortages is an important management skill. The ability to match work volume to available staffing choices helps a health care manager keep operating costs in line with the annual operating budget.

A simple calculation that can be made on a quarterly or annual basis is to measure a hospital's labor ratio. This ratio shows how much earned revenue (money made) is spent to cover labor expenses (money spent). An example of this calculation is shown in Figure 9–22. A hospital that carefully manages labor costs on a daily or weekly basis

Figure 9–22 | Annual labor ratio

$$\frac{\text{Net Operating Revenue for 12 months}}{\text{Total Labor Expenses for 12 months (Salary, Benefits, Contract Charges)}}$$

$$\frac{\$8,478,900}{\$20,000,000} = .42 \times 100 = 42\%$$

will find that the annual labor ratio runs between 35% and 40%. Conversely, a hospital that does not actively manage work hours and staffing needs may have an annual labor ratio between 45% and 50%, numbers that are generally considered high in the health care industry.

If a 42% ratio appears positive, why would one bother with attempting additional improvements? In this example, if the hospital reduces labor expenses by 2% (for a total labor ratio of 40%), it would realize an annual savings of $400,000, or a daily savings of $1,095.85. As a result of this potential for savings, line managers (such as HIM managers) are tasked with finding ways to maintain their annual labor budget and helping to keep the hospital's annual labor ratio low.

Other HIM activities that use labor analytics to measure productivity include productivity tracking of medical transcription (how quickly recorded physician reports are typed and proofed) and productivity tracking of coding (how quickly health records are coded using ICD-9-CM, CPT, and other nomenclatures). Using the coding example, a supervisor may also want to calculate the accuracy rate of the coding staff, a labor analytic for the coding team. This is important because some coding staff members who work quickly may also create many errors. By contrast, some coding staff members may be highly accurate but too slow. Neither scenario is cost-effective for the organization. In light of this, the supervisor will need to determine the coding team's strengths and weaknesses and develop an action plan to help all coders become as quick and accurate as possible. The supervisor may ask the coders to track their outcomes on a template while they are engaged in the coding activity. From these data, the supervisor can track both speed and accuracy. To calculate speed, the supervisor may track the start and stop times for a set of charts. To calculate accuracy, the supervisor could count the total number of accurate codes and divide them by the total number of codes discovered for that coding set. Calculation of the accuracy rate using this scenario is shown in Figure 9–23.

Ensuring a smooth and speedy process for coding and transcription can present unique challenges to the HIM professional. Most coding cannot be considered final until the coder has read the transcribed operative reports and discharge summaries. If a delay exists in either transcribing the reports or reading the transcribed reports, a resultant delay

Figure 9-23 | Labor analytic: calculating accuracy ratio

Data collection:

Coder Name/Chart Type/Chart Count/Time to Code/Errors

Calculation:

The individual coder coded eleven (11) inpatient charts for a total of 60 different codes for the set. An audit of the work reveals that 12 of the codes were either in error or missing.

Accuracy count: 60 − 12 = 48 accurate

Convert to percentage: 48/60 = 0.8($\times$100) = 80%

Accuracy rate: subtract 48 from 60

Error rate: subtract 12 from 60

Note: using 12 as the numerator calculates the error rate; using 48 as the numerator calculates the accuracy rate. This allows a choice of which labor analytic to report—accuracy rate or error rate. This report may be described in these two examples:

Coder/Date/Chart Type/Chart Count/Coding Time/Accuracy:

Kelly/01/01/07/Inpatient/11/1 hr., 13min./80%
Lorraine/01/28/07/Inpatient/20/1 hr., 2 min./94%

---

will occur in coding the health records. Understanding the cause of the delay can contribute to resolving the issue and increasing productivity. For example, delays in transcription may be a result of numerous causes: perhaps the physician never dictated a recording, or the transcriptionist could not understand what was said by the person who was dictating (because of heavy accents, eating while dictating, etc.). By addressing these causes, the HIM professional can ensure that the operative reports and discharge summaries are available to the coder in a timely fashion and thus influence the timeliness of reimbursement.

Statistical Tools Per the predominant form of reimbursement in the United States, a hospital cannot send a bill to the patient's insurance company or a third-party payer until the health record has been coded. Therefore, problems with the transcription process can affect the coding process, which in turn affects the billing process. Today's HIM manager has introduced statistical solutions to solve process problems. Determining the sequence of events and taking measurements at significant points along the way form the foundation of productivity analysis. The statistical tools used to reach these measurements include: control charts, trend charts, and process capability ratios.

Control Charts Among the variety of statistical tools that are available, the control chart is the most commonly used. A control chart is a graph with statistically generated upper and lower control limits used to measure key processes over time. Control charts focus attention on a variation in the process and help a team determine whether a variation is normal or the result of special circumstances. The control chart was invented in the 1920s by Walter Shewhart of Bell Laboratories and was originally referred to as a Shewhart chart. A variety of software applications are available for control chart management, including the Statistical Process Control (SPC) tool used in the Six Sigma process. These software applications greatly aid in the creation and use of control charts.

In the following example, the HIM professional selects a control chart to identify problems with regard to dictation not being completed in a timely manner. The control chart is a simple plotted graph that has three key components: performance data are plotted over time (using sampling techniques); a solid centerline on the graph indicates the average of all of the plotted samples; and a dotted line at the top and bottom of the chart defines the upper and lower sample limits (see Figure 9-24).

The control chart reveals a variation in the plotted points, which may be expected because each physician has his own personal method of completing the required dictation. The focus should be on variation that goes beyond common experiences (what Six Sigma refers to as common cause variation) and extends to unusual experiences

Figure 9–24 | **Control chart**

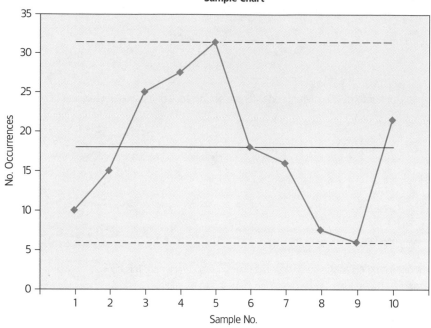

(= special cause variation). In some cases, the HIM professional will discover a special cause (e.g., a dictation that goes off-line for 12 hours at a stretch) and can fix the problem. In other instances, the chart may reveal no special cause variation, only a common cause variation (e.g., physicians eating while dictating results in an unusable recording). In that case, reducing the common cause variation (removing food items from the dictation room or moving dictation stations to the examination rooms) can save time and money.

Using control charts to discover bugs in a process is an excellent way to manage the day-to-day running of a busy HIM department. However, when using control charts one must be aware of two types of errors that can occur. The first, a Type I error, occurs when a sample point falls outside the upper or lower control limits, but there is no special cause to explain it. The manager may invest a great deal of time and energy trying to find out what went wrong, but no

explanation exists. The second, a Type II error, indicates that a special cause exists, but the sampling isn't sensitive enough to discover it, so it remains unnoticed (and unresolved).

Clearly, there is a need for good sampling techniques, and certain rules are central to collecting samples for the control chart: timeliness of samples, sample size, and randomness in sample collection. Considerations for each of these rules are listed in Table 9–9. One can more easily understand the need for these rules by using an example. Assume that a hospital has experienced an increase in patients stricken with hospital-acquired bladder infections at a higher than expected rate. Sample data are collected on nursing catheter techniques. A special cause, an on-call nurse who received bad training in sterile technique, is the source of the hospital-acquired bladder infections. However, this nurse is only on the floor during periods of high census, and then for just a single-shift period. If samples

Table 9–9 | **Rules for Collecting Samples for Control Chart Purposes**

Timeliness	How frequently should samples be taken? As often as needed to capture all of the conditions. Spacing out the sampling over a certain time period (a week or a month) can help to ensure that all circumstances will be captured. Within a health care setting, be certain to sample all shifts in a process that runs 24 hours a day.
Size	The larger the sample size, the more likely special causes will be discovered in the result. A minimum of 25–30 samples is recommended as a way to allow enough variations to be able to detect the cause of process problems. Cost should be considered when determining how large the sample will be.
Collection	Randomness in collecting the samples must be incorporated to avoid disguising the cause of a problem. For example, if the problem is the result of a single employee's technique, collecting samples on all employees on all shifts for a particular time window will allow the control chart to capture the special cause.

Figure 9–25 | Trend chart

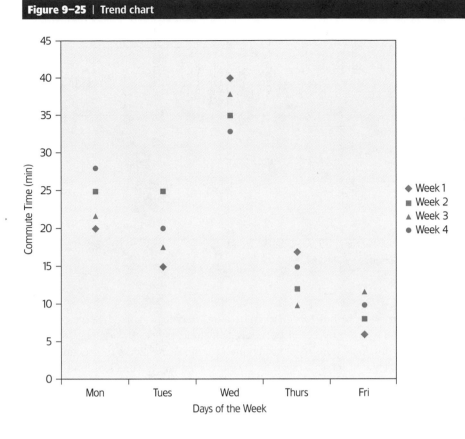

were taken around the clock, and at varying times, this particular nurse who is only on the floor on an occasional basis would be captured on the control chart, leading to the discovery that he is the source of these infections.

Trend Charts Similar to a control chart is the **trend chart**, a graphical presentation of data that shows patterns or shifts according to time. A downward trend contains a section of data points that decrease over a time period, whereas an upward trend shows the opposite. Trend charts differ from control charts because trend charts focus on time patterns; control charts, on the other hand, focus on acceptable limits of a process. Trend charts can be useful, however, to discover patterns in a process over time. Similar to control charts, software applications are available for creating trend charts.

Trend charts have applications in the HIM environment. For example, a coding supervisor in a heart hospital may want to track how long it takes the coding team to code health records of cardiac patients. The supervisor can collect the coding times of the coders by day of the week and then graph the results into a month-long trend chart to evaluate the results. Over time, trends can be revealed that are otherwise invisible in a daily process.

Trend charts are readily understandable by the general public and, therefore, applicable for everyday use. For example, a trend chart would be useful for a person who

commutes to work, following the same route each day, and experiences variations in commute time. By collecting data concerning the commute time each day of the week for a one-month period, the person could plot those data on a trend chart to determine trends or cyclical patterns. Figure 9–25 illustrates a trend chart for this example. From this plotted data, the person can reach decisions about how much time to budget for commuting each day of the week.

Process Capability Analysis Another type of statistical tool seen in HIM and many quality improvement departments is **process capability analysis**, a process control technique. The first rule of using process control techniques is to ensure that the performance being monitored is predictable and brought under statistical control (i.e., there are no special cause variations). The first step is to complete a series of control chart reviews. After determining that the process is essentially working, the second step involves implementing the process capability analysis to ensure continued improvement to the process. It is important to be sensitive to the fact that those statistics that are the foundation of process capability only work in very predictable environments. If large variations exist, the results from a process capability analysis can be misleading. Therefore, if the control chart shows a wide range of variability, it is not appropriate to move to the process capability portion of analysis.

Figure 9-26 | Process capability chart

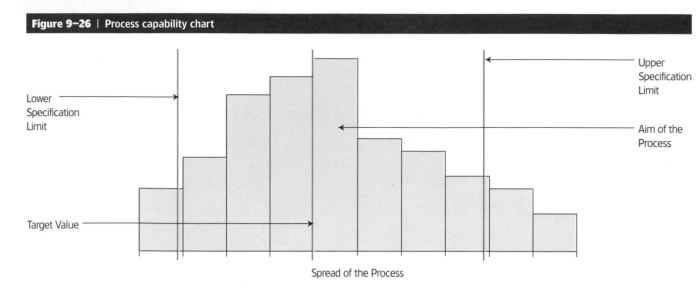

When is it appropriate to use process capability analysis? Lean manufacturing concepts can help to provide an answer. Although it is beyond the scope of this chapter to educate the reader in full on lean manufacturing concepts, a brief description and application can assist the reader's understanding. In lean manufacturing, time is money, and the goal is to take a basically stable and predictable work process and improve it to be more efficient. A simple example illustrates the concept.

A HIM supervisor of imaging feels that he has a stable work group. The team owns the process of converting paper charts to imaged documents from beginning to end, and in general takes about 10 hours to convert a chart to a final image once all of the process steps are taken (cycle time). The supervisor thinks that he can improve the process, possibly reducing the cycle time to eight hours. The supervisor may decide to use a process capability ratio diagram, in which a model is built of each step (component) of the imaging process (see Figure 9-26). This model will demonstrate how much time is spent at each component.

Measuring how much time is spent on each step helps to determine the component parts that make up the total cycle time. In this way, possible cycle time delays

(bottlenecks) can be identified and resolved. Some common sources of bottlenecks include: physical workspace restrictions (e.g., not enough room for the clerks to prepare the charts, or excessive clutter leading to time lost hunting for pages that have become loose or damaged) and delay time due to personnel matters (e.g., smoking breaks and impromptu meetings). Each of these elements will have an effect upon execution time.

The point of process capability analysis is to identify the process, measure each step within the process, and identify areas for improvement. It is helpful for a manager or supervisor to be aware of a management theory known as the Pareto principle. In 1892, an economics professor, Vilfredo Federico Domasco Pareto, developed a theory of wealth distribution that stated that the wealth in any country is held by a few; the majority of citizens struggle for the remaining dollars. This is commonly known as the 80/20 Rule. One hundred years later, the Pareto principle is applied to quality improvement activities in an effort to identify and resolve problems in a process that speeds efficiency. In this context, an 80% improvement in process can be realized by reworking or eliminating the 20% that is causing unacceptable performance. The use of control charts and process capability analysis can help identify the hidden 20%.

Conclusion

As this chapter shows, statistics involves multiple features. One central feature is the ability that statistics has to define the nature of health care, from large national studies of disease prevalence rates to small departmental-based statistical studies of the productivity of a coding team. To be an effective participant in the health care system, the HIM professional must possess a basic understanding of the many features of statistics. Furthermore, the professional should be acquainted with a wide variety of statistical applications, moving confidently through the steps of data collection, evaluation, and display.

CHAPTER SUMMARY

Numbers and mathematical concepts have played a role in society for thousands of years. The past few centuries have seen the development of health care statistics, ranging from the elementary level to the complex level. These statistics are categorized by type, with descriptive statistics playing the largest role in health care. Measures of central tendency appear frequently in the health care field (e.g., in support of research studies), as well as in mainstream fields (e.g., in press releases and journalism pieces). How data are collected, used in calculations and formulae, and presented are integral to the practice of statistics in any field, including health care. Relationships among data variables are the focus of regression analysis, an advanced statistical tool used in the emerging fields of clinical and applied informatics. Regression analysis is a fundamental element of grouper programs. Models such as the Pearson product-moment correlation, the ANOVA test, and the chi-square are all used in regression analysis. Health information management statistics focus on the use of statistical formulae on a routine basis. HIM managers rely upon productivity measures to determine how effectively the organization is managed. Statistical tools such as control charts, trend charts, and process capability analysis are used to solve process problems, improve productivity, and contribute to the organization's financial well-being.

CASE STUDIES

The following scenarios deal with the rules for graphical presentations:

1. George is a new coding manager. He was hired in December. He assured his employer that he would bring about major productivity gains in coding charts within 30 days if he was hired. George is making his first presentation to the Reimbursement Committee. Annie created a graph for him (see Figure 9–27), but George didn't like it and created another instead (see Figure 9–28). Explain why George's graph isn't working.

Figure 9–27 | Annie's graph

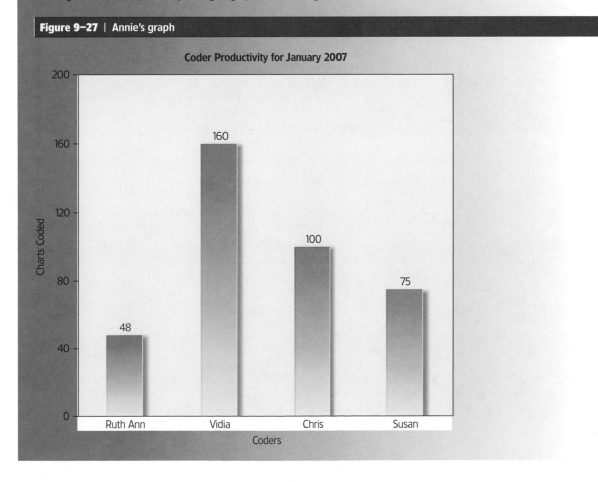

Figure 9–28 | George's graph

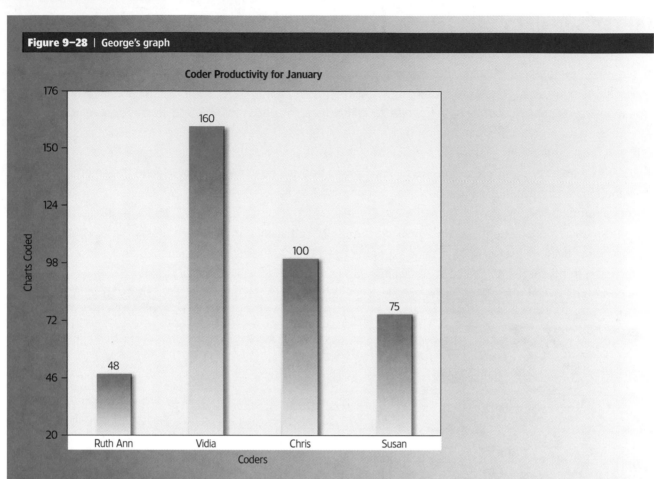

Coder Productivity for January

2. Denise has collected information on hospital reimbursement compared to length-of-stay days for 12 physicians. She decides to display her data as a pie chart because she has done a pie chart before and is comfortable creating one (see Figure 9–29). How would you advise her?

Figure 9–29 | Denise's pie chart

LOS vs DRG Reimb 063005

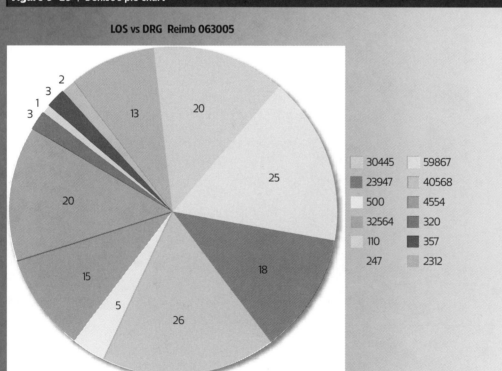

3. Jillian is completing her first graphical presentation for the Medical Staff Review Committee. She has decided to use a pie chart because there are only four categories and she wants the physicians to focus on percentages rather than actual counts. The pie chart she created for the meeting is shown in Figure 9–30. What needs to be fixed?

Figure 9–30 | Jillian's pie chart

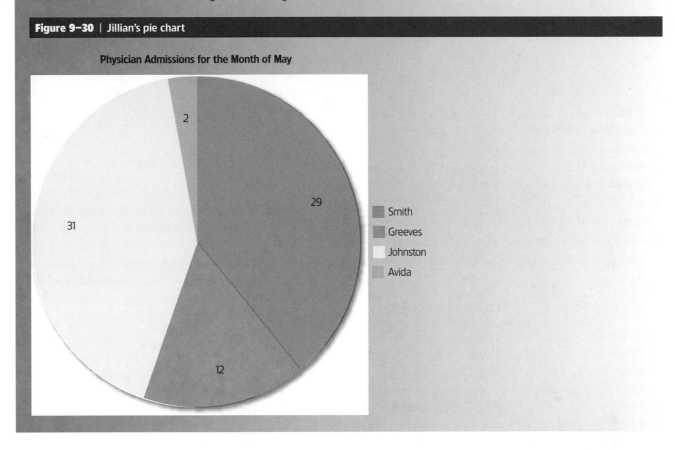

Physician Admissions for the Month of May

REVIEW QUESTIONS

1. How is a population different from a sample for statistical purposes?

2. What is the difference between morbidity and mortality rates?

3. Identify the steps involved in collecting mortality statistics from the local to the federal level, the sources of data, and how the statistics are typically presented.

4. What is the general pattern that guides the construction of rate formula?

5. In presenting graphical data, why is it necessary to set the y-axis at zero?

6. List four types of commonly used graphs and discuss the unique aspect of each.

7. Explain how a research study could be statistically reliable while lacking validity.

8. What is the value of labor analytics?

9. Describe how a process capability ratio diagram can help with scenarios found in an HIM department.

10. What is the Pareto principle?

ENRICHMENT ACTIVITIES

1. Team Debate: Public health notification of contagious diseases takes place today, but what isn't in place today are methods to ensure that *rapid* notification occurs. At this time, hospitals, private practices, and public health agencies are forming task forces to try to create notification models. Your team should consider the obstacles involved in timely notification to the Centers for Disease Control and Prevention of a *suspected* bioterrorist action. Identify possible delay areas and notification breakdown points and propose a solution to remedy each obstacle.

2. **A. Real-World Statistics Part I:**
   Medicare Part D, Selecting the Best Plan

   Contact two senior citizens (friends, family, or a resident in a retirement community) and, using the online tools found on Medicare's Web site (http://www.medicare.com), look up prescription card providers by their zip codes. Evaluate three or more drugs for each senior citizen. Find out which of the prescription plan providers offers the best price for each senior citizen. Search for "Medicare's Prescription Drug Finder" on the Medicare Web site to aid you with this activity.

   Example:

   ### Step I: Data Collection

   Mary Jones is 85 years old, a Medicare beneficiary, and makes about $8,000 a year from Social Security. She takes Fosamax, Encarda, and Prozac. Compare her prescription drug costs:

   Provider A = $85.00 for a 30-day supply of 70 mg Fosamax

   Provider B = $110.00 for a 30-day supply of 70 mg Fosamax

   Provider C = $78.00 for a 30-day supply of 70 mg Fosamax

   ### Step II: Data Calculations

   For Ms. Jones's first drug, Provider C offers the best price. Now we can complete the comparison for her remaining prescriptions and determine which provider offers the best price overall for this client.

   Note: Be sure the supply is consistent among the three providers. Some companies will quote a 30-day supply and others will offer a 90-day supply. In that case, divide the 90-day supply by 3 to get a consistent 30-day supply quote.

   ### Step III: Data Display

   At this point, your statistical research is just a collection of numbers and would be difficult for your senior citizen clients to follow. Create a table and show the prices that were offered for each drug by prescription plan provider. Also identify how much the annual card fee is for each provider, because this will impact the client's annual "out-of-pocket" costs. Include a narrative summary of your findings and explain to the reader the findings of your research.

   ### Example Table 1:

   Client: Mary Jones

Provider:	Fosamax 70 mg	Encarda 5 mg	Prozac 20 mg
Illinois First	$85.00	$32.00	$62.00
Hitcha Hard	$110.00	$78.00	$99.00
Best Deal on Drugs	$78.00	$30.00	$45.00

   Summary: Best Deal on Drugs consistently offers the best price on Ms. Jones's three medications. The annual fee for this card is $25.00. Compared to the Hitcha Hard price, Ms. Jones is realizing a 29% savings on her Fosamax prescription.

   B. Real-World Statistics Part II:
   Patient Safety in Long-Term Care

   This is your first day as the new HIM data analyst at Baptist Hospital. Your boss is going into a meeting to talk about re-evaluating the discharge planning procedures for the hospital as a result of several complaints from patients' families. Their concerns center on the fact that their loved ones are not receiving adequate care in some of the nursing homes in the community, and this is causing an increase in hospital stays.

   The hospital's medical staff also has concerns that the nursing homes to which they have historically sent their patients do not meet the Baptist Hospital's high standards of care. They see their patients returning to the hospital with pneumonia, congestive heart failure, and decubitus ulcers, among other conditions—all signs of poor care.

   Your boss has asked you to research three nursing homes in your community (research the city/state of your choice). Select three facilities to profile and provide a detailed summary of which one is the best of the three, along with what findings led you to make that conclusion. Use the statistics you find on Medicare's Web site (http://www.medicare.gov) to compare nursing homes using many different criteria. Search for "Nursing Home Compare" on Medicare's Web site to aid you with this activity.

   Using what you have learned about different types of graphs and the rules of good graphical construction, design a graph to display your research. Provide a complete narrative summary (one-half page to one page in length) to explain your conclusions. Your findings should be easy to understand and backed up with statistics; which statistics you choose to compare and contrast are up to you. If you need help using graphing software, an easy-to-use graph wizard can be found by visiting the National Center for Education Statistics Web site for kids (http://nces.ed.gov/nceskids).

3. Brainstorm with other students to identify subject matter that can be measured using a Likert scale. After selecting subject matter, create a short survey using the Likert scale as a basis for those who will answer your survey. Ask your classmates to complete your survey and return it to you. Using the returned surveys, tabulate the results and create a visual image (graphical representation) of those results. Share the results and the visual image with your instructor and classmates.

WEB SITES

Centers for Medicare and Medicaid Services, http://www.cms.hhs.gov

Federal Statistics, http://www.fedstats.gov

Medicare Nursing Home Compare,
    http://www.medicare.gov/NHCompare

Medicare Prescription Drug and Assistance Program,
    http://www.medicare.gov/Prescription/Home

National Association for Public Health Statistics and Information
    Systems, http://www.naphsis.org

National Cancer Institute, http://www.cancer.gov/statistics

National Center for Education Statistics, http://www.nces.ed.gov

National Center for Health Statistics, http://www.cdc.gov/nchs

SPSS Analytical Software, http://www.spss.com

U.S. Bureau of Labor Statistics, http://www.bls.gov

REFERENCES

American Health Information Management Association. (2005). *Health information management and technology pocket glossary*. Chicago: Author.

Koch, G. (2000). *Basic allied health statistics and analysis* (2nd ed.). Albany, NY: Delmar.

Campbell, C., Schmitz, H., & Waller, L. (1998). *Financial management in a managed care environment*. Albany, NY: Delmar.

Mattingly, R. (1997). *Management of health information*. Albany, NY: Delmar.

Peden, A. (1998). *Comparative records for health information management*. Albany, NY: Delmar.

Statistics.com. (2005). http://www.statistics.com.

NOTES

1. See, e.g., MINN. STAT ANN. § 144.222 (2007); S.D.CODIFIED LAWS ANN. §34-25-32.1 (2007); TENN. CODE ANN. § 68-3-208 (2007); VA. CODE ANN. § 32.1–264 (Michie 2007), all relating to the reporting of fetal deaths.

2. American Health Information Management Association. (2005). *Health information management and technology pocket glossary*. Chicago: Author.

10

Research

CERTIFICATION CONNECTION

RHIA

Health care research
Patient care-related studies

RHIT

Health care research

LEARNING OBJECTIVES

After reading this chapter, the learner should be able to:

1. Trace the development of research over time.

2. Compare and contrast qualitative and quantitative research methods.

3. Describe various types of research studies.

4. List the steps involved in research study design.

5. Understand the role that institutional review boards play in protecting human subjects involved in research studies.

6. Understand the role that institutional animal care and use committees play in protecting animal subjects involved in research studies.

7. Describe the emerging trends associated with protecting human subjects or animals used in research.

8. Trace the development of the epidemiology field over time.

9. Understand the basics of epidemiology, including the relationships among the agent, host, and environment in the progression of disease.

10. Compare and contrast descriptive, analytic, and experimental epidemiology.

Outline

Research Principles

Historical Overview
Methodology

Research Study Process

Research Design
Publication Process

Institutional Review Boards

Historical Overview
Review Process
Emerging Trends

Epidemiology

Historical Overview
Epidemiological Basics

Key Concepts

Agent

Analysis and results

Analytic epidemiology

Applied research

Assent

Blind study

Case-control study

Clinical research

Clinical trials

Cohort study

Common rule

Conclusion and discussion

Conflict of interest

Control

Controlled clinical trials

Cross-sectional study

Data aggregation studies

Data Safety Monitoring Board

Data Safety Monitoring Plan

De-identified data

Descriptive epidemiology

Descriptive research

Double-blind study

Efficacy

Efficiency

Endemic

Environment

Epidemics

Epidemiologists

Epidemiology

Evaluation research

Experimental epidemiology

Experimental research

Host

Human subject

Hypothesis

Incidence rate

Institutional animal care and use committees

Institutional review board

Laboratory research

Limited data set

Literature review

Methods

Minimum risk

Mortality rates

Observational studies

Outcomes research

Pandemics

Placebos

Primary prevention

Prospective

Pure research

Qualitative form

Qualitative research

Quantitative form

Quantitative research

Randomization

Relative risk ratio

Reliability

Research

Research methodology

Retrospective

Risk

Risk factors

Scientific method

Secondary prevention

Social and behavioral research

Study rationale

Survey

Tertiary prevention

Validity

Variables

Vector

INTRODUCTION

Two disciplines of significant importance in health care are research and epidemiology. Both areas serve to advance knowledge of numerous topics, leading to new applications, treatments, and modalities that may improve patient care and assist the well-being of communities and the world at large. Research and epidemiology possess a symbiotic relationship; knowledge and use of research principles are essential to the proper design of epidemiological studies, and knowledge and use of epidemiological principles assist in the proper design of research studies.

Both areas are intimately connected with health information management in the modern age. Health information management professionals are extremely knowledgeable about health care data content and structure, including its collection, analysis, storage, and retrieval. Each of these functional areas is an essential component of both research and epidemiology. In light of this connection, two roles envisioned by the American Health Information Management Association (AHIMA)—the clinical data specialist and the research and decision support analyst—are now in operative form throughout the United States. Some health information management professionals design and conduct studies that concern the clinical, financial, and administrative aspects of health information management, and others support studies in different areas. Whether acting in the direct capacity of conducting one's own studies, or in the support capacity of assisting another's research or epidemiological efforts, the knowledge and skills a health information management professional possesses with regard to health care data content and structure, database management, and statistics offer considerable advantages to researchers at all levels.

The discipline of health information management requires professionals to understand the concepts of research and epidemiology. This chapter provides that understanding, beginning with a discussion of research principles and moving to an introduction to the research process. A discussion of institutional review boards follows, with a section on the history and basics of epidemiology completing the chapter.

Research Principles

Research refers to a careful, diligent, and exhaustive search designed to discover new facts and relationships; revise accepted conclusions, theories, or laws in light of newly discovered facts and relationships; gain solutions to problems; or discover specific answers to specific questions—all in a reliable, objective, and organized way. The ultimate goal of research is to discover the truth. This discovery serves the purposes of learning what is new, what has previously had no conclusive answer, and what solutions can be reached to address problems, both big and small.

Variations in research are widespread. Research studies may be conducted on a wide range of topics, such as biology, sociology, and psychology, and over a wide range of subjects, including cells, viruses, laboratory rats, and human beings. A variety of persons and institutions rely on research results to accomplish their goals, including those involved in biomedical research, such as national research bodies, drug companies, genetic engineering firms, academic institutions, and individual researchers. Although variations exist, all research involves seeking answers to relevant questions and using the scientific method as the basis of study.

Historical Overview

Long before the concept or idea of research was realized, societies relied upon superstition, tradition, and authority to answer the questions and problems that perplexed mankind. Organized religion established itself as the power over both the temporal and spiritual arenas of life; as a result, established doctrines and dogma served to answer these questions and problems. This approach served the Western world for centuries, through the Middle Ages. Those few persons who questioned doctrine and dogma during the Middle Ages were branded heretics and suffered dire consequences for taking what were considered new and threatening positions on issues and problems.

With the advent of the Renaissance, pioneers of research emerged who relied on observations and facts to question the teachings of organized religion and draw their own conclusions. These pioneers included Galileo Galilei and Copernicus, who challenged the immobility of the earth and its place in the universe, and artists such as Michelangelo, Raphael, and Leonardo da Vinci, who incorporated the study of anatomy into their drawings and other works. Through the centuries, additional pioneers emerged who focused not only on clinical observations of disease but on the effectiveness of remedies employed to combat disease, such as the need for clean water as a way to stop the transmission of cholera. Pioneers like Louis Pasteur and Edward Jenner succeeded in creating vaccinations to prevent transmission of infectious diseases.

One significant pioneer in research was Florence Nightingale. Working as a nurse who tended to the injuries of soldiers engaged in the Crimean War, Nightingale recorded detailed observations of the effects that her nursing actions had upon soldiers. By doing so, she not only reached conclusions based on her observations, she effected changes in nursing practice. Furthermore, she established the rationale that detailed observation, combined with meticulous recordkeeping, could serve as the basis for both conclusion and change.

Advancements continued through the 18th and 19th centuries. The invention of the microscope by Antonj van Leeuwenhoek enhanced the ability of physicians and scientists to draw conclusions from observable facts. Clinical trials were conducted in Europe and North America, validating the concepts of hand washing by health care personnel and the use of ether for surgery. New equipment, such as radiology machines, was also invented, which served to advance medical knowledge.

During the 20th century, advances in medicine mirrored advancements in scientific research. The establishment of medical colleges was accompanied by the recognition that clinical research was an important component of the teaching of medicine. By creating a symbiotic relationship, medical colleges enhanced their students' ability to apply scientific observations to the patient's bedside. Of particular significance to advancing research was the availability of funds to support these efforts. These funds came in the form of government investment in biomedical research and private investment in the pharmaceutical industry.

Whereas many scientific advancements were considered spectacular achievements in medicine, other scientific endeavors were accompanied by troubling tales of unethical conduct by clinical researchers. These questionable scientific endeavors occurred across the globe and continued throughout much of the century, leading to widespread condemnation and calls for reform. Many of these reforms crystallized in the creation of institutional review boards, discussed in more detail later in this chapter.

At the dawn of the 21st century, the research industry can be categorized as robust and thriving. More persons and institutions are involved with research than ever before, and the advancements brought about by research border on astounding. New frontiers in research, such as genetic studies and new treatments developed through the use of banked tissue specimens, will likely continue into the near future.

Methodology

Research methodology refers to the manner in which problems are solved through careful, diligent, and exhaustive search. The scientific method is used in the modern tradition. The **scientific method** refers to the process of discovery by systematic investigation. This formal process is designed to develop or contribute to generalizable knowledge through rigorous observation, analysis, and reasoning. By employing the scientific method, scientists and researchers allow future scientists and researchers to replicate their research and reproduce the same conclusion.

Research can be categorized in a number of ways. Some research is considered **pure**, meaning that it is abstract and general, seeking to generate knowledge for knowledge's sake. By contrast, other research is considered **applied**, meaning that it is designed to answer a practical question. Still other categories include **experimental research**, meaning the use of variables, control, and randomization in an experiment, or **descriptive research**, referring to the description of individuals, groups, or situations as a means to apply the knowledge gained to future individuals, groups, or situations. Finally, research may be of a **clinical** nature—meaning that it is performed in the real world, where control over variables may be difficult—or of a **laboratory** nature—meaning that it is performed in the laboratory setting under tight control. Although the student may encounter any of these research categories, the combination of applied, experimental, and clinical research is most frequently seen in the health care context.

Qualitative and Quantitative Research The two main research methods are qualitative and quantitative research. Although they are discussed individually here, these methodologies are not always utilized separately and may be integrated into a single study. The reasons to integrate the two methodologies vary and may include: serving as a means to add power to the study's findings, gaining a comprehensive understanding of the study topic through the use of different techniques, and compensating for the weakness of one methodology with the strength of a second methodology. Whether they are separated or integrated, it is important to understand both methods; they serve as the basis of the research activities conducted by health professionals.

Qualitative research refers to the methodology that relies upon generating descriptive theory from data gleaned from an investigation. Those investigators using the qualitative research method develop hypotheses that may be vague or general within a broad topic, focusing on the phenomenon present in a given setting and not upon an experiment constructed for study purposes. With the focus resting on what naturally occurs in a given setting, the investigator is able to ground her data upon the real life of the study participants, thereby placing the obtained data within context.

Several features are significant to qualitative research. First, a phenomenological perspective is employed, emphasizing how a study participant in a given setting constructs the world around herself. Second, because the data are obtained in context, they have the potential to reveal complexity. If data are collected over a long period of time, they can generate answers to the "why" questions associated with causality. Third, the investigator typically operates without the benefit of standardized instruments, using herself as the instrument to both question participants and collect data. Fourth, much of the study analysis is performed using words, instead of numbers, to detect patterns or themes. Finally, the investigator interprets these data as a way to understand why study participants, groups, societies, and organizations act in a certain manner and manage life situations the way they do. From this interpretation, and by taking the bottom-up approach, the investigator is able to *build* a theory.

Quantitative research refers to the methodology that relies upon testing theories to establish facts, show causal explanations and relationships among variables, and make predictions. Much of quantitative research is grounded upon experimentation that requires a defined model and a detailed plan of operation. This research may take the form of experiments, structured surveys, structured interviews, or structured observations. The investigator seeks to answer a specific research question using analysis of statistical data to *prove* a theory.

Several features are significant to quantitative research. First, one or more variables are present in the study that may be manipulated or measured. Variables are those things that may vary or change and therefore can be manipulated or measured. As those variables change (i.e., the manipulation), an effect may or may not be produced, which in turn can be measured. Second, an element of control is present. In a research context, control refers to the investigator's ability to eliminate interfering and irrelevant influences so that only the variables may be manipulated and therefore measured. Quantitative research studies often involve the use of control groups who share the same experiences as the experimental group, with the exception of receiving the experimental treatment or device. Third, investigators often employ randomization in their studies as a means to reduce bias and increase the validity of results. Randomization means that every subject in a research population is given an equal chance of either being selected for the study sample (referred to as *random selection*) or being assigned to either the experimental group or the control group (referred to as *random assignment*). If variables, control, and randomization are all present, the study employs a true experimental design. If manipulation of one or more variables is present but either control or randomization is not, the study employs a quasi-experimental design. If no manipulation of a variable is included, the study employs a nonexperimental design.

The health care professions have relied upon quantitative research more often than qualitative research. This may be the case for a variety of reasons, including the ease and speed of analyzing statistical data over the more laborious process of analyzing narrative data; the higher availability of funding for studies that seek to prove a theory as opposed to those that seek to establish a theory; and the comfort found in using structured and defined models in lieu of a generalized design. Further information comparing quantitative and qualitative research can be found in Table 10–I.

During recent decades, health care providers have begun to recognize the value of qualitative research more readily, as seen by the value qualitative research added to development of an understanding of the AIDS crisis in America. Much of the initial research conducted involving HIV and AIDS focused on the quantitative approach, permitting scientists to develop hypotheses about why the immune systems of some people failed, and a profile of individuals and groups who contracted the virus or disease. The qualitative research on the personal experiences and actions of those at risk of developing HIV or AIDS was what really made a difference in containing the spread of the epidemic. By focusing on these aspects, qualitative research studies were able to identify the practices that placed individuals in danger and could then recommend practices, such as the use of condoms and testing of blood products, that could be effective in controlling the spread of disease. Because these qualitative studies by definition employed a phenomenological perspective, researchers

Table 10-1 | Comparison of Qualitative and Quantitative Analysis

	Qualitative	Quantitative
Purpose	Develop concepts; describe multiple realities	Test theories to establish facts; show causal explanations; make predictions
Design	General in nature	Predetermined and structured; defined model; detailed plan of operation
Data	Descriptive; deal with qualities; harder to manage	Quantifiable and statistical; easy to manage
Subject Samples	Small volume	Large volumes; control groups
Investigator's Relationship with Subjects	Intense contact with participant over long period	Circumspect contact over a short period
Techniques	Observations; open-ended interviewing; narrative display of data	Experiments, structured surveys, interviews, or observations; statistical data analysis
Instruments	Investigator may serve as the instrument; audio or digital recording	Scales, tests, inventories, questionnaires
Data Analysis	Inductive, coding, event listing, ongoing activity	Deductive, statistical manipulation done at conclusion of study
Outcome	Verifies existing theory or develops new theory (requiring additional investigation)	Answer specific research questions through statistics
Problems	Nonstandardization of procedures; difficulty managing large amounts of data; time consuming	Difficulty controlling variables; difficulty relating experiments to real life

Source: Bailey, D. (1997). *Research for the health professional* (2nd ed., pp. 49–51). Philadelphia: F. A. David & Co.

were able to develop educational tools to explain the disease, its development, and risks in a manner that would resonate with the most at-risk populations as well as the general population. As more funding becomes available to support qualitative research, and as an understanding develops that qualitative research presents applications in the health care arena, more health care professionals may engage in this kind of research or expand the qualitative research they presently pursue.

Study Types Because research covers a broad spectrum of areas and activities, the types of studies that are available to support research vary greatly. This section contains descriptions of several study types, using health care as a basis for illustration.

Some forms of research rely upon data aggregation studies. Data aggregation studies involve the collection of data from large numbers of medical records without focusing on direct patient contact. The collected data comprise the sum total of a data element across a patient population as opposed to the data found in a specific episode of patient care. These data are then analyzed to facilitate comparisons or elicit evidence of patterns. Data aggregation studies can determine a baseline range for use in future studies that utilize direct patient contact. Data aggregation studies can also be used to demonstrate the effectiveness, superiority, or equivalence of therapies or treatments, or to improve the performance of health care providers.

Clinical research involves the use of experimental studies conducted as clinical trials. Clinical trials are investigations that assess the difference between two clinical populations with respect to the outcome of therapy or treatments. Unlike other types of scientific research involving cells, viruses, or laboratory rats, clinical trials involve the use of human beings. Because human beings are involved, the Food and Drug Administration (FDA) requires the satisfactory completion of clinical trials before it will approve a new treatment as safe and effective. Two overriding objectives are present in clinical trials: to determine whether applying a certain form of treatment to people results in a better clinical outcome than not applying the treatment, and to determine what harmful effects, if any, are associated with a certain form of treatment. These trials may be therapeutic—focusing on different treatment protocols—or prophylactic—focusing on different methods of disease prevention. Clinical trials attempt to determine the efficacy and the efficiency of a given therapeutic agent or procedure. In this context, efficacy refers to the benefits that accrue to the individual receiving care, and efficiency refers to the resources consumed by the treatment. By focusing on efficacy and efficiency, clinical trials work to advance health care knowledge, both in general and with regard to application. Clinical trials may also determine the effectiveness, superiority, or equivalence of therapies or treatments. As such, they require the use of comparisons among groups of participants. A summary of the different types of clinical trials is found in Table 10-2.

Table 10-2 | Different Types of Clinical Trials

	Controlled clinical trial	Cohort study	Case-control study
Type	Experimental/random assignment	Longitudinal	Known groups
Time Frame	Prospective, relatively short	Prospective, relatively long	Retrospective
Purpose	Draw scientific conclusions	Provide strength of evidence for further research	Provide strength of evidence for further research

Clinical trials sometimes progress in phases. Phase I clinical trials focus on safety and dosage issues and generally last no more than one and a half years. Phase II clinical trials focus on efficacy and last approximately two years. Phase III clinical trials focus on reproducing the findings or results from a previous phase but on a larger scale. Phase III clinical trials may last three to four years.

Clinical trials that utilize randomization are referred to as controlled clinical trials. These controlled clinical trials serve as the basis for drawing scientific conclusions. For example, a controlled clinical trial may wish to compare two treatments given to two different groups of participants. Applying randomization, groups of participants would be randomly divided into subgroups so that each group receives different treatments. This randomization is performed by computer programs that generate pseudorandom numbers; each participant will have the same chance as other participants of receiving one of the two treatments. The researcher then records data about the results of each treatment and any side effects experienced by the participants.

Variations exist within the universe of controlled clinical trials. Some clinical trials involve the use of placebos: something that resembles treatment, such as a pill containing inert ingredients, which ensures that the participant does not know that she is in a control group. If the effects of active treatment are superior to those of placebo therapy, the researcher may reach conclusions concerning the active treatment. Another variation involves the use of two active treatments without the use of placebos. If the effects of one treatment are superior to the other, or if the effects are equivalent, the researcher may reach conclusions concerning the treatments.

A further variation involves the use of blinding. In a blind study, the participant is not informed about which kind of therapy (assuming more than one type) she is receiving, except for what is required for informed consent, during the course of the clinical trial. In a double-blind study, neither the patient nor the clinicians involved are aware of which participants have been assigned to receive the experimental intervention. Blinding and double blinding are useful in research because they help minimize the effects of bias on study outcomes, meaning that neither the participant nor the clinician "sees what they want or expect to see" in the experiment. Double-blind studies in which patients are randomized are considered the gold standard of clinical research design.

Not all clinical trials involve randomization. Perhaps the required sample size for a specific study is hard to recruit, or it is unethical to conduct an experiment (e.g., studying risk factors such as cigarette smoking, occupational exposure to mineral fibers, or exposure to infectious disease agents). In these instances, the researcher instead designs and conducts observational studies. Observational studies are investigations that are based on observation rather than experimentation. Observational studies are not used to draw scientific conclusions. Rather, observational studies serve to provide strength of evidence that, in turn, can be used as the basis for additional experiments.

A cross-sectional study, also called a prevalence study, refers to studies that examine the current rates of disease frequency against other factors. For example, a cross-sectional study may use the same group of individuals to compare the current rate of exposure to a disease with the frequency in which the disease is present. Similarly, a cross-sectional study may compare the rates of disease frequency in certain places against the frequency of factors in those same places at various points in time.

Two types of observational studies are cohort and case-control studies. A cohort study is a study that follows two or more groups in a population that are or are not exposed to the risk factor under investigation. In other fields, cohort studies are referred to as longitudinal studies. A cohort study may be prospective in nature—looking into the future for both exposure and onset of disease—or retrospective in nature—looking at exposure and onset of disease that have already occurred. Prospective studies are chosen if a population is available that can be tracked over a long time interval, whereas retrospective studies are chosen if existing records are available that permit classification of individuals based on both exposure to a risk factor and disease history. Utilizing either approach, the researcher allows an adequate time interval (e.g., 5 to 10, to even 20 years, in some instances) to observe how many events of interest occur in the study groups or whether exposure to certain factors in the environment may influence development of disease. The relative frequency of the occurring event is called the *incidence*, which can then be calculated into a rate, the incidence rate. For example, a researcher may study the risk of cigarette smoking as it relates to the events of high blood pressure within two study groups of 1,000 patients each. If, over a 10-year period, the observed incidence of high blood pressure in the group containing cigarette smokers is 100/1,000, and, in a second group containing nonsmokers it is 10/1,000, the researcher can calculate the relative risk that cigarette smoking poses to the development of high blood pressure.

The second type of observational study is the case-control study. In a case-control study, the researcher focuses on the event to be studied and not on the risk factor. Two groups are involved: one group that includes those persons who have the disease to be studied, and a second group that includes those without the disease to be studied (the control group), but who are similar in other characteristics. A case-control study is retrospective in nature and uses naturally occurring groups. Other fields refer to case-control studies as known-group studies. Using the cigarette smoking/blood pressure example, a researcher would use two groups of patients for a case-control study: those with a diagnosis of high blood pressure and those without. Those patients without the diagnosis of high blood pressure would serve as the control group. The researcher would then ask a series of questions to the patients in each group concerning their current and past smoking habits. From these answers, the researcher can calculate an odds ratio.

An entirely different form of study is survey research. A survey is a collection of facts, figures, or opinions taken from individuals or groups that are objects of an investigation. Surveys serve multiple purposes, as illustrated in Table 10–3. Surveys vary in both scope and complexity, ranging from ones that involve small groups attempting to provide easily defined, objective facts to ones that involve enormous groups attempting to provide subtle answers to highly personal questions. Other differences exist with regard to the manner in which data are collected—either using personal interviews, telephone interviews, or questionnaires delivered in traditional written form or electronically. This variety can be further complicated by the level of analysis used to examine the data that are gathered in the survey. Some surveys support their conclusions using the simplest of statistical measures, whereas others use the most sophisticated. The choice of scope, complexity, and analytical level depends in large measure upon the nature of the research problem and the use to which the information will be put. The scope, complexity, and analytical level factors all contribute to the strength of survey research.

Surveys are often employed in social and behavioral research (SBR) studies. SBR studies focus on research dealing with human attitudes, beliefs, and behaviors. Surveys are not the only instruments relied upon for SBR studies; questionnaires, interviews, focus groups, and direct or participant observation techniques may also be employed. Questions of a social or behavioral nature may be incorporated into other study types, as well as a means to reveal additional data. For example, researchers may inquire into health histories, family pedigrees, and quality-of-life assessments to obtain data that supplement the primary purpose of the research.

One of the most rapidly growing study types is outcomes research. Outcomes research, sometimes referred to as evidence-based research, is clinical research conducted to evaluate the outcome of non-validated treatment practices, existing standards of practice, or already-approved drugs or devices against each other and/or against placebo controls. Outcomes research developed in large part as a result of a response to the high cost of health care in the United States and other developed countries in the last half of the 20th century. Clinicians, health care providers, governmental entities, and third-party payers sought to determine if the wide geographic variations in the style and cost of medical care and management of patients with apparently similar conditions was explained by variations in training, local habits, and differing opinions, or were based on firm evidence of what form of care and management produced the best patient results. Essentially, these groups sought to answer whether those who received and/or paid for health care services were getting their money's worth.

The research community responded to this concern by reviewing the outcomes patients achieved from these various practices, drugs, and/or devices. These outcomes focused on both physiologic changes and end results that affect the patient's symptom relief, daily functioning, or survival. For example, a patient with an enlarged prostate who receives drug therapy may see a resulting outcome of reduced prostate size (physiologic) and/or an improvement in urinary

Table 10–3	Purposes of Survey Research	
Description	Data about characteristics, attitudes, or beliefs used to describe the distribution of these attributes in a population. This answers the questions of "what" the survey population thinks, believes, or does.
Explanation	Data that examine "why" a survey population thinks, behaves, or believes a certain way.
Prediction	Data gathered from a survey population to forecast future outcomes, trends, or behaviors.
Exploration	Data gathered in the preliminary stages of research to investigate unknowns. These data may shape the design and focus of later research efforts.

frequency or urgency (end result). By studying outcomes, the research community is able to present scientific data about which practices, drugs and/or devices result in outcomes for the patient (whether an improved outcome or not) and details about what those outcomes are. In turn, the medical community can use this scientific data to develop outcomes measures for use in the course of clinical care and determine areas needed for quality improvement. Additional materials addressing outcomes measures can be found in Chapter 7, "Quality Health Care Management." Outcomes research has been embraced at many levels, including federal, state, and local governments, educational institutions, and research entities. Many of these groups seeks to improve the quality, efficiency, and outcomes of patient care.

Evaluation research differs from the research types already addressed in that it assesses systems and/or strategies and provides feedback on their worth or merit. For example, evaluation research may be used to determine if a certain program reached its intended beneficiaries, how well the program functioned, and whether, and at what cost, the program achieved its intended goals. In this example, the data gained in evaluation research would be used as feedback to determine the worth or merit of the program. Virtually any organization, institution, or system can be subject to evaluation research, including private and governmental agencies. In the academic world, evaluation research is sometimes employed as part of traditional social research.

The most well-known example of evaluation research in the health care field is the work of Abraham Flexner in evaluating the quality of medical school education at the beginning of the 20th century. Flexner used specific criteria to examine the quality and effectiveness of these schools, reaching the conclusion that many schools produced poorly educated physicians. The recommendations contained in Flexner's report offered feedback to those involved with medical school. Those recommendations also resulted in numerous changes, including the closure of some medical schools, the development of teaching relationships between medical schools and hospitals, and rigorous examinations for state licensure of physicians. Although this was among the earliest uses of evaluation research, it was not until the end of the 20th century that evaluation research became more frequently used.

Research Study Process

To read and understand or engage in research studies, one must understand the multiple steps involved in study design. These multiple steps are illustrated in Figure 10–1, along with the means of publication used for the dissemination of research results.

Research Design

Using proper research design increases the possibility of achieving solid results. Proper research design offers other benefits, including minimizing the number of patients necessary to demonstrate statistical validity, thereby reducing the number of persons enrolled in studies that carry the potential for risk from an experimental drug or device.

The first step in research design is to identify a topic for study. Typically, the topic identifies a problem that needs to be solved or a question that needs to be answered. Topics may originate from a number of sources, including problems encountered in a work environment, ideas generated as a result of a review of professional literature or attendance at a professional conference, perceived inadequacies of older ideas or methods, or from other research projects. In some instances, research topics may share similarities with existing research studies but contain modifications. For example, an existing research

Figure 10–1 | Steps in a research study

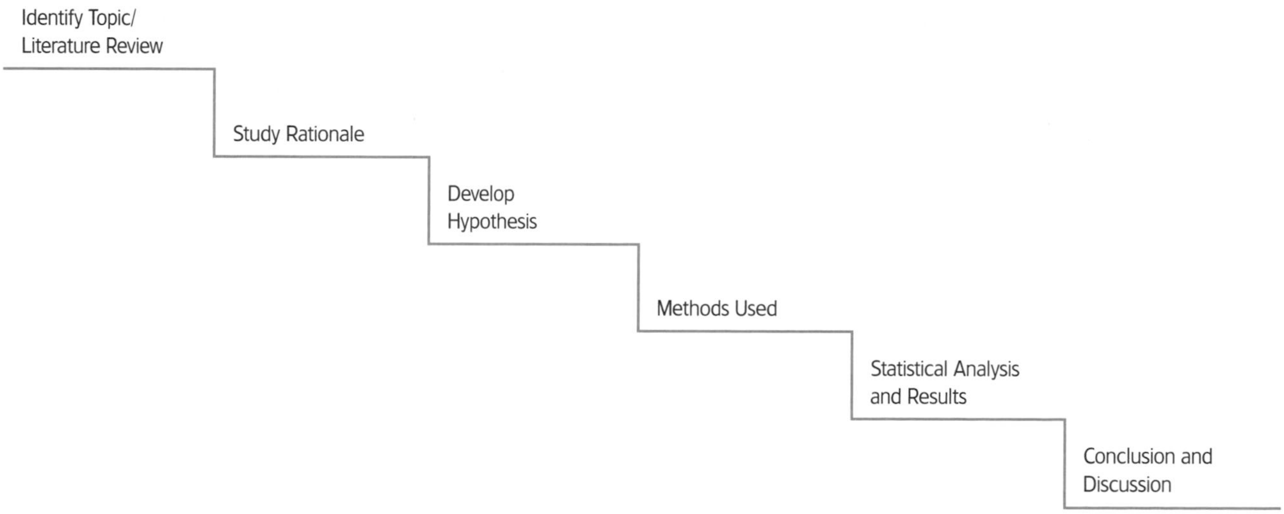

Identify Topic/
Literature Review

Study Rationale

Develop
Hypothesis

Methods Used

Statistical Analysis
and Results

Conclusion and
Discussion

study conducted on the study habits of high school students may be replicated using a different age group, such as college students, as subjects.

The second step in research design involves a literature review. A **literature review** determines what research has already been performed on the topic in question, differentiates the study hypothesis from the hypotheses of prior studies, and provides a solid foundation for proceeding with the study. The literature review leads to the creation of a **study rationale**. A study rationale demonstrates why a certain study should be performed. This rationale consists of a clear statement of the need for the research and its potential impact on medical care. The literature review process has greatly changed in the last decade as use of the Internet to gather information from bibliographic databases has largely replaced manual review of printed annual bibliographic databases. Additionally, more sources for literature review exist than ever before, including newly released government documents and abstracts, and indices of professional journals. All literature reviews should be comprehensive; they serve as the basis for the study rationale.

The next step is to develop a hypothesis. A **hypothesis** is a tentative assertion that is assumed by the researcher until the assumption is tested. A hypothesis is more than a hunch because it is formulated after the literature review and development of the study rationale. This allows the tentative assertion to complement the aims and objectives of the research topic that was previously identified. Generally presented in a question format, a hypothesis is specific in nature and will either be supported or not supported at the conclusion stage of the study. For example, a hypothesis that asks "Can the clinical course of a specific disease be altered?" is not as clear as a more specific one that asks "Is a certain therapy useful in slowing disease progression or increasing survival in patients with a specific disease?"[1]

The methods used by the researcher follow the study rationale. **Methods** refers to the procedures and processes employed; they may include—but are not limited to—identifying the research population, the recruitment strategies, and the informed consent process if human beings are involved; the location and time window for the research; the administration/types of treatment; and the assessments of effectiveness and safety. Whether the study is prospective (i.e., looking forward) or retrospective (i.e., looking backward) is also identified, as is the data collection process utilized.

Several data collection techniques are used in research. Data may be collected from observable, measurable phenomena, such as measuring sweat gland activity as a means of determining a patient's preoperative anxiety levels. Alternatively, data may be collected by trained observers focused on the relevant behaviors of a given research situation. Still other techniques include interviews and written questionnaires or reviews of existing records and artifacts.

Data may be collected using written tests, measures, and inventories. Whatever technique is chosen, the importance of using that technique consistently cannot be overstated.

If research includes the use of human beings as subjects, an additional step is involved—namely, the approval of an institutional review board (IRB). Researchers submit research plans and informed consent documents to IRBs for approval before engaging in data collection. Once these are approved, the researcher proceeds with the remaining steps in the process. More information about IRBs can be found later in this chapter.

The next steps are **analysis and results**. Sometimes these steps occur separately, but they may also be combined. The analysis section of any research study report indicates the statistical methods of analysis employed in the study. These statistical methods may include the use of automated programs if more powerful statistical analysis is necessary. Statistical analysis may be presented in **quantitative form** (i.e., expressed with regard to amounts or quantities) or in **qualitative form** (i.e., expressed with regard to quality). The results section demonstrates what happened in the study, correlating to the hypothesis presented in an earlier step of the research design process. This section also includes any findings of statistical significance in the research. Frequently, the results are displayed through the use of tables, graphs, charts, and diagrams, many of which are addressed in detail in Chapter 9, "Health Statistics."

The final steps are **conclusion and discussion**. At this stage, the researcher interprets the results of the study and attempts to integrate those results into other findings within the field. This integration frequently addresses whether the results fit or fail to fit the expectations derived from prior studies or theories, and whether the results of the study in question advance knowledge in the field or contribute to better health care. This stage answers whether or not support exists for the hypothesis put forth at the beginning of the research effort.

Publication Process

Following the steps of study design will result in a completed research study. At this point, the researcher seeks to share the study's results through publication of the research report, often by submitting it to respected research journals for consideration. In the past, the exclusive means of publication was in print form. As a result of the advent of the Internet, however, some research journals are disseminated solely through electronic means, which presents new opportunities for publication. Examples of online research journals include *British Medical Journal, Online Journal of Issues in Nursing, Journal of Clinical Investigation,* and *Perspectives in Health Information Management.* Whether a journal exists in electronic or traditional printed form, selecting the correct journal for publication is important; journals may be highly

Table 10–4 | **Research Journal Manuscript Requirements**

1. Title

2. Abstract
   a. Study arm
   b. Research design
   c. Setting and source of subjects
   d. Measurements made
   e. Results
   f. Conclusions and implications

3. Introduction

4. Methods

5. Results

6. Analysis and Discussion

Source: Crombie, I. K. & Davies, H. T. O. (1996). Research in healthcare. Chicester, UK: John Wiley & Sons.

specialized and warrant the use of certain forms of writing over others (e.g., technical reports vs. general relevance articles). Furthermore, journals may specify requirements for the structure of a manuscript for submission, as seen in Table 10–4. In almost all cases, marked competition exists among researchers to be published in the most prestigious research journals.

Several criteria are used by research journals to decide whether reported research results may be considered valid, resulting in a study's acceptance for publication. The focus rests initially on the need the study addresses, with particular emphasis placed on the hypothesis under study. Although it is considered at the outset of study design, the need for the study is articulated in the completed study report so that the evaluator can determine how this study differs from others or adds to the literature in existence on the study point in question. The study report further delineates the hypothesis under study, generally providing background information about what is known and unknown in support of the hypothesis and how the hypothesis will be tested.

Evaluators also review the composition of the study groups included in the research design, looking for equivalency between the control group and the comparison group. This equivalency focuses on inclusion/exclusion criteria of those in both groups, which may vary depending on the subject matter of the study. For example, a case-control study looks for the presence or absence of disease whereas a cohort study looks for the presence or absence of exposure. The equivalency review also focuses on the amount of information available to those in both groups and whether that information came from the same source. The purpose of this equivalency examination is to detect the existence of bias in the study design.

Evaluators also review the submitted study to determine sample size and power. Although actual numbers may vary from study to study, a sufficient number of partici-

pants must be studied if results are to be considered valid. The power of the sample size should be sufficient to answer the hypothesis posed in the study. If the power is inadequate, it is impossible to draw inferences or conclusions from the study (e.g., whether causal relationships exist between exposure and disease).

Evaluators examine whether accurate study measures were employed so that they can evaluate the reliability and validity of the data contained in the study. Reliability, the repeatability of a measurement, is evaluated to see if the conditions of measurement were standardized. Validity, the accuracy of a measurement, is evaluated to see if the measurement represents reality. The extent to which an evaluator can determine the reliability and validity of the measures used in the study will greatly strengthen its credibility.

Finally, the analysis technique and the discussion section are of particular concern to the evaluator. The analysis technique must relate to the type of study performed. For example, prospective studies should address incidence or mortality rates and relative risk measures, including confidence limits for risk ratios and other relevant tests. The discussion section states not only the study's finding but also the inferences and conclusions that can be drawn from the study's data. This section compares and contrasts the study in question against previous studies and addresses the significance of the research along with its wider implications.

Institutional Review Boards

Typically associated with a university or an academic medical center or hospital, an institutional review board is a group that is formally designated by an institution to safeguard the rights and welfare of human subjects by reviewing, approving, and monitoring medical research. IRBs are a fairly recent phenomenon, arising from reactions to real and perceived abuses in medical research in the last half of the 20th century. IRBs govern research involving human subjects that is conducted pursuant to or supported by federal funding, or otherwise subject to federal regulations. As a matter of efficiency, institutions will often assign responsibility for review of all research protocols involving human subjects to their IRBs, regardless of a connection to federal funding or federal regulation.

The determination of what protocols these IRBs must review rests on the connection the research has to a human subject. Under federal regulation, a human subject is defined as a living individual from whom an investigator conducting research obtains data, materials (organs, tissues, or fluids), or identifiable private information.[2] In some states, the term *human subject* is defined by law or regulation to include deceased individuals and fetal remains (e.g., material obtained as part of an autopsy). In those states,

IRBs must review research protocols that involve materials obtained from the deceased's remains.

IRBs are typically composed of a mix of persons with different backgrounds. Although a minimum of only five members is required, many IRBs are considerably larger. Members of both sexes and various professions are included, with at least one member serving who is not affiliated with the institution sponsoring the IRB, one member whose expertise lies in scientific areas, and one member whose primary expertise lies beyond scientific areas. Members must be knowledgeable and experienced in dealing with vulnerable populations and sensitive to community attitudes. Finally, members must be knowledgeable of the applicable laws and regulations, institutional commitments, and accepted standards of professional conduct. Members are required to engage in continuing education in the protection of human research participants; many of these educational programs are now offered online.

Historical Overview

Institutional review boards arose in response to medical research abuses that occurred in the middle and late 20th century in both Europe and the United States. Among the most notorious were medical research experiments conducted on concentration camp victims by Nazi doctors and scientists during World War II, which involved torture, mutilation, and other atrocities. Almost equally notorious was a study conducted by the U.S. Public Health Service from 1932 through 1971, which documented the natural history of syphilis in African-American men through enrollment of these human subjects without their consent. Whereas the Nazi experiments were conducted on individuals who had no way to refuse consent, the Public Health Service experiments were conducted on persons who were deliberately misinformed about the treatment they received and denied medicines readily available to treat syphilis. Lesser-known abuses include studies involving mentally retarded children who were deliberately infected with viral hepatitis, senile patients who were injected with live cancer cells, persons who were unknowingly exposed to radiation levels during the Cold War, Hispanic women who were supplied unknowingly with placebos in lieu of oral contraceptives, and students who were led to administer increasing levels of electric shocks to fellow students as part of a learning and memory study.

Each of these abusive studies, and others not listed here, brought to light ethical concerns over the proper manner in which to conduct research studies. As discussed in detail in Chapter 4, "Ethical Standards," concepts such as autonomy, beneficence, justice, rights, and veracity are all central tenets in the health care world. When abusive studies violated these concepts through such actions as withholding information from patients, employing coercive or deceptive tactics, or taking advantage of a vulnerable population, persons within and outside the health care world reacted with outrage. Immediately following World War II, the world community conducted legal trials—relying upon the principles of the Nuremberg Code—to both punish wrongdoers and educate the world community about the atrocities committed and the need for voluntary consent of human subjects to engage in any form of experimentation. During the next decade, the world community—working through the World Health Organization—developed the Declaration of Helsinki, which provided guidelines for physician use when human subjects are involved in a research study. This declaration, in modified form, is in use to this day.

Whereas ethical concerns occupied the thoughts of many, others focused their concerns upon developing the means to establish and enforce ethical protections at a legal level. This effort evolved into regulation of the research study industry. In the 1970s, the U.S. Congress responded by passing the National Research Act, which authorized implementing regulations and the forming of a commission to identify basic ethical principles that underlie human research studies. Called the National Commission for the Protection of Human Subjects in Biomedical and Behavioral Research, and known as the National Commission, this new group published what many consider the landmark document in human subject research ethics: the Belmont Report.

The Belmont Report[3] asserted that three main principles form the ethical basis for all research involving human subjects: respect for persons, beneficence, and justice. Several requirements arose from each of these principles. For example, requirements for treating individuals as autonomous agents, obtaining informed consent, and respecting the privacy of research subjects derive from the principle of respect for persons. Requirements for studies to seek a balance between benefits and risks to the patient, along with strong research design that maximizes benefits and reduces harms, derive from the beneficence principle. Requirements to select subjects equitably and avoid exploitation of vulnerable populations derive from the principle of justice. According to the authors of the Belmont Report, these three principles carry equal force and weight used to evaluate the ethical nature of any research study involving human subjects.

The Belmont Report also provides the ethical basis for the federal regulations that govern research involving human subjects. These regulations[4] require: (1) review of all research involving human subjects by an Institutional Review Board; (2) informed consent obtained from human research subjects; and (3) an assurance by the institution that it will comply with these federal regulations. The Office for Human Research Protections (OHRP), an agency within the U.S. Department of Health and Human Services (DHHS), administers these regulations.

The Privacy Rule governs protected health information collected and used in the research environment.

New regulations have been introduced to the research environment as a result of the Health Insurance Portability and Accountability Act (HIPAA). The most significant regulation is the Privacy Rule, which protects individually identifiable health information that has been electronically maintained or transmitted by a covered entity as well as such information when it takes any other form. This information is referred to as protected health information (PHI) and is discussed in further detail in Chapter 3, "Legal Issues." Within the research context, IRBs have applied the HIPAA regulations in general, and the Privacy Rule in particular, to determine whether PHI can be used as the researcher suggests in the protocol, whether the patient has authorized such use, and whether a waiver of authorization is warranted under the protocol's circumstances. This examination by the IRB may result in changes made to submitted research protocols.

HIPAA

The regulations offer two exceptions to IRB review: the use of de-identified data or a limited data set.

Furthermore, HIPAA offers two alternatives to researchers who are interested in collecting and using data about human subjects without undergoing the IRB's review of the protocol's provisions on the issues of use, authorization, and waiver. The first alternative, often referred to as the HIPAA safe harbor provision, allows use of **de-identified data**, which refers to data with all identifiers removed so that no one can reasonably identify the patient based on what remains. The second alternative allows researchers to utilize a **limited data set**, a form of data in which direct identifiers have been removed; other data—such as city, state, zip code, and dates of service, birth, or death—remain. A list of the direct identifiers that must be excluded or removed are found in Table 10–5. To employ limited data sets, researchers are required under HIPAA to enter into data use agreements with the covered entity that provides the limited data set.

Although the HIPAA regulations are the most recent effort to establish and enforce ethical protections at a legal level, they certainly will not be the last. Because of the ease with which data can be accessed in electronic form, regulators at the federal and state levels, along with professional associations and consumer watchdog groups, may

Table 10–5 | Limited Data Set Direct Identifiers
Name
Address
Telephone number
Fax number
E-mail address
Social security number
Medical record number
Health plan beneficiary number
Account numbers
Certificate/license numbers
Biometric identifiers
Vehicle ID/license plate numbers
Internet protocol (IP) address numbers
Web universal resource locators (URLs)
Device identifiers and serial numbers
Full-face photographic images and comparable images

Source: 45 C.F.R. 164.51(c) (2007).

take action in the future to strengthen ethical and legal protections even further. Such efforts have already been seen at the state level; legislatures have passed laws addressing requirements for informed consent and confidentiality protections as part of conducting the research process in their states.

Review Process

As part of the safeguard role played by the IRB, an investigator's research protocol undergoes rigorous review pursuant to criteria listed in federal regulations. These regulations, jointly promulgated by several federal departments and agencies, are referred to as the **common rule** and address protections for human subjects involved in research. At minimum, an investigator's research plan and informed consent documents are considered to determine the scientific benefits of the proposed research and any potential risk to the subject, including the risk of breach of confidentiality. The risks identified are then weighed against the anticipated benefits that the research offers, with a view to determining minimum risk. **Minimum risk** is defined as the probability and magnitude of harm or discomfort anticipated in the research; these risks should be no greater than the probability and magnitude of harm or discomfort ordinarily encountered in daily life or during the performance of routine physical or psychological examinations or tests. If the risks are minimized and determined to be reasonable in relation to the potential benefits, the balance resets in favor of approving the research.

The risk/benefit analysis is but one of many assessments conducted by the IRB during the review of a research protocol. The recruitment and selection of subjects is reviewed to determine if it is equitable in terms of gender, race, and ethnicity. If advertisements will be used to recruit study participants, they are examined to determine whether they are coercive or make false promises or claims. The qualifications of the study's investigators and its scientific validity are also reviewed, particularly as the scientific validity relates to the risks the human subjects may be exposed to as part of the study. Any use of investigational devices or drugs are identified and examined to determine whether appropriate federal regulations are met and to ensure that the consent document clearly indicates that the device or drug is of an investigational nature. HIPAA review is also performed, with special care placed upon the use of protected health information and the subjects' authorization for its use by the research team.

Of particular importance are the confidentiality protections specified in the protocol. These protections are examined by the IRB, with focus on determining what type of identifiable private information will be collected and how long it will be kept, who will have access to identifiable private information, how limitations on access will be assured, how the study proposes to prevent inadvertent disclosures, and what procedures will be employed to dispose of or destroy the data when they are no longer needed. Special emphasis is placed upon the safeguards to be employed once data are collected. These safeguards frequently take the form of a Data Safety Monitoring Plan (DSMP) or the use of a Data Safety Monitoring Board (DSMB) to review the data to be collected, stored, and analyzed as part of the study. DSMPs and DSMBs evaluate study data to ensure participant safety and study integrity. DSMPs are mechanisms used by the study investigators, with information reported to the IRB; DSMBs are sometimes composed of IRB members or, more often than not, are an autonomous group that provides information to the IRB. Utilizing either approach, the data are reviewed to determine evidence of study-related adverse events; data quality, timeliness, and

completeness; evidence of efficacy and adherence to protocols; compliance with recruitment and retention goals specified in the protocols; and any factors that would implicate confidentiality.

The process that will be used to obtain the human subject's informed consent and the consent documents themselves are reviewed carefully. Specific regulatory requirements for research study consent forms are listed in Table 10–6. Particular emphasis is placed upon the need for language in the consent form that can be understood at a sixth- to eighth-grade reading level. If investigators intend to bank or archive biological specimens for future research, this future purpose and use must be specified in the consent documents.

In very limited circumstances, an IRB may waive the informed consent requirement.[5] If research is to be conducted by state or local governmental officials and is designed to study, examine, or evaluate public benefit or service programs, the procedures for obtaining those programs, or possible changes in methods or levels of payment for benefit or services under these programs, informed consent will be waived. Other categories qualifying for informed consent include those in which the only record linking the subject with the research is the informed consent and the subject risks harm if a breach of confidentiality occurs; the research poses minimal risk and involves no procedures for which written consent would normally be required outside of the research context; or the research involves minimal risk, a waiver would not adversely affect the rights and welfare of the subject, the research could not practicably be carried out without a waiver, and the subject will be provided with additional information after participating in the research.

Protocols are reviewed by the IRB for conflicts of interest involving investigators or collaborators. A conflict of interest is present when a professional's interests or

Table 10–6	Research Study Informed Consent Requirements
1. Indication that the study involves research, including its purpose; expected duration of participation; a description of any experimental drug, device, or procedure; and a description of the procedures to be followed.
2. A clear and accurate description of the risks relating solely to research.
3. A description of the benefits offered by the research.
4. Disclosure of any alternative procedures or treatments available to the subject.
5. A description of the measure to be employed to protect confidentiality of health information.
6. For research involving more than minimal risk, an explanation of who bears financial responsibility for medical care in the event of injury, and whether compensation will be offered for participation in the study.
7. Point-of-contact data for further information regarding subject rights, the study itself, or any research-related injury.
8. A clear statement that participation in the research study is voluntary, that the subject may discontinue participation at any time, and that refusal to participate will not result in penalty or loss of benefits.

Source: 45 C.F.R. Part 46116(a) and 21 C.F.R. Part 50.25(a) (2007).

commitments compromise her judgment, research report, or communications to research subjects, participants, patients, or clients. Conflicts can be of a personal or financial nature or they may involve competing loyalties. These conflicts may increase the potential for bias, harm, or wrongdoing because the professional's independence is compromised. Investigators must disclose in their protocol materials any significant financial interests they hold so that the IRB can decide whether those interests bear on the protection of human subjects or could affect the design, conduct, or publication of research. In some instances, the conflicts of interest will result in the IRB not approving the research protocol or recommending that the investigator be barred from investments related to her research field. In less drastic instances, the IRB will determine that the conflict of interest must be disclosed to the study participants in the informed consent documents.

Although the review discussed thus far applies to all protocols, some research protocols submitted to IRBs may involve specific areas of concern and warrant an enhanced level of review. If a vulnerable population is involved, the IRB will examine the protocol to determine whether additional safeguards have been included that serve to protect the rights and welfare of this population. Examples of vulnerable populations include prisoners, minors, pregnant women, handicapped or mentally disabled persons, or persons who are educationally or economically disadvantaged. Employees of the institution that sponsors the IRB may also be seen as a vulnerable population warranting special protection, because employees may view participation in a research study as a condition of employment. IRBs check for any indication that the member of the vulnerable population would be forced to participate in the research through coercion, undue influence, or manipulation. If minors are involved, informed consent is obtained from the minor's parents or legal guardian, and assent is obtained from the minor. **Assent** refers to the minor's agreement to

participate in the research. If genetic research is involved, the IRB will require that the protocol and consent documents clearly identify and communicate the risks of harm to the subject. These risks are not as easy to describe as the risks found in traditional research because they may be of a psychological, social, or economic nature rather than a physical nature.

Three types of IRB review are allowed under federal regulations. The standard by which most IRBs operate is to submit protocols to full committee review. This means that review of all documentation is conducted by a quorum of the members of the full committee at a regularly scheduled meeting. In many locations, the full IRB will employ a primary reviewer system in conjunction with the full committee process. This system establishes a select number of IRB members to conduct a thorough review of the protocol and report their findings and recommendations at a meeting of the full committee. The other members of the full committee also receive information about the protocol, but it may be in abbreviated form or at a more basic level than that received by the primary reviewers. A majority vote of the members of the full committee is required to take action. Typically, they may approve, disapprove, or modify the research protocols submitted. In some instances, they may approve a protocol contingent upon the investigator's concurrence that the IRB's modification requests be incorporated into the revised document. Alternatively, the IRB may table any decision and revisit the protocol once any information that is essential for decision making is added to the protocol.

A second form of review is expedited review. Expedited review refers to the review of studies that pose no more than minimal risk to the human subject and fall within certain categories as defined by federal regulations. These categories are listed in Table 10–7. The determination that no more than a minimal risk exists rests with the reviewer—either

Table 10–7 | Research Categories Qualifying for Expedited Review

1. Studies involving drugs or medical devices that do not require an investigational drug (IND) or investigational device exemption (IDE) application; a clear and accurate description of the risks relating solely to research.
2. Where blood is collected by finger stick, heel stick, ear stick, or venipuncture.
3. Where biological specimens are collected prospectively by noninvasive means.
4. Where data are collected by noninvasive procedures routinely employed in clinical practice, excluding the use of anesthesia, sedation, X-rays, or microwaves.
5. Where data will be collected from previously existing documents, records, or specimens, or will be collected for non-research purposes.
6. Where data will be collected from voice, video, digital, or image recordings made for research purposes.
7. Research on individual/group characteristics or behavior.
8. Continuing review of studies previously approved by an IRB if enrollment was closed, all subjects have completed the research-related activities, and long-term follow-up is the only activity remaining.
9. Continuing review of studies not involving an IDE or IND previously approved by an IRB, where no other categories apply.

Source: **45 C.F.R. Part 46116(a) and 21 C.F.R. Part 50.25(a) (2007).**

Table 10-8 | Human Subject Research Categories Exempted from IRB Review

1. Research conducted in educational settings involving normal educational practices, such as instructional strategies.

2. Research involving the use of educational tests, survey procedures, interview procedures, or observation of public behavior wherein the subject is not placed at civil, criminal, or financial risk.

3. Research involving individually identifiable persons who are elected or appointed as public officials or candidates for office.

4. Research involving existing, publicly available data, records, pathology specimens, or diagnostic specimens wherein the data are de-identified.

5. Research of public service or public benefit programs by heads of governmental departments or agencies.

6. Research evaluating the taste and quality of food and consumer acceptance studies.

Source: 45 C.F.R. Part 46 (2007).

the IRB chairperson or an experienced IRB member—and not with the investigator or research study sponsor. Once the minimal risk and category determinations are made, the IRB chairperson or designate conducts the review according to the regulatory requirements, either approving, modifying, or referring the protocol to full committee review. Expedited review cannot result in a determination to disapprove the protocol because that authority rests with the full committee.

The final form of review involves those research studies that fall within the six categories that have been exempted from review by federal regulation. These categories are listed in Table 10-8. Research protocols that fall within these categories are typically submitted to the IRB; the chairperson or a staff member then reviews the protocol to determine whether the exemption applies. Similar to the expedited process, the determination of whether the exemption applies rests with the IRB and not with the investigator or research study sponsor. Even if the research at issue falls within one of these six categories, research will not be exempt if the research populations involve prisoners as subjects.

IRB activity does not cease once protocols are approved. To the contrary, the IRB engages in a series of actions involving the previously approved protocols. For example, the IRB must monitor the progress of the protocol at least once a year, examining the number of subjects accrued, whether the informed consent document remains the same as it did at the time of initial review, and whether any adverse events, unexpected problems, or complaints exist. This process is referred to as continuing review. The IRB—or a Data Safety Monitoring Board, if one exists—will review and evaluate data gained from the research to ensure participant safety and study integrity. Additionally, the IRB possesses an obligation to review all amendments and modifications to a previously approved protocol if the investigator proposes any changes that would impact the subjects. Finally, the IRB often reports to regulatory authorities instances of noncompliance with or deviations from the protocol, whether an adverse event or unanticipated problem occurred, and data safety monitoring summaries.

Review of Research on Animals Research that investigators propose to conduct on human subjects will frequently be conducted using animal subjects first. As a result of past abusive research practices involving animals, federal laws and regulations are in place to establish safeguards. Chief among these safeguards are **institutional animal care and use committees** (IACUC). Similar to institutional review boards, these bodies are associated with universities or academic medical centers or hospitals. They are charged with reviewing all activities that involve the use of a live vertebrate animal, including research, research training, and biological testing.

Composition of the IACUC is prescribed by regulations, with five members serving as a minimum. At least one member must be a veterinarian, another a scientist with laboratory animal research experience, and a third a member of the community who has no affiliation with the institution. Members will often include persons with expertise in ethics and those who have been active in the animal welfare community. Membership in an organization's IRB and its IACUC does not overlap.

Similar to the IRB's process, IACUC members review each research protocol to determine its scientific validity and whether the choice of species is justified. Members also evaluate the benefits the research poses for mankind, whether the animals' living conditions are appropriate, whether anesthesia should be used, whether an excessive number of animals is involved, and whether suffering can be avoided or minimized. They categorize the research they review into one of three established categories, which are explained in more detail in Table 10-9.

Table 10-9 | Categories for Animal Research

Category	Definition
A	No potential for suffering is involved.
B	If the potential for suffering exists, it can be alleviated by anesthetic agents or analgesics.
C	Potential suffering exists, which cannot be alleviated by anesthetic agents or analgesics.

Reports of the IACUC are also required and are kept by the National Institute of Health's Office of Laboratory Animal Welfare (OLAW), the federal regulatory body tasked with implementing policy and regulations on the use of animals in research.

The National Institutes of Health (NIH) regulatory requirements include a provision for assurance that animal research supported by NIH grants, awards, or contracts meets acceptable standards of care, use, and treatment. Institutions that use animals in research and are supported by these NIH funds may meet this assurance either by becoming accredited by a recognized professional laboratory animal accrediting body or by establishing their own committees to conduct an oversight of animal care programs. The American Association of Accreditation of Laboratory Animal Care (AAALAC), an independent body that provides accrediting services, is widely respected and relied upon by many institutions in America as their accrediting body for research involving the use of animals. Although some institutions rely upon their own committees to provide oversight, the majority of institutions in the United States apply for accreditation with the AAALAC.

Emerging Trends

Several trends have emerged over the last decade that relate to the protection of human subjects or animals used in research. Each of these trends has varied with regard to the strength with which it has taken hold, but none appears to be waning. These trends include accreditation of research programs, new roles for research staff members, recognition of the need for continuing education in the research field, deployment of new technologies, and application of ethical and legal concepts and principles to emerging areas of medicine.

Whereas the accreditation of research programs involving the use of animals dates back to the early 1960s, the accreditation of research programs involving human subjects is a more recent phenomenon. The two prominent bodies that review and accredit human subject research programs are the National Commission on Quality Assurance (NCQA) and the Association for the Accreditation of Human Research Protection Programs (AAHRPP). The NCQA's main focus has been on accrediting human subject research programs associated with the Veteran's Administration; the AAHRPP's main focus has been on major research universities. Both bodies operate to advance the quality of IRBs by engaging in an accreditation process.

The accrediting body possesses several options when determining the outcome of the accreditation process. The highest level, full accreditation, is given to those institutions that meet every standard evaluated by the accrediting body. Qualified accreditation is conferred on those institutions that meet almost all standards, and where the deficiencies are minor and administrative in nature. Accreditation pending is conferred on those institutions that do not meet the full or qualified status but convey the ability and willingness to work toward meeting the standards evaluated by the accrediting body. Accreditation withheld applies to those institutions that do not meet a large number of standards and are either unwilling or unable to address the outstanding issues.

One trend recognizes the ongoing transition in the role that staff members play with regard to the work of IRBs and IACUCs. When little regulation existed at the federal or state levels governing research, many of those in decision-making positions viewed staff members as merely keepers of paper and trackers of schedules. As regulations have grown more complex, however, this view has changed and a new role has been created: the research information manager. Although this role currently exists under a variety of different job titles, the role itself attends to the business end of managing the research paperwork, works to secure and protect health information and records, monitors regulatory compliance by team members, and coordinates the institution's efforts toward gaining and maintaining accreditation status. In some institutions, the research information manager serves as the initial reviewer of HIPAA-related issues for all research protocols using human subjects, freeing the IRB member to serve in a secondary review capacity on the issues related to HIPAA. Because this role requires knowledge of regulatory schemes, the management of data in both electronic and traditional forms, and concepts of privacy and confidentiality, it is uniquely suited to a health information management professional.

Another emerging trend is the recognition that key members of a research team should undergo continuing education concerning the protection of human subjects in clinical research. For those research teams whose funding is secured by grants from NIH, this ongoing education requirement is a mandated feature. Some institutions have built upon this mandated feature and require ongoing education for all research teams, regardless of how funding is secured. Furthermore, some institutions have expanded the definition of key members of the research team to include the members of the IRB and those who staff it. Several online tutorials have been established through which researchers, IRB members, and staff can fulfill this requirement. Some of these online tutorials offer certification for those who complete the course.

Another trend emerged simultaneously with the trend in changing roles and the need for ongoing education: the role that new technologies could play in accomplishing the business work of the IRB and IACUC. Similar to the deployment of the electronic health record (EHR) for clinical care, some institutions have attempted to deploy an electronic means with which IRBs can complete their work. This approach requires that all documents be in an electronic form so that IRB members can review them, make remarks, vote, and take any other necessary actions without the use of paper documents. Though this approach is still relatively new, it offers advantages similar to those offered by the EHR—namely, easier methods of communication, better data retrieval and storage options, immediate and simultaneous access to data by multiple persons, and ease in recovering information in the event of a disaster. For institutions whose IRB is composed of multiple committees, this approach provides staff with the ability to track the status of various protocols easily and compare and contrast the work of these committees over time.

One trend that addresses the research itself is the application of ethical and legal concepts and principles to emerging areas of medicine. Much of what is occurring in the field of genetic research implicates more than one person, because confirming a genetic basis for a medical condition indicates that at least one of a patient's parents carries the gene in question. As a result, some researchers have faced ethical dilemmas regarding whether they should contact family members of the patient who consented to be part of a research study. Because the parent is not a subject of the study and did not consent to participate in it, the researcher arguably violates the parent's right to privacy if contact is made. However, if contact is not made and the parent is at risk of developing the condition that is the subject of the genetic research study, does the researcher violate ethical principles of doing no harm? Answers to questions such as this are still in the formative stage, resulting in a wide variety of opinions.

Advances in medicine are not limited to the field of genetic research. For example, technology now allows scientists to develop blood cell treatments for cancer based on human tissue specimens. This new ability raises questions related to informed consent and individual property rights. If the tissue in this scenario were obtained as part of a protocol from an earlier date, without full disclosure to the patient that stored tissue specimens may be used for purposes not known at the time consent was obtained, the patient may rightfully claim that her tissue was improperly used, she was subjected to deceptive practices, and/or she is entitled to both ownership and any financial profit associated with the new blood cell treatment. Even if disclosure of a future unspecified purpose was given at the time informed consent was obtained, the law remains unclear about whether the patient retains some right to the financial benefits derived from the treatment based on the tissue specimens that came from the patient's body.

A further interchange between medicine, law, and ethics that has emerged is the number of lawsuits filed as a result of either negative outcomes from clinical trials or the denial of a participant's wish to continue in a clinical trial and obtain an experimental drug. This increase in lawsuits may be due to the sheer number of clinical trials in existence, public distrust of pharmaceutical companies, concerns about the ethics of investigators and institutions involved in research studies, or any combination thereof. Issues raised in these lawsuits center on flaws in the informed consent process, deception about the level to which a drug or device is experimental, and breach of an individual's right to be treated with dignity while participating in a research trial. These issues, and others not listed here, form the basis for much of the discussion concerning ethics and law as they relate to the protection of human subjects involved in research.

Epidemiology

One area that is closely related to research is epidemiology. Epidemiology refers to the determination of the occurrence and distribution of human health problems, the establishment of their root causes, and the factors that influence their distribution. In other words, epidemiology is the study of how and why diseases occur in different groups of human beings. The underlying premise of epidemiology is that disease occurrence is not random; rather, disease is present or absent due to certain characteristics that may be identified through study. This area of health care combines the investigation of the root causes of disease with the discovery and formulation of measures to control the spread of disease. Additionally, epidemiology helps disseminate knowledge about the interplay between the causes of disease (e.g., biologic or toxicologic) and their relationship with factors that increase an individual's or group's risk for succumbing to disease, such as sociologic processes. Specific objectives of epidemiology are listed in Table 10–10.

Professionals involved in this area of study are called epidemiologists. Epidemiologists engage in research and investigation using high-tech computers, software applications, and research labs to perform their work. They also utilize less sophisticated methods in their work, often relying upon simple communication techniques among individuals affected by disease, those who care for them, and the epidemiologists themselves to gain information about why some persons are affected by disease while others are not. In turn, this can lead to an understanding of how to prevent disease from occurring and how to contain any existing disease so that it does not spread to others.

Table 10–10	Epidemiology Objectives
1. Investigate the root causes of disease and identify associated risk factors.
2. Examine the extent to which disease is found in a given population.
3. Through study, determine the natural progression of disease.
4. Discover and formulate measures to control the spread of disease.
5. Disseminate knowledge to the health care community and the public at large as a means to improve human health.

Source: Gordis, L. (2000). Epidemiology (2nd ed.). Philadelphia: W. B. Saunders.

Table 10–11 | Predominant Causes of Death in the United States

1900		2000	
Causes of Death	**Crude Death Rate per 100,000 Population per Year**	**Causes of Death**	**Crude Death Rate per 100,000 Population per Year**
All causes	1,719.0	All causes	873.1
Pneumonia and influenza	202.2	Diseases of the heart	258.2
Tuberculosis	194.4	Malignant neoplasms	200.9
Diarrhea, enteritis, and ulceration of the intestine	142.7	Cerebrovascular diseases	60.9
Diseases of the heart	137.4	Chronic lower respiratory diseases	44.3
Senility, ill-defined or unknown	117.5	Accidents (unintentional injuries)	35.6
Intracranial lesions of vascular origin	109.6	Diabetes mellitus	25.2
Nephritis	88.6	Influenza and pneumonia	23.7
All accidents	72.3	Alzheimer's disease	18.0
Cancer and other malignant tumors	64.0	Nephritis, nephritic syndrome, and nephrosis	13.5
Diphtheria	40.3	Septicemia	11.3

Sources: U.S. National Center for Health Statistics. (2003). *Vital statistics of the United States,* http://www.cdc.gov/nchs/data; Williams, S. J., & Torrens, P. R. (2002). *Introduction to health services* (6th ed.). Albany, NY: Delmar.

Epidemiologists look not only at outbreaks of disease today but also at past outbreaks to learn how to address present problems. For example, acute infectious disease was the major cause of death in the United States at the beginning of the 20th century, and chronic disease was the major cause of death by the end of the same century. Table 10–11 contrasts the predominant causes of death between these two periods. Using the knowledge gained over the past century with regard to preventing, containing, and curing acute infectious diseases, epidemiologists can act to prevent the development of acute infectious diseases (through means such as vaccination) and address incidences of acute infectious diseases in developing countries (through means such as treatment).

Epidemiologists are drawn from many different fields. Some possess medical degrees, and others are veterinarians, dentists, laboratory scientists, statisticians, and public health and health information management professionals. Each brings a specialized area of training or expertise to the field, and all share in the skill of gathering information for testing and analysis. Because epidemiology focuses on population groups instead of individuals, all epidemiologists must be familiar with statistics so that rates of illness and disease within population groups can be compared and patterns detected. They must be aware of database management techniques because much of the data they collect, store, and retrieve relies upon automated methods. Furthermore, they must possess complex reasoning and problem-solving skills because many epidemiological discoveries require complicated solutions.

Although epidemiologists share many attributes, they may differ in the types of work they perform and with whom they perform it. Some epidemiologists choose specialty fields, such as environmental studies, nutrition, aging, and pediatrics; others specialize in the type of work they perform: data gathering or statistical review. Epidemiologists serve in a wide variety of organizations in both the public and private sectors. Governmental entities at the national, state, and local levels all employ epidemiologists, as do educational institutions, hospitals, pharmaceutical companies, and private foundations. Some of the more well-known employers of epidemiologists include the National Institutes of Health and the Centers for Disease Control and Prevention.

Epidemiology intersects with health information management with regard to collecting and managing data. Some collected data involve retrospective studies that include access to medical records containing patient-identifiable data. Other data are collected on a prospective basis from patients in various care settings. However they are collected, these data must be managed so that specific incidences of disease can be identified. This identification in turn can lead to tracking disease trends and making projections about future outbreaks with the goals of preventing and controlling disease and monitoring the overall health status of a population. As a result of being involved in epidemiology, health information management professionals can help advance the well being of many communities.

Table 10-12	History of Epidemiology				
Time Period	Ancient World	Middle Ages	19th Century	20th Century	21st Century
Area	Greece and Rome	Europe	Europe	Move toward global involvement	Move toward global involvement
Diseases	Plagues	Black Plague	Cholera, tuberculosis	Influenza pandemic	Influenza pandemic
Focus	Infectious diseases	Infectious diseases	Infectious diseases	Infectious and noninfectious diseases	Infectious and noninfectious diseases

Historical Overview

Long before the terms *epidemiology* and *epidemiologists* were created, efforts to identify the root causes of disease and prevent their spread were under way in all parts of the world. Table 10-12 illustrates the historical development of epidemiology. The ancient Greeks made a connection between the location of villages on wet lowlands and the incidences of infectious diseases, and they sought to prevent such incidences by positioning villages on higher ground where infectious diseases were less prevalent. The ancient Romans made a connection between dirty water and incidences of diseases, and they created public baths as a means to flush away sewage. During the Middle Ages, many countries in Europe used an early version of quarantine as a way to combat the plague, or Black Death.

As medical science advanced, so did the area of study that came to be known as epidemiology. Scientists began to identify outbreaks of disease as epidemics and to study them accordingly. The early years of epidemiology centered on the discovery of biological causes of infectious diseases and the manner in which such diseases could be controlled or prevented. For example, the 19th century ushered in John Snow's determination that water and personal contact were the transmitters of cholera and William Budd's determination of the contagious nature of tuberculosis. Such determinations led to the control techniques of immunization and quarantine. Other examples include the study of smallpox, typhoid, tuberculosis, anthrax, rabies, and trachoma, and the resultant focus on tracing the sources of these diseases and instituting preventive measures to stop recurrences. Scientists such as Edward Jenner, Louis Pasteur, and Robert Koch became famous for their work in developing vaccines as a means to prevent the spread of infectious diseases.

Infectious diseases remained the focus of epidemiology well through the 19th and early 20th centuries; episodes of epidemics—diseases that affected many persons in a community, area, or region at the same time, arising from a common source and clearly in excess of normal expectancy—were quite prevalent. One variation on this effort was the tracking of infectious disease prevalence across geographic areas. Scientists studied the connections between ship landings in U.S. coastal cities and the existence of yellow fever epidemics. They also studied how infectious diseases that existed in one geographic location were introduced to new geographic locations, such as when sailors brought bacteria and diseases like measles and smallpox to island nations. They further studied pandemics, epidemics that spread quickly over a wide geographic area. Of particular importance to the development of epidemiology as a science was the influenza pandemic of 1918, which spread across and between continents worldwide and resulted in millions of deaths. Scientists who studied this pandemic were able to gather data that showed patterns of occurrence across nations and to connect those patterns with the fact that many persons were displaced, relocating, or far from home at the end of World War I.

As the field of epidemiology matured, many epidemiologists began to expand their attention beyond infectious diseases to address noninfectious diseases. Some focused on making connections between nutritional deficits and occupations, such as sailors who suffered from scurvy, while others made the connection between nutritional deficits and geographic locations, such as poor southerners in the United States whose diet lacked vitamin B. Still others focused on occupational diseases, such as coal miners suffering from black lung disease. Later on in the 20th century, epidemiologists began to turn their attention to chronic and degenerative diseases such as cancer, arthritis, and cardiovascular disorders. For example, the work of epidemiologists Richard Doll and Austin Bradford Hill resulted in the conclusion of a connection between cigarette smoking and lung cancer. This, in turn, led to efforts by the epidemiological and medical communities to educate the public about this link and thereby reduce the incidence of lung cancer.

Today, epidemiology's focus includes both infectious and noninfectious diseases as well as disorders that involve congenital defects, nutrition, and mental illness. New diseases, such as severe acute respiratory system (SARS) and acquired immunodeficiency syndrome (AIDS); mutations of existing diseases, such as Avian flu; and diseases that have existed for thousands of years, such as leprosy, all demand the attention of epidemiologists. Other diseases that are less well known to the public share this attention, resulting in a wide variety of problems for epidemiologists to solve.

Epidemiological Basics

To fully comprehend the field of epidemiology, one must first understand the elements that constitute the field. These elements include who is being studied, the concept of risk identification, the sources of data used in studies, the main focus of epidemiology, the nature of disease progression, and the different types of epidemiological investigation.

Among the most basic elements of epidemiology is the population group being studied. This population group may vary in size and characteristics; however, all members of the group have at least one common element, such as the presence of or exposure to a certain disease. Focus rests on the population group as a whole, including those who manifest a disease and those who do not. This approach differs from research that focuses on a statistically valid sample of a whole group so that conclusions may be reached, and also from clinical medicine that focuses on individual patients or a series of patients.

Another basic element is the concept of risk identification. This concept encompasses the term risk, which refers to the probability of an unfavorable event occurring. Epidemiologists identify risk by determining which factors are associated with or increase the risk of acquiring a disease and label these risk factors. Risk factors vary depending on the disease studied but may reside in the physical environment (e.g., radiation) or the social environment (e.g., death of a loved one). Risk factors may also be behavioral in nature (e.g., life-threatening habits such as smoking) or inherited (e.g., hemoglobin S, which increases the risk of infection). After identifying the risk, epidemiologists attempt to determine the probability of an individual acquiring a disease. This involves calculating risk for populations as a whole and then identifying how similar or different an individual person is from the population as a whole. Epidemiologists also calculate the relative risk ratio, an estimate of how much the risk of acquiring a disease increases with an individual's exposure to a known risk factor or a particular causal agent. For example, a relative risk ratio of three indicates that an individual is three times more likely to acquire a disease if exposed to a known risk factor or particular causal agent than an individual who is not exposed.

Epidemiology draws from a number of sources to obtain data to support a study or reach a conclusion. These sources may include data that are reported to state and local health departments and agencies pursuant to legal requirements, such as incidences of infectious diseases, morbidity, or mortality. With the support of governmental agencies, epidemiologists may gather data from surveys, such as those conducted by the U.S. National Health Survey on Morbidity. Epidemiologists may also conduct their own studies—including controlled experiments—that utilize a prospective or retrospective approach.

A main focus of epidemiology is the prevention of disease. Such prevention can be addressed on three levels: primary, secondary, and tertiary. Primary prevention looks at healthy population groups and suggests actions to be taken that will prevent members of the healthy population groups from developing a given disease. General health promotion—such as nutrition and hygiene education—plus specific protective measures—such as immunizations and sanitation—are examples of primary prevention measures. Secondary prevention focuses on identifying, through screening techniques, those people who are in the preclinical and clinical stages of a disease and applying intervention techniques early in the disease progression process. By doing so, secondary prevention efforts attempt to prevent mortality, slow progression, limit disability, and reduce complications and costs. Examples of secondary prevention measures include routine screenings for glaucoma and cervical cancer by health care professionals and breast self-examinations by females. Tertiary prevention focuses on limiting the level of disability and increasing the probability of rehabilitation for persons in an advanced stage of disease or disability. Undergoing physical therapy to restore motion to affected limbs and engaging in psychosocial and vocational rehabilitation programs are examples of tertiary prevention.

Whether they are addressed at the primary, secondary, or tertiary levels, prevention efforts may be applied widely or narrowly. When they are applied widely, prevention efforts can be targeted at an entire population; applied narrowly, prevention efforts can be targeted at a high-risk population group. For example, efforts to educate the population about the connection between levels of physical activity and obesity are widely used, but efforts to screen those who are at high risk for developing heart disease because of family history and levels of cholesterol are more narrowly applied.

An equally important focus of epidemiology is the formation of health planning and policy. Epidemiological data about the occurrence and distribution of diseases often lead to the identification of the health needs of a population, whether preventive or curative, and estimates of the demands that are required to meet those needs. Planners and policy makers employ this data to develop objectives and approaches to improve the public health. For example, certain services or programs may be initiated, maintained, expanded, reduced, or deleted because of epidemiological data. By focusing their efforts on outcomes, planners and policy makers can impact the state of health of an entire population.

Disease Progression A significant basic element of epidemiology is the study of the natural history or progression of a disease. This history or progression begins with a description of the forces that created the disease stimulus and continues through the human being's response, including the changes that take place as a result of the human being's response, such as death, disability, defect, or recovery. Three factors serve as the basis for this portion of epidemiological study: the agent, the host, and the environment.

In epidemiology, the **agent** is the factor that causes a disease. The agent may take the form of a presence—such as cases where lead is consumed, leading to lead poisoning—or it may take the form of an absence—such as cases of insufficient calcium and vitamin D that lead to rickets. Six types of agents exist: physical, chemical, nutrient, biologic, genetic, and psychological. Physical agents include the mechanical forces or frictions that may cause injury and certain atmospheric abnormalities, such temperature extremes, fire, excessive radiation, or trauma. Chemical agents include dusts, fumes, vapors, and gases, and may affect the host by way of inhalation, ingestion, or contact. Poison, alcohol, and smoke are examples of chemical agents. Nutrient agents include the basic dietary elements, either in overabundant or insufficient quantities. Biologic agents include living organisms such as bacteria, viruses, and fungi, to name only a few. Genetic agents include those traits that are transmitted from parent to child through genes. Psychological agents include the stressful social circumstances that exist in the environment, which affect a person's physiology by psychosomatic means.

The **host** is the living being upon whom the agent acts, such as the human being. How susceptible or resistant the host is to the agent will in part determine the occurrence and distribution of disease within a population. Many variables can influence a human's susceptibility to disease, including genetic background, personal habits, customs, and lifestyle. For example, good nutrition habits, personal cleanliness, interaction with other people, and the availability of sanitation measures may all influence the start, kind, and direction of a given disease. The host may influence the resistance to the onset of disease through defenses designed to protect the human being (e.g., skin and coughing). Furthermore, such attributes as heredity, constitutional composition, ethnic origin, sex, age, marital status, and socioeconomic indicators may also play a role in susceptibility or resistance to disease.

The **environment** is the aggregate of the things, conditions, or influences that surround the host. The environment may be physical, biological, social, or economic. The physical environment may include geography (e.g., climate, season, or weather), topography (e.g., soil or water), or the presence of physical and chemical pollutants. The biological environment includes living animals and plants, which may harbor agents of disease. The socioeconomic environment includes variations in the standard of living, different levels of economic deprivation, and attitudes and beliefs that promote health.

How the agent, host, and environment interact determines in large measure the level of health within a given population. This interaction can be more clearly understood by picturing a child's seesaw, with the environment serving as the base or fulcrum and the agent and host sitting on either end of the board. If the balance changes between the agent

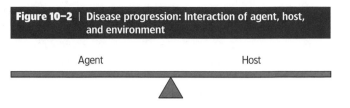

Figure 10-2 | Disease progression: Interaction of agent, host, and environment

Agent   Host

and host, the level of health may change; see Figure 10-2. For example, when the balance shifts in favor of the host, the level of health is higher; when the balance favors the agent, disease occurs more frequently. The base of the seesaw itself may decrease if the environment deteriorates, thereby influencing both the agent and the host.

The level of health in a given population is also influenced by the means of disease transmission. Diseases are transmitted either directly (person to person) or indirectly (through a common vehicle that comes in contact with two or more people). A classic example of direct transmission is seen in Figure 10-3, which shows the dispersal of droplets following a sneeze. Indirect transmission may be the result of single, multiple, or continuous exposures to a common vehicle or the result of action due to a vector. A **vector** is an agent capable of transmitting a pathogen from one organism to another organism, such as the fleas that transmitted the Black Plague to humans in the Middle Ages through their bites and the mosquitoes who harbor malaria and infect humans today. Because diseases may be transmitted in a variety of ways, epidemiologists focus on this element when examining the progression of disease.

Types of Epidemiology   Because epidemiology focuses on the occurrence and distribution of diseases, their root causes, and preventive measures, the field must by necessity encompass several levels of inquiry. The three levels most commonly seen are descriptive, analytic, and experimental epidemiology. Table 10-13 contrasts the three levels of epidemiological inquiry.

Figure 10-3 | Droplets following a sneeze

(Courtesy of Lester V. Bergman/Corbis)

Table 10-13 | Three Levels of Epidemiological Inquiry

Title	Descriptive	Analytic	Experimental
Studies	Observational	Observational	Controlled experiment
Focus	Person, place, and time	Development of hypotheses of causal factors	Prove causal relationships

Descriptive Epidemiology Descriptive epidemiology refers to the activities that are involved in investigating and describing the occurrence and distribution of disease within a population. Because occurrence and distribution are the focus, descriptive epidemiology addresses amounts or rates of disease. Descriptive epidemiology tries to answer the "who," "where," and "when" questions associated with epidemiology. Descriptive epidemiology involves observing a population to see what occurs; it does not attempt to manipulate the study population in any way. The populations under study may differ in whole or in part, such as smaller segments of the same large group. The focus rests on three characteristics: persons, place, and time.

The characteristics of person, place, and time assume that diseases are not randomly distributed. With regard to the person characteristic, factors such as age, sex, race, and ethnic origin may all play a role in the distribution of disease. With regard to the place characteristic, diseases may be endemic, habitually peculiar to a particular locality, or concentrated in certain areas without recurrence on a routine basis. For example, diseases may cluster around a geographic area. With regard to the time characteristic, the presence of diseases may fluctuate based on season (e.g., more respiratory diseases in the winter months) or over many years (e.g., the decrease in acute infectious diseases as the cause of death in the United States over the last century).

Descriptive epidemiology seeks to take available data from various sources and apply them to the variable characteristics of person, place, and time. Data such as incidence rates, the rates of newly occurring cases, and mortality rates, the rates of death from a disease, are commonly used in the early stages of investigation. If application of the data to the characteristics is not uniform, epidemiologists can make certain inferences. Using the observational approach, epidemiologists who have studied hypertension have found that hypertension is more prevalent among the black population in the United States than the white population. From that observation, epidemiologists examine the agent-host-environment relationship to create hypotheses to be used in analytic and experimental epidemiology. Epidemiologists use the data and inferences to assist in the planning and programming of health services for a given population and for the community at large.

Analytic and Experimental Epidemiology Analytic and experimental epidemiology move beyond descriptive epidemiology to pinpoint the determinants, reasons, and mechanisms of disease. Both types of epidemiology try to answer the "how" and "why" questions associated with epidemiology. Using cross-sectional, case-control, and cohort studies, epidemiologists often can determine whether a relationship exists between the presence of a disease and a specific phenomenon. Further study may reveal whether this relationship is causal in nature.

Analytic epidemiology refers to the investigative technique used to determine a statistical correlation between a specific factor and a given disease. If the underlying premise of epidemiology is that disease occurrence is not random, then establishing statistical relationships among two or more factors and a given disease will indicate whether the relationships are a result of chance alone or more than chance. Applying statistical tests, such as the chi-square test or a correlation coefficient, can help to establish whether chance alone explains the relationship between a specific factor and a given disease or if a frequency greater than chance is present, thereby making the relationship statistically significant.

Analytic epidemiology tests the hypothesis created by descriptive epidemiology to reach a conclusion, using both prospective and retrospective studies to establish a statistical correlation between a specific factor and a given disease. As such, analytic epidemiology relies upon the observational approach to reach a conclusion because the groups under study are not created as part of the study but exist apart from it. Similar to descriptive epidemiology, analytic epidemiology does not attempt to manipulate the groups under study but merely observes them. Among the most well-known examples of analytic epidemiology is the testing of the hypothesis that cigarette smoking contributes to the development of lung cancer. Using studies, epidemiologists have established a statistical association between cigarette smoking and lung cancer, observing that groups of persons who do not smoke have a lower rate of developing lung cancer than those groups of persons who do smoke.

Experimental epidemiology refers to the investigative technique used to determine the cause of disease using controlled experiments. This form of epidemiology takes the hypothesis from descriptive epidemiology and the statistical correlation from analytic epidemiology and tests both in a controlled manner. By doing so, the experiment works to differentiate those characteristics present in the observational approach from the specific factor under study to determine if the specific factor is the cause of disease. Experimental epidemiology is most useful for establishing a causal relationship between the presence of disease and a specific phenomenon. Experimental epidemiology relies upon both clinical trials and community trials

Figure 10-4 | Causal relationships

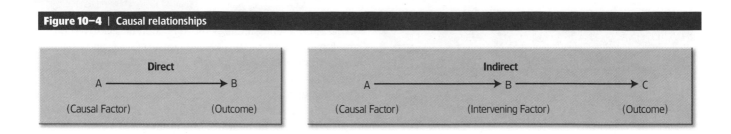

to reach conclusions about causal relationships, which means that the epidemiologist is not merely a observer but one who manipulates the study population in some respect, such as by exposing some of the group to a risk factor that is the cause of disease and leaving others unexposed.

There are two types of causal relationships established through analytic and experimental epidemiology: direct and indirect. Direct causal relationships refer to those relationships in which a factor causes a disease, with no other factor intervening. Infectious organisms, such as bacteria and viruses that cause disease, are examples of a direct causal relationship. Indirect causal relationships refer to those relationships in which a variable intervenes between the causal factor and the disease (outcome). For example, cigarette smoking damages the respiratory epithelium (causal factor), which results in susceptibility to infection (intervening variable), which may lead to chronic bronchitis (disease outcome). Figure 10-4 illustrates these two concepts. In some instances, epidemiologists are able to establish a single cause for disease occurrence, whereas other instances indicate multiple causes. The number of causes for disease occurrence in turn influences the means and methods used to prevent and contain the presence of disease.

Conclusion

During the last half century, research and epidemiology have played valuable roles in the many advancements seen in medicine and public health. Research and epidemiology promise to play significant roles in the future as well; more individuals and organizations will become involved in both activities, more funding opportunities will arise, and the deployment of various technologies will present better opportunities to retrieve data collected as part of research and epidemiologic studies. Because of the complexities that accompany these developments, it is important that those who work in health care possess an understanding of research and epidemiology—both activities will continue to impact the delivery of health care well into the future.

CHAPTER SUMMARY

Pioneers in research began to come forth during the Renaissance, focusing on clinical observations and employing remedies to combat illnesses. Significant developments in research have occurred during the last two centuries, resulting in the creation of research methodologies that apply to many topics, including medicine. Qualitative and quantitative research are two forms of research methodologies, and research studies that follow these methods employ an established series of steps. Abuses in research led to the creation of institutional review boards, which are groups formally designated by an institution to safeguard the rights and welfare of human subjects. IRBs review research protocols and weigh the risks and benefits they pose to human subjects. Epidemiology as a science emerged during the last century as a means to investigate the root causes and progressions of diseases. Three types of epidemiology are recognized: descriptive, analytic, and experimental. New methods to control disease have developed as a result of the intersection of research and epidemiology.

CASE STUDY

You are part of a research team studying the safety of a new medical device to be used on human beings. Your role is to obtain the informed consent of potential study enrollees, explaining to potential study enrollees the risks and benefits of the study and any available alternatives to using the new medical device. You encounter a potential study enrollee who indicates that she wants to participate in the study but does not wish to read the materials, including the consent form, nor hear from you a description of the study and other important information. The potential study enrollee simply asks, "Where do I sign?" How should you proceed? What ethical principles are involved?

REVIEW QUESTIONS

1. Which research method seeks to build a theory and which seeks to prove a theory?

2. What are the overriding objectives of clinical trials?

3. What are blind and double-blind studies?

4. Why would a researcher design and conduct observational studies?

5. How do prospective and retrospective studies differ?

6. What benefits are offered by proper research design?

7. What is an institutional review board, and what does it consider?

8. What is the name of the landmark document in the area of human research ethics?

9. How is an institutional animal care and use committee similar to an institutional review board?

10. How does epidemiology intersect with health information management?

11. How does a pandemic differ from an epidemic?

12. What are the basic elements of epidemiology?

13. How does epidemiology differ from research and clinical medicine?

ENRICHMENT ACTIVITIES

1. Using the Internet, locate at least three recently concluded health care research studies. Identify whether each research study was a clinically controlled trial or an observational study, and provide information if applicable on the use of placebos, blinding, and cohort and case–control studies. Report this information to your instructor in written form, making sure to provide the appropriate Web site address for each study.

2. Search the Internet to learn more about epidemiology, using such search words as "epidemic," "pandemic," "vaccine," and "epidemiologist." When viewing the information you find, determine how epidemiology has changed over time. Report this information and your conclusion to your instructor in

written form, making sure to provide the appropriate Web address for each site.

3. Select one of the following Web links that address the protection of human subjects in research and complete the online training found there. Upon completion of the training, print the completion certificate. Provide one copy of the certificate to your instructor and retain one copy for your professional portfolio. When you design your resume, make sure to include this certification among your list of accomplishments.
http://cme.cancer.gov/clinicaltrials/learning/humanparticipant-protections.asp
http://tutorials.rgs.uci.edu/

WEB SITES

Association for the Accreditation of Human Research Protection Programs, http://www.aahrpp.org

National Commission on Quality Assurance, http:/www.ncqa.org

National Institute of Health Trials Finder, http://ClinicalTrials.gov

National Science Foundation, http://www.nsf.gov

Office for Human Research Protections, http://ohrp.osophs.dhhs.gov

World Health Organization, http://www.who.int

REFERENCES

Bailey, D. (1997). *Research for the health professional* (2nd ed.). Philadelphia: F. A. Davis & Co.

Crombie, I. K., & Davies, H. T. O. (1996). *Research in health care.* Chichester, UK: John Wiley & Sons.

DeSalle, R. (Ed.). (1999). *Epidemic!* New York: The New Press.

Fos, P. J., & Fine, D. J. (2000). *Designing health care for populations.* San Francisco, CA: Jossey–Bass.

Fowler, F., Jr. (1988). *Survey research methods.* Beverly Hills, CA: Sage Publications.

Gallin, J. J. (2002). *Principles and practice of clinical research.* San Diego, CA: Academic Press.

Gordis, L. (2000). *Epidemiology* (2nd ed.). Philadelphia: W. B. Saunders Co.

Leedy, P. D. (1993). *Practical research planning and design* (5th ed.). New York: Macmillan.

Mausner, J., & Bahn, A. (1970). *Epidemiology: An introductory text.* Philadelphia: W. B. Saunders Co.

The National Commission for the Protection of Human Subjects of Biomedical and Behavioral Research. (1978). *The Belmont report.* Washington, DC: Department of Health, Education, and Welfare.

Silverman, J., Suckow, M., & Murthy, S. (Eds.). (2000). *The IACUC handbook.* Boca Raton, FL: CRC Press.

U.S. Department of Health and Human Services and the Applied Research Ethics National Association. (1992). *Institutional animal care and use committee guidebook.* Washington, DC: Author.

Valanis, B. (1992). *Epidemiology in nursing and health care* (2nd ed.). Norwalk, CT: Appleton & Lange.

NOTES

1. Adapted from Jordan, T. (2002). *Understanding medical information: A user's guide to informatics and decision making.* New York: McGraw-Hill.

2. 45 C.F.R. Part 46.102(f) (2007).

3. The National Commission for the Protection of Human Subjects of Biomedical and Behavioral Research. (1978). *The Belmont report.* Washington, DC: Department of Health, Education, and Welfare.

4. 45 C.F.R. Part 46.111 and 21 C.F.R. Part 56.11 (2007).

5. 45 C.F.R.46.116, 21 C.F.R. 50.23-.24 (2007) (specifying waiver of informed consent requirements to include no more than minimal risk and fall within named categories).

Management Organization

CERTIFICATION CONNECTION

RHIA

Benchmarking
Best practices
Change management
Communications
Operational planning
Negotiation
Present data
Process engineering
Productivity standards
Project management
Strategic planning
Workflow design

RHIT

Communications
Ergonomics
Labor relations
Policies and procedures
Productivity standards
Strategic planning
Work processes

LEARNING OBJECTIVES

After reading this chapter, the learner should be able to:

1. Understand the general principles of management: planning, organizing, directing, controlling, and leading.

2. Compare and contrast strategic planning with managerial, operational, and disaster planning.

3. Explain the interrelationships between planning, organizing, directing, controlling, and leading.

4. Describe the role that the leading function plays within an organization.

5. Trace the development of management theories over time.

6. Compare and contrast specialized management theories.

Outline

Principles of Management

Planning
Organizing
Directing
Controlling
Leading

Management Theories

Historical Overview
Specialized Management Theories

Key Concepts

Affinity diagram

Assigning work

Brainstorming

Budget

Cause-and-effect
diagram

Change management

Classical management

Communication

Controlling

Critical path

Data

Decision making

Delegating

Delegating authority

Disaster planning

Disaster recovery plan

Dysfunctional conflicts

Environmental analysis

Ergonomics

Explicit knowledge

Five "why"s

Flowchart

Force field analysis

Functional conflicts

Gantt chart

Goals

Humanistic
management

Information

Internal analysis

Job

Job analysis

Job description

Job enrichment

Job evaluation

Job satisfaction

Knowledge

Knowledge management

Knowledge management
system

Leading

Leadership

Maintenance factors

Management

Management by
objectives

Meeting

Mental imaging

Mission statement

Motivation

Motivators

Multivoting

Negotiation

Nominal group technique

Objectives

Operational planning

Organizational chart

Organizational design

Organizational structure

Organizing

Pareto chart

Participatory
management

Personal power

PERT

Physical layout

Planning

Policy

Positional power

Procedure

Process improvement

Project management

Risk assessment

Scientific management

Signals

Strategic planning

SWOT technique

Tacit knowledge

Theory X

Theory Y

Theory Z

Total quality
management

Vision statement

Wisdom

Work distribution chart

Work motivation

Work simplification

INTRODUCTION

Management is both an art and a science. The art of management addresses both the exercise of judgment in given situations and the learning managers gain from experience and use to mold future behavior. The science of management involves the principles that can be learned from textbooks and guides and applied to specific situations. This chapter focuses on the science of management, with references to the art of management used sparingly.

Management is the process of using activities to create objectives and of teaming with people to meet those objectives through the efficient and effective use of resources. In analyzing this definition, three basic components are at play. First, management is a process generally defined to include planning, organizing, directing, controlling, and leading. Second, management requires resources both external and internal to the manager. Third, management must meet objectives, attain goals, and produce results.

This chapter attempts to explain the principles of management from an overview perspective. The level of information necessary to give the reader a thorough understanding of management is beyond the scope of this book. Nonetheless, it is possible to gain an awareness and understanding of management principles from the materials presented. This level of awareness and understanding will assist those who plan to move into the management ranks by laying the groundwork for future study, and it will assist those who in the future will be managed by others by giving them a basis from which to identify clearly the manager's role in an organization.

Principles of Management

As with many frequently used words, the word "management" is familiar to most people. On an individual level, people manage their own homes and budgets. On a group level, people learn of management through their exposure to organizations in various contexts. Regardless of the orientation people bring to the word management, the classic approach to management provides a useful basis from which to begin discussion. This approach involves understanding the following abstract concepts or functions: planning, organizing, directing, and controlling. In more recent years, the concept of leadership has been introduced to the management discussion.

Planning

In a broad sense, planning refers to those activities that outline what needs to be done and how to accomplish that effort. By taking such actions, planning results in better use of both time and money. Planning encompasses the establishment of a basic mission through strategic planning, goal setting through management planning, and method identification through operational planning. The relationship of these three planning approaches is illustrated in Figure II–I. Additionally, disaster planning encompasses efforts to minimize the effect disruptions or destructions may have upon organizations. Several planning tools exist and are explained in detail in the following sections.

Strategic Planning Strategic planning is defined as "the process of determining the long-term vision and goals of an enterprise and how to fulfill them."[1] It involves looking beyond the day-to-day operations of an organization to a larger vision of the organization's future and deciding how to create and implement the goals necessary to achieve that future. Strategic planning focuses on the "why" element of planning, providing those individuals and groups internal

Figure 11–1 | Relationship of planning approaches

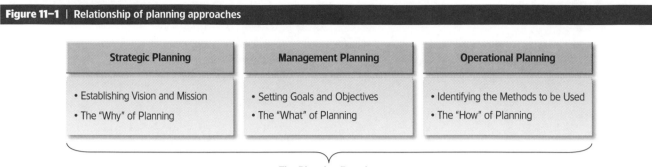

Strategic Planning	Management Planning	Operational Planning
• Establishing Vision and Mission	• Setting Goals and Objectives	• Identifying the Methods to be Used
• The "Why" of Planning	• The "What" of Planning	• The "How" of Planning

The Planning Function

and external to the organization with a clear understanding of the organization's purpose.

Central to the strategic planning process are mission and vision statements. A **mission statement** is the documentation and confirmation of the purpose of the organization. The mission statement should describe the fundamental reason an organization exists, inspire and direct change, connect and motivate people, and serve as the reference point for the strategic planning process. The three elements of a mission statement are described in Table 11–1. An example of a mission statement containing these three elements is found in Figure 11–2. A **vision statement** is an idealized goal that proposes a new future for an organization. Long-range objectives are then developed from the mission and vision statements. Together, the mission and vision statements will help create the strategy to be employed in transforming the long-range objectives into action and reality. In turn, the vision, goals, and implementation strategy developed in strategic planning should lead to optimal business results.

The strategic planning process involves both key elements and multiple steps. The key elements of strategic planning—constants, catalysts, choices, content, contract, and continuity—are defined in Table 11–2. The steps in the strategic planning process include: (1) assessing the organization's competitive position; (2) determining the alternatives that allow the organization to move ahead; (3) assessing the feasibility of these alternatives; and (4) selecting the alternatives and implementing them. Both the key elements and steps lead to the development of a plan that sets the future direction of the organization.

The success of strategic planning efforts can generally be traced to the effort put into organizing resources to support the planning process and completing analyses of the organization. When organizing resources, it is important

that senior management demonstrate support for the strategic planning effort, thereby sending a message to employees that strategic planning is essential to the well-being and survival of the organization. A planning team approach is typically used, relying on members of senior level management to staff the team. Often a facilitator from outside the organization is used if the organization has no internal expertise to call upon to coordinate the planning process. Finally, task groups are formed to assist the planning process, completing the data gathering and analysis present in the planning function.

Analyses of the organization generally are of two types. **Environmental analysis** is an assessment of the organization's external environment, including an evaluation of national, political, economic, social, legal, and technological forces that may affect the organization. **Internal analysis** is an assessment of the organization's internal environment in order to gain an understanding of the organization's functions and to develop a factual portrait of the organization. These two analyses are combined in a summary report, designed to identify areas of agreement and disagreement and to indicate trends for the future direction and success of the organization.

In assessing the results of the environmental and internal analyses, managers frequently use the SWOT technique. The **SWOT technique** is actually another form of analysis used to identify *strengths, weaknesses, opportunities,* and *threats* an organization may face in relation to the competitive marketplace. When using this technique, managers typically review the strengths and weaknesses as the first step and then move to opportunities and threats. When used in concert, the components of the SWOT technique can support the basis of the strategic plan developed by the organization.

As a general matter, strategic planning is primarily a function of setting and accommodating reasonably projected possibilities and expectations. Although predicting the future is not a science, careful thought and analysis can produce an awareness of the probability of future events for which plans can and should be made. This is what is meant by the phrase "creating the future." Increases or decreases in

Table 11–1 | Elements of a Mission Statement

1. The purpose or ultimate outcome of the organization

2. The critical functions performed to achieve the organization's purpose

3. The core values or guides to behavior used when engaging in the critical functions

Figure 11–2 | Example of a mission statement

The primary reason the Department of Family Practice exists is to:

Increase the availability of quality primary health care to residents of the United States through the advancement and demonstration of the principles of family medicine as an academic discipline.

In support of this purpose, the most critical functions we perform are:

- The provision of quality family practice education across the continuum of medical education
- The conduct of original research, which advances the knowledge base of the specialty and improves the quality of care delivered
- The delivery of family practice-based medical care, which meets the needs of patients and serves as a model for primary care education and research
- The promotion of the principles of family practice at the local, state, and national levels
- The enhancement of faculty skills and careers consistent with individual and department needs

The core values and principles that guide the department in this mission are:

- Relationships that respect diversity and foster collegiality
- Integration of biomedical, humanistic, and psychosocial principles in teaching, research, and patient care
- Commitment to the principles and practices of continuous quality improvement
- Collaboration with other specialties and organizations in the pursuit of common goals
- Advocacy for quality of life for all members of the department
- Responsiveness to unmet societal and community needs

resources, projections of workload, the useful life of physical resources, demographic changes, and similar issues can be projected with varying degrees of accuracy and should be used in the strategic planning process. To remain meaningful, any strategic plan must undergo continual review, evaluation, and revision.

Management Planning Management planning focuses on the results to be achieved through the planning process; it is the answer to the "what" element of planning. Objectives and goals are the foundation of management planning. Although sometimes used interchangeably, subtle differences exist between them. **Objectives** are the broad statements defining the future, whether of the organization or department. Objectives cover a long period of time—for example, 1, 5, or 10 years—and are not reformulated each time a

problem arises. **Goals** are statements of the process by which the future will be reached. Goals specify a course of action in support of the objectives. Used in conjunction, objectives and goals provide a definition of the future and how the organization or department will get there.

One popular approach to management planning is management by objectives. Under the **management by objectives** (MBO) approach, performance objectives are jointly planned by managers and employees, with periodic reviews of progress and rewards based on this progress. MBO works well in environments composed of highly motivated staff. It involves the following elements: (1) specific objectives created at each organizational level; (2) participatory decision making in creating and meeting goals; (3) target dates included in the objectives; (4) communication and feedback at all levels; (5) performance evaluation and feedback; and (6) rewards and recognition of results achieved.[2] As these elements indicate, MBO is results oriented, clarifying who is to perform what function, within what time frame, with the appropriate level of recognition provided.

In practice, management by objectives involves a flow of planning that moves both upward from the bottom of the organizational hierarchy and downward from the top management. In this fashion, everyone in the organization participates in management by creating objectives.

Certain characteristics are typically present in objectives and goals. First, they are consistent with the organization's mission and vision as defined in the strategic plan.

Table 11–2 | Key Elements of Strategic Planning

Constants	Articulation of the organization's vision and mission
Catalysts	Identification of emerging trends and assessment of stakeholder expectations
Choices	Selection of key results areas
Content	Development of priority goals
Contract	Design of implementation strategies and measures of success
Continuity	Documentation of achievement, the monitoring of the plan, and the refinement of the process

Source: Federal Judicial Center. (2004). *Strategic planning of the U.S. Courts.*

Second, the objectives and goals are measurable by established criteria, allowing the organization to determine whether it has met its objectives and goals. Third, they are fully stated, meaning that they require little or no explanation to understand them. Fourth, they may result in a challenge to the status quo within the organization. In sum, these characteristics define the results that the organization wishes to achieve.

Operational Planning Not every organization subscribes to the view that strategic planning is necessary; some rely instead upon operational planning as the planning method of choice. Alternatively, operational planning may be used as an outgrowth or extension of strategic and management planning. During strategic planning, focus rests on the reason the organization exists, or its so-called "purpose." During management planning, goals and objectives that are consistent with this purpose are chosen for the organization. During operational planning, the manager's focus narrows to creating specific plans for a department or cost center. In other words, operational planning is concerned with creating short-term plans that specify the details of how the strategic plans will be implemented. As such, operational planning answers the "how" element of planning.

One of the first steps of the operational planning function is the budgeting process. Budget involves all money matters, including the planning for, allocation of, requests for, accountings of, and control of financial resources. In the operational planning process, these resources are external to the manager and must be harnessed if the objectives and goals are to be met. In essence, the budgeting process supports planning by allocating resources through a financial plan. Additional information concerning budgets can be found in Chapter 14, "Financial Management."

Once the specific objectives and budget are in place, the manager creates policies and procedures so that the plan may be implemented. A policy is a decision-making guide that establishes the parameters for taking action and meeting objectives. By definition, a policy establishes boundaries or limitations on the direction the organization will take in the future. A procedure is a series of interrelated steps that are documented and used to provide standardization to routine tasks or structured problems. A procedure provides the necessary detail for meeting one aspect of an objective or goal.

Operational planning sometimes relates to an unanticipated event or condition, such as the implementation of a new and unexpected policy change, an adjustment to an emergency, or the realization of an aspect of strategic planning. Because of the immediacy of operational planning, more detailed information is usually available, and, as a result, the plans can and should become more specific. For example, an organization's strategic plan to remain competitive in its marketplace may call for a move to a new building. The realization of this move identified in the strategic plan involves the use of operational planning. The operational planning aspect of the move involves making the plan more detailed and specific. Multiple questions must be answered. Where will the space be located? How will it be subdivided? What technical services will be required? What equipment, furniture, and furnishings are required? What funding is needed and available? What temporary or permanent staffing changes will be required? Accurate and specific answers to these and many other questions will determine the efficacy and relevance of the operational planning process in this scenario.

Disaster Planning During the past few decades, health care organizations have increased their reliance on technology and automated systems to improve patient care and increase productivity. While these benefits are very real, this increased reliance is accompanied by the potential for financial loss or threats to organizational survival if these technologies or systems are disrupted or destroyed. Disaster planning focuses on how to minimize the effect these disruptions or destructions may have on organizations through the use of a disaster recovery plan. A disaster recovery plan is a comprehensive written statement of consistent actions to be taken before, during, and after a disaster, with the goal to ensure continuity of operations and availability of critical resources. Disaster recovery plans address not only technology and automated systems, they also incorporate the broader areas of operations, finance, and administration.

Creating a disaster recovery plan involves multiple steps, as illustrated in Figure 11–3. Among the first steps is the performance of a risk assessment. A risk assessment is a method used to measure an organization's level of preparedness to prevent and recover from a disaster. While no person can predict when a disaster will occur, one can assess the probability of a disaster occurring by examining

Figure 11–3 | **Steps in a disaster recovery plan**

1. Ensure top management support.
2. Establish a planning committee.
3. Perform a risk assessment.
4. Prioritize processing and operations.
5. Identify practical alternatives.
6. Collect data.
7. Draft a written plan.
8. Develop testing criteria.
9. Test the plan.
10. Evaluate/revise the plan.
11. Approve and distribute the plan.

Table 11-3 | Threat Examples

Natural Threats	Flooding
	Earthquake
	Fire
	Storms
	Tornado
Technical Threats	Power failure/fluctuation
	Electromagnetic interference
	Telecommunication failure
	Software/hardware malfunction
Human Threats	Improper handling of data
	Malicious destruction of assets
	Unauthorized access to data
	Sabotage
	Toxic waste/chemical spill
	Theft
	Bomb threats

Source: Wold, G. H., & Shriver, R. F. (1991). *Disaster proof your business.* Chicago: Probus.

potential exposures to natural, technical, and human threats. Examples of natural, technical, and human threats are illustrated in Table 11-3. Once risks are identified, the impact of these risks upon the organization or a given department must be measured.

Among the most significant steps in creating a disaster recovery plan is the prioritization of processes and operations. As part of the prioritization effort, managers should identify the critical needs of their department, including the necessary functions, procedures, and equipment needed to continue operations should there be any form of disaster. To do so, managers must have first documented all of the functions performed in the department and identified the necessary equipment, applications, and reports necessary to complete these functions. From there, managers can rank the functions in priority order: essential, important, and nonessential. This ranking will allow managers to determine the minimum number of staff necessary to perform each ranked function, the minimum size of off-premise facility if one is needed to continue operations, and the minimum type and number of pieces of equipment to be available in an off-premise facility.

During the course of developing the plan, managers must identify and evaluate alternative methods for conducting business. These methods often include backup plans to support data replication and other automation efforts; communication strategies for employees, customers, and suppliers to use; and the availability of vendor- or organization-supplied equipment at alternate sites. After each department within the organization identifies and evaluates those methods that may assist their functioning in the event of a disaster, a higher level of review is conducted. This review is designed to eliminate duplications or contradictions, align each department's methods with the organization as a

whole, and assign responsibilities to individuals and teams to coordinate the recovery process. From this point, a comprehensive written document can be developed that outlines how the organization will address the numerous unpredictable and sometimes unpreventable hazards that might endanger its operation or survival.

It is essential that any disaster recovery plan be tested upon its formation and on a periodic basis. Testing offers many benefits, including verifying the feasibility, compatibility, and adequacy of the measures identified and incorporated into the plan. To the extent that testing identifies deficiencies in the plan, measures to modify or improve the plan can be taken. Testing also provides the organization, and those external customers who rely upon the organization, with assurance that the organization can recover in the event of a disaster.

Many different testing approaches exist. Some managers employ a checklist approach, comparing the essential elements contained in the plan against the reality of what is available to the organization. Other managers employ a structured walk-through approach, leading a discussion of the responsibilities of the parties involved and the steps to be followed for each essential element of the plan. Some managers simulate a disaster during non-business hours, testing as many of the essential elements of the plan as possible. Other managers employ a parallel testing approach, conducting business at a parallel site using an organization's historical transactions (i.e., yesterday's transactions) and comparing the reports generated at the alternate site against the organization's backup files. Finally, some managers conduct full-interruption testing, during which they purposefully disrupt an organization's operations for a short time period to determine whether the entire plan will allow the organization to recover smoothly. Full-interruption testing is costly, making it a less viable choice for many managers. Each of these approaches can be employed separately or in combination with one another to determine the effectiveness of a disaster recovery plan.

After completing testing and curing any deficiencies, the highest level of the organization should approve the disaster recovery plan. This level could be the highest level of an organization's management or an organization's oversight board. Proper dissemination of the plan follows, with educational sessions conducted as needed. Such dissemination may include notification and distribution of the plan to regulatory agencies and insurance companies, both of which may have established requirements for an organization to meet.

While each of these steps applies to any organization or entity, it is important to note that additional requirements may be imposed in specific industries based on laws, rules, and regulations. In the health care context, the

implementing regulations of the Health Insurance Portability and Accountability Act (HIPAA) specifically address the
contents of a covered entity's disaster recovery plan.[3]
Found under the administrative safeguards section of the
Security Rule, these provisions address who is responsible
for the information systems and various business operations in the event of a disaster; which information systems,
protected health information, and business functions are
involved; and when the disaster recovery plan should be
invoked. The plan must establish procedures to restore
any data lost through a disaster, whether the loss is from
server-based systems, computer infrastructure, or communications systems such as faxes, electronic mail, and voice
mail. The plan must also be reviewed and tested on a
periodic basis.

Planning Tools One challenging aspect of the planning
function is scheduling the time needed to accomplish the
objectives and goals and to follow the policies and procedures. Many scheduling tools exist, including calendars,
agendas, and charts. This section concentrates on two of
the most commonly used planning tools, the Gantt chart
and the PERT network.

The Gantt chart is an outgrowth of the work of an
engineer named Henry Gantt. As part of his work in

studying ways to increase worker efficiency, Gantt created a
mechanism for comparing the progress of a project at different points in time. A Gantt chart is defined as a graphic
representation of the time relationships in a project. The
chart lists different activities in the project on one axis and
lists time periods on the other axis.

Gantt charts are particularly applicable to projects that
pose limited changes to the process; involve simple, repetitive tasks; or require simple and direct communication.
Gantt charts are less applicable if the steps involved are
highly interdependent. Gantt charts allow the supervisor to
readily identify which activities precede one another, which
should occur simultaneously, and which should follow one
another. They also can be used to determine whether projects
are running ahead of, behind, or on schedule. A sample
Gantt chart is illustrated in Figure 11–4. Where a Gantt chart
uses different colors to identify the actual and proposed
start and completion dates, the color difference can assist
the manager in assessing whether an activity is on schedule.

A second planning tool is the Program Evaluation and
Review Technique, or PERT. PERT is the outgrowth of work
performed by the U.S. Navy to reduce the time frame projected to complete the Polaris Ballistic Missile Project in
1958. PERT is particularly applicable to projects that have
multiple variables.

Like a Gantt chart, PERT tracks activities according to a
time sequence. It differs from a Gantt chart in that it shows
the interdependence between activities. On a PERT network,
the longest sequence of events to be completed will have the
largest effect upon the project. This longest sequence is

Figure 11–4 | Sample Gantt chart

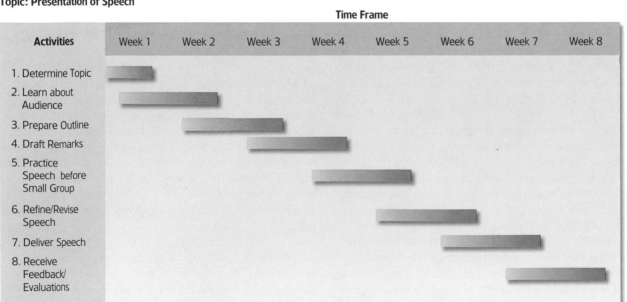

Figure 11–5 | Sample PERT network

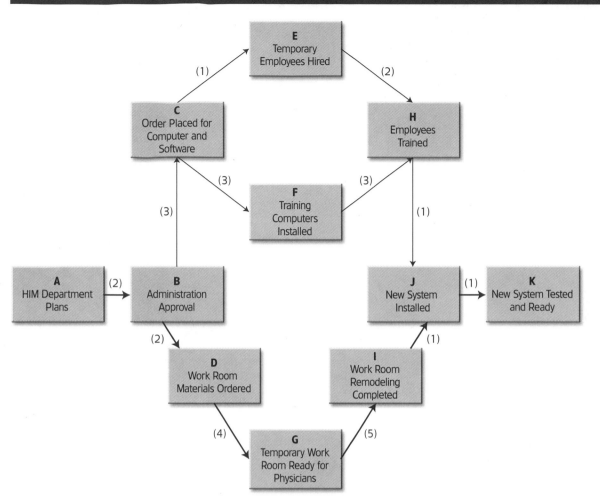

called the **critical path** and requires the most attention from the manager. A sample PERT network is illustrated in Figure 11–5. As the illustration indicates, a network of interrelated activities must be planned to accomplish the goal.

Organizing

Organizing refers to determining what tasks should be done and who will do them, establishing the reporting structure, and deciding at what level decisions will be made. In other words, it means to bring together basic resources in an orderly manner and arrange them in an acceptable fashion to ensure that the goals and objectives identified in the planning function are achieved. Organizing focuses on design and structure, the people involved, the type of work, the procedures used in performing the work, and the environment in which the work is performed.

Design and Structure Considerable changes have occurred in the business and health care communities during the last decade, as organizations have merged, restructured, and—in some cases—ceased to exist. With all of these changes taking place, considerable focus has been brought upon the question of how to design and structure organizations that will survive tumultuous business cycles, respond to

customer needs, and allow organizations to grow and thrive. **Organizational design** refers to "the planning and fitting together of the people and activities involved in doing the work of an organization."[4] An organization greatly influences its level of performance when it creates a design that aligns with its vision, strategy, and systems, including decision support systems, reward systems, and human resource systems.

A number of forces influence what type of design an organization needs and when or whether the organization needs to change its design. Among those forces are changes in technology; the need to modernize work processes; a desire to save costs, increase efficiencies, and make the organization more flexible; increased emphasis upon customer service; and recognition of the need to take into consideration quality-of-life issues in the workplace. A more comprehensive listing of influences is illustrated in Figure 11–6.

Organizational structure refers to the manner in which the work and responsibilities are divided within the organization. Organizations may be structured in multiple ways, with some organizations combining structures to form

Figure 11–6 | Forces influencing organizational design

Universal Macro Forces	Modern Flexibilities	Health Care Context Factors	Key Design Drivers
Legislation and Regulation	Strategic Options	Patient Needs	Efficiency and Economy
Budget	Design Principles and Best Practices	Reimbursement Mechanisms	Customer Satisfaction
Technology	Administrative Resources and Systems	Labor Market/Human Resources	Adaptability and Flexibility
		Organizational Culture and Management Style	Technological Innovation
		Labor Market/Human Resources	
		Organizational Culture and Management Style	

hybrids. Structures that are common to organizations include those based on function, product or service, teams, or customer orientation. Functional structure divides work and responsibilities according to the major technical or professional functions performed by those within the organizational units. Product or service structure divides work and responsibilities around the organization's products or services. Team-based structure divides work and responsibilities around the organization's major work processes, allowing team members to perform all major activities within a business process from beginning to end. Customer-oriented structure divides work and responsibilities around the characteristics of an organization's customers or markets. The strengths and weaknesses of these structures are illustrated in Figure 11–7.

Organizing People   Organizing people to accomplish goals and objectives requires establishing the divisions and subdivisions of the organization, including the assignment of teams and the interdependencies of divisions, subdivisions, and teams. Most often, this structure is illustrated by an **organizational chart**. An organizational chart is a document—paper based or electronic—that maps how positions within a department or organization are tied together along the principal lines of authority. This document reflects formal reporting relationships as opposed to the significant informal and informational relationships present in organizations.

Organizational charts take various forms, including top-down, left-to-right, and circular. The top-down organizational chart, illustrated in Figure 11–8, is the chart familiar to most

Figure 11–7 | Strengths and weaknesses of organizational structures

Type	Functional	Product or Service	Customer Orientation	Team Orientation
Strengths	• People within the same group share the same knowledge and language, and increase one another's expertise • One large pool to balance work within	• Team spirit along product lines • Independence among managers • Good pool of talent from which to draw management staff	• Unique needs of customers well served • Organization is aware of customer needs and preferences	• Increases flexibility and/or speed in handling projects, requests • Reduces layers and numbers of management • Greater worker involvement
Weaknesses	• Turf issues • Difficult to assign accountability • Creates specialization, which can limit flexibility and inhibit change • Different departments with different priorities	• Duplication of effort • Less sharing of resources • Customers must work with multiple services within one organization • Slow to recognize when services should be changed, dropped, or added	• Duplication of effort • Less sharing of resources • Different ways to serve different customer segments may result in difficulty in managing organization overall	• Time–consuming process to implement • Requires expertise in each team as opposed to functional experts outside the team

Figure 11–8 | Top-down organizational chart (U.S. Department of Health and Human Services)

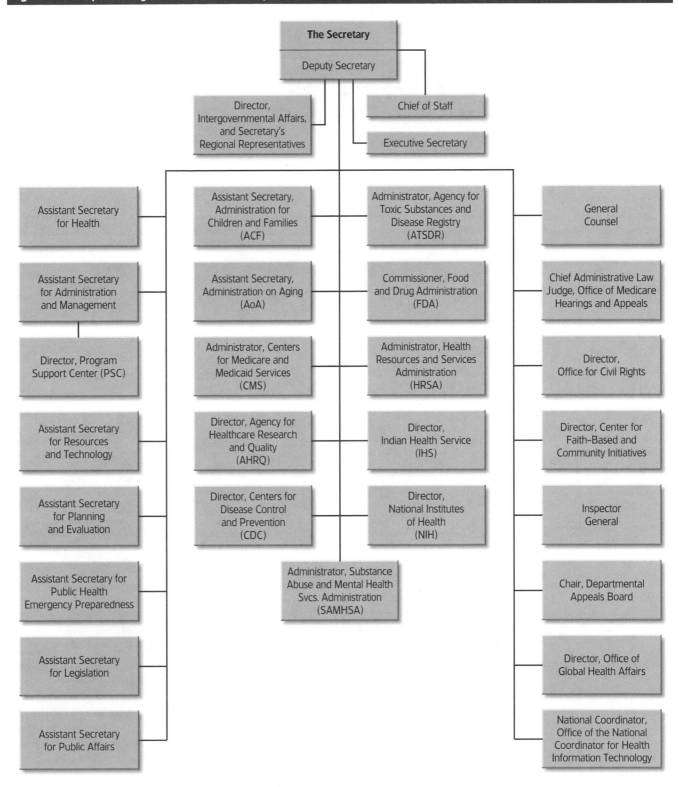

managers. The top-down chart places the major positions of the organization at the top, with subordinate positions placed in lower levels. By contrast, a left-to-right organizational chart places the major positions of the organization in the middle left section of the page, thereby suggesting that the so-called "top" position is not supreme. Although not as familiar as the top-down chart, left-to-right charts primarily facilitate reading, as the normal reading pattern is from left to right. This type of chart is illustrated in Figure 11–9. Finally, the circular organizational chart places the so-called "top" position in the center, with subordinate positions surrounding the center. The circular chart suggests that all of the positions

Figure 11–9 | Left-to-right organizational chart (U.S. Environmental Protection Agency, Office of Water)

Figure 11–10 | Circular organizational chart (National Institute of Standards and Technology)

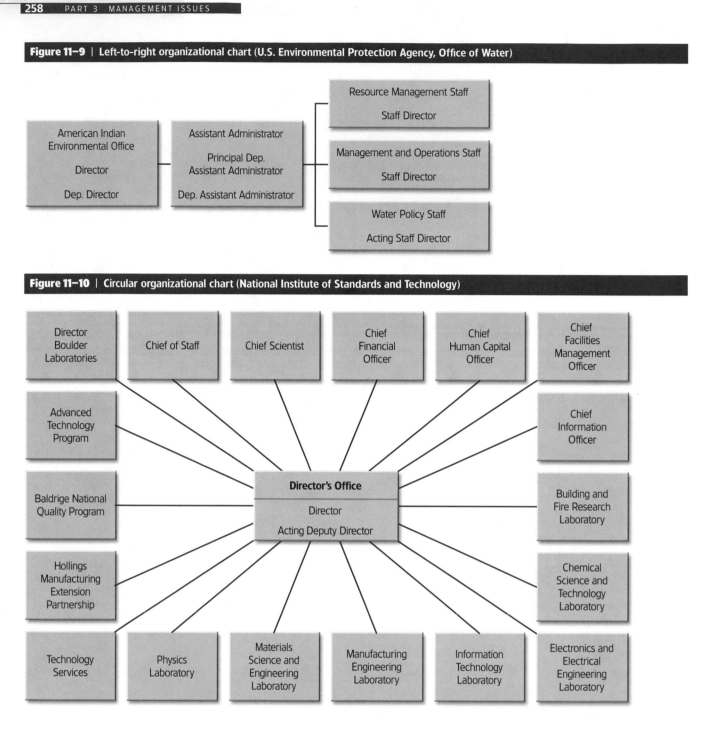

within the organization are of equal importance, thereby discouraging the view of a top and bottom to the organization. This type of chart is illustrated in Figure 11–10.

Despite their helpfulness, organizational charts possess certain limitations. Organizational charts do not reflect clearly what authority is delegated from one level to another nor do these charts always reflect the organization's structure as it really is. Managers do not always update the organizational chart to reflect changes within the organization as they should, thus rendering the organizational chart obsolete. Additionally, some confuse the authority relationships shown on an organizational chart with status in the organization. Although charts attempt

to conform to levels of importance, issues such as salary and bonus levels make it almost impossible to reflect status on an organizational chart.

Organizing people is also accomplished through the identification of a job and through job analysis. A **job** refers to the tasks and responsibilities that, on the whole, are regarded as the regular assignment of an individual. **Job analysis** determines the content of a job. Job analysis is accomplished by examining each of the tasks that makes up a job and by determining the requirements for successful performance of each task. The job analysis in turn leads to the development of a job evaluation and a job description.

Figure 11–11 | Sample job description

Data Quality Manager
Sample Position Description

Position Title: Data Quality Manager
Immediate Superior: Vice President, Quality

General Purpose: The Data Quality Manager is responsible for developing, implementing, and maintaining a data quality management (compliance) plan for coding and reimbursement, health records and documentation, and quality data in all divisions of the organization.

Responsibilities:

- Assessing current compliance activities, identifying areas of high risk, and evaluating risk factors in coding and documentation practices
- Developing, implementing, and maintaining a standardized, organization-wide, quality data management (compliance) plan and program to ensure compliance with external regulatory and accreditation requirements, ensure consistency of quality data for the organization's internal data needs, and identify, investigate and prevent violations
- Developing, implementing, and maintaining standardized, organization-wide policies and procedures to monitor the success of the quality data management plan, review areas of risk, investigate identified issues, report data analyses, and take appropriate steps to correct violations
- Establishing, implementing, and maintaining a formalized review process for compliance, including a formal review (audit) process
- Optimizing receipt of high-quality data from parent and contract hospitals by active participation and leadership in quality monitoring and improvement efforts
- In partnership with appropriate personnel, developing and implementing standardized, organization-wide coding guidelines and documentation requirements and developing and implementing training and educational programs for physicians and coders
- Providing consulting services in the area of data quality management to individuals, special projects, and executive and clinical departments throughout the organization

Qualifications:

- Bachelor's degree in health information management or a related field and at least 10 years of professional experience, 5 of which are in data quality; or a master's degree or its equivalent and at least 7 years of experience in a clinical, operational, or data quality improvement function
- Credentialed as an RHIA or RHIT and a CCS
- Experience in operational management
- Experience in project management
- Knowledge of health information systems and database management
- Knowledge of applied statistics, process analysis, and outcomes analysis

---

Copyright by the American Health Information Management Association. Reprinted and adapted with permission.

A job evaluation compares tasks within jobs to one another and provides a basis for grading or ranking jobs. It helps to place the job in an accurate position on the organizational chart and establishes the basis for salary structure. A job description is a written statement summarizing what an employee does, how it is done, and why it is done. In other words, it identifies the activities, skills, and performance requirements for a particular position. Job descriptions are used in a multitude of ways, including recruitment, employee orientation, to clarify relationships within an organization, and to serve as a basis for a performance evaluation. An example of a job description is given in Figure 11–11. Further information concerning job descriptions can be found in Chapter 12, "Human Resource Management."

Organizing people also includes the delegation of authority. Delegating authority means to transfer some of a manager's decision-making authority to subordinates. Note that not all of the manager's decision-making authority is given away; some is retained so that the manager can evaluate the subordinates' decisions and exercise veto authority where necessary. Delegation works well if the manager shares information with the subordinates, enabling the subordinates to successfully solve their problems.

Organizing the Type of Work Organizing the type of work involved may be done in several ways: by function, by location, by product, by client, by project, or by process. The manager may choose one of these ways or a combination of ways. In many organizations, the top level is organized by function; the middle level by product, client, or location; and the lower level by the process to be followed in completing the work.

One tool used in organizing work is the work distribution chart. A **work distribution chart** records the work activities performed, the time it takes to perform the work, the individual performing the work, and the amount of time each individual spends on each activity. This information can then be used to analyze what work takes the most time, whether there is any misdirected effort or improper use of skills, whether tasks are spread evenly or too thinly, and whether employees perform too many unrelated tasks. Armed with this analysis, the manager can then determine whether work should be redistributed among staff or remain the same.

Organizing Work Performance The act of organizing work performance concentrates on the development of procedures. Procedures are the series of interrelated steps that are documented and used to give standardization to routine tasks or structured problems. They flow from the policies described in the "Planning" section of this chapter. Within a department, procedures are gathered into a manual or handbook, which is then made available to each employee for his use.

Two common formats for written procedures are the narrative style and the flowchart style. The narrative style describes the interrelated steps in sentences or paragraphs. One disadvantage of this style is that the employee will need to read the entire procedure, even if the employee is only searching for one specific point. An example of a narrative style procedure is illustrated in Figure 11-12. By

Figure 11-12 | Narrative style procedure

Narrative Procedure
Troubleshooting Computer Printer

Problem: Printer stops due to paper jam

Steps:

1. Review the message which states where paper jam is located.

2. If the message indicates the paper tray area, open the paper tray, check for problem (e.g., wrinkled or damaged paper), and correct it. Reinsert the paper tray and press "print."

3. If the message indicates the rear door, open it, check for problem (e.g., wrinkled or damaged paper), and correct it. Close rear door and press "print."

4. If neither approach solves the problem and no immediate solution is available, call for repairs.

5. Once problem is solved or repaired, operate printer.

contrast, the flowchart style describes the interrelated steps in a visual manner, using standard systems flowchart symbols. Becoming familiar with the symbols may be a disadvantage, but, once learned, the flowchart is easy to follow. An example of a flowchart style procedure is illustrated in Figure 11-13.

Organizing the Work Environment Organizing the work environment involves both the physical layout of the space where the work is performed and the ergonomics associated therein. When organized successfully, the work environment will comply with the requirements of both the Americans with Disabilities Act (ADA) and the Occupational Safety and Health Administration (OSHA).

A **physical layout** is a model of space in actual miniaturized detail of the physical environment at issue. It illustrates the people and objects involved in the process of work and should support the work flow.

Ergonomics refers to the design of products, processes, and systems to meet the requirements and capacities of those people who use them. Ergonomics focuses on such areas as furniture, noise control, lighting, high-technology equipment, and aesthetics. Ergonomics is particularly important in a technologically intensive environment where stress on the human body may result in workplace injuries. Through the use of ergonomic principles, manufacturers may design equipment—such as workstations—to fit human anatomy and physiology, with the desired result of eliminating stressors that reduce productivity and quality.

Organization of the work environment is not limited to the considerations present in a traditional work space. With the advent of nontraditional work environments, such as those involving telecommuters, employers have learned that questions of physical layout, ergonomics, and safety hazards apply in any context in which the employee performs the work. This realization arises from the fact that employees are being paid to perform their functions and duties under their employer's direction and control, whether that performance occurs in a traditional setting or not. Accordingly, those burdens imposed by law upon employers to maintain a safe working environment in a traditional setting also have application in a nontraditional setting. For example, if an employee performs work at home pursuant to a telecommuting policy, and the employer knows or has reason to know that the home environment presents safety hazards (e.g., no clear method of egress in the event of a fire), the employer should insist on action by the employee to create and maintain a safe work environment at home if telecommuting is to be employed. Employers who permit telecommuting have handled questions relating to physical layout, ergonomics, and safety in several ways, ranging from the use of checklists that are reviewed and signed by employees to the performance of home inspections. An

Figure 11–13 | Flowchart style procedure

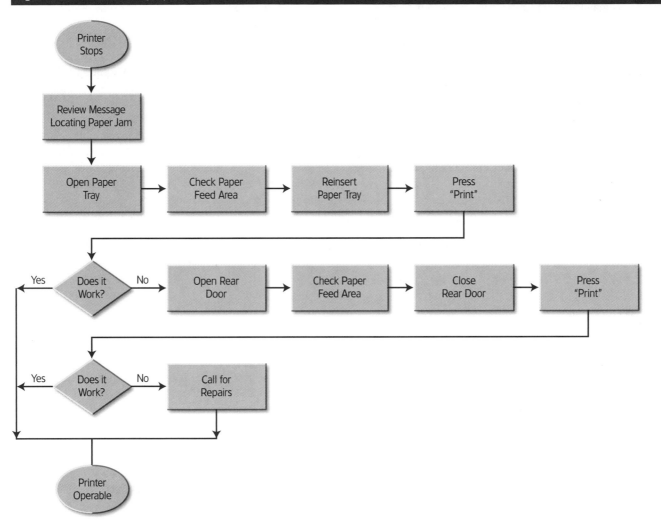

example of a safety checklist employed in a telecommuting environment is illustrated in Figure 11–14.

Directing
Directing is the continuous process of decision making, instructing others, and giving orders. The directing activity involves the translation of planning into specific behaviors and activities. The focus of directing is on the functional component, as opposed to the interpersonal aspects, of an activity.

Decision Making Organizations benefit enormously when employees at all levels are skilled at decision making. It is especially important for managers and supervisors to possess this skill, as their decisions affect so many individuals and groups. While the amount of decision-making responsibility possessed by managers and supervisors may vary, the effectiveness of the decisions they make influences greatly the organization's success.

Figure 11–14 | Telecommuting safety checklist

Telecommuting Safety Checklist

☐ Fire safety, including smoke detectors, fire extinguishers, and a fire evacuation plan.

☐ Ergonomics, including use of correct office furniture, lighting, and equipment.

☐ Security, including password protections, virus scanning, and firewalls.

☐ Space design that allows for ingress and egress without tripping or blocking.

☐ Electrical safety, including use of grounded outlets and appropriate numbers of electrical circuits.

☐ Accident and injury reporting mechanisms.

Source: Office of Personnel Management. (2003). *Telework: A management priority; A guide for managers, supervisors, and Telework coordinators.* **http://www.telework.gov/**

Decision making is the act of reaching a conclusion. While some managers and supervisors may reach decisions as a result of instinct, impulse, or whim, the skill involved in decision making generally follows a logical thought process. This process involves answering a series of questions: why should a decision be made, what are the alternative solutions, which solution is the best, when and how should the solution be implemented, and what are the results of the decision?

A number of factors must be considered when identifying why a decision needs to be made. The individual making the decision must understand the context from which the need for the decision arises. For example, it is important to know that an event has taken place that requires a response, or that a situation is developing that may alter the status quo, requiring a proactive approach. It is also necessary for the decision maker to understand who else should be involved in the process and how he will approach the task at hand. Finally, it is helpful for the individual to know the kinds and amounts of resources that will be invested in making the decision.

Armed with this information, the individual can then develop alternative solutions. Some alternatives are identified through the use of selected criteria while others may be identified pursuant to a brainstorming technique. Some constraints exist in developing these alternatives, such as considering organizational strategy, policy, or values. For example, organizational policy may dictate the limits within which certain alternatives are possible and which ones are considered off-limits, while overall organizational strategies or values may compel the development of some alternatives over others.

Once the alternatives are identified and developed, the decision maker must choose the one solution that offers the best advantages to the organization. Optimally, the chosen solution will offer the best results at the least cost. In selecting between competing alternatives, the decision maker must remain consistent with the organization's objectives. For example, an organization's objectives may include maximizing long-term profits or increasing market share within a short time frame. With the organization's objectives in mind, the alternatives are compared against multiple criteria, such as performance, durability, reliability, and cost, with each criterion considered equally or given different weight, depending on the circumstances present. The manager or supervisor then chooses the alternative solution that correlates most closely to the organization's objectives and identified criteria.

Implementation of the selected solution can be as difficult a task as arriving at the optimum solution itself. Obstacles may not have been anticipated nor adequate measures to resolve the obstacles discussed. To increase the likelihood of implementation success, the decision maker must decide when to begin the implementation process. Some decisions require a minimum amount of time and effort to implement while others require extraordinary effort over a lengthy period of time. The decision maker must also decide how to conduct the implementation process. As a first step, the decision maker may assign responsibility for follow-through, charging an individual with the job of championing the decision within and beyond the organization. The decision maker may provide incentives for staff within the organization to make the implementation process work smoothly. Finally, the decision maker must make the required resources readily available.

The end of the decision-making process involves an evaluation. This evaluation should include measures that were identified at the beginning of the decision-making process to represent success. Using these measures, the manager or supervisor may evaluate the actual results and, where appropriate, make adjustments as needed.

Instructing Others Among the most basic of directional activities is the instruction of others. As a generality, managers instruct others either by assigning or delegating work activities.

Assigning work means matching an individual employee with specific work that needs to be performed. Work assignments depend largely on the nature of the task involved, varying from routine repetitive assignments to variable routine assignments to special project assignments. Routine repetitive assignments work well in large office environments where employees perform specialized functions. Variable routine assignments work well in smaller office environments where employees are often generalists who deliver different services or perform different tasks during a single shift. Special project assignments work well in environments where employees possess specialized knowledge or where the work performed lends itself to a project orientation.

The likelihood that a given assignment will achieve the desired result is directly related to the manner in which the assignment is made. Among the first considerations is the selection of the right person for the job. Suggested criteria include the employee's knowledge, skills, experience, and maturity. These criteria may lead to the selection of an employee with proven strengths or may lead to the selection of an employee who needs to overcome obstacles and improve performance. Additionally, consideration is given to the level of detail to be provided in the instruction. Such detail includes identifying the activities required of each task, the resources available, the methods the employee should use or avoid, any product or performance standards, and deadlines for work completion.

While assigning work involves asking an employee to perform work that is within the scope of his employment, delegating involves asking an employee to perform work that falls within the scope of the manager's own job description and position level. Delegating means to entrust another person with selected powers and functions; that person then acts on behalf of the person making the request. When delegating, the manager decides what work can be delegated and to whom. While some tasks require skills that are unique to the manager or involve proprietary or confidential information, other tasks do not require unique skills or involve these forms of information and therefore are appropriate for delegating. Rather, these tasks may involve operational detail, such as data collection, proofreading, or making calculations, or they may involve representation duties, such as delegating a staff member to attend a meeting on the manager's behalf. Choosing the person to whom to delegate a task often requires use of the same criteria as the assignment of work: evaluating an employee's knowledge, skills, experience, and maturity. It also involves consideration of that employee's current workload, since what is being delegated is in addition to the employee's current level of work and may require redistribution of the chosen employee's work to others.

Delegating can involve risks and rewards for both the manager and the employee. Managers are sometimes concerned that the amount of time necessary to provide instructions, perform periodic checks, and review final work products delegated to an employee will outweigh the amount of time the manager would expend if performing the work himself. Employees are sometimes concerned that any failure to perform the delegated work accurately and timely will result in the loss of trust or opportunity for advancement, or even in permanent damage to the working relationship. While risks certainly exist, delegating also offers rewards to both the manager and employee. Delegating offers the manager the opportunity to handle higher-level assignments and responsibilities when his routine tasks are delegated to others. Delegating offers the employee the opportunity to broaden his range of skills and experiences, thereby placing his in a better position for future advancement and promotion.

Work Simplification One example of directing is work simplification. **Work simplification** is a method used to find easier and better ways of doing work. It focuses on the most effective way to eliminate waste of time, energy, materials, and cost while still maintaining safety. Although sometimes confused with the process of speeding up work, work simplification focuses on the methods used to accomplish the work, not merely on the time it takes to accomplish the work.

E-HIM

Work simplification performed before conversion to an electronic health record system can identify inefficiencies in paper-based processes and prevent those inefficiencies from being adapted to and repeated in an electronic world.

Many steps are involved in work simplification; these are illustrated in Table 11–4. In determining which work

Table 11–4 | Steps to Work Simplification

1. Choosing the work to be improved
2. Collecting data from those involved
3. Recording the data on work process flowcharts
4. Analyzing the details to select the improvements
5. Incorporating the improvements into the work process

should be the subject of work simplification, the manager may focus on some very obvious problems, such as backlogs, unfinished work, and the use of overtime. The manager may also focus on less obvious problems, such as the activities associated with beginning or ending a specific job, to see if they can be streamlined into the process. Managers may also apply work simplification steps when converting to an electronic health record system as a way to avoid adapting inefficient paper-based processes to an electronic world. When collecting data from those involved, the manager should not merely rely on a supervisor's description of the process but, rather, should study the process himself as it is performed by the employee.

When the data is collected, the manager should record it on a work process flowchart. Once only available in manual form, flowcharts are now available via computer programs. Regardless of which form is chosen, the flowchart includes the following elements: (1) an identification section stating what process is being studied, when the study begins and ends, and who is the person performing the process; and (2) a body containing work classification symbols and a brief description of each step in the process, and any time or quantity measurements.

After the flowchart has been completed, the manager should analyze the data collected to determine improvements. The analysis should examine the necessity of each step in the process flow and seek opportunities to eliminate, combine, change, or simplify the process. In conducting this analysis, the guiding principle should be to determine whether there is a better way to perform the process, not to change the process merely for the sake of change.

Finally, the manager should incorporate the improvements into the work process. First, the flowchart should be revised to include the improvement. Second, the improved procedure should be tested by an employee. Assuming that the test is successful, the written procedure should be modified and distributed to the affected staff. Finally, the manager should check the revised work process periodically to determine whether the improvement as actually implemented improved the process.

Controlling

Controlling refers to the act of ensuring that activities are accomplished as planned and correcting any significant deviations from the plan. While controlling may be among the least exciting principles of management, it is arguably the most critical because, when done well, the manager can identify a problem and take action before the problem becomes uncorrectable. It is directly related to the planning function, in that controlling measures whether the planning has been effective; it differs from the planning function, however, in that controlling requires managers to react quickly and appropriately to unexpected deviations from the plan and to correct any planning errors previously made. Managers perform the controlling function by identifying the types of controls to be used, setting standards, and monitoring performance.

Types of Controls As a general matter, managers employ any or all of three types of controls in the workplace: input controls, process controls, and output controls. Input controls are designed to anticipate problems and prevent them from occurring. Examples include employing routine maintenance on costly equipment at periodic intervals to avoid equipment failure or downtime and employing internal inventory control systems to ensure that supplies needed to support daily operations are readily available. Process controls are designed to measure and evaluate work in progress. Examples include formal and informal assessments, through periodic checking or sampling, of employee performance according to established standards for quality and timeliness. Output controls are designed to evaluate final results. Output controls are not designed necessarily to correct past work but are designed to serve as guides to future activities by highlighting problems in work efficiency or effectiveness. A classic example of an output control is an employee performance appraisal. Most employee performance appraisal systems measure past performance against established standards. Therefore, the content of an employee performance appraisal cannot change past performance, but it can serve as a feedback mechanism for improving the employee's future performance by identifying areas of solid and weak performance and opportunities for improvement.

Implementation of any of these controls varies according to individual situations and circumstances. Some controls may need to be used continuously, such as standing plans for use in emergency or disaster situations. When developed, standing plans are considered input controls. When implemented, standing plans become process controls. Other controls, such as audits or budget reviews, should be employed on a periodic basis. Still other controls should be used only when needed, for example, when a special report is necessary to identify the cause of a problem and an attendant solution or to identify an opportunity and the mechanism to take advantage of it.

Setting Standards Setting standards ensures that work is performed, and performed properly. Issues of quality and quantity are central to setting productivity and performance standards. In setting standards, managers must first measure the work.

Quality of work can be measured through inspection, incident reports, and audits. Under the inspection approach, a manager inspects all or selected work performed ("spot-checking") and notes deviations. The number or type of deviations will help to determine the quality of work performed.

Quality can also be measured through incident reports. Incident reports are records made of deviations from the norm. These reports do not require observation by the manager; rather, they can be made merely through awareness of a deviation from a norm. Ideally, incident reports contain only factual information and not opinions or interpretations of an event noted as a deviation from the norm.

Quality can also be measured by audits. Audits are techniques used to look retrospectively at a specific activity, measure it, and compare it to established guidelines. When a pattern emerges indicating that established guidelines were not met, the manager determines what further action should be taken, including the education and training of staff and work simplification of processes.

Quantity of work can be measured both manually and electronically. In a manual system, work may be measured by work sampling or employee logs. In work sampling, a sample is taken at random from a large group or from an individual, based on the theory that the sample will tend to resemble the distribution pattern of the group as a whole or the total work of the individual. The accuracy or validity of a work sampling increases with the number of observations. The higher the number of observations involved in the sample, the higher the accuracy or validity of the sample.

Using the employee log approach, a log is set up for each type of work that is performed. The employee notes on the log each work unit in which he is engaged. The information is tallied and can then be plotted on a graph.

Quantity can also be measured electronically. Integrated computerized information systems can provide managers with comprehensive data about the quantity of work performed by staff. Depending on the type of data maintained in the database and how the programming query is developed, managers can obtain reports that provide quantity totals for each employee or team. One such example is the employee log; in addition to tallying information manually, an employee log can be created using an integrated computerized information system.

Once quality and quantity determinations are made, a standard can be established for all employees who perform the same work. For example, a manager may establish that a certain number of deviations relating to quality and quantity are acceptable for the work performed. An employee whose work shows a higher number of deviations than the one established in the standard may receive the attention of management.

Effective performance standards can also be based on cost or time. Cost standards address the total cost or cost per unit limits within which a product is produced or a service is delivered. Time standards address the deadlines by which results are to be accomplished or the amount of time, as measured by minutes, hours, or days, that it should take to produce the desired results.

Monitoring Performance As with setting standards, monitoring performance involves a series of steps. The first step is to capture data by measuring the actual activity. Managers capture data manually using work sheets, survey forms, and questionnaires, and electronically through the extraction of data stored in an electronic database. Once the data are captured, managers analyze and compare the data against the standard that has been set for the activity. Historically, managers used manual systems to analyze the data. With the advent of integrated computerized information systems, raw data can be examined electronically and exceptions to the standards can be recorded on exception reports. These exceptions form what is called the variation or deviation.

Because actual performance will not always conform to the standard that has been set for an activity, variations or deviations are to be expected. Evaluating whether the variation or deviation between the analyzed data and the standard are significant is the next step in controlling. Depending on the circumstances involved, it may be relatively easy to determine whether the variation is significant; under some circumstances, however, managers must exercise considerable judgment. Once the manager has determined the significance of the variance, he should take appropriate action. Constant attention must be paid to variations or deviations, since failure to take appropriate action, early enough in time, may result in a problem that is uncorrectable.

Leading

Leading is the management function involved in motivating employees, directing others, resolving conflicts, and selecting effective communication channels. Leading emphasizes the role of setting the tone for the organization and encouraging staff by example. It differs from the directing function described previously in that leading focuses on the interpersonal aspects of an activity. By contrast, the directing function focuses on the functional component of an activity.

Leadership refers to the ability to get work done with and through others while simultaneously winning their respect, confidence, loyalty, and willing cooperation. Leadership is both an ability and a process. As an ability, leadership means to inspire and influence others to receive a positive result. This inspiration and influence motivates

Table 11–5	Leader	
L	Legal Responsibility	Compliance
E	Ethics	Integrity
A	Accountability	Trust; checks and balances
D	Direction	Strategic and operational planning
E	Education	Education and training
R	Resource Management	Stewardship of available resources

Source: **Administrative Office of the U.S. Courts. (2002).** *Annual report of the director*.

others to follow a leader, setting the leader apart from nonleaders. As a process, leadership means to influence the behavior of group members in accomplishing the planned objectives. Both aspects can be seen in the description of a leader found in Table 11–5.

A leader's power derives from either the leader's position in the organization or the perception of others. Positional power rests on the authority inherent in the job status, title, or rank. This type of power is accorded to those with a higher status in an organization and is limited by the individual's rank or job title. Personal power rests on the positive regard that others accord an individual. This type of power emphasizes perception and belief. Those individuals who possess the skills, expertise, breadth of experience, or additional qualities that others believe are valuable and important possess personal power. Unlike positional power, which is given to an individual, personal power is earned and recognized by others. Neither type of power is necessarily related to the other; some individuals who possess positional power lack personal power, while others who are relatively low in positional power may possess a high level of personal power. Figure 11–15 compares both types of power.

Motivating Successful leaders must understand motivation theory in order to encourage others to achieve and foster their enthusiasm and feelings of investment in the organization. Motivation is the need or drive that stimulates a person to some action or behavior. Abraham Maslow's

Figure 11–15 | **Power type comparison**

Positional Power	Personal Power
Given by virtue of job status, title, or rank	Earned and recognized by others
Limited by individual's rank or job title	Continues to grow as others view individual's exercise of power positively
Accorded to those higher in an organization's structure	Available at any level of an organization

Figure 11–16 | Maslow's hierarchy of needs

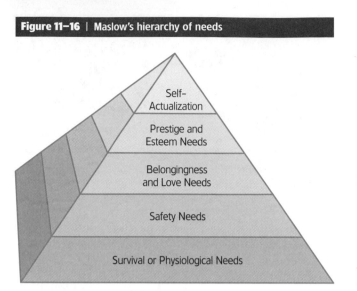

hierarchy of needs theory is among the best known of the motivation theories. This theory posits that human needs exist in a hierarchical fashion. If viewed from the perspective of a pyramid, the hierarchy would be explained as follows, with the most elementary need listed first: (1) physiological; (2) safety; (3) social; (4) esteem; and (5) self-actualization. One moves up the pyramid as each lower need is satisfied. Using this reasoning, an employee's need for self-actualization does not become active until after those needs listed in lower order are satisfied. Maslow's hierarchy of needs theory is illustrated in Figure 11–16.

In applying this hierarchy of needs to motivation, it is important to understand that motivation springs from needs not yet fulfilled. As one need is fulfilled, another need emerges that must be fulfilled. To the extent that needs are interrelated, it may be important to attempt to fulfill, at the same time, more than one need or parts of more than one need combined with an entirely separate need.

Scientist Frederick Herzberg refined Maslow's hierarchy of needs theory further, developing what is often referred to as the "two-factor theory." The two-factor theory separates work motivation and job satisfaction into two entities. Under this theory, **work motivation** includes those things that stimulate an employee to exceed basic performance expectations. When motivated to work, an employee works better, faster, or more accurately than the minimum required by a supervisor. **Job satisfaction** refers to those things that keep an employee from actively seeking other employment. The concept that the two entities are separate is illustrated by the employee who is satisfied with his job but does not work above and beyond the minimum level required under the job performance standards.

To succeed in developing work motivation and job satisfaction among staff, a leader must understand two factors: motivators and maintenance. **Motivators** are those forces that cause people to do more than just get by. Motivators

are internal to the nature of work and include opportunities for personal or professional growth, achievement, autonomy, advancement, responsibility, and recognition. Under Herzberg's theory, motivators are what affect the attitude and performance of employees, making the difference in job satisfaction. By contrast, **maintenance factors** are those forces that help people who are performing at acceptable levels continue to do so. Maintenance factors are external to the nature of work, meaning that they relate more to the circumstances surrounding how the work is performed and less to the nature of the work itself. Some examples of maintenance factors include interpersonal relationships, job security, organizational policies and procedures, working conditions, technical supervision, and salary/benefits. Under Herzberg's theory, maintenance factors can be the source of job dissatisfaction, leading to reduced work motivation and poor job performance.

Herzberg applied both the motivators and maintenance factors to Maslow's hierarchy of needs, concluding that motivators relate to higher-order needs while maintenance factors relate to lower-order needs. A comparative table illustrating this application is shown in Figure 11–17. According to Herzberg's theory, a leader should concentrate on motivators, rather than maintenance factors, to improve employee work performance.

The challenge for a leader is to develop situations that permit all employees to satisfy their needs within the work environment without frustrating the needs of one or more members of a team. One method of answering this challenge is through job enrichment. **Job enrichment** entails modifying the job itself by introducing into it additional motivating factors that meet an employee's higher-order needs, making the job more meaningful and rewarding. This

Figure 11–17 | Comparison of Maslow and Herzberg

Maslow	Herzberg
Higher-Order Needs	**Motivators**
Self-Actualization	Personal and/or Professional Growth Achievement Autonomy Responsibility
Self-Esteem	Recognition Advancement
Lower-Order Needs	**Maintenance Factors**
Social	Interpersonal Relationships Technical Supervision
Security	Policies and Procedures Job Security
Physiological/Survival	Working Conditions Salary/Benefits

increase in meaning and reward enhances the employee's commitment and involvement in the work performed. Where circumstances make modifying the job itself difficult, a leader can concentrate on changing the way an employee looks at the job. For example, a leader can heighten the perceived importance of the work performed by increasing the employee's amount of direct contact with internal and external customers or by providing more information to the employee on what meaning the organization, customers, or regulatory bodies give to the work. Other job enrichment strategies include: increasing the amount of autonomy and freedom an employee has, increasing the degree to which the employee sees the results of his labor in terms of the end product or intended service, and increasing the degree to which the employee can identify with the product or service he provides.

Directing Others One thing that sets leaders apart from managers is the clear focus and direction that leaders provide an organization. Leaders accomplish this by fostering the development of a common vision that is understood and accepted by everyone in the organization. This clear focus logically leads to the development of a mission, which identifies what an organization needs to accomplish and how to measure its success. The leader provides direction by making clear to employees what is expected of them, both on a daily basis and over the longer term, and what organizational priorities exist so that employees may make appropriate decisions about the work they are to perform.

Providing clear focus and direction also includes taking additional action. By clarifying roles and responsibilities, a leader increases ownership, helps to alleviate conflicts, and eliminates unnecessary ambiguity. By linking an employee group or team to the organization's mission, the leader helps employees understand how their work ties into that of the organization and its objectives. This link also educates others who may be important to the organization's success about the employee group's or team's work, thereby increasing the understanding and support needed to accomplish the organization's objectives.

Resolving Conflicts One of a leader's major tasks is to manage or resolve conflicts. The leader succeeds in this task by anticipating and trying to resolve conflicts, disagreements, and confrontations in a constructive manner. Conflict is an inevitable part of an organization, because interpersonal relationships are involved. Although most people consider conflict uncomfortable, it may be a necessary part of an organization's method of avoiding stagnation.

Conflict may be categorized in two ways. First, conflict may be considered functional. Functional conflicts are conflicts of a constructive nature that support the goals of the organization. Functional conflict can occur when teams or groups possess conflicting priorities or activities. The focus of functional conflict is upon the priority or activity, not the

Table 11–6 | Conflict Resolution Options

Accommodation	Encourages participants to place another individual's concerns and needs above their own
Force	Satisfies one participant's needs at the expense of another participant's needs
Compromise	Encourages participants to relinquish something of value
Collaboration	Attempts to gain advantage for all participants; a so-called "win-win situation"
Avoidance	Resolution is not attempted for a certain period of time if high emotions are involved and a cooling-off period is needed, or if insufficient information is available to make a discussion of value

Source: Mattingly, R. (1997). *Management of health information: Functions and applications*. Albany, NY: Delmar.

interpersonal relationships. Second, conflict may be considered dysfunctional. Dysfunctional conflicts are conflicts that result in destructive behavior and prevent the organization from achieving its goals. Dysfunctional conflict can occur when personality differences cause conflicts among teams or groups. The focus of dysfunctional conflict is upon the interpersonal relationships, not the priority or activity.

It is generally easier for managers to handle functional conflict than dysfunctional conflict, since managing personal chemistry differences among employees is inherently more problematic. Conflict resolution options can be effective mechanisms to employ when resolving both functional and dysfunctional conflicts. Several standard conflict resolution options are illustrated in Table 11–6.

Among the most effective mechanisms used to resolve conflicts is negotiation. Negotiation refers to the process of conferring, discussing, or bargaining to reach an agreement. Negotiation methods vary widely, from taking hard-bargaining positions to seeking reciprocity through favors and keeping score to issuing threats. Principled negotiation, however, has proven to be the most successful method, because it focuses on principles as the means to reach outcomes rather than forcing outcomes through the use of power. The seven principles of this form of negotiation are illustrated in Table 11–7.

Table 11–7 | Principles of Negotiation

Focus on the interests
Protect the relationship
Use good communication
Rely on legitimacy
Consider the options
Weigh the alternatives
Make commitments

Each principle adds value to the negotiating process. By focusing on interests, the dynamic changes from one of staking positions to one of seeking out the interests that underlie a given position. In this manner, the focus rests on what is really sought by each party rather than on what may be expressed on the surface level. The principle of protecting the relationship centers on the issue of respect for those persons involved in the negotiation. This demonstration of respect works to build a partnership around solving the problem. By using good communication techniques, the expression of different points of view and persuasion can be injected into the negotiation process. The legitimacy principle focuses on the fairness aspect of negotiation. Use of an established external standard or criterion can allow the parties to measure the fairness of any given proposal. By exploring the full range of options, more creative solutions may be identified. Once identified, each option or alternative can be weighed, leading to the identification of the best viable alternative. Finally, the making of commitments allows the parties to formalize the results of their negotiations and convey those results to others.

Effective Communication Managers cannot lead without being able to communicate their ideas well. Because of the time constraints facing all leaders, everything that is said and done must count. Ultimately, the leader is responsible for the success or failure of the communication effort. Communication is the process of sharing meaning through the intentional or unintentional sending and receiving of messages. Communication involves many facets, including: (1) knowing who needs what information and communicating that information in a concise and timely way; (2) choosing the most appropriate communication medium, oral or written, for the recipient's use; (3) knowing how to listen effectively; and (4) helping others to communicate effectively, so that communication occurs at all levels of the organization and with all needed people.

Leaders may communicate with others efficiently without communicating effectively. Effective communication is measured by looking at whether the communication produced the desired results. To be effective, the leader must put time and effort into making certain that the communication is received by those for whom it was intended, is understood to mean what it was intended to mean, is remembered for a reasonably long period of time, and is used the way the leader intended the message to be used. Leaders who master these elements of communication can be both effective and efficient.

In exercising communication skills, the leader works to ensure a consistent and timely flow of high-quality information within the organization and to all of its internal and external stakeholders. The leader accomplishes this by employing multiple behaviors. First, the leader represents and articulates viewpoints in a manner that influences the dialogue positively. The viewpoints and ideas expressed should be focused messages that inspire support or action from others. Second, the leader relates to all internal and external stakeholders, communicating with individuals up, down, across, and beyond the organization. Third, the leader maximizes his listening skills, increasing the possibility of problems being solved in a timely fashion. Fourth, the leader conveys information in a clear, organized, and understandable manner while maintaining quality standards in all forms of communication. Finally, the leader provides continuous, constructive feedback to internal and external stakeholders by employing descriptive language and separating facts from opinions, inferences, and assumptions.

Management Theories

The theories used by managers to direct and control the activities of subordinates greatly determine the climate of that portion of an organization for which the managers are responsible. A historical overview of these theories provides a basis for discussion of specialized management theories. A chart showing the progression of various management theories is found in Figure 11–18.

Historical Overview

The first efforts toward a management approach or theory originated in the early part of the 20th century. At that time, individuals such as Frederick Taylor, Henri Fayol, Frank and Lillian Gilbreth, and Henry Gantt began studying management from a scientific perspective. They conducted extensive studies of aspects of production by observing, measuring, and relating the contributions of each aspect. In these studies, they attempted to prove or disprove a particular hypothesis or assumption by means of controlled experimentation. In doing so, they sought to increase efficiency and productivity of an operation through scientific means. Their approach is referred to as scientific management; it became widely accepted by managers and influenced the academic community.

While the scientific management approach gained acceptance in America, a different approach developed in Europe. Based on the work of sociologist Max Weber and others, the classical management approach focused on the organization as a whole, rather than on individual functions, to improve performance. The organizational focus was on a well-run bureaucracy, where managers were expected to make decisions to enhance the organization and workers were expected to follow orders. This approach posited that workers were merely cogs in a wheel or one more function to be managed, and that attention to sentiment or emotion was unnecessary because both were irrelevant in the workplace. Although it was not entirely accepted, numerous managers thought this approach appropriate for the work environment.

Figure 11–18 | Progression of management theories

Features	Scientific Management	Classical Management	Humanistic Management	Participatory Management	Total Quality Management
Time Period	1900–1920s	1920–1930s	1930–1940s	1950–1970s	1970–1990s
Proponents	Frederic Taylor, Henri Fayol, Frank and Lillian Gilbreth, Henry Gantt	Max Weber	Elton Mayo	Douglas McGregor, Peter Drucker	W. Edwards Deming, Walter Shewhart, Joseph Juran, Kaoru Ishikawa
Focus	Science as a means to improve performance	Remove sentiment and emotion from the workplace	Social relationships in the workplace	Motivating through use of expectations and information	Customer expectations and needs
Examples	Time studies	Well-run bureaucracy	Hawthorne studies	Theories X, Y, and Z	Continuous improvement process

Although scientific and classical management efforts often resulted in higher productivity and efficiency, neither focused on the human aspect of management. The failure to address the human aspect of management led to the development of the humanistic management approach. Under the leadership of Elton Mayo in his famous Hawthorne studies for Western Electric in the 1930s, managers became more aware of the need to focus on social relationships in the workplace. Humanistic management supports the proposition that an organization's objectives can be achieved and productivity increased when managers use human relations skills to work with people. The emphasis is placed on satisfying the needs of employees, motivating employees to improve productivity, and using communication tools and work groups effectively. Through cooperative efforts rather than mere engineering of products, the humanistic management approach stressed the importance of social relationships to work productivity.

During the 1950s, behavioral scientists developed a bridge between the scientific, classical, and humanistic management approaches through the concept of participatory management. Participatory management involves the use of expectations and information within an organization to motivate people to work. Proponents of participatory management include Douglas McGregor (Theory X and Theory Y) and Peter Drucker (management by objectives, addressed earlier in this chapter).

McGregor's theories held that the nature of a manager's expectations of employees influences the way the manager treats employees and how employees respond to the manager. He developed two alternate theories to test his assumptions. Theory X holds that the average employee dislikes work, possesses relatively little ambition, wishes to avoid responsibility, prefers to be directed by others, and wants security above everything else. Consequently, managers who subscribe to this theory use fear as a motivator and keep close surveillance over their employees to achieve organizational objectives. Alternatively, Theory Y holds that work may be a source of employee satisfaction and that employees, under proper conditions, will not only accept but seek responsibility. Theory Y emphasizes an employee's potential to act maturely and show self-motivation. Consequently, managers who subscribe to this theory emphasize motivation through objectives and permit employees to experience personal satisfaction as they contribute to the achievement of objectives. More recently, Theory Z has emerged as an advancement of Theory Y. Theory Z holds that the responsibilities sought by employees, and over which they are capable of self-control, are culturally related. As societal needs and goals change, those things that motivate employees will change as well. Consequently, managers who subscribe to this theory look to individual and aggregate quality-of-life issues when developing motivators for employees. While these theories can be considered generalizations, and no one theory applies to every situation, the three theories illustrate the concept that employees will live up to—or down to—the expectations of the managers in their organization.

Another theory that has gained wide credence in the last two decades is total quality management (TQM). TQM is a customer-focused management philosophy that challenges an organization to exceed customer expectations while still maintaining a cost-competitive market position. It involves continuous improvement of processes and the entire organization's participation to be successful. With TQM, emphasis is placed on measuring the customer's needs and expectations and measuring the capability of the organization to meet those needs and expectations.

TQM originated from the statistical control theories and evaluation of production processes introduced by Americans W. Edwards Deming, Walter Shewhart, and Joseph Juran. These theories and processes were further developed in Japan, by Kaoru Ishikawa, which led to numerous organizational success stories. Corporate America later embraced TQM, applying its principles to both manufacturing and health care settings.

Specialized Management Theories

While management as a discipline is a relatively recent academic development, the late 20th and early 21st centuries have seen newer management theories and practices emerge. These newer management theories and practices attempt to respond to the striking changes occurring in the workplace, including those resulting from technological innovations, the availability of information, and the increase in global competitiveness. While more theories and practices exist than can be addressed in one textbook, this section focuses on those theories that have greatly impacted the health care environment during the last two decades. All are subsets of management theory and practice, and they are addressed separately because of the differences they pose with one another and with general management principles.

Change Management The change management theory developed as a result of the magnitude and frequency of changes in the health care and business environments, and the need to anticipate and respond to those changes. Change management generally refers to a large-scale change in an organization's operation or structure. It involves numerous management activities such as planning, designing, and implementing, and focuses on developing procedures, processes, systems, routines, or tools that require a change in human performance. The end result of change management in an organization is that people will perform their jobs differently in order to achieve a stated goal or objective.

Change management can be broken into two parts: the change and the transition. The change addresses the outcome sought by the organization, for example, moving to a customer service orientation or a flatter organizational structure. The transition addresses the psychology the organization must deal with, for example, letting go of the reality and identity that previously existed within the organization so that a new reality and identity can be forged. The transition to change poses the most difficult challenge to managers and organizations. Organizations who focus on both aspects of change management increase their potential for success. Examples of reasons for organizational change are listed in Table 11-8.

It is important to understand that people react to change much as they react to other significant events and activities in their lives. For some, change is welcome; for others, change is somewhat difficult; for still others, change is catastrophic. Many who find change difficult or worse are experiencing the loss of something familiar and are faced with something unfamiliar. They must go through the stages

Table 11-8	Reasons for Organizational Change
External Pressures	Reimbursement issues; government regulation; demands of accreditation agencies
Leadership	Vacancy, retirement, or replacement of key personnel
Policies and Procedures	Influence of new information or strategic approach
Structure	Reorganization or privatization of services
Technology	Advances in the field affecting private industry and government; new applications for existing technology

of denial, resistance, bargaining, and depression before they reach the stage of acceptance. Recognizing these stages is the first step to managing the change successfully.

Managing change requires activity at multiple levels of operation. At the individual level, managers find that the individual's history and personality, along with the type and consequences of change, will influence the response to change. At the team level, managers find that the team's purpose and the composition of its members will influence the response to change. At the organizational level, managers find that the complexity level is great and that multiple models and approaches may be used, depending on the particular circumstances.

Change is an ongoing phenomenon; changes may overlap with one another, occur simultaneously, or occur in a rapid series. Without proper planning, change can lead to dysfunction or even crisis in an organization. Employing life cycle management, worst-case scenarios, and the theory of change as normal may assist in handling the reaction. In life cycle management, a life expectancy is given to a product or process. Within the life cycle, the manager can begin to acclimate staff to the need for future change, so that it is not seen as unexpected or poorly understood. Worst-case scenarios allow the manager to build contingency clauses into change management plans. These contingencies can include alternate methods and procedures in the event of unforeseen circumstances. Because these alternatives are developed before they are actually employed, they permit the manager to change plans smoothly, or to minimize difficulties facing staff and the organization. The "change as normal" theory requires managers to educate staff that organizational change is a constant and that the status quo is only temporary until a better way of performing work or doing business is discovered. Utilizing this approach, the organization's values remain unchanged; it is the procedures and processes the organization employs that will remain in constant transition.

Project Management One discipline within the larger framework of management is project management (PM).

Figure 11–19 | Elements of project management

1. Unique undertaking that results in a single output or product.

2. A plan comprised of a series of activities that are interrelated.

3. Involves multiple resources.

4. Composed of a life cycle: concept, development, implementation, and termination.

5. Executive or other major stakeholder as project sponsor.

6. May have funding limits.

7. A project manager tasked with seeing the project through to fruition.

Project management refers to temporary endeavors undertaken to produce a definite product or service. PM differs from the general definition of management in that it focuses on complex projects that require a more intensive effort to manage, are of a limited duration, involve a sponsor and specific staff, and generally involve something new or unique. Elements typically associated with project management are listed in Figure 11–19.

Managers use PM to solve problems, identify opportunities, define what needs to be done, and commit to achieving a specific goal. Projects can be of a substantial nature, such as converting to and implementing a new software program affecting multiple users, or of a less substantial nature, such as developing an archive shipment for records to be stored off-site. Project management is most successfully used in situations where upper management support is present, clear goals and objectives exist, adequate resources are available, communication is clear and precise, team members are knowledgeable and committed to one another, and priorities and politics are not conflicting.

Project management encompasses many functions. Initially, the project manager must understand the scope function. This requires knowledge of all activities to be performed, the end product that will result, and the resources needed to achieve this result. Project integration is one of the most significant functions, because it requires the project manager to integrate people, resources, and technologies effectively and efficiently within both time and financial limits. Also important is strategic planning. By creating an overall strategy or vision, the project manager facilitates integration and controls actions. The project manager must also be able to allocate resources effectively, assigning the right resources to the right tasks. Functional areas concerning quality, time, and cost require management attention, as do identifying, analyzing, and responding to risk factors associated with the project. Finally, the project manager must attend to the communication function. The project manager routinely works to build consensus or confidence in decisions at critical junctions in a project by practicing active

communication skills. This communication may involve individuals and groups at many levels, including upper management, members of the project team, and other stakeholders.

Project management software applications can aid the project manager greatly. Software programs can help identify which activities are most critical, the number of resource units required (by day) under the schedule, and the activities for which a critical resource is required. Many project managers use software scheduling programs to plot the time frame needed to complete the project, the time frame for activities within the project, and the windows of time when activities may overlap. Many of these software-scheduling programs create a physical representation of the project timeline using Gantt charts.

The successful management of projects can be measured in several ways, including whether they were completed on time and within cost, produced the desired performance or technology level, were achieved using the assigned resources effectively and efficiently, involved minimum if any scope changes, did not disturb the main work flow of an organization, or did not change the corporate culture but served to enhance it. Essential to successful completion are accurate estimates of time, resources, and cost. The easiest way to determine the sequence and time needed to complete a project is through the use of a Gantt chart or PERT network. Estimates of resources and cost may be obtained by including others—beyond the project manager—since many individuals and departments may be involved in a project.

Project management is not without its obstacles, and many constraints may affect a project. At times, the project's complexity can overwhelm the effort. The special requirements of customers or changes in technology may impact the project adversely. Some risks may not be detected soon enough or avoided adequately, increasing the chance of a poor outcome. Pricing of the goods needed may rise beyond what was planned for, or the scope of the project may change drastically.

Management support may disappear or organizational restructuring may obviate the need for the project completely. While contingency plans can be developed to cover some uncertainties, the project manager must retain flexibility, practice active communication skills, and be prepared to make concessions or trade-offs in order to overcome obstacles.

In summary, project management must assist an organization's competitiveness. PM can accomplish this if projects are aligned with the organization's strategic plan, goals, and objectives; if they demonstrate a return on the effort expended; if they balance an organization's needs with its desired levels of risk and growth; and if they are staffed and supplied with the resources required for the task at hand.

Process Improvement In many respects, an organization's processes demonstrate its effectiveness. Where processes follow a logical pattern, they can support an organization's goals and improve performance. Conversely, processes that stumble along without attention from management and staff cost the organization in terms of efficiency and effectiveness. The realization of these and other costs have resulted in the development of process improvement theory as a subset of management.

Process improvement refers to the efforts to implement changes to business processes as a means to improve performance. Sometimes referred to as process reengineering, process redesign, or process innovation, the goal of process improvement is to facilitate some form of change, focusing on the business processes and various activities within each process and eliminating those activities that do not add value to the business. Process improvement has been shown to increase the speed, productivity, and profitability of organizations. It differs from performance improvement in that performance improvement focuses on patient care, whereas process improvement can apply to any business process, regardless of its connection to patient care. It is similar to total quality management in that both deal with process improvement; TQM, however, focuses on continuous improvement as opposed to improvement on a one-time basis. Both management theories employ the Plan-Do-Study-Act (PDSA) cycle as a model for action.

Under the PDSA cycle, one begins the planning stage by identifying, evaluating, and analyzing the process appropriate for improvement. Next is the doing stage, which involves implementing actions that correct the root cause(s) of a process problem. This is followed by the study stage, which measures and reviews the results of the actions taken to determine if they achieved the target sought. Finally, focus rests on the act stage, where successful improvement efforts are integrated into daily operations and, where appropriate, are transferred or shared with other organizations. The activity that occurs in each of these stages is critical to the success of the process improvement effort.

The need for creativity is present at each of these stages, with idea generation often used as a means to boost creativity. Ideas may be generated through several methods. With brainstorming, ideas are offered about a particular process or topic in an unrestrained manner by all members of a group. All ideas are recorded, with analysis and editing waiting until a later stage. The strength of this method is that it allows for gathering a variety of ideas in a short time frame. With mental imaging, the group visualizes a detailed picture of an ideal situation, identifying both the key relationships and obstacles that will need to be addressed in order to influence eventual success. The strength of this method is that the desired outcome—and the conditions needed to make that happen—is clearly identified for everyone in the group to share. Using the five "why"s method, the root causes of a problem are discovered by asking the question "why" at least five times in a given discussion. The strength of this method is that it assists in understanding how different causes might be related and focuses on the process rather than the personalities involved.

Once ideas are generated, they must be prioritized in some fashion. Several decision-making tools can assist in this prioritizing process, including multivoting, nominal group technique, and force field analysis. In multivoting, the highest priority items are determined by allowing each

---

Figure 11–20 | Multivoting tool

Members of five teams participate in meetings on a regular basis. The members find these meetings unproductive and seek a solution. A representative of each team participates in a brainstorming session to identify how to improve the situation. They identify the following list:

1. Lack of agenda
2. Meeting focus unclear
3. Too many topics addressed
4. No meeting facilitator
5. Problems not mentioned
6. No administrative support
7. No desired meeting outcome
8. Key information not included
9. Unproductive
10. Unrelated topics addressed
11. Too much "dog and pony" show
12. Unclear charts/figures/tables
13. No decision/result reached
14. No action plan created

By dividing the list of 14 in half, each team member may cast seven votes as a way to reduce the list to a more manageable size:

III	1.	Lack of agenda
IIII	2.	Meeting focus unclear
I	3.	Too many topics addressed
I	4.	No meeting facilitator
II	5.	Problems not mentioned
I	6.	No administrative support
IIIII	7.	No desired meeting outcome
II	8.	Key information not included
I	9.	Unproductive
II	10.	Unrelated topics addressed
I	11.	Too much "dog and pony" show
II	12.	Unclear charts/figures/tables
IIIII	13.	No decision/result reached
IIIII	14.	No action plan created

The resulting vote indicates that the group will focus on those items receiving the highest votes: 1, 2, 7, 13, and 14.

Figure 11-21 | Nominal group technique tool

An organization with a new leader has asked selected staff to identify a list of problems troubling the organization. At a brainstorming session, the group identifies the following:

A. Ineffective organizational design and structure
B. Unclear vision, mission, goals, and objectives
C. Poor communications within the organization
D. Poor communications outside the organization
E. Lack of feedback on work produced
F. Lack of training

The selected staff are instructed to prioritize each of the six items, labeled A–F on separate slips of paper, using "6" as the highest and "1" as the lowest. They use each number only once.
The result:

Problem	Person					Total	Priority	
	1	2	3	4	5			
A	5	6	5	6	4	26	1	← Highest Priority
B	6	5	4	5	5	25	2	
C	4	3	6	4	6	23	3	
D	3	4	2	2	3	14	4	
E	1	2	3	1	1	8	6	← Lowest Priority
F	2	1	1	3	2	9	5	

group member to vote for items he believes have the highest priority. The number of votes per group member is determined by halving the total number of ideas or items on a list, for example, by allowing fifteen votes for a thirty-item list. Those items on the list with the highest number of votes are then pursued by the group. This tool is illustrated in Figure 11–20. Multivoting is particularly applicable to large groups who wish to participate in the decision-making process or to long lists that require separations between vital and trivial ideas or items.

Nominal group technique is more appropriate for smaller groups or smaller lists of ideas or items. Using this technique, a list of ideas is labeled alphabetically, and each group member prioritizes the list by writing a number beside each lettered idea. A tally is computed of the numbers given to each lettered idea, identifying by score the priority from highest to lowest. This tool is illustrated in Figure 11–21.

Force field analysis is a tool applicable to identifying and visualizing the relationships of significant influencing forces. Once the problem or process to analyze is identified, the group lists the key forces that promote or hinder solving or streamlining the process, with promoting and hindering forces listed separately. Each force is then prioritized according to the impact it possesses. Effort is then expended on strengthening those forces that promote solving the problem or streamlining the process, and on weakening those forces that hinder the desired outcome. This tool is illustrated in Figure 11–22.

Figure 11-22 | Force field analysis tool

Force Field Analysis

One goal of an organization's Wellness Program is to reduce smoking among its employees. An employee meets with a counselor to identify the key factors or forces involved in his smoking.

Goal: Stop Smoking

Promoting Forces	Hindering Forces
Better health →	← Habits
Save money →	← Addiction to nicotine
Food tastes better →	← Gain weight when quitting
Won't have to exit building →	← Way to handle stress
No second-hand smoke for family/loved ones →	← Need to have something in mouth

After completing this analysis, the employee prioritizes which forces to strengthen and which to weaken.

Where the root cause of a problem is particularly difficult to understand, analysis tools may be used, such as flowcharts, affinity diagrams, cause-and-effect diagrams, and Pareto charts. A **flowchart** is a diagram, often using geometric symbols, that shows the steps in a sequence of operations. This graphical representation of a process can identify both critical stages and problem areas. Standard flowchart symbols exist and are used as shown in Figure 11–23. An **affinity diagram** organizes information into a visual pattern to show the relationship between factors in a problem. Affinity diagrams begin with specific ideas and move toward broad categories; an affinity diagram is illustrated in Figure 11–24.

Figure 11–23 | Standard flowchart symbols

Symbol	Meaning	Examples
	Start/Stop	"Receive Trouble Report" "Machine Operable"
	Decision Point	Approve/Disapprove Yes/No Accept/Decline
	Activity	"Open Access Panel"
	Document	"Fill Out Trouble Report"
	Connector (to another part of the diagram or page)	

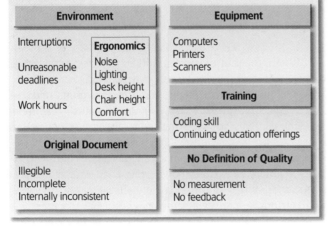

Figure 11–24 | Sample affinity diagram

The Health Information Department has convened its coding staff to discuss how to reduce coding errors. The brainstorming session yields the following list of factors affecting the error rate:

Noise	Computers	No feedback
Printers	Lighting	Work hours
Comfort	No measurements	Interruptions
Unreasonable deadlines	Desk height	Incomplete
Internally inconsistent	Chair height	Scanners
Continuing ed. offerings	Illegible	Coding skills

The coding staff creates an affinity diagram to identify areas for further analysis:

Environment
Interruptions
Unreasonable deadlines
Work hours

Ergonomics
Noise
Lighting
Desk height
Chair height
Comfort

Equipment
Computers
Printers
Scanners

Training
Coding skill
Continuing education offerings

Original Document
Illegible
Incomplete
Internally inconsistent

No Definition of Quality
No measurement
No feedback

Figure 11–25 | Sample cause-and-effect diagram

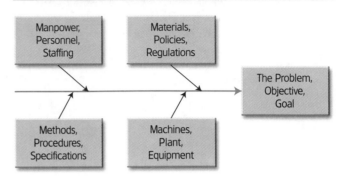

A **cause-and-effect diagram**, sometimes referred to as a fish bone diagram, identifies major categories of factors that influence an effect, along with the subfactors within each major category. The cause-and-effect diagram begins with broad causes and works toward specifics, often using the categories of 4Ms (methods/manpower/materials/machinery) or 4Ps (policies/procedures/people/plant). One such diagram is illustrated in Figure 11–25. A **Pareto chart** is a bar graph used to identify and separate major and minor problems. It is based on the Pareto principle, which posits that 20 percent of problems pose 80 percent of the impact. This chart orders categories according to frequency, in descending order from left to right, and is illustrated in Figure 11–26.

Armed with these ideas and tools for analysis and decision making, processes can be transformed from their present "as is" state to a "should be" state. This involves addressing those areas of disconnect found in the process review that impede efficiency or effectiveness, such as missing or unnecessary steps, substandard equipment or materials,

Figure 11–26 | Sample Pareto chart

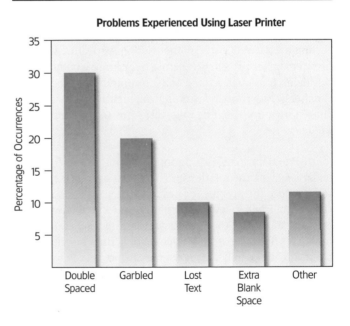

assignment of work to the wrong group or person, or performing work at the wrong time—for example, in a series rather than on parallel tracks. At times, the efficiency to be gained is the result of improving the execution of the work through additional training or by automating a previously manual process. A series of recommendations that address these impediments, supported by cost-benefit analyses and a timeline, form the design of the implementation plan.

The transition to implementation of a particular process improvement may vary according to the challenges involved. Widespread resistance to change may exist, or special expertise in certain areas may be needed. The impact upon staff and systems may be substantial, and new infrastructure may be necessary. Finally, the depth and breadth of communication requirements necessary to ensure that the improvement is accepted in the work environment can be formidable. Each of these challenges can be met and overcome with proper planning, attention to detail, and wise use of resources. The results are improved processes, which can be measured and integrated into an organization's daily operation.

Knowledge Management Knowledge has always been an important factor in the success of organizations and entities. Leaders have applied their expertise and operational knowledge to reach decisions and take action. Workers have applied their knowledge to carry out these decisions and make decisions of their own. During the last half-century, the concept of managing knowledge has been formally recognized as a subset of management theory and practice. **Knowledge management** refers to the strategies, policies, actions, and tools involved in creating an environment that facilitates the creation, transfer, and sharing of knowledge within an organization. By managing knowledge, the organization stands to gain a competitive advantage and sustain that advantage over time.

Before one can understand the concept of knowledge management, one must first understand the definition of knowledge. **Knowledge** is the understanding and use—often in the forms of mental models, scripts, and schemata—of a range of information. Knowledge can be thought of as one element in a continuum, moving from signals to data to information to knowledge to wisdom. Figure 11–27 illustrates this continuum. **Signals** refer to objects serving to convey data, whereas **data** generally refer to raw facts and figures. Considered by themselves, these raw facts and figures are meaningless. By contrast, **information** refers to organized and classified data put into context, or so-called "meaningful" data. A full understanding and use of this information is referred to as knowledge. **Wisdom**, in turn, refers to the ability to judge matters soundly, especially as they relate to life, conduct, and practical affairs. It is at the knowledge stage of the continuum that the principles of knowledge management apply.

Figure 11–27 | The knowledge continuum

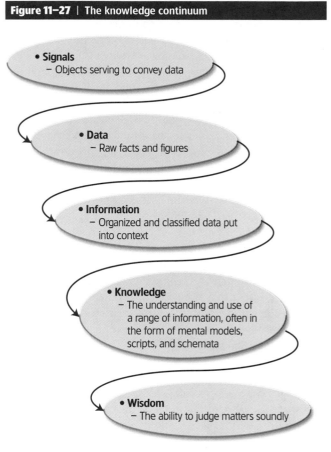

A basic principle of knowledge management is the concept of capturing and categorizing knowledge into one of two categories: explicit and tacit. **Explicit knowledge** refers to knowledge that can be recorded, archived, codified, or embedded into products. Patents, trademarks, business plans, customer lists, organizational charts, procedures, formulas, and marketing research are all examples of explicit knowledge. **Tacit knowledge** refers to personal knowledge, or that knowledge contained in people's heads. For example, an individual's learning or experiences are classified as tacit knowledge. Both of these forms of knowledge are sometimes referred to as intellectual capital or knowledge assets.

Once identified as explicit or tacit, the value of the knowledge is then determined. Valuable explicit knowledge is channeled into some form of recorded, archived, codified, or embedded structure. This contrasts with valuable tacit knowledge, which resides with a given individual. To the extent that tacit knowledge can be readily articulated, it can be transformed into explicit knowledge, available for dissemination. To the extent that tacit knowledge cannot be readily articulated, however, strategies to provide infrastructure support, empowerment management support, and retention and replacement support are used to leverage that knowledge for the organization's benefit.

Consider the knowledge associated with the concepts of innovation and leadership. Both concepts are highly tacit and complex, and are not readily articulated or easily transferable to others. Nonetheless, they are highly valued by individuals and organizations. Because of this high value given to both concepts, knowledge management theory would support efforts to record an individual's innovation and leadership experiences for sharing with others. To the extent that these experiences cannot be articulated and shared, knowledge management theory would support efforts to retain and empower the individual who holds this knowledge.

By contrast, consider the knowledge associated with business processes. These processes are generally explicit, may or may not be complex, and are often readily articulated and easily transferable to others. Because of the high value given to business processes, knowledge management theory would support recording them for sharing with others. To the extent that these business processes can be improved, resulting in greater efficiencies for the organization, knowledge management theory would support this process improvement action.

It is at this point that the principle of knowledge transfer applies. Mechanisms and processes—whether formal or informal—are put into place that allow other individuals and groups, both within and beyond the organization, to integrate this knowledge with their own knowledge. The actions involved with knowledge transfer or sharing are often referred to as knowledge management systems. A **knowledge management system** (KMS) is a mechanism or process that captures knowledge, uses and refines that knowledge to assist understanding, and transfers or shares that knowledge with others. These systems may work to address entirely new problems or address old problems in new ways, or they may be useful for circumstances that could occur in the future.

Some knowledge management systems utilize technology, while other systems do not. The type of technology used varies with the type of knowledge to be transferred. Document management systems, data mining tools, automated alert systems, searching and indexing software programs, and online analytical processing systems are examples of technologies that are useful for facilitating the transfer of explicit knowledge. Electronic mail, groupware, instant messaging, and related technologies are examples of technologies that are helpful for facilitating the transfer of tacit knowledge. To justify its use and expense, the type of technology chosen should relate to an organization's strategic plan, goals, and objectives.

While technology often facilitates knowledge management, technology is not required for a successful knowledge management system. In fact, some knowledge management systems do not use technology at all or do so sparingly. These systems focus on people-related or other "soft" issues of management, including organizational behaviors or culture (tacit knowledge) or business practices and processes (explicit knowledge) that do not readily lend themselves to technology solutions. For example, to transfer tacit knowledge, an organization may facilitate joint activities between employees who currently possess the valued knowledge with those who do not, allowing for dialogue and reflection to share knowledge and direct experiences to create new knowledge. To transfer explicit knowledge, an organization may have employees who currently possess the valued knowledge exchange documents or engage in simulations or experiments with those employees who do not. For either tacit or explicit knowledge, an organization may engage in a best practices analysis, using flowcharts and benchmarking approaches as guides. While all of these activities can be aided by technology, they can just as easily be conducted without the aid of technology.

As this discussion shows, knowledge management encompasses a broad range of principles, tools, and techniques. This broadness is a strength, since knowledge management can be applied to any discipline, business, or organization. Aligning knowledge management systems to organizational strategies, goals, and objectives serves to maximize the organization's effectiveness and positions the organization for competitive advantage.

Effective Meeting Management   One constant in every form of management is the need to conduct meetings. A **meeting** is a purposeful coming together of people or things. The purposes of meetings vary, ranging from transmitting information or announcing a decision to serving as forums for sharing ideas, making joint decisions, and planning actions to achieve results. Because meetings have become more frequent, the topics discussed at them more complex, and the categories of persons attending them more broad, it is important that managers understand how to manage meetings effectively.

Among the first considerations in meeting management is assisting the attendees in understanding the focus of the meeting. The focus can be developed by defining the purpose and desired outcome(s) of the meeting. The purpose is the intention or aim of the meeting (specific purposes were listed earlier in this discussion). Desired outcomes are the tangible results that can be achieved by the end of the meeting. Examples include a better understanding of a topic, a plan with assigned action items, a list of recommendations, or a decision. The focus is further developed by determining the topics to be covered; the best format in which to discuss each topic; the length, time, and place of the meeting; and who should participate. Once these elements are determined, an agenda can be created and distributed to the participants in advance of the meeting. When the meeting begins, the focus can be reemphasized through a restatement of the purpose and desired outcome(s) and a review of the agenda. Ground rules for how the meeting will be managed (e.g., the structure or climate), key information to be delivered (e.g., what precipitated a need for the meeting or what budget amount is involved), and who will handle note taking are often discussed at this stage.

The heart of meeting management involves concentrating on the content and process of the meeting while encouraging the participation of attendees. Concentrating on the content requires paying attention to what participants contribute to the discussion and relating it to the desired outcome(s) of the meeting. Utilizing techniques that address content, such as periodically summarizing key points or reinforcing constructive contributions, can help the participants reach consensus on the meeting's topic. Concentrating on the process requires attention to format or how the meeting is flowing. Utilizing techniques that address process, such as quickening or slowing the meeting's pace or reminding the participants of the progress made to date, can help the participants remain focused on the meeting's topic. Encouraging participation requires the use of a variety of techniques,

including clarifying or paraphrasing ideas, employing messages of positive reinforcement, and encouraging diverse points of view. The end result of this concentration should be that the participants reach some form of a decision or result.

Once the decision or result is reached, the next stage involves action. This stage is among the most critical, because participants may find that they have expended enormous amounts of time and energy only to leave the meeting without a clear understanding of what should occur next. To avoid this problem, it is important that participants understand before they leave the meeting how to bring the decision or result to the action level. This can be accomplished by assigning action items as soon as possible, identifying who is accountable for each action, setting deadlines, and establishing methods for monitoring progress. By memorializing in meeting minutes or summaries both the decision or results reached and the manner of accomplishing them, participants can gauge how effective the meeting was and evaluate how to improve future meeting effectiveness.

Conclusion

Whether management principles serve as the basis for an individual's work as a manager or as the basis for an awareness of how an organization conducts its business, the theories and practices supporting these principles provide the foundation for lifelong understanding and knowledge. Planning, organizing, directing, controlling, and leading all play a role in successful management. The development of management theory over time, particularly the development of specialized management theories, shows a response to the striking changes that have occurred in the workplace during the past century, as well as to the changes that will occur in the future.

CHAPTER SUMMARY

The principles of management—planning, organizing, directing, controlling, and leading—are central to the success of each manager within an organization and to the organization itself. Managers use planning to outline what needs to be done and how to actually do it. They organize all identified tasks and assign them to individuals or groups. They direct work through decision making, instructing others, and simplifying work processes. They control work to ensure that activities are accomplished as planned and correct any significant deviations from the plan. They lead by focusing on the interpersonal aspects of an activity, thereby motivating employees and reducing conflicts. When engaging in these activities, managers follow any number of management theories, including specialized theories such as change management, project management, process improvement, knowledge management, and effective meeting management. These management theories greatly determine the climate of that portion of an organization for which the managers are responsible.

CASE STUDY

You are a first-line supervisor in the health information department at Anywhere Hospital. Your authority allows you to control or manipulate certain factors about the jobs of the employees you supervise, but not all factors. Some factors over which you have *limited* control include salary and benefits, organization policies and procedures, and interpersonal relationships. Some factors over which you have a *larger level* of control include achievement, responsibility, autonomy, and professional growth. Using Herzberg's two-factor theory, can you be an effective supervisor for the staff?

REVIEW QUESTIONS

1. What planning elements are identified with the terms "why," "what," and "how"?

2. What are the steps in the strategic planning process?

3. What is a SWOT analysis?

4. What are the limitations present in organizational charts?

5. How does directing differ from leading?

6. How do positional power and personal power differ?

7. What are the stages a person goes through before accepting change?

8. How does project management differ from management in general?

9. What is process improvement?

10. Do all knowledge management systems require the use of technology? Why or why not?

11. What management techniques can be used to assist attendees in concentrating on the content and process of a meeting?

ENRICHMENT ACTIVITIES

1. Develop a Gantt chart for one of your class projects.

2. Recall an instance where a decision you reached failed in the implementation stage. Alternatively, recall an instance where a decision reached by an organization failed in the implementation stage. Examine why each implementation failed. If you could reduce such failure in the future, what particular change would you make in the decision-making process?

3. Think of a situation in which you felt that others expected you to fail. Alternatively, think of a situation in which you felt that others expected you to succeed. Ask yourself: How could you tell what others' expectations were? How did those expectations influence your behavior? How might your expectations and assumptions affect the way you influence others?

4. Interview an individual who holds a position of authority in an organization, preferably a health information management professional, concerning the process involved in introducing a significant change to a department or organization. Determine the process that was in place before the change, and identify how the change was introduced, what length of time occurred before the change was fully implemented, what problems were encountered, and how the problems were solved. While gathering this information, identify how the concepts of planning, organizing, directing, controlling, and leading were applied to the change.

WEB SITES

American Management Association, http://www.amanet.org

Association for Project Management, http://www.apm.org

Association for Work Process Improvement, http://www.tawpi.org

Change Management Association, http://www.cmassociation.org

Project Management Institute, http://www.pmi.org

United States Process Improvement Association, http://www.uspia.org

REFERENCES

Amatayakul, M. K. (1980). *Tools of management*. Chicago: American Health Information Management Association.

Bridges, W. (1991). *Managing transitions: Making the most of change*. Reading, MA: Addison-Wesley.

French, W. (1990). *Human resources management* (2nd ed.). Boston: Houghton Mifflin.

Gebelein, S., Nelson-Neuhaus, K., Skube, C., Lee, D., Stevens, L., Hellerik, L., et al. (Eds.). (1996). *Successful manager's handbook*. Minneapolis, MN: Personnel Decisions, Inc.

Haimann, T. (1989). *Supervisory management for healthcare organizations* (4th ed.). St. Louis, MO: Catholic Health Association of the United States.

Lee, S. M. (1981). *Management by multiple objectives*. Princeton, NJ: Petrocelli Books.

Liebler, J., & McConnell, C. (1999). *Management principles for health professionals*. Gaithersburg, MD: Aspen Publishers.

Mattingly, R. (1997). *Management of health information: Functions and applications*. Albany, NY: Delmar.

Mourier, P., & Smith, M. (2001). *Conquering organizational change.* Atlanta: CEP Press.

Odiorne, G. S. (1985). *The human side of management.* San Francisco: Jossey-Bass.

Phillips, D. T. (1992). *Lincoln on leadership.* New York: Warner Books.

Silva, K. (1994). *Meetings that work.* New York: Business One Irwin/Mirror Press.

Slevin, D. P. (1989). *The whole manager.* New York: American Management Association.

Tompkins, N. C. (1996). *Personnel management for the small business.* Boston: Crisp Publications.

Wold, G. H., & Shriver, R. F. (1991). *Disaster proof your business.* Chicago: Probus.

Zangwill, W. I. (1976). *Success with people: The Theory Z approach to mutual achievement.* Homewood, IL: Dow-Jones Irwin.

NOTES

1. Bean, W. C. (1993). *Strategic planning that makes things happen* (p. 13). New York, New York. Reed Business Information Inc.

2. Mattingly, R. (1997). *Management of health information: Functions and applications* (p. 86). Albany, NY: Delmar.

3. 45 C.F.R. § 164.308 (2006).

4. Davis, M., & Weckler, D. (1996). *A practical guide to organization design.* Boston: Crisp Publications.

12

Human Resource Management

CERTIFICATION CONNECTION

RHIA

Counseling
Disciplinary action
Employment laws
Job analysis
Job descriptions
Recruitment
Retention
Supervision
Team building
Training

RHIT

Job descriptions
Job functions
Performance appraisals
Staffing analysis
Staff orientation
Team leadership
Teams
Training

LEARNING OBJECTIVES

After reading this chapter, the learner should be able to:

1. Define the concept of employment and differentiate between the various types of employees.

2. Understand the elements of the staffing process.

3. Explain the concept of the at-will employment doctrine.

4. Trace the development of employee rights.

5. List and describe the various civil rights and workplace protection laws that relate to human resource management.

6. Compare and contrast the supervisory functions involved with performance evaluations, prevention of problem behaviors, discipline and grievance, teambuilding, developing others, and telecommuting.

7. Describe the perspectives of the business community toward the concept of workforce diversity.

Outline

Employment

Staffing

Recruitment
Selection
Compensation
Orientation and Training
Retention
Separation

Employee Rights

Overview
Employment Law Application

Supervision

Performance Evaluations
Problem Behaviors
Discipline and Grievance
Developing Others
Team Building
Telecommuting

Workforce Diversity

Key Concepts

At-will employment
Career development
Coaching
Compensation
Conduct problems
Disability
Diversity
Employee
Employers
Employment
Essential job functions
Full-time employee
Functional limitation
Grievance
Hostile work environment
Human resource management
Incentives
Independent contractor

Job description
Leased employees
Living wage laws
Mentoring
Nonessential job functions
Orientation
Part-time employee
Performance evaluation
Performance problems
Position summary
Qualifications
Quid pro quo
Reasonable accommodation
Recognition programs
Recruitment
Regular employee
Retention
Reward programs
Salary

Selection
Separation
Serious health condition
Sexual harassment
Staffing
Statutory employee
Substantially equal
Supervision
Supplemental benefits
Team
Team building
Telecenters
Telecommuting
Training
Undue hardship
Unemployment insurance
Wages
Workers' compensation
Workplace barrier

INTRODUCTION

Management requires both external and internal resources. One of the most significant of these resources is human resources. Human resource management involves the strategic use of human beings within an organization to enhance an organization's efficiency and effectiveness. Human resource management activities cover a broad range, from ensuring effective recruitment and retention to engaging in corrective/disciplinary action to handling an employee's separation from the organization to promoting employee well-being within an organization.

No matter how well a manager understands management principles and tools, work cannot be accomplished in an optimum fashion without an understanding of human resource issues. Human resource issues cover a broad spectrum; this chapter addresses in detail issues related to staffing, employee rights, and supervision—key elements of human resource management. A discussion of workplace diversity concludes the chapter.

Employment

At the heart of human resource management is the concept of employment. Employment is the process of providing work, engaging services or labor, and paying for the work performed. Those persons, businesses, or organizations that provide the work, engage the services or labor, and pay for the work performed are employers. The vast majority of individuals who are engaged in these services or labor are employees. As a generality, an employee is an individual hired by another, such as a business firm, to work for wages or a salary.[1] Employees are covered by a host of laws at the federal, state, and local levels, ranging from insurance and pension benefits to workplace safety requirements and protections from discrimination. Employee rights derived from these laws are addressed later in this chapter.

Many types of employees exist, and the meaning of each employee type carries with it certain benefits and protections under federal and state laws. A regular employee, sometimes referred to as a common law employee, is one who has a continuing relationship with the employer. To create a continuing relationship, it is not necessary for the work to be performed on a daily basis; rather, the work must be performed according to some frequency—for example, several days per month. Employees are generally classified as full-time if they work 30 hours per week or more, part-time if they work less than 30 hours per week. Many part-time employees are paid on an hourly basis and, under some state laws, may receive different benefits than full-time employees. At one time, employers used the term "permanent employee" interchangeably with "regular employee"; however, permanent employee has since lost favor, because it implies that an employee has some right to stay with the business or organization indefinitely without change. Absent the protections brought by unions, employees are generally considered employed at will, a concept addressed in more detail later in this chapter.

Leased employees, sometimes referred to as temporary employees, are employed by a service firm and are assigned to work at a business or an organization. Both the work product and the manner in which the work is performed by the leased employee are subject to the control of the business or organization. While leased employees may work at the premises and under the direction of a business or organization, they receive their paychecks and benefits from the service firm. Leased employees often perform work for a fixed period, typically on a specific project. Once the project is completed or the fixed period ends, the leased employee is assigned to work at another business or organization. Leased employees are expected to abide by the rules and regulations of the business or organization where they are assigned to work, but under many state laws the employees must look to the service firm and not to the client business or organization for benefits such as unemployment insurance compensation.

Not all individuals who work with businesses and organizations can be classified as employees. Many businesses and organizations use independent contractors to complete work. An **independent contractor** is an individual who agrees to perform certain work according to her own means, manner, and methods of performance. This personal control over means, manner, and methods does not mean that the business or organization does not exercise any form of control—merely that the amount of control is limited. In the employer-independent contractor relationship, the level of control exercised by a business or organization is limited to the results or products of the independent contractor's work. By contrast, in the employer-employee relationship, the employer has control over the means, manner, and methods of completing work, along with the end result or product of that work. Many independent contractors offer their services to multiple businesses and organizations, thereby solidifying their independence from any one employer.

A classification of worker that does not fall into the category of employee or independent contractor is a statutory employee. A **statutory employee** is one who has been designated by specific laws as subject to the tax withholding requirements imposed upon employers but who might not otherwise be considered an employee. The issue of control has no relevance to this definition, since those groups of workers who have been designated as statutory employees are categorized as such because of the specific type of work they perform. The benefits and protections offered to these statutory employees vary greatly. Groups of workers who have been classified as statutory employees under these laws include delivery drivers, life insurance agents, and traveling salespeople who sell business-to-business.

Many legal consequences result from the classification of workers as employees, independent contractors, or statutory employees. Whether a given worker receives certain benefits and protections rests largely on her classification. While some consistency exists within federal law, contrasts with state law are not unusual. For example, a worker may be properly classified as not an employee pursuant to the tax requirements of federal law but be classified as an employee under state law for workers' compensation or unemployment insurance purposes. As a general rule, the strictest law is the law that takes precedence over the other laws in any given situation. Accordingly, it is important that each employer becomes familiar with the variations among federal, state, and local laws when classifying workers and providing benefits and protections.

Staffing

Staffing is the process of assigning workers to all positions in an organization. This process includes recruiting, selecting, training, orienting, and compensating members of an organization's workforce. Staffing also includes the processes of retaining employees and, where appropriate, terminating employees. Managers frequently are involved in some or all of this process.

Recruitment

Recruitment is the process of finding employees for an organization. The recruitment process entails a number of steps. After developing a job description and determining that a position should be filled, the recruitment process starts. Multiple recruitment sources exist for each position. Internal candidates may be available within the organization, assuming that the organization adheres to a policy of promoting from within. In order for internal candidates to apply for a position, the job must be posted. Job posting may consist of placing a job opening notice on a bulletin board in a central area frequented by employees or on a Web site available to employees, or by circulating the notice among staff.

Candidates may also be available from outside of the organization. Employers might look outside of the organization if special skills or qualifications are required for the position or if the organization is looking for new ideas and talents. Employers typically attract outside applicants through the use of advertisements, which are short summaries of the job description. Advertisements may be made in newspapers, on the radio or television, or on Web sites available to the general public, or they may be posted in newspapers and professional journals directed toward a particular group of readers.

The number of applicants any given advertisement may attract is unpredictable; therefore, employers may tap other sources as needed to attract applicants. Employers may contact public or private employment agencies, employment search firms, and educational institutions in search of applicants. They may also engage in field recruiting, a process in which the employer sends recruiters into the field—for example, to a college campus or a meeting of a professional association—in an effort to locate potential employees.

Selection

Selection is the process an organization engages in to choose who it will employ. The selection process may involve any or all of the following components: reference check, personal interview, background check, and selection test. In addition, federal law places requirements upon employers to verify the identity and employment authorization of every employee hired.

A reference check involves contacting a candidate's prior employers and others listed by the candidate to obtain

Figure 12–1 | **Reference check contact list**

Figure 12–1 | **Reference check contact list**

Applicant Name: _____

Professional/Personal Reference Name: _____

Date: _____

1. How well do you know the applicant?

2. When did the applicant work for/with you?

3. What work did the applicant perform?

4. Does anything in particular stand out about the applicant's work performance and/or work habits?

5. This position requires the applicant to be a member of a team (alternate: work independently). How well do you think the applicant will be a team player (alternate: will work independently)?*

6. The applicant will also be dealing with the public and providing customer service (alternate: solving complex problem situations). Have you observed how the applicant has dealt with the public or provided customer service (alternate: solved complex problem situations)?*

7. Given the chance, would you hire the applicant again?

8. Is there anything else you wish to add?

* Optional questions

information. A reference check serves two purposes: (1) to verify the information the candidate has represented about herself, and (2) to gather additional information about the candidate that may be useful in the hiring decision. The reference check should reveal the candidate's prior salary and position, the dates of employment, and the reason for leaving the previous job. An example of a reference check contact listing is shown in Figure 12–1. Unfortunately, many employers hesitate to release any information beyond simple factual data because they fear being the subject of a future lawsuit brought on defamation grounds.

A personal interview may take place at multiple stages before a candidate is hired. The screening interview occurs early in the selection process. The goal of this interview is to assess a candidate's basic qualifications and screen out those candidates who are not qualified. Additional interviews are conducted so that the employer can reach a final decision and offer a position. Interviews are important in the selection process because they allow the employer to assess the candidate beyond what is listed on paper, and because they allow the candidate to express her attitude toward the organization and the job in particular.

Background checks can take various forms, including examining a candidate's criminal or credit history and comparing it to the hiring standards that the organization maintains. Some background checks are more extensive, involving fingerprint, name, and tax checks. The extent of the background check depends on the level of employee hired: the higher the level of authority that will be granted to the new hire, the more extensive the background check

may be. Levels of authority that may require a more extensive background check include positions involving: (1) policy making, determining, and implementing; (2) higher-level management duties and assignments or major program responsibility; (3) independent spokespersons or non-management positions with authority for independent action; and (4) education, public contact, or other duties demanding the highest degree of public trust.

Background checks legitimately take place only with the candidate's consent, since the candidate must supply detailed information above and beyond what is contained in a resume in order for the background check to occur. Such information may include the candidate's date of birth or social security number. Background checks are most useful in excluding candidates from consideration for positions. An example of a form used to obtain consent to engage in a background check is illustrated in Figure 12–2.

Merely obtaining information from a background check does not necessarily satisfy the employer's obligations under the law. If the information obtained results in denial of employment, the employing organization must take additional action. For example, the Fair Credit Reporting Act (FCRA) requires the employing organization to inform the individual of the type of adverse information contained in the credit check report, provide a copy of the report and a description of the individual's rights under the FCRA, and give the person an opportunity to contest the information. If the organization is a public institution subject to the Privacy Act of 1974, the employee who is selected for the position may obtain a copy of her background investigation report.

Selection tests are administered to help employers place applicants in suitable jobs. Examples include skill tests, job knowledge tests, medical exams, drug tests, mental ability tests, physical abilities tests, and personality tests. They often are administered at different stages of the selection process. Some tests, such as skill tests or job knowledge tests, may be conducted during the early stage of the process. Others, such as medical exams or drug tests, may be administered at the latter end of the process because of the cost the employer must bear.

Selection tests are fraught with legal and ethical concerns and have been subject to great criticism and scrutiny. Organizations that employ selection tests should ensure that these tests are fully validated and demonstrate a relationship to successful performance before administering them. If used carefully and with due consideration for the person being tested, selection tests are helpful devices in the selection process.

Armed with the information gained via the above methods, the employer is in the position to compare each candidate against the pre-established selection criteria and determine who should be offered a position with the organization. Once the position is offered and accepted, the

Figure 12–2 | **Consent to engage in background check**

Selection for an interview will be based on the candidate's employment experience, educational background, other relevant information and the needs of the organization. As part of the selection process, a preliminary background check will be made with your consent. Please provide the following information:

Name (List all names used): _____

_____ Social Security Number: _____

Date of Birth: _____ Place of Birth: _____

Driver's License No. _____ State: _____

Current Residence: _____

Phone No.: _____ (Home) _____ (Work)

List any other states or countries of former residence: _____

_____

Any documents submitted by you will be maintained by the organization, will not be returned, and will not be available for review. If you receive an appointment to the position, all information submitted will be incorporated into your personnel file. By signing below, you acknowledge that you have reviewed this document and consent to a preliminary background check, including a criminal record search.

_____
Signature

_____
Date

employer is required by federal law to verify the identity and employment authorization of every employee hired.[2] This is accomplished through the use of the federal Employment Eligibility Verification form, commonly known as the I-9 form. An example of the I-9 form is illustrated in Figure 12–3.

Compensation

Compensation refers to the wages, salaries, incentives, and supplemental benefits provided to staff. A well-developed and administered compensation program can be effective in supporting an organization's goals and objectives because it influences employee recruitment, satisfaction, motivation, and retention.

As a general rule, the term wages refers to an hourly rate of pay and is the basis used for many blue-collar workers. Wage-earning employees ordinarily are paid only for the hours they actually work or for the quantity of work produced. If they work beyond the scheduled number of hours, wage-earning employees frequently receive overtime or call-in pay.

The term salary refers to a rate of pay given on a weekly, monthly, or yearly schedule and is the basis used for white-collar workers. Salaried employees are paid the same amount each pay period regardless of any modest difference in total working hours from one pay period to another or in the quantity of work performed. Salaried employees are subject to fewer cumbersome work rules, such as the use of time clocks, or cumbersome work restrictions, such as the docking of pay for attendance problems.

Incentives refer to the additional compensation an employee receives beyond the base salary or wage. Incentives often take the form of commissions, bonuses, or stock options. Incentives pose both positive and negative points to the employee. On the positive side, incentives do not inflate the salary structure and can be tied to profits and revenues. On the negative side, incentives can cause financial insecurity for employees and are not tied to employee benefits such as pensions and insurance.

Supplemental benefits are services and programs offered to employees beyond the base salary or wage. They include legally required benefits, such as social security and workers' compensation payments, and optional benefits, such as pensions and health insurance. Employees may pay a portion of the cost of these benefits, but, typically, the majority of the cost is borne by the employer.

Orientation and Training

Orientation is a program designed to help acclimate new employees to an organization and allow for a productive beginning on the job. Training refers to those experiences designed to further the learning of behaviors that contribute to the organization's goals. Often, both concepts are employed together in a new employee orientation and training program.

An effective new orientation and training program generally has several goals. First, the organization wants the new employee to learn about its mission, vision, goals, and

Figure 12–3 | Federal Employment Eligibility Verification form (I-9 form)

Department of Homeland Security
U.S. Citizenship and Immigration Services

OMB No. 1615-0047; Expires 03/31/07
Employment Eligibility Verification

INSTRUCTIONS
PLEASE READ ALL INSTRUCTIONS CAREFULLY BEFORE COMPLETING THIS FORM.

Anti-Discrimination Notice. It is illegal to discriminate against any individual (other than an alien not authorized to work in the U.S.) in hiring, discharging, or recruiting or referring for a fee because of that individual's national origin or citizenship status. It is illegal to discriminate against work eligible individuals. Employers **CANNOT** specify which document(s) they will accept from an employee. The refusal to hire an individual because of a future expiration date may also constitute illegal discrimination.

Section 1- Employee.
All employees, citizens and noncitizens, hired after November 6, 1986, must complete Section 1 of this form at the time of hire, which is the actual beginning of employment. **The employer is responsible for ensuring that Section 1 is timely and properly completed.**

Preparer/Translator Certification. The Preparer/Translator Certification must be completed if Section 1 is prepared by a person other than the employee. A preparer/translator may be used only when the employee is unable to complete Section 1 on his/her own. However, the employee must still sign Section 1 personally.

Section 2 - Employer.
For the purpose of completing this form, the term "employer" includes those recruiters and referrers for a fee who are agricultural associations, agricultural employers or farm labor contractors.

Employers must complete Section 2 by examining evidence of identity and employment eligibility within three (3) business days of the date employment begins. If employees are authorized to work, but are unable to present the required document(s) within three business days, they must present a receipt for the application of the document(s) within three business days and the actual document(s) within ninety (90) days. However, if employers hire individuals for a duration of less than three business days, Section 2 must be completed at the time employment begins. **Employers must record: 1)** document title; **2)** issuing authority; **3)** document number, **4)** expiration date, if any; and **5)** the date employment begins. Employers must sign and date the certification. Employees must present original documents. Employers may, but are not required to, photocopy the document(s) presented. These photocopies may only be used for the verification process and must be retained with the I-9. **However, employers are still responsible for completing the I-9.**

Section 3 - Updating and Reverification.
Employers must complete Section 3 when updating and/or reverifying the I-9. Employers must reverify employment eligibility of their employees on or before the expiration date recorded in Section 1. Employers **CANNOT** specify which document(s) they will accept from an employee.

- If an employee's name has changed at the time this form is being updated/reverified, complete Block A.
- If an employee is rehired within three (3) years of the date this form was originally completed and the employee is still eligible to be employed on the same basis as previously indicated on this form (updating), complete Block B and the signature block.
- If an employee is rehired within three (3) years of the date this form was originally completed and the employee's work authorization has expired **or** if a current employee's work authorization is about to expire (reverification), complete Block B and:

- examine any document that reflects that the employee is authorized to work in the U.S. (see List A **or** C),
- record the document title, document number and expiration date (if any) in Block C, and
- complete the signature block.

Photocopying and Retaining Form I-9. A blank I-9 may be reproduced, provided both sides are copied. The Instructions must be available to all employees completing this form. Employers must retain completed I-9s for three (3) years after the date of hire or one (1) year after the date employment ends, whichever is later.

For more detailed information, you may refer to the Department of Homeland Security (DHS) Handbook for Employers, (Form M-274). You may obtain the handbook at your local U.S. Citizenship and Immigration Services (USCIS) office.

Privacy Act Notice. The authority for collecting this information is the Immigration Reform and Control Act of 1986, Pub. L. 99-603 (8 USC 1324a).

This information is for employers to verify the eligibility of individuals for employment to preclude the unlawful hiring, or recruiting or referring for a fee, of aliens who are not authorized to work in the United States.

This information will be used by employers as a record of their basis for determining eligibility of an employee to work in the United States. The form will be kept by the employer and made available for inspection by officials of the U.S. Immigration and Customs Enforcement, Department of Labor and Office of Special Counsel for Immigration Related Unfair Employment Practices.

Submission of the information required in this form is voluntary. However, an individual may not begin employment unless this form is completed, since employers are subject to civil or criminal penalties if they do not comply with the Immigration Reform and Control Act of 1986.

Reporting Burden. We try to create forms and instructions that are accurate, can be easily understood and which impose the least possible burden on you to provide us with information. Often this is difficult because some immigration laws are very complex. Accordingly, the reporting burden for this collection of information is computed as follows: **1)** learning about this form, 5 minutes; **2)** completing the form, 5 minutes; and **3)** assembling and filing (recordkeeping) the form, 5 minutes, for an average of 15 minutes per response. If you have comments regarding the accuracy of this burden estimate, or suggestions for making this form simpler, you can write to U.S. Citizenship and Immigration Services, Regulatory Management Division, 111 Massachuetts Avenue, N.W., Washington, DC 20529. OMB No. 1615-0047.

NOTE: This is the 1991 edition of the Form I-9 that has been rebranded with a current printing date to reflect the recent transition from the INS to DHS and its components.

EMPLOYERS MUST RETAIN COMPLETED FORM I-9
PLEASE DO NOT MAIL COMPLETED FORM I-9 TO ICE OR USCIS

Form I-9 (Rev. 05/31/05)Y

Figure 12–3 | *(continued)*

Department of Homeland Security
U.S. Citizenship and Immigration Services

OMB No. 1615-0047; Expires 03/31/07

Employment Eligibility Verification

Please read instructions carefully before completing this form. The instructions must be available during completion of this form. ANTI-DISCRIMINATION NOTICE: It is illegal to discriminate against work eligible individuals. Employers CANNOT specify which document(s) they will accept from an employee. The refusal to hire an individual because of a future expiration date may also constitute illegal discrimination.

Section 1. Employee Information and Verification. To be completed and signed by employee at the time employment begins.

Print Name: Last	First	Middle Initial	Maiden Name

Address *(Street Name and Number)*   Apt. #   Date of Birth *(month/day/year)*

City   State   Zip Code   Social Security #

I am aware that federal law provides for imprisonment and/or fines for false statements or use of false documents in connection with the completion of this form.

I attest, under penalty of perjury, that I am (check one of the following):

☐ A citizen or national of the United States
☐ A Lawful Permanent Resident (Alien #) A _____
☐ An alien authorized to work until _____
(Alien # or Admission #) _____

Employee's Signature   Date *(month/day/year)*

Preparer and/or Translator Certification. *(To be completed and signed if Section 1 is prepared by a person other than the employee.) I attest, under penalty of perjury, that I have assisted in the completion of this form and that to the best of my knowledge the information is true and correct.*

Preparer's/Translator's Signature   Print Name

Address *(Street Name and Number, City, State, Zip Code)*   Date *(month/day/year)*

Section 2. Employer Review and Verification. To be completed and signed by employer. Examine one document from List A OR examine one document from List B and one from List C, as listed on the reverse of this form, and record the title, number and expiration date, if any, of the document(s).

List A	OR	**List B**	**AND**	**List C**
Document title:				
Issuing authority:				
Document #:				
Expiration Date *(if any)*:				
Document #:				
Expiration Date *(if any)*:				

CERTIFICATION - Iattest, under penalty of perjury, that I have examined the document(s) presented by the above-named employee, that the above-listed document(s) appear to be genuine and to relate to the employee named, that the employee began employment on *(month/day/year)* _____ and that to the best of my knowledge the employee is eligible to work in the United States. (State employment agencies may omit the date the employee began employment.)

Signature of Employer or Authorized Representative	Print Name	Title
Business or Organization Name	Address *(Street Name and Number, City, State, Zip Code)*	Date *(month/day/year)*

Section 3. Updating and Reverification. To be completed and signed by employer.

A. New Name *(if applicable)*	B. Date of Rehire *(month/day/year) (if applicable)*

C. If employee's previous grant of work authorization has expired, provide the information below for the document that establishes current employment eligibility.

Document Title: _____ Document #: _____ Expiration Date (if any): _____

I attest, under penalty of perjury, that to the best of my knowledge, this employee is eligible to work in the United States, and if the employee presented document(s), the document(s) I have examined appear to be genuine and to relate to the individual.

Signature of Employer or Authorized Representative	Date *(month/day/year)*

NOTE: This is the 1991 edition of the Form I-9 that has been rebranded with a current printing date to reflect the recent transition from the INS to DHS and its components.

Form I-9 (Rev. 05/31/05)Y Page 2

Figure 12–3 | *(continued)*

LISTS OF ACCEPTABLE DOCUMENTS

LIST A		LIST B		LIST C
Documents that Establish Both Identity and Employment Eligibility	**OR**	**Documents that Establish Identity**	**AND**	**Documents that Establish Employment Eligibility**

LIST A — Documents that Establish Both Identity and Employment Eligibility

1. U.S. Passport (unexpired or expired)

2. Certificate of U.S. Citizenship *(Form N-560 or N-561)*

3. Certificate of Naturalization *(Form N-550 or N-570)*

4. Unexpired foreign passport, with *I-551 stamp or* attached *Form I-94* indicating unexpired employment authorization

5. Permanent Resident Card or Alien Registration Receipt Card with photograph *(Form I-151 or I-551)*

6. Unexpired Temporary Resident Card *(Form I-688)*

7. Unexpired Employment Authorization Card *(Form I-688A)*

8. Unexpired Reentry Permit *(Form I-327)*

9. Unexpired Refugee Travel Document *(Form 1-571)*

10. Unexpired Employment Authorization Document issued by DHS that contains a photograph *(Form I-688B)*

OR

LIST B — Documents that Establish Identity

1. Driver's license or ID card issued by a state or outlying possession of the United States provided it contains a photograph or information such as name, date of birth, gender, height, eye color and address

2. ID card issued by federal, state or local government agencies or entities, provided it contains a photograph or information such as name, date of birth, gender, height, eye color and address

3. School ID card with a photograph

4. Voter's registration card

5. U.S. Military card or draft record

6. Military dependent's ID card

7. U.S. Coast Guard Merchant Mariner Card

8. Native American tribal document

9. Driver's license issued by a Canadian government authority

For persons under age 18 who are unable to present a document listed above:

10. School record or report card

11. Clinic, doctor or hospital record

12. Day-care or nursery school record

AND

LIST C — Documents that Establish Employment Eligibility

1. U.S. social security card issued by the Social Security Administration *(other than a card stating it is not valid for employment)*

2. Certification of Birth Abroad issued by the Department of State *(Form FS-545 or Form DS-1350)*

3. Original or certified copy of a birth certificate issued by a state, county, municipal authority or outlying possession of the United States bearing an official seal

4. Native American tribal document

5. U.S. Citizen ID Card *(Form I-197)*

6. ID Card for use of Resident Citizen in the United States *(Form I-179)*

7. Unexpired employment authorization document issued by DHS *(other than those listed under List A)*

Illustrations of many of these documents appear in Part 8 of the Handbook for Employers (M-274)

structure. It also tries to inform the new employee of the organization's general employment policies, accepted methods of communication, expectations for conduct, and confidentiality needs. Additionally, the employee learns how she fits within the organization and the department in which she is placed. Finally, the employee is provided specific job training, designed to expose the employee to policies and procedures necessary for the task, the work flow, and the available resources.

Orientation and training programs differ by organization. Some orientation and training programs last less than one day, while other programs are conducted over several weeks or months. During orientation, the employee receives information by way of group meetings and discussions, handbooks, videotapes, and tours, or a combination of these and other methods. Entrance interviews may be included, allowing the employer to evaluate the new employee's expectations against the employer's design of the position.

During training, the employee is presented with new experiences designed to make her competent to perform the tasks that may be assigned to her. This training may be skills training, involving a short-term focus and technical in nature, or career development training, involving a future-oriented focus and less technical in nature. The training may occur on the job site, at off-site conferences, or through computer-assisted instruction. Whichever method is employed, the employee learns behaviors that contribute to the organization's goals.

Training needs are not exclusive to new employees but are also required for established employees who must adapt to new technologies and other changes in the workplace. Organizations engage frequently in numerous educational and training opportunities for their staff. The types of training opportunities are as varied as types of employers. Opportunities for skill development and professional growth may be provided through in-house training, as well as access to local training events and distance education. Other opportunities may include providing paid time to attend meetings of professional associations or using a cooperative private television network to view programs of specific interest.

Traditionally, the process of identifying training needs has been the province of a manager or supervisor, with limited responsibilities placed upon the employee to identify or take responsibility for upgrading her knowledge, skills, and abilities. As the business and health care environments have changed, this traditional process has lost favor and responsibilities have shifted to a more shared approach. This shared approach requires the manager and supervisor to set clear expectations and standards for the employee to meet, and it requires the employee to commit to upgrading her knowledge, skills, and abilities so that she remains employable. This partnership approach recognizes that both sides possess a vested interest in maximizing employee performance and provides both the individual and the organization with a greater ability to adjust to the rapid pace of change and the increased complexities of modern society.

Retention

With so much effort, time, and money invested in hiring, orienting, and training an individual, it is in an organization's best interest to take steps to keep the individual on staff. **Retention** refers to the ability of an organization to retain employees. Central to retention efforts are organizational programs that foster personal loyalty, professionalism, high morale, and organizational pride.

One of the most effective means to improve employee retention is to establish and maintain a recognition and reward program. **Recognition programs** provide formal acknowledgment and approval of an employee's efforts and accomplishments. **Reward programs** provide formal compensation in return for an employee's service or merit. Recognition or rewards may be provided for many reasons, including reaching a professional milestone, meeting or exceeding a goal, completing a difficult assignment, or reaching a sales target. These programs may take a public or private form and may occur either at fixed times, such as during an annual awards ceremony, or on an impromptu basis. Implementation of these programs demonstrates that the organization values the employee because of her efforts or contributions and may result in improving employee morale.

Another effective means to improve employee retention is to foster a learning environment in the workplace. This learning environment may range from formal training sessions to on-the-job education to employing formal career-development strategies. A learning environment provides employees with an opportunity to improve as individuals and members of a team. By enlarging their knowledge, skills, and abilities, employees may achieve and maintain high levels of performance and strengthen the organization as a whole. Organizations that integrate learning into their culture emphasize that they value employees by investing the organization's time and money in the employee's future, thereby fostering personal loyalty and organizational pride.

Compensation is a key factor in employee retention. Organizations must provide competitive salaries and benefits to their workers or risk losing them. In addition to setting fair salaries, wages, and benefits when employees initially join the organization, managers should establish mechanisms to increase compensation over time. Organizational policies frequently indicate when employees will be eligible for an increase or a raise and how those increases or raises are earned and calculated. Additionally, organizational policies may address how a manager might respond to an employee who is considering accepting a position elsewhere by providing a financial incentive to stay with the organization.

Programs that recognize the balance between home and work life are often used by organizations as a means to increase employee retention. These programs may address work schedules, such as flexible workdays or hours, or the work environment, such as working from home or at off-site centers. They may focus on goodwill gestures, such as providing clothing with the organization's logo to employees, scheduling an organization's holiday parties during regular work hours instead of on the employee's personal time, or providing a certificate or extra time off for a job well done. Programs such as these allow current and future employees to differentiate between employers and organizations and identify those employers and organizations with whom they want to work. Such gestures set organizations apart from one another and instill organizational loyalty and pride.

Separation

Whether because of new opportunities, retirement, conflicts within a team, department, or organization, corporate downsizing, the results of disciplinary action, or for a multitude of other reasons, individuals will end their employment with an organization. The process of ending employment is referred to as **separation**.

While the reasons for separation may vary, they generally fall into one of two categories: voluntary or involuntary. Voluntary separation involves the employee's resignation from a position or the expiration of a fixed term of employ-

ment. As the term implies, these types of separations are often the result of employee choice. Involuntary separations involve the employer's decision to end a person's employment and are the result of the employer's choice.

Whether the separation is voluntary or involuntary, good practice suggests that the employer provide the employee with a separation package. This package may address severance pay, explanation of benefits, status of insurance, access to retirement funds, restrictions on the exiting employee—such as the existence of a non-compete agreement—and other issues of importance to both the employer and employee. Simultaneously, the employee should return to the employer any equipment, organizational property, and identification badges. Some organizations condition return of these items before release of the employee's final paycheck. Additionally, employers may conduct an exit interview. Often attended by a member of the organization's human resources staff, exit interviews are meetings between the departing employee and her supervisor. They are designed to solicit information from the departing employee that may be used to improve the organization. Questions frequently used in exit interviews are presented in Figure 12–4.

Figure 12–4 | Questions frequently asked in exit interviews

Nature of Work

1. Did the job meet your expectations? Did significant differences exist between what you perceived the job to be and what it was?
2. What elements of your position did you like and why?
3. What elements of your position did you dislike and why? What did you like least about working here?
4. Did you feel your training and orientation for this position were sufficient? What three training areas would have increased your success in the job?
5. Were your training, skills, and experience utilized? Did you feel you used your skills to your highest potential in this position?
6. Did you have a clear understanding of the organization's mission and your role in the operations of the organization?

Supervision

1. How did you view your manager? How much of a factor was your supervision in your decision to resign?
2. Were you provided adequate instruction and/or proper equipment to perform your job duties in a satisfactory manner?
3. Were sufficient duties delegated to you?
4. Were you told when you did things well or needed improvement?
5. Were you counseled adequately on performance? Did you feel that your job performance appraisals were a fair and accurate representation of you work?

Advancement and Compensation

1. How do you feel about the promotional opportunities in this organization and your personal chances for promotion?
2. Did this job fit with your career plans?
3. Was the compensation fair for the level of responsibility? Rate your benefits.
4. Were salary increases keyed to performance?
5. How did your compensation compare with salaries elsewhere?

Reason For Leaving

1. If you are beginning another job, what attracts you most to this new job? What does your new job have that your current one lacks?
2. Is this new job a promotion? With higher pay?
3. What was the major factor influencing you to leave this organization?
4. What actions, if any, could this organization have taken to influence you not to leave this organization?

Employee Rights

Important to any discussion involving management is the issue of employee rights. Legislation that affects the working relationship between employers and employees has a great impact on human resource management. A comprehensive list of the federal laws regulating the workforce is contained in Table 12–1. Several of the most significant laws affecting the employer-employee relationship are discussed in this section.

Overview

Traditionally, all employees were considered at-will employees. **At-will employment** is an employment arrangement that allows the employer to terminate the employee at any time and allows the employee to leave the employer at any time. Under this arrangement, the employer may hire, fire, promote, and demote any employee it chooses as long as there is no employment contract (such as a labor agreement) or federal, state, or local law to the contrary. This means that employers may have a good reason, a bad

Table 12–1   Federal Employment Laws
Age Discrimination in Employment Act (ADEA)
Americans with Disabilities Act (ADA)
Civil Rights Act of 1964
Davis Bacon Act
Drug-Free Workplace Act
Employee Polygraph Protection Act
Employment Retirement Income Security Act (ERISA)
Equal Employment Opportunity (EEO) Act and implementing guidelines concerning sexual harassment and employee selection practices
Equal Pay Act
Fair Credit Reporting Act
Fair Labor Standards Act
Family and Medical Leave Act (FMLA)
Immigration Reform and Control Act (IRCA)
National Labor Relations Act
Medical and Health Care Continuation Act
Newborns and Mother's Health Protection Act
Occupational Safety and Health (OSH) Act
Older Workers' Benefit Protection Act
Pregnancy Discrimination Act
Privacy Act
Rehabilitation Act of 1973
Vietnam–Era Veterans Readjustment Assistance Act (VEVRAA)
Worker Adjustment and Retraining Notification (WARN) Act

Source: Mattingly, R. (1997). *Management of health information: Functions and applications*. Albany, NY: Delmar.

reason, or no reason to hire, fire, promote, or demote an employee, as long as such action does not violate the law. Some states have placed restrictions on the employment-at-will doctrine, asserting that phrases contained in an employer's handbook may create an implied contract of employment, thereby limiting the employer's right to hire, fire, promote, and demote.

Following the advent of labor unions, Congress passed the National Labor Relations Act. Also known as the Wagner Act, this law guarantees workers broad rights to organize and bargain collectively with their employer. It also provides workers with rights to engage in concerted efforts and activities such as strikes and picket lines. The act bans employment discrimination to discourage unionization, employer domination of unions, and an employer's refusal to bargain in good faith with a union.

Once considered unusual, the health care field has seen an increasing development in union activity. Some commentators directly relate this rise in union activity to a combination of the cost containment measures employed by hospitals and the decrease in reimbursement brought about by various prospective payment systems. In dealing with both issues, many hospitals have reduced the number of staff they employ and have correspondingly increased their patient-staff ratio. Others have focused on the lack of open communication by hospital management about noneconomic matters (e.g., an institution's goals or plans for change). In those instances where hospital management has not responded to staff complaints about dissatisfaction in the quality of work life, or has failed to communicate widely with staff, unions have filled the void.

Several civil rights laws enacted on the federal level have broadened the protections afforded employees. For example, Title VII of the Civil Rights Act of 1964 bans discrimination in compensation, terms, and conditions of employment based on race, religion, color, sex, or national origin. The Equal Pay Act prohibits an employer from paying the workers of one sex less than the rate paid to the opposite sex for jobs substantially similar or identical in skill, effort, and responsibility and performed under similar working conditions. The Sexual Harassment Guidelines issued pursuant to Title VII require the employer to maintain a sexual harassment-free work environment. Under the Family and Medical Leave Act (FMLA), employers must offer to their employees up to a total of 12 weeks of leave during a 12-month period for the birth of a child; the placement of a child for adoption or foster care; a serious health condition of the employee; or to care for a spouse, child, or parent with a serious health condition. The Age Discrimination in Employment Act (ADEA) bars employment discrimination against persons aged 40 or older with respect to hiring, promotion, demotion, compensation, transfer, and other terms and conditions of employment. The Americans with Disabilities Act (ADA) bars employment discrimination against qualified individuals with a disability and requires employers to provide qualified individuals with reasonable accommodations to assist them in performing the essential functions of the job, absent a financial hardship to the employer. The Worker Adjustment and Retraining Notification (WARN) Act requires employers to provide 60 days of warning before closing offices or beginning massive layoffs. Finally, the Employee Retirement Income Security Act (ERISA) prevents an employer from discharging an employee who would otherwise attain immediate vested pension rights or who exercised her rights under ERISA.

Employment protections are also provided under the Occupational Safety and Health (OSH) Act. This federal act sets mandatory standards for safety and health for all employees in general industry, maritime operations, construction, and agriculture. It requires employers to operate a place of employment that is free from recognized hazards that are likely to cause serious injury or a fatality.

Employment protections may also be provided under federal laws not traditionally targeted toward employment. For example, the Consumer Credit Protection Act protects workers whose earnings have been subjected to a wage garnishment from being fired. Similarly, an employee who exercises a public duty, such as attending federal jury duty, is protected from firing by the Jury System Improvement Act. Both the Federal Railroad Safety Act and the Federal Employer's Liability Act prohibit employers from firing an employee who files a complaint, furnishes facts, or testifies about a railroad accident. Finally, the Uniformed Services Employment and Reemployment Rights Act (USERRA) and the Military Selective Service Act offer protections to veterans and military personnel who are called up for short-term emergency duty or extended reserve duty.

Employee protections may also arise as a result of actions by the head of the executive branch. The president is the head of the executive branch in the federal system, while the governor is the head of the executive branch in the state system. Executive orders interpret, implement, or provide administrative effect to a provision of the constitution or law. Executive orders gain the effect of law after they are published in the *Federal Register,* in the case of the federal system, or in a comparable publication on the state level. At the federal level, Executive Order 11246 bars discrimination in federal government employment and mandates each executive department and agency to maintain equal employment opportunity programs.[3]

A broad range of laws and regulations also exist at the state and local levels. Laws and regulations govern wage and hour issues, workers' compensation, and unemployment insurance. These laws and regulations also commonly influence policy decisions within an organization. Some states have chosen to create their own civil rights and occupational safety and health enforcement operations to supple-

ment federal coverage. For instance, some states protect workers from discharge for refusing to violate criminal laws—such as participating in illegal schemes—or for observing the general public policy of a state—such as refusing to perform unethical research. Lastly, local governments may pass ordinances influencing the work environment, such as living wage laws that require employers to pay employees more than the federal minimum wage.

As shown above, no one law encompasses all of the rights afforded to an employee. In many instances, multiple laws may offer protection on the same subject matter. For example, laws at the federal, state, and local levels may all offer civil rights protections to employees in a given locality. Or several laws at one level of government may cover the same subject matter—for example, multiple federal laws that provide protections to veterans. As a general rule, the strictest law is the law that takes precedence over the other laws. Accordingly, managers and supervisors must be mindful of employment laws at the federal and state levels as well as those in their local business community.

Employment Law Application

Employers who are committed to complying fully with employment laws ensure equal opportunity and safe workplace conditions for both job applicants and current employees. Applying these laws in the work context requires an understanding of the doctrines and principles involved. The following paragraphs address the major employee protections laws found in the modern work context.

Discrimination Virtually all private employers, employment agencies, and labor organizations in the United States are affected by Title VII of the Civil Rights Act and its subsequent amendments, the Equal Employment Opportunity (EEO) Act and the Civil Rights Act of 1991. These acts protect current and potential employees from discrimination throughout all stages of employment: recruiting, selecting, compensating, orienting, training, disciplining, and discharging. Such discrimination may be based on gender or marital status; race or color; religion or national origin; age; or disability or physical handicap. The principles of nondiscrimination were codified into law so that people would be considered on the basis of individual capacities and not on the basis of any characteristics generally attributable to a group.

Sex Discrimination Discrimination based on gender or marital status is commonly referred to as sex discrimination. Sex discrimination may take the form of unequal pay for equal work, sexual harassment, or discrimination with regard to childbirth leave or pregnancy-related conditions, as shown in Table 12–2. Prohibitions against sex discrimination are meant to stop hiring, promotion, and work practices that are based on gender stereotypes. Wage inequities between the genders for equal work are prohibited by Title VII, the Equal Pay Act, and the Fair Labor Standards Act. All three

Table 12–2	Forms of Sex Discrimination
Unequal pay for equal work
Sexual harassment
Discrimination in childbirth leave
Discrimination in pregnancy-related conditions

laws apply to jobs that are considered **substantially equal**, meaning they are performed under similar working conditions and require equal skill, effort, and responsibility. Wage differences are allowed where they reflect a legitimate, pre-established seniority system, merit system, or system that measures earnings by quantity or quality of production. For example, a health care organization hired six male lab technicians in year one and four female lab technicians in year five. Although all 10 lab technicians currently perform the same job, the 6 male lab technicians receive greater hourly pay rates than the 4 female lab technicians because of their seniority and number of years with the organization.

Sexual discrimination also encompasses sexual harassment. **Sexual harassment** refers to unwelcome sexual advances, requests for sexual favors, and verbal or physical conduct of a sexual nature made in return for job benefits, promotions, or continued employment. This type of sexual harassment is considered **quid pro quo** sexual harassment, or "this for that." Sexual harassment may also arise in a hostile working environment. In a **hostile work environment**, the unwelcome sexual conduct must be sufficiently pervasive or severe enough to alter the terms or conditions of employment. Examples of a hostile work environment include sharing sexually explicit photos, making sex-related or gender-demeaning jokes, or repeatedly requesting dates from a person who clearly is not interested. One instance of the above examples is generally not enough to be considered a hostile work environment; rather, a combination or repetition of these and other examples may bring a workplace to the level of a hostile work environment. Claims of sexual harassment may be based on either the quid pro quo or hostile work environment, or both. Furthermore, sexual harassment can occur between people of different or the same genders.

Employers seeking to prevent and eliminate sexual harassment can do so by developing a comprehensive policy, publicizing that policy, investigating any complaints promptly and adequately, and taking action appropriate to the situation. Practical actions, which include disseminating written materials that indicate that sexual harassment of any kind is not tolerated; training managers, supervisors, and employees in identifying sexual harassment; and providing mechanisms to address complaints in confidence and without reprisals, offer support to the premise that an employer or organization is complying with the law.

Another form of sexual discrimination involves childbirth leave or pregnancy-related conditions. The Pregnancy Discrimination Act bars discrimination based on pregnancy, childbirth, and related medical conditions. The Family Medical Leave Act (FMLA) allows an employee to take up to 12 weeks of unpaid leave in any 12-month period for the birth, adoption, or foster care of a child; to care for a child, spouse, or parent with a serious health condition; or to recuperate from a serious health condition that makes it impossible to work. A **serious health condition** is any injury, illness, impairment, or physical or mental condition requiring either inpatient care at a hospital, hospice, or residential medical care facility, or continuing treatment by a health care provider. Employers are permitted under the FMLA to seek medical certification concerning the need for leave when the leave request involves a serious health condition. Whereas the Pregnancy Discrimination Act applies only to women, the FMLA applies to both women and men.

Racial, Religious, and National Origin Discrimination Discrimination based on race or color constitutes unlawful discrimination under Title VII of the Civil Rights Act. Immutable characteristics of race, such as skin color, hair texture, or certain facial features, cannot be used by an employer to consider job applicants or current employees in any stage, term, condition, or privilege of employment. Such discrimination may take many forms, including harassment. Examples of harassment include the use of ethnic slurs, racial jokes, offensive or derogatory comments, or other verbal or physical conduct based on an individual's race or color. Title VII also bars discrimination based on a condition that predominantly affects one race, absent a showing of a business necessity and a relationship to a job. For example, sickle cell anemia is a condition that occurs predominantly in African Americans. Without a business necessity and a relationship to the job, an employer's policy excluding individuals with sickle cell anemia from the workplace would violate Title VII.

Religious discrimination in employment is barred pursuant to the provisions of Title VII, making it illegal to consider adherence to a particular faith the basis on which to deny an applicant a job. Furthermore, Title VII requires employers to reasonably accommodate the religious practices of employees and job applicants unless doing so causes an undue hardship. Religious practices or beliefs include moral or ethical beliefs concerning what is right or wrong that are sincerely held with the strength of traditional religious views. The employer may not require the individual employee or applicant to establish or prove the truth, validity, or reasonableness of her religious beliefs; rather, the employer must attempt to provide reasonable accommodation if the beliefs are sincerely held by the employee or applicant. The burden of identifying that a conflict exists between the employee's or applicant's religious beliefs and a job requirement rests on the employee or applicant. For example, an employer who is notified by an employee that her religion requires her to worship on workdays must make reasonable accommodation for the employee's religious belief unless to do so would impose an undue hardship.

Title VII of the Civil Rights Act bars discrimination based on national origin, including birthplace, ancestry, culture, or linguistic characteristics common to a specific ethnic group. Such discrimination may include denying employment based on an individual's accent or manner of speaking or harassment through the use of ethnic slurs and other verbal or physical conduct relating to an individual's national origin. Furthermore, the Immigration Reform and Control Act prohibits discrimination based on whether the person is or is not a U.S. citizen. Together, these two laws serve as the basis for protecting workers from discrimination based on national origin. For example, a rule requiring that employees speak only English on the job may violate Title VII unless the employer shows that the requirement is necessary for conducting business. An employer who conducts business with the public may, however, require employees to be fluent in English so that they can interact with customers. The difference is that English is not mandated as the *only* language an employee may speak on the job.

Age Discrimination As with the examples of discrimination previously addressed, federal law offers protections to workers who are 40 years of age or older. The Age Discrimination in Employment Act (ADEA) bars discrimination because of a person's age and applies during both the employment and preemployment stages, making it unlawful to include age preferences, limitations, or specifications in job notices or advertisements. As a general premise, an employer may not make employment decisions in which the employee's age is a substantial factor. This prohibition is qualified, however, since the ADEA allows employers to consider age if they can show that age is a bona fide occupational qualification reasonably necessary to the normal operation of the particular business.

The Older Workers Benefit Protection Act (OWBPA) bars discrimination in benefits because of a person's age. The OWBPA requires employers who request employees to sign releases or waivers in connection with an offer of early retirement to do so in writing, to provide the employee sufficient time to consider the offer, and to provide the employee with the opportunity to seek advice from a lawyer. Further, the OWBPA provides the employee a time window in which to repudiate an offer of early retirement to which the employee had previously agreed. Large-scale early retirement programs and mass termination programs that involve releases or waivers require even more from employers; the employer must provide a longer time frame for employees to consider the agreement and provide those employees with data concerning the ages of all individuals in the same job classification who are not eligible for these programs.

Disability Discrimination Disability discrimination is covered under both the Rehabilitation Act and the Americans

Table 12–3	Application of the ADA
1. Determining qualification
2. Determining disability
3. Determining reasonable accommodation

with Disabilities Act (ADA). Both acts apply to employees, job applicants, customers, and other visitors to an organization, as well as to a wide range of businesses that serve the public. Within the employment context, these acts operate to protect employees and job applicants from discrimination based on a disability, the perception of a disability, or a past record of impairment, such as an illness that has been cured, controlled, or is in remission.

Evaluating the applicability of the ADA to a given situation is a three-step process: determining qualification, disability, and reasonable accommodation. This process is illustrated in Table 12–3. Initially, the employer must determine that the individual in question is qualified for a position. To be qualified, an individual must possess the requisite qualifications for the job. This means that the individual can perform the essential functions of the job with or without reasonable accommodation. Essential functions are those duties that are so fundamental to the position that the job cannot be performed adequately without them. Being qualified also means that the individual possesses the required education, degrees, certificates, professional licenses, and any other qualifications, along with the knowledge, skills, and abilities to perform the job. The burden rests on the individual to demonstrate that she possesses the requisite job qualifications and can perform the essential functions. If the individual cannot perform the essential functions or show that she possesses the requisite job qualifications, she is not considered qualified for the job and the ADA evaluation process ends.

It is not always apparent whether an individual will be able to perform the essential functions of the job. In those instances, medical information will be necessary. When requesting medical information, the employer should identify the essential functions of the job and provide a written list of those functions to the individual's health care provider. The individual's health care provider should respond with advice concerning whether the individual can perform the essential functions with or without reasonable accommodation. If the health care provider recommends reasonable accommodation, the health care provider should address specific suggestions for reasonable accommodation in the response.

After determining that the individual is qualified, the employer must decide whether the individual possesses a disability. **Disability** refers to a physical or mental impairment that substantially limits one or more of the major life activities of an employee; a record of such an impairment;

or being regarded as having such an impairment. Guidance for this determination can be obtained from the regulations of the Equal Employment Opportunity Commission (EEOC), which indicate that the issue turns on: (1) the nature and severity of the impairment; (2) the duration or expected duration of the impairment; and (3) the permanent or long-term impact of the impairment.[4] The EEOC has already established certain impairments as constituting disabilities, such as cerebral palsy, epilepsy, muscular dystrophy, mental retardation, and HIV/AIDS infection, to name only a few. The burden rests on the individual to show that her impairment is a disability. Not all impairments constitute disabilities since they may not substantially limit one or more major life activities. The employer may also consider corrective or mitigating measures when determining the existence of a disability. If there is no disability, the ADA evaluation process ends.

The most challenging aspect for an employer complying with the ADA is determining the reasonable accommodations for qualified individuals with disabilities without incurring undue hardship to the employer. A **reasonable accommodation** is any change in the work environment or in the manner in which things are customarily done that enables a qualified person with a disability to have equal employment opportunities. As with the question of disability, medical documentation may be necessary to determine the individual's functional limitations, if any. A **functional limitation** is a physical or mental limitation of a major life activity caused by a disability. An analysis of a functional limitation is important to the extent it bears a relationship with a workplace barrier. A **workplace barrier** is any workplace obstacle, whether physical or procedural, that prevents an employee from performing the duties of the job, whether those duties are considered essential or marginal. Work areas where the duties of the job are performed, such as an office or cubicle, should be examined for potential barriers. Non-work areas frequented by the employee, such as conference rooms, entryways, and lounges, should also be considered. If a workplace barrier exists that limits the individual's ability to perform the job, and a reasonable accommodation would overcome that barrier, the employer should provide the reasonable accommodation, absent undue hardship to the employer. **Undue hardship** refers to a specific accommodation that creates significant difficulty or expense for the employer. The employer may consider the nature and cost of the requested accommodation plus its impact on the employer's operations when considering the issue of undue hardship.

Under the ADA, an employer is not required to propose reasonable accommodations but only provide them, making the employee or job applicant bear the burden of suggesting workable and affordable changes to the workplace or hiring process. If it appears that the individual needs an accommodation, the employer may initiate the

Table 12–4 | Reasonable Accommodation Process

Submission of Request	From employee or job applicant identifying the disability and seeking an accommodation; employer confirms the request in writing
Determining an Individual's Qualification	Does the individual possess the requisite qualifications for the job? Can the individual perform the essential functions of the job?
Substantiating the Disability and Need for Accommodation	Does the individual have a physical or mental impairment that substantially limits a major life activity? Do the individual's functional limitations due to disability relate to a workplace barrier?
Potential Reasonable Accommodations	Employer and individual search for and evaluate potential reasonable accommodations
Select and Provide Reasonable Accommodations	Employer selects, funds, and provides reasonable accommodation; employer and individual monitor effectiveness of reasonable accommodation

process by asking whether the individual wants an accommodation. After receiving such a request, the employer should confirm the request in writing and make a determination whether the individual is both qualified and disabled before addressing the question of reasonable accommodation. The steps of the reasonable accommodation process are listed in Table 12–4.

The search for potential reasonable accommodations will vary based on the circumstances of the situation. In an ideal situation, the employer and the requesting individual work together to identify the potential reasonable accommodations. Reasonable accommodations generally do not include personal-use items since they are also required for the individual's use in a non-employment setting. Examples of personal-use items usually not considered as a reasonable accommodation to be supplied by the employer include eyeglasses, hearing aids, wheelchairs, and crutches. Examples of reasonable accommodations that an employer may provide are found in Table 12–5.

Once potential reasonable accommodations are identified, the employer should evaluate them to determine whether they will overcome the workplace barrier and also whether the costs constitute an undue hardship. An employee's preference for a particular reasonable accommodation may be considered, but an employer is not bound to provide a preferred reasonable accommodation if the one provided is effective. Ultimately, it is the employer's right and responsibility to choose the accommodations it determines are the

Table 12–5 | Examples of Reasonable Accommodations

Supplying and/or altering office equipment or devices, including automation and information technology
Altering or modifying the workplace, including lights and chairs
Relocating a job within the office
Telecommuting provided that the employer has adopted a formal written telecommuting policy
Obtaining reader or interpreter services
Changing the means by which instructions are provided
Restructuring the job
Relocating the individual to another existing vacant position for which the individual is qualified and can perform the essential functions

most appropriate in the given situation. If no potential reasonable accommodations exist that address the issues of workplace barrier and undue hardship, the ADA evaluation process ends.

Once a decision on reasonable accommodations is reached, the employer should notify the individual or her designee in writing. This writing should address whether or not a reasonable accommodation will be provided, what the reasonable accommodation will be, and when the reasonable accommodation will be available. If the employer decides to deny the request for reasonable accommodation, the writing should provide the reasoning for the decision. Once a reasonable accommodation is implemented, the employer should test the effectiveness of the accommodation, assess whether it meets expectations, and make any adjustments as needed. Continued monitoring is necessary, because some individuals may no longer need an accommodation if their circumstances change.

In summary, accommodations assist qualified disabled employees and job applicants by allowing them to remain functional and independent in the workplace. Absent undue hardship, the employer should try to provide accommodation, within reason and within a specified time period, for a qualified disabled employee to perform essential functions of the job or for a qualified disabled job applicant to complete the application and interview process.

Workplace Protections In addition to the workplace protections offered by antidiscrimination laws, employee rights are provided under laws and regulations governing health, safety, pay, hours, and conditions of the workplace. These laws and regulations offer protections to employees in the form of both prohibitions on certain practices and entitlements to certain conditions or treatment in the workplace.

Health and Safety Workplace health and safety issues are governed primarily by the Occupational Safety and Health

Act. This act created the Occupational Safety and Health Administration (OSHA) under the U.S. Department of Labor as the central agency charged with enforcing safety precautions in the workplace. OSHA covers virtually every private employer in the United States and issues regulations governing workplace safety. In general, these regulations guide employers in providing a workplace free of dangers that may cause physical harm to those who work there.

Many states also address workplace safety issues through their own OSHA laws and regulations, some of which may be more stringent than the federal OSHA requirements. In addition, a large number of states have laws addressing the use, storage, and handling of hazardous substances in the workplace. Many state and local government workers are governed by OSHA laws and regulations issued at the state level rather than the federal level.

To comply with federal and state OSHA requirements, an employer must develop and implement a health and safety program to achieve employee protections. Recommended components of a health and safety program are listed in Table 12–6. Within the health care environment, some employees engaged in direct patient care may encounter hazardous work conditions, particularly in the context of exposure to communicable diseases. Health care providers can minimize risks to employees by operating effective infection control practices, forming effective infection control committees, and applying safety precautions such as those involving the handling of bodily fluids. The workplace is primarily an office environment in the health information management field. Typically, an office environment does not pose the same hazardous work conditions as those present in a direct patient care environment. Nonetheless, efforts should be made toward an ergonomics education program that addresses both workstation design and employee work habits. Such efforts may alleviate repetitive stress disorders such as carpal tunnel syndrome or tendonitis. Health and safety checklists and report forms provide the means to identify and correct problems. Specific hazardous conditions, such as those created by secondhand smoke, can be addressed by policies that prohibit introduction of the

Table 12–6 | Recommended Components of a Health and Safety Program

Clear designation of responsibilities of management and line staff
Provisions for conducting inspections and abating hazards, including health and safety checklists
Establishment of a safety committee; designation of a safety manager; or identification of a safety liaison with the building landlord
Training of all management and line staff, including health and safety education
Record keeping and reporting
Self-evaluation of the health and safety program

hazard into the workplace (e.g., smoking prohibition in all interior spaces and any outdoor area located in front of air-intake ducts).

Certain record-keeping and reporting requirements are borne by employers as a result of OSHA regulations. These include keeping injury and illness logs, safety training records, and medical records of employees who have been exposed to hazardous substances or harmful physical agents.

Hours, Pay, and Conditions of Employment Several federal statutes address the hours, pay, and conditions under which employees work. The Federal Labor Standards Act (FLSA) offers workers specific protections against excessive work hours and substandard wages. Often referred to as the "minimum wage law," the FLSA establishes the minimum wage that must be paid to employees. The FLSA also establishes the maximum number of hours that an employee may work in a given time frame. For example, the FLSA mandates a 40-hour workweek and includes overtime pay provisions for those employees who work in excess of 40 hours. Overtime pay is generally calculated at one and a half times the regular rate at which an employee is normally compensated.

Some employees are considered exempt from the minimum wage/maximum hour provisions of the FLSA. Although the subject of much litigation, employees fall under the exempt category if they are paid a salary as opposed to wages; exercise discretion in performing their work; are primarily responsible for managing a business or department; routinely manage others; and possess the authority to hire and fire other employees. Conversely, employees who are paid wages as opposed to salary; do not exercise discretion in performing their work; are not responsible for managing a business, department, or other employees; and do not possess the authority to hire and fire other employees do not fall under the exempt category. Many positions that are classified as executive, administrative, or professional are considered exempt under the FLSA.

The FLSA's overtime provisions place an obligation upon the employer to exercise control over the workplace in terms of the total number of hours an employee works. In a traditional work environment where employees work face-to-face with supervisors, management can exercise this control more easily. Exercising this control in nontraditional work environments, however, such as ones involving telecommuting, is far more difficult; the supervisor may be unaware of any additional hours the employee is working at home beyond the scheduled hourly total. Nonetheless, the same principle applies to a telecommuting context as to the traditional work environment: if the employer knows or has reason to believe that the employee is continuing to work beyond the amount requested by the employer, those additional hours must be counted as overtime and are subject to overtime pay. This principle applies because the law places the burden upon the employer to exercise control over the

work environment, whether that environment is a traditional one or not.

The Equal Pay Act (EPA) also provides wage protections, specifically for workers who perform the same or substantially similar jobs. Subsumed within the definition of wages are fringe benefits such as bonuses, expense accounts, profit-sharing plans, or leave benefits. Assuming that jobs are substantially similar or identical in terms of skill, effort, and responsibility, the EPA requires equal pay between the sexes. Not all pay differences between the sexes violate the EPA, however, since some pay differences are attributable to matters other than sex—such as seniority or merit pay systems—or are based on quantity or quality of production.

Conditions of employment are addressed by the Family Medical Leave Act (FMLA), the Employee Retirement Income Security Act (ERISA), and federal laws governing unionization of the workforce. The FMLA allows eligible employees to take up to 12 weeks of unpaid leave during any 12-month period for the birth or adoption of a child; placement of a child in foster care; or for a serious health condition of the employee or the employee's spouse, child, or parent. Additionally, the FMLA provides that the employer must allow the employee to return to the same or a similar position as held before taking leave. The employer must also continue to make the same benefit contributions during the leave period as were required before the employee took leave. Many states have laws similar in scope to the FMLA, as do local municipalities in the form of leave ordinances.

ERISA addresses employee pensions and other benefit programs. ERISA offers protections by establishing minimum standards for pension and welfare plans and barring discriminatory treatment of persons with regard to their entitlement and use of benefits. For ERISA purposes, welfare plans include health and life insurance plans. ERISA does not require employers to establish pension and welfare plans; it merely regulates those employers who do establish them.

Federal law governing unionization of the workforce was designed initially to protect employees from abuses by their employers. Additional federal laws granted protections to employers from the excesses of unions and to union members from the unions themselves. These protections were addressed through the creation of the National Labor Relations Board. The Board establishes fair collective bargaining procedures and identifies unfair labor practices. The Board also oversees labor union representation elections and hears disputes related to labor law. Many unions work to negotiate better working conditions, benefits, and employment contracts for their members. Unions also work to resolve workplace disputes through structured grievance procedures.

While federal law addresses many conditions of employment, state law addresses others, including workers' compensation and unemployment insurance programs. Both programs are intricate and complex, making an extensive discussion of them beyond the scope of this chapter. An overview of each program follows.

Workers' compensation is a program designed to replace income and provide medical expenses to employees who are injured, become ill, or die as a result of their jobs. This program benefits not only employees and their dependents but also offers protection to employers from being sued for those injuries, illnesses, or deaths that occur on the job and are covered by the workers' compensation program. The benefits paid to employees are financed by employer contributions. Although national in scope, most employees are governed by workers' compensation programs that arise from state law and are administered by individual states. If a federal civilian employee is involved, work injury benefits are governed by the Federal Employees Compensation Act. Accordingly, great variations exist with regard to who is eligible for benefits, what conditions are covered, and the proper process for filing claims. General guidelines addressing how to handle an employee injury in the workplace are provided in Table 12–7.

Unemployment insurance is a program designed to provide regular income to those who have lost their jobs. Funding for this program comes from a tax on employers; unlike workers' compensation, this tax is paid by the employer to both state and federal governmental entities who jointly run the program. Unemployment insurance covers a broad spectrum of the workforce, as long as minimum requirements are met. Some employees are disqualified from receiving benefits due to their behavior on the job or because of the time they left employment. Many states have strict rules with regard to filing a claim, the time periods before receiving unemployment income, or appealing a benefit decision.

Conditions of employment also encompass the concept of employee privacy. This concept is broad based and includes such issues as the use of drug and lie detector tests and the surveillance and monitoring techniques available for use with telephone calls, voice mail, computer files, and electronic mail. The perspective on employee privacy is, in essence, a contrast between two views. While employees may expect to possess

as many rights to privacy in the workplace as they do outside of the workplace, many employers believe that they themselves possess legitimate interests in employing these tests and techniques as a way to maintain a safe, harassment-free work environment. Federal and state laws generally fall somewhere in the middle of these two views, offering limited protections to employees while granting employers some authority to engage in these activities.

HIPAA

Some employers are considered covered entities under HIPAA, subjecting them to the provisions of the Privacy Rule.

Employee privacy is also implicated by the regulations of the Health Insurance Portability and Accountability Act (HIPAA). Some employers are considered covered entities under HIPAA, making them subject to virtually all provisions of the Privacy Rule. Other employers are not considered covered entities, per se, but fall within protections of the Privacy Rule because they offer some form of a health plan or group health plan as a benefit to their employees. Unless the plan is self-administered, with less than 50 participants, the HIPAA Privacy Rule will apply to the health information received by those employers pursuant to such a plan. Accordingly, issues related to marketing restrictions and the use and disclosure of protected health information become concerns for employers who are not considered covered entities per se. In both of these situations, the Privacy Rule requires employers to establish firewalls or procedural and operational separations between health-related functions and general employment-related functions. Failure to protect such information may result in sanctions or other penalties. Additional information concerning HIPAA can be found in Chapter 3, "Legal Issues"; Chapter 5, "Health Data Content and Structures"; and Chapter 13, "Information Systems and Technology."

Supervision

Inherent in the concept of human resource management is the role of supervision. **Supervision** is the process by which an individual directs others to perform work on time with available resources (money, materials, and manpower) and in a manner that meets or exceeds performance standards. It is the concern of the supervisor to address work schedules, budget constraints, resource availability, and policy requirements. The key to supervision is in understanding that work is done by other people rather than by performing all of the work oneself. Although circumstances exist that require supervisors to pitch in and perform the same work as those who are supervised, this is the exception and not the rule.

Table 12–7	Workplace Injury Guidelines
Report the accident to a supervisor immediately.
Document the circumstances surrounding the accident and provide a copy of the document to the supervisor.
Obtain a written account of the accident from eyewitnesses, if any.
Obtain medical attention if the situation warrants.
Complete any paperwork requirements of the organization's human resources department.

Supervisors engage in the planning, organizing, controlling, directing, and leading functions outlined in Chapter 11. When planning and organizing others' work, supervisors specify the objectives for employees to follow, identify the resources needed and available, and develop the work schedules. In controlling and directing others' work, supervisors ensure that employees understand what work should be performed, by whom it should be performed, when it should be performed, and what specifications or standards apply. Supervisors check employee work periodically to ensure that it is proceeding according to plan and, where it is not, supervisors resolve problems so that work may resume. By leading others, supervisors influence group behavior to accomplish planned objectives.

Supervisors possess a multitude of responsibilities, which vary among organizations. Supervisory functions that are common to many organizations include creating and conducting performance evaluations, addressing problem behaviors, disciplining employees, addressing grievances, developing others, and building teams. In addition to these functions, some supervisors monitor employee performance conducted in nontraditional work environments, such as those involved with telecommuting. A discussion of these functions follows.

Performance Evaluations

In addition to understanding the general principles of management, a supervisor must also understand how to evaluate and appraise the work performances of others. A **performance evaluation** is a formal opportunity to review and evaluate an employee on a periodic basis. Performance evaluations serve a number of purposes, as illustrated in Table 12–8.

Table 12–8 | Purposes of a Performance Evaluation

Evaluate an employee's performance against established performance standards
Measure an employee's accomplishments toward goals set at the last evaluation
Measure an employee's technical knowledge, organizational skills, directions required, and ability to work with and through others
Recognize an employee's contributions to the organization
Encourage open lines of communications between employee and supervisor
Encourage employee participation in organization evaluations and development
Establish future objectives and commitments for the employee and supervisor
Determine salary increases based on satisfactory performances
Suggest areas for training and education that benefit the organization and the employee's career choices

Performance evaluations do not operate in a vacuum; rather, they operate in tandem with job descriptions and performance standards. A **job description** is a written statement summarizing what an employee does, how it is done, and why it is done. In other words, it identifies the activities, skills, and performance requirements for a position. Job descriptions are used in a multitude of ways. They serve as a way to set the appropriate salary or wage for a given position and as the basis for advertisements used in the recruiting process. Interviewers use them to explain to prospective candidates the type of work to be performed in the job. Managers may use them to plan employee orientation sessions. Supervisors may turn to them to resolve performance problems with employees, to clarify relationships within an organization, and to serve as a basis for a performance evaluation.

Job descriptions outline the work of an individual and are composed of a position summary, a listing of both essential and nonessential job functions, and the qualifications deemed necessary to perform the work. A **position summary** identifies the job's purpose, describes how it contributes to accomplishing the overall objectives of the organization, and distinguishes the job from others in the organization. **Essential job functions** are those functions and duties that are required for a particular job; in other words, the core functions and duties of the job. Essential job functions are often listed in the order of their importance, and subheadings may be used to define related activities. **Nonessential job functions** are those functions and duties that are desirable but not required for a particular job. **Qualifications** are the necessary skills, education, experience, and licensure required for the position. In addition, many job descriptions describe the level of authority delegated to the position, the working relationships that are considered key to carrying out the functions described for the position, and the job setting, including the location and the physical and social conditions of the setting.

E-HIM

Conversion to an electronic health record system requires revisions to job descriptions, particularly job qualifications.

Like many documents used in the workplace, job descriptions are subject to revision for a variety of reasons, including changes in laws and regulations applying to the workplace or the use of technology in the workplace. Major changes in operations—such as conversion to the use of an electronic health record system—may require revisions to job descriptions; new qualifications for employees may be added while other qualifications may be identified as obsolete.

While job descriptions assist the performance evaluation process by describing the activities to be evaluated, they do not describe the results that must be achieved. Performance standards serve that purpose. Performance standards establish expectations for the quantity, quality, and timeliness of work to be performed; are developed for each function of a job; and contain some form of measurement. Methods for setting standards and monitoring performance are addressed more fully in Chapter II, "Management Organization."

Armed with the job description and performance standards, the supervisor knows what activities of the employee's job should be evaluated and how to do so. The next step is to make the actual comparison: the work the employee performed and the results achieved are compared against the requirements found in the job description and the performance standards set at the beginning of the review period. When making this comparison, the supervisor may focus on the employee's work methods and habits and the types of behaviors exhibited. This comparison is typically articulated in a written document that the employee can review and understand. The written performance evaluation document often contains ratings that may be numerically or narratively based.

Consider the performance evaluation of a supervisor in the areas of planning, organizing, directing, controlling, and leading. When evaluating planning, the manager may look to see if the supervisor provided sufficient time to complete projects, addressed contingencies, determined the proper amount and type of resources needed, and developed a successful course of action for each assignment. When evaluating organizing, the manager may look to see if the supervisor completed her work efficiently, grouped tasks logically, and matched the work to be performed with the resources available. When evaluating directing, the manager may look at whether the supervisor made decisions promptly and accepted responsibility for those decisions willingly. When evaluating controlling, the manager may look at whether the supervisor kept assigned work and projects on track by monitoring progress and taking required corrective action where necessary. When evaluating leading, the manager may look at whether the supervisor provided direction to others as well as whether others were willing to accept and support the supervisor's leadership efforts.

While performance evaluations cannot substitute for routine feedback on performance given throughout the performance window, they can memorialize an employee's work performance over the time period in question. Some performance evaluations are composed of the views of management alone, while other evaluations are a compilation of the views of management and the employee herself using a self-evaluation tool. Other performance evaluations include content from all levels of the organization in which the employee has contact. These so-called 360-degree evalua-

Table 12–9 | Performance Evaluation Checklist

Establish a date for regular, timely, objective evaluation of the employee's performance.

Document the evaluation with specific examples of acceptable or unacceptable performance.

Emphasize positive comments where possible.

Address problem areas and possible situations.

Encourage dialogue with employees and discuss specific goals for the next review period.

Place a copy of the performance evaluation, signed by both the employee and supervisor, in the employee's personnel file.

tion instruments provide the broadest level of feedback to an employee. A performance evaluation checklist is illustrated in Table 12–9.

Performance evaluations are considered both a tool and a process of human resource management. While most performance evaluations include some sort of written document (the tool), many also include formal meetings between a supervisor and an employee (the process). These formal meetings may involve discussions of the salient points of the performance evaluation document or they may be used as part of a goal-setting session for the coming performance period. Another part of the process is the mechanism provided to respond to or appeal a performance evaluation that the employee believes is unfair or inaccurate. Such mechanisms may involve strict rules, including limited time periods in which to lodge an appeal or content requirements addressing the areas of disagreement.

Problem Behaviors

During the course of a formal evaluation process or at some other time, the supervisor may observe or receive reports of an employee exhibiting problem behaviors. Addressing problem behaviors is among the most difficult tasks facing supervisors. Because it can be such an unpleasant experience, supervisors sometimes delay dealing with these problems, hoping that the problems will improve over time. That approach almost never works and problems sometimes even exacerbate. When handled with dignity and fairness, supervisors can confront and deal with problem behaviors, benefiting the supervisor, the employee experiencing the problem, and any additional employees in the work group.

Before a supervisor can address problem behaviors with an employee, the supervisor must first assess whether the problem is related to the employee's job performance or the employee's conduct on the job. **Performance problems** relate directly to and impact the employee's ability to carry out critical job duties and meet required job standards. Examples include an employee who submits reports that are inaccurate or incomplete or shows repeated discourtesy to customers. **Conduct problems** relate to the employee's ability to comply with organizational rules governing employee behavior. Examples include repeated tardiness, insubordination, theft of property, or drinking on the job.

It is not always easy to separate the two issues in the workplace, as the same behavior could be considered a conduct problem or a performance problem. Consider an employee who is consistently rude when using the telephone to communicate with other people. This rudeness could be considered a conduct problem if it is simply unpleasant; it could also be considered a performance problem if it impacts customer service or the ability of coworkers to achieve desired work results. Consider the employee who consistently turns in reports late because she is often late for work. The lateness associated with turning in reports is a performance issue; the lateness associated with coming in late for work is a conduct problem. Consider the employee who plays the radio loudly and disturbs others in the surrounding work area. The noise level is a conduct problem if others dislike the type of music being played; the loud volume is a performance problem if the noise level is such that coworkers cannot concentrate on their work duties. The challenge to the supervisor is deciding which type of problem should be dealt with first, since both problems are intertwined.

When addressing performance problems, the supervisor's focus rests on assisting employees with improving their unacceptable performance. This assistance can take many forms. The supervisor may provide training and reemphasize performance standards related to the employee's job in order to resolve performance problems. When resolving conduct problems, on the other hand, the supervisor may review organizational rules and policies or refer an employee to an employee assistance program or professional counseling. For either set of problems, the supervisor established a time window in which employees can improve their performance. If problems persist or performance remains below standard after the supervisor offers assistance and the time for improvement expires, appropriate formal action may be necessary.

Discipline and Grievance

Whereas many problem behaviors can be addressed successfully through training or counseling, some problem behaviors warrant disciplinary action, particularly those behaviors dealing with conduct. The major purpose of a disciplinary policy is to provide a mechanism to administer equitable and consistent discipline when dealing with unsatisfactory conduct in the workplace. By administering discipline fairly and consistently, the supervisor may be able to correct the problem, prevent its recurrence, and prepare the employee for satisfactory performance in the future. To the extent that disciplinary action is warranted, it is in the organization's best interest to ensure that it is delivered in a prompt, uniform, and impartial manner.

Table 12–10 | **Steps in the Disciplinary Process**

1. Oral warning
2. Written warning
3. Written reprimand
4. Suspension without pay
5. Demotion
6. Termination of employment

Multiple steps are involved in the disciplinary process and are illustrated in Table 12–10. Which step, or how many steps, a supervisor should use depends on the situation involved. Oral warnings may be warranted when the problem behavior is not of a severe nature and prior directions to the employee have not been followed. If the problem behavior is serious or the oral warning did not result in changed behavior, a written warning may be in order. For severe problems, a written reprimand may be warranted. Written reprimands differ from written warnings in that written reprimands are often placed in the employee's personnel file whereas written warnings are often not. Suspending an employee without pay may be warranted when an employee's behavior resulted in a violation of rules or a minor illegal act. Demotion is particularly suitable for situations involving a mismatch between job requirements and an employee's skills and abilities. Demotion is typically only used when the employee has previously received more than one unsatisfactory performance evaluation. Termination of employment is an alternative of last resort and may be used when the problem behavior resulted in a major illegal act or where little possibility exists that the employee will be able to perform the job at an acceptable level or conform to the organization's conduct norms in the near future.

Disciplinary action may be considered progressive in nature, meaning that a supervisor could use all of the steps as listed above with respect to any category of problem. For example, a first offense may call for a verbal warning, a next offense may be followed by a written warning, another offense may lead to a suspension, while yet another offense may lead to termination of employment. Even with a progressive disciplinary policy in place, certain types of employee problems are serious enough to justify a suspension pending investigation, or immediate termination of employment, without first going through the usual progressive disciplinary steps.

Employees who have been subject to disciplinary action may consider pursuing a grievance. A **grievance** is a complaint regarding the policies and procedures of an organization or a protest of treatment perceived to be unjust by an employee. The grievance policies of many organizations provide employees the right to select a representative to assist them in preparation and representation of a grievance and the right to appeal any decision reached on the grievance.

These policies often include time constraints in which to pursue a grievance, and failure to adhere to the time limits may jeopardize the employee's right to appeal the grievance to a higher level.

Consider an employee who perceives unfair treatment by her immediate supervisor. Depending on the specifications of the organization's policies, the employee may initiate the grievance by consulting with her immediate supervisor verbally to settle her complaint. If the employee does not settle her complaint or is not satisfied with the verbal settlement, the employee may proceed with a formal written grievance to that same supervisor. If the supervisor fails to respond timely or the employee is not satisfied with the response, the employee may appeal the immediate supervisor's decision to a higher-level manager. Such appeals may involve formal meetings before a decision is issued or may be conducted solely based on the paperwork submitted. Depending on the number of levels of management within an organization, such appeals may continue to be brought until the appeals process is exhausted.

As with disciplinary action, supervisors often view the grievance process as an unpleasant one. Supervisors can take action to avoid generating grievances by treating all employees fairly and equitably and applying organization policies uniformly. Supervisors can also encourage employees to communicate their dissatisfactions to the supervisor before the dissatisfaction rises to the level of a grievance. Further, supervisors who keep employees informed and the lines of communication open may see a decrease in employee dissatisfaction, resulting in a decrease in grievances.

Once a grievance is filed, it is important that the supervisor resolve the grievance through prompt investigation and action. Supervisors should follow the organization's established grievance procedures strictly, adhering to the time limits found in those policies. Finally, the supervisor must ensure that the employee who filed a grievance is not penalized for doing so.

Developing Others

One of the most rewarding tasks for any supervisor is to witness the blossoming of an employee for whom she had some developmental responsibility. Part of a supervisor's responsibility in many organizations is to develop those employees with whom she works. Supervisors develop others in a variety of ways, from employing formal career development strategies to acting as a coach or mentor.

Career Development Over time, many organizations have incorporated strategic plans and farsighted strategies into their management practices. One strategy that has received considerable positive acceptance in the business and health care communities is career development. Career development refers to the planned efforts and activities employed to align an individual's career needs with an organization's workforce requirements. In other words, it refers to creating opportunities for staff to advance and develop professionally within the organization.

Hallmarks of a successful career development program vary, but certain key factors are often present. First, employee development should be linked with business strategy. By doing so, career development is seen as a business necessity that relates to competitive advantage rather than as an extra that may be trimmed when budgets are tight. Second, career development aligns individual needs with organizational workforce requirements quite clearly, providing the potential for significant gains on both sides. Third, this development is employed as part of an overall human resource strategy, allowing for consistency in performance management and supervision. Fourth, accountability mechanisms are present, so that the effects wrought through career development can be sustained over time. Finally, development becomes institutionalized, so that those at every level of the organization are aware of the program, know how to take advantage of it, and can rely on its existence over time.

Several approaches are used in career development on an organizational level. Some organizations identify career paths for employees to follow upon initial association with the employer. These career paths may stand alone or they may be closely aligned with the concept of succession planning for key positions within the organization. Organizations that employ succession planning often identify both the interested individual and the path for the individual to follow. Mentoring systems may also be employed to encourage employee advancement. Employee self-assessment tools may be made available, such as career planning workshops, workbooks, or computer software applications. Formal development programs may also be utilized, along with tuition reimbursement, job rotation, and enrichment systems, as a means to encourage employee development.

At the supervisory level, those persons tasked with career development of the employees they supervise may engage in a variety of behaviors and activities. Supervisory behaviors and activities may include identifying employee potential, aligning individual career goals with organizational needs when providing career counseling, helping employees understand the link between their current job performance and future development, particularly as it relates to the employees' performance evaluations, inspiring staff to work to their highest potential, and ensuring that resources are available to support employee development. Supervisors often play a role in creating growth opportunities that are consistent with employee and organizational goals and providing exposure for employees to other people who can advance their careers or otherwise assist them. Finally, supervisors may assist employees in identifying options, setting goals, and developing an action plan. In each of these ways, the supervisor can help an employee to advance within the organization and can assist the organization in strengthening the skills and abilities of current staff. In turn, these efforts may result in improved employee retention and an environment where people will want to work.

Coaching At various times during a supervisor's career, she will need to act as a coach. Coaching is "the process of equipping people with the tools, knowledge, and opportunities they need to develop themselves and become more effective."[5] Coaching focuses on the learning process, assisting the employee with developing the knowledge and skills needed to perform the functions assigned to her current position. Armed with this knowledge and skill, the employee should be able to improve her performance.

Coaching can be formal or informal and may take many forms. Coaches sometimes use encouragement, feedback, demonstration, personal examples, or developmental activities to help employees attain higher levels of performance. Coaches may model behavior for an employee to follow or may assist an employee through problems or crises. Using a positive and constructive manner, coaches may help employees recognize their strengths and weaknesses and address critical developmental issues or barriers in a candid and timely way.

Coaches often assist individuals who are struggling with performance standards, including those standards that are part of a new job or are due to new competencies being added to established positions. New competencies may be a result of a change in an organization's direction, such as when a health care facility implements an electronic health record. In such an instance, the coach assists the individual with moving from the competencies needed in a paper-based system to the competencies needed in an electronic system by identifying the new competencies, comparing those competencies with the competencies possessed by the individual, and identifying strategies for the individual to either build new skills or apply existing skills to the new competencies.

Mentoring Mentoring refers to the act of advising another through an established formal relationship. The person who is considered the advisor in the relationship is called the mentor; the person who receives the advice is called the mentee. Mentors respond to the problems and concerns of the mentee by providing expert advice that will have a practical application. Mentoring differs from coaching in that mentoring focuses on sharing the mentor's expertise, personal experiences, and past opportunities, whereas coaching focuses on the process of learning, particularly in creating learning opportunities for the employee who is being coached. It also differs in that mentoring focuses beyond the employee's current job to some point in the future, whereas coaching focuses on the employee's current job.

Much of the advice provided by mentors is directed at competencies a mentee must possess to be considered qualified for or successful in a given position. Both championing change and communicating effectively are generally considered competencies for managers and supervisors. The behaviors discussed below are examples of practical behaviors the mentee may engage in that will strengthen those required competencies.

Consider the mentor who is advising the mentee on how to champion and manage change. The mentor could suggest that the mentee participate in or serve as the chairperson of a process improvement team or a committee responsible for implementing a change in the department or organization. Similarly, the mentor could suggest that the mentee seek out projects that require initiating and planning change within the organization or interview someone who has led an organizational change effort successfully. Finally, the mentor could suggest that the mentee identify change champions in her organization and work with them to support and initiate a change.

Consider the mentor who is advising the mentee on how to communicate effectively. The mentor could suggest that the mentee identify methods currently used to convey information in the organization, evaluate the strengths and weakness of those methods, and propose or implement better methods. Similarly, the mentor could suggest that the mentee seek out assignments that require her to make presentations to groups, offer to represent his supervisor at a meeting, or volunteer to serve on committees or task forces that provide opportunities to speak and write. Finally, the mentor could suggest that the mentee speak with peers or direct reports about communication breakdowns within the organization and generate ideas to avoid such breakdowns in the future.

As these behaviors indicate, the focus of the mentor/mentee relationship is on the future. By engaging in and succeeding at the suggested behaviors, the mentee is better positioned to be considered for other roles or positions that may become available in the future, within or beyond the organization.

Team Building

Although teams have always been present in one way or another throughout business history, only during the last few decades has the concept of team building been widely applied in business and health care settings. This development can be traced to the emergence of the concepts of participatory management and Theory Y, both of which postulate that employees, under proper conditions, will not only accept but seek responsibility in their work positions. While these theories were gaining prominence, the classic theory of organizational management, with top-down styles of management and multiple layers of bureaucratic control existing within an organization, was losing popularity. In its place, theories of flexible organizational design, which included flattened levels of bureaucracy, communicating information and ideas to all levels of an organization involved in a project, and pushing decision making to lower levels of an organization, were gaining acceptance. These theories posited that applying team-building concepts to the business and health care environments would result in greater efficiencies, reduced costs to the organization, and a greater ability to deal with the rapid pace of change and the increased complexities of modern society.

A **team** is a group of people working together in a coordinated effort. Several types of teams exist, often classified on the basis of their objectives. A problem-solving team generally involves employees of the same department who are tasked with finding solutions to defined problems, often with a focus on improving work processes and methods. The authority given to problem-solving teams varies, as some do not possess the authority to implement the suggestions they develop. Cross-functional teams generally involve employees from several departments or work areas who are assigned a specific task; task forces and committees are examples of these. Self-directed work teams generally are problem-solving teams who also possess some responsibilities traditionally held by management, such as controlling the pace of work or determining work assignments.

No matter what type of team is employed, several characteristics are common to effective teams. These characteristics include a shared purpose; strong leadership; well-understood operating rules and procedures; motivation to perform work of high quality and quantity; recognition of the importance of sharing information; expressions of support and loyalty to fellow team members, the organization, and its management; and the ability to exercise self-control and guidance. When these characteristics are in place, teams can achieve high levels of performance and influence individuals, departments, and organizations for the better.

Supervisors play a strong role in building and guiding teams. **Team building** is the process by which a selected group of people is organized and developed so that each team member's actions work interdependently toward a common objective. When building a team, the supervisor selects and trains individual group members; educates them concerning the team's goals, the level of the team members' involvement, and the means of communication both within and beyond the team; and identifies available resources and the applicable performance standards from which the team will be judged. Once the team is developed, the supervisor works to increase its effectiveness. This is often accomplished by facilitating interaction between group members, solving problems that the team has not been able to address successfully, addressing conflict within the team, and creating a high level of awareness and commitment to the team's goals.

Consider the efforts of a supervisor in building and guiding a team tasked with identifying the work functions that are suitable to telecommuting for an office environment located in a health care institution. The supervisor would select individuals with broad knowledge of the interrelation of an office's functions or expertise in specific office functions to serve as team members. The supervisor would educate the team concerning its goals (e.g., identifying suitable functions), the level of team member involvement (e.g., review of functions from operational, technical, and policy perspectives), and resources and performance standards (e.g., what software programs are available offsite and the quantity and quality of work to be performed). The supervisor would guide the team's efforts by facilitating team meetings, addressing conflicts between what is desirable and what is practical, and reporting the status of the team's work to management and others within the institution. The supervisor's efforts would continue until the team had accomplished its task and the functions identified as suitable were woven into the office's telecommuting policy.

Telecommuting

Supervisors play a key role in the success of any telecommuting endeavor, since it is generally the supervisor who sets the parameters of the telecommuting arrangement. These parameters may include the eligibility of employees to participate in telecommuting, the location where the telecommuting is performed, the amount of time spent telecommuting, the type and amount of training necessary to support telecommuting, the manner in which telecommuting work will be monitored and measured, and compliance with regulatory matters, such as health and safety issues.

Telecommuting is "any arrangement in which an employee regularly performs officially assigned duties at home or other work sites geographically convenient to the residence of the employee."[6] These alternative arrangements have been referred to under many names, including flexiwork, telework, flexiplace, and virtual offices. They generally involve the use of telecommunication services and devices, such as computers, cellular phones, facsimile machines, advanced communications links, and Internet access.

Determining eligibility for telecommuting is a significant supervisory function. Eligibility for telecommuting varies by employer, with employers at the federal level mandated by law to offer telecommuting options to eligible employees. Some positions or job functions may not be appropriate for telecommuting if they involve access to material that cannot be removed from the primary workplace or if they require the employee's physical presence on the job. In the business world, telecommuting has succeeded for positions that involve thinking and writing (such as data analysis, report writing, or grant review), positions that involve telephone-intensive tasks (such as customer service representatives), and positions that involve

Figure 12–5 | Telecommuting screening tool

Rate yourself or your employee using the following scale:

5 (Always) 4 (Usually) 3 (Sometimes) 2 (Rarely) 1 (Never)

1. ___ Employee works without regular monitoring/ supervision.
2. ___ Employee independently identifies required work products.
3. ___ Employee successfully plans work production schedule.
4. ___ Employee communicates roadblocks to successful completion of a task or project in sufficient time to allow for alterations that improve the opportunity for success.
5. ___ Employee meets deadlines.
6. ___ Employee is computer literate.

Source: Office of Personnel Management. (2003). *Telework: A management priority; A guide for managers, supervisors, and Telework coordinators.* http://www.telework.gov/

computer-oriented tasks (such as programming, data entry, or word processing). In the health information management field, functions such as medical transcription and coding have been performed successfully through telecommuting.

After determining which positions and job functions are appropriate to be performed off-site from both technical and policy perspectives, the supervisor must determine which candidate is suitable for telecommuting. A screening tool can assist this effort by assessing characteristics that have been identified as leading to success in telecommuting. An example of a screening tool is illustrated in Figure 12–5.

Employees who conduct all or some of their work away from the primary workplace may do so in a variety of settings, including in the employee's home, at telecenters, or at other locations where there exist both connectivity to the primary office and a setting conducive to accomplishing the work requirements. Telecenters are facilities, rented or leased by the employer, that provide business-like settings that may include workstations, docking stations, conference rooms, and other amenities that enable employees to perform work away from the primary workplace. These telecenters may be rented by a single employer, amounting to a satellite office located near a concentration of employee residences, or by multiple employers who share the contiguous workspace in a single location that their employees may access. Other locations may include virtual offices, which allow employees to use technology to contact the primary workplace, customers, or suppliers from an airport, a hotel, the employee's car, or other off-site locations.

When implementing telecommuting programs, the supervisor must determine the amount of time the employee

spends telecommuting. Some employees telecommute on a full-time basis, meaning that the employee completes all or almost all work duties outside of a traditional office setting. This type of telecommuting offers the employer the potential for cost savings through avoidance of office rent that otherwise would have been expended for that employee in the primary workplace setting. It is particularly useful for employers who wish to retain valued employees who cannot remain in the geographical area of the primary workplace. Some employees telecommute on a part-time basis, using a regular schedule to perform work off-site one or more days a week or several days a month. This type of telecommuting also offers the employer the potential for cost savings, since part-time teleworkers can rotate and share office space. Some employees telecommute on an irregular basis, when telecommuting is designed to accommodate a specific employee or employer need. For example, employees who experience a medical problem, seek reasonable accommodation to a disability, or need to focus on a special project may meet those needs through telecommuting on an irregular basis. Employers may benefit also by incorporating this type of telecommuting into their disaster recovery planning effort.

Supervisors must also focus on the type and amount of training necessary to support telecommuting. To some extent, this training is a form of change management, because the introduction of telecommuting is a significant organizational change. Supervisors must engage in awareness training, educating employees at every level of the organization about the business case for telecommuting and how it will be integrated into the workplace. Supervisors should deliver specific training relating to policies, procedures, and techniques to be employed in telecommuting. Supervisors should educate telecommuting employees about the means and mechanisms for good communication between the primary workplace and the telecommuting site as a way to prevent obstacles to success. Finally, participation in question and answer sessions may assist employees in understanding the telecommuting process, including typical barriers and their attendant solutions. Once telecommuting has commenced, supervisors should remain aware of the need to educate these employees about changes to organizational policies, procedures, and techniques on a continuous basis.

Supervisors must also examine the manner in which telecommuting work will be monitored and measured. After establishing clearly the work to be performed and the results to be accomplished, the supervisor must establish a mechanism for monitoring and measuring that work. Mechanisms to measure performance may focus on quantity, quality, timeliness, or cost-effectiveness. Once the mechanisms are in place, the supervisor must provide a means to monitor them and provide feedback to the employee. Because telecommuting employees are not close at hand, the supervisor may employ a variety of means to provide feedback, such as e-mails, phone calls, and faxes. Additionally, supervisors must ensure that they recognize the achievements of

Figure 12–6 | Telecommuting safety checklist

- Fire safety, including smoke detectors, fire extinguishers, and a fire evacuation plan
- Ergonomics, including use of correct office furniture, lighting, and equipment
- Security, including password protections, virus scanning, and firewalls
- Space design that allows for ingress and egress without tripping or blocking
- Electrical safety, including use of grounded outlets and appropriate numbers of electrical circuits
- Accident and injury reporting mechanisms

Source: Office of Personnel Management. (2003). *Telework: A management priority; A guide for managers, supervisors, and Telework coordinators.* http://www.telework.gov/

telecommuters as well as those employees who commute to the primary workplace.

Supervisors also play a role in maintaining compliance with regulations, rules, and policies that govern the workplace. As addressed earlier in this chapter and in Chapter II, the law imposes obligations upon employers to maintain a safe working environment, whether their staff work in a traditional or nontraditional setting. Issues relating to physical layout, ergonomics, and safety hazards fall within the purview of the supervisor's role in maintaining a safe work environment. Wage and hour laws also apply in nontraditional settings, protecting employees from working excessive hours without the benefit of overtime pay. Review of time, pay, and attendance issues, such as core hours, days, duty station, and sick and vacation time, all are subject to institutional policies and fall within the supervisor's responsibilities. Figure 12–6 shows an example of a telecommuting safety checklist. Furthermore, antidiscrimination laws and regulations apply to workers in a telecommuting environment in the same manner in which they apply to workers in a traditional environment. Employees who suffer work-related injuries or damages while telecommuting are eligible for benefits under state and federal workers' compensation programs. Finally, laws, rules, and regulations that govern access to and confidentiality of protected health information also apply to the telecommuting environment. This is of particular importance because the employer has no mechanism to control who enters an employee's home and, therefore, must have a means to safeguard sensitive data, records, and information from unauthorized disclosure. Supervisors frequently address these access and confidentiality issues by reemphasizing confidentiality policies and standards and requiring those who telecommute to adhere to confidentiality and nondisclosure agreements.

An essential step for all supervisors who are involved in the telecommuting process is the completion of a

telecommuting agreement with the employee. This agreement should stipulate the parameters of the telecommuting program, including the areas previously addressed in this discussion. Additionally, the agreement should address the work product to be produced, the delivery dates for each work product, the need for and timing of status reports, the equipment to be provided by the employer or employee, and safety guidelines. The agreement should be in writing and signed by the supervisor, the employee, and any manager identified in the organization's telecommuting policy.

Workforce Diversity

Diversity refers to the myriad of differences between and among people in a defined setting. These differences include race, gender, ethnic or cultural background, age, sexual orientation, religion, and physical or mental capability. These differences may also include educational levels, class, job function, personality, and marital status. In the workplace setting, these differences have the potential to touch upon virtually all major organizational policies, practices, and processes that affect the lives of employees.

Diversity is viewed from a variety of perspectives in the business community of the 21st century. Some view a diverse workforce as necessary to bring a competitive edge to an organization. In light of fiscal constraints and the need to do more with less, businesses have increased their reliance on individuals and work groups within their organizations to take initiative, assume risks, and be accountable and responsible for work performed and products produced. This increased reliance presses decision making farther down the organizational hierarchy. Research has shown that "the more varied the group, the better the decision-making capability and the more solid and reliable the results."[7] In turn, solid and reliable decisions and results translate into organizational success.

Others in the business community view the need for a diverse workforce as the result of legal initiatives, such as the Civil Rights Act of 1964, the Equal Employment Opportunity Commission (EEOC), and affirmative action. Seen from this viewpoint, diversity is a matter of legal compliance, with efforts to increase and maintain a diverse workforce viewed as the means to both protect human rights and avoid litigation and its attendant expenses to the business.

Still others view diversity from the perspective of changes in the business world. Many organizations recognize that customer service is central to their business and therefore hire a diverse workforce that best reflects their customers across a continuum of time. As trade barriers decrease around the globe and technologies allow for expansion into markets worldwide, businesses are competing on a global scale. This global competition leads businesses to understand the need for cross-cultural understanding and partnerships. Finally, the demographic changes forecasted for the United States during the 21st century indicate that the future pool of talented employees will come from a wide range of persons in the workforce,[8] leading some businesses to make diversity a crucial component of their strategic business plan to attract and retain employees.

Whether viewed from these or other perspectives, achieving workforce diversity requires organizational effort. This effort begins at the highest management level, with the organization's leaders emphasizing the importance of diversity to the organization's strategic plan and cultivating conditions necessary to achieve the envisioned diversity. Managers at all levels of the organization can research current employment conditions to determine baseline data from which to measure progress. Educational efforts may be employed where needed to manage change and address diversity-related behaviors such as racial or gender stereotyping. The organization's policies, practices, and procedures are examined and, where needed, aligned with the vision of a diverse workforce. Major human resource activities such as recruitment, orientation, and training are included in this examination; these activities send powerful messages to new employees about the seriousness of the organization's diversity efforts. Each of these steps should be revisited on a regular basis, both as a way to achieve results and as a way to avoid stagnation.

As a practical matter, managers and supervisors who value diversity often view differences as an asset and demonstrate sensitivity to individual differences. They create environments where differences are accepted, actively solicit input from staff in a wide variety of functions across the department and even the organization, and view issues and opportunities from multiple viewpoints before reaching decisions. Further, they challenge organizational policies and practices that may be exclusionary and take appropriate action to address intolerant or prejudiced behavior or speech.

Conclusion

For any organization to be successful, those within it must understand the role of human resource management. In the course of any given day, managers and supervisors are presented with situations that call upon their knowledge of human resource management. Furthermore, the organization as an entity responds to questions and demands that require a full integration of human resource management principles with organizational policies and procedures. Achieving this understanding and integration will assist organizations, managers, and supervisors to recognize and address human resource management problems and, where possible, prevent their initial occurrence and potential for reoccurrence.

CHAPTER SUMMARY

The study of human resource management—the strategic use of human beings within an organization to enhance an organization's efficiency and effectiveness—at heart includes the concept of employment. Within employment are encompassed the activities of staffing: recruitment, selection, compensation, orientation and training, retention, and separation. Each of these activities involves not only the considerations and obligations of the employer, but also employee rights. Laws at the federal, state, and local levels all provide protections for employees and place responsibilities upon employers. The vast majority of these laws were passed in the last 50 years and apply to virtually all employees within the United States. The broad range of human resource management includes both supervision—with its focus on performance evaluations, discipline and grievance, developing others, teambuilding, and telecommuting—and workforce diversity, which requires organizational effort to succeed.

CASE STUDY

Laura Losos is employed as a data quality analyst at Anywhere Hospital and has received an exemplary performance evaluation for each of the last five years. She and her department recently began using a new computer application, and you have observed a marked decrease in Laura's ability to complete work accurately and timely. In addition, Laura has not been in compliance with the hospital's policies concerning attendance. As a supervisor, what steps might you take to address these problems?

REVIEW QUESTIONS

1. Name the components of the selection process.

2. What is the purpose of a reference check?

3. Name the components of a compensation program.

4. What are the goals of an effective new employee orientation and training program?

5. How can the content of an employer's handbook affect the employment-at-will doctrine?

6. What is the most challenging aspect for an employer complying with the ADA, and why?

7. Name the types of problem behaviors supervisors deal with, and differentiate between them.

8. How does mentoring differ from coaching?

9. What advantages are available to employers who allow telecommuting on a full-time, part-time, or irregular basis?

ENRICHMENT ACTIVITIES

1. Think of an incident from your recent experience when differences in age, gender, or culture probably contributed to a problem between you and another person. Write out the details of the situation, along with several questions that you could ask a person of the same group with which you experienced the problem. These questions should focus on how you could handle such situations better in the future.

2. Think of someone from your past who coached you to success. What qualities did the coach possess or what skills did the coach employ to assist you? How did the coach set or communicate goals to you? How did the coach evaluate your efforts and provide you with feedback? What reward or recognition did you receive for your efforts? Write out the answers to these questions and determine how you can use this experience to act as a coach for someone else in the future.

WEB SITES

American Management Association, http://www.amanet.org

Equal Employment Opportunity Commission, http://www.eeoc.gov

International Public Management Association for Human Resources, http://www.ipma-hr.org

Internal Revenue Service, http://www.irs.ustreas.gov

International Telework Association and Council, http://www.workingfromanywhere.org

Office of Personnel Management, http://www.opm.gov

Society for Human Resource Management, http://www.shrm.org

U.S. Government Telework site, http://www.telework.gov

REFERENCES

Bennet, M., Polden, D. J., & Rubin, H. J. (2004). *Employment relationships law & practice*. New York: Aspen Publishers.

McConnell, C. R. (2003). *The effective health care supervisor* (5th ed.). Sudbury, MA: Jones & Bartlett.

Practice Brief. (2002). *Establishing a telecommuting or home-based employee program* (updated). Chicago: American Health Information Management Association.

Sack, S. M. (2000). *The employee rights handbook*. New York: Warner Books.

Steingold, F. S. (1999). *The employer's legal handbook* (3rd ed.). Berkeley, CA: Nolo Press.

NOTES

1. Many of the definitions addressed in this section may be found in *Webster's new world college dictionary* (4th ed.). (2001). Foster City, CA: IDG Books Worldwide, Inc. Because the Internal Revenue Service (IRS) is the governmental agency responsible for determining whether monies should be routinely withheld from employee paychecks, its classification of the different types of employees is also used in this discussion; see http://www.irs.ustreas.gov.

2. The Immigration Reform and Control Act (IRCA) of 1986 obligates every employer to verify, within three days of hire, the identity and employment authorization of every employee hired. 8 U.S.C. § 1324-1365 (2005).

3. Exec. Order No. 11246, 30 Fed. Reg. 12319 (1965).

4. 42 C.F.R. § 1630 (2006).

5. Peterson, D., & Hicks, M. D. (1996). *Leader as coach* (p. 14). Minneapolis, MN: Personnel Decisions International.

6. Public Law 106-346, Dept. of Transportation and Related Agencies Appropriations Act (2001).

7. Lebo, F. (1996). *Mastering the diversity challenge* (p. 3). Delray Beach, FL: St. Lucie Press.

8. Judy, R., & D'Amico, C. (1997). *Workforce 2020*. Washington, DC: Hudson Institute.

13

Information Systems and Technology

CERTIFICATION CONNECTION

RHIA

Database architecture
Data/record storage
Data security
Electronic health record
Evaluate/recommend applications
Hardware
Interoperability
Organization–wide systems
Software applications
Standards
Technology applications

RHIT

Access logs/systems
Data/record storage
Design/generate reports
Electronic health record
Hardware
Imaging technology
Internet
Intranet
Networks
Security of PHI
Security policies
Software applications

LEARNING OBJECTIVES

After reading this chapter, the learner should be able to:

1. Compare and contrast the computer concepts of hardware and software.

2. Recognize the basic units of a personal computer and a computer room.

3. Differentiate between the software concepts of operating systems, application programs, utility programs, and programming languages.

4. Define the term *information systems life cycle* and explain its application in project management.

5. Understand communication technologies such as networks, the Internet, and security measures.

6. Define the term *informatics* and describe its application in the health care field.

7. Distinguish between the terms *electronic health, e-health organizations*, and *e-health consumers*.

8. Describe the technology applications of telemedicine, voice recognition, and digital imaging.

9. Understand the functionalities of an electronic health record.

Outline

Information Systems

Computer Concepts
Information Systems Life Cycle
Communication Technologies
Security

Informatics

Technology Applications and Trends

Electronic Health Records

Key Concepts

Application program
Application service providers
Authentication
Authorship
Backup regime
Bit
Byte
Cable modems
CD-ROM drive
Central processing units
Clinical information system
Computer room
Computer virus
Crackers
Digital imaging
Disaster recovery plans
Disk drive
Domain name
DSL
Educational informatics
E-health
E-health consumers
E-health organizations
E-learning
E-prescribing
Electronic health record
Encryption
Extensible markup language
Extranet
Firewall
Flash drive

Floppy disk
Hackers
Hard drive
Hardware
Health care informatics
Health care information systems
Hypertext markup language
Informatics
Information brokering
Information security policies
Information systems
Information systems life cycle
Interactive voice recognition
Internet
Internet protocol
Internet protocol address
Internet service provider
Intranet
ISDN
Keyboard
Laptop computer
Links
Local area network
Mainframe
Metropolitan area network
Mobile
Modem

Monitor
Mouse
Network
Operating system
Peripheral
Permission
Personal computer
Personal digital assistant
Portal
Printers
Programming language
Public health informatics
Releases
Scanners
Security
Security Rule
Servers
Software
Standard generalized markup language
Standards
Telehealth
Telemedicine
Utility program
Versions
Virtual private network
Virus scan
Voice recognition technology
Wide area network
Wireless
World Wide Web

INTRODUCTION

Once upon a time, functions of the health information management department were entirely paper based. That time is long past. With the advent of the electronic master patient index, automated transcription systems, clinical data repositories, federal regulations relating to electronic transmission of billing data, and the electronic health record, today's health information manager must become intimately aware of information technology and all that it offers to the health information field. This awareness serves to assist the practitioner in protecting the health information housed in information technology.

Furthermore, the relationship between the Health Information Services (HIS) department and the Information Technology (IT) department in many institutions has grown close. In some institutions, the HIS department reports to the chief information officer (CIO). In other institutions, the HIS department is split between the reimbursement and revenue cycle functions reporting to the chief financial officer (CFO) and the records, data, and information collection/analysis functions reporting to the CIO. Still others have recognized that IT cannot be managed without the knowledge of HIS professionals, while at the same time HIS functions cannot be managed without IT solutions. Administrators in many institutions have come to clearly understand the differences between the IT role of deploying electronic solutions to issues and the HIS role of expertise in data definition, capture, management, use, analysis, and interpretation. Combined, the development and understanding of these relationships have brought HIS and IT into close alliance.

Because of this interrelationship and the need to ensure proper use of health information, the health information professional must possess a basic understanding of information technology. To understand information technology, one must start at the elementary level. A basic description of computer concepts begins this chapter, with an explanation of the names and functions of a computer's parts, pieces, and basic software concepts. Discussion of the information systems life cycle and communication technologies follows, with concentration on the Internet. Security issues, including the impact of the HIPAA Security Rule, are addressed, along with informatics. A discussion of technology applications and trends completes the chapter.

Information Systems

A frequently used phrase in the business world is information systems, referring to the collection of components (facts or data) that work in concert to achieve a common objective. Within the health care context, the collection of facts and data used to provide specific meaningful information support and improve health services management is referred to as health care information systems. Health care information systems cover a broad range of applications, serving both clinical and administrative functions, as shown in Figure 13–1. An understanding of the computer concepts supporting these systems, the existence of the information systems life cycle, the communication technologies that enable information systems, and the security measures necessary to support these systems are essential to managing an information system successfully.

Figure 13-1 | Typical component applications

Health Care Information System

Clinical	Administrative
• Physician Order	• Admitting
• Monitoring	• Finance
• Nursing	• Risk Management
• Radiology	• Quality Assurance
• Laboratory	• Scheduling
• Pharmacy	• Contract Management

Computer Concepts

Computer concepts can be broken into three main areas: hardware, software, and units of measure. Hardware refers to all of the physical electronic components of a computer system—in other words, those things that one can touch. By contrast, software is the term for the programs that tell the computer what to do and how to do it. Although these two terms are easily distinguishable, they are interconnected in the sense that software requires hardware to exist.

Hardware Many different types of hardware exist, and the following definitions introduce the basic units of a personal computer and a computer room. A personal computer (PC) is a computer that contains a central processing unit (Figure 13-2). Central processing units (CPUs), sometimes called microprocessors or processors, are the most important piece of hardware for personal computers. A CPU is responsible for executing programs, performing calculations,

Figure 13-2 | A personal computer

and moving data between memory and long-term storage media. A CPU is important because it determines what programs can run on a computer and how fast those programs can run. The speed of the CPU is measured in a unit of frequency called megahertz (MHz). The higher the megahertz number, the faster the CPU works. The memory of a CPU stores data that is not being processed.

In addition to the CPU, a personal computer typically includes other peripheral equipment (types of hardware pieces), some of which are shown in Figure 13-3. A monitor displays the output of a computer. Similar to a television screen, a monitor can vary by size, picture resolution, and the colors it displays. Also included is a mouse, which is a small hand control with buttons that control the position of the cursor on the monitor screen. A keyboard is a device used to input numbers, characters, and commands into a computer. Keyboards resemble typewriters but with lighter-sprung keys fitted into a shallow tray. A disk drive is a device that reads and writes data from a rotating disk. Four types of disk drives are hard drives, floppy disk drives, CD-ROM drives, and flash drives. A hard drive is a magnetic storage device that stores individual data on the surface of a rapidly rotating metal disk that is coated with a film of magnetizable material. This drive is sealed in the factory to prevent contamination and is contained within the computer cabinet. Newer technology now permits hard drives to exist external to the CPU, allowing portability of the hard drive. A floppy disk is a removable flexible disk made of plastic coated with a magnetic oxide layer. A CD-ROM drive, short for "compact disk read-only memory," is an optical storage medium that uses the same technology as music compact disks and can store vast amounts of information. This storage capacity makes an ideal medium to deliver software programs (Figure 13-4). A flash drive, sometimes referred to as a jump drive, is a small, lightweight, removable data storage device to which data can be written (Figure 13-5). Inserted into a USB port, a flash drive offers a dense form of storage that is impervious to scratches and dust. Printers reproduce on paper the text and image found on the computer. Scanners convert printed pages or graphic images into a file, which can be stored in a computer and retrieved by an end user.

Some of the items listed in the paragraph above are considered peripherals. A peripheral is a form of computer hardware that is added to a host computer to expand its capabilities. Peripherals are generally considered optional in nature. For that reason, devices like monitors and disk drives are not referred to as peripherals when they are not truly optional. Examples of peripherals include the mouse, scanner, printer, plotter, and microphones.

The personal computers available at employee workstations are often powerful computers capable of following multiple instructions at the same time. This was not always the case; at one time the terminal at an employee's workstation

Figure 13-3 | Computer hardware

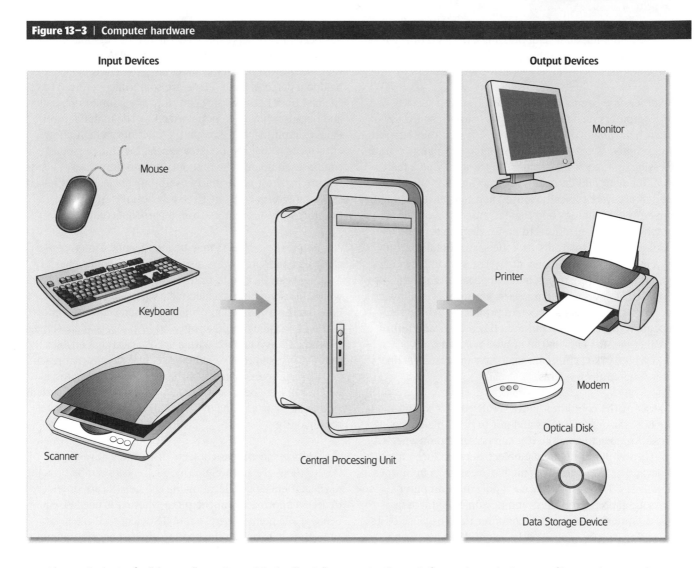

Input Devices

Mouse

Keyboard

Scanner

Central Processing Unit

Output Devices

Monitor

Printer

Modem

Optical Disk

Data Storage Device

was the equivalent of a "dummy" monitor with the "brain" computer housed in a separate room that held computer equipment (a **computer room**). This brain computer is referred to as a **mainframe,** a computer containing a powerful central processing unit that controls the activity of the dummy monitor. Under this setup, the monitor could only display data sent to it from the mainframe or send messages

to the mainframe through the use of keystrokes typed on a keyboard. This relationship between the mainframe computer and the dummy monitor made computers impractical for personal use until the advent of powerful personal computers in the 1990s.

Some mainframe computers are still in use in the business world. These mainframes may perform massive administrative functions such as processing census data or utility bills. They may also work at a lower administrative level,

Figure 13-4 | CD-ROM storage device

Figure 13-5 | Flash drive storage device

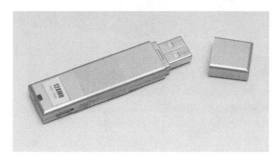

operating videoconferencing technology in multiple sites within one building or several buildings. Because of the revolution of personal computers and technology changes, mainframes have been largely replaced with servers.

Servers are computers that provide shared services to other computers on a network. Servers store resources and display them when you request them. Because they support many computer workstations, servers require a large central processing unit, an efficient operating system, and a high level of memory and data storage. Traditionally, one or more servers were typically housed in a central computer room; newer technology and the decreased size of servers have led many organizations to house them in server closets. Servers play many roles: as a file server holding data files, a mail server supporting an electronic mail program, an application server storing many applications, a database server supporting shared databases, a print server allowing all of a network's users access to a printer, a Web server accepting requests from remote Web browsers and returning Web pages for view in the browser, or a fax server enabling networked computer users to send faxes via one or more shared fax modems.

Most of the computer hardware discussed so far relates to stationary objects and not to portable or mobile objects. An object is **mobile** if it can be carried or wheeled from place to place. As mobile objects have reduced in both size and price, they have become more common in business and industry. Two commonly used portable computer objects are laptop computers and personal digital assistants. A **laptop computer** is a computer that, because of its smaller size, can be conveniently balanced on a person's knees (Figure 13–6). The laptop includes a shell-type case containing a keyboard, a liquid crystal display (LCD) monitor, and a hard disk, floppy disk, CD-ROM drive, or other rewriteable disc system. A laptop computer is powered by internal rechargeable batteries; as such, it is designed to offer several hours of operation away from an electrical

Figure 13–6 | A laptop computer

outlet. Within the health care context, the use of laptops has been largely supplanted by the use of personal digital assistants. A **personal digital assistant** (PDA) is a computer that, because of its even smaller size, can conveniently be held in a person's hand. PDAs are sometimes referred to as "palms" both because they can fit in the palm of one hand and because they were popularized by the manufacturer Palm Computing, Inc. Among its functions, a PDA allows entry of text that can be later synched with a personal computer to upload the text entries into databases. This feature makes it particularly useful for physicians and other caregivers who must see a series of patients in physical locations remote from a personal computer.

While these objects may be mobile, one cannot conclude that they are always also wireless. A mobile object by itself may not be able to transmit and receive data to a network but may require connectivity via cable or telephone line to receive updated information or send collected information to a large computer network. An object is considered **wireless** if it is equipped with a special card that enables it to broadcast and receive radio or cellular signals that reach a network via access points. As this definition illustrates, a wireless object does not require a physical connection such as a cable or telephone line to receive or transmit information continuously.

Mobile and wireless objects offer many advantages. Due to their size and weight, mobile objects can be brought to the patient's bedside, allowing the health care provider to access information at the place where it is needed. By being at the point of care, a mobile object facilitates data collection, eliminating the need to create handwritten notes for later entry into a stationary computer. By eliminating the need for cable, wireless objects may reduce costs to the health care provider; installing cable is labor intensive, may disrupt patient care, and may be difficult to accomplish in older buildings. Additionally, wireless objects may reduce errors if they are able to deliver up-to-date information and access to reference materials and prescription order processing applications.

Mobile and wireless objects do raise some concerns. Mobile objects are particularly prone to theft and loss due to their smaller size and lighter weight. Battery life varies considerably among mobile objects and according to use patterns and processing demands. Memory limitations are also present, as is the limited ability to display and see information due to screen size limits. Data may be lost if the mobile objects are damaged or stolen or if a battery dies before data can be shared with another computer. Finally, some wireless devices may be unable to transmit and receive information in certain locations if dead zones are present.

Software Software, like hardware, involves multiple areas including operating systems, application programs, utility programs, and programming languages. An operating system is the software that controls how the computer works. The type of operating system found on any given computer manages all of the hardware located in the computer and dictates what specific applications will work with the operating system. For example, two computers may contain the same type of CPU but run different operating systems, meaning that the two computers may be unable to run the same software application programs. Examples of commonly used operating systems include: Mac OS, used with Macintosh computers; UNIX and Solaris, used on network computers and computers that serve as major gateways to the Internet; and Windows, used on IBM-compatible computers.

An application program performs tasks on behalf of the end user. Application programs are typically self-contained, storing data within files of a special format that it can create, open for editing, and save to disk. Application programs create the screens end users see and the reports that are printed. Examples of application programs include word processing, accounting, mail, personnel evaluation, and games. By contrast, a utility program performs simple operations on files created by other programs. Utility programs generally are used to automate frequently required tasks.

A programming language is a created language used to write application and utility programs. Programming languages are readable by human beings but act by translating into binary machine code instructions for the computer to follow. Hundreds of different programming languages exist, with no one language remaining dominant for any length of time. Examples of commonly used programming languages include Visual Basic, PERL, C++, and Java. Programming languages also exist to enable users to interact with others on the Internet. Hypertext markup language (HTML) is a programming language that allows for the display of information in a similar format on different operating systems and system hardware. The body of text is surrounded by custom codes called tags, which allow the text to be formatted. Whereas HTML works well with text, it doesn't work well with raw data. Extensible markup language (XML) works with raw data, allowing it to be treated in a similar fashion. XML is based on a separate language called standard generalized markup language (SGML).

Units of Measure and Standards The capacity of a computer indicates how much storage it contains. Analogous to the paper world, a computer's storage capacity can be thought of in the same way as a file room's storage capacity. Instead of being measured by traditional measures, such as linear feet or square footage, the basic unit of measure for computer storage is a bit, a single digit representing either the number 1 or 0. A group of eight bits is called a byte. A byte is used to measure memory size (e.g., kilobyte and megabyte) and data transfer speed (e.g., kilobytes per second). Table 13-1 illustrates the various quantities used with

Table 13-1 | Units of Measure

Term	Abbreviation	Approximate Number of Characters
Bit	b	1
Byte	B	8
Kilobyte	KB	1,000
Megabyte	MB	1,000,000
Gigabyte	GB	1,000,000,000
Terabyte	TB	1,000,000,000,000

computer measurement. Understanding the units of measurement applicable to a computer system can assist with proper purchasing and maintenance of equipment.

Understanding the units of measure can also assist in understanding how computers operate. Computers work by receiving, processing, and storing data. Computers rely on binary code to represent alphanumeric characters. This binary code, the series of numbers 1 or 0 referred to as bits, is combined into bytes. Each byte represents a particular character—for example, binary code 00001101 represents the number 13. When bytes are processed in sequence, they have specific meaning. It is that meaning that provides the instructions directing what work the computer will perform.

Standards are the technical specifications or other precise criteria to be used consistently as rules, guidelines, or other definitions of characteristics in order to ensure that materials, products, processes, or services are fit for their purposes. The importance of standards cannot be overstated, since it is the mutual adherence to these standards that permit the interchange of hardware components and the exchange of data between different manufacturer's computers. An international organization, the International Organization for Standardization (ISO), has promulgated standards for hardware connectors, character sets, network protocols, and programming languages, among other standards.

Information Systems Life Cycle

An additional concept relating to computers is the information systems life cycle. Information systems life cycle refers to the succession of stages of an information system. It is a subset of management in the sense that managers actively practice review and decision making with regard to the hardware and software maintained by an organization. The life cycle stages typically include design and development, implementation and testing, operation and maintenance, and obsolescence. The cycle begins with recognition of the need for new or replacement computer hardware or software. Some organizations develop time frames for the cyclical replacement of their computer hardware and budget

Figure 13-7 | Information systems life cycle

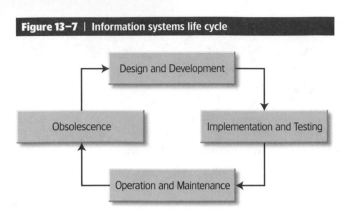

Table 13-3 | Elements of an IT Project Justification Statement

1	The project's primary users, sponsors, and stakeholders
2	The project's objective and scope
3	The business need, particularly related to requirements or outcomes to be accomplished
4	The problem, deficiency, or opportunity presented
5	A cost/benefit analysis or a business case in economic terms
6	The interfaces, performance measures, and operational procedures to solve the problem, deficiency, or opportunity

accordingly. Others perform a routine assessment of software applications and functional needs, identifying areas for future development. An example of this life cycle approach is illustrated in Figure 13-7.

To gain an understanding of the information systems life cycle process, it is instructive to apply it in context. An effective method of doing so is to illustrate the life cycle process through the use of project management in the information technology setting. The following illustration focuses on the life cycle process of an IT project, as opposed to the principles of project management, which are discussed in detail in Chapter 11, "Management Organization." No particular IT project is identified in this exercise, allowing the learner to focus on the six life cycle phases typically present in IT projects, which are listed in Table 13-2.

The steps begin with an identification of the need for and justification of the new IT project. Identification of the need may come about in many ways, including the existence of a problem or deficiency requiring a solution, a new opportunity gleaned from industry trends, changes in legislation affecting the organization, or the need to economize, to name only a few reasons. Justifying the project often involves preparation of a project justification statement, once referred to as a mission needs statement. This statement identifies the problem or deficiency facing the organization, defines the scope of the effort required to resolve the problem or deficiency, and provides an economic justification for the project. The details often contained in a project justification statement are listed in Table 13-3. The manner in which an entity is organized will determine the

distribution of this document and the number of concurrences required to approve the request.

Once approved, the project moves to the requirements phase where the project team defines and documents the project's requirements. These requirements include attributes that the solution must possess if it is to operate successfully in its intended environment and satisfy the end users' needs; examples include functional, performance, security, interface, system, and interoperability requirements. By identifying these needs accurately and timely, the possibility for "requirements creep" is minimized and the focus and direction of the project is established.

This information sets the stage for the alternatives analysis phase. Here, the focus is on identifying and analyzing alternate solutions to determine which is most advantageous to the project. Such analysis includes a comparison of the costs, benefits, schedule, and performance risk against the established project requirements. Additional considerations, such as disaster recovery and security issues, may be included. If no one alternative solution meets all of the stated requirements, the solution that meets a majority of the requirements is reviewed to determine whether it provides the best benefit to the organization.

Phase three presents a choice of whether to procure commercial off-the-shelf software (COTS) or develop an internal system to fit the organization's needs. Considerations such as the time frame in which the product or service is needed, access to source code, the ability to support development and testing efforts, the ability and cost of creating modifications and enhancements over time, and the need for ongoing support over the life of the product or service all influence the decision. If a COTS solution is chosen, procurement actions follow, many of which are described in detail in Chapter 14, "Financial Management." If an internal system development solution is chosen, considerable resources must be available within the organization to support this approach.

Phase four involves development and testing of the chosen solution. Development involves creating source code (in the context of software applications), preparing

Table 13-2 | Life Cycle Phases of IT Projects

Project identification and justification
Definition of requirements
Alternatives analysis
Design/procurement
Development and testing
Implementation and support

supporting documentation, and conducting internal testing and validation. Testing of either a procured or internally developed solution includes using or creating a set of standardized instruction manuals for users of the software or hardware to determine whether the solution can perform in the applicable environment. Typically, this testing is concluded with preparation of a test analysis report, an installation and operations guide, and an implementation plan.

Implementation and support is the last phase in the life cycle of the IT project. Implementation may occur over a period of time, particularly if multiple institutions within a larger organization all choose to implement the same solution. Upon full deployment and training for all end users, implementation is considered complete, subject only to future enhancements and modifications. These future improvements are referred to as versions, if they provide new functionality, or releases, if they provide routine maintenance, patches, or fixes to existing functionality. Releases are often categorized as part of user support, that portion of the phase that includes the normal maintenance of a product or service. Support can also include changes required due to statutory mandates, emergency or normal modification requests, information systems architecture changes (such as changes to an operating system), and improvements to address poor performance. Some support systems offer a help desk feature to assist end users with operation and maintenance of the product or service, or a post-implementation review to determine the extent and degree to which the solution meets the end users' needs. The relationship between implementation and support is illustrated in Figure 13–8.

Although the project is complete at the end of this phase, the life cycle is not. At some point, the particular solution that was selected may become obsolete, the need for this solution may extinguish, or an entirely new problem, deficiency, or opportunity may arise. Whatever the cause, the life cycle begins anew with a needs identification and project justification, followed by the remaining phases of the life cycle.

Communication Technologies

Understanding the basics of computer concepts serves as the means to understanding the technologies involved in their communications. Communication technologies

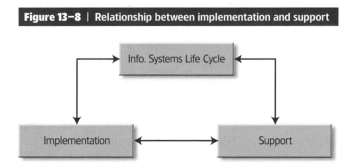

Figure 13–8 | Relationship between implementation and support

applicable to computers include networks, the Internet, intranets, and extranets.

A network is a collection of computers connected together by way of cables or wireless links so that they can exchange data with one another. Besides computers, networks can include printers, fax modems, scanners, CD-ROM drives, tape backup units, and plotters. For example, the computers at several workstations within a department can be connected to a single printer or scanning station.

Many different types of networks exist. A local area network (LAN) connects computers that are located within a small area—for example, in the same office or firm found within the same or closely adjacent areas or buildings. The industry standard for a LAN is the Ethernet, a medium that controls the signals computers send to one another. A metropolitan area network (MAN) connects an array of computers across a campus or city, often employing wireless infrastructure or optical fiber connections to link between sites. A wide area network (WAN) connects computers that are widely separated geographically, typically by cities, countries, or continents; the Internet is an example of a WAN. Because of this wide geographic spread, a WAN uses long-distance communication technologies to connect the computers. A virtual private network (VPN) is a WAN that connects private subscribers (e.g., employees of the same company) together using the public Internet as the transport medium while ensuring through encryption technology that the private subscribers' traffic is not readable by the Internet at large. A VPN can be used with two widely separated LANs belonging to the same firm or organization through the use of a tunneling protocol.

The Internet is a worldwide network of smaller networks. The Internet began in the late 1960s as part of the U.S. Department of Defense's efforts to provide a decentralized network of communication that could not be destroyed at any one nerve center in the event of a nuclear attack. It gradually grew to include educational and other institutions and eventually expanded to the public at large. Although the Internet is not owned by any one entity or organization, many of the smaller networks that comprise the Internet are managed by governments, corporations, educational institutions, and not-for-profit organizations. Certain nongovernmental bodies maintain the Internet, such as the Internet Architecture Board, the Internet Engineering Task Force, and the Internet Assigned Numbers Authority.

The Internet is organized into three levels of carriers, considered in a tree-like fashion. The trunk consists of the Internet backbone, the high-speed, high-capacity networks that carry Internet traffic around the world. These networks include military networks and commercial fiber optic networks owned by large telecommunications companies. The branches are mid-level networks and the twigs are stub networks. Individuals and organizations that wish to access the Internet do so through Internet service providers. An **Internet service provider** (ISP) is a company that provides Internet services, such as hosting Web sites, and sells access to the Internet. Very few ISPs connect directly to the Internet backbone. Most ISPs are resellers who lease connections to the Internet from one of the aforementioned large telecommunications companies and share this bandwidth among their paying customers.

Connecting to the Internet involves not only the use of an ISP but also a communications device. Common communications devices include modems and high-speed devices such as Integrated Services Digital Networks (ISDNs). A **modem** is a device that allows a computer to transfer information over a telephone line. Since a modem is a device, it falls within the definition of hardware. It works by converting digital computer data into analog sound signals. Traditional modems dial a telephone number to establish a connection over a public telephone line, commonly referred to as "dial-up and connect." Modems that are attached to the outside of the computer are called external modems; modems that sit inside the computer are referred to as internal modems. Other types of modems include: fax (facsimile) modems that work to transform documents and scanned pictures into the standard fax data format for transmission; null modems that work via a cable allowing two computers to communicate directly; and software modems that work via software rather than hardware.

High-speed devices such as ISDN, cable modems, and digital subscriber line (DSL) technology are popular alternatives to traditional modems because they increase the speed of access to the Internet. **ISDN** is a public digital data network intended to supplant traditional telephone systems. An adapter is required to link a personal computer to the ISDN line found on traditional telephone wiring, allowing one to send and receive digital signals. **Cable modems** work via cable television connections, allowing one to transmit and receive all data as digital signals. Cable modems require the use of security software because, unlike dial-up modems, turning on a computer with a cable modem automatically connects one to the Internet. **DSL** also transmits all data as digital signals but does not require access to television connections. Rather, DSL uses traditional telephone wiring but transmits the data at higher frequencies than those used for voice transmission. DSL technologies vary by the relative speeds of incoming and outgoing signals and the distance from the exchange over which they can operate.

Although the Internet crosses over many different types of hardware, users are able to communicate because of the **Internet Protocol** (IP), which controls all of the traffic on the Internet. It uses an **Internet Protocol address** scheme, which is a unique number that is assigned to each host computer connected to the Internet so as to distinguish computers from one another. The IP address works with the Domain Name Service (DNS) to translate the numeric IP

Table 13–4	Recognized Domain Names within the United States
.aero	airline, airport, computer reservations, and related industries
.biz	a business
.com	a commercial organization
.coop	a business cooperative
.edu	an educational institution
.gov	a governmental entity
.info	a global identifier
.int	an international organization
.mil	a branch of the U.S. military
.museum	an accredited museum (worldwide)
.name	a category for individuals
.net	a network organization
.org	a not-for-profit organization
.pro	professional status

address into a human readable host name, for example www.delmarcengagelearning.com. The **domain name** is the name given to a server or group of servers connected to the Internet. For example, in an e-mail address, the wording following the @ symbol constitutes the domain name. Domain names recognized in the United States are listed in Table 13–4.

The Internet became universally available in the early 1990s with the advent of the World Wide Web (the Web). The **World Wide Web** (WWW) is a set of technology standards that enables the publishing of multimedia documents to be read by anyone with access to the Internet. These multimedia documents include text, images, sound, and video. In order for the Web to operate, three software components must be used: (1) the hypertext markup language (HTML) that describes what a Web page should look like; (2) a Web browser that can interpret HTML—such as Netscape Navigator and Internet Explorer—and display it on a computer screen; and (3) the hypertext transfer protocol (HTTP) that enables a browser to send requests for pages across the Internet and return HTML descriptions to it. Pages on the Web are identified with unique labels called uniform resource locators (URLs), such as http://www.thomson.com.

E-HIM

Internet access has greatly impacted health care providers and patients by fostering the ability to obtain and exchange health information.

Access to the Web has greatly impacted both the practice of medicine and the patient's knowledge base. Health care providers use the Internet for access to medical information, the latest health care news, libraries of medical data and clinical alerts, and patient records. Providers may further research poison center databases and the results of clinical studies, for example. This access and research can enhance the health care provider's ability to care for his patients. Patients use the Internet to research their conditions, register for clinical trials, learn about their prescriptions, schedule participation in screening programs, and purchase durable medical equipment. In addition to these activities, providers and patients may communicate directly with each other to improve a patient's care. This direct communication constitutes electronic health (e-health) practice, discussed in more detail further in this chapter.

One recent development involving the interplay between the Web and health care providers is the use of portals. A portal is a Web site that offers free entry to numerous other sites through the use of links. Links are Internet Protocol addresses that are activated to provide a connection between a browser and another site on the Internet. Familiar examples of portals used in the commercial sector include Yahoo!, Lycos, and MSN, among others. Portals are often seen as advantageous because of their low cost and their ability to integrate with different information systems already in existence. Portals are used in the health care setting for many purposes, including allowing facilities with multiple campuses and locations the ability to bridge the sites where data are stored and display that data in a ready manner at one site on the Internet. Some health care facilities use portals as the means for patients to access their own health information, make appointments, and order medication refills while at the same time allowing the provider to review that same information as well as medical research articles.

Two additional communication technologies are the intranet and extranet. An intranet is similar to the Internet in that it uses the three software components of the World Wide Web. It differs, however, in that an intranet operates as a private network that is accessible only within one organization. So, although there is only one public Internet, as many intranets can exist as there are organizations. It is not uncommon to find that a personal computer within an organization displays mechanisms to access both the Internet and an intranet. An extranet is an intranet system that allows selected external users limited access to the private networks. The external user selected typically has a prior relationship with the organization operating the intranet (e.g., as a supplier). Authentication methods are employed to address security concerns.

Security

Within a computer context, security is defined as the means to regulate access to and ensure preservation of data. Communication technology is implicated with regard to access. Within the health information management context, security is implicated through a disruption of the health care facility's computer system, an interruption or discontinuation of a

Table 13-5 | Information Technology Security Measures

Authentication	The process of ensuring that people are who they say they are
Permission	The level of access to an operating system or application given to a person or group of persons
Encryption	The mechanism to prevent third parties from eavesdropping on a communication
Damage Prevention	Preventing malicious attempts to damage data or bring down a computer
Disaster Recovery	The plans used to resume immediate computer operations in the event of a problem

telemedicine session, unauthorized access to patient medical records, or the destruction or modification of patient information, among other examples. Such unauthorized access, destruction, or modification leads to privacy violations, particularly a breach of confidentiality.

Security measures can be divided into five main areas: authentication, permission, encryption, damage prevention, and disaster recovery; these are listed in Table 13-5. All five areas are needed in order to ensure security of any given computer system. Authentication is the process of ensuring that people are who they say they are when using a computer. This is performed typically by examining some identifying information such as a password or a digital signature. Permission is the level of access granted by the operating system to a person or group of persons. Permission levels may apply to individual files or entire directories. Encryption is the mechanism employed so that no third party can eavesdrop on the communication. Encryption involves encoding data so that it may be read only by authorized persons.

The remaining two areas, damage prevention and implementing disaster recovery plans, involve multiple mechanisms. The prevention of malicious attempts to damage data or bring down a computer may include either of two mechanisms: firewalls and virus scanning. A firewall is special hardware or software placed between a computer and the Internet that serves to monitor all traffic passing between them. A firewall allows the end user to access the Internet but prevents unauthorized users from obtaining access to the end user's computer. Firewalls are considered the first level of protection and are the most common security measure taken by firms or organizations connected to the Internet. Firewalls are particularly important for use with high-speed devices that provide access to the Internet, since high-speed devices often involve automatic access to the Internet once the computer is turned on. A virus scan is the process of searching a hard drive or network data stream to detect the presence of computer viruses. A computer virus is a small computer program capable of copying itself from one computer to another. Almost exclusively written to cause damage on the computers they infect, computer viruses are spread either through the downloading of files from the Internet or by being hidden in an attachment to an electronic mail message. Antivirus software used in virus scanning detects and removes viruses. Unfortunately, the development of new viruses is on the rise, making it necessary to update antivirus software on a regular basis.

Firewalls and virus scans operate to protect organizations from hackers and crackers. **Hackers** are persons who gain unauthorized access to computer systems and networks. **Crackers** are criminal hackers. Often considered to be one and the same, hackers and crackers work by creating a denial of service through system overload, mounting spam attacks (the repetitive sending of junk e-mail), spoofing IP addresses to take control of another person's server, requesting personal information using a false e-mail address as a way to commit identity theft or fraud (phishing), creating computer viruses, and setting traps to capture the passwords of legitimate users. These cyber attacks can have considerable impact on the operational and financial aspects of an organization.[1]

Disaster recovery plans are the blueprints used to resume immediate computer operations in the event of a problem. As part of these plans, a firm or organization institutes a rigorous **backup regime**, copying on a regular basis the data stored on a computer or server so that it can be restored should the original data be destroyed. Such a backup regime would specify what data should be backed up (e.g., protected health information or application software), the frequency of the backup process, on what media the backups are stored, how they are tested, and the storage location. The firm or organization would also arrange for the use of duplicate computer equipment at an alternative or mobile site. Disaster recovery plans are applicable whether the problem is theft; mechanical failure or software failure at the firm's or organization's current site; or a natural disaster such as flood, fire, or tornado requiring the use of a temporary base. These plans are also mandated by accrediting organizations such as the Joint Commission and the Accreditation Association for Ambulatory Health Care.[2]

The use of application service providers (ASPs) creates an often overlooked security issue. **Application service providers** are organizations that provide customers, for a fee, with access to software applications located on servers away from the customer's site. Using desktop computers or wireless devices, the customer communicates with these applications to perform such functions as storing patient-specific health information, claims processing, appointment scheduling, and accounting. Application service providers are particularly useful for health care providers who lack the technology support staff to install and maintain internal applications and for those who find the cost of purchasing, installing, and maintaining software applications prohibitively expensive. If not resolved by contract terms, security issues such as who has access (permission levels) to the data stored on the ASP's servers will place the health care provider in a vulnerable position.

HIPAA

The Security Rule establishes security safeguards for protected health information that a covered entity creates, receives, maintains, or transmits in an electronic format.

HIPAA Security Rule Layered above all of these levels of security are the security control provisions found in the final rule issued pursuant to the Health Insurance Portability and Accountability Act (HIPAA).[3] This **Security Rule** establishes security safeguards for protected health information (PHI) that a covered entity creates, receives, maintains, or transmits in an electronic format. These safeguards serve to: (1) protect the confidentiality of data so that only those persons authorized may see the data; (2) ensure data integrity by protecting it from unauthorized creation, modification, or deletion; and (3) allow data to be available when it is needed. These safeguards are categorized in three ways—administrative, physical, and technical—with each category containing both standards and implementation specifications. Table 13–6 compares these three categories.

Eighteen different security standards exist. These standards specify the use of integrity controls and encryption technology when transmitting electronic protected health information; information access management techniques such as authorization, establishment, and modification of access privileges (permission levels); workforce security standards such as clearance checks of personnel

Table 13–6	HIPAA Security Safeguards		
	Administrative Safeguards	**Physical Safeguards**	**Technical Safeguards**
Number of Standards	9	4	5
Specifications	12 required and 11 addressable implementation specifications	4 required and 6 addressable implementation specifications	4 required and 5 addressable implementation standards
Statutory Provision	Section 164.308	Section 164.310	Section 164.312

and termination procedures; and access controls such as automatic logoff and emergency access procedures.

These security standards in turn create 42 implementation specifications, which fall within two categories: required and addressable. Required specifications means that a covered entity must implement the standard, allowing no flexibility for the covered entity to determine what is reasonable in the implementation process. Addressable specifications means that the covered entity is not bound to implement the specification as identified by Department of Health and Human Services (DHHS) but has some flexibility to determine reasonableness in implementation. This additional flexibility does not mean that the covered entity can ignore the specification if it decides it is unreasonable. Rather, the addressability component is designed such that a covered entity that finds a specification unreasonable must document that unreasonableness and identify what other steps it has taken to protect personally identifiable health information that it considers reasonable.

The essence of administrative safeguards under HIPAA is to help covered entities take actions and create policies and procedures to manage the development, implementation, and maintenance of security measures to protect personally identifiable health information. These actions, policies, and procedures should be designed to assist the covered entity in preventing, detecting, containing, and correcting security violations. Each covered entity is required to perform a risk analysis of its security practices, which should identify the way protected health information in an electronic format is accessed and any potential vulnerabilities to that information. Examples of activities a covered entity may engage in to comply with the administrative safeguards include monitoring computer access activity by end users (e.g., login access attempts); protecting PHI from viruses and software attacks; changing passwords on a periodic basis; and creating contingency plans for continuing operations in the event of a disaster, emergency situation, or loss of data.

The essence of physical safeguards under HIPAA is to help covered entities protect their electronic information systems and related building and equipment from unauthorized intrusions and natural and environmental hazards. This focus on systems, facilities, and equipment addresses security from a macro level and differs from administrative safeguards, which addresses security from a micro level. For example, the physical safeguards would restrict an individual's access to facilities housing electronic information systems, whereas the administrative safeguards would restrict an individual's access to the data residing in a database. Examples of activities a covered entity may engage in to comply with the physical safeguards include establishing access levels to physical space based on a person's role or function; ensuring that workstations are properly secure (including portable devices); establishing disposal policies and procedures for disks, tapes, storage devices, and other equipment; and establishing regular backup routines.

The essence of technical safeguards under HIPAA is to help covered entities employ technological solutions to secure electronic PHI. This focus on technology should assist the covered entity in limiting unauthorized access and ensuring data integrity. Examples of activities a covered entity may engage in to comply with the technical safeguards include employing encryption technology with its electronic mail (e-mail) system; examining activity occurring on its computer networks; assigning unique identifiers to end users as a way to identify and track their use of electronic information systems; and employing account validation or password identification schemes to authenticate a user's identity.

In addition, the Security Rule addresses training requirements for staff concerning the vulnerability of protected health information in a covered entity's possession and the procedures to be followed to protect such information. While the rule itself does not specify what training should be provided to which employee, a training program on computer security basics is necessary for all staff, including managers, agents, contractors, and maintenance personnel. This training could address such topics as virus protection, password management, physical/workstation security, the mechanism to report known or suspected breaches, monitoring procedures, and sanctions, both at the individual and organizational levels. Once training has been delivered, the covered entity must document that it was provided plus document how it will periodically review, validate, and update the training program.

Woven throughout the Security Rule is the requirement that a covered entity establish effective information security policies. Information security policies are those policies that define the framework around which an information security program is managed.[4] These policies answer the "who, what, where, when, why, and how" questions of information security. Information security policies may have common elements, such as specification of roles and responsibilities, standards to which employees must adhere, and the level of compliance that is expected with those standards. These policies may be applied at different levels, such as organizational, system specific, or issue specific.

HIPAA

While proceeding from different angles, both the Privacy and Security Rules serve to protect data from unauthorized uses and disclosures.

The relationship between the HIPAA Security and Privacy Rules is symbiotic in their protection of personally identifiable health information. Both rules employ similar

Table 13-7 | HIPAA Security Officer Actions

Design, implement, manage, and enforce HIPAA security directives
Address organization's needs for access controls, disaster recovery, business continuity, and information risk management
Perform risk assessments and audits
Lead incident response team to security breach
Lead awareness and training efforts for workforce
Improve IT security within organization and with vendors, consultants, and other third parties

INFORMATICS

The study of both the structure and general properties of information and the design and implementation of technology to use and communicate that information is the focus of informatics.

terminology and the parallel treatment of business associates and three major safeguards. The HIPAA Privacy Rule serves to protect this information by providing patients with more control over their own health information through safeguards and limitations imposed upon covered entities. These safeguards and limitations specify the actions covered entities may engage in or are prohibited from engaging in while protecting the information, particularly with regard to the use and release of information. The HIPAA Security Rule serves to protect this same information by specifying the technical requirements, policies, and procedures that covered entities can use to protect data from known threats and vulnerabilities Although both rules proceed from different angles, they both serve the ultimate goal of protecting data from unauthorized uses and disclosures.

The Security Rule also mirrors the Privacy Rule in the way that it assigns responsibility for compliance with HIPAA's mandated security directives to an individual within the covered entity. This Security Officer is tasked with the responsibility of developing and implementing information security policies, procedures, and technology systems required under the rule to maintain the confidentiality, integrity, and availability of both protected health information and the organization's health care information systems. The Security Officer accomplishes this through a variety of actions, many of which are included in Table 13-7.

Informatics

Whereas information technology has its roots in the 20th century, a fairly new discipline within information technology arose in the last third of that century: informatics. **Informatics** refers to the discipline focusing on the study of both the structure and general properties of information and the design and implementation of technology to use and communicate that information. Informatics is a broad and wide discipline that can encompass computer programming, database management, mathematical modeling, statistics, and research design, to name only a few areas. The discipline arose in Europe, took its name as an adaptation of the French term *informatique*, and moved rapidly to the United States and worldwide. Informatics resulted from the convergence of the late-20th-century explosions in the volume and type of information stored electronically and the availability of new computer technologies.

Multiple subsets of this discipline exist, and many are listed in Table 13-8. Of particular interest for readers of this text is **health care informatics,** which concentrates on how to use technology to facilitate acquiring, processing, interpreting, using, and communicating health care data. Health care informatics intersects with health information management in that both concern health care data. They differ in that the focus of informatics is on the *technology* and its uses, whereas health information management focuses on the *data* itself, with the technology seen as an aid and not an end in itself. By focusing on the data itself, the health

Table 13-8 | Subsets of the Informatics Discipline

Medical Informatics	Application of technology to support specialized activities associated with a range of health care workers and the practice of medicine
Health Care Informatics	Application of technology to facilitate acquiring, processing, interpreting, using, and communicating health care data
Clinical Informatics	Application of technology to enhance clinical information management at the point of patient care, using information processes, systems, and tools to improve the effectiveness, quality, and value of care
Dental Informatics	Application of technology to support specialized activities associated with improving dental practice, research, education, and management
Public Health Informatics	Application of technology to support public health practice, research, and learning
Nursing Informatics	Application of technology to support specialized activities associated with nursing practice and support activities
Consumer Health Informatics	Application of technology to analyze consumer needs for information and the methods for making that information accessible, according to consumer preferences
Educational Informatics	Application of technology to facilitate the learning process

information management professional must understand the media in which data is generated, stored, or retrieved (whether electronic or not) and move beyond it to issues of managing that data to achieve protection, security, and compliance with ethical and legal requirements.

Informatics has been instrumental in developing numerous applications that comprise the clinical information systems component of a health care information system. These applications allow the clinician to access information quickly and accurately, thereby eliminating the duplication of data collection efforts by numerous health care providers. These applications support a variety of health care professionals and functional areas. For example, a monitoring application uses technology to monitor biometric measurements in critical care and other specialty areas. The monitoring application integrates the technology used to collect the data (e.g., blood glucose monitors) with the technology used by the clinician or support staff at a separate location (e.g., the laboratory system) to display the biometric measurements in a graphic manner and compare them to the patient's past biometric measurements in order to discover trends or to alert the clinician to significant abnormal findings.

Two significant contributions of informatics to health care are the development of computerized physician order entry (CPOE) and pharmacy applications, commonly referred to in combination as **e-prescribing**. CPOE refers to applications that permit physicians to enter directly into a computer system orders for medications and treatments. These orders are transmitted promptly to the appropriate functional area—for example, pharmacy, laboratory, or radiology—for action. Pharmacy applications not only assist in the ordering of medications but also in the dispensing and administrating of the medications; they automate the labor-intensive process of pharmacist review of patient history and allergies, clinical progress, medication profile, laboratory values, and potential drug interactions. This component is a decision support function. E-prescribing has contributed to promoting patient care and containing costs because it reduces the margin of error in the delivery of patient care, as in the case of deciphering illegible handwriting, and provides an automated means to track usage, costs, and inventory.

One of the newest subsets of informatics involves public health. **Public health informatics** refers to the application of technology to public health practice, research, and learning. This technology is used to develop communication, surveillance, information, and learning systems related to public health. In addition to computer programming, public health informatics draws upon the fields of epidemiology, microbiology, toxicology, organizational theory, communications, political science, law, and statistics to accomplish its objectives. Those objectives address the improvement of the health of populations as a whole instead of the health of a

specific individual, and the prevention of disease or injury through the altering of conditions or environments that pose risks to the population. Because public health exists in a governmental context, the effectiveness of public health informatics is dependent upon addressing the legislative, regulatory, and policy directives; the balancing of competing priorities; and battling the existence of chronic underfunding present in public health. Doing so will lead to growth of this subset of the informatics discipline.

Another subset of informatics involves education. **Educational informatics**, sometimes referred to as **e-learning**, is the application of technology to facilitate the learning process. An elementary example of educational informatics applications is computer-assisted instruction (CAI), whether delivered in a classroom setting or across a distance via the Internet. Several methodologies are used with CAI, including tutorials, simulations, drills and practice, instructional games, and computerized tests. Several technologies are also used with CAI, including text-only instruction; interactive media including CM-ROMs, DVDs, and interactive videos; virtual reality; and Web-based instruction.

While each subset of informatics described in this section illustrates a technological application, the subsets should be considered in the context of their relationship to the discipline that is assisted technologically. By doing so, informatics can be seen as the aid that it is, albeit a powerful aid with great potential to move beyond its present applications and into additional disciplines.

Technology Applications and Trends

The latest applications and trends in technology have greatly influenced the delivery of health care. Whereas inpatient hospitalization was once the standard practice for surgery and treatment of serious illness and disease, advances in technology have allowed patients to safely undergo procedures in ambulatory care centers and return home the same day. Electronic health has seen steady growth. In particular, new applications such as telemedicine, voice recognition technology, interactive voice recognition, and digital imaging systems have brought new efficiencies to the health care field. The long-awaited transformation from paper-based medical records to electronic health records is taking place across the United States. All of these elements combined have resulted in rapid change in the health care industry.

Electronic health (**e-health**) refers to health improvement and disease management techniques that utilize the Web and other interactive electronic communication tools.[5] E-health applies to both consumers and businesses. Entities and organizations that collect and display individually

Figure 13–9 | E-health

E-Health Organizations

Business to Business	Business to Consumer
Use the Internet to electronically deliver systems and services to health care providers	Use the Internet to electronically deliver systems and services to consumers

identifiable health information over the Internet are known as **e-health organizations**. Patients who participate in e-health are known as **e-health consumers**, defined as individuals whose individually identifiable health information is collected, maintained, or displayed over the Internet. As e-health has developed, two main types of e-health organizations have become prominent: business to business (B2B) and business to consumer (B2C). Examples of both types of organizations are found in Figures 13–9 and 13–10.

Another new trend is **information brokering**, the business of buying and selling information as a commodity. Information brokering began in earnest in Europe in the 20th century, with entrepreneurs creating businesses which provided selected information to those who subscribed to their services for a fee. Information brokering in the healthcare context is still in the early stages and has focused on the need for privacy of protected health information from intrusion by those lacking a patient's authorization. As the practice of brokering information develops, more robust applications will no doubt emerge.

Telemedicine, sometimes referred to as **telehealth**, is the use of electronic communications and information technologies to provide or support clinical care at a distance. Telemedicine connects the patient to the health care provider through the use of multimedia communications and information technologies. These electronic communications

and information technologies take the form of full-motion video, audio capabilities including radio and telephone, still images, facsimile, and color screens to facilitate face-to-face contact. Application packages can include image capture, blood pressure and pulse meters, analog-based audio stethoscopes, and digital dermascopes built into the video system.

Telemedicine works well in remote areas where access to health care professionals may be limited and in urban and suburban areas where specialists in the field are located some distance from the patient. Telemedicine can improve communication between health care providers and reduce transportation expenses. Using telemedicine, health care providers may diagnose, treat, and monitor patients located at a distance from the providers themselves. Examples of use include the transfer of diagnostic images such as CAT scans, MRIs, and X-rays to a specialist for a second opinion; the use of video visits for housebound patients; and video-conferencing between a counselor and a patient located some distance apart.

In addition to influencing how health care is delivered, telemedicine impacts who pays for health care. As telemedicine grew into accepted medical practice, third-party payers began reimbursing practitioner-to-practitioner teleconsultations. In 1999, Medicare issued reimbursement rules that allowed reimbursement for teleconsultations in rural health professional shortage areas.[6] The acceptance of telemedicine practice by the federal government resulted in wider acceptance of reimbursement by private third-party payers.

Other examples of efficiency include voice recognition technology (VRT) and interactive voice recognition (IVR). Also referred to as continuous speech recognition, **voice recognition technology** is a computer application that uses voice patterns to allow a computer to record and automatically translate voice into written language in real time. In other words, VRT allows a computer to convert the spoken

Figure 13–10 | E-health relationships

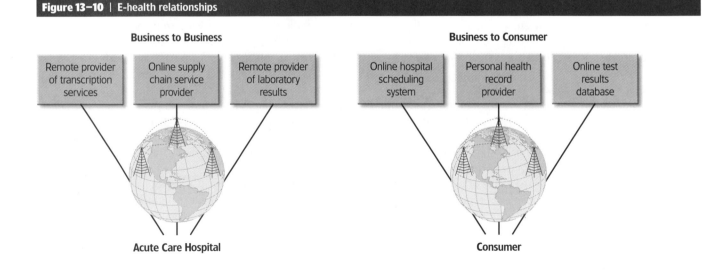

Business to Business

Remote provider of transcription services · Online supply chain service provider · Remote provider of laboratory results — **Acute Care Hospital**

Business to Consumer

Online hospital scheduling system · Personal health record provider · Online test results database — **Consumer** word into a word processing document. VRT is particularly applicable to dictation, where the voice of the person dictating is transcribed into streams of printable text. Effective VRT systems allow the health care provider to generate self-transcribed reports at an acceptable level of accuracy.

Interactive voice recognition is a computer application that allows a person to use a telephone to gain access by voice alone to information in a computer. It differs from VRT in that, using interactive voice recognition, the voice is interactive with the computer. For example, the voice can give a command to the computer and activate devices. In a housebound setting, IVR can activate a recirculator pump to heat water in a shower and open the curtains in a bedroom, preventing a physically disabled individual from risking injury by performing those tasks himself. IVR has also been used in settings where the housebound patient must check his status. For example, a computer equipped with IVR can be programmed with a motion detection device set at 30-minute intervals. If the computer does not detect movement within the time frame, IVR is activated to seek confirmation from the patient that he is all right. If no confirmation occurs, the computer automatically contacts persons on a call list, such as the attending physician, the home health nurse, or a family member. Such contact would indicate the need to check on the patient's well-being.[7]

E-HIM

Digital imaging facilitates the use of information by multiple persons simultaneously.

Not all technology applications are directed toward the delivery of patient care. Digital imaging, for example, involves the use of technology to store patient information. **Digital imaging** is a system in which paper documents are scanned on devices that work similar to a photocopier, allowing the image to be saved to an optical disc, a compact disk (CD), or magnetic tape. Once the image is electronically indexed, it can be viewed through a server or Web browser.

Many advantages are gained through the use of a digital imaging system: multiple users may simultaneously access the same image at the same time; viewers can be assured of the image's integrity because it cannot be altered; viewers can readily locate the image as compared to locating a paper-based file; the need for and cost of storage space is lessened; images can be readily recovered in the event of a disaster; images can be readily transferred to remote locations quickly and easily; and audit trail capabilities allow for tracing the path of access to a given image. Equally important is the opportunity for faster coding and chart completion, which can result in better accounts receivable management.

Digital imaging should not be confused with the electronic health record (EHR). An EHR contains clinical applica-

tions that provide enhanced medical decisions, and it allows the end user to retrieve the clinical content stored within the documents displayed. Digital imaging, by contrast, is the electronic storage of paper records and text, with all of those problems inherent with paper records and text (e.g., illegible handwriting and difficulty in collecting data in a standardized, organized manner). Digital imaging allows for retrieval of the documents in the record but not of the clinical content stored within the document. Digital imaging is, however, often seen as a bridge or stepping-stone to the future implementation of an electronic health record.

Electronic Health Records

One of the most exciting trends in technology is the advent of an electronic health record. Sometimes described as a computerized patient record or patient record system, an **electronic health record** (EHR) is defined as:

> [A]n electronic record that resides in a system specifically designed to support users by providing accessibility to complete and accurate data, alerts, reminders, clinical decision support systems, links to medical knowledge and other aids.[8]

Another descriptor for an EHR, as defined by the Institute of Medicine, is as follows:

> A **clinical information system** has a central focus of clinical data, not financial or billing information. Such systems may be limited in their scope to a single area of clinical information (e.g., lab data) or they may be comprehensive and cover virtually every facet of clinical information pertinent to patient care (e.g., computer-based patient record systems).[9]

A third descriptor for an EHR is that of the Computer-based Patient Record Institute (CPRI), now a part of the Healthcare Information and Management Systems Society (HIMSS): a system that integrates data from multiple sources, captures data at the point of care, and supports health care providers in their decision making.[10] For purposes of clarity, this discussion refers to the patient record created and maintained in an electronic format as an electronic health record or EHR.

Many views have developed over time to describe the functionality of an EHR. These views range from how much data to include (e.g., all patient data vs. limited patient data); whether to offer decision support capabilities (e.g., clinical guideline-driven prompts); whether the EHR should be enterprise specific or community specific; and whether the EHR should differ based on practice settings (e.g., hospital, ambulatory care, or nursing home). Only recently has the Institute of Medicine identified the core functionalities that constitute an electronic health record.[11] These functionalities are illustrated in Table 13–9.

Table 13-9 | Functionalities of an EHR

Health information and data

Results management

Electronic communications

Clinical decision support

Order entry and management

Patient support

Reporting and population health management

Administrative processes

Among the most functional elements of the EHR is health information and data, which centers on the patient and is found in a defined data set. This defined data set encompasses items such as medical and nursing diagnoses, medication lists, allergies, demographics, clinical narratives, and laboratory results. These items would be available to the clinician at the point of care, thereby increasing support for sound clinical decisions.

Of similar importance is the functionality of results management. Results of all types—for example, laboratory or radiology results, available in electronic form—reduce the lag time between when the results are created and when they are available to the clinician. As a result, the clinician is in a better position to recognize and treat medical problems and to avoid redundant testing. Furthermore, electronic availability allows multiple providers access to the same information, thereby improving the coordination of care.

The functionality of order entry and management has already demonstrated multiple benefits to direct patient care. Among the most significant benefits is the reduction in the incidence of medication errors; the e-prescribing component of an EHR can allow for checks of proper dosage amounts, and of drug-allergy and drug-drug interactions. Other patient care benefits include reducing the ambiguities caused by illegible handwriting, improving the time to fill orders, and eliminating lost orders. Management of electronic orders also offers nonpatient care benefits such as the reduction of purchasing costs for preprinted forms and consistency of prescribing practices among physicians with a pharmacy's formulary.

Similarly, where EHRs have included clinical decision support features, patient care has benefited. Clinical decision support features include items such as preventive service reminders, alerts concerning possible drug interactions, and clinical guideline-driven prompts. In addition to assisting in the diagnosis and treatment of patients, clinical decision support features can be used to identify and track the frequency of adverse events, hospital-acquired infections, disease outbreaks, and bioterrorism events.

Benefits have also been shown as a result of the remaining four functional elements of an EHR. Electronic communication (e.g., e-mail and Web messaging) can facilitate communication both among health care providers and with patients, creating a greater continuity of care. Patient support in the form of patient education can be effective in allowing the patient to better understand and manage a chronic illness, particularly when the management occurs in a home setting, away from the supervision of a clinician. Administrative processes conducted in an electronic form, such as the scheduling of hospital admissions and procedures and the validation of insurance eligibility, can result in more timely service to patients and improved access to services. Finally, having available in an electronic format the data necessary to meet the reporting requirements of public health agencies, accrediting organizations, and quality/safety oversight boards can reduce the labor-intensive and time-consuming process of abstracting data from claims, paper records, and surveys.

In addition to the advantages listed above relating to the functionality of an EHR, other advantages also exist. For example, immediate access to real-time information is available to multiple caregivers at multiple locations simultaneously; the quality of documentation improves; the need for and cost of storage space is lessened; work flow processes improve; paperwork is reduced; and information can be easily recovered in the event of a disaster. All of these advantages lead to the more effective use of health care resources. Furthermore, one recent survey of hospitals revealed that information technology applications such as the EHR have advanced the quality of patient care through more timely diagnosis and intervention, reduction of medical errors, and better communication within the care team.[12]

While the views on the functionality of an EHR have differed over time, one constant has been that many of the concepts of a traditional health record are applicable to the EHR. For example, accrediting and licensing requirements dealing with the content of a medical record apply, whether the content is on paper or in an electronic format. Similarly, retention requirements apply in both contexts. Where they differ, of course, is with regard to the medium used. This difference is seen in both subtle and direct ways.

Differences applying to the EHR include the areas of authorship and authentication. **Authorship** refers to the identification of the health care provider who makes an entry in a record. Under a paper-based system, authorship would include an entry in writing or by dictation. Using an EHR, authorship would include an entry by keyboard or keyless data entry. **Authentication** refers to the act of ensuring the entry in the record for both accuracy and authorship. Under a paper-based system, authentication would include a written signature or initials. Using an EHR, authentication would include a computer-generated signature code. Both authorship and authentication would seemingly be more accurate in an EHR system, since the timeliness of an entry and the identity of the person making the entry can be established automatically, assuming that computer passwords are not shared and that biometric identification techniques or other control techniques are used.

Many of the steps necessary to implement an electronic health record rely on the computer concepts and communications technologies addressed earlier in this chapter. Fundamental to an EHR are hardware and software concepts and network technologies. Applied together, these concepts and technologies deliver the functionality and data of an EHR.

Conclusion

Every health information management professional is impacted in some manner by information technology. That impact is seen not only in emerging areas such as the use of the Internet and telemedicine to support patient care but also in more traditional areas such as an office setting where technologies can be used to create efficiencies. An effective partnership between health information management and information technology can lead to overall reductions in health care costs, new efficiencies, and improvements in the delivery of patient care.

CHAPTER SUMMARY

The interrelationship between health information management and information technology has grown steadily over recent decades, particularly with the development and implementation of the electronic health record. Key understandings of the computer concepts of hardware, software, and units of measure and standards all support the deployment of these technologies and the application of the information systems life cycle to the health care field. Different forms of communications technologies—for example, Internet, intranets, extranets, and issues of security, including the requirements of the Health Insurance Portability and Accountability Act—all serve to increase focus on the interrelationship between HIM and IT. Informatics as a discipline has emerged recently, with applications to the health care field such as e-prescribing's promise of improved patient care and contained costs through the reduction of errors. Emerging trends that employ information technology, such e-health and telemedicine, offer numerous advantages to both health care providers and those they treat.

CASE STUDY

You have been appointed a member of the project management team at Anywhere Hospital charged with determining an information technology solution to a change in legislation that affects the hospital. Many members of the team are from patient care disciplines with limited understanding of the life cycle process involved in IT project management. You have been tasked with educating your fellow team members about the life cycle process in IT project management. Develop a presentation to meet your task.

REVIEW QUESTIONS

1. Why is it necessary for the health information professional to possess a basic understanding of information technology?

2. What is a server? List some examples.

3. Differentiate between the terms *laptop computer* and *personal digital assistant*.

4. How can a piece of computer hardware be mobile but not wireless?

5. Is an application program the same as a utility program? Why or why not?

6. What is the concept of computer capacity and how is it analogous to the paper world?

7. What is the Internet and how does one connect to it?

8. Define the term *security* and list five main security measures.

9. What is telemedicine? Provide technological examples of its use.

10. What are voice recognition technology and interactive voice recognition? How do they differ from each other?

11. How does digital imaging differ from an electronic health record?

ENRICHMENT ACTIVITY

Obtain several examples of policies governing the implementation of the HIPAA Security Rule from local health care facilities. For each policy, examine its strengths and weaknesses. For example, are training requirements addressed?

WEB SITES

American Health Information Management Association, http://www.ahima.org

American Medical Informatics Association, http://www.amia.org

Healthcare Information and Management Systems Society, http://www.himss.org

Medical Records Institute, http://www.medrecinst.com

Telemedicine Information Exchange, http://www.tie.telemed.org

REFERENCES

Amatayakul, M. (2002, April). A reasonable approach to physical security. *Journal of AHIMA, 73/4,* 16A–16C.

Amatayakul, M. (2004). *Electronic health records: A practical guide for professionals and organizations* (2nd ed.). Chicago: American Health Information Management Association.

Beaver, K., & Herold, R. (2004). *The practical guide to HIPAA privacy and security compliance.* Boca Raton, FL: Auerbach.

Joint Healthcare Information Technology Alliance. Various reports. Available at http://www.jhita.org.

Joint Working Group on Telemedicine. (1997). *Telemedicine report to Congress.* Retrieved February 7, 2007, from http://www.ntia. doc.gov/reports/telemed

Jordan, T. J. (2002). *Understanding medical information: A user's guide to informatics and decision making.* New York: McGraw-Hill.

O'Carroll, P., Yasnoff, W., Ward, M. E., Ripp, L., & Martin, E. (Eds.). (2003). *Public health informatics and information systems.* New York: Springer-Verlag.

Practice Brief. (2002). *HIPAA privacy and security training.* Chicago: American Health Information Management Association. Available from http://www.ahima.org.

Practice Brief. (2003). *Document imaging as a bridge to the EHR.* Chicago: American Health Information Management Association. Available from http://www.ahima.org.

Pountain, D. (2001). *The new Penguin dictionary of computing.* London: Penguin.

Sardinas, J. L, Jr., & Muldoon, J. D. (2001, December). Are you vulnerable to hackers? How to protect patient information. *Journal of AHIMA, 72/10,* 47–53.

Sells, D. H., Jr. (2000). *Security in the health care environment.* Germantown, MD: Aspen Publishers.

NOTES

1. According to the Computer Security Institute, 85 percent of organizations surveyed had experienced cyber attacks. See Computer Security Institute, *Computer Crime and Security Survey,* available at http://www. gocsi.com.

2. The Joint Commission and the Accreditation Association for Ambulatory Health Care.

3. 45 C.F.R.§164.306 et seq. (2006).

4. Beaver, K., & Herold, R. (2004). *The practical guide to HIPAA privacy and security compliance.* Boca Raton, FL: Auerbach.

5. Hughes, G. (2001, September). Opportunities in e-health. *Journal of AHIMA, 72/8,* 73–74.

6. 42 U.S. C. § 1395i, mm (2006).

7. Technology that assists the disabled is available through many sources, including government agencies. Examples include: Illinois Assistive Technology Project, available at http://www.iltech.org; Missouri Assistive Technology, available at http://www.dolir.state.mo.gov/matp/.

8. Institute of Medicine. (1991). *The computer-based patient record: An essential technology for health care* (pp. 11–12). Washington, DC: National Academies Press. (Available at http://www.nap.edu.)

9. Ibid.

10. The Healthcare Information and Management Systems Society, available at http://www.himss.org.

11. Institute of Medicine. (2003). *Key capabilities of an electronic health record system: Letter report.* Washington, DC: National Academies Press. (Available at http://www.nap.edu.)

12. Issue Brief. (2006, May). *New hospital information technology: Is it helping to improve quality?* Mathematica Policy Research, Inc. The six areas of information technology surveyed include: (1) electronic lab results; (2) electronic clinical notes systems; (3) electronic images available throughout hospitals; (4) electronic lab orders; (5) electronic reminders for guideline-based interventions; and (6) e-prescribing.

14

Financial Management

CERTIFICATION CONNECTION

RHIA

Budgets
Contracts
Cost-benefit analysis
Return on investment

RHIT

Budgets
Resource management

LEARNING OBJECTIVES

After reading this chapter, the learner should be able to:

1. Understand the three parts of the finance cycle.

2. Identify the uses and users of accounting information.

3. Compare and contrast a balance sheet, income statement, and cash flow statement.

4. Differentiate between managerial accounting and financial accounting.

5. Define a budget and describe the ways in which organizations rely upon them.

6. Trace the stages in the procurement process.

7. Identify the contents of a request for proposal.

Outline

Overview

Accounting

Managerial Accounting
Financial Accounting

Budgets

Procurement

Request for Proposal

Key Concepts

Acceptance process

Account

Accountant

Accounting

Accrual accounting

Asset

Auditors

Audits

Audit trails

Balance sheet

Bond rating

Bookkeeper

Bookkeeping

Bottom-up process

Budget

Budget organization plan

Capital

Capital expenditure budget

Cash accounting

Cash budget

Cash flow statement

Chief financial officer

Contract dispute

Controller

Cost accounting

Cost-benefit analysis

Credits

Debits

Delegation of authority

Disbursements

Expense budget

Expenses

Finance

Financial accounting

Financial Accounting Standards Board

Financial management

Forecasting

General ledger

Generally accepted accounting principles

Income statement

Internal controls

Journal

Liability

Managerial accounting

Master budget

Owner's equity

Procurement

Purchase order

Receipts

Request for information

Request for proposal

Request for quotation

Return on investment analysis

Revenue

Safeguarding of assets

Sales budget

Separation of duties

Source document

Specifications

Statistics budget

Top-down process

Treasurer

Variances

INTRODUCTION

The fiscal health of an organization is affected by its employees on a daily basis. Whether they hold traditional finance jobs, positions with some level of financial responsibility, or largely nonfinancial positions, an organization's employees play a direct role in managing the organization's fiscal health and supporting its goals. Many examples illustrate this premise. Accountants assess the organization's financial performance, and capital budget officers oversee planning for large tangible projects. Department managers address budget and payroll issues on a routine basis. With every instance of employee hiring, the manager influences an organization's financial health. If a manager allows a position to remain vacant, the payroll budget is affected positively, but the operational area may be impacted negatively. If a manager hires an employee at the highest salary level within a salary range, the payroll budget is affected negatively, but the operational area may be impacted positively.

Others play a role in the organization's financial health as well, whether they recognize this role or not. For example, those responsible for sharing information concerning a patient's condition influence the speed at which this sharing occurs. If information is shared faster than normal, costs may be reduced; if information is shared slower than normal, costs may be increased. Reimbursement to the organization is affected by the accuracy and timeliness with which coding is performed; if coding occurs accurately and quickly, reimbursement is maximized; if coding occurs less accurately and takes more time, reimbursement is minimized.

It is important for all members of a health care organization, from the line staff to the supervisors to the senior executives, to share an understanding of financial management. This chapter provides an awareness and understanding of finance; it introduces the accounting function, along with the concepts of internal controls and audits. A discussion of budgeting and procurement functions follows, including an explanation of the request for proposal process.

Overview

Finance is the science of money, credit, and banking. Within the business world, finance refers to raising, managing, and making money for an organization. Finance can be thought of as a cycle that primarily focuses on: (1) assessing the financial performance and health of an organization; (2) applying that information to create a plan for future performance; and (3) executing that plan. This cycle is illustrated in Figure 14–I. Once the organization completes the plan's execution, the cycle begins again.

Equally as important as understanding how the finance cycle functions is knowledge of the players who are involved in that cycle: the chief financial officer, treasurer, controller, accountant, and bookkeeper. The chief financial officer (CFO) oversees the organization's finances. Reporting to the CFO are the treasurer and the controller. The treasurer oversees the organization's assets and financial planning; obtains the organization's financing; and manages its cash, credit, and inventories. The controller assesses the organization's performance and accounts for assets, liabilities, and costs. The controller selects the organization's accounting method; enforces that method through internal monitoring and audits; is responsible for both managerial and financial accounting; and pays the organization's taxes. The accountant keeps, examines, and adjusts the financial records of an organization, whereas the bookkeeper records entries in the financial records of an organization. Working together, they perform the finance cycle of assessment, planning, and execution.

Figure 14–1 | The finance cycle

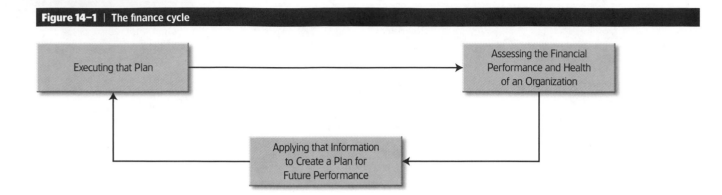

The finance cycle in the health care world shares many of the same features that are present in the corporate world. Among those features is the concept of **capital**, money that is invested in a business to help that business grow. Capital may be raised for the benefit of for-profit organizations through the issuance of stocks and bonds and by borrowing money; for not-for-profit organizations, capital may be raised through issuance of bonds and borrowing money. When organizations issue bonds, the level of risk associated with the bond is determined by its bond rating. A **bond rating** indicates the likelihood that the bond issuer will pay back both the principal and interest to the buyer. The higher the rating, the more likely the bonds will be repaid. Bond issuers who are facing financial problems often must pay very high interest rates as a means to attract purchasers. Accordingly, those issuers receive a low bond rating, which in turn affects their ability to sell bonds and raise capital. In the context of the finance cycle, raising capital bridges the assessment and execution activities.

Another feature shared with the corporate world is the use of cost-benefit analysis. A **cost-benefit analysis** refers to the systematic method of assessing the economic desirability of alternatives based upon evaluating initial and ongoing expenses (costs) against an expected return (benefits). Initial and ongoing expenses may be estimated by using survey methods or drawing inferences from economic behavior. Cost-benefit analyses can be simple or highly complex, depending upon the significance of the activity/project/product being evaluated. For example, a cost-benefit analysis of an electronic health record system would include an estimate of all quantifiable costs and benefits over the life cycle, a discussion of all non-quantifiable costs and benefits over the same period, and an analysis of the baseline and all potential alternatives using present value analysis to develop cost-benefit ratios. For each alternative, a life cycle cost estimate would be developed focusing on system-related costs, along with an estimate of the benefits for each alternative focusing on the benefits realized in executing the organization's mission. From this, a recommended alternative emerges. In the context of the finance cycle, a cost-benefit analysis falls within the assessment activity.

E-HIM

Health care organizations frequently engage in return on investment and cost-benefit analyses before migrating to an electronic health record system.

A third feature shared with the corporate world is a return on investment (ROI) analysis. A **return on investment analysis** refers to the process of evaluating an investment by comparing the magnitude and timing of expected gains against investment costs. ROI is sometimes referred to under other titles, such as return, rate of return, or rate of profit. Regardless of the title, an ROI analysis is helpful because it presents data in a quantifiable way that can be used to determine whether it is financially prudent to proceed with purchase or investment decisions or other types of decisions. For example, an investment of $100 generates $20 in interest; a second investment of $1,000 generates $50 in interest. In gross figures, $50 is larger than $20, which may lead one to view the second investment more favorably than the first investment. Using an ROI analysis, however, it is clear that the $100 investment ($20 \div 100 = 20\%$ ROI) is more favorable than the $1,000 investment ($50 \div 1,000 = 5\%$). Many organizations apply ROI as part of the assessment portion of the finance cycle. In the HIM world, ROI has been applied repeatedly to organizational efforts to migrate to an electronic health record system, as has the concept of cost-benefit analysis.

In order for the finance cycle to operate, one must understand the difference between accounting and budgeting. Accounting is a backward-looking activity—it reviews actual transactions after they have taken place. That review constitutes the assessment portion of the financing cycle. Documents prepared as part of that activity are frequently reported outside the business. By contrast, budgeting is a forward-looking activity—it determines what is expected to take place in the future based on the organization's strategy and goals. Budgeting is the plan creation portion of the financing cycle. Documents prepared as part of that activity are for internal management use only and are not made public. The execution portion of the finance cycle belongs to the organization's managers and can be performed in as many ways as there are organizations. The finance cycle is integral to **financial management**, the efficient and effective use of financial resources to achieve the organization's mission.

Accounting

Accounting is a distinct discipline that has its own standards, practices, and language. **Accounting** is the system used to record, state, or audit business transactions; it is also known as the "language" of finance because it is used to record financial transactions. Accounting is used by numerous individuals and groups on a regular basis. Each investor in a business venture relies on financial reports to inform her of the status of her investment. Government regulators examine financial statements on a routine basis to determine a business's financial condition. Businesspeople examine accounting reports to determine the amount of profit earned, the impact of that profit on the business, and the sources and uses of cash flow. Accrediting organizations review financial reports to determine compliance with financial regulations. Bond rating agencies use financial reports as the basis for determining the financial viability of an organization. Individuals rely on accounting principles and terms to understand personal investments and financial affairs, such as deciphering their retirement fund reports. A lack of understanding of accounting by any of these individuals or groups can hamper their decision-making ability.

Two types of accounting exist: managerial accounting and financial accounting. Both forms of accounting involve the creation and use of reports as part of the ordinary course of business and for specific functions.

Managerial Accounting

Managerial accounting—sometimes referred to as **cost accounting**—refers to the day-to-day management of an organization's cash, credit, inventory, liabilities, and expenses. The information generated in managerial accounting is primarily used to manage an organization's operations; as such, it focuses on the little picture of an organization or its divisions. Managerial accounting encompasses the design of the organization's bookkeeping system, the establishment of the internal controls, and the verification of the recorded information through audits.

Bookkeeping is the record-keeping aspect of accounting. Steps in the bookkeeping process are illustrated in Figure 14-2. Bookkeepers record transactions onto a series of documents called journals, accounts, and general ledgers. A **journal** is a book or document in which each transaction is entered in chronological order. A journal can be considered a running activity log for a given time period (e.g., one day). An **account** is a separate recording made for each asset and liability, whereas a **general ledger** is the complete set of accounts established and maintained by the organization. Bookkeepers record a given transaction in the journal and later post the transaction in the account to which the transaction applies. For example, when an organization purchases medical supplies, the bookkeeper first records the transaction in a journal, then posts the same transaction in the account for medical supplies, and, finally, updates the entries contained in the general ledger. For many years, bookkeeping was a manual function that was subject to recording errors and timeliness issues. As a result of the advent of computer programs and bar-coding information on products, recording errors and timeliness questions have been reduced.

Internal controls are the accounting policies, procedures, precautions, and forms established to prevent and

Figure 14-2 | **Steps in the bookkeeping process**

Recording Transactions

Preparing and Collecting Source Documents

Recording Original Entries

Performing End-of-Period Procedures

Preparing the Adjusted Trial Balance

Closing the Books

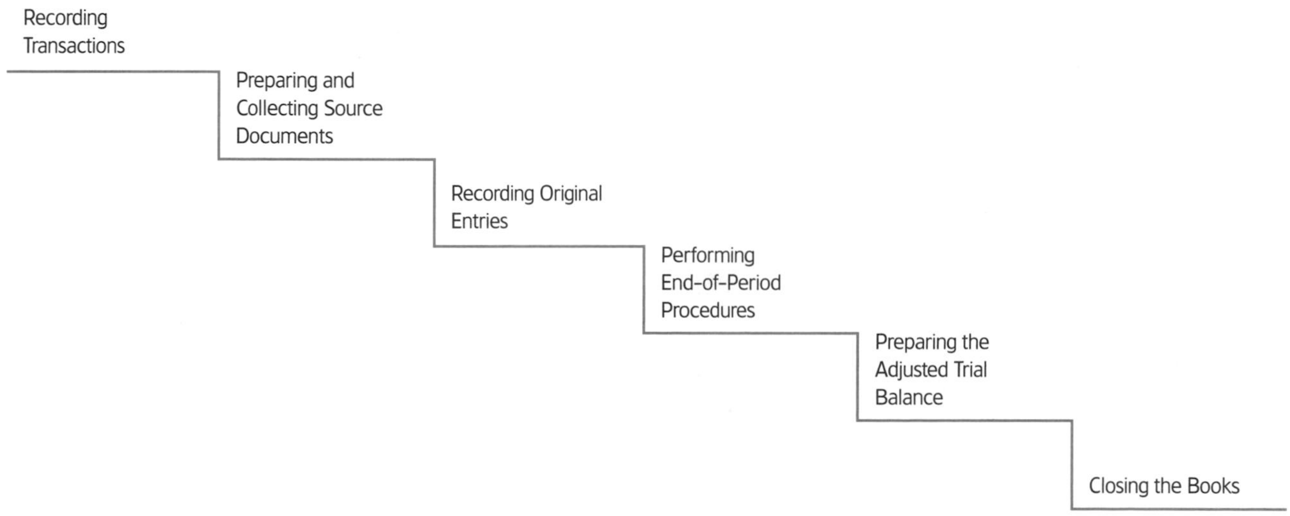

minimize errors and fraud, establish business practices that are in compliance with applicable laws and regulations, ensure accurate and reliable financial reports, and increase operational efficiency and effectiveness. These policies, procedures, precautions, and forms extend beyond the bookkeeping system and are not limited to a single event; rather, they are a series of activities and actions that extend throughout an entity's operations and on an ongoing basis. Internal controls frequently are memorialized into an internal controls document. Internal controls serve to prevent mistakes from occurring and, when they do occur, to keep them to an absolute minimum. By contrast, audits serve to discover mistakes after their occurrence. Said simply, internal controls are preventative work; audits are detective work.

Management possesses the responsibility for good internal controls. This responsibility manifests by managers instilling an attitude in the workplace that business processes must follow applicable laws, rules, and regulations. From that point, managers set the objectives, establish control mechanisms and activities, ensure that staff receive training and guidance, and monitor and evaluate the control process. An environment in which staff members are encouraged to ask questions and raise concerns to managers helps to bring to light the need for potential changes to internal controls.

Three elements of internal controls that exist within many organizations are delegation of authority, separation of duties, and safeguarding of assets (Figure 14–3). **Delegation of authority** refers to establishing limits upon the authority of individuals to act within the organization. For example, such delegations may include granting a person authority for transactions without a countersignature up to a specified amount and requiring a countersignature on transactions over that amount. **Separation of duties** refers to the effort to separate different parts of the same transaction among various individuals and departments so that no one person may control an entire transaction from start to finish. Examples include developing a system to ensure that enough staff members are competent and qualified to carry out the responsibilities of the organization and enforcing mandatory vacation policies for employees in sensitive positions. **Safeguarding of assets** refers to the careful control of valuable assets so that those persons lacking authority cannot gain access to them. Examples include establishing a system for the separate storage of duplicate records, restricting access to computer networks

through the use of firewalls and other security measures, and conducting surprise inspections and inventory counts.

Managers must ensure that their organizations' internal controls are reasonable and cost effective. No amount of internal controls will provide absolute assurance that irregularities will not occur, even with the most honest employees and a past history of no irregularities. Furthermore, consideration should be given so that the cost of the controls imposed will not exceed the value of the benefit derived from the controls. Where additional assurance is sought, cyclical audits may fill the role.

Audits are the activities associated with the inspection of an organization's accounts, reports, and statements. Audits serve the function of verifying whether an organization's work has been performed in compliance with governing law and whether the reports and statements issued by the organization provide a true and fair view of the organization's financial affairs during a specified window of time. Audits focus on systemic weaknesses within an organization, relying upon a sample of transactions processed during the full audit period to reach a conclusion about the organization's financial affairs.

Accountants who perform these inspections are referred to as **auditors**. Auditors may be employed independently of the organization (external auditors) or within the organization's personnel structure (internal auditors). Many organizations benefit from using both external and internal auditors. For example, the work done by external auditors is often considered objective and unbiased, which provides confidence to investors, lenders, and regulatory authorities. Internal auditors can provide an initial line of defense against mistakes and fraud within an organization and identify any weaknesses in internal accounting systems.

Verification of the information recorded by an organization is performed using audit trails. **Audit trails** are paths that clearly show the sequence of events leading to an entry in a given account. In other words, they are the methods used to trace an event to its creation. When using an audit trail, the auditor begins with the **source document**—the paperwork that evidences the terms and conditions of the transaction—and follows it through the steps in the bookkeeping process. By the end of this activity, the auditor should be able to reconstruct the path that was used to record information. If such information is correct, the information is verified; if incorrect, the discrepancy in the information is noted and followed up with appropriate action.

Audits vary in both length and results. Depending on the size of the organization and the scope of the audit period, audits may take several weeks or more to complete. Upon completion, the auditors will issue a report detailing their opinion concerning the financial health and practices

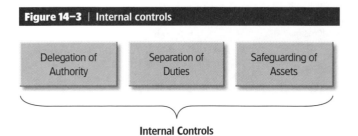

Figure 14–3 | Internal controls

Delegation of Authority

Separation of Duties

Safeguarding of Assets

Internal Controls

of the organization and its compliance with the law. These reports fall within two categories: unqualified and qualified. An unqualified report is of the highest level and indicates that the auditors are satisfied with the organization's financial health and practices, as well as its legal compliance. A qualified report is of a lesser level and indicates that the auditors were dissatisfied in some manner with the organization's financial health and practices or its legal compliance. This dissatisfaction may be referred to as a finding, a material weakness, a misstatement, or a reportable condition; additionally, the auditor's report may contain recommendations for correcting problems. Any of these terms are considered serious matters that warrant review and action by the organization that is the subject of the audit.

Financial Accounting

Financial accounting refers to the periodic assessment of an organization's financial health on a monthly, quarterly, or annual basis. The information generated by managerial accounting serves as the basis for the information that relates to financial accounting. This information is primarily displayed in a series of financial reports: the balance sheet, the income statement, and the cash flow statement. These financial reports are used by individuals and groups outside the organization to assess the financial performance and viability of the organization. As such, financial accounting is focused on the big picture of an organization.

To the uninitiated, balance sheets, income statements, and cash flow statements would appear to apply only to for-profit organizations. However, not-for-profit organizations also rely on these reports. The differences between the reports made for not-for-profit and for-profit organizations rest on the not-for-profit organization's exemption from income taxes and on the requirement to account for the use of donated funds. In other respects, the concepts and components of these reports apply similarly to both types of organizations.

A **balance sheet** is a financial report that summarizes the true financial condition of an organization, showing its assets, liabilities, and the owners' equity in the organization at a specified point in time. The balance sheet provides a dollar value for the assets an organization possesses, as well as where it obtained the money to buy these assets. A sample balance sheet is illustrated in Figure 14–4.

An **income statement** is a financial report that summarizes revenue and expenses of an organization at a specified point in time, noting profits along with extraordinary gains and losses. The income statement indicates what the organization earned and how much was spent over the interval of time covered by the statement. A sample income statement is illustrated in Figure 14–5.

A **cash flow statement** is a financial report that summarizes the cash inflows and outflows of an organization at a specified point in time. The cash flow statement demonstrates how much money the organization possesses at the beginning and end of a reporting period, and how it achieved those balances. A sample cash flow statement is illustrated in Figure 14–6.

To understand these three reports, one must first understand the difference between cash accounting and accrual accounting. **Cash accounting** records an activity only when cash is received (**receipts**) and paid (**disbursements**), regardless of when services were performed. For example, assume that a physician provides services to a patient in her office in Month 1 but receives payment for those services in Month 3. Per the cash accounting method, the physician would not record any receipts until Month 3. However, the physician would record disbursements for such things as rent, supplies, utilities, and salaries during Month 1 because those things were necessary to conduct business at the time the patient was seen in the office. In this scenario, the physician loses money during Month 1.

In contrast, **accrual accounting** records an activity at the time the activity occurs, regardless of when the cash is received or paid. Using the same example, the physician would record the income (**revenue**) to be received from the patient during Month 1, without waiting to receive that money. The physician would also record the same rent, supplies, utilities, and salaries (here referred to as **expenses**) that were paid out during Month 1. If the physician treats a sufficient number of patients during Month 1, as compared to the office's expenses, she will break even or may even show a profit.

Organizations generally choose between these two methods of accounting by determining which method best suits their interests. For organizations that can synchronize the receipt and payment of cash readily, cash accounting may be the preferred method. For those organizations that experience broad fluctuations between the receipt and payment of cash, accrual accounting may be the best method. These two methods are further illustrated in Table 14–1.

Also important to financial accounting are the **generally accepted accounting principles** (GAAP). These principles are issued by the **Financial Accounting Standards Board** (FASB), the body that governs the accounting profession. These principles constitute, in essence, the official "rule book" of accounting and are represented in thousands of pages of rules and guidelines. GAAP applies to financial accounting but not managerial accounting; financial reports that are issued for the benefit of those outside the organization are thus issued in a consistent fashion. This consistency allows individuals and groups to compare organizations within the same field.

Other basic elements of accounting include assets, liabilities, owner's equity, credits, and debits. An **asset** is

Figure 14–4 | Sample consolidated balance sheet

XYZ CORPORATION
CONSOLIDATED BALANCE SHEET
(in millions)

	Year Ended December 31	
	2005	**2004**
Assets		
Current Assets		
Cash and cash equivalents	20	48
Accounts receivable	190	188
Unbilled revenue	133	118
Miscellaneous receivables	7	13
Accounts receivable—affiliates	59	8
Materials and supplies	199	199
Other current assets	57	18
Total current assets	665	592
Property & Plant, Net	5157	4853
Investments and Other Assets		
Plant decommissioning fund	250	235
Intercompany note receivable	61	–
Total other income	922	848
Total investments and other assets	1233	1083
Total Assets	7055	6528
Liabilities and Stockholders' Equity		
Current Liabilities		
Current maturities of long-term debt	4	3
Short-term debt	80	375
Accounts and wages payable	408	327
Taxes accrued	59	51
Other current liabilities	96	108
Total current liabilities	647	864
Long-term Debt, Net	2698	2059
Deferred Credits & Other Liabilities		
Accumulated deferred income taxes	166	106
Accumulated deferred investment tax credits	96	108
Regulatory liabilities	802	776
Asset retirement obligations	466	431
Accrued pension and other postretirement benefits	203	219
Other deferred credits and liabilities	72	80
Total deferred credits and liabilities	1805	1720
Stockholder's Equity		
Common stock	511	511
Preferred Stock	113	113
Other paid-in capital	733	718
Retained earnings	548	543
Total stockholders' equity	1905	1885
Total Liabilities and Stockholders' Equity	7055	6528

Figure 14–5 | Sample consolidated statement of income

XYZ CORPORATION
CONSOLIDATED STATEMENT OF INCOME
(in millions)

	Year Ended December 31		
	2005	**2004**	**2003**
Operating Revenue			
Ongoing operations	2426	2197	2191
Other	183	163	145
Total operating revenue	2609	2360	2336
Operating Expenses			
Purchase of widgets	865	614	593
Other operations	108	100	91
Maintenance	771	785	747
Widget contract settlements			−51
Depreciation and amortization	324	294	284
Taxes other than income	229	222	213
Total operating expenses	2297	2015	1877
Other Income and Expenses			
Miscellaneous income	28	25	23
Miscellaneous expense	−7	−7	−7
Total other income	21	18	16
Interest Charges	116	104	105
Income before Income Taxes	217	259	370
Income Taxes	193	208	251
Net Income	24	51	119

something of value that can be used to serve an organization's needs. For example, the organization's real property, cash on hand, inventories, and goodwill are all considered assets because they may be used to pay the organization's debts. By contrast, a liability is a debt or obligation owed by an organization. For example, the amount of money an organization owes its employees as salary is considered a liability. Owner's equity is the ownership capital base of a business—for example, the amount an owner invests in the start-up of a health care organization is considered owner's equity. Credits and debits are increases and decreases in assets and liabilities, respectively. The easiest way to understand credits and debits is to apply these concepts to one's personal financial situation. For example, assume that a bank's bookkeeper enters a credit to you, the customer, when you deposit money with the bank. Conversely, the bank's bookkeeper enters a debit to you when you remove money from the bank. A similar process occurs when you record entries in your checkbook: deposits are credits and checks that you write are debits. Credits and debits should balance each other out, so that the sum of credit balance accounts equals the sum of debit balance accounts.

Budgets

A budget is an organization's revenue and expenditure plan. As the definition indicates, a budget is a planning tool that encapsulates an organization's financial plan (goals and expectations) for a future window of time. Often the window of time is a one-year period; however, some organizations develop budgets for two-, three-, and five-year periods. The shorter the time window, the more definite and detailed the budget can be. Conversely, longer-term budgets are less definite and contain less detail.

An organization can often create and operate the budget process of its financial plan using a management tool called a budget organization plan. This tool documents the organization's budgetary processes and procedures and generally contains three elements: organizational structure, duties and responsibilities, and operating processes. The organizational structure element describes the framework of the decision-making process for budgetary planning, review, approval, management, and oversight within

Figure 14–6 | Sample consolidated statement of cash flow

XYZ CORPORATION
CONSOLIDATED STATEMENT OF CASH FLOW
(in millions)

	Year Ended December 31		
	2005	**2004**	**2003**
Cash Flow from Operating Activities			
Net income	24	51	119
Adjustments to reconcile net income			
to net cash provided by operating activities			
Depreciation and amortization	324	294	284
Amortization of debt issuance cost	28	31	33
Deferred income taxes and investment tax credits	5	5	4
Long-term contract settlements	33	111	37
Other	11	43	−36
Changes in assets and liabilities			
Receivables	−82	7	−4
Materials and supplies	0	−24	−13
accounts and wages payable	75	9	−21
taxes accrued	8	0	−52
Assets, other	−36	−27	−41
Liabilities, other	−4	20	20
Postretirement obligations	−16	−99	−25
Net cash provided by operating activities	370	421	305
Cash Flows from Investing Activities			
Capital expenditures	−721	−458	−414
Other	−5	−56	−23
Net cash used in investing activities	−726	−514	−437
Cash Flows from Financing Activities			
Dividends on common stock	−280	−315	−288
Dividends on preferred stock	−6	−6	−6
Capital insurance cost	−5	−4	−6
Changes in short-term debt	−239	281	−44
Redemption long-term debt	−5	−442	−429
Issuance long-term debt	643	404	698
Other	14	2	6
Net cash provided by (used in) financing activities	122	−80	−69
Net change in cash and cash equivalents	−234	−173	−201
Cash and cash equivalents at beginning of year	48	15	9
Cash and cash equivalents at end of year	−186	−158	−192

the organization. The duties and responsibilities element details the roles of the governing board, executives, and subordinates within the organization, including the delegation of authority. The operating processes element describes the operating procedures to be followed by respective levels in the organization to manage the budget. While serving as a master document for use by those within the organization, a budget organization plan is subject to revision on an as-needed basis to reflect changes in any of the elements.

Budgets are created in one of two ways: the bottom-up process and the top-down process. The **bottom-up process** allows lower-level and middle-level managers the opportunity to contribute to the development of priorities and objectives within the budget process; this participatory effort allows these managers to feel a sense of ownership with regard to the budget. The managers share their concerns, suggestions, and ideas with the organization's budget committee or upper management, who then develop or approve the final budget. Utilizing the **top-down process,**

Table 14–1 | Accounting Methods: Cash Basis versus Accrual Basis

Dr. Lopez is a family practitioner who has recently opened his practice. Total billed revenues for July were $15,000. Currently, all of his patients are insured by Medicare or commercial insurers. Third-party payers typically pay two months after care is delivered, so his actual receipts in July equal zero. Dr. Lopez pays his nursing staff $1,500 twice a month. The rest of his expenses—rent, utilities, supplies, insurance, and bookkeeping—are paid monthly and total $6,000.

Income Statement: Cash Basis, for the Month of July		Income Statement: Accrual Basis, for the Month of July	
Receipts	Disbursements	Revenue	Disbursements
$0	$3,000 (staff salary and benefits)	$15,000	$3,000 (staff salary and benefits)
	$6,000 (other practice expenses)		$6,000 (other practice expenses)
$0	$9,000	$15,000	$9,000
Net income for July: **−$9,000**		Net income for July: **$6,000**	

Source: Campbell, C., Schmitz, H., & Waller, L. (1998). *Financial management in a managed care environment.* Albany, NY: Delmar.

upper-level management or the budget committee communicate to lower-level and middle-level managers the priorities and objectives for the budget year and distribute the final budget. The lower-level and middle-level managers in turn disseminate this information to the line staff.

Once budgets are approved, the budget execution process begins. Budget transactions such as purchases and expenditures occur and are recorded in journals, accounts, and general ledgers. Formal reviews of all spending activity are conducted on a periodic basis and, when appropriate, funds are moved among spending classes if initial funding amounts prove insufficient. Supplemental funding requests may be made in the event that total funding levels are insufficient to conduct critical operations. If supplemental funding proves unavailable, spending plans are adjusted to reduce expenditures. Depending upon the requirements of an organization, departments may issue reports to higher levels within their organization to reflect how their expenditures match with the previously developed spending plan.

Budgets begin by looking at historical information: past performance in terms of revenue, expenses, earnings, and cash flow. This historical information can be found in the financial reports discussed in the section on financial accounting. Using this historical information, estimates are created for future performance in terms of revenue, expenses, earnings, and cash flow. These estimates are influenced by current economic conditions as well as by predictions of future economic conditions and trends. With this exercise, the organization is well placed to allocate its resources (funding-specific activities) to carry out its business plan in the future.

Several types of budgets are used within any given organization. An **expense budget** focuses on the costs of the organization, such as administrative costs, research and development costs, and marketing costs. A **cash budget** focuses on the amount of cash flow within the organization on a weekly, monthly, or quarterly basis; this enables the organization to know how much money it will have on hand to cover payments to be made during those time frames. A **capital expenditure budget** focuses on an organization's major long-term projects, such as expansions, replacements, and improvements to the physical plant. A **sales budget** focuses on the projected sales of products or services, such as the number of prescriptions that will be filled by a pharmacy. A **statistics budget** focuses on the volume and type of health care services provided in the past and compares it to an estimate of future needs for health care services. These and any other budgets are rolled into the **master budget**, the large blueprint for the organization's financial plan.

In the health information management (HIM) field, within an acute care organization, budgets focus mainly upon expenses; limited revenue is generated by most HIM departments. Generated revenue may take the form of charges to an organization's outside users (e.g., for copy services) or to those internal departments that use HIM services (e.g., transcription services). These charges seldom permit an HIM department to be self-sustaining for budget purposes. For this reason, a focus on expenses often results in the development of a spending plan. Such plans are generally tied to both the organization's and department's goals for the budget year.

Organizations rely on a budget as a means of management control. The chief executive officer and the president of the organization focus on the master budget, whereas lower-level managers focus on the area of the budget for which they hold responsibility. This management control allows organizations to assess whether actual performance meets budget targets and to decide whether to hold individual managers responsible for any variance between the two numbers or revise the budget as needed.

Variances are inconsistencies between two numbers or statements. Variances are typically identified using the routine reporting process in which actual results are compared against budget amounts. If variances exist, managers must first examine the report to determine whether the data were reported correctly. If they were, the manager investigates the cause(s) of the variance and determines what actions to take. Such actions may require modifications to the financial plan.

Organizations use budgets for other purposes as well. Budgeting imposes deadlines and discipline on the planning process, forcing individuals to develop a course of action to achieve objectives. Budgeting helps an organization stay true to its vision, mission, and values—these serve as the framework for developing the budget. Budgeting helps organizations develop financial models that in turn help managers make day-to-day decisions. Budgeting helps managers focus on changes in the business environment that could impact the organization. With regard to new organizations, budgeting is instrumental in writing the business plan that will be used to raise capital.

Managers and staff need to understand budget concepts and know when budgets are created within their organization. At minimum, managers and staff play a role in helping the organization stay within its budget. Depending on the degree of delegation of authority employed within the organization, managers and staff may also play a role in budget development.

A function complementary to budgeting is forecasting. **Forecasting** refers to a financial projection of how an organization is likely to perform in the future. Forecasting differs from budgeting in that budgeting addresses how an organization *hopes* it will perform based on what should happen, whereas forecasting addresses how an organization *thinks* it will perform based on what is actually happening. For that reason, the budgeting phases precede the forecasting phase. Budgeting and forecasting do, however, share the same mechanical processes.

Procurement

Procurement refers to the activities that are involved in purchasing goods and contracting services. These activities begin when someone in an organization identifies the need to purchase an item or contract for a service and continues through identification of vendors, solicitation and evaluation of bids, contract award and monitoring, and acceptance and payment. These activities are illustrated in Figure 14–7. Procurement activities often occur on a continuous cycle (e.g., purchase of routine supplies), whereas other procurement activities may occur on a singular basis (e.g., building acquisition).

Procurement is an important component of financial management because it contributes to an organization's ability to make profits and contain costs. In view of the many opportunities for fraud and waste that exist during the procurement process, and because significant amounts of money are often involved, the procurement function employs several forms of internal control. For example, the separation of duties involved in the purchase of goods necessitates the use of one person to authorize the purchase, a second person to receive the goods, and a third person to keep records and arrange payment. Organizations are ever vigilant concerning the procurement function because it poses the potential to assist or damage the organization's chances for financial success.

Identification of the need to purchase goods or contract for services is an ongoing function within an organization. Some goods or services are in constant need, whereas others arise as a result of the planning and budgeting process. Sometimes the identification of services is clear, such as the need to purchase supplies whose quality

Figure 14–7 | Steps in the procurement process

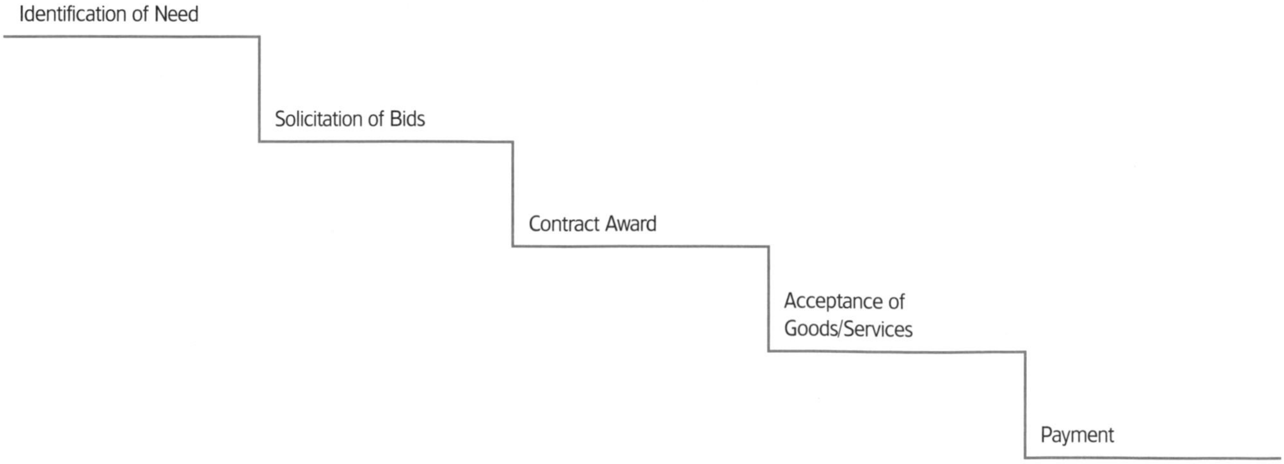

are impacted by freshness; other times, the identification is less clear, such as when an organization needs additional manpower to accomplish its mission and must decide between contracting for temporary personnel services and hiring regular staff. In general, the identification of the need to purchase goods or contract for services requires the creation of specifications. **Specifications** are features required of a product or service and may take the form of quality, price, quantity, service, delivery, or performance. The level of specifications may vary greatly and, on occasion, may need to be redefined to meet budget requirements or cost-effectiveness standards.

Once the need for goods or services and their specifications are identified, those individuals involved in purchasing can begin the solicitation process. Solicitation begins by identifying potential suppliers of the goods or services needed. Information for this purpose may come from a variety of sources, including sales personnel, advertisements, and industry journals and magazines. Personal interviews, site visits, reference checks, and financial analyses may play a role in this process. Because of the abundance of information that is now available electronically, the Internet provides an additional resource for identifying potential suppliers and compare information.

Organizations employ standard procedures for all activities involved in the procurement process, particularly those that relate to the evaluation of bids. In the government sector and within certain industries, evaluation is performed pursuant to the competitive bid process, wherein a minimum number of bids are solicited during a specified time period and reviewed before an award can be made. These bids are routinely submitted in writing and indicate to what extent the supplier responded to the specifications outlined by the organization. Evaluation of these bids follows, using an organization's established criteria such as choosing the lowest qualified bid. Rating methods are frequently employed as part of the evaluation process, examples of which are seen in Table 14–2.

Once the decision is made, a contract must be awarded to the winning bidder. This contract is a legally binding document; for that reason, it often takes the form of a purchase order. A **purchase order** is a document that formalizes the

purchase transaction between a buyer and supplier/vendor. Organizations often restrict the number of persons who are authorized to sign purchase orders as a means to control the commitment of the organization's funds. This authority is generally outlined in the organization's internal control document. The successful bidder is then notified and the purchase order is routed, either electronically or through traditional paper means, to the respective departments within the organization. The buyer monitors the order placed on a routine basis, including communication with the supplier/vendor to identify whether the goods or services will be delivered in a timely manner.

Once the ordered goods arrive or the services contracted for begin, the buyer must examine the goods or evaluate the services to determine whether they comply with the purchase order. This examination or evaluation is referred to as the **acceptance process**. If discrepancies are discovered (e.g., quantity or quality), the buyer notifies the supplier/vendor. Depending upon the degree of discrepancy, this notification may involve rejection of the goods or services or a request for correction. If the goods or services comply with the purchase order in all respects, they are accepted.

At this stage, the invoice submitted by the supplier/vendor is examined against the original purchase order and the receiving record for discrepancies. If no discrepancies are found, the invoice is paid in the ordinary course. If discrepancies are discovered, the buyer notifies the supplier/vendor and often engages in negotiations. Once negotiations cease, the buyer determines what amount will be paid against the invoice received. Depending upon the difference between the invoice amount and the amount paid, the supplier/vendor may exercise its legal rights to recover the difference.

Files must be established and maintained for every purchase action. Such files may be kept in electronic form, traditional paper form, or some combination thereof, and they should contain records of each step of the procurement process. In view of the fact that many procurement files contain proprietary information, these files must be managed and secured with access allowed only on a need-to-know basis. The specific content of any procurement file may vary and is often based on standards that are established according to an objective criteria (e.g., dollar value). Retention requirements for these types of records are based on statutes and regulations at both the federal and state levels, as well as rules imposed by the organization itself. Similar to health data, business record retention policies must encompass all forms of media in which the business record is created or stored, including paper and electronic records.

Maintenance and retention of procurement files are of particular importance in the event of a contract dispute. A **contract dispute** refers to a written claim, demand, or assertion made by a contracting party. Typically, this dispute includes a detailed statement of the legal and factual basis

Table 14–2	Rating Methods	
Method	**Examples**
Pass/fail	
Color ratings	Blue, yellow, green
Adjectival ratings	Fair, satisfactory, good, excellent
Numerical weights (expressed as percentages)	Total amounts to equal no more than 100 percent
Ordinal rankings	1st, 2nd, 3rd, etc. in importance

of the problem and a proposal for resolution. The disputing party may assert a number of claims, including payment of money in a sum certain, adjustment or interpretation of contract terms, a request for an equitable adjustment, or another form of specific relief arising from or relating to the contract. Resolution of a contract dispute varies by organizational setting. Some organizations refer all disputes to counsel at the moment the dispute arises, whereas other organizations require contracting officers to hold informal discussions in an attempt to resolve the contract dispute by mutual agreement and refer to counsel only those disputes in which the parties fail to resolve their differences.

Many of the activities involved in procurement rely upon communication between the respective parties. Though this seems like an elementary concept, good communication between the parties leads to faster procurement of goods or services and quicker payment. If communication problems occur, established protocols are employed as a means to resolve issues swiftly.

Request for Proposal

Although it is not employed on a routine basis, a request for proposal is a significant activity in the procurement process. A **request for proposal** (RFP) is a formal document that indicates both an organization's intent to procure products or services based upon specifications and provisions included in the document and the guidelines to be used by those who wish to bid for the contract. RFPs are often preceded by a **request for information** (RFI), which is a formal document seeking information about products or services available in the marketplace that can meet the organization's needs. Though they are often confused with each other, an RFI is distinguished from an RFP by the fact that it is not an invitation to bid, does not contain a high level of information, is often sent to a wide list of potential vendors, and is not binding on the part of either buyers or sellers. By contrast, RFPs are highly detailed documents that constitute an invitation to bid and are typically sent to a narrow list of potential vendors who are bound by the pricing schedules included in their responses. In addition to providing useful information that will later be incorporated into an RFP, the RFI can be used as a tool to prescreen vendors.

An alternative to a request for proposal is a request for quotation. A **request for quotation** (RFQ) is a formal document that seeks pricing information from a group of vendors for specific products or services. RFQs are most appropriate for use in situations where the specifications of a product or service are known but prices are unknown. Because the specifications are known, it is generally unnecessary for the organization issuing the RFQ to meet with potential vendors to discuss the RFQ content. The advantage of issuing an RFQ before an RFP is that the RFQ can establish general price ranges, which informs the organiza-

tion issuing the documents of price ceilings to expect when responses to the RFP are later received.

Content of an RFP typically follows a set pattern, beginning with introductory language that provides details on the organization requesting the proposal. This introductory language may be simple—merely identifying the organization, its location, and its points of contact—or it may be more detailed and include organizational charts, operating statistics, number of personnel, or financial information. This section is followed by another that provides the substantive content of the solicitation, including the functional requirements (indicated as desired or mandatory) and specifications of the products to be delivered or the work to be performed under the contract. These requirements and specifications may address software and hardware descriptions, training plans, documentation to be provided, incidental deliverables such as manuals and reports, performance guarantees, price schedules, and a reference list of past or current clients who have used the vendor's products or services. If appropriate, the RFP may address the need for an on-site demonstration, the vendor's role in installation and implementation of a product, and the testing plan.

The next sections of the RFP address its general contractual aspects. Packaging and marking specifications may be addressed, as well as the requirements for inspection, acceptance, quality assurance, and reliability. Frequently, the RFP specifies the time, place, and method of delivery or performance and includes provisions for warranties, performance bonds, payment schedules, and penalties in the event of nonperformance. Instructions on how to respond to the RFP are often provided, sometimes to the level of specifying the order or organization of different portions of the response (e.g., administrative, management, technical, past performance, and cost or pricing data).

The final section of the RFP lists the criteria to be considered during evaluation of all bids. These criteria invariably include price or cost plus any significant subfactors that will be considered when making the award. The relative importance of each evaluation criterion is addressed; however, numerical weights or other scoring systems that are used to rank offers need not be disclosed in the RFP. If minimum requirements exist in relation to any of the evaluation criteria, the RFP describes them.

At this point, the RFP can be released to potential vendors. Very strict rules apply to any contact between the organization that is soliciting responses and the vendors who are deciding whether to respond. If questions are raised concerning the RFP at this point, all potential vendors must receive the same data concerning both the question and the answer provided. Some organizations will hold a vendor's conference so that all questions—as well as any answers—may be heard by everyone at the same time. Discussions may be held to address technical capabilities or to clarify errors in the response. If it is important for the potential vendors to observe the physical space in which a project will be completed (e.g., building space), a walkthrough will be conducted wherein all vendors will be present at the same time.

Upon receipt of the responses, the organization that has solicited bids begins its analysis. Any bids received in an untimely manner will not be considered unless the RFP contains specific criteria with regard to late submissions. Site visits or vendor presentations may be held to demonstrate the vendor's product or service. Reference checks may be conducted, and an initial assessment of significant criteria (e.g., price, reliability, etc.) will follow. The number of vendors who meet the criteria in the RFP are then narrowed, typically to three. At this stage, the soliciting organization may begin the negotiation process and seek a "best and final" offer from the narrowed list of vendors. This last set of offers will constitute the final set of bids for review. The bid that best meets the evaluation criteria will be selected, and the organization will then award the contract.

Conclusion

As this chapter shows, financial management involves multiple features. To be an effective participant in the health care system, one must possess an understanding of the many features of financial management. Of particular importance are the budget and procurement processes; both can be influenced greatly by the actions of individuals and can affect an organization's financial well being.

CHAPTER SUMMARY

Sound financial management contributes greatly to an organization's overall success. Accounting practices are the hallmark of a financially progressive business, and the accounting discipline requires knowledge of certain principles, practices, concepts, and terms. Managerial accounting involves the design of an organization's bookkeeping system, the establishment of internal controls, and the verification of recorded information through audits. Financial accounting focuses on the big picture of an organization by periodically assessing its financial health. The budget-planning tool permits an organization to align its revenue and expenditures with its mission and goals. The procurement activity serves as a way for an organization to create profits and contain costs.

CASE STUDY

Review the accounting methods used by Dr. Lopez as illustrated in Table 14–1 in this chapter. Contrast the profitability that Dr. Lopez faces by using the cash basis of accounting with the profitability he faces by using the accrual basis of accounting for the month of July. What if Dr. Lopez did not accept third-party insurance and required all patients to pay at the time of service? Would there be any difference between the cash basis and accrual basis of accounting? Why or why not?

REVIEW QUESTIONS

1. Identify the roles of the persons involved in the finance life cycle.

2. How do internal controls and audits differ from each other?

3. How does cash accounting differ from accrual accounting?

4. Explain generally accepted accounting principles.

5. List and describe the different types of budgets.

6. How does forecasting differ from budgeting?

7. How does a request for proposal differ from a request for information and a request for quotation?

ENRICHMENT ACTIVITIES

1. Visit the Web site of the Financial Accounting Standards Board (http://www.fasb.org) and review the sections entitled "Frequently Asked Questions" and "Facts about FASB." Using these sections, compose a summary that describes the Financial Accounting Standards Board, its activities, and how the public can interact with it. Share your summary with your instructor and fellow students.

2. The concepts of return on investment and cost-benefit analyses are sometimes hard to understand. These two concepts are often used when health care providers migrate to an electronic health record. Search the Internet using the term *cost-benefit analysis* or *return on investment* in combination with the term *electronic health record*. Review a sample of the many entries addressing these topics, including entries that involve governmental entities, professional associations, and commercial companies. Discuss your findings with your instructor and fellow students.

WEB SITES

American Accounting Association, http://www.aaahq.org

American Institute of Certified Public Accountants, http://www.aicpa.org

Association of Chartered Accountants in the U.S., http://www.acaus.org

Financial Accounting Standards Board, http://www.fasb.org

Financial Executives International, http://www.fei.org

Financial Managers Society, http://www.fmsinc.org

Government Financial Officers Association, http://www.gfoa.org

Institute of Management Accountants, http://www.imanet.org

National Association of State Auditors, Comptrollers, and Treasurers, http://www.nasact.org

National Center for Research Resources, http://www.ncrr.nih.gov

REFERENCES

Bossert, J. L. (Ed.). (1994). *Supplier management handbook.* Milwaukee, WI: ASQC Quality Press.

Campbell, C., Schmitz, H., & Waller, L. (1998). *Financial management in a managed care environment.* Albany, NY: Delmar.

Francia, A. J. (1994). *Managerial accounting.* Houston, TX: Dame Publications.

Mattingly, R. (1997). *Management of health information.* Albany, NY: Delmar.

Peden, A. (1998). *Comparative records for health information management.* Albany, NY: Delmar.

Sullivan, P. (2003). Use financial, management reports to increase your profitability. *Illinois Bar Journal, 91*(5), 257.

Zenz, G. J. (1994). *Purchasing and the management of materials* (7th ed.). New York: John Wiley & Sons.

15

Reimbursement Methodologies

CERTIFICATION CONNECTION

RHIA

Compliance/reporting
PPS
Reimbursement systems
Revenue cycle management

RHIT

Payment systems
PPS
Reimbursement systems
Revenue cycle management

LEARNING OBJECTIVES

After reading this chapter, the learner should be able to:

1. Understand the concept of reimbursement methodologies as they relate to a health care organization's financial well-being.

2. Define the term *third-party payer* and identify examples in the governmental and nongovernmental sectors.

3. Describe the different forms of managed care organizations.

4. Compare and contrast the many payment methodologies used in health care.

5. Explain the processes involved in revenue cycle management.

Outline

Third-Party Payers

Governmental Payers
Nongovernmental Payers

Payment Methodologies

Fee for Service
Prospective Payment Systems
Resource-Based Relative Value Systems
Capitation

Revenue Cycle Management

Key Concepts

Balance billing

Blue Cross/Blue Shield

Capitation

Case mix

Certificate-of-need
program

CHAMPVA

Chargemaster

Claim

Closed-panel
arrangement

Compliance programs

Cost allocation

Coverage

CPT

Diagnosis-related group

EPO

Explanation of benefits

Fee for service

HCPCS

Health system

HEDIS

HMO

IDS

Inflation

Insured

Insurer

Managed care

Medicaid

Medical necessity

Medicare

POS

PPO

Premium

Private health insurance

Prospective payment
system

Reimbursement
methodologies

Resource-based relative
value scale

Revenue cycle
management

Third-party
administrators

Third-party payers

TRICARE

Unbundling

Usual, customary, and
reasonable costs

Workers' compensation

INTRODUCTION

One of the most significant developments in modern health care is the concept of reimbursement methodologies. Reimbursement methodologies are the theories and practices utilized to pay for the services provided by health care professionals. Using these theories and practices, the focus rests on the financial aspect of the interaction between the health care provider and the patient—the so-called "financial transaction." Attention is given to the type of services provided and the need or lack thereof for these services; however, this attention is directed from a financial perspective and not a treatment perspective. The efficient and effective management of applicable reimbursement systems can further an organization's mission and improve its financial well-being; if reimbursement systems are not managed efficiently and effectively, an organization's mission and financial well-being may suffer. For these reasons, it is essential that health information management professionals understand the role reimbursement methodologies play in the modern health care system.

This chapter begins with a discussion of reimbursement methodologies, including an explanation of third-party payers—both governmental and nongovernmental—and their role in financing the delivery of health care in the United States. The emergence of managed care is explained, with attention given to the various forms employed. A description of the methods used in the reimbursement function is provided, followed by an explanation of revenue cycle management. The awareness and understanding to be gained from a study of this chapter can provide the framework each employee needs to assist a health care organization's efforts in achieving its mission and improving its financial well-being.

Third-Party Payers

As discussed in Chapter 1, "Health Care Delivery Systems," the four stages of health care development illustrated that—for a significant portion of this country's history—the patient paid directly for health care services. Because the patient shouldered the financial burden for health care, many individuals went without care for lack of ability to pay. Over time, third-party payers in both the public and private sectors entered the scene. Third-party payers are organizations or entities that are willing to pay for health care services rendered the patient by the health care provider, according to a preexisting arrangement made using set criteria. Utilizing this definition, the first party is the patient receiving care, the second party is the professional or institution providing the care, and the third party is the organization paying for that care. The emergence of third-party payers in the 20th century increased the availability of health

care by providing a mechanism for payment of services that had previously been nonexistent for many patients. The reimbursement methodologies employed by these third-party payers have contributed dramatically to the costs—and the attendant effort to control costs—of health care services in the United States.

Third-party payers operate at both governmental and nongovernmental levels. Governmental payers are divided between programs offered at the federal and state levels. Among the most powerful of third-party payers is the federal government. The federal government represents 40 percent of the market, and few, if any, health care providers can ignore patients who are insured through programs operated by the federal government.[1] Equally powerful is the influence of private insurance companies and managed care organizations that cover individuals, groups, and institutions across the nation.

Table 15-1 | Coverage Differences between Medicare Parts A and B

Part A	Part B
Ninety days of inpatient care in a benefit period, with no limit to the number of benefit periods a beneficiary may use	Physician-ordered supplies and services
A lifetime reserve of 60 days of inpatient care, once the 90 days are exhausted	Outpatient hospital services
One hundred days of post-hospitalization care in a skilled nursing facility	Rural health clinic visits
Home health agency visits	Home health visits for persons with Part A

Source: Information adapted from Williams, S., & Torrens, P. (2002). *Introduction to health services* (6th ed.). Albany, NY: Delmar.

Governmental Payers

The largest health care reimbursement program operated by the federal government is the Medicare program. Medicare is the program designed to provide financing for persons over age 65, regardless of financial need. Medicare's reimbursement strategy is to reduce overall reimbursement to health care providers, thereby stabilizing the budget. The strategy attempts to reduce the costs of traditional health services while combating fraud and abuse. Medicare is divided between Part A, generally covering inpatient hospital care and long-term care; Part B, generally covering physician fees, outpatient hospital services, and home health care services; Part C, an expanded coverage option for those fees not paid for under Parts A and B; and Part D, covering prescription care. Part C is sometimes referred to as Medicare+Choice, because it offers the patient choices of additional health insurance plans such as medical savings accounts (MSA), health maintenance organizations (HMO), and fee-for-service plans. Table 15-1 illustrates the differences between Parts A and B, the most familiar areas of Medicare.

Next in size is the Medicaid program, which is designed to provide financing for poor and impoverished persons. Medicaid is a joint federal-state program, with funding supplied by the federal government and administration supplied by state governments. Substantial differences exist among the ways that states administer, finance, and reimburse under Medicaid. Because of this wide variance in administration of the Medicaid program and the low level of reimbursement found throughout the states, many health care providers restrict the number of patients they see from the Medicaid program or elect not to serve any patients from the program at all.

Eligibility for the Medicare and Medicaid programs differ. Medicare eligibility is determined by federal regulations issued by the Centers for Medicare and Medicaid Services (CMS). Medicaid eligibility is determined by a combination of regulations issued at both the federal and state levels. Tables 15-2 and 15-3 illustrate the eligibility requirements of the Medicare and Medicaid programs, respectively.

The programs offered for the members of the armed services and their families comprise the next largest component of the federal government's role in health care. Two programs, TRICARE and CHAMPVA, encompass virtually every health care service related to military duty. TRICARE offers financing and the provision of care for (1) active-duty members of the armed services, and (2) retired members of the military and their dependents who receive care at nonmilitary treatment facilities. The component of TRICARE that relates to retired service members and their families was formerly known as Civilian Health and Medical Program of the Uniformed Services (CHAMPUS). The Civilian Health and Medical Program of the Department of Veterans Affairs (CHAMPVA) is the system designed to finance and provide care for (1) veterans of the armed services who are permanently and totally disabled, (2) survivors of veterans who died from service-related conditions, and (3) survivors of military personnel who died in the line of duty.

Table 15-2 | Medicare Eligibility Requirements

1. Applicant is 65 years or older and is receiving, or is eligible for, retirement benefits from Social Security or the Railroad Retirement Board, or

2. Applicant is 65 years or older and has received Railroad Retirement disability benefits for the prescribed time and meets the Social Security Act disability requirements, or

3. Applicant or spouse had Medicare—government employment, or

4. Applicant is under sixty-five years old and has End-Stage Renal Disease (ESRD).

Source: Centers for Medicare and Medicaid Services, 2006, http://www.cms.hhs.gov.

Table 15-3 | Medicaid Eligibility Requirements

1. Applicant must be either a pregnant woman, a member of a low-income family, or must be aged, blind, or disabled. A few states also cover single, healthy adults.

2. Applicant must meet state income and resource standards, and certain other requirements.

3. Applicant must be a resident of the state, and be a United States citizen or a qualified immigrant. Legal immigrants can also qualify under certain circumstances depending on their date of entry into the country. Illegal aliens cannot qualify, except for emergency care.

Source: Centers for Medicare and Medicaid Services, 2006, http://www.cms.hhs.gov.

Another program offered by the federal government is the Indian Health Service (IHS), which is designed to provide health services to native American Indians and native Alaskans. The IHS provides care through its own facilities and, when those facilities are not present or lack the ability to provide specific treatments, through contracts with local health care institutions and providers.

Workers' compensation is a program offered at both the federal and state levels. Workers' compensation refers to insurance coverage for employees who suffer work-related injuries and illnesses. In addition to covering health care costs, workers' compensation programs compensate employees for lost wages due to work-related injuries and illnesses. Federal employees are governed by the Federal Employees' Compensation Act (FECA); nonfederal employees are governed by the laws of the respective state in which they work.

State and local governments also offer health care services to their citizens in the form of public hospitals, mental health institutions, and long-term care and rehabilitation facilities, among others. State and local governments finance the services needed by those patients who patronize their hospitals, institutions, and facilities because those patients are generally unable to pay for their own care and have limited or no private insurance coverage. These patients may have delayed seeking medical treatment until they became critically ill, thereby increasing the costs to care for them. Typically, the demand for services outstrips the ability of state and local governments to finance those services.

Nongovernmental Payers

Private insurance companies, employers, and managed care organizations comprise the entities that finance health care services within the private sector. Utilizing private health insurance, the insured (the one holding the policy/receiving the care) prepays a specific amount or fee (the premium) to an insurer on a regular basis (e.g., monthly). In exchange, the insurance company (insurer) agrees to pay the health care provider's charges for the treatment rendered to the insured, up to previously specified limits. The insurer is able to do so because it has pooled the premiums from a large group of insured members and can draw from this pool to pay the charges. This arrangement is memorialized as a legal contract for services between the insured and the insurance company.

Private health care insurance companies range from small companies that are centered in one or two states to large companies that cover all of the states in the nation. The single largest trade association of private health care insurers in the United States is the Blue Cross/Blue Shield Association. This association coordinates the activities of locally operated Blue Cross and Blue Shield plans. These plans provide coverage for hospital and related services (Blue Cross) and physician services (Blue Shield). Although the association and its locally operated plans are not-for-profit organizations, many private health care insurers are for-profit organizations.

When determining whether and how much to pay the health care provider for charges that have been submitted, the private insurance company examines two elements: coverage and medical necessity. Coverage refers to those health care services that have previously been identified as reimbursable under the insurance plan. Medical necessity refers to the principle requiring health care providers to make reasonable efforts to limit the treatments and services rendered to the patient to those that are necessary to accomplish the intended purpose of care (e.g., diagnosis). Treatment and services that are primarily for the convenience of the patient are not considered medically necessary. Considerable disagreement exists over what health care providers and private insurance companies consider appropriate health care services for coverage purposes and what is considered medically necessary. Similar disagreement also exists between health care providers and governmental payers. Table 15–4 provides examples of services excluded from coverage under the Medicare program.

Table 15–4	Summary of Coverage Exclusions for Medicare Benefits	
• Routine personal checkups	• Orthopedic shoes or supportive devices
• Eyeglasses or contact lenses	• Custodial care
• Routine eye examinations	• Cosmetic surgery and related services
• Hearing aids or examinations	• Most dental care and dentures
• Most immunizations (shots)	• Routine foot care and flat foot care
• Outpatient occupational and physical therapy furnished incident to a physician's services	• Certain services of an assistant-at-surgery
• Home health services furnished under a plan of care, if the agency does not submit the claim	• Some experimental or investigation devices
• Custodial care	• Care that is used to cause death (assisted suicide)
• Certain hospital services	

Source: 42 C.F.R. § 411.15 (2007)

The same concepts of payments, coverage, and medical necessity are also present in employer-based self-insurance. Utilizing this scenario, the employee (the insured) pays premiums to the employer (insurer) on a regular basis, typically through the payroll withholding process. In exchange, the employer pays the health care provider's charges up to previously specified limits. Employers with a large work force often favor the self-insurance approach, viewing it as a cost-saving mechanism because the overhead of the private insurance company is not factored into the premium. Additionally, the employer can retain the funds pooled as premiums until such time as payment is necessary. Finally, the employer can contract with an independent organization to administer its self-insurance plan, often at financially favorable rates, as a means to minimize its own overhead costs. These independent organizations are called **third-party administrators** and possess expertise in all or a portion of the claims process.

The activities associated with coverage and necessity are part of the billing process. After treating the patient, the health care provider submits a **claim** to the third-party payer, which is a statement seeking to be paid for the services rendered and/or supplies provided to the patient. This statement describes the services and/or supplies with sufficient particu-larity, including classification codes and other supporting information where necessary, so that the third-party payer can determine whether the services and/or supplies are reimbursable under the health plan (coverage) and whether they are truly necessary to accomplish the intended purpose of care (necessity). At that point, the third-party payer issues an **explanation of benefits (EOB)**, which is a statement sent to both the health care provider and the patient explaining what amounts the third-party payer paid associated with the claim statement. An example of an EOB sent to a health care provider is found in Figure 15–1. To the extent that the third-party payer did not pay all charges submitted by the health care provider, the patient is generally responsible for the remaining amount. Additional information about the billing process is discussed later in this chapter, in the section entitled "Payment Methodologies."

Managed Care Organizations Among the most significant developments on the third-party payer scene in the latter half of the 20th century was the emergence of the managed care industry. **Managed care** refers to health plans that integrate fully the financial and delivery aspects of health care. The concept is that a defined, enrolled population will receive health care services through either a

Figure 15–1 | Explanation of benefits

Service Date	Type of Service	Charge(s) Submitted	Not Covered or Discount	Amount Covered	Patient Co-payment Co-insurance Deductible	Covered Balance	Plan Liability
Insured Name **Mallory, Michael**		Insured Patient ID 999510226-82		Patient Name **Mallory, Christina**			
Provider Name: L.D. HEATH, MD – In-Network Provider Reference Number: 987552							
11/14/2007	90221 Hosp Care Detailed	$97.00	$4.00	$93.00	$18.60 co-ins	$74.40	$74.40
11/15/2007	99238 Hosp Discharge	$98.00	$3.00	$95.00	$19.00 co-ins	$76.00	$76.00
						Total Paid:	$150.40
Insured Name **Manaly, Richard**		Insured Patient ID 999236189		Patient Name **Manaly, Richard**			
Provider Name: D.J. SCHWARTZ – Out-of-Network Provider Reference Number: 987523							
10/20/2007	99213 Est.Pat.Level 3	$78.00	$6.00	$72.00	$14.40 co-ins	$57.60	$57.60
						Total Paid:	$57.60
Insured Name **Ruhl, Robert**		Insured Patient ID 999321168-02		Patient Name **Ruhl, Mary**			
Provider Name: J.D. HEATH, MD – In-Network Provider Reference Number: 987524							
11/5/2007	99221 Hosp Care Detailed	$97.00	$4.00	$93.00	$18.60 co-ins	$74.40	$74.40
11/06/07 to 11/09/07	99231 Hosp Subsequent Care	$192.00	$12.00	$180.00	$36.00 co-ins	$144.00	$144.00
11/10/2007	99238 Hosp Discharge	$98.00	$3.00	$95.00	$19.00 co-ins	$76.00	$76.00
						Total Paid:	$294.40

prepayment or discounted fee-for-services arrangement. The focus of managed care is to approach health care services by facilitating cost containment and control utilization while maintaining a high quality of care. Begun as an alternative delivery system designed to contain costs, managed care has emerged as a significant force in the health care industry.

In essence, managed care is a method that is used to assume and transfer risk. Risk is assumed through aggressive medical management and transferred through payment structures such as capitation and prospective payment systems. The health care provider assumes the risk of delivering care in an efficient and effective manner, and the managed care organization retains the risk of underwriting the use of health care for those enrolled. This division of risk is designed to make each side accountable for that part of the risk it can manage effectively.

Managed care began as an outgrowth of the Health Maintenance Organizations Act of 1973 (HMO Act).[2] This Act supplied federal subsidies to new managed care organizations to allow them to compete with traditional commercial health insurance plans. This competition provided consumers with alternatives and—at the same time—made health care providers more price conscious. Employers with 25 employees or more were required by the Act to offer their employees the option to choose a managed care organization for their health care insurance coverage. Although the Act imposed this requirement, the number of managed care organizations that were available to employees varied greatly across the nation, with significant availability in California, Washington, and Minnesota, and limited availability in other parts of the country.

Two factors greatly influenced the growth of managed care during the next three decades: inflation and legislative change. Inflation refers to the persistent rise in the average level of prices. During the 1980s and 1990s, charges for health care rose considerably, taxing the ability of governmental and nongovernmental payers to fund the care provided. One perceived answer to the inflationary pressures in health care was the use of managed care organizations; they were seen as the way to reduce health insurance premium costs and to lower hospital utilization. Accordingly, businesses took aggressive measures to encourage employees to choose a managed care organization for their health insurance coverage. Governmental payers, such as Medicaid, offered managed care plans to recipients of governmental benefits.

During this same time period, efforts for legislative change relating to the costs of health care also occurred. In 1982, Congress passed the Tax Equity and Fiscal Responsibility Act (TEFRA), making managed care available to Medicare beneficiaries. In 1985, Congress passed the Preferred Provider Health Care Act, easing restrictions on preferred provider organizations and the use of their network physi-

cians. Congress amended the HMO Act in 1988, easing restrictions on health maintenance organizations.[3] The relaxations provided by these three laws enabled managed care organizations to compete more readily with commercial health insurance plans. Critics maintained that Congress had not gone far enough and urged the adoption of universal health care coverage for all United States citizens. The Clinton administration proposed such comprehensive legislation in 1994, using managed care plans as the basis for the reform model, but a wide coalition of interest groups worked successfully to defeat its passage. Although it was ultimately unsuccessful, the proposed legislation served to raise awareness of the potential cost savings to be gained from managed care plans.

The current trend is toward continued growth of managed care plans. By 1998, some states saw 45 percent of their population enrolled in managed care plans.[4] Managed care strategies have been adopted by virtually every state government to deliver some form of health care service. At the federal level, Medicare (through Part C) and Medicaid both offer some form of managed care to their beneficiaries.

Certain features are present in all managed care plans. A primary care provider (PCP) is the physician who serves as the gatekeeper or coordinator for all of the patient's care. The patient works through the PCP to learn what additional care or testing is needed beyond what the PCP can provide. The theory is that the PCP will assist in reducing inappropriate or duplicative utilization of health care services and costs. Additionally, the emphasis in managed care is on preventive care and wellness education, with the theory being that the probability of a patient becoming critically ill is lessened, thereby reducing the costs of care over time. Another common feature is the use of phrases different from those used in private health insurance companies. In the managed care vernacular, patients are referred to as "members" or "subscribers" at the administrative level and as "patients" at the treatment level.

Similar to other third-party payers, managed care organizations are subject to federal and state regulation. At the federal level, the Office of Managed Care (OMC) in the Centers for Medicare and Medicaid Services regulates HMOs in which Medicare and Medicaid beneficiaries are enrolled. The OMC evaluates HMOs with regard to issues of management, fiscal soundness, and quality of health care provided, using the Contractor Performance Monitoring System (CPMS). Those HMOs that meet the OMC's requirements under CPMS receive federally qualified status, a designation that is valued by employers who choose managed care plans with which to contract. At the state level, insurance laws or laws specifically targeted to managed care also apply. These laws are administered by the state's insurance commissioner or HMO regulatory agency and generally address issues of fiscal soundness.

Managed care organizations are also subject to the requirements of accrediting bodies. Strong incentive exists to meet these requirements because accreditation serves as recognition of the delivery of high quality health care services. Three accrediting bodies address managed care organizations: the National Committee for Quality Assurance (NCQA); the Joint Commission (JC), formerly known as the Join Commission on Accreditation of Healthcare Organizations (JCAHO); and the Accreditation Association for Ambulatory Health Care (AAAHC). These accrediting bodies address issues of management, fiscal soundness, and the quality of health care provided.

Of particular value to employers is a set of performance measures created by NCQA called the Health Plan Employer Data and Information Set (HEDIS). HEDIS measures five performance areas: access and patient satisfaction, quality, finance, membership and utilization, and health plan management. Employers use HEDIS to compare health plans, to hold health plans accountable for meeting these measures, and to understand the value of what they purchase when contracting with a managed care organization.

As important as the origins and current trends of managed care are, it is also important to understand the different models that are used. An HMO is only one form of managed care; other forms include preferred provider organizations, exclusive provider organizations, point-of-service plans, and integrated delivery systems. These forms of managed care are addressed further in the following section and in Table 15–5.

Health Maintenance Organizations A health maintenance organization is a prepaid, organized system for providing comprehensive health care services within a geographic area to all persons under contract; this type of organization emphasized preventive medicine. The members of an HMO are required to use participating or approved providers for all of their health needs and to seek the HMO's approval for services through the HMO's utilization program. An HMO can be organized under a variety of models including the staff model, the group model, the network model, the independent practice association model, and the mixed model.

In the staff model, the HMO actually owns the facilities where care is provided. Physicians are employees of the HMO, not independent contractors, and they are only allowed to treat those patients who are members of the HMO plan. This is referred to as a closed-panel arrangement. Because the physicians are employees, they do not join in any profits that the organization generates. If the HMO owns only the clinical facilities in which patients see their physician, the HMO contracts with others to provide the remaining services such as hospital, emergency, and surgical care.

With the group model, the HMO contracts with an independent multispecialty medical group that provides all physician services to members of the HMO plan. Similar to the staff group model, the HMO contracts with other organizations for services that are not available through the independent multispecialty group; these physicians are part of a closed-panel arrangement. The contract with the independent multispecialty medical group generally includes significant financial incentives for the physicians to provide proper patient care and financial management.

With the network model, the HMO contracts with more than one independent multispecialty group to deliver services. The physicians are not in a closed-panel arrangement, meaning that they can provide care to others who are not enrolled in the particular HMO with which the group has a contract.

With the independent practice association model (IPA), the HMO contracts with an organized group of independent practitioners to deliver services. This organized group or association serves as the buffer between the HMO and the individual physician, acting on the individual physician's behalf during contract negotiations and receiving payments from the HMO for distribution to the individual physician. The individual physicians are not in a closed-panel arrangement and can maintain their own individual practices.

With the mixed model, the HMO operates under more than one arrangement. For example, the HMO may begin as an IPA model but gradually obtain facilities or physician practices. Mixed models may also occur as a result of the merger or acquisition of two or more HMOs.

Table 15–5	Forms of Managed Care
Health Maintenance Organizations (HMOs)	A prepaid, organized system for providing comprehensive health care services within a geographic area to all persons under contract, emphasizing preventive medicine.
Preferred Provider Organizations (PPOs)	An entity composed of health care providers who contract with an employer or private health insurance company to deliver services at a discounted rate in return for a promise of a high volume of patients.
Exclusive Provider Organizations (EPOs)	An entity similar to a PPO except that the patient must stay within the provider network to receive care.
Point-of-Service Plans (POS)	A health plan that allows the patient to choose the type of provider from whom he will receive care, at or near the point in time when he will receive the care.
Integrated Delivery System (IDS)	A network of organizations that provides a full spectrum of coordinated health care services.

Figure 15-2 | Contrast between an IDS and a health system

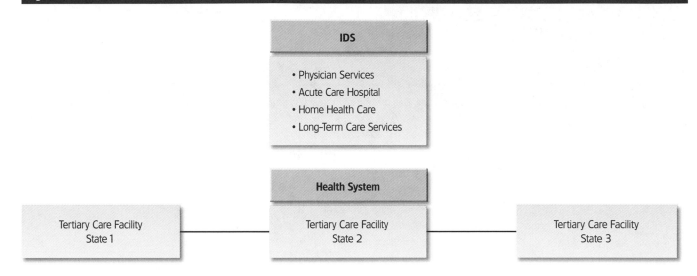

Preferred and Exclusive Provider Organizations A preferred provider organization (PPO) is an entity composed of health care providers who contract with an employer or private health insurance company to deliver services at a discounted rate in return for the promise of a high volume of patients. The strength of a PPO is that the patient may choose to receive care from a large number of providers (e.g., physicians, hospitals, pharmacies, etc.) who are part of the PPO network, with the expectation of limited out-of-pocket expenses. The patient is not limited to the providers within the PPO network. However, if the patient chooses to receive care from an out-of-network provider, the patient experiences higher out-of-pocket expenses.

An exclusive provider organization (EPO) is an entity similar to a PPO except that the patient must stay within the provider network to receive care. If the patient receives care outside the provider network, the patient is responsible for paying the out-of-network provider's charges in full.

Point-of-Service Plans A point-of-service plan (POS) is a health plan that allows the patient to choose the type of provider from whom he will receive care, at or near the point in time when he will receive the care. This stands in contrast to other forms of managed care, which require the patient to choose the type of provider (e.g., HMO, PPO) during the time of open enrollment at the place of employment. For example, the patient may choose an HMO physician (and incur no out-of-pocket expenses), a PPO network physician (and incur limited out-of-pocket expenses), or an out-of-network physician (and incur higher out-of-pocket expenses). Such freedom to choose appeals to many patients and allows them greater control over their fiscal expenditures for health care.

Integrated Delivery Systems An integrated delivery system (IDS) is a network of organizations that provide coordinated health care services. An IDS concentrates on vertical integration, meaning that the network provides a full spectrum of

services that cover the continuum of care. An IDS could include organizations that offer hospital services, physician services, long-term care services, and home health services, to name a few. The IDS offers the patient "one-stop shopping," thereby maximizing the patient's convenience. The IDS should not be confused with a health system; a health system concentrates on delivering a single type of service (e.g., acute care hospitals) to a geographic region. Such integration is horizontal in nature. By offering a single type of service, the health system hopes to increase efficiency and effectiveness. The contrast between an IDS and a health system is illustrated in Figure 15-2.

Payment Methodologies

The methods used to reimburse health care providers have varied over time. Originally, patients paid for services or went without for lack of ability to pay. Later, third-party payers bore the economic risks associated with reimbursement, primarily doing so under the fee-for-service method. Health care costs rose as a result of the fee-for-service method, making the need to share the economic burden even more evident. Accordingly, new payment methodologies arose, which resulted in a shift in economic burden from the payer to the health care provider and patient. These payment methodologies are listed in Table 15-6. As these new methodologies came into play, the nation experienced a slowdown in the increase of health care expenditures on a routine basis.

Fee for Service

The predominant method of payment used in the United States during the 20th century was the fee-for-service (FFS) method. Utilizing FFS, the health care provider charged the patient a specific price for each identifiable and distinct unit of service delivered. The number of

Table 15–6 | Types of Payment Methodologies

Fee For Service	• Specific price paid per unit of service delivered • Retrospective payment method • Usual, customary, and reasonable costs payment formula • Economic risk with the payer
Prospective Payment Systems	• Prices predetermined before delivery of service • Applicable to acute care, skilled nursing facilities, outpatient, home health, and inpatient rehabilitation settings • Case mix analysis • Economic risk with the health care provider
Resource–Based Relative Value System	• Prices predetermined before delivery of service • Applicable to physician services • Economic risk with the health care provider
Capitation	• Formula of a set amount, regardless of quantity or nature of services rendered • Economic risk with the health care provider • Increased economic risk to health care provider if services rendered exceed set amount paid

units of service that were delivered determined the total amount that was charged to the patient. A unit of service was defined on a per-procedure or per-service-provided basis for health care professionals such as doctors and dentists, and on a per-day basis for institutions such as acute care hospitals and long-term care facilities. Once services were rendered, the health care provider developed a **chargemaster**, which is a tally or master listing of all the elements involved in providing the service to be billed (e.g., medical equipment and supplies, room and board, laboratory tests, anesthesia, etc.). A listing of a selected group of services contained in a chargemaster is found in Table 15–7. The patient would then pay the health care provider according to the bill received. If the patient had insurance, the private health insurance company or the patient's employer would pay the health care provider according to the terms of the insurance plan. Any charges not paid by the private insurance company or the patient's employer became the responsibility of the patient (**balance billing**). As described above, this method is a retrospective payment system.

Table 15–7 | Select Group of Charges and Prices Included in a Chargemaster

Item Number	Description	Price
43801836	CHEMO ADM INF EA ADD HR	205.00
10406214	CHEMO INF UPTO 1st HR	526.00
10406239	CHEMO IV PUSH	310.00
62101571	KIDNEY FUNCTION W/PHARM	946.30
62101415	KIDNEY IMAGE STATIC	757.90
40683716	KIDNEY STONE ANALYSIS	15.31
19104249	ZITHROMAX 100MG5ML	40.25
19104256	ZITHROMAX 1 GM PKT RC	121.00
19004298	ZITHROMAX 500 MG VIAL	160.77

This method created little to no financial incentive for health care providers to contain charges, thereby increasing health care expenditures over time. Utilizing FFS, charges could rise if the fees for each unit of service increased, if more units of service were provided, or if more expensive units of service were substituted for less expensive ones. Furthermore, no mechanism existed to police the practice of unbundling. **Unbundling** means to bill for a package of health care procedures on an individual basis rather than on a combined basis. For example, a health care provider may bill separately for groups of laboratory tests that are performed together. As a result of submitting separate charges for each individual encounter, service, procedure, or day of care provided, the health care provider receives a larger level of payment.

An increase in the charges issued by health care providers was not always the result of profit motives. For decades, health care providers subsidized care for indigent persons through the fees charged to wealthier persons. Uncertainty over the outcomes of treatment and the possibility of litigation for inadequate or inappropriate treatment added pressure to the health care provider to do more, not less. Although consumers often benefited from insurance coverage, they were insulated from paying charges directly to the health care provider and, therefore, demanded more services.

In an effort to manage costs related to FFS, third-party payers began to base hospital and physician payments on a cost basis, relying on **usual, customary, and reasonable costs** (UCR). Although no universal formula exists, UCR is generally calculated to include: (1) the health care provider's usual charge for a given procedure or service; (2) the amount customarily charged for the same procedure or service by other health care providers in the area; and (3) the reasonable costs of procedures or services for a given patient following medical review of the case. This formula results in a reasonable compensation for the service billed in that geographic area of the country. Utilizing UCR, the health care provider is reimbursed only for the costs incurred, not for the amount billed, with limited allowance for overhead expenses such as general administration and maintenance costs.

This cost reimbursement method requires health care providers to determine how to allocate overhead expenses to a given charge in order to obtain reimbursement for those overhead expenses. This activity is referred to as cost allocation and involves the identification of non-revenue-generating and revenue-generating departments within an organization. For example, the hospital's administration section, chaplain services, and health information services departments are considered non-revenue-generating departments; they do not provide direct patient care. The costs to operate these areas nonetheless exist and are therefore allocated in some fashion to those departments that generate revenue by providing direct patient care. Several cost allocation methods exist, including the step-down method, the double-distribution method, and the simultaneous equations method.

To monitor this allocation of overhead expenses, Medicare began requiring hospitals to file Medicare cost reports. Because of the volume of cost reports filed nationwide and the potential for mistakes, Medicare hires fiscal intermediaries to examine these reports and issue rules for counting and including costs. With regard to hospitals that receive reimbursement under Medicare, the need to file Medicare cost reports on an annual basis has become as important as the need to file tax returns. Whereas hospitals attempt to minimize taxes when filing returns, hospitals attempt to maximize revenues through proper allocation of overhead expenses when filing cost reports. This maximization of revenues has lessened the effectiveness of the cost reimbursement method as a way to manage costs.

Monitoring cost allocations is not a matter solely for third-party payers such as Medicare; each department within an organization has an obligation to determine whether the costs associated with its area are allocated properly. Within the health information management (HIM) context, this determination involves examining what areas of the organization receive HIM services and to what extent HIM costs are allocated to other areas.

A second approach to containing costs was the development of certificate-of-need programs. A certificate-of-need program requires health care facilities to justify to a state agency the need to purchase new equipment, buy or create new buildings, or offer new services. The concept behind these programs is that by mandating review of actions before they take place, a state can act to reduce health care expenses overall (e.g., duplication of services or equipment will be prevented or reduced). Although they are seen by some within the health care community as an irritant at best and improper state action at worst, these programs have contributed to controlling costs to some extent.

As health care expenditures nationwide increased at greater and greater rates, third-party payers reacted. Using their market power, third-party payers began to dictate reimbursement rates and define reimbursable units of service. Third-party payers demanded discounted rates from health care providers and, when that did not contain costs sufficiently, moved to set the rates themselves. Gradually, new alternatives to the fee-for-service model emerged. Among the new reimbursement models were the prospective payment system, the resource-based relative values system, and capitation.

Prospective Payment Systems

A prospective payment system (PPS) is a payment method that establishes rates, prices, or budgets for future reimbursement before the health care provider delivers services or incurs costs. This system bases reimbursement on a case basis as opposed to a service basis. For example, treatment of a patient with a particular condition is set at a predetermined rate. If the health care provider treats a patient with this particular condition, the health care provider receives the predetermined rate, regardless of the number of services rendered in the course of treatment. If the actual cost to treat the patient exceeds the predetermined rate, the health care provider loses money. If the actual cost to treat the patient is lower than the predetermined rate, the health care provider receives the difference or surplus. Utilizing the prospective payment system, the health care provider is given an incentive to increase efficiency and therefore improve financial performance.

Medicare introduced the prospective payment system for inpatient hospital services in 1983 as a strategy to reduce costs. To make PPS work, Medicare adopted the diagnosis-related group (DRG) model developed by Yale University. This model is a classification system that groups patients who are medically related by diagnosis, treatment, and length of stay, using the International Classification of Diseases, ninth revision, clinical modifications codes (ICD-9-CM). DRGs provide a means of relating the type and volume of patients a hospital treats (case mix) to the costs incurred by the hospital. This relationship between case mix and costs allows hospitals to reach strategic decisions concerning the types of services they will continue to offer their patient population. Twenty-three diagnostic categories were originally formed, from which 467 diagnosis-related groups were created; over time, more than 500 diagnosis-related groups have been created. A predetermined rate was established for each DRG, and Medicare pays hospitals according to that rate.[5] Adjustments are made to the PPS rates on an annual basis. Further adjustments are made for cost outliers, patient transfers, capital costs, and medical education. Additional information concerning diagnosis-related groups is found in Chapter 6, "Nomenclatures and Classification Systems."

Medicare considered PPS such a success in the inpatient hospital setting that it expanded its application to other settings. Currently, PPS applies to skilled nursing facilities (SNF PPS) using resource utilization groups, version III (RUG-III); outpatient settings (OPPS) using ambulatory payment classification groups (APC); home health settings (HH PPS) using home health resource groups (HHRG); and inpatient rehabilitation facilities (IRF PPS) using case mix groups (CMG).

Other third-party payers saw the advantages presented by PPS and adopted it as a payment method; nearly half of the states have applied PPS to their Medicaid programs.[6] Blue Cross plans and other private health insurance companies have also adopted this payment method.

Important changes followed the implementation of the prospective payment system in the inpatient hospital setting. The health care industry saw a shift in the utilization of services from acute care hospitals to outpatient settings, including physician offices. The average length of stay for hospital inpatients decreased, and occupancy rates dropped. Some financially weak hospitals failed or merged with more financially viable organizations. Critics maintained that access to health care services decreased overall; some health care providers chose to avoid treating patients with complex diseases or who were at critical stages of illness because of the potential for financial loss. In addition, some critics charged that hospitals attempted to maximize reimbursement improperly by assigning patients to the highest-paying DRG (upcoding) even if documentation did not support such an assignment.

Resource-Based Relative Value Systems

As effective as PPS was in creating change in acute care hospitals, it was not able to control total Medicare costs; some nonhospital services were still reimbursed on a cost basis. Particular concern was focused on the increase in charges for physician services. To address this situation, Medicare adopted a DRG-type system for reimbursement of physician services called the resource-based relative value scale (RBRVS).

In addition to slowing the increase in Part B physician expenditures, the goal of RBRVS was to discourage the use of procedures and encourage the use of physician time, reduce specialist fees for services deemed overvalued, and limit the occurrence of balance billing to patients. To do this, RBRVS measures three input factors: the physician's time and skill, the physician's overhead and practice expenses, and the physician's malpractice insurance. Each factor is measured in relative value units (RVU) and fed into a formula to create values for each service rendered. These values are multiplied by geographic cost indices and compiled into a fee schedule published by CMS and revised annually. Payments made to nonphysician caregivers such as nurse practitioners, clinical social workers, nurse midwives, and physician assistants are tied to the RBRVS.

The RBRVS is based on a coding system used in physician offices called current procedural terminology (CPT)

codes, which was developed by the American Medical Association. The RBRVS system uses an expanded version of CPT called the Healthcare Common Procedure Coding System (HCPCS, pronounced "Hicpics"). The expanded version includes codes for nonphysician services.

Other third-party payers have been slower to adopt RBRVS than they were to adopt the DRG system. Although usage is not universal, many Blue Cross/Blue Shield plans use RBRVS, as do some managed care organizations that employ the IPA-model HMO and the PPO model. Gradually, private health insurance companies are abandoning the use of the usual, customary, and reasonable costs reimbursement system and are adopting RBRVS to reimburse physicians.

Certain changes followed the implementation of RBRVS. The growth in Medicare spending for physician services has slowed during the last decade. Certain specialties and subspecialties have seen slower growth, and balance billing has been reduced. However, some critics maintain that the upcoding phenomenon found in PPS has also occurred under RBRVS.

Capitation

As previously discussed, both PPS and RBRVS involve the shift of economic risk to the health care provider. As a result of the growth of managed care companies, one particular reimbursement methodology has taken on large importance: capitation. Capitation is a payment method wherein a specific amount is paid to a health care provider for a group of specified health services on a periodic basis, regardless of the quantity or nature of the services rendered. The amount is determined by assessing payment per member or subscriber per fixed period (e.g., per member per month). Utilizing capitation, health care providers are not reimbursed for services rendered over the set amount. For this reason, health care providers are given an incentive to only provide those services necessary to the patient. Accordingly, health care providers bear the economic risk if services rendered exceed the amount paid.

To better understand capitation, the following example is instructive. Dr. X is paid a per-member per-month (PMPM) amount of $50.00 for the patients assigned to him pursuant to the contract he has signed with a network model health maintenance organization. One hundred patients are assigned to him, so that he receives $5,000.00 on a monthly basis. Thus, Dr. X receives $60,000 during a 12-month period. Dr. X must deduct from the total an amount to pay salaries for office staff and other expenses. Some patients make multiple visits per year, whereas others only receive care once a year. Utilizing this scenario, Dr. X may benefit financially if the number of patients who make multiple visits can be offset by the number of patients who receive care only once a year. If, however, the patients assigned to Dr. X are individuals who suffer from chronic diseases or illnesses associated with advancing age and require close monitoring via multiple visits, Dr. X may be at financial risk.

The economic incentive and financial risk aspects of the capitation method have engendered fierce criticism. Patients have questioned whether their health care provider acts in the patient's interest or in the provider's interest when determining the amount of patient care provided. Health care providers have criticized capitation as a method that should not be applied to the treatment of patients with chronic diseases and illnesses, because these diseases and illnesses are resource intensive and are not as easily subject to the cost-containment aspects of capitation. Despite these criticisms, capitation appears to have become not only an established reimbursement method but one that is increasing in use.

Revenue Cycle Management

During the last quarter century, a dramatic shift occurred as a result of the introduction of new payment methodologies into the health care system. These new methodologies impacted almost every sector of the health care system, adding complexity and administrative burden to an already complicated structure of billing systems, accounting and regulatory requirements, and quality standards. Health care providers responded to these complex methodologies by focusing on how to best manage the reimbursement process as a means to maximize revenue. These efforts have culminated into an area of financial management known as revenue cycle management. **Revenue cycle management** refers to the efficient and effective use of administrative and clinical functions to capture, manage, and collect revenue related to the delivery of patient services.

A number of processes are involved in revenue cycle management, as illustrated in Figure 15–3. For most health care providers, the process begins even before treatment or services are rendered; specific information must first be collected about the patient and his method of payment. Once treatment or services are rendered, the claims processing activity begins. Special emphasis is placed on capturing all charges that relate to the patient's care and listing them in the chargemaster so that they can be billed to the third-party payer or the patient. Once billed, the third-party payer processes the invoice and pays according to previously established standards. The revenue received at this stage is reconciled against the health care provider's records, and any remaining balance is billed to the patient if no third-party payer is present. Upon collection of this balance, the cycle is complete.

Although this description appears very streamlined on the surface, it actually is fraught with many levels of complexity and opportunities for mismanagement. For example, many items that should be captured on a chargemaster may be omitted or deleted because of improper posting, misunderstanding, or ignorance by any of the multitude of individuals who are involved in a single patient's treatment. Identifying ways to lessen the opportunity for these types of errors is a major task within many health care organizations. Electronic order entry systems offer great promise (as opposed to traditional paper-based systems) to reduce these problems. Furthermore, chargemasters require continuous updates; new services and procedures may be offered by health care providers, and code sets must be modified on a regular basis.

Another element of complexity is dependency upon the content of the health record to support the postings contained in the chargemaster. This content should be both accurate and complete with regard to the conditions treated and the services provided to the patient. Using this content, the health information management professional is able to evaluate the data contained in the record and assign appropriate diagnosis and procedure codes. In turn, these codes are used as part of the invoice process and determine in large measure the amount of reimbursement a health care

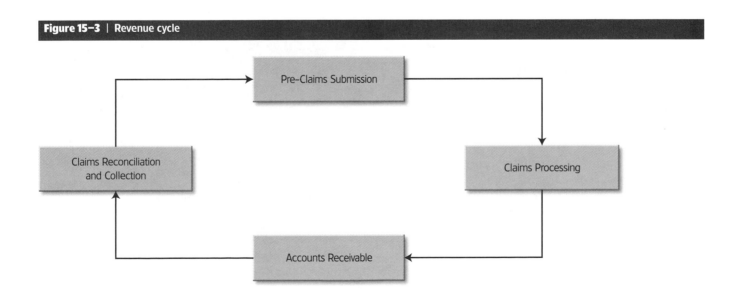

Figure 15–3 | Revenue cycle

organization will receive. Unfortunately, the quality of this content varies among health care organizations—with some documentation missing and other documentation incomplete—thus contributing to possible underpayments and revenue loss. The responsibility for this variation in quality rests with virtually all members of the health care organization; each plays a role in sharing or documenting information.

In light of the quality issues associated with documentation of the health record, many health information management professionals have responded by concentrating on improving those factors that fall within their control. Many focus on reducing the number of hours or days that elapse between the date a report is dictated and the date it is transcribed. Still more focus on the coding activity. These HIM professionals seek to reduce the time period between when a patient is discharged or treated and when codes are assigned, and between when codes are assigned and when they are entered into the billing system. Each of these activities can contribute to reducing the revenue cycle time.

Reducing revenue cycle time—although a laudable goal—can at times challenge the need for complete data to support coding efforts. Without supporting documentation, the coding process may be delayed or codes may be assigned improperly. Pressure to meet time standards for coding—lacking a counterbalance with regard to clinical data quality—may result in instances of noncompliance with regulatory requirements and the imposition of penalties.

One aid to compliance, which also adds to the level of complexity, is the use of internal auditing systems. Commonly referred to as "scrubbers," these automated systems operate to review each claim against a series of edits so that any discrepancies can be identified and corrected before submission to the third-party payer. Similar processes can be conducted by hand but often are not, because of the cost-effectiveness of automated systems. Failure to identify and correct these discrepancies may result in the rejection or denial of claims and attendant lost revenue.

The Transactions Rule requires covered entities that transmit certain patient data electronically to use specific electronic transactions and code sets.

Adding another layer of complexity are the standards and requirements imposed by the Health Insurance Portability and Accountability Act (HIPAA). HIPAA requires covered entities to employ specific standards for the electronic exchange of detailed health information. The Final Rule on Standards for Electronic Transactions and Code Sets, known as the Transactions Rule, identifies 10 electronic transactions and six code sets, as seen in Tables 15–8 and 15–9, for use by

Table 15–8   HIPAA Electronic Transaction Standards
Health Care Claims or Equivalent Encounter Information
Referral Certification and Authorization
Health Care Payment and Remittance Advice
Enrollment and Disenrollment in a Health Plan
Claims Attachments
Health Care Claim Status
Coordination of Benefits
Eligibility for a Health Claim
Health Plan Premium Payments
First Report of Injury

Source: 45 C.F.R. § 162. 1101–1801 (2007).

these covered entities. This rule allows all those involved with the revenue cycle process—including health care providers, third-party payers, claims clearinghouses, and health plans—to communicate with one another using common standards and sets, thereby facilitating the processing and payment of claims. Additional information concerning HIPAA rules is provided in Chapter 3, "Legal Issues," and Chapter 5, "Health Data Content and Structures." HIPAA's administrative, physical, and technical safeguards are discussed in Chapter 13, "Information Systems and Technology."

Once claims are transmitted electronically, a new time period in the revenue cycle begins: the time between transmission and receipt of payment. Health care organizations monitor this time period closely because this revenue stream is essential to maintain operations. Much of the time that elapses during this period is a result of actions taken by the third-party payer, who must process the received claim, issue a remittance advice to the health care organization, and issue an explanation of benefits to the patient. This remittance advice may indicate that the claim has been paid, denied, or rejected. If the indication shows payment, an amount is transferred electronically to

Table 15–9   HIPAA Code Sets
1   *International Classification of Diseases* (9th ed.) *Clinically Modified* (ICD-9-CM), Volumes 1 and 2
2   *International Classification of Diseases* (9th ed.) *Clinically Modified* (ICD-9-CM), Volume 3, Procedures
3   National Drug Codes (NDC)
4   Code on Dental Procedures and Nomenclature
5   Healthcare Common Procedural Coding System (HCPCS) in combination with Current Procedural Terminology (4th ed.) (CPT-4) for physician and other health care services
6   Healthcare Common Procedural Coding System (HCPCS) for medical supplies, durable medical equipment, orthotic and prosthetic devices, and all other substances and items used in health care services

Source: 45 C.F.R. § 162.1002 (2007).

the health care provider according to the payment methodology applicable to the third-party payer; if the indication shows denial or rejection, the health care provider must determine whether to correct and resubmit the claim to the third-party payer or write off a portion of the patient's account. Finally, any amount not paid by the third-party payer (e.g., copayments or deductibles) is then billed to the patient.

The potential for fraud and abuse is present within the revenue cycle process. The Office of the Inspector General of the U.S. Department of Health and Human Services has responded to this potential by instituting and emphasizing preventive programs to be operated by the Centers for Medicare and Medicaid Services. Examples include the Correct Coding Initiative (CCI), designed to promote national correct coding methodologies, and the Payment Error and Prevention Program (PEPP), designed to reduce the Medicare payment error rate. CMS also coordinates with OIG to publish numerous guidance materials that explain and clarify its regulations. These materials identify risk areas and offer suggestions for proper billing practices and internal controls. Health information management professionals routinely keep abreast of these initiatives by reviewing guidance materials and comparing that guidance against current practices that are employed in their institutions. More information concerning the actions of the OIG can be found in Chapter 3, "Legal Issues."

Prevention programs are not limited to use by third-party payers such as CMS—they include programs undertaken by health care providers themselves. Often referred to as **compliance programs**, these programs ensure the use of effective internal controls that promote adherence to applicable local, state, and federal laws and regulations and to the program requirements of federal, state, and private health plans. More information concerning the use of compliance programs can be found in Chapter 3, "Legal Issues." The challenge for health care organizations is to balance any potential delay these compliance programs may pose against the need to reduce the revenue cycle time. Those organizations that achieve this balance are able to position themselves for prompt remittance of payment along with the assurance of a shield from or a reduction in liability.

Conclusion

In today's competitive health care environment, it is essential for health information professionals to understand how applicable reimbursement systems influence an organization's financial health and further the organization's mission. Understanding the different payment methodologies used in health care today is necessary; almost all of an organization's reimbursement is derived from one or more of these methods. Knowing the revenue cycle process and its complexity can aid the professional in increasing an organization's financial health.

CHAPTER SUMMARY

Reimbursement methodologies are the means used to pay for the services provided by health care professionals. Reimbursement is performed primarily by third–party payers in both the public and private sectors, with the U.S. government operating the largest set of health care reimbursement programs in the nation. Nongovernmental payers, such as private insurance companies, employers, and managed care organizations, finance health care in the private sector. Managed care organizations have played a significant role in the financing of health care in the latter half of the 20th century, with several models operating across geographic regions. Payment methods have differed over time, moving from the once predominant method of fee for service to such methods as prospective payment systems and capitation. With the focus on containing costs, many health care entities have seen a dramatic shift take place with regard to managing the revenue cycle. Efforts to improve the revenue cycle process are largely dependent upon the content of the health record, adding new complexities to the role of the health information management professional.

CASE STUDY

You are the director of health information management services at Anywhere Hospital. Because of increased awareness of the role the revenue cycle process plays in your facility, you have resolved to minimize any delays that are within your level of control. Identify the measures you can take to improve the revenue cycle.

REVIEW QUESTIONS

1. How do TRICARE and CHAMPVA differ from each other?

2. What do the terms *insured, insurer,* and *premium* mean?

3. Why do employers with a large workforce favor the self-insurance approach?

4. What are the different ways in which an HMO can be organized?

5. What is the difference between an integrated delivery system and a health system?

6. What reasons would support the increase in health care charges in a fee-for-service situation?

7. What is a prospective payment system, and which third-party payers use this system?

8. To what type of services does a resource-based relative value scale apply?

9. What is capitation?

10. Provide some examples of how a health information management professional can improve the revenue cycle process.

ENRICHMENT ACTIVITIES

1. Using the Internet, research information about at least two managed care organizations in your geographic area. Determine which model the managed care organizations follow. Compare the information you have gathered with the concepts covered in this chapter, and discuss them with your instructor.

2. Review Table 15–4, Summary of Coverage Exclusions for Medicare Benefits. Do you agree or disagree with the items on this list? If you believe that any item on the list should be included as a Medicare benefit, formulate a persuasive argument and share it with your instructor.

WEB SITES

Alliance of Claims Assistance Professionals, http://www.claims.org

American Association of Health Plans, http://www.aahp.org

American Medical Billing Association, http://www.ambanet.net

Blue Cross and Blue Shield Association, http://www.bcbsa.com

Centers for Medicare and Medicaid Services, http://www.cms.hhs.gov/medicare

International Claim Association, http://www.claim.org

National Association of Insurance Commissioners, http://www.naic.org

National Uniform Billing Committee, http://www.nubc.org

National Uniform Claims Committee, http://www.nucc.org

Resource-Based Relative Value System, http://www.rbrvs.com

TRICARE, http://www.tricare.osd.mil

REFERENCES

Campbell, C., Schmitz, H., & Waller, L. (1998). *Financial management in a managed care environment.* Albany, NY: Delmar.

Jones, L. M. (2001). *Reimbursement methodologies for healthcare services.* Chicago: American Health Information Management Association.

Mattingly, R. (1997). *Management of health information.* Albany, NY: Delmar.

Peden, A. (1998). *Comparative records for health information management.* Albany, NY: Delmar.

Williams, S., & Torrens, P. (2002). *Introduction to health services* (6th ed.). Albany, NY: Delmar.

NOTES

1. Campbell, C., Schmitz, H., & Waller, L. (1998). *Financial management in a managed care environment.* Albany, NY: Delmar.

2. 42 U.S.C. § 300e et seq. (2007).

3. Health Maintenance Organization Amendments of 1988, 42 U.S.C. § 300e (2007).

4. In 1998, California and Oregon showed 46 percent and 45 percent of their populations, respectively, enrolled in health maintenance organizations. Six other states—Rhode Island, Massachusetts, Utah, Colorado, New York, and New Hampshire—followed, with between 30 percent and 34 percent of their populations enrolled in health maintenance organizations. Source: Welch, J. (1998). Managed care: The dominant paradigm in U.S. healthcare. *Journal of AHIMA, 69*(4), 22.

5. Several types of hospitals are excluded from the Medicare PPS and are paid according to the usual, customary, and reasonable costs. These hospitals include: children's hospitals, cancer hospitals, psychiatric and rehabilitation hospitals and units within larger medical facilities, and long-term care hospitals (defined as hospitals with an average length of stay of 25 days or longer).

6. Campbell, Schmitz, & Waller (1998), p. 141.

Common HIM Abbreviations

AAAHC	Accreditation Association for Ambulatory Health Care
AAALAC	Association for Assessment and Accreditation of Laboratory Animal Care
AAHRPP	Association for the Accreditation of Human Research Protection Programs
AAIDD	American Association on Intellectual and Developmental Disabilities
AAMR	American Association for Mental Retardation
AAMRL	American Association of Medical Record Librarians
ABC	Alternative Billing Codes
ACA	American Correctional Association
ACS	American College of Surgeons
ADA	American Dental Association
ADA	Americans with Disabilities Act
ADEA	Age Discrimination in Employment Act
ADT	Admission, Discharge, and Transfer
AHA	American Health Association
AHCPR	Agency for Health Care Policy and Research
AHIC	American Health Information Community
AHIMA	American Health Information Management Association
AHRQ	Agency for Healthcare Research and Quality
AIDS	Acquired Immunodeficiency Syndrome
ALOS	Average Length of Stay
AMA	American Medical Association
AMIA	American Medical Informatics Association
AMRA	American Medical Record Association
ANSI	American National Standards Institute
AOA	American Osteopathic Association
APC	Ambulatory Payment Classification
APR-DRG	All-Patient Refined Diagnosis-Related Groups

(Continued)

ARLNA	Association of Record Librarians of North America
ART	Accredited Record Technician
ASC	Accredited Standards Committee
ASP	Application Service Providers
AVHIMA	American Veterinary Health Information Management Association
A&D	Admission & Discharge
A&C	Adults & Children
BCBS	Blue Cross/Blue Shield
CAAHEP	Commission on Accreditation of Allied Health Education Programs
CAHIIM	Commission on Accreditation for Health Informatics and Information Management Education
CAHPS	Consumer Assessment of Healthcare Providers and Systems
CAI	Computer-Assisted Instruction
CAP	College of American Pathologists
CARF	Commission on Accredited Rehabilitation Facilities
CATCH	Comprehensive Assessment for Tracking Community Health
CCA	Certified Coding Associate
CCS	Certified Coding Specialist
CCS-P	Certified Coding Specialist–Physician–Based
CDC	Centers for Disease Control and Prevention
CDM	Charge Description Master
CD-ROM	Compact Disk Read-Only Memory
CERT	Centers for Education and Research on Therapeutics
CFO	Chief Financial Officer
CFR	Code of Federal Regulations
CHAMPUS	Civilian Health and Medical Program of the Uniformed Services
CHAMPVA	Civilian Health and Medical Program of the Department of Veterans Affairs
CHAP	Community Health Accreditation Program
CHIMA	Canadian Health Information Management Association
CHP	Certified in Healthcare Privacy
CHPS	Certified in Healthcare Privacy and Security
CHS	Certified in Healthcare Security
CMS	Centers for Medicare and Medicaid Services
CoP	Communities of Practice
COTS	Commercial Off-the-Shelf Software
CPHQ	Certified Professional in Healthcare Quality
CPMS	Contractor Performance Monitoring System
CPOE	Computerized Physician Order Entry
CPRI	Computer-Based Patient Record Institute
CPT	Current Procedural Terminology
CPU	Central Processing Unit
CSA	Component State Associations
CTR	Certified Tumor Register

CTT	Census-Taking Time
DC	Discharge
DD	Discharge Days
DEEDS	Data Elements for Emergency Department Systems
DHHS	Department of Health and Human Services
DIPC	Daily Inpatient Census
DIS	Discharge
DNS	Domain Name Services
DOA	Dead on Arrival
DOJ	Department of Justice
DRG	Diagnosis-Related Group
DSL	Digital Subscriber Lines
DSMB	Data Safety Monitoring Board
DSMP	Data Safety Monitoring Plan
ECT	Electroconvulsive Therapy
EDI	Electronic Data Interchange
EEOC	Equal Employment Opportunity Act
e-HIM	Electronic Health Information Management
EHR	Electronic Health Records
EOB	Explanation of Benefits
EPA	Equal Pay Act
EPO	Exclusive Provider Organization
E-R	Entity-Relationship
ERISA	Employee Retirement Income Security Act
ERM	Enterprise Risk Management
FAHIMA	Fellow of the American Health Information Management Association
FASB	Financial Accounting Standards Board
FCA	False Claims Act
FCRA	Fair Credit Reporting Act
FDA	Food and Drug Administration
FECA	Federal Employees Compensation Act
FFS	Fee-for-Service
FLSA	Fair Labor Standards Act
FMLA	Family Medical Leave Act
FORE	Foundation of Research and Education
GAAP	Generally Accepted Accounting Principles
GUI	Graphical User Interface
HCFA	Health Care Financing Administration
HCPCS	Healthcare Common Procedure Coding System
HCUP	Healthcare Cost and Utilization Project
HEDIS	Health Plan Employer Data and Information Set
HEW	Department of Health, Education, and Welfare

(Continued)

HFAP	Healthcare Facilities Accreditation Program
HHRG	Home Health Resource Groups
HIM	Health Information Management
HIMSS	Healthcare Information and Management Systems Society
HIPAA	Health Insurance Portability and Accountability Act
HIPDB	Healthcare Integrity and Protection Data Bank
HISB	Health Care Informatics Standards Board
HIV	Human Immunodeficiency Virus
HL7	Health Level Seven
HMO	Health Maintenance Organization
HQA	Hospital Quality Alliance
HSA	Health Savings Account
HSRP	Heart/Stroke Recognition Program
HTML	Hypertext Markup Language
HTTP	Hypertext Transfer Protocol
IACUC	Institutional Animal Care and Use Committee
ICD	International Classification of Diseases
ICF	International Classification of Functioning, Disability, and Health
ICIDH	International Classification of Impairments, Disabilities, and Handicaps
IDS	Integrated Delivery Systems
IFHRO	International Federation of Health Records Organizations
IHS	Indian Health Service
IP	Internet Protocol Inpatient
IPSD	Inpatient Service Days
IPA	Independent Practice Associations
IQ	Intelligence Quotient
IRB	Institutional Review Board
ISDN	Integrated Services Digital Network
ISO	International Standards Organization
ISP	Internet Service Provider
IVR	Interactive Voice Recognition
JC	Joint Commission (formerly known as the Joint Commission on Accreditation of Healthcare Organizations)
JCAH	Joint Commission on Accreditation of Hospitals
JCMIH	Joint Commission on Mental Illness and Health
KMS	Knowledge Management System
LAN	Local Area Network
LCD	Liquid Crystal Display
LOINC	Logical Observation Identifiers Names and Codes
LOS	Length of Stay
MAN	Metropolitan Area Network
MBO	Management by Objectives

MCO	Managed Care Organization
MDC	Major Diagnostic Category
MDS	Minimum Data Set
MEDPAR	Medicare Provider Analysis and Review
MEPS	Medical Expenditure Panel Survey
MeSH	Medical Subject Headings
MPI	Master Patient Index
NAHQ	National Association for Healthcare Quality
NAQAP	National Association of Quality Assurance Professionals
NB	Newborn
NCCHC	National Commission on Correctional Health Care
NCHICA	North Carolina Healthcare Information and Communications Alliance
NCHS	National Center for Health Statistics
NCQA	National Committee for Quality Insurance
NCRA	National Cancer Registrars Association
NCVHS	National Committee on Vital and Health Statistics
NDC	National Drug Codes
NEDSS	National Electronic Disease Surveillance System
NEI	National Employer Identifier
NHII	National Health Information Infrastructure
NHIN	National Health Information Network
NIC	Nursing Intervention Classification
NIH	National Institutes of Health
NIMH	National Institute of Mental Health
NLRB	National Labor Relations Board
NOC	Nursing Outcome Classification
NPI	National Provider Identifier
NVSS	National Vital Statistics System
OASIS	Outcome and Assessment Information Set
OB	Obstetrical
OBRA	Omnibus Budget Reconciliation Act
OHRP	Office for Human Research Protections
OIG	Office of Inspector General
OLAP	Online Analytical Processing
OMC	Office of Managed Care
ONCHIT	Office of the National Coordinator for Health Information Technology
OP	Outpatient
OQL	Object Query Language
OSCAR	Online Survey, Certification, and Reporting
OSHA	Occupational Safety and Health Administration
OWBPA	Older Workers Benefit Protection Act
PACT	Post-Acute Transfer Policy

(Continued)

PATH	Physicians at Teaching Hospitals
PCP	Primary Care Provider
PDA	Personal Digital Assistant
PDCA	Plan-Do-Check-Act
PDSA	Plan-Do-Study-Act
PEPP	Payment Error and Prevention Program
PHI	Protected Health Information
PHS	Public Health Service
PM	Project Management
PMRI	Patient Medical Record Information
POS	Point-of-Service
PPO	Preferred Provider Organization
PPS	Prospective Payment System
PRO	Peer Review Organization
PSDA	Patient Self-Determination Act
PSRO	Professional Standards Review Organization
QI	Quality Indicator
QIO	Quality Improvement Organization
RBRVS	Resource-Based Relative Value Scale
RFI	Request for Information
RFP	Request for Proposal
RFQ	Request for Quotation
RHIA	Registered Health Information Administrator
RHIO	Regional Health Information Organization
RHIT	Registered Health Information Technician
ROI	Return on Investment
RRA	Registered Record Administrator
RRL	Registered Record Librarian
RVU	Relative Value Units
SBR	Social and Behavioral Research
SDO	Standards Development Organization
SGML	Standard Generalized Markup Language
SNDO	Standard Nomenclature of Diseases and Operations
SNF	Skilled Nursing Facility
SNOMED International	Systemized Nomenclature of Medicine, International
SNOMED-CT	Systemized Nomenclature of Medicine, Clinical Terms
SNOMED-RT	Systemized Nomenclature of Medicine, Reference Terminology
SNOP	Systematized Nomenclature of Pathology
SNVDO	Standard Nomenclature of Veterinary Diseases and Operations
SOM	Semantic Object Model
SOW	Scope of Work
SQL	Structured Query Language

SPC	Statistical Process Control
SURS	Surveillance and Utilization Review System
SWOT	Strengths, Weaknesses, Opportunities, and Threats
TECH-net	Technology Exchange for Cancer Health Network
TEFRA	Tax Equity and Fiscal Responsibility Act
THINC	Taconic Health Information Network and Community
TQM	Total Quality Management
TRF-in	Transfer in
TRF-out	Transfer out
TRIP	Translation of Research into Practice
UACDS	Uniform Ambulatory Care Data Set
UCR	Usual, Customary, and Reasonable
UHDDS	Uniform Hospital Discharge Data Set
UMLS	Unified Medical Language System
UNICEF	United Nations Children's Fund
URL	Uniform Resource Locator
USERRA	Uniformed Services Employment and Reemployment Rights Act
VA	Department of Veterans Affairs
VMDB	Veterinary Medical Database
VPN	Virtual Private Network
VRT	Voice Recognition Technology
WAN	Wide Area Network
WARN	Worker Adjustment and Retraining Notification
WEDI	Workgroup for Electronic Data Interchange
WWW	World Wide Web
XML	Extensible Markup Language

B

Web Resources

By Subject Matter

Accrediting Entities

Accreditation Association for Ambulatory Healthcare, http://www.aaahc.org

Accreditation Council for Graduate Medical Education, http://www.acgme.org

American Association of Nurse Anesthetists, http://www.aana.com

American College of Healthcare Executives, http://www.ache.org

American College of Surgeons, http://www.facs.org

American Correctional Association, http://www.corrections.com/aca

American Dental Association, http://www.ada.org

American Dietetic Association, http://www.eatright.org

American Medical Association, http://www.ama-assn.org

American Nurses Association, http://www.nursingworld.org

American Osteopathic Association, http://www.osteopathic.org

American Society of Clinical Pathologists, http://www.ascp.org

Association for the Accreditation of Human Research Protection Programs, http://www.aahrpp.org

College of American Pathologists, http://www.cap.org

Commission on Accreditation for Health Informatics and Information Management Education, http://www.cahim.org

Commission on Accreditation of Rehabilitation Facilities, http://www.carf.org

Community Health Accreditation Program, Inc., http://www.chapinc.org

Joint Commission, http://www.jointcommission.org

National Commission on Correctional Health Care, http://www.ncchc.org

National Committee for Quality Assurance, http://www.ncqa.org

Bioethics

Human Genome Project, http://www.ornl.gov/hgmis

Johns Hopkins Bioethics Institute, http://www.med.jhu.edu/bioethics_institute

Midwest Bioethics Center, http://www.midbio.org

National Catholic Bioethics Center, http://www.ncbcenter.org

National Reference Center for Bioethics Literature, http://www.georgetown.edu/research/nrcbl

United Network for Organ Sharing, http://www.unos.org

Codes of Ethics

American Association of Medical Assistants, http://www.aama-ntl.org

American Association for Medical Transcription, http://www.aamt.org

American Dental Hygienists' Association, http://www.adha.org

American Health Information Management Association, http://www.ahima.org

American Medical Association, http://www.ama-assn.org

American Nurses Association, http://www.nursingworld.org

American Occupational Therapy Association, http://www.aota.org

American Pharmaceutical Association, http://www.aphanet.org

American Physical Therapy Association, http://www.apta.org

American Society for Clinical Laboratory Science, http://www.ascls.org

American Society of Radiologic Technologists, http://www.asrt.org

American Speech-Language-Hearing Association, http://www.asha.org

Coding Entities/Materials

Coding and Reimbursement Network, http://www.codingandreimbursement.net

Current Dental Terminology, http://www.ada.org

Current Procedural Terminology, http://www.ama-assn.org

eWebCoding, http://www.ewebcoding.com

National Correct Coding Initiative, http://www.cms.hhs.gov/medlearn.ncci.asp

National Drug Code, http://www.fda.gov/cder.ndc

Resource-Based Relative Value System, http://www.rbrvs.com

E-Health-Related Entities

American Health Information Management Association, http://www.ahima.org

American National Standards Institute, http://www.ansi.org

American Society for Testing and Materials, http://www.astm.org

California Regional Health Information Organization, http://www.calrhio.org

Colorado Health Information Exchange, http://www.ccbh.ehealthinitiative.org/profiles

Community Health Information Technology Alliance, http://www.chita.org

Data Interchange Standards Association, http://www.disa.org

Electronic Privacy Information Center, http://www.epic.org

Foundation for eHealth Initiative, http://www.ehealthinitiative.org

Health Level Seven, http://www.hl7.org

Indiana Health Information Exchange, http://www.ihie.com

National Association for Public Health Statistics and Information Systems, http://www.naphsis.org

North Carolina Healthcare Information and Communications Alliance, Inc., http://www.nchica.org

President's Information Technology Advisory Committee, http://www.nitrd.gov/pitac

Taconic Health Information Network and Community, http://www.ccbh.ehealthinitiative.org

Telemedicine Information Exchange, http://www.tie.telemed.org

Volunteer eHealth Initiative of Tennessee, http://www.volunteer-ehealth.org

Workgroup for Electronic Data Interchange, http://www.wedi.org

Finance/Reimbursement Entities

Alliance of Claims Assistance Professionals, http://www.claims.org

American Accounting Association, http://www.aaahq.org

American Institute of Certified Public Accountants, http://www.aicpa.org

American Medical Billing Association, http://www.ambanet.net

Association of Chartered Accountants in the U.S., http://www.acaus.org

Blue Cross/Blue Shield Association, http://www.bcbsa.com

Financial Accounting Standards Board, http://www.fasb.org

Financial Executives International, http://www.fei.org

Financial Managers Society, http://www.fmsinc.org

Government Financial Officers Association, http://www.gfoa.org

Institute of Management Accountants, http://www.imanet.org

International Claim Association, http://www.claim.org

National Association of State Auditors, Comptrollers, and Treasurers, http://www.nasact.org

National Uniform Billing Committee, http://www.nubc.org

National Uniform Claims Committee, http://www.nucc.org

Pennsylvania Health Care Cost Containment Council, http://www.phc4.org

Risk and Insurance Management Society, Inc., http://www.rims.org

TRICARE, http://www.tricare.osd.mil

Governmental Entities/Materials

Administration on Aging, http://www.aoa.dhhs.gov

Administrative Simplification Provisions of the Health Insurance Portability and Accountability Act, http://www.aspe.hhs.gov/admnsimp/

Agency for Healthcare Research and Quality, http://www.ahrq.gov

Centers for Disease Control and Prevention, http://www.cdc.gov

Centers for Medicare and Medicaid Services, http://www.cms.hhs.gov

Equal Employment Opportunity Commission, http://www.eeoc.gov

Federal Register, http://www.gpoaccess.gov

Federal Statistics, http://www.fedstats.gov

Health Resources and Services Administration, http://www.hrsa.gov

HIPAA Privacy and Security Regulations, http://www.hhs.gov/ocr

Home Health Compare Reports, http://www.medicare.gov/hhcompare/home.asp

Hospital Compare Reports, http://www.hospitalcompare.hhs.gov/hospital/home.asp

Indian Health Service, http://www.ihs.gov

Internal Revenue Service, http://www.irs.ustreas.gov

Malcolm Baldridge National Quality Program, http://www.quality.nist.gov

Medicare Prescription Drug and Assistance Program, http://www.medicare.gov/Prescription/Home

Medline Retrieval Service PubMed, http://www.pubmed.gov

National Cancer Institute, http://www.cancer.gov/statistics

National Center for Education Statistics, http://www.nces.ed.gov

National Center for Health Statistics, http://www.cdc.gov/nchs

National Committee on Vital and Health Statistics, http://www.ncvhs.hhs.gov

National Drug Code, http://www.fda.gov/cder.ndc

National Institutes of Health, http://www.nih.gov

National Institute of Health Trials Finder, http://ClinicalTrials.gov

National Library of Medicine's Internet Grateful Med, http://www.nlm.nih.gov/pubs/techbull/tbindex/gm/html

National Library of Medicine's Unified Medical Language System, http://www.nlm.nih.gov/research/umlsmain.html and http://www.nlm.nih.gov/research/umls/umlshelp.html

National Science Foundation, http://www.nsf.gov

Nursing Home Compare Reports, http://www.medicare.gov/nhcompare/home.asp

Occupational Safety and Health Administration, http://www.osha.gov

Office for Civil Rights, U.S. Department of Health and Human Services, http://www.hhs.gov/ocr

Office for Human Research Protections, http://ohrp.osophs.dhhs.gov

Office of Inspector General Compliance Guidelines and Annual Work Plan, http://oig.hhs.gov/publications/workplan.html

Office of the National Coordinator for Health Information Technology, http://www.hhs.gov/healthit

Office of Personnel Management, http://www.opm.gov

President's Information Technology Advisory Committee, http://www.nitrd.gov/pitac

Social Security Administration, http://www.ssa.gov

TRICARE, http://www.tricare.osd.mil

U.S. Bureau of Labor Statistics, http://www.bls.gov

U.S. Department of Health and Human Services, http://www.hhs.gov

U.S. Government Telework site, http://www.telework.gov

Veteran Administration Health Care System, http://www.va.gov

Health Care Associations

American Academy of Physician Assistants, http://www.aapa.org

American Academy of Professional Coders, http://www.aapc.com

American Association of Medical Assistants, http://www.aama-ntl.org

American Association for Medical Transcription, http://www.aamt.org

American Association for Respiratory Care, http://www.aarc.org

American Dental Association, http://www.ada.org

American Dental Hygienists' Association, http://www.adha.org

American Health Information Management Association, http://www.ahima.org

American Hospital Association, http://www.aha.org

American Medical Association, http://www.ama-assn.org

American Medical Informatics Association, http://www.amia.org

American Music Therapy Association, http://www.musictherapy.org

American Nurses' Association, http://www.ana.org

American Occupational Therapy Association, http://www.aota.org

American Osteopathic Association, http://www.osteopathic.org

American Pharmaceutical Association, www.aphanet.org

American Physical Therapy Association, http://www.apta.org

American Society for Clinical Laboratory Science, http://www.ascls.org

American Society of Radiologic Technologists, http://www.asrt.org

American Spinal Injury Association, http://www.asia-spinalinjury.org

American Veterinary Medical Association, http://www.avma.org

Association of American Medical Colleges, http://www.aamc.org

Association of State and Territorial Health Officials, http://www.astho.org

Association for Public Health Laboratories, http://www.aphl.org

Canadian Health Information Management Association, http://www.chra.ca.org

Healthcare Information and Management Systems Society, http://www.himss.org

International Federation of Health Records Organizations, http://www.ifhro.org

Joint Commission, http://www.jointcommission.org

Medicare Prescription Drug and Assistance Program, http://www.medicare.gov/Prescription/Home

Medline Retrieval Service PubMed, http://www.pubmed.gov

Midwest Bioethics Center, http://www.midbio.org

National Alliance for Health Information Technology, http://www.hospitalconnect.com

National Association for Healthcare Quality, http://www.nahq.org

National Association for Public Health Statistics and Information Systems, http://www.naphsis.org

National Association of Emergency Medical Technicians, http://www.naemt.org

National Association of Medical Staff Services, http://www.namss.org

National Athletic Trainers Association, http://www.nata.org

National Cancer Registrars Association, http://www.ncra-usa.org

National Commission on Correctional Health Care, http://www.corrections.com/ncchc

National Medical Association, http://www.nmanet.org

Society of Diagnostic Medical Sonography, http://www.sdms.org

Management-Focused Entities

American College of Health Care Administrators, http://www.achca.org

American Management Association, http://www.amanet.org

Association for Project Management, http://www.apm.org

Association for Work Process Improvement, http://www.tawpi.org

Change Management Association, http://www.cmassociation.org

International Public Management Association for Human Resources, http://www.ipma-hr.org

International Telework Association and Council, http://www.workingfromanywhere.org

Office of Personnel Management, http://www.opm.gov

Project Management Institute, http://www.pmi.org

Society for Human Resource Management, http://www.shrm.org

U.S. Bureau of Labor Statistics, http://www.bls.gov

U.S. Government Telework site, http://www.telework.gov

U.S. Process Improvement Association, http://www.uspia.org

Quality-Care-Focused Organizations

Academy of Certified Case Managers, http://www.academyccm.org

Agency for Health Care Research and Quality, http://www.ahrq.gov

American Society for Quality, http://www.asq.org

Case Management Society of America, http://www.cmsa.org

Commission for Case Manager Certification, http://www.ccmcertification.org

Consumer Checkbook, http://www.checkbook.org

HealthGrades, http://www.healthgrades.com

Institute of Medicine, http://www.iom.edu

Joint Commission, http://www.jointcommission.org

Juran Institute, http://www.juran.com

Leap Frog Group, http://www.leapfroggroup.org

National Association for Healthcare Quality, http://www.nahq.org

National Committee for Quality Assurance, http://www.ncqa.org

NCQA's Health Plan Report Card, http://www.hprc.ncqa.org

Select Quality Care, http://www.selectqualitycare.com

Six Sigma, http://www.isixsigma.com

The W. Edwards Deming Institute, http://www.deming.org

Records-Related Entities

American Health Information Management Association, http://www.ahima.org

American Record Management Association, http://www.arma.org

Medical Records Institute, http://www.medrecinst.com

Chart Filing and Tracking Systems, http://www.adldata.com, http://www.filingtoday.com, http://www.hale-systems.com, and http://www.bibberosystems.com

Paper-Based and Electronic Personal Health Records, http://www.HealthFrame.com, http://www.checkupsoftware.com, and http://www.medicalert.org,

Miscellaneous Resources

American Correctional Association, http://www.corrections.com/aca

Living Wills, http://www.uslivingwillregistry.com

National Health Law Program, http://www.healthlaw.org

SPSS Analytical Software, http://www.spss.com

WebMD, http://www.WebMD.com

World Health Organization, http://www.who.int

Alphabetical Order

A

Academy of Certified Case Managers, http://www.academyccm.org

Accreditation Association for Ambulatory Healthcare, http://www.aaahc.org

Accreditation Council for Graduate Medical Education, http://www.acgme.org

Administration on Aging, http://www.aoa.dhhs.gov

Administrative Simplification Provisions of the Health Insurance Portability and Accountability Act, http://www.aspe.hhs.gov/admnsimp/

Agency for Healthcare Research and Quality, http://www.ahrq.gov

Alliance of Claims Assistance Professionals, http://www.claims.org

American Academy of Physician Assistants, http://www.aapa.org

American Academy of Professional Coders, http://www.aapc.com

American Accounting Association, http://www.aaahq.org

American Association of Medical Assistants, http://www.aama-ntl.org

American Association for Medical Transcription, http://www.aamt.org

American Association for Respiratory Care, http://www.aarc.org

American Association of Nurse Anesthetists, http://www.aana.com

American College of Health Care Administrators, http://www.achca.org

American College of Healthcare Executives, http://www.ache.org

American College of Surgeons, http://www.facs.org

American Correctional Association, http://www.corrections.com/aca

American Dental Association, http://www.ada.org

American Dental Hygienists' Association, http://www.adha.org

American Dietetic Association, http://www.eatright.org

American Health Information Management Association, http://www.ahima.org

American Hospital Association, http://www.aha.org

American Institute of Certified Public Accountants, http://www.aicpa.org

American Management Association, http://www.amanet.org

American Medical Association, http://www.ama-assn.org

American Medical Billing Association, http://www.ambanet.net

American Medical Informatics Association, http://www.amia.org

American Music Therapy Association, http://www.musictherapy.org

American National Standards Institute, http://www.ansi.org

American Nurses' Association, http://www.ana.org

American Occupational Therapy Association, http://www.aota.org

American Osteopathic Association, http://www.osteopathic.org

American Pharmaceutical Association, http://www.aphanet.org

American Physical Therapy Association, http://www.apta.org

American Record Management Association, http://www.arma.org

American Society for Clinical Laboratory Science, http://www.ascls.org

American Society for Quality, http://www.asq.org

American Society for Testing and Materials, http://www.astm.org

American Society of Clinical Pathologists, http://www.ascp.org

American Society of Radiologic Technologists, http://www.asrt.org

American Speech-Language-Hearing Association, http://www.asha.org

American Spinal Injury Association, http://www.asia-spinalinjury.org

American Veterinary Medical Association, http://www.avma.org

Association for the Accreditation of Human Research Protection Programs, http://www.aahrpp.org

Association for Project Management, http://www.apm.org

Association for Public Health Laboratories, http://www.aphl.org

Association for Work Process Improvement, http://www.tawpi.org

Association of American Medical Colleges, http://www.aamc.org

Association of Chartered Accountants in the U.S., http://www.acaus.org

Association of State and Territorial Health Officials, http://www.astho.org

B

Blue Cross/Blue Shield Association, http://www.bcbsa.com

C

California Regional Health Information Organization, http://www.calrhio.org.

Canadian Health Information Management Association, http://www.chra.ca.org

Case Management Society of America, http://www.cmsa.org

Centers for Disease Control and Prevention, http://www. cdc.gov

Centers for Medicare and Medicaid Services, http://www.cms.hhs.gov

Change Management Association, http://www.cmassociation.org

Chart Filing and Tracking Systems, http://www.adldata.com, http://www.filingtoday.com, http://www.hale-systems. com, and http://www.bibberosystems.com

Coding and Reimbursement Network, http://www.codingandreimbursement.net

College of American Pathologists, http://www.cap.org

Colorado Health Information Exchange, http://www.ccbh.ehealthinitiative.org/profiles

Commission for Case Manager Certification, http://www.ccmcertification.org

Commission on Accreditation for Health Informatics and In-formation Management Education, http://www.cahim.org

Commission on Accreditation of Rehabilitation Facilities, http://www.carf.org

Community Health Accreditation Program, Inc., http://www.chapinc.org

Community Health Information Technology Alliance, http://www.chita.org

Consumer Checkbook, http://www.checkbook.org

Current Dental Terminology, http://www.ada.org

Current Procedural Terminology, http://www.ama-assn.org

D

Data Interchange Standards Association, http://www.disa.org

E

Electronic Privacy Information Center, http://www.epic.org

Equal Employment Opportunity Commission, http://www.eeoc.gov

eWebCoding, http://www.ewebcoding.com

F

Federal Register, http://www.gpoaccess.gov

Federal Statistics, http://www.fedstats.gov

Financial Accounting Standards Board, http://www.fasb.org

Financial Executives International, http://www.fei.org

Financial Managers Society, http://www.fmsinc.org

Foundation for eHealth Initiative, http://www.ehealthinitiative.org

G

Government Financial Officers Association, http://www.gfoa.org

H

Healthcare Information and Management Systems Society, http://www.himss.org

HealthGrades, http://www.healthgrades.com

Health Level Seven, http://www.hl7.org

Health Resources and Services Administration, http://www.hrsa.gov

HIPAA Privacy and Security Regulations, http://www.hhs.gov/ocr

Home Health Compare Reports, http://www.medicare.gov/hhcompare/home.asp

Hospital Compare Reports, http://www.hospitalcompare.hhs.gov/hospital/home.asp

Human Genome Project, http://www.ornl.gov/hgmis

I

Indian Health Service, http://www.ihs.gov

Indiana Health Information Exchange, http://www.ihie.com.

Institute of Management Accountants, http://www.imanet.org

Institute of Medicine, http://www.iom.edu

Internal Revenue Service, http://www.irs.ustreas.gov

International Claim Association, http://www.claim.org

International Federation of Health Records Organizations, http://www.ifhro.org

International Public Management Association for Human Resources, http://www.ipma-hr.org

International Telework Association and Council, http://www.workingfromanywhere.org

J

Johns Hopkins Bioethics Institute, http://www.med.jhu.edu/bioethics_institute

Joint Commission, http://www.jointcommission.org

Juran Institute, http://www.juran.com

L

Leap Frog Group, http://www.leapfroggroup.org

Living Wills, http://www.uslivingwillregistry.com

M

Malcolm Baldridge National Quality Program, http://www.quality.nist.gov

Medical Records Institute, http://www.medrecinst.com

Medicare Nursing Home Compare, http://www.medicare.gov/NHCompare

Medicare Prescription Drug and Assistance Program, http://www.medicare.gov/Prescription/Home

Medline Retrieval Service PubMed, http://www.pubmed.gov

Midwest Bioethics Center, http://www.midbio.org

N

National Alliance for Health Information Technology, http://www.hospitalconnect.com

National Association for Healthcare Quality, http://www.nahq.org

National Association for Public Health Statistics and Information Systems, http://www.naphsis.org

National Association of Emergency Medical Technicians, http://www.naemt.org

National Association of Medical Staff Services, http://www.namss.org

National Association of State Auditors, Comptrollers, and Treasurers, http://www.nasact.org

National Athletic Trainers Association, http://www.nata.org

National Cancer Institute, http://www.cancer.gov/statistics

National Cancer Registrars Association, http://www.ncra-usa.org

National Catholic Bioethics Center, http://www.ncbcenter.org

National Center for Education Statistics, http://www.nces.ed.gov

National Center for Health Statistics, http://www.cdc.gov/nchs

National Commission on Correctional Health Care: http://www.ncchc.org

National Committee for Quality Assurance, http://www.ncqa.org

National Committee on Vital and Health Statistics, http://www.ncvhs.hhs.gov.

National Correct Coding Initiative, http://www.cms.hhs.gov/medlearn.ncci.asp

National Drug Code, http://www.fda.gov/cder.ndc

National Health Law Program, http://www.healthlaw.org

National Institutes of Health, http://www.nih.gov

National Institute of Health Trials Finder, http://ClinicalTrials.gov

National Library of Medicine's Internet Grateful Med, http://www.nlm.nih.gov/pubs/techbull/tbindex/gm.html

National Library of Medicine's Unified Medical Language System, http://www.nlm.nih.gov/research/umlsmain.html and http://www.umlsinfo.nlm.nih.gov/research/umls/umlshelp.html

National Medical Association, http://www.nmanet.org

National Reference Center for Bioethics Literature, http://www.georgetown.edu/research/nrcbl

National Science Foundation, http://www.nsf.gov

National Uniform Billing Committee, http://www.nubc.org

National Uniform Claims Committee, http://www.nucc.org

NCQA's Health Plan Report Card, http://www.hprc.ncqa.org

North Carolina Healthcare Information and Communications Alliance, Inc., http://www.nchica.org

Nursing Home Compare Reports, http://www.medicare.gov/nhcompare/home.asp

O

Occupational Safety and Health Administration, http://www.osha.gov

Office for Civil Rights, U.S. Department of Health and Human Services, http://www.hhs.gov/ocr

Office for Human Research Protections, http://ohrp.osophs.dhhs.gov

Office of Inspector General Compliance Guidelines and Annual Work Plan, http://oig.hhs.gov/publications/workplan.html

Office of the National Coordinator for Health Information Technology, http://www.hhs.gov/healthit

Office of Personnel Management, http://www.opm.gov

P

Pennsylvania Health Care Cost Containment Council, http://www.phc4.org

Personal Health Records, http://www.HealthFrame.com, http://www.checkupsoftware.com, and http://www.medicalert.org,

President's Information Technology Advisory Committee, http://www.nitrd.gov/pitac

Project Management Institute, http://www.pmi.org

R

Resource-Based Relative Value System, http://www.rbrvs.com

Risk and Insurance Management Society, Inc., http://www.rims.org

S

Select Quality Care, http://www.selectqualitycare.com

Six Sigma, http://www.isixsigma.com

Social Security Administration, http://www.ssa.gov

Society for Human Resource Management, http://www.shrm.org

Society of Diagnostic Medical Sonography, http://www.sdms.org

SPSS Analytical Software, http://www.spss.com

T

Taconic Health Information Network and Community, http://www.ccbh.ehealthinitiative.org.

Telemedicine Information Exchange, http://www.tie.telemed.org

TRICARE, http://www.tricare.osd.mil

U

United Network for Organ Sharing, http://www.unos.org

U.S. Bureau of Labor Statistics, http://www.bls.gov

U.S. Department of Health and Human Services, http://www.hhs.gov

U.S. Government Telework site, http://www.telework.gov

U.S. Process Improvement Association, http://www.uspia.org

V

Veteran Administration Health Care System, http://www.va.gov

Volunteer eHealth Initiative of Tennessee, http://www.volunteer-ehealth.org

W

WebMD, http://www.WebMD.com

W. Edwards Deming Institute, The, http://www.deming.org

Workgroup for Electronic Data Interchange, http://www.wedi.org.

World Health Organization, http://www.who.int

C

Sample HIPPA Notices of Privacy Practices

These sample notices are included to illustrate the many variations a Notice of Privacy Practices may take. Such notices are required by regulation in virtually all patient care settings, including physician practices, allied health professional practices, inpatient and outpatient facilities, stand-alone service centers, and pharmacies. Each Notice of Privacy Practices presents similar information in a different manner, and no one approach is recommended over another. Source material for these notices can be found in the HIPAA regulations beginning with 45 C.F.R. § 164.500. These regulations are included in Appendix E, "Selected HIPAA Regulations."

Sample HIPAA Notice of Privacy Practices #1

NOTICE OF PRIVACY PRACTICES

THIS NOTICE DESCRIBES HOW MEDICAL INFORMATION ABOUT YOU MAY BE USED AND DISCLOSED AND HOW YOU CAN GET ACCESS TO THIS INFORMATION. PLEASE REVIEW IT CAREFULLY.

This Notice of Privacy Practices describes how we may use and disclose your protected health information (PHI) to carry out treatment, payment, or health care operations (TPO) and for other purposes that are permitted or required by law. It also describes your rights to access and control your protected health information. "Protected health information" is information about you, including demographic information, that may identify you and that relates to your past, present, or future physical or mental health or condition and related health care services.

Uses and Disclosures of Protected Health Information

Your PHI may be used and disclosed by your physician, our office staff, and others outside of our office that are involved in your care and treatment for the purpose of providing health care services to you, to pay your health care bills, to support the operation of the physician's practice, and any other use required by law.

Treatment:
We will use and disclose your PHI to provide, coordinate, or manage your health care and any related services. This includes the coordination or management of your health care with a third party. For example, we would disclose your PHI, as necessary, to a home health agency that provides care to you. For example, your PHI may be provided to a physician to whom you have been referred to ensure that the physician has the necessary information to diagnose or treat you.

Payment:
Your PHI will be used, as needed, to obtain payment for your health care services. For example, obtaining approval for a hospital stay may require that your relevant PHI be disclosed to the health plan to obtain approval for the hospital admission.

Health Care Operations:
We may use or disclose, as needed, your PHI in order to support the business activities of your physician's practice. These activities include, but are not limited to, quality assessment activities, employee review activities, training of medical students, licensing, and conducting or arranging for other business activities.

For example, we may disclose your PHI to medical school students that see patients at our office. In addition, we may use a sign-in sheet at the registration desk where you will be asked to sign your name and indicate your physician. We may also call you by name in the waiting room when your physician is ready to see you. We may use or disclose your PHI, as necessary, to contact you to remind you of your appointment.

We may use or disclose your protected health information in the following situations without your authorization. These situations include: as required by law, Public Health issues; Communicable Diseases; Health Oversight; Abuse or Neglect; Food and Drug Administration requirements; Legal Proceedings; Law Enforcement; Coroners, Funeral Directors, and Organ Donation; Research; Criminal Activity; Military Activity and National Security; Workers' Compensation; Inmates; Required Uses and Disclosures. Under the law, we must make disclosures to you and when required by the Secretary of the Department of Health and Human Services to investigate or determine our compliance with the requirements of Section 164.500.

Other Permitted and Required Uses and Disclosures will be made only with your consent, authorization, or opportunity to object unless required by law.

You may revoke this authorization, at any time, in writing, except to the extent that your physician or the physician's practice has taken an action in reliance on the use or disclosure indicated in the authorization.

Your Rights
Following is a statement of your rights with respect to your PHI.

You have the right to inspect and copy your protected health information. Under federal law, however, you may not inspect or copy the following records: psychotherapy notes; information compiled in reasonable anticipation of, or use in, a civil, criminal, or administrative action or proceeding, and PHI that is subject to law that prohibits access to PHI.

You have the right to request a restriction of your protected health information. This means you may ask us not to use or disclose any part of your PHI for the purposes of treatment, payment, or health care operations. You may also request that any part of your PHI not be disclosed to family members or friends who may be involved in your care or for notification purposes as described in this Notice of Privacy Practices. Your request must state the specific restriction requested and to whom you want the restriction to apply.

Your physician is not required to agree to a restriction that you may request. If your physician believes it is in your best interest to permit use and disclosure of your PHI, your PHI will not be restricted. You then have the right to use another health care professional.

You have the right to request to receive confidential communications from us by alternate means or at an alternative location. You have the right to obtain a paper copy of this notice from us upon request, even if you have agreed to accept this notice alternatively, i.e., electronically.

You may have the right to have your physician amend your protected health information. If we deny your request for amendment, you have the right to file a statement of disagreement with us and we may prepare a rebuttal to your statement and will provide you with a copy of any such rebuttal.

You have the right to receive an accounting of certain disclosures we have made, if any, of your protected health information.

We reserve the right to change the terms of this notice and will inform you by mail of any changes. You then have the right to object or withdraw as provided in this notice.

Complaints

You may complain to us or to the Secretary of Health and Human Services if you believe your privacy rights have been violated by us. You may file a complaint with us by notifying our privacy contact of your complaint. **We will not retaliate against you for filing a complaint.**

This notice was published and become effective on or before April 14, 2003.

We are required by law to maintain the privacy of, and provide individuals with, this notice of our legal duties and privacy practices with respect to PHI, If you have any objections to this form, please ask to speak with our HIPAA Compliance Officer in person or by phone.

Your signature below is only acknowledgement that you have received this Notice of our Privacy Practices:

Print Name: _____   Signature: _____

Date: _____

Sample HIPAA Notice of Privacy Practices #2

NOTICE OF PRIVACY PRACTICES

THIS NOTICE DESCRIBES HOW MEDICAL INFORMATION ABOUT YOU MAY BE USED AND DISCLOSED AND HOW YOU CAN GET ACCESS TO THIS INFORMATION. PLEASE REVIEW IT CAREFULLY.

Understanding Your Health Information:

To make an accurate diagnosis or render a correct treatment or service, your health care provider relies upon the protected health information (PHI) contained in your health or medical record. These records are created each time you visit your health care provider. Certain types of PHI are typically contained in these records, including a list of your symptoms, results of examinations and tests, all diagnoses, treatment options, and plans for future care or treatment.

The PHI contained in your health or medical record serves many purposes, including those that benefit you directly:

- Creating a chronological document of the care you receive

- Creating the foundation for planning your future care and treatment

- Communicating among and between the many health care providers involved in your care today and in the future

- Documenting any disabilities for which you may seek benefits

- Creating the ability for you or a third-party payer to verify whether the services billed for were actually provided

And those that benefit you indirectly:

- Improving the education of health professionals across many disciplines

- Assisting the health care community in its medical research efforts

- Strengthening efforts of public health officials to control disease and monitor the overall health status of a community

- Assisting health care organizations with facility planning and marketing of services

- Analyzing and improving patient care and outcomes

Who Will Follow This Notice

This notice describes our practices and those of all our employees, staff, and personnel.

Our Responsibilities

We understand that your PHI (medical information about you and your health) is private. We are committed to protecting your PHI. We create a record of the care and services you receive here. We need this record to provide you with quality care and comply with certain legal requirements. This notice applies to all of the records of your care generated by us.

This notice will tell you about the ways in which we may use and disclose PHI about you. We also describe your rights and certain obligations we have regarding the use and disclosure of PHI.

Examples of How We May Use or Disclose Your PHI

The following categories describe different ways that we use and disclose PHI. For each category of uses or disclosures, we will explain what we mean and try to give some examples. Not every use or disclosure in a category will be listed. However, all of the ways we are permitted to use and disclose PHI will fall within one of the categories.

We will use your PHI for treatment

We may use your PHI to provide you with medical treatment or services. We may disclose information about you to doctors, nurses, technologists, or other health care professionals involved in your care.

For example, PHI obtained by a member of the health care team, including but not limited to a specialist, technologist, etc., will be recorded in your record and used to determine the course of treatment that should work best for you. Our specialist will document in your record his or her findings.

We will also provide your physician and any subsequent health care provider with copies of various reports and films, upon request, that should assist him or her in your treatment.

We will use your PHI for regular health operations

We may use and disclose PHI for our operations. These uses and disclosures are necessary to run our organization and make sure that all of our patients receive quality care. For example, we may use PHI to review our treatment and services and to evaluate the performance of our care, the necessity of services, and the effectiveness and expansion of services offered.

We may use and disclose PHI to contact you as a reminder that you have an appointment at our facility. We may also contact you to provide you with instructions to prepare for your exam or to reschedule your exam. If you are unavailable, we may leave a message on your answering machine at the phone number provided to us. This message will be limited to a reminder of the date, time, and facility location.

Unless you object, we may use and disclose your name, location in the facility, general condition, and religious affiliation for religious purposes. This will be provided to clergy and, except for religious affiliation, to those who ask for you by name.

We will use your PHI for payment

We may use and disclose PHI, as needed, to obtain payment for your bill. For example, we may provide your insurer or third-party payer with PHI so that they can certify or approve your treatment before it begins.

Business associates

Our organization sometimes asks business associates to assist us with our work. Examples include an outside billing service and outside personnel who provide maintenance service on our medical equipment. It may be necessary for us to disclose your PHI to our business associates so that they can perform the job we have asked them to perform. As part of our effort to protect your PHI, we require each business associate to sign a contract and pledge to use appropriate safeguards when handling your PHI.

Communication with family

We may disclose to your family member or other relative, your close personal friend, or any other person you identify, your PHI to the extent it is relevant to that person's involvement in your care or payment related to your care.

Correctional institution

If you are an inmate of a correctional institution, we may disclose to the institution or its agents PHI necessary for your health and the health and safety of other individuals.

Law enforcement

If presented with a valid subpoena or if required by law, we may disclose PHI for law enforcement purposes.

Military and veterans

If you are a member of the armed forces, we may release PHI about you as required by military command authorities. We may also release PHI about foreign military personnel to the appropriate foreign military authority.

Notification

We may use or disclose information to notify or assist in notifying a family member, personal representative, or another person responsible for your care, of your location and general condition.

Public health

As required by law, we may disclose your PHI to public health or legal authorities charged with preventing or controlling disease, injury, or disability.

Research

We may disclose PHI to researchers when their research has been approved by an institutional review board that has reviewed the research proposal and established protocols to ensure the privacy of your health information.

Workers' compensation

We may disclose PHI to the extent authorized by and to the extent necessary to comply with laws relating to workers' compensation or other similar programs established by law.

Other uses of PHI

Other uses and disclosures of PHI not covered by this notice or the laws that apply to us will be made only with your written permission. If you provide us permission to use or disclose PHI about you, you may revoke that permission, in writing, at any time. If you revoke your permission, we will no longer use or disclose PHI about you for the reasons covered by your written authorization. You understand that we are unable to take back any disclosures we have already made with your permission, and that we are required to retain our records of the care that we provided to you.

Your Rights

PHI compiled by your health care provider or organization belongs to you. The medium in which this PHI is stored, the health or medical record, is the physical property of the health care provider. Your rights include the ability to:

- Request a copy of your health or medical record.

- Request a paper copy of the notice of privacy practices. You may obtain a copy of this notice at our Web site or by requesting a paper copy from the receptionist at this facility.

- Request a restriction on certain uses and disclosures of your PHI.

- Request an accounting of disclosures of your PHI.

- Request an amendment to your health or medical record.

- Request that we communicate your PHI by alternative means or at alternative locations.

- Revoke your authorization to use or disclose PHI except to the extent that we have already taken action.

Our Obligations Regarding Use and Disclosure of PHI

We recognize the importance of the privacy of your PHI and shall abide by both the requirements of the law and the terms of this notice with respect to the PHI we collect and maintain about you. If we are unable to agree to any of your requests to restrict the use and/or disclosure of your PHI, we will notify you. We will make a good faith effort to accommodate any reasonable request to communicate PHI by alternative means or at alternative locations.

There may be reasons in the future to change our practices and this notice, and we reserve the right to do so. We also reserve the right to make the revised or changed notice effective for PHI we already have about you as well as any information we receive in the future. We will post a copy of the current notice in our facility. In addition, each time you register at our facility, we will make available to you a copy of the current notice in effect.

For More Information or to Report a Problem

If you have questions or would like additional information, you may contact the Privacy Officer in person or by phone. If you believe your privacy rights have been violated, you can file a complaint with the Privacy Officer or with the Secretary of Health and Human Services. You will not be retaliated against for filing a complaint.

Effective Date: April 14, 2003

Sample HIPAA Notice of Privacy Practices #3

NOTICE OF PRIVACY PRACTICES

THIS NOTICE DESCRIBES HOW MEDICAL INFORMATION ABOUT YOU MAY BE USED AND DISCLOSED AND HOW YOU CAN GET ACCESS TO THIS INFORMATION. PLEASE REVIEW IT CAREFULLY.

We are required by law to maintain the privacy of Protected Health Information (PHI) and to provide you with notice of our legal duties and privacy practices with respect to PHI. PHI is information that may identify you and that relates to your past, present, or future physical or mental health or condition and related health care services. This Notice of Privacy Practices (Notice) describes how we may use and disclose PHI to carry out treatment, payment, or health care operations and for other specified purposes that are permitted or required by law. The Notice also describes your rights with respect to your PHI. We are required to provide this notice to you by the Health Insurance Portability and Accountability Act (HIPAA) of 1996.

We are required to follow the terms of this Notice. We will not use or disclose your PHI without your written authorization, except as described or otherwise permitted by this Notice. We reserve the right to change our practices and this Notice and to make the new Notice effective for all PHI we maintain. Upon request, we will provide any revised notice to you.

EXAMPLES OF HOW WE USE AND DISCLOSE PROTECTED HEALTH INFORMATION ABOUT YOU

THE FOLLOWING CATEGORIES DESCRIBE DIFFERENT WAYS THAT WE USE AND DISCLOSE YOUR PHI. WE HAVE PROVIDED YOU WITH EXAMPLES IN CERTAIN CATEGORIES; HOWEVER, NOT EVERY USE OR DISCLOSURE IN A CATEGORY WILL BE LISTED.

Treatment

We may use your PHI to provide and coordinate the treatment, medications, and services you receive. We many disclose your PHI to members of the health care team, including but not limited to physicians, specialists, technologists, and pharmacists, and to third parties, such as a home health agency, who are involved in your care. Based on the PHI they receive, these members of the health care team may contact you regarding the care you receive. For example, a pharmacist may contact you regarding refill reminders, therapeutic substitution, drug recommendations, other product recommendations, counseling and drug utilization review (DUR), product recalls, or disease state management.

Payment

We may use your PHI for various payment-related functions. For example, we may contact your insurer, medical benefit manager, or other health care payer to determine whether it will pay for your treatment and the amount of your co-payment. We will bill you or a third-party payer for the cost of treatment delivered to you. The information on or accompanying the bill may include information that identifies you, as well as the treatment you received.

Health Care Operations

We may use your health information for certain operational, administrative, and quality assurance activities. For example, we may use information in your health record to monitor the performance of the health care team providing treatment to you. This information will be used in an effort to continually improve the quality and effectiveness of the health care and service we provide.

We may disclose PHI to business associates if they need to receive this information to provide the service we have asked them to perform and they will agree to abide by specific HIPAA rules relating to the protection of health information.

We may also use your PHI to provide you with information about benefits and alternative treatments available to you and, in limited situations, about health-related products or services that may be of interest to you. If you register your e-mail address with us, you may elect to receive this information via e-mail.

WE ARE PERMITTED TO USE OR DISCLOSE YOUR PHI FOR THE FOLLOWING PURPOSES. HOWEVER, WE MAY NEVER HAVE ANY REASON TO MAKE SOME OF THESE DISCLOSURES.

To Communicate with Individuals Involved in your Care or Payment for Your Care

We may disclose to a family member, other relative, close personal friend, or any other person you identify PHI directly relevant to that person's involvement in your care or payment related to your care.

Food and Drug Administration (FDA)

We may disclose to the FDA, or persons under the jurisdiction of the FDA, PHI relative to adverse events with respect to drugs, foods, supplements, products and product defects, or post-marketing surveillance information to enable product recalls, repairs, or replacement.

Health Oversight Activities

We may disclose your PHI to an oversight agency for activities authorized by law. These oversight activities include audits, investigations, inspections, and credentialing, as necessary for licensure and for the government to monitor the health care system, government programs, and compliance with civil rights laws.

Judicial and Administrative Proceedings

If you are involved in a lawsuit or a dispute, we may disclose your PHI in response to a court or administrative order. We may also disclose your PHI in response to a subpoena, discovery request, or other lawful process that is not accompanied by a court or administrative order, but only if reasonable efforts have been made, either by the requesting party or us, to tell you about the request or to obtain an order protecting the information requested.

Organ or Tissue Procurement Organizations

Consistent with applicable law, we may disclose your PHI to organ procurement organizations or other entities engaged in the procurement, banking, or transplantation of organs for the purpose of tissue donation and transplant.

Research

We may disclose your PHI to researchers when their research has been approved by an institutional review board or privacy board that has reviewed the research proposal and established protocols to ensure the privacy of your information.

Fund-Raising

We may contact you as part of a fund-raising effort.

Coroners, Medical Examiners, and Funeral Directors

We may release your PHI to a coroner or medical examiner. This may be necessary, for example, to identify a deceased person or determine the cause of death. We may also disclose PHI to funeral directors consistent with applicable law to enable them to carry out their duties.

Disaster Relief

We may use or disclose your PHI to assist a public or private entity authorized by law or by its charter that participates in disaster relief efforts.

Public Health

As required by law, we may disclose your PHI to public health or legal authorities charged with preventing or controlling disease, injury, or disability.

Law Enforcement

We may disclose your PHI for law enforcement purposes as required by law or in response to a valid subpoena or court order.

Correctional Institution

If you are or become an inmate of a correctional institution, we may disclose to the institution or its agents PHI necessary for your health and the health and safety of other individuals.

National Security, Intelligence Activities, and Protective Services for the President and Others

We may release PHI about you to authorized federal officials for conduct of lawful intelligence, counterintelligence, protection to the president and foreign heads of state, and other national security activities authorized by law.

Military and Veterans

If you are a member of the armed forces, we may release PHI about you as required by military command authorities. We may also release PHI about foreign military personnel to the appropriate foreign military authority.

Workers' Compensation

We may disclose your PHI to the extent authorized by and to the extent necessary to comply with laws relating to workers' compensation or other similar programs established by law that provide benefits for work-related injuries or illnesses without regard to fault.

Victims of Abuse and Neglect

We may disclose PHI about you to a government authority if we reasonably believe you are a victim of abuse or neglect. We will only disclose this type of information to the extent required by law, if you agree to the disclosure, or if the disclosure is allowed by law and we believe it is necessary to prevent serious harm to you or someone else.

Other Uses and Disclosures of PHI

We will obtain your written authorization before using or disclosing your PHI for purposes other than those provided for above (or as otherwise permitted or required by law). You may revoke an authorization in writing at any time. Upon receipt of the written revocation, we will stop using or disclosing your PHI, except to the extent that we have already taken action in reliance on the authorization.

As Required by Law

We will disclose your PHI when required to do so by federal, state, or local law.

YOUR HEALTH INFORMATION RIGHTS

Obtain a Paper Copy of the Notice upon Request

You may request a copy of our current Notice at any time as provided. Even if you have agreed to receive the Notice electronically, you are still entitled to a paper copy. You may obtain a paper copy from the receptionist, the Privacy Office, or our Web site.

Request a Restriction on Certain Uses and Disclosures of PHI

You have the right under 45 CFR § 164.522 to request additional restrictions on our use or disclosure of your PHI. You may do so by sending a written request to the Privacy Office. We are not required to agree to those restrictions. We cannot agree to restrictions on uses or disclosures that are legally required, or which are necessary to administer our business.

Inspect and Obtain a Copy of PHI

In most cases, 45 CFR § 164.524 gives you the right to access and copy the PHI that we maintain about you. To inspect or copy your PHI, you must send a written request to the Privacy Office. We may charge you a fee for the costs of copying, mailing, and supplies that are necessary to fulfill your request. We may deny your request to inspect and copy in certain limited circumstances.

Request an Amendment of PHI

If you feel the PHI we maintain about you is incomplete or incorrect, you may request that we amend it as provided for by CFR § 164.528. To request an amendment, you must send a written request to the Privacy Office. You must include a reason that supports your request. In certain cases, we may deny your request for amendment.

Receive an Accounting of Disclosures of PHI

You have the right under 45 CFR § 164.528 to receive an accounting of disclosures we have made of your PHI after April 14, 2003, for most purposes other than treatment, payment, or health care operations. The right to receive an accounting is subject to certain exceptions, restrictions, and limitations. To request an accounting, you must submit a request in writing to the Privacy Office. Your request must specify the time period. The time period may not be longer than six years and may not include dates before April 14, 2003.

Request Communication of PHI by Alternative Means or at Alternative Locations

For instance, you may request that we contact you at a different residence or post office box. To request confidential communication of your PHI, you must submit a request in writing to the Privacy Office. Your request must tell us how or where you would like to be contacted. We will accommodate all reasonable requests.

Where to Obtain Forms for Submitting Written Requests

You may obtain forms for submitting written requests from any store or mail service location or by contacting the Privacy Office. You can also visit our Web site to obtain these forms.

Minors

If you are a minor who has lawfully provided consent for treatment and you wish for us to treat you as an adult for purposes of access to and disclosure of records related to such treatment, please notify the Privacy Office.

For More Information or to Report a Problem

If you have questions or would like additional information about our privacy practices, you may contact our Privacy Office. If you believe your privacy rights have been violated, you can file a complaint with the Privacy Officer or with the Secretary of Health and Human Services. You can also file a complaint through our Web site and we will route your complaint to the Privacy Office. There will be no retaliation for filing a complaint.

Effective Date

This Notice is effective as of April 13, 2003.

Selected Laws Affecting HIM

This sample listing includes federal statutes and regulations that directly govern the collection, use, and dissemination of health information, plus those applicable to the subareas of health care fraud and abuse, health care technology, and personnel management. Although an attempt is made to be inclusive, the nature of changes in the law makes this listing by definition comprehensive only to an extent.

Age Discrimination in Employment Act	29 U.S.C. §§ 621–634
Agency for Health Care Policy and Research Reauthorization Act	42 U.S.C. § 201
Americans with Disabilities Act	42 U.S.C. §§ 12101–12213
Bankruptcy Abuse Prevention and Consumer Protection Act	11 U.S.C. § 351
Cancer Registries Amendment Act	42 U.S.C. § 280e
Civil Rights Act (Title VII)	42 U.S.C. § 2000
Comprehensive Alcohol Abuse and Alcoholism Prevention, Treatment, and Rehabilitation Act	42 U.S.C. § 290ee-3 42 C.F.R. Ch. 1, Part 2, §§ 2.1–2.67
Comprehensive Telehealth Act	42 U.S.C. § 1395i, mm
Deficit Reduction Act	42 U.S.C. §§ 1396, 10701-1, 1092e
Drug Abuse Prevention, Treatment, and Rehabilitation Act	42 U.S.C. § 290dd-3
Electronic Signatures in Global and National Commerce Act	15 U.S.C. §§ 7001–7031
Emergency Medical Treatment and Active Labor Act	42 U.S.C. §§ 1395 et seq.
Employee Retirement Income Security Act	29 U.S.C. §§ 1001–1191, 1201–1242, 1301–1461
Equal Employment Opportunity Act	42 U.S.C. § 2000a
Equal Pay Act	29 U.S.C. § 201
Fair Credit Reporting Act	15 U.S.C. § 1681
Fair Labor Standards Act	29 U.S.C. § 201 et seq.
Family Medical Leave Act	29 U.S.C. §§ 2601 et seq., 6381 et seq.
Federal Business Records Act	28 U.S.C. § 1732
Federal Employees' Compensation Act	5 U.S.C. § 8101 et seq.
Federal Employers Liability Act	45 U.S.C. § 51 et seq.
Federal Railroad Safety Act	49 U.S.C. § 20101 et seq.
Food and Drug Act	21 U.S.C. §§ 301–360bb
Health Care Fraud and Abuse Statutes	
Antikickback statutes (Stark I and II)	42 U.S.C. § 1395nn(b)
	42 U.S.C. § 1320a-7b(b)

False Claims Act	31 U.S.C. § 3729–33 (civil)
	31 U.S.C. § 3729–3731 (criminal)
Mail fraud	18 U.S.C. §§ 1341, 1342
Health Care Quality Improvement Act	42 U.S.C. §§ 11101–11152
	42 C.F.R. §§ 60.1–.14
Healthcare Research and Quality Act	42 U.S.C. § 29 et seq.
Health Insurance Portability and Accountability Act	42 U.S.C. § 1320d
General Administrative Requirements	45 C.F.R. § 160.101–.552
Administrative Requirements	45 C.F.R. § 162.100–.1802
Security and Privacy Requirements	45 C.F.R. § 164.102–.534
HIV Health Services Program	42 U.S.C. § 300(ff)
Health Maintenance Organizations Act	42 U.S.C. § 300e et seq.
Health Professions Education Extension Act	42 U.S.C. § 799
Identity Theft and Assumption Deterrence Act	18 U.S.C. § 1028
Immigration Reform and Control Act	8 U.S.C. § 1324–1365
Institutional Review Boards	
FDA	42 C.F.R. § 50.1 et seq.
DHHS	42 C.F.R. § 46.101 et seq.
Malcolm Baldridge National Quality Improvement Act	15 U.S.C. §3711a
Medicaid Program	42 U.S.C. § 1396
Medicare Conditions of Participation	42 U.S.C. § 1395(e) et seq.
General health	42 C.F.R. § 482.1–.66.
Mental health	42 C.F.R. § 483.100–138
Long-term care facilities	42 C.F.R. § 483.100–.75
Home health	42 C.F.R. Ch. IV, §§ 484.1–.265
Specialized providers	42 C.F.R. § 485.50–.729
Medicare Prescription Drug, Improvement and Modernization Act	42 U.S.C. § 1395w
Military Selective Service Act	50 U.S.C. §§ 451–471a
National Bureau of Standards Act	15 U.S.C. § 271 et seq.
National Labor Relations Act	29 U.S.C. §§ 151–169
National Library of Medicine Act	42 U.S.C. § 201
National Research Act	42 U.S.C. § 201
Occupational Safety and Health Act	29 U.S.C. §§ 651–678
Older Workers Benefit Protection Act	29 U.S.C. § 621
Patient Self-Determination Act (governing living wills and advance directives)	7 U.S.C. § 1421 et seq.
	42 C.F.R. §§ 417.436
	42 C.F.R. §§ 431.20
	42 C.F.R. §§ 434.28
Pregnancy Discrimination Act	42 U.S.C. §2000e
Privacy Act	5 U.S.C. § 552a
Safe Medical Devices Act	21 U.S.C. §§3601, 383
Social Security Act	42 U.S.C. § 301 et seq.
Tax Equity and Fiscal Responsibility Act	26 U.S.C. §§ 291, 6700 et seq.
Telecommunications Act (governing telemedicine)	47 U.S.C. §§ 254(b) & (h)
Uniformed Services Employment and Reemployment Rights Act	38 U.S.C. §§ 4301–4333
Utilization Review Act	42 C.F.R. Part 456, Subparts B & C

Selected HIPAA Regulations

These selected regulations were issued pursuant to the Health Insurance Portability and Accountability Act (HIPAA) of 1996. They guide health care organizations, providers, and consumers in complying with issues related to the collection, use, dissemination, and transmission of health information. A full listing of HIPAA regulations is so voluminous as to be beyond the scope of this book. Those regulations most pertinent to health information management are included in this appendix and address the final Rules and Standards found in Part 162 governing National Provider Identifier, Standard Employer Identifier, Transactions Standards, and Code Sets, and in Part 164 governing Privacy and Security.

Part 162 Administrative Requirements

Subpart D—Standard Unique Health Identifier for Health Care Providers

§ 162.402 Definitions.
Covered health care provider means a health care provider that meets the definition at paragraph (3) of the definition of "covered entity" at §160.103 of this subchapter.

§ 162.404 Compliance dates of the implementation of the standard unique health identifier for health care providers.

(a) *Health care providers.* A covered health care provider must comply with the implementation specifications in §162.410 no later than May 23, 2007.

(b) *Health plans.* A health plan must comply with the implementation specifications in §162.412 no later than one of the following dates:

  (1) A health plan that is not a small health plan—May 23, 2007.

  (2) A small health plan—May 23, 2008.

(c) *Health care clearinghouses.* A health care clearinghouse must comply with the implementation specifications in §162.414 no later than May 23, 2007.

§ 162.406 Standard unique health identifier for health care providers.

(a) *Standard.* The standard unique health identifier for health care providers is the National Provider Identifier (NPI). The NPI is a 10-position numeric identifier, with a check digit in the 10th position, and no intelligence about the health care provider in the number.

(b) *Required and permitted uses for the NPI.* (1) The NPI must be used as stated in §162.410, §162.412, and §162.414.

  (2) The NPI may be used for any other lawful purpose.

§ 162.408 National Provider System.
National Provider System. The National Provider System (NPS) shall do the following:

(a) Assign a single, unique NPI to a health care provider, provided that—

  (1) The NPS may assign an NPI to a subpart of a health care provider in accordance with paragraph (g); and

  (2) The Secretary has sufficient information to permit the assignment to be made.

(b) Collect and maintain information about each health care provider that has been assigned an NPI and perform tasks necessary to update that information.

(c) If appropriate, deactivate an NPI upon receipt of appropriate information concerning the dissolution of the health care provider that is an organization, the death of the health care provider who is an individual, or other circumstances justifying deactivation.

(d) If appropriate, reactivate a deactivated NPI upon receipt of appropriate information.

(e) Not assign a deactivated NPI to any other health care provider.

(f) Disseminate NPS information upon approved requests.

(g) Assign an NPI to a subpart of a health care provider on request if the identifying data for the subpart are unique.

§ 162.410 Implementation specifications: Health care providers.

(a) A covered entity that is a covered health care provider must:

    (1) Obtain, by application if necessary, an NPI from the National Provider System (NPS) for itself or for any subpart of the covered entity that would be a covered health care provider if it were a separate legal entity. A covered entity may obtain an NPI for any other subpart that qualifies for the assignment of an NPI.

    (2) Use the NPI it obtained from the NPS to identify itself on all standard transactions that it conducts where its health care provider identifier is required.

    (3) Disclose its NPI, when requested, to any entity that needs the NPI to identify that covered health care provider in a standard transaction.

    (4) Communicate to the NPS any changes in its required data elements in the NPS within 30 days of the change.

    (5) If it uses one or more business associates to conduct standard transactions on its behalf, require its business associate(s) to use its NPI and other NPIs appropriately as required by the transactions that the business associate(s) conducts on its behalf.

    (6) If it has been assigned NPIs for one or more subparts, comply with the requirements of paragraphs (a)(2) through (a)(5) of this section with respect to each of those NPIs.

(b) A health care provider that is not a covered entity may obtain, by application if necessary, an NPI from the NPS.

§ 162.412 Implementation specifications: Health plans.

(a) A health plan must use the NPI of any health care provider (or subpart(s), if applicable) that has been assigned an NPI to identify that health care provider on all standard transactions where that health care provider's identifier is required.

(b) A health plan may not require a health care provider that has been assigned an NPI to obtain an additional NPI.

§ 162.414 Implementation specifications: Health care clearinghouses.

A health care clearinghouse must use the NPI of any health care provider (or subpart(s), if applicable) that has been assigned an NPI to identify that health care provider on all standard transactions where that health care provider's identifier is required.

§ 162.600 Compliance dates of the implementation of the standard unique employer identifier.

(a) *Health care providers.* Health care providers must comply with the requirements of this subpart no later than July 30, 2004.

(b) *Health plans.* A health plan must comply with the requirements of this subpart no later than one of the following dates:

    (1) *Health plans other than small health plans* —July 30, 2004.

    (2) *Small health plans* —August 1, 2005.

(c) *Health care clearinghouses.* Health care clearinghouses must comply with the requirements of this subpart no later than July 30, 2004.

§ 162.605 Standard unique employer identifier.

The Secretary adopts the EIN as the standard unique employer identifier provided for by 42 U.S.C. 1320d–2(b).

§ 162.610 Implementation specifications for covered entities.

(a) The standard unique employer identifier of an employer of a particular employee is the EIN that appears on that employee's IRS Form W–2, Wage and Tax Statement, from the employer.

(b) A covered entity must use the standard unique employer identifier (EIN) of the appropriate employer in standard transactions that require an employer identifier to identify a person or entity as an employer, including where situationally required.

(c) Required and permitted uses for the Employer Identifier.

    (1) The Employer Identifier must be used as stated in § 162.610(b).

    (2) The Employer Identifier may be used for any other lawful purpose.

§ 162.910 Maintenance of standards and adoption of modifications and new standards.

(a) *Designation of DSMOs.* (1) The Secretary may designate as a DSMO an organization that agrees to conduct, to the satisfaction of the Secretary, the following functions:

        (i) Maintain standards adopted under this subchapter.

        (ii) Receive and process requests for adopting a new standard or modifying an adopted standard.

(2) The Secretary designates a DSMO by notice in the Federal Register.

(b) *Maintenance of standards.* Maintenance of a standard by the appropriate DSMO constitutes maintenance of the standard for purposes of this part, if done in accordance with the processes the Secretary may require.

(c) *Process for modification of existing standards and adoption of new standards.* The Secretary considers a recommendation for a proposed modification to an existing standard, or a proposed new standard, only if the recommendation is developed through a process that provides for the following:

(1) Open public access.

(2) Coordination with other DSMOs.

(3) An appeals process for each of the following, if dissatisfied with the decision on the request:

   (i) The requestor of the proposed modification.

   (ii) A DSMO that participated in the review and analysis of the request for the proposed modification, or the proposed new standard.

(4) Expedited process to address content needs identified within the industry, if appropriate.

(5) Submission of the recommendation to the National Committee on Vital and Health Statistics (NCVHS).

§ 162.915 Trading partner agreements.

A covered entity must not enter into a trading partner agreement that would do any of the following:

(a) Change the definition, data condition, or use of a data element or segment in a standard.

(b) Add any data elements or segments to the maximum defined data set.

(c) Use any code or data elements that are either marked "not used" in the standard's implementation specification or are not in the standard's implementation specification(s).

(d) Change the meaning or intent of the standard's implementation specification(s).

§ 162.920 Availability of implementation specifications.

A person or an organization may directly request copies of the implementation standards described in subparts I through R of this part from the publishers listed in this section. The Director of the Office of the Federal Register approves the implementation specifications described in this section for incorporation by reference in subparts I through R of this part in accordance with 5 U.S.C. 552(a) and 1 CFR part 51. The implementation specifications described in this paragraph are also available for inspection by the public at the Centers for Medicare & Medicaid Services, 7500 Security Boulevard, Baltimore, Maryland 21244 or at the National Archives and Records Administration

(NARA). For information on the availability of this material at NARA, call 202-741-6030, or go to: *http://www.archives.gov/federal_register/code_of_federal_regulations/ibr_locations.html.* Copy requests must be accompanied by the name of the standard, number, if applicable, and version number. Implementation specifications are available for the following transactions:

(a) *ASC X12N specifications.* The implementation specifications for ASC X12N standards may be obtained from the Washington Publishing Company, PMB 161, 5284 Randolph Road, Rockville, MD 20852-2116; Telephone (301) 949-9740; and Fax: (301) 949-9742. They are also available through the Washington Publishing Company on the Internet at *http://www.wpc-edi.com/.* The transaction implementation specifications are as follows:

(1) The ASC X12N 837—Health Care Claim: Dental, Version 4010, May 2000, Washington Publishing Company, 004010X097 and Addenda to Health Care Claim: Dental, Version 4010, October 2002, Washington Publishing Company, 004010X097A1, as referenced in §162.1102 and §162.1802.

(2) The ASC X12N 837—Health Care Claim: Professional, Volumes 1 and 2, Version 4010, May 2000, Washington Publishing Company, 004010X098 and Addenda to Health Care Claim: Professional, Volumes 1 and 2, Version 4010, October 2002, Washington Publishing Company, 004010X098A1, as referenced in §162.1102 and §162.1802.

(3) The ASC X12N 837—Health Care Claim: Institutional, Volumes 1 and 2, Version 4010, May 2000, Washington Publishing Company, 004010X096 and Addenda to Health Care Claim: Institutional, Volumes 1 and 2, Version 4010, October 2002, Washington Publishing Company, 004010X096A1 as referenced in §162.1102 and §162.1802.

(4) The ASC X12N 835—Health Care Claim Payment/Advice, Version 4010, May 2000, Washington Publishing Company, 004010X091, and Addenda to Health Care Claim Payment/Advice, Version 4010, October 2002, Washington Publishing Company, 004010X091A1 as referenced in §162.1602.

(5) ASC X12N 834—Benefit Enrollment and Maintenance, Version 4010, May 2000, Washington Publishing Company, 004010X095 and Addenda to Benefit Enrollment and Maintenance, Version 4010, October 2002, Washington Publishing Company, 004010X095A1, as referenced in §162.1502.

(6) The ASC X12N 820—Payroll Deducted and Other Group Premium Payment for Insurance Products, Version 4010, May 2000, Washington Publishing Company, 004010X061, and Addenda to Payroll Deducted and Other Group Premium Payment for Insurance Products, Version 4010, October 2002, Washington Publishing Company, 004010X061A1, as referenced in §162.1702.

(7) The ASC X12N 278—Health Care Services Review—Request for Review and Response, Version 4010, May 2000, Washington Publishing Company, 004010X094 and Addenda to Health Care Services Review—Request for Review and Response, Version 4010, October 2002, Washington Publishing Company, 004010X094A1, as referenced in §162.1302.

(8) The ASC X12N–276/277 Health Care Claim Status Request and Response, Version 4010, May 2000, Washington Publishing Company, 004010X093 and Addenda to Health Care Claim Status Request and Response, Version 4010, October 2002, Washington Publishing Company, 004010X093A1, as referenced in §162.1402.

(9) The ASC X12N 270/271—Health Care Eligibility Benefit Inquiry and Response, Version 4010, May 2000, Washington Publishing Company, 004010X092 and Addenda to Health Care Eligibility Benefit Inquiry and Response, Version 4010, October 2002, Washington Publishing Company, 004010X092A1, as referenced in §162.1202.

(b) *Retail pharmacy specifications.* The implementation specifications for retail pharmacy standards may be obtained for a fee from the National Council for Prescription Drug Programs (NCPDP), 9240 E. Raintree Drive, Scottsdale, AZ 85260; Telephone (480) 477–1000; and FAX (480) 767–1042. They may also be obtained through the Internet at *http://www.ncpdp.org.* The transaction implementation specifications are as follows:

(1) The Telecommunication Standard Implementation Guide Version 5, Release 1 (Version 5.1), September 1999, National Council for Prescription Drug Programs, as referenced in §162.1102, §162.1202, §162.1302, §162.1602, and §162.1802.

(2) The Batch Standard Batch Implementation Guide, Version 1, Release 1 (Version 1.1), January 2000, supporting Telecommunication Standard Implementation Guide, Version 5, Release 1 (Version 5.1) for the NCPDP Data Record in the Detail Data Record, National Council for Prescription Drug Programs, as referenced in §162.1102, §162.1202, §162.1302, and §162.1802.

(3) The National Council for Prescription Drug Programs (NCPDP) equivalent NCPDP Batch Standard Batch Implementation Guide, Version 1, Release 0, February 1, 1996, as referenced in §162.1102, §162.1202, §162.1602, and §162.1802.

§ 162.923 Requirements for covered entities.

(a) *General rule.* Except as otherwise provided in this part, if a covered entity conducts with another covered entity (or within the same covered entity), using electronic media, a transaction for which the Secretary has adopted a standard under this part, the covered entity must conduct the transaction as a standard transaction.

(b) *Exception for direct data entry transactions.* A health care provider electing to use direct data entry offered by a health plan to conduct a transaction for which a standard has been adopted under this part must use the applicable data content and data condition requirements of the standard when conducting the transaction. The health care provider is not required to use the format requirements of the standard.

(c) *Use of a business associate.* A covered entity may use a business associate, including a health care clearinghouse, to conduct a transaction covered by this part. If a covered entity chooses to use a business associate to conduct all or part of a transaction on behalf of the covered entity, the covered entity must require the business associate to do the following:

(1) Comply with all applicable requirements of this part.

(2) Require any agent or subcontractor to comply with all applicable requirements of this part.

§ 162.925 Additional requirements for health plans.

(a) *General rules.* (1) If an entity requests a health plan to conduct a transaction as a standard transaction, the health plan must do so.

(2) A health plan may not delay or reject a transaction, or attempt to adversely affect the other entity or the transaction, because the transaction is a standard transaction.

(3) A health plan may not reject a standard transaction on the basis that it contains data elements not needed or used by the health plan (for example, coordination of benefits information).

(4) A health plan may not offer an incentive for a health care provider to conduct a transaction covered by this part as a transaction described under the exception provided for in §162.923(b).

(5) A health plan that operates as a health care clearinghouse, or requires an entity to use a health care clearinghouse to receive, process, or transmit a standard transaction may not charge fees or costs in excess of the fees or costs for normal telecommunications that the entity incurs when it directly transmits, or receives, a standard transaction to, or from, a health plan.

(b) *Coordination of benefits.* If a health plan receives a standard transaction and coordinates benefits with another health plan (or another payer), it must store the coordination of benefits data it needs to forward the standard transaction to the other health plan (or other payer).

(c) *Code sets.* A health plan must meet each of the following requirements:

(1) Accept and promptly process any standard transaction that contains codes that are valid, as provided in subpart J of this part.

(2) Keep code sets for the current billing period and appeals periods still open to processing under the terms of the health plan's coverage.

§ 162.930 Additional rules for health care clearinghouses.

When acting as a business associate for another covered entity, a health care clearinghouse may perform the following functions:

(a) Receive a standard transaction on behalf of the covered entity and translate it into a nonstandard transaction (for example, nonstandard format and/or nonstandard data content) for transmission to the covered entity.

(b) Receive a nonstandard transaction (for example, nonstandard format and/or nonstandard data content) from the covered entity and translate it into a standard transaction for transmission on behalf of the covered entity.

§ 162.940 Exceptions from standards to permit testing of proposed modifications.

(a) *Requests for an exception.* An organization may request an exception from the use of a standard from the Secretary to test a proposed modification to that standard. For each proposed modification, the organization must meet the following requirements:

(1) *Comparison to a current standard.* Provide a detailed explanation, no more than 10 pages in length, of how the proposed modification would be a significant improvement to the current standard in terms of the following principles:

(i) Improve the efficiency and effectiveness of the health care system by leading to cost reductions for, or improvements in benefits from, electronic health care transactions.

(ii) Meet the needs of the health data standards user community, particularly health care providers, health plans, and health care clearinghouses.

(iii) Be uniform and consistent with the other standards adopted under this part and, as appropriate, with other private and public sector health data standards.

(iv) Have low additional development and implementation costs relative to the benefits of using the standard.

(v) Be supported by an ANSI-accredited SSO or other private or public organization that would maintain the standard over time.

(vi) Have timely development, testing, implementation, and updating procedures to achieve administrative simplification benefits faster.

(vii) Be technologically independent of the computer platforms and transmission protocols used in electronic health transactions, unless they are explicitly part of the standard.

(viii) Be precise, unambiguous, and as simple as possible.

(ix) Result in minimum data collection and paperwork burdens on users.

(x) Incorporate flexibility to adapt more easily to changes in the health care infrastructure (such as new services, organizations, and provider types) and information technology.

(2) *Specifications for the proposed modification.* Provide specifications for the proposed modification, including any additional system requirements.

(3) *Testing of the proposed modification.* Provide an explanation, no more than 5 pages in length, of how the organization intends to test the standard, including the number and types of health plans and health care providers expected to be involved in the test, geographical areas, and beginning and ending dates of the test.

(4) *Trading partner concurrences.* Provide written concurrences from trading partners who would agree to participate in the test.

(b) *Basis for granting an exception.* The Secretary may grant an initial exception, for a period not to exceed 3 years, based on, but not limited to, the following criteria:

(1) An assessment of whether the proposed modification demonstrates a significant improvement to the current standard.

(2) The extent and length of time of the exception.

(3) Consultations with DSMOs.

(c) *Secretary's decision on exception.* The Secretary makes a decision and notifies the organization requesting the exception whether the request is granted or denied.

(1) *Exception granted.* If the Secretary grants an exception, the notification includes the following information:

(i) The length of time for which the exception applies.

(ii) The trading partners and geographical areas the Secretary approves for testing.

(iii) Any other conditions for approving the exception.

(2) *Exception denied.* If the Secretary does not grant an exception, the notification explains the reasons the Secretary considers the proposed modification would not be a significant improvement to the current standard and any other rationale for the denial.

(d) *Organization's report on test results.* Within 90 days after the test is completed, an organization that receives an exception must submit a report on the results of the test, including a cost-benefit analysis, to a location specified by the Secretary by notice in the Federal Register.

(e) *Extension allowed.* If the report submitted in accordance with paragraph (d) of this section recommends a modification to the standard, the Secretary, on request, may grant an extension to the period granted for the exception.

Subpart J—Code Sets

§ 162.1000 General requirements.

When conducting a transaction covered by this part, a covered entity must meet the following requirements:

(a) *Medical data code sets.* Use the applicable medical data code sets described in § 162.1002 as specified in the implementation specification adopted under this part that are valid at the time the health care is furnished.

(b) *Nonmedical data code sets.* Use the nonmedical data code sets as described in the implementation specifications adopted under this part that are valid at the time the transaction is initiated.

§ 162.1002 Medical data code sets.

The Secretary adopts the following maintaining organization's code sets as the standard medical data code sets:

(a) For the period from October 16, 2002 through October 15, 2003:

  (1) *International Classification of Diseases, 9th Edition, Clinical Modification, (ICD-9-CM), Volumes 1 and 2* (including The Official ICD-9-CM Guidelines for Coding and Reporting), as maintained and distributed by HHS, for the following conditions:

    (i) Diseases.

    (ii) Injuries.

    (iii) Impairments.

    (iv) Other health problems and their manifestations.

    (v) Causes of injury, disease, impairment, or other health problems.

  (2) *International Classification of Diseases, 9th Edition, Clinical Modification, Volume 3: Procedures* (including The Official ICD-9-CM Guidelines for Coding and Reporting), as maintained and distributed by HHS, for the following procedures or other actions taken for diseases, injuries, and impairments on hospital inpatients reported by hospitals:

    (i) Prevention.

    (ii) Diagnosis.

    (iii) Treatment.

    (iv) Management.

  (3) *National Drug Codes* (NDC), as maintained and distributed by HHS, in collaboration with drug manufacturers, for the following:

    (i) Drugs.

    (ii) Biologics.

  (4) *Code on Dental Procedures and Nomenclature,* as maintained and distributed by the American Dental Association, for dental services.

  (5) The combination of *Health Care Financing Administration Common Procedure Coding System (HCPCS),* as maintained and distributed by HHS, and *Current Procedural Terminology, Fourth Edition (CPT-4),* as maintained and distributed by the American Medical Association, for physician services and other health care services. These services include, but are not limited to, the following:

    (i) Physician services.

    (ii) Physical and occupational therapy services.

    (iii) Radiologic procedures.

    (iv) Clinical laboratory tests.

    (v) Other medical diagnostic procedures.

    (vi) Hearing and vision services.

    (vii) Transportation services including ambulance.

  (6) *The Health Care Financing Administration Common Procedure Coding System (HCPCS),* as maintained and distributed by HHS, for all other substances, equipment, supplies, or other items used in health care services. These items include, but are not limited to, the following:

    (i) Medical supplies.

    (ii) Orthotic and prosthetic devices.

    (iii) Durable medical equipment.

(b) For the period on and after October 16, 2003:

  (1) The code sets specified in paragraphs (a)(1), (a)(2),(a)(4), and (a)(5) of this section.

  (2) *National Drug Codes (NDC),* as maintained and distributed by HHS, for reporting the following by retail pharmacies:

    (i) Drugs.

    (ii) Biologics.

  (3) *The Healthcare Common Procedure Coding System (HCPCS),* as maintained and distributed by HHS, for all other substances, equipment, supplies, or other items used in health care services, with the exception of drugs and biologics. These items include, but are not limited to, the following:

    (i) Medical supplies.

    (ii) Orthotic and prosthetic devices.

    (iii) Durable medical equipment.

§ 162.1011 Valid code sets.

Each code set is valid within the dates specified by the organization responsible for maintaining that code set.

Part 164 Security and Privacy

Subpart A—General Provisions

§ 164.102 Statutory basis.

The provisions of this part are adopted pursuant to the Secretary's authority to prescribe standards, requirements, and implementation specifications under part C of title XI of the Act and section 264 of Public Law 104–191.

§ 164.103 Definitions.

As used in this part, the following terms have the following meanings:

Common control exists if an entity has the power, directly or indirectly, significantly to influence or direct the actions or policies of another entity.

Common ownership exists if an entity or entities possess an ownership or equity interest of 5 percent or more in another entity.

Covered functions means those functions of a covered entity the performance of which makes the entity a health plan, health care provider, or health care clearinghouse.

Health care component means a component or combination of components of a hybrid entity designated by the hybrid entity in accordance with §164.105(a)(2)(iii)(C).

Hybrid entity means a single legal entity:

(1) That is a covered entity;

(2) Whose business activities include both covered and non-covered functions; and

(3) That designates health care components in accordance with paragraph §164.105(a)(2)(iii)(C).

Plan sponsor is defined as defined at section 3(16)(B) of ERISA, 29 U.S.C. 1002(16)(B).

Required by law means a mandate contained in law that compels an entity to make a use or disclosure of protected health information and that is enforceable in a court of law. *Required by law* includes, but is not limited to, court orders and court-ordered warrants; subpoenas or summons issued by a court, grand jury, a governmental or tribal inspector general, or an administrative body authorized to require the production of information; a civil or an authorized investigative demand; Medicare conditions of participation with respect to health care providers participating in the program; and statutes or regulations that require the production of information, including statutes or regulations that require such

information if payment is sought under a government program providing public benefits.

§ 164.104 Applicability.

(a) Except as otherwise provided, the standards, requirements, and implementation specifications adopted under this part apply to the following entities:

(1) A health plan.

(2) A health care clearinghouse.

(3) A health care provider who transmits any health information in electronic form in connection with a transaction covered by this subchapter.

(b) When a health care clearinghouse creates or receives protected health information as a business associate of another covered entity, or other than as a business associate of a covered entity, the clearinghouse must comply with §164.105 relating to organizational requirements for covered entities, including the designation of health care components of a covered entity.

§ 164.105 Organizational requirements.

(a) (1) *Standard: Health care component.* If a covered entity is a hybrid entity, the requirements of subparts C and E of this part, other than the requirements of this section, §164.314, and §164.504, apply only to the health care component(s) of the entity, as specified in this section.

(2) *Implementation specifications:*

(i) *Application of other provisions.* In applying a provision of subparts C and E of this part, other than the requirements of this section, §164.314, and §164.504, to a hybrid entity:

(A) A reference in such provision to a "covered entity" refers to a health care component of the covered entity;

(B) A reference in such provision to a "health plan," "covered health care provider," or "health care clearinghouse," refers to a health care component of the covered entity if such health care component performs the functions of a health plan, health care provider, or health care clearinghouse, as applicable;

(C) A reference in such provision to "protected health information" refers to protected health information that is created or received by or on behalf of the health care component of the covered entity; and

(D) A reference in such provision to "electronic protected health information" refers to electronic protected health information that is created, received, maintained, or transmitted by or on behalf of the health care component of the covered entity.

(ii) *Safeguard requirements.* The covered entity that is a hybrid entity must ensure that a health care component of the entity complies with the applicable requirements of this section and subparts C and E of this part. In particular, and without limiting this requirement, such covered entity must ensure that:

(A) Its health care component does not disclose protected health information to another component of the covered entity in circumstances in which subpart E of this part would prohibit such disclosure if the health care component and the other component were separate and distinct legal entities;

(B) Its health care component protects electronic protected health information with respect to another component of the covered entity to the same extent that it would be required under subpart C of this part to protect such information if the health care component and the other component were separate and distinct legal entities;

(C) A component that is described by paragraph (a)(2)(iii)(C)(2) of this section does not use or disclose protected health information that it creates or receives from or on behalf of the health care component in a way prohibited by subpart E of this part;

(D) A component that is described by paragraph (a)(2)(iii)(C)(2) of this section that creates, receives, maintains, or transmits electronic protected health information on behalf of the health care component is in compliance with subpart C of this part; and

(E) If a person performs duties for both the health care component in the capacity of a member of the workforce of such component and for another component of the entity in the same capacity with respect to that component, such workforce member must not use or disclose protected health information created or received in the course of or incident to the member's work for the health care component in a way prohibited by subpart E of this part.

(iii) *Responsibilities of the covered entity.* A covered entity that is a hybrid entity has the following responsibilities:

(A) For purposes of subpart C of part 160 of this subchapter, pertaining to compliance and enforcement, the covered entity has the responsibility of complying with subpart E of this part.

(B) The covered entity is responsible for complying with §164.316(a) and §164.530(i), pertaining to the implementation of policies and procedures to ensure compliance with applicable requirements of this section and subparts C and E of this part, including the safeguard requirements in paragraph (a)(2)(ii) of this section.

(C) The covered entity is responsible for designating the components that are part of one or more health care components of the covered entity and documenting the designation in accordance with paragraph (c) of this section, provided that, if the covered entity designates a health care component or components, it must include any component that would meet the definition of covered entity if it were a separate legal entity. Health care component(s) also may include a component only to the extent that it performs:

(*1*) Covered functions; or

(*2*) Activities that would make such component a business associate of a component that performs covered functions if the two components were separate legal entities.

(b) (1) *Standard: Affiliated covered entities.* Legally separate covered entities that are affiliated may designate themselves as a single covered entity for purposes of subparts C and E of this part.

(1) *Implementation specifications:*

(i) *Requirements for designation of an affiliated covered entity.* (A) Legally separate covered entities may designate themselves (including any health care component of such covered entity) as a single affiliated covered entity, for purposes of subparts C and E of this part, if all of the covered entities designated are under common ownership or control.

(B) The designation of an affiliated covered entity must be documented and the documentation maintained as required by paragraph (c) of this section.

(ii) *Safeguard requirements.* An affiliated covered entity must ensure that:

(A) The affiliated covered entity's creation, receipt, maintenance, or transmission of electronic protected health information complies with the applicable requirements of subpart C of this part;

(B) The affiliated covered entity's use and disclosure of protected health information comply with the applicable requirements of subpart E of this part; and

(C) If the affiliated covered entity combines the functions of a health plan, health care provider, or health care clearinghouse, the affiliated covered entity complies with §164.308(a)(4)(ii)(A) and §164.504(g), as applicable.

(c) (1) *Standard: Documentation.* A covered entity must maintain a written or electronic record of a designation as required by paragraphs (a) or (b) of this section.

(2) *Implementation specification: Retention period.* A covered entity must retain the documentation as required by paragraph (c)(1) of this section for 6 years from the date of its creation or the date when it last was in effect, whichever is later.

Subpart B [Reserved]

Subpart C—Security Standards for the Protection of Electronic Protected Health Information

Authority: 42 U.S.C. 1320d-2 and 1320d-4.

§ 164.302 Applicability.

A covered entity must comply with the applicable standards, implementation specifications, and requirements of this subpart with respect to electronic protected health information.

§ 164.304 Definitions.

As used in this subpart, the following terms have the following meanings:

Access means the ability or the means necessary to read, write, modify, or communicate data/information or otherwise use any system resource. (This definition applies to "access" as used in this subpart, not as used in subpart E of this part.)

Administrative safeguards are administrative actions, and policies and procedures, to manage the selection, development, implementation, and maintenance of security measures to protect electronic protected health information and to manage the conduct of the covered entity's workforce in relation to the protection of that information.

Authentication means the corroboration that a person is the one claimed.

Availability means the property that data or information is accessible and useable upon demand by an authorized person.

Confidentiality means the property that data or information is not made available or disclosed to unauthorized persons or processes.

Encryption means the use of an algorithmic process to transform data into a form in which there is a low probability of assigning meaning without use of a confidential process or key.

Facility means the physical premises and the interior and exterior of a building(s).

Information system means an interconnected set of information resources under the same direct management control that shares common functionality. A system normally includes hardware, software, information, data, applications, communications, and people.

Integrity means the property that data or information have not been altered or destroyed in an unauthorized manner.

Malicious software means software, for example, a virus, designed to damage or disrupt a system.

Password means confidential authentication information composed of a string of characters.

Physical safeguards are physical measures, policies, and procedures to protect a covered entity's electronic information systems and related buildings and equipment, from natural and environmental hazards, and unauthorized intrusion.

Security or Security measures encompass all of the administrative, physical, and technical safeguards in an information system.

Security incident means the attempted or successful unauthorized access, use, disclosure, modification, or destruction of information or interference with system operations in an information system.

Technical safeguards means the technology and the policy and procedures for its use that protect electronic protected health information and control access to it.

User means a person or entity with authorized access.

Workstation means an electronic computing device, for example, a laptop or desktop computer, or any other device that performs similar functions, and electronic media stored in its immediate environment.

§ 164.306 Security standards: General rules.

(a) *General requirements.* Covered entities must do the following:

(1) Ensure the confidentiality, integrity, and availability of all electronic protected health information the covered entity creates, receives, maintains, or transmits.

(2) Protect against any reasonably anticipated threats or hazards to the security or integrity of such information.

(3) Protect against any reasonably anticipated uses or disclosures of such information that are not permitted or required under subpart E of this part.

(4) Ensure compliance with this subpart by its workforce.

(b) *Flexibility of approach.* (1) Covered entities may use any security measures that allow the covered entity to reasonably and appropriately implement the standards and implementation specifications as specified in this subpart.

    (2) In deciding which security measures to use, a covered entity must take into account the following factors:

        (i) The size, complexity, and capabilities of the covered entity.

        (ii) The covered entity's technical infrastructure, hardware, and software security capabilities.

        (iii) The costs of security measures.

        (iv) The probability and criticality of potential risks to electronic protected health information.

(c) *Standards.* A covered entity must comply with the standards as provided in this section and in §164.308, §164.310, §164.312, §164.314, and §164.316 with respect to all electronic protected health information.

(d) *Implementation specifications.* In this subpart:

    (1) Implementation specifications are required or addressable. If an implementation specification is required, the word "Required" appears in parentheses after the title of the implementation specification. If an implementation specification is addressable, the word "Addressable" appears in parentheses after the title of the implementation specification.

    (2) When a standard adopted in §164.308, §164.310, §164.312, §164.314, or §164.316 includes required implementation specifications, a covered entity must implement the implementation specifications.

    (3) When a standard adopted in §164.308, §164.310, §164.312, §164.314, or §164.316 includes addressable implementation specifications, a covered entity must—

        (i) Assess whether each implementation specification is a reasonable and appropriate safeguard in its environment, when analyzed with reference to the likely contribution to protecting the entity's electronic protected health information; and

        (ii) As applicable to the entity—

            (A) Implement the implementation specification if reasonable and appropriate; or

            (B) If implementing the implementation specification is not reasonable and appropriate—

                (*1*) Document why it would not be reasonable and appropriate to implement the implementation specification; and

                (*2*) Implement an equivalent alternative measure if reasonable and appropriate.

(e) *Maintenance.* Security measures implemented to comply with standards and implementation specifications adopted under §164.105 and this subpart must be reviewed and modified as needed to continue provision of reasonable and appropriate protection of electronic protected health information as described at §164.316.

§ 164.308 Administrative safeguards.

(a) A covered entity must, in accordance with §164.306:

    (1) (i) *Standard: Security management process.* Implement policies and procedures to prevent, detect, contain, and correct security violations.

        (ii) *Implementation specifications:*

            (A) *Risk analysis* (Required). Conduct an accurate and thorough assessment of the potential risks and vulnerabilities to the confidentiality, integrity, and availability of electronic protected health information held by the covered entity.

            (B) *Risk management* (Required). Implement security measures sufficient to reduce risks and vulnerabilities to a reasonable and appropriate level to comply with §164.306(a).

            (C) *Sanction policy* (Required). Apply appropriate sanctions against workforce members who fail to comply with the security policies and procedures of the covered entity.

            (D) *Information system activity review* (Required). Implement procedures to regularly review records of information system activity, such as audit logs, access reports, and security incident tracking reports.

    (2) *Standard: Assigned security responsibility.* Identify the security official who is responsible for the development and implementation of the policies and procedures required by this subpart for the entity.

    (3) (i) *Standard: Workforce security.* Implement policies and procedures to ensure that all members of its workforce have appropriate access to electronic protected health information, as provided under paragraph (a)(4) of this section, and to prevent those workforce members who do not have access under paragraph (a)(4) of this section from obtaining access to electronic protected health information.

        (ii) *Implementation specifications:*

            (A) *Authorization and/or supervision* (Addressable). Implement procedures for the authorization and/or supervision of workforce members who work with electronic protected health information or in locations where it might be accessed.

            (B) *Workforce clearance procedure* (Addressable). Implement procedures to determine that the access of a workforce member to electronic protected health information is appropriate.

(C) *Termination procedures* (Addressable). Implement procedures for terminating access to electronic protected health information when the employment of a workforce member ends or as required by determinations made as specified in paragraph (a)(3)(ii)(B) of this section.

(4) (i) *Standard: Information access management.* Implement policies and procedures for authorizing access to electronic protected health information that are consistent with the applicable requirements of subpart E of this part.

(ii) *Implementation specifications:*

(A) *Isolating health care clearinghouse functions* (Required). If a health care clearinghouse is part of a larger organization, the clearinghouse must implement policies and procedures that protect the electronic protected health information of the clearinghouse from unauthorized access by the larger organization.

(B) *Access authorization* (Addressable). Implement policies and procedures for granting access to electronic protected health information, for example, through access to a workstation, transaction, program, process, or other mechanism.

(C) *Access establishment and modification* (Addressable). Implement policies and procedures that, based upon the entity's access authorization policies, establish, document, review, and modify a user's right of access to a workstation, transaction, program, or process.

(5) (i) *Standard: Security awareness and training.* Implement a security awareness and training program for all members of its workforce (including management).

(ii) *Implementation specifications.* Implement:

(A) *Security reminders* (Addressable). Periodic security updates.

(B) *Protection from malicious software* (Addressable). Procedures for guarding against, detecting, and reporting malicious software.

(C) *Log-in monitoring* (Addressable). Procedures for monitoring log-in attempts and reporting discrepancies.

(D) *Password management* (Addressable). Procedures for creating, changing, and safeguarding passwords.

(6) (i) *Standard: Security incident procedures.* Implement policies and procedures to address security incidents.

(ii) *Implementation specification: Response and Reporting* (Required). Identify and respond to suspected or known security incidents; mitigate, to the extent practicable, harmful effects of security incidents that are known to the covered entity; and document security incidents and their outcomes.

(7) (i) *Standard: Contingency plan.* Establish (and implement as needed) policies and procedures for responding to an emergency or other occurrence (for example, fire, vandalism, system failure, and natural disaster) that damages systems that contain electronic protected health information.

(ii) *Implementation specifications:*

(A) *Data backup plan* (Required). Establish and implement procedures to create and maintain retrievable exact copies of electronic protected health information.

(B) *Disaster recovery plan* (Required). Establish (and implement as needed) procedures to restore any loss of data.

(C) *Emergency mode operation plan* (Required). Establish (and implement as needed) procedures to enable continuation of critical business processes for protection of the security of electronic protected health information while operating in emergency mode.

(D) *Testing and revision procedures* (Addressable). Implement procedures for periodic testing and revision of contingency plans.

(E) *Applications and data criticality analysis* (Addressable). Assess the relative criticality of specific applications and data in support of other contingency plan components.

(8) *Standard: Evaluation.* Perform a periodic technical and nontechnical evaluation, based initially upon the standards implemented under this rule and subsequently, in response to environmental or operational changes affecting the security of electronic protected health information, that establishes the extent to which an entity's security policies and procedures meet the requirements of this subpart.

(b) (1) *Standard: Business associate contracts and other arrangements.* A covered entity, in accordance with §164.306, may permit a business associate to create, receive, maintain, or transmit electronic protected health information on the covered entity's behalf only if the covered entity obtains satisfactory assurances, in accordance with §164.314(a) that the business associate will appropriately safeguard the information.

(2) This standard does not apply with respect to—

(i) The transmission by a covered entity of electronic protected health information to a health care provider concerning the treatment of an individual.

(ii) The transmission of electronic protected health information by a group health plan or an HMO or health insurance issuer on behalf of a group health plan to a plan sponsor, to the extent that the requirements of §164.314(b) and §164.504(f) apply and are met; or

(iii) The transmission of electronic protected health information from or to other agencies providing the services at §164.502(e)(1)(ii)(C), when the covered entity is a health plan that is a government program providing public benefits, if the requirements of §164.502(e)(1)(ii)(C) are met.

(3) A covered entity that violates the satisfactory assurances it provided as a business associate of another covered entity will be in noncompliance with the standards, implementation specifications, and requirements of this paragraph and §164.314(a).

(4) *Implementation specifications: Written contract or other arrangement* (Required). Document the satisfactory assurances required by paragraph (b)(1) of this section through a written contract or other arrangement with the business associate that meets the applicable requirements of §164.314(a).

§ 164.310 Physical safeguards.

A covered entity must, in accordance with §164.306:

(a) (1) *Standard: Facility access controls.* Implement policies and procedures to limit physical access to its electronic information systems and the facility or facilities in which they are housed, while ensuring that properly authorized access is allowed.

(2) *Implementation specifications:*

(i) *Contingency operations* (Addressable). Establish (and implement as needed) procedures that allow facility access in support of restoration of lost data under the disaster recovery plan and emergency mode operations plan in the event of an emergency.

(ii) *Facility security plan* (Addressable). Implement policies and procedures to safeguard the facility and the equipment therein from unauthorized physical access, tampering, and theft.

(iii) *Access control and validation procedures* (Addressable). Implement procedures to control and validate a person's access to facilities based on their role or function, including visitor control, and control of access to software programs for testing and revision.

(iv) *Maintenance records* (Addressable). Implement policies and procedures to document repairs and modifications to the physical components of a facility which are related to security (for example, hardware, walls, doors, and locks).

(b) *Standard: Workstation use.* Implement policies and procedures that specify the proper functions to be performed, the manner in which those functions are to be performed, and the physical attributes of the surroundings of a specific workstation or class of workstation that can access electronic protected health information.

(c) *Standard: Workstation security.* Implement physical safeguards for all workstations that access electronic protected health information, to restrict access to authorized users.

(d) (1) *Standard: Device and media controls.* Implement policies and procedures that govern the receipt and removal of hardware and electronic media that contain electronic protected health information into and out of a facility, and the movement of these items within the facility.

(2) *Implementation specifications:*

(i) *Disposal* (Required). Implement policies and procedures to address the final disposition of electronic protected health information, and/or the hardware or electronic media on which it is stored.

(ii) *Media re-use* (Required). Implement procedures for removal of electronic protected health information from electronic media before the media are made available for re-use.

(iii) *Accountability* (Addressable). Maintain a record of the movements of hardware and electronic media and any person responsible therefore.

(iv) *Data backup and storage* (Addressable). Create a retrievable, exact copy of electronic protected health information, when needed, before movement of equipment.

§ 164.312 Technical safeguards.

A covered entity must, in accordance with §164.306:

(a) (1) *Standard: Access control.* Implement technical policies and procedures for electronic information systems that maintain electronic protected health information to allow access only to those persons or software programs that have been granted access rights as specified in §164.308(a)(4).

(2) *Implementation specifications:*

(i) *Unique user identification* (Required). Assign a unique name and/or number for identifying and tracking user identity.

(ii) *Emergency access procedure* (Required). Establish (and implement as needed) procedures for obtaining necessary electronic protected health information during an emergency.

(iii) *Automatic logoff* (Addressable). Implement electronic procedures that terminate an electronic session after a predetermined time of inactivity.

(iv) *Encryption and decryption* (Addressable). Implement a mechanism to encrypt and decrypt electronic protected health information.

(b) *Standard: Audit controls.* Implement hardware, software, and/or procedural mechanisms that record and examine activity in information systems that contain or use electronic protected health information.

(c) (1) *Standard: Integrity.* Implement policies and procedures to protect electronic protected health information from improper alteration or destruction.

(2) *Implementation specification: Mechanism to authenticate electronic protected health information* (Addressable). Implement electronic mechanisms to corroborate that electronic protected health information has not been altered or destroyed in an unauthorized manner.

(d) *Standard: Person or entity authentication.* Implement procedures to verify that a person or entity seeking access to electronic protected health information is the one claimed.

(e) (1) *Standard: Transmission security.* Implement technical security measures to guard against unauthorized access to electronic protected health information that is being transmitted over an electronic communications network.

(2) *Implementation specifications:*

(i) *Integrity controls* (Addressable). Implement security measures to ensure that electronically transmitted electronic protected health information is not improperly modified without detection until disposed of.

(ii) *Encryption* (Addressable). Implement a mechanism to encrypt electronic protected health information whenever deemed appropriate.

§ 164.314 Organizational requirements.

(a) (1) *Standard: Business associate contracts or other arrangements.* (i) The contract or other arrangement between the covered entity and its business associate required by § 164.308(b) must meet the requirements of paragraph (a)(2)(i) or (a)(2)(ii) of this section, as applicable.

(ii) A covered entity is not in compliance with the standards in § 164.502(e) and paragraph (a) of this section if the covered entity knew of a pattern of an activity or practice of the business associate that constituted a material breach or violation of the business associate's obligation under the contract or other arrangement, unless the covered entity took reasonable steps to cure the breach or end the violation, as applicable, and, if such steps were unsuccessful—

(A) Terminated the contract or arrangement, if feasible; or

(B) If termination is not feasible, reported the problem to the Secretary.

(2) *Implementation specifications* (Required).

(i) Business associate contracts. The contract between a covered entity and a business associate must provide that the business associate will—

(A) Implement administrative, physical, and technical safeguards that reasonably and appropriately protect the confidentiality, integrity, and availability of the electronic protected health information that it creates, receives, maintains, or transmits on behalf of the covered entity as required by this subpart;

(B) Ensure that any agent, including a subcontractor, to whom it provides such information agrees to implement reasonable and appropriate safeguards to protect it;

(C) Report to the covered entity any security incident of which it becomes aware;

(D) Authorize termination of the contract by the covered entity, if the covered entity determines that the business associate has violated a material term of the contract.

(ii) *Other arrangements.* (A) When a covered entity and its business associate are both governmental entities, the covered entity is in compliance with paragraph (a)(1) of this section, if—

(*1*) It enters into a memorandum of understanding with the business associate that contains terms that accomplish the objectives of paragraph (a)(2)(i) of this section; or

(*2*) Other law (including regulations adopted by the covered entity or its business associate) contains requirements applicable to the business associate that accomplish the objectives of paragraph (a)(2)(i) of this section.

(B) If a business associate is required by law to perform a function or activity on behalf of a covered entity or to provide a service described in the definition of business associate as specified in § 160.103 of this subchapter to a covered entity, the covered entity may permit the business associate to create, receive, maintain, or transmit electronic protected health information on its behalf to the extent necessary to comply with the legal mandate without meeting the requirements of paragraph (a)(2)(i) of this section, provided that the covered entity attempts in good faith to obtain satisfactory assurances as required by paragraph (a)(2)(ii)(A) of this section, and documents the attempt and the reasons that these assurances cannot be obtained.

(C) The covered entity may omit from its other arrangements authorization of the termination of the contract by the covered entity, as required by paragraph (a)(2)(i)(D) of this section if such authorization is inconsistent with the statutory obligations of the covered entity or its business associate.

(b) (1) *Standard: Requirements for group health plans.* Except when the only electronic protected health information disclosed to a plan sponsor is disclosed pursuant to §164.504(f)(1)(ii) or (iii), or as authorized under §164.508, a group health plan must ensure that its plan documents provide that the plan sponsor will reasonably and appropriately safeguard electronic protected health information created, received, maintained, or transmitted to or by the plan sponsor on behalf of the group health plan.

(2) *Implementation specifications* (Required). The plan documents of the group health plan must be amended to incorporate provisions to require the plan sponsor to—

(i) Implement administrative, physical, and technical safeguards that reasonably and appropriately protect the confidentiality, integrity, and availability of the electronic protected health information that it creates, receives, maintains, or transmits on behalf of the group health plan;

(ii) Ensure that the adequate separation required by §164.504(f)(2)(iii) is supported by reasonable and appropriate security measures;

(iii) Ensure that any agent, including a subcontractor, to whom it provides this information agrees to implement reasonable and appropriate security measures to protect the information; and

(iv) Report to the group health plan any security incident of which it becomes aware.

§ 164.316 Policies and procedures and documentation requirements.

A covered entity must, in accordance with §164.306:

(a) *Standard: Policies and procedures.* Implement reasonable and appropriate policies and procedures to comply with the standards, implementation specifications, or other requirements of this subpart, taking into account those factors specified in §164.306(b)(2)(i), (ii), (iii), and (iv). This standard is not to be construed to permit or excuse an action that violates any other standard,

implementation specification, or other requirements of this subpart. A covered entity may change its policies and procedures at any time, provided that the changes are documented and are implemented in accordance with this subpart.

(b) (1) *Standard: Documentation.* (i) Maintain the policies and procedures implemented to comply with this subpart in written (which may be electronic) form; and

(ii) If an action, activity or assessment is required by this subpart to be documented, maintain a written (which may be electronic) record of the action, activity, or assessment.

(2) *Implementation specifications:*

(i) *Time limit* (Required). Retain the documentation required by paragraph (b)(1) of this section for 6 years from the date of its creation or the date when it last was in effect, whichever is later.

(ii) *Availability* (Required). Make documentation available to those persons responsible for implementing the procedures to which the documentation pertains.

(iii) *Updates* (Required). Review documentation periodically, and update as needed, in response to environmental or operational changes affecting the security of the electronic protected health information.

§ 164.318 Compliance dates for the initial implementation of the security standards.

(a) *Health plan.* (1) A health plan that is not a small health plan must comply with the applicable requirements of this subpart no later than April 20, 2005.

(2) A small health plan must comply with the applicable requirements of this subpart no later than April 20, 2006.

(b) *Health care clearinghouse.* A health care clearinghouse must comply with the applicable requirements of this subpart no later than April 20, 2005.

(c) *Health care provider.* A covered health care provider must comply with the applicable requirements of this subpart no later than April 20, 2005.

§ 164.106 Relationship to other parts.

In complying with the requirements of this part, covered entities are required to comply with the applicable provisions of parts 160 and 162 of this subchapter.

Subpart D [Reserved]

Subpart E—Privacy of Individually Identifiable Health Information
Authority: 42 U.S.C. 1320d–2 and 1320d–4, sec. 264 of Pub. L. 104–191, 110 Stat. 2033–2034 (42 U.S.C. 1320d–2(note)).

§ 164.500 Applicability.

(a) Except as otherwise provided herein, the standards, requirements, and implementation specifications of this subpart apply to covered entities with respect to protected health information.

(b) Health care clearinghouses must comply with the standards, requirements, and implementation specifications as follows:

(1) When a health care clearinghouse creates or receives protected health information as a business associate of another covered entity, the clearinghouse must comply with:

    (i) Section 164.500 relating to applicability;

    (ii) Section 164.501 relating to definitions;

    (iii) Section 164.502 relating to uses and disclosures of protected health information, except that a clearinghouse is prohibited from using or disclosing protected health information other than as permitted in the business associate contract under which it created or received the protected health information;

    (iv) Section 164.504 relating to the organizational requirements for covered entities;

    (v) Section 164.512 relating to uses and disclosures for which individual authorization or an opportunity to agree or object is not required, except that a clearinghouse is prohibited from using or disclosing protected health information other than as permitted in the business associate contract under which it created or received the protected health information;

    (vi) Section 164.532 relating to transition requirements; and

    (vii) Section 164.534 relating to compliance dates for initial implementation of the privacy standards.

(2) When a health care clearinghouse creates or receives protected health information other than as a business associate of a covered entity, the clearinghouse must comply with all of the standards, requirements, and implementation specifications of this subpart.

(c) The standards, requirements, and implementation specifications of this subpart do not apply to the Department of Defense or to any other federal agency, or non-governmental organization acting on its behalf, when providing health care to overseas foreign national beneficiaries.

[65 FR 82802, Dec. 28, 2000, as amended at 67 FR 53266, Aug. 14, 2002; 68 FR 8381, Feb. 20, 2003]

§ 164.501 Definitions.

As used in this subpart, the following terms have the following meanings:

Correctional institution means any penal or correctional facility, jail, reformatory, detention center, work farm, halfway house, or residential community program center operated by, or under contract to, the United States, a State, a territory, a political subdivision of a State or territory, or an Indian tribe, for the confinement or rehabilitation of persons charged with or convicted of a criminal offense or other persons held in lawful custody. Other persons held in lawful custody includes juvenile offenders adjudicated delinquent, aliens detained awaiting deportation, persons committed to mental institutions through the criminal justice system, witnesses, or others awaiting charges or trial.

Data aggregation means, with respect to protected health information created or received by a business associate in its capacity as the business associate of a covered entity, the combining of such protected health information by the business associate with the protected health information received by the business associate in its capacity as a business associate of another covered entity, to permit data analyses that relate to the health care operations of the respective covered entities.

Designated record set means:

(1) A group of records maintained by or for a covered entity that is:

    (i) The medical records and billing records about individuals maintained by or for a covered health care provider;

    (ii) The enrollment, payment, claims adjudication, and case or medical management record systems maintained by or for a health plan; or

    (iii) Used, in whole or in part, by or for the covered entity to make decisions about individuals.

(2) For purposes of this paragraph, the term record means any item, collection, or grouping of information that includes protected health information and is maintained, collected, used, or disseminated by or for a covered entity.

Direct treatment relationship means a treatment relationship between an individual and a health care provider that is not an indirect treatment relationship.

Health care operations means any of the following activities of the covered entity to the extent that the activities are related to covered functions:

(1) Conducting quality assessment and improvement activities, including outcomes evaluation and development of clinical guidelines, provided that the obtaining of generalizable knowledge is not the primary purpose of any studies resulting from such

activities; population-based activities relating to improving health or reducing health care costs, protocol development, case management and care coordination, contacting of health care providers and patients with information about treatment alternatives; and related functions that do not include treatment;

(2) Reviewing the competence or qualifications of health care professionals, evaluating practitioner and provider performance, health plan performance, conducting training programs in which students, trainees, or practitioners in areas of health care learn under supervision to practice or improve their skills as health care providers, training of non-health care professionals, accreditation, certification, licensing, or credentialing activities;

(3) Underwriting, premium rating, and other activities relating to the creation, renewal or replacement of a contract of health insurance or health benefits, and ceding, securing, or placing a contract for reinsurance of risk relating to claims for health care (including stop-loss insurance and excess of loss insurance), provided that the requirements of §164.514(g) are met, if applicable;

(4) Conducting or arranging for medical review, legal services, and auditing functions, including fraud and abuse detection and compliance programs;

(5) Business planning and development, such as conducting cost-management and planning-related analyses related to managing and operating the entity, including formulary development and administration, development or improvement of methods of payment or coverage policies; and

(6) Business management and general administrative activities of the entity, including, but not limited to:

  (i) Management activities relating to implementation of and compliance with the requirements of this subchapter;

  (ii) Customer service, including the provision of data analyses for policy holders, plan sponsors, or other customers, provided that protected health information is not disclosed to such policy holder, plan sponsor, or customer;

  (iii) Resolution of internal grievances;

  (iv) The sale, transfer, merger, or consolidation of all or part of the covered entity with another covered entity, or an entity that following such activity will become a covered entity and due diligence related to such activity; and

  (v) Consistent with the applicable requirements of §164.514, creating de-identified health information or a limited data set, and fundraising for the benefit of the covered entity.

Health oversight agency means an agency or authority of the United States, a State, a territory, a political subdivision of a State or territory, or an Indian tribe, or a person or entity acting under a grant of authority from or contract with such public agency, including the employees or agents of such public agency or its contractors or persons or entities to whom it has granted authority, that is authorized by law to oversee the health care system (whether public or private) or government programs in which health information is necessary to determine eligibility or compliance, or to enforce civil rights laws for which health information is relevant.

Indirect treatment relationship means a relationship between an individual and a health care provider in which:

(1) The health care provider delivers health care to the individual based on the orders of another health care provider; and

(2) The health care provider typically provides services or products, or reports the diagnosis or results associated with the health care, directly to another health care provider, who provides the services or products or reports to the individual.

Inmate means a person incarcerated in or otherwise confined to a correctional institution.

Law enforcement official means an officer or employee of any agency or authority of the United States, a State, a territory, a political subdivision of a State or territory, or an Indian tribe, who is empowered by law to:

(1) Investigate or conduct an official inquiry into a potential violation of law; or

(2) Prosecute or otherwise conduct a criminal, civil, or administrative proceeding arising from an alleged violation of law.

Marketing means:

(1) To make a communication about a product or service that encourages recipients of the communication to purchase or use the product or service, unless the communication is made:

  (i) To describe a health-related product or service (or payment for such product or service) that is provided by, or included in a plan of benefits of, the covered entity making the communication, including communications about: the entities participating in a health care provider network or health plan network; replacement of, or enhancements to, a health plan; and health-related products or services available only to a health plan enrollee that add value to, but are not part of, a plan of benefits.

  (ii) For treatment of the individual; or

(iii) For case management or care coordination for the individual, or to direct or recommend alternative treatments, therapies, health care providers, or settings of care to the individual.

(2) An arrangement between a covered entity and any other entity whereby the covered entity discloses protected health information to the other entity, in exchange for direct or indirect remuneration, for the other entity or its affiliate to make a communication about its own product or service that encourages recipients of the communication to purchase or use that product or service.

Payment means:

(1) The activities undertaken by:

  (i) A health plan to obtain premiums or to determine or fulfill its responsibility for coverage and provision of benefits under the health plan; or

  (ii) A health care provider or health plan to obtain or provide reimbursement for the provision of health care; and

(2) The activities in paragraph (1) of this definition relate to the individual to whom health care is provided and include, but are not limited to:

  (i) Determinations of eligibility or coverage (including coordination of benefits or the determination of cost sharing amounts), and adjudication or subrogation of health benefit claims;

  (ii) Risk adjusting amounts due based on enrollee health status and demographic characteristics;

  (iii) Billing, claims management, collection activities, obtaining payment under a contract for reinsurance (including stop-loss insurance and excess of loss insurance), and related health care data processing;

  (iv) Review of health care services with respect to medical necessity, coverage under a health plan, appropriateness of care, or justification of charges;

  (v) Utilization review activities, including precertification and preauthorization of services, concurrent and retrospective review of services; and

  (vi) Disclosure to consumer reporting agencies of any of the following protected health information relating to collection of premiums or reimbursement:

    (A) Name and address;

    (B) Date of birth;

    (C) Social security number;

    (D) Payment history;

    (E) Account number; and

    (F) Name and address of the health care provider and/or health plan.

Psychotherapy notes means notes recorded (in any medium) by a health care provider who is a mental health professional documenting or analyzing the contents of conversation during a private counseling session or a group, joint, or family counseling session and that are separated from the rest of the individual's medical record. *Psychotherapy notes* excludes medication prescription and monitoring, counseling session start and stop times, the modalities and frequencies of treatment furnished, results of clinical tests, and any summary of the following items: Diagnosis, functional status, the treatment plan, symptoms, prognosis, and progress to date.

Public health authority means an agency or authority of the United States, a State, a territory, a political subdivision of a State or territory, or an Indian tribe, or a person or entity acting under a grant of authority from or contract with such public agency, including the employees or agents of such public agency or its contractors or persons or entities to whom it has granted authority, that is responsible for public health matters as part of its official mandate.

Research means a systematic investigation, including research development, testing, and evaluation, designed to develop or contribute to generalizable knowledge.

Treatment means the provision, coordination, or management of health care and related services by one or more health care providers, including the coordination or management of health care by a health care provider with a third party; consultation between health care providers relating to a patient; or the referral of a patient for health care from one health care provider to another.

[65 FR 82802, Dec. 28, 2000, as amended at 67 FR 53266, Aug. 14, 2002; 68 FR 8381, Feb. 20, 2003]

§ 164.502 Uses and disclosures of protected health information: General rules.

(a) *Standard.* A covered entity may not use or disclose protected health information, except as permitted or required by this subpart or by subpart C of part 160 of this subchapter.

  (1) *Permitted uses and disclosures.* A covered entity is permitted to use or disclose protected health information as follows:

    (i) To the individual;

    (ii) For treatment, payment, or health care operations, as permitted by and in compliance with §164.506;

(iii) Incident to a use or disclosure otherwise permitted or required by this subpart, provided that the covered entity has complied with the applicable requirements of §164.502(b), §164.514(d), and §164.530(c) with respect to such otherwise permitted or required use or disclosure;

(iv) Pursuant to and in compliance with a valid authorization under §164.508;

(v) Pursuant to an agreement under, or as otherwise permitted by, §164.510; and

(vi) As permitted by and in compliance with this section, §164.512, or §164.514(e), (f), or (g).

(2) *Required disclosures.* A covered entity is required to disclose protected health information:

(i) To an individual, when requested under, and required by §164.524 or §164.528; and

(ii) When required by the Secretary under subpart C of part 160 of this subchapter to investigate or determine the covered entity's compliance with this subpart.

(b) *Standard: Minimum necessary* —(1) *Minimum necessary applies.* When using or disclosing protected health information or when requesting protected health information from another covered entity, a covered entity must make reasonable efforts to limit protected health information to the minimum necessary to accomplish the intended purpose of the use, disclosure, or request.

(2) *Minimum necessary does not apply.* This requirement does not apply to:

(i) Disclosures to or requests by a health care provider for treatment;

(ii) Uses or disclosures made to the individual, as permitted under paragraph (a)(1)(i) of this section or as required by paragraph (a)(2)(i) of this section;

(iii) Uses or disclosures made pursuant to an authorization under §164.508;

(iv) Disclosures made to the Secretary in accordance with subpart C of part 160 of this subchapter;

(v) Uses or disclosures that are required by law, as described by §164.512(a); and

(vi) Uses or disclosures that are required for compliance with applicable requirements of this subchapter.

(c) *Standard: Uses and disclosures of protected health information subject to an agreed upon restriction.* A covered entity that has agreed to a restriction pursuant to §164.522(a)(1) may not use or disclose the protected health information covered by the restriction in violation of such restriction, except as otherwise provided in §164.522(a).

(d) *Standard: Uses and disclosures of de-identified protected health information.* (1) Uses and disclosures to create de-identified information. A covered entity may use protected health information to create information that is not individually identifiable health information or disclose protected health information only to a business associate for such purpose, whether or not the de-identified information is to be used by the covered entity.

(2) *Uses and disclosures of de-identified information.* Health information that meets the standard and implementation specifications for de-identification under §164.514(a) and (b) is considered not to be individually identifiable health information, i.e., de-identified. The requirements of this subpart do not apply to information that has been de-identified in accordance with the applicable requirements of §164.514, provided that:

(i) Disclosure of a code or other means of record identification designed to enable coded or otherwise de-identified information to be re-identified constitutes disclosure of protected health information; and

(ii) If de-identified information is re-identified, a covered entity may use or disclose such re-identified information only as permitted or required by this subpart.

(e) (1) *Standard: Disclosures to business associates.* (i) A covered entity may disclose protected health information to a business associate and may allow a business associate to create or receive protected health information on its behalf, if the covered entity obtains satisfactory assurance that the business associate will appropriately safeguard the information.

(ii) This standard does not apply:

(A) With respect to disclosures by a covered entity to a health care provider concerning the treatment of the individual;

(B) With respect to disclosures by a group health plan or a health insurance issuer or HMO with respect to a group health plan to the plan sponsor, to the extent that the requirements of §164.504(f) apply and are met; or

(C) With respect to uses or disclosures by a health plan that is a government program providing public benefits, if eligibility for, or enrollment in, the health plan is determined by an agency other than the agency administering the health plan, or if the protected health information used to determine enrollment or eligibility in the health plan is collected by an agency other than the agency administering the health plan, and such activity is authorized by law, with respect to the collection and sharing of individually identifiable health information for the performance of such functions by the health plan and the agency other than the agency administering the health plan.

    (iii) A covered entity that violates the satisfactory assurances it provided as a business associate of another covered entity will be in noncompliance with the standards, implementation specifications, and requirements of this paragraph and §164.504(e).

(2) *Implementation specification: documentation.* A covered entity must document the satisfactory assurances required by paragraph (e)(1) of this section through a written contract or other written agreement or arrangement with the business associate that meets the applicable requirements of §164.504(e).

(f) *Standard: Deceased individuals.* A covered entity must comply with the requirements of this subpart with respect to the protected health information of a deceased individual.

(g) (1) *Standard: Personal representatives.* As specified in this paragraph, a covered entity must, except as provided in paragraphs (g)(3) and (g)(5) of this section, treat a personal representative as the individual for purposes of this subchapter.

(2) *Implementation specification: adults and emancipated minors.* If under applicable law a person has authority to act on behalf of an individual who is an adult or an emancipated minor in making decisions related to health care, a covered entity must treat such person as a personal representative under this subchapter, with respect to protected health information relevant to such personal representation.

(3) (i) *Implementation specification: unemancipated minors.* If under applicable law a parent, guardian, or other person acting in loco parentis has authority to act on behalf of an individual who is an unemancipated minor in making decisions related to health care, a covered entity must treat such person as a personal representative under this subchapter, with respect to protected health information relevant to such personal representation, except that such person may not be a personal representative of an unemancipated minor, and the minor has the authority to act as an individual, with respect to protected health information pertaining to a health care service, if:

    (A) The minor consents to such health care service; no other consent to such health care service is required by law, regardless of whether the consent of another person has also been obtained; and the minor has not requested that such person be treated as the personal representative;

    (B) The minor may lawfully obtain such health care service without the consent of a parent, guardian, or other person acting *in loco parentis,* and the minor, a court, or another person authorized by law consents to such health care service; or

    (C) A parent, guardian, or other person acting *in loco parentis* assents to an agreement of confidentiality between a covered health care provider and the minor with respect to such health care service.

  (ii) Notwithstanding the provisions of paragraph (g)(3)(i) of this section:

    (A) If, and to the extent, permitted or required by an applicable provision of State or other law, including applicable case law, a covered entity may disclose, or provide access in accordance with §164.524 to, protected health information about an unemancipated minor to a parent, guardian, or other person acting *in loco parentis;*

    (B) If, and to the extent, prohibited by an applicable provision of State or other law, including applicable case law, a covered entity may not disclose, or provide access in accordance with §164.524 to, protected health information about an unemancipated minor to a parent, guardian, or other person acting *in loco parentis;* and

    (C) Where the parent, guardian, or other person acting *in loco parentis,* is not the personal representative under paragraphs (g)(3)(i)(A), (B), or (C) of this section and where there is no applicable access provision under State or other law, including case law, a covered entity may provide or deny access under §164.524 to a parent, guardian, or other person acting *in loco parentis,* if such action is consistent with State or other applicable law, provided that such decision must be made by a licensed health care professional, in the exercise of professional judgment.

(4) *Implementation specification: Deceased individuals.* If under applicable law an executor, administrator, or other person has authority to act on behalf of a deceased individual or of the individual's estate, a covered entity must treat such person as a personal representative under this subchapter, with respect to protected health information relevant to such personal representation.

(5) *Implementation specification: Abuse, neglect, endangerment situations.* Notwithstanding a State law or any requirement of this paragraph to the contrary, a covered entity may elect not to treat a person as the personal representative of an individual if:

  (i) The covered entity has a reasonable belief that:

  (A) The individual has been or may be subjected to domestic violence, abuse, or neglect by such person; or

  (B) Treating such person as the personal representative could endanger the individual; and

  (ii) The covered entity, in the exercise of professional judgment, decides that it is not in the best interest of the individual to treat the person as the individual's personal representative.

(h) *Standard: Confidential communications.* A covered health care provider or health plan must comply with the applicable requirements of §164.522(b) in communicating protected health information.

(i) *Standard: Uses and disclosures consistent with notice.* A covered entity that is required by §164.520 to have a notice may not use or disclose protected health information in a manner inconsistent with such notice. A covered entity that is required by §164.520(b)(1)(iii) to include a specific statement in its notice if it intends to engage in an activity listed in §164.520(b)(1)(iii)(A)–(C), may not use or disclose protected health information for such activities, unless the required statement is included in the notice.

(j) *Standard: Disclosures by whistleblowers and workforce member crime victims*—(1) *Disclosures by whistleblowers.* A covered entity is not considered to have violated the requirements of this subpart if a member of its workforce or a business associate discloses protected health information, provided that:

  (i) The workforce member or business associate believes in good faith that the covered entity has engaged in conduct that is unlawful or otherwise violates professional or clinical standards, or that the care, services, or conditions provided by the covered entity potentially endangers one or more patients, workers, or the public; and

  (ii) The disclosure is to:

  (A) A health oversight agency or public health authority authorized by law to investigate or otherwise oversee the relevant conduct or conditions of the covered entity or to an appropriate health care accreditation organization for the purpose of reporting the allegation of failure to meet professional standards or misconduct by the covered entity; or

  (B) An attorney retained by or on behalf of the workforce member or business associate for the purpose of determining the legal options of the workforce member or business associate with regard to the conduct described in paragraph (j)(1)(i) of this section.

(2) *Disclosures by workforce members who are victims of a crime.* A covered entity is not considered to have violated the requirements of this subpart if a member of its workforce who is the victim of a criminal act discloses protected health information to a law enforcement official, provided that:

  (i) The protected health information disclosed is about the suspected perpetrator of the criminal act; and

  (ii) The protected health information disclosed is limited to the information listed in §164.512(f)(2)(i).

[65 FR 82802, Dec. 28, 2000, as amended at 67 FR 53267, Aug. 14, 2002]

§ 164.504 Uses and disclosures: Organizational requirements.

(a) Definitions. As used in this section:

Plan administration functions means administration functions performed by the plan sponsor of a group health plan on behalf of the group health plan and excludes functions performed by the plan sponsor in connection with any other benefit or benefit plan of the plan sponsor.

Summary health information means information, that may be individually identifiable health information, and:

  (1) That summarizes the claims history, claims expenses, or type of claims experienced by individuals for whom a plan sponsor has provided health benefits under a group health plan; and

  (2) From which the information described at §164.514(b)(2)(i) has been deleted, except that the geographic information described in §164.514(b)(2)(i)(B) need only be aggregated to the level of a five digit zip code.

(b)–(d)

(e) (1) *Standard: Business associate contracts.* (i) The contract or other arrangement between the covered entity and the business associate required by §164.502(e)(2) must meet the requirements of paragraph (e)(2) or (e)(3) of this section, as applicable.

  (ii) A covered entity is not in compliance with the standards in §164.502(e) and paragraph (e) of this section, if the covered entity knew of a pattern of activity or practice of the business associate that constituted a material breach or violation of the business associate's obligation under the contract or other arrangement, unless the covered entity took reasonable steps to cure the breach or end the violation, as applicable, and, if such steps were unsuccessful:

(A) Terminated the contract or arrangement, if feasible; or

(B) If termination is not feasible, reported the problem to the Secretary.

(2) *Implementation specifications: Business associate contracts.* A contract between the covered entity and a business associate must:

(i) Establish the permitted and required uses and disclosures of such information by the business associate. The contract may not authorize the business associate to use or further disclose the information in a manner that would violate the requirements of this subpart, if done by the covered entity, except that:

(A) The contract may permit the business associate to use and disclose protected health information for the proper management and administration of the business associate, as provided in paragraph (e)(4) of this section; and

(B) The contract may permit the business associate to provide data aggregation services relating to the health care operations of the covered entity.

(ii) Provide that the business associate will:

(A) Not use or further disclose the information other than as permitted or required by the contract or as required by law;

(B) Use appropriate safeguards to prevent use or disclosure of the information other than as provided for by its contract;

(C) Report to the covered entity any use or disclosure of the information not provided for by its contract of which it becomes aware;

(D) Ensure that any agents, including a subcontractor, to whom it provides protected health information received from, or created or received by the business associate on behalf of, the covered entity agrees to the same restrictions and conditions that apply to the business associate with respect to such information;

(E) Make available protected health information in accordance with §164.524;

(F) Make available protected health information for amendment and incorporate any amendments to protected health information in accordance with §164.526;

(G) Make available the information required to provide an accounting of disclosures in accordance with §164.528;

(H) Make its internal practices, books, and records relating to the use and disclosure of protected health information received from, or created or received by the business associate on behalf of, the covered entity available to the Secretary for purposes of determining the covered entity's compliance with this subpart; and

(I) At termination of the contract, if feasible, return or destroy all protected health information received from, or created or received by the business associate on behalf of, the covered entity that the business associate still maintains in any form and retain no copies of such information or, if such return or destruction is not feasible, extend the protections of the contract to the information and limit further uses and disclosures to those purposes that make the return or destruction of the information infeasible.

(iii) Authorize termination of the contract by the covered entity, if the covered entity determines that the business associate has violated a material term of the contract.

(3) *Implementation specifications: Other arrangements.*
(i) If a covered entity and its business associate are both governmental entities:

(A) The covered entity may comply with paragraph (e) of this section by entering into a memorandum of understanding with the business associate that contains terms that accomplish the objectives of paragraph (e)(2) of this section.

(B) The covered entity may comply with paragraph (e) of this section, if other law (including regulations adopted by the covered entity or its business associate) contains requirements applicable to the business associate that accomplish the objectives of paragraph (e)(2) of this section.

(ii) If a business associate is required by law to perform a function or activity on behalf of a covered entity or to provide a service described in the definition of *business associate* in §160.103 of this subchapter to a covered entity, such covered entity may disclose protected health information to the business associate to the extent necessary to comply with the legal mandate without meeting the requirements of this paragraph (e), provided that the covered entity attempts in good faith to obtain satisfactory assurances as required by paragraph (e)(3)(i) of this section, and, if such attempt fails, documents the attempt and the reasons that such assurances cannot be obtained.

(iii) The covered entity may omit from its other arrangements the termination authorization required by paragraph (e)(2)(iii) of this section, if such authorization is inconsistent with the statutory obligations of the covered entity or its business associate.

(4) *Implementation specifications: Other requirements for contracts and other arrangements.* (i) The contract or other arrangement between the covered entity and the business associate may permit the business associate to use the information received by the business associate in its capacity as a business associate to the covered entity, if necessary:

    (A) For the proper management and administration of the business associate; or

    (B) To carry out the legal responsibilities of the business associate.

(ii) The contract or other arrangement between the covered entity and the business associate may permit the business associate to disclose the information received by the business associate in its capacity as a business associate for the purposes described in paragraph (e)(4)(i) of this section, if:

    (A) The disclosure is required by law; or

    (B) (*1*) The business associate obtains reasonable assurances from the person to whom the information is disclosed that it will be held confidentially and used or further disclosed only as required by law or for the purpose for which it was disclosed to the person; and

        (*2*) The person notifies the business associate of any instances of which it is aware in which the confidentiality of the information has been breached.

(f) (1) *Standard: Requirements for group health plans.* (i) Except as provided under paragraph (f)(1)(ii) or (iii) of this section or as otherwise authorized under §164.508, a group health plan, in order to disclose protected health information to the plan sponsor or to provide for or permit the disclosure of protected health information to the plan sponsor by a health insurance issuer or HMO with respect to the group health plan, must ensure that the plan documents restrict uses and disclosures of such

information by the plan sponsor consistent with the requirements of this subpart.

(ii) The group health plan, or a health insurance issuer or HMO with respect to the group health plan, may disclose summary health information to the plan sponsor, if the plan sponsor requests the summary health information for the purpose of:

    (A) Obtaining premium bids from health plans for providing health insurance coverage under the group health plan; or

    (B) Modifying, amending, or terminating the group health plan.

(iii) The group health plan, or a health insurance issuer or HMO with respect to the group health plan, may disclose to the plan sponsor information on whether the individual is participating in the group health plan, or is enrolled in or has disenrolled from a health insurance issuer or HMO offered by the plan.

(2) *Implementation specifications: Requirements for plan documents.* The plan documents of the group health plan must be amended to incorporate provisions to:

(i) Establish the permitted and required uses and disclosures of such information by the plan sponsor, provided that such permitted and required uses and disclosures may not be inconsistent with this subpart.

(ii) Provide that the group health plan will disclose protected health information to the plan sponsor only upon receipt of a certification by the plan sponsor that the plan documents have been amended to incorporate the following provisions and that the plan sponsor agrees to:

    (A) Not use or further disclose the information other than as permitted or required by the plan documents or as required by law;

    (B) Ensure that any agents, including a subcontractor, to whom it provides protected health information received from the group health plan agree to the same restrictions and conditions that apply to the plan sponsor with respect to such information;

    (C) Not use or disclose the information for employment-related actions and decisions or in connection with any other benefit or employee benefit plan of the plan sponsor;

    (D) Report to the group health plan any use or disclosure of the information that is inconsistent with the uses or disclosures provided for of which it becomes aware;

    (E) Make available protected health information in accordance with §164.524;

(F) Make available protected health information for amendment and incorporate any amendments to protected health information in accordance with §164.526;

(G) Make available the information required to provide an accounting of disclosures in accordance with §164.528;

(H) Make its internal practices, books, and records relating to the use and disclosure of protected health information received from the group health plan available to the Secretary for purposes of determining compliance by the group health plan with this subpart;

(I) If feasible, return or destroy all protected health information received from the group health plan that the sponsor still maintains in any form and retain no copies of such information when no longer needed for the purpose for which disclosure was made, except that, if such return or destruction is not feasible, limit further uses and disclosures to those purposes that make the return or destruction of the information infeasible; and

(J) Ensure that the adequate separation required in paragraph (f)(2)(iii) of this section is established.

(iii) Provide for adequate separation between the group health plan and the plan sponsor. The plan documents must:

(A) Describe those employees or classes of employees or other persons under the control of the plan sponsor to be given access to the protected health information to be disclosed, provided that any employee or person who receives protected health information relating to payment under, health care operations of, or other matters pertaining to the group health plan in the ordinary course of business must be included in such description;

(B) Restrict the access to and use by such employees and other persons described in paragraph (f)(2)(iii)(A) of this section to the plan administration functions that the plan sponsor performs for the group health plan; and

(C) Provide an effective mechanism for resolving any issues of noncompliance by persons described in paragraph (f)(2)(iii)(A) of this section with the plan document provisions required by this paragraph.

(3) *Implementation specifications: Uses and disclosures.* A group health plan may:

(i) Disclose protected health information to a plan sponsor to carry out plan administration functions that the plan sponsor performs only consistent with the provisions of paragraph (f)(2) of this section;

(ii) Not permit a health insurance issuer or HMO with respect to the group health plan to disclose protected health information to the plan sponsor except as permitted by this paragraph;

(iii) Not disclose and may not permit a health insurance issuer or HMO to disclose protected health information to a plan sponsor as otherwise permitted by this paragraph unless a statement required by §164.520(b)(1)(iii)(C) is included in the appropriate notice; and

(iv) Not disclose protected health information to the plan sponsor for the purpose of employment-related actions or decisions or in connection with any other benefit or employee benefit plan of the plan sponsor.

(g) *Standard: Requirements for a covered entity with multiple covered functions.* (1) A covered entity that performs multiple covered functions that would make the entity any combination of a health plan, a covered health care provider, and a health care clearinghouse, must comply with the standards, requirements, and implementation specifications of this subpart, as applicable to the health plan, health care provider, or health care clearinghouse covered functions performed.

(2) A covered entity that performs multiple covered functions may use or disclose the protected health information of individuals who receive the covered entity's health plan or health care provider services, but not both, only for purposes related to the appropriate function being performed.

§ 164.506 Uses and disclosures to carry out treatment, payment, or health care operations.

(a) *Standard: Permitted uses and disclosures.* Except with respect to uses or disclosures that require an authorization under §164.508(a)(2) and (3), a covered entity may use or disclose protected health information for treatment, payment, or health care operations as set forth in paragraph (c) of this section, provided that such use or disclosure is consistent with other applicable requirements of this subpart.

(b) *Standard: Consent for uses and disclosures permitted.* (1) A covered entity may obtain consent of the individual to use or disclose protected health information to carry out treatment, payment, or health care operations.

(2) Consent, under paragraph (b) of this section, shall not be effective to permit a use or disclosure of protected health information when an authorization, under §164.508, is required or when another condition must be met for such use or disclosure to be permissible under this subpart.

(c) *Implementation specifications: Treatment, payment, or health care operations.* (1) A covered entity may use or disclose protected health information for its own treatment, payment, or health care operations.

(2) A covered entity may disclose protected health information for treatment activities of a health care provider.

(3) A covered entity may disclose protected health information to another covered entity or a health care provider for the payment activities of the entity that receives the information.

(4) A covered entity may disclose protected health information to another covered entity for health care operations activities of the entity that receives the information, if each entity either has or had a relationship with the individual who is the subject of the protected health information being requested, the protected health information pertains to such relationship, and the disclosure is:

    (i) For a purpose listed in paragraph (1) or (2) of the definition of health care operations; or

    (ii) For the purpose of health care fraud and abuse detection or compliance.

(5) A covered entity that participates in an organized health care arrangement may disclose protected health information about an individual to another covered entity that participates in the organized health care arrangement for any health care operations activities of the organized health care arrangement.

§ 164.508 Uses and disclosures for which an authorization is required.

(a) *Standard: authorizations for uses and disclosures—* (1) *Authorization required: general rule.* Except as otherwise permitted or required by this subchapter, a covered entity may not use or disclose protected health information without an authorization that is valid under this section. When a covered entity obtains or receives a valid authorization for its use or disclosure of protected health information, such use or disclosure must be consistent with such authorization.

(2) *Authorization required: Psychotherapy notes.* Notwithstanding any provision of this subpart, other than the transition provisions in §164.532, a covered entity must obtain an authorization for any use or disclosure of psychotherapy notes, except:

    (i) To carry out the following treatment, payment, or health care operations:

      (A) Use by the originator of the psychotherapy notes for treatment;

      (B) Use or disclosure by the covered entity for its own training programs in which students, trainees, or practitioners in mental health learn under supervision to practice or improve their skills in group, joint, family, or individual counseling; or

      (C) Use or disclosure by the covered entity to defend itself in a legal action or other proceeding brought by the individual; and

    (ii) A use or disclosure that is required by §164.502(a)(2)(ii) or permitted by §164.512(a); §164.512(d) with respect to the oversight of the originator of the psychotherapy notes; §164.512(g)(1); or §164.512(j)(1)(i).

(3) *Authorization required: Marketing.* (i) Notwithstanding any provision of this subpart, other than the transition provisions in §164.532, a covered entity must obtain an authorization for any use or disclosure of protected health information for marketing, except if the communication is in the form of:

    (A) A face-to-face communication made by a covered entity to an individual; or

    (B) A promotional gift of nominal value provided by the covered entity.

    (ii) If the marketing involves direct or indirect remuneration to the covered entity from a third party, the authorization must state that such remuneration is involved.

(b) *Implementation specifications: General requirements—* (1) *Valid authorizations.* (i) A valid authorization is a document that meets the requirements in paragraphs (a)(3)(ii), (c)(1), and (c)(2) of this section, as applicable.

    (ii) A valid authorization may contain elements or information in addition to the elements required by this section, provided that such additional elements or information are not inconsistent with the elements required by this section.

(2) *Defective authorizations.* An authorization is not valid, if the document submitted has any of the following defects:

    (i) The expiration date has passed or the expiration event is known by the covered entity to have occurred;

    (ii) The authorization has not been filled out completely, with respect to an element described by paragraph (c) of this section, if applicable;

    (iii) The authorization is known by the covered entity to have been revoked;

    (iv) The authorization violates paragraph (b)(3) or (4) of this section, if applicable;

    (v) Any material information in the authorization is known by the covered entity to be false.

(3) *Compound authorizations.* An authorization for use or disclosure of protected health information may not be combined with any other document to create a compound authorization, except as follows:

    (i) An authorization for the use or disclosure of protected health information for a research study may be combined with any other type of written permission for the same research study, including another authorization for the use or disclosure of protected health information for such research or a consent to participate in such research;

(ii) An authorization for a use or disclosure of psychotherapy notes may only be combined with another authorization for a use or disclosure of psychotherapy notes;

(iii) An authorization under this section, other than an authorization for a use or disclosure of psychotherapy notes, may be combined with any other such authorization under this section, except when a covered entity has conditioned the provision of treatment, payment, enrollment in the health plan, or eligibility for benefits under paragraph (b)(4) of this section on the provision of one of the authorizations.

(4) *Prohibition on conditioning of authorizations.* A covered entity may not condition the provision to an individual of treatment, payment, enrollment in the health plan, or eligibility for benefits on the provision of an authorization, except:

(i) A covered health care provider may condition the provision of research-related treatment on provision of an authorization for the use or disclosure of protected health information for such research under this section;

(ii) A health plan may condition enrollment in the health plan or eligibility for benefits on provision of an authorization requested by the health plan prior to an individual's enrollment in the health plan, if:

(A) The authorization sought is for the health plan's eligibility or enrollment determinations relating to the individual or for its underwriting or risk rating determinations; and

(B) The authorization is not for a use or disclosure of psychotherapy notes under paragraph (a)(2) of this section; and

(iii) A covered entity may condition the provision of health care that is solely for the purpose of creating protected health information for disclosure to a third party on provision of an authorization for the disclosure of the protected health information to such third party.

(5) *Revocation of authorizations.* An individual may revoke an authorization provided under this section at any time, provided that the revocation is in writing, except to the extent that:

(i) The covered entity has taken action in reliance thereon; or

(ii) If the authorization was obtained as a condition of obtaining insurance coverage, other law provides the insurer with the right to contest a claim under the policy or the policy itself.

(6) *Documentation.* A covered entity must document and retain any signed authorization under this section as required by §164.530(j).

(c) *Implementation specifications: Core elements and requirements—*(1) *Core elements.* A valid authorization under this section must contain at least the following elements:

(i) A description of the information to be used or disclosed that identifies the information in a specific and meaningful fashion.

(ii) The name or other specific identification of the person(s), or class of persons, authorized to make the requested use or disclosure.

(iii) The name or other specific identification of the person(s), or class of persons, to whom the covered entity may make the requested use or disclosure.

(iv) A description of each purpose of the requested use or disclosure. The statement "at the request of the individual" is a sufficient description of the purpose when an individual initiates the authorization and does not, or elects not to, provide a statement of the purpose.

(v) An expiration date or an expiration event that relates to the individual or the purpose of the use or disclosure. The statement "end of the research study," "none," or similar language is sufficient if the authorization is for a use or disclosure of protected health information for research, including for the creation and maintenance of a research database or research repository.

(vi) Signature of the individual and date. If the authorization is signed by a personal representative of the individual, a description of such representative's authority to act for the individual must also be provided.

(2) *Required statements.* In addition to the core elements, the authorization must contain statements adequate to place the individual on notice of all of the following:

(i) The individual's right to revoke the authorization in writing, and either:

(A) The exceptions to the right to revoke and a description of how the individual may revoke the authorization; or

(B) To the extent that the information in paragraph (c)(2)(i)(A) of this section is included in the notice required by §164.520, a reference to the covered entity's notice.

(ii) The ability or inability to condition treatment, payment, enrollment or eligibility for benefits on the authorization, by stating either:

(A) The covered entity may not condition treatment, payment, enrollment, or eligibility for benefits on whether the individual signs the authorization when the prohibition on conditioning of authorizations in paragraph (b)(4) of this section applies; or

(B) The consequences to the individual of a refusal to sign the authorization when, in accordance with paragraph (b)(4) of this section, the covered entity can condition treatment, enrollment in the health plan, or eligibility for benefits on failure to obtain such authorization.

(iii) The potential for information disclosed pursuant to the authorization to be subject to redisclosure by the recipient and no longer be protected by this subpart.

(3) *Plain language requirement.* The authorization must be written in plain language.

(4) *Copy to the individual.* If a covered entity seeks an authorization from an individual for a use or disclosure of protected health information, the covered entity must provide the individual with a copy of the signed authorization.

§ 164.510 Uses and disclosures requiring an opportunity for the individual to agree or to object.

A covered entity may use or disclose protected health information, provided that the individual is informed in advance of the use or disclosure and has the opportunity to agree to or prohibit or restrict the use or disclosure, in accordance with the applicable requirements of this section. The covered entity may orally inform the individual of and obtain the individual's oral agreement or objection to a use or disclosure permitted by this section.

(a) *Standard: Use and disclosure for facility directories—* (1) *Permitted uses and disclosure.* Except when an objection is expressed in accordance with paragraphs (a)(2) or (3) of this section, a covered health care provider may:

(i) Use the following protected health information to maintain a directory of individuals in its facility:

(A) The individual's name;

(B) The individual's location in the covered health care provider's facility;

(C) The individual's condition described in general terms that does not communicate specific medical information about the individual; and

(D) The individual's religious affiliation; and

(ii) Disclose for directory purposes such information:

(A) To members of the clergy; or

(B) Except for religious affiliation, to other persons who ask for the individual by name.

(2) *Opportunity to object.* A covered health care provider must inform an individual of the protected health information that it may include in a directory and the persons to whom it may disclose such information (including disclosures to clergy of information regarding religious affiliation) and provide the individual with the opportunity to restrict or prohibit some or all of the uses or disclosures permitted by paragraph (a)(1) of this section.

(3) *Emergency circumstances.* (i) If the opportunity to object to uses or disclosures required by paragraph (a)(2) of this section cannot practicably be provided because of the individual's incapacity or an emergency treatment circumstance, a covered health care provider may use or disclose some or all of the protected health information permitted by paragraph (a)(1) of this section for the facility's directory, if such disclosure is:

(A) Consistent with a prior expressed preference of the individual, if any, that is known to the covered health care provider; and

(B) In the individual's best interest as determined by the covered health care provider, in the exercise of professional judgment.

(ii) The covered health care provider must inform the individual and provide an opportunity to object to uses or disclosures for directory purposes as required by paragraph (a)(2) of this section when it becomes practicable to do so.

(b) *Standard: Uses and disclosures for involvement in the individual's care and notification purposes—*(1) *Permitted uses and disclosures.* (i) A covered entity may, in accordance with paragraphs (b)(2) or (3) of this section, disclose to a family member, other relative, or a close personal friend of the individual, or any other person identified by the individual, the protected health information directly relevant to such person's involvement with the individual's care or payment related to the individual's health care.

(ii) A covered entity may use or disclose protected health information to notify, or assist in the notification of (including identifying or locating), a family member, a personal representative of the individual, or another person responsible for the care of the individual of the individual's location, general condition, or death. Any such use or disclosure of protected health information for such notification purposes must be in accordance with paragraphs (b)(2), (3), or (4) of this section, as applicable.

(2) *Uses and disclosures with the individual present.* If the individual is present for, or otherwise available prior to, a use or disclosure permitted by paragraph (b)(1) of this section and has the capacity to make health care decisions, the covered entity may use or disclose the protected health information if it:

  (i) Obtains the individual's agreement;

  (ii) Provides the individual with the opportunity to object to the disclosure, and the individual does not express an objection; or

  (iii) Reasonably infers from the circumstances, based the exercise of professional judgment, that the individual does not object to the disclosure.

(3) *Limited uses and disclosures when the individual is not present.* If the individual is not present, or the opportunity to agree or object to the use or disclosure cannot practicably be provided because of the individual's incapacity or an emergency circumstance, the covered entity may, in the exercise of professional judgment, determine whether the disclosure is in the best interests of the individual and, if so, disclose only the protected health information that is directly relevant to the person's involvement with the individual's health care. A covered entity may use professional judgment and its experience with common practice to make reasonable inferences of the individual's best interest in allowing a person to act on behalf of the individual to pick up filled prescriptions, medical supplies, X-rays, or other similar forms of protected health information.

(4) *Use and disclosures for disaster relief purposes.* A covered entity may use or disclose protected health information to a public or private entity authorized by law or by its charter to assist in disaster relief efforts, for the purpose of coordinating with such entities the uses or disclosures permitted by paragraph (b)(1)(ii) of this section. The requirements in paragraphs (b)(2) and (3) of this section apply to such uses and disclosure to the extent that the covered entity, in the exercise of professional judgment, determines that the requirements do not interfere with the ability to respond to the emergency circumstances.

§ 164.512 Uses and disclosures for which an authorization or opportunity to agree or object is not required.

A covered entity may use or disclose protected health information without the written authorization of the individual,

as described in §164.508, or the opportunity for the individual to agree or object as described in §164.510, in the situations covered by this section, subject to the applicable requirements of this section. When the covered entity is required by this section to inform the individual of, or when the individual may agree to, a use or disclosure permitted by this section, the covered entity's information and the individual's agreement may be given orally.

(a) *Standard: Uses and disclosures required by law.* (1) A covered entity may use or disclose protected health information to the extent that such use or disclosure is required by law and the use or disclosure complies with and is limited to the relevant requirements of such law.

  (2) A covered entity must meet the requirements described in paragraph (c), (e), or (f) of this section for uses or disclosures required by law.

(b) *Standard: Uses and disclosures for public health activities—*
  (1) *Permitted disclosures.* A covered entity may disclose protected health information for the public health activities and purposes described in this paragraph to:

  (i) A public health authority that is authorized by law to collect or receive such information for the purpose of preventing or controlling disease, injury, or disability, including, but not limited to, the reporting of disease, injury, vital events such as birth or death, and the conduct of public health surveillance, public health investigations, and public health interventions; or, at the direction of a public health authority, to an official of a foreign government agency that is acting in collaboration with a public health authority;

  (ii) A public health authority or other appropriate government authority authorized by law to receive reports of child abuse or neglect;

  (iii) A person subject to the jurisdiction of the Food and Drug Administration (FDA) with respect to an FDA-regulated product or activity for which that person has responsibility, for the purpose of activities related to the quality, safety or effectiveness of such FDA-regulated product or activity. Such purposes include:

    (A) To collect or report adverse events (or similar activities with respect to food or dietary supplements), product defects or problems (including problems with the use or labeling of a product), or biological product deviations;

    (B) To track FDA-regulated products;

    (C) To enable product recalls, repairs, or replacement, or lookback (including locating and notifying individuals who have received products that have been recalled, withdrawn, or are the subject of lookback); or

(D) To conduct post marketing surveillance;

(iv) A person who may have been exposed to a communicable disease or may otherwise be at risk of contracting or spreading a disease or condition, if the covered entity or public health authority is authorized by law to notify such person as necessary in the conduct of a public health intervention or investigation; or

(v) An employer, about an individual who is a member of the workforce of the employer, if:

(A) The covered entity is a covered health care provider who is a member of the workforce of such employer or who provides health care to the individual at the request of the employer:

(1) To conduct an evaluation relating to medical surveillance of the workplace; or

(2) To evaluate whether the individual has a work-related illness or injury;

(B) The protected health information that is disclosed consists of findings concerning a work-related illness or injury or a workplace-related medical surveillance;

(C) The employer needs such findings in order to comply with its obligations, under 29 CFR parts 1904 through 1928, 30 CFR parts 50 through 90, or under state law having a similar purpose, to record such illness or injury or to carry out responsibilities for workplace medical surveillance; and

(D) The covered health care provider provides written notice to the individual that protected health information relating to the medical surveillance of the workplace and work-related illnesses and injuries is disclosed to the employer:

(1) By giving a copy of the notice to the individual at the time the health care is provided; or

(2) If the health care is provided on the work site of the employer, by posting the notice in a prominent place at the location where the health care is provided.

(2) *Permitted uses.* If the covered entity also is a public health authority, the covered entity is permitted to use protected health information in all cases in which it is permitted to disclose such information for public health activities under paragraph (b)(1) of this section.

(c) *Standard: Disclosures about victims of abuse, neglect or domestic violence*—(1) *Permitted disclosures.* Except for reports of child abuse or neglect permitted by paragraph (b)(1)(ii) of this section, a covered entity may disclose protected health information about an individual whom the covered entity reasonably believes to be a victim of abuse, neglect, or domestic violence to a government authority, including a social service or protective services agency, authorized by law to receive reports of such abuse, neglect, or domestic violence:

(i) To the extent the disclosure is required by law and the disclosure complies with and is limited to the relevant requirements of such law;

(ii) If the individual agrees to the disclosure; or

(iii) To the extent the disclosure is expressly authorized by statute or regulation and:

(A) The covered entity, in the exercise of professional judgment, believes the disclosure is necessary to prevent serious harm to the individual or other potential victims; or

(B) If the individual is unable to agree because of incapacity, a law enforcement or other public official authorized to receive the report represents that the protected health information for which disclosure is sought is not intended to be used against the individual and that an immediate enforcement activity that depends upon the disclosure would be materially and adversely affected by waiting until the individual is able to agree to the disclosure.

(2) *Informing the individual.* A covered entity that makes a disclosure permitted by paragraph (c)(1) of this section must promptly inform the individual that such a report has been or will be made, except if:

(i) The covered entity, in the exercise of professional judgment, believes informing the individual would place the individual at risk of serious harm; or

(ii) The covered entity would be informing a personal representative, and the covered entity reasonably believes the personal representative is responsible for the abuse, neglect, or other injury, and that informing such person would not be in the best interests of the individual as determined by the covered entity, in the exercise of professional judgment.

(d) *Standard: Uses and disclosures for health oversight activities*—(1) *Permitted disclosures.* A covered entity may disclose protected health information to a health oversight agency for oversight activities authorized by law, including audits; civil, administrative, or criminal investigations; inspections; licensure or disciplinary actions; civil, administrative, or criminal proceedings or actions; or other activities necessary for appropriate oversight of:

(i) The health care system;

(ii) Government benefit programs for which health information is relevant to beneficiary eligibility;

(iii) Entities subject to government regulatory programs for which health information is necessary for determining compliance with program standards; or

(iv) Entities subject to civil rights laws for which health information is necessary for determining compliance.

(2) *Exception to health oversight activities.* For the purpose of the disclosures permitted by paragraph (d)(1) of this section, a health oversight activity does not include an investigation or other activity in which the individual is the subject of the investigation or activity and such investigation or other activity does not arise out of and is not directly related to:

(i) The receipt of health care;

(ii) A claim for public benefits related to health; or

(iii) Qualification for, or receipt of, public benefits or services when a patient's health is integral to the claim for public benefits or services.

(3) *Joint activities or investigations.* Notwithstanding paragraph (d)(2) of this section, if a health oversight activity or investigation is conducted in conjunction with an oversight activity or investigation relating to a claim for public benefits not related to health, the joint activity or investigation is considered a health oversight activity for purposes of paragraph (d) of this section.

(4) *Permitted uses.* If a covered entity also is a health oversight agency, the covered entity may use protected health information for health oversight activities as permitted by paragraph (d) of this section.

(e) *Standard: Disclosures for judicial and administrative proceedings*—(1) *Permitted disclosures.* A covered entity may disclose protected health information in the course of any judicial or administrative proceeding:

(i) In response to an order of a court or administrative tribunal, provided that the covered entity discloses only the protected health information expressly authorized by such order; or

(ii) In response to a subpoena, discovery request, or other lawful process, that is not accompanied by an order of a court or administrative tribunal, if:

(A) The covered entity receives satisfactory assurance, as described in paragraph (e)(1)(iii) of this section, from the party seeking the information that reasonable efforts have been made by such party to ensure that the individual who is the subject of the protected health information that has been requested has been given notice of the request; or

(B) The covered entity receives satisfactory assurance, as described in paragraph (e)(1)(iv) of this section, from the party seeking the information that reasonable efforts have been made by such party to secure a qualified protective order that meets the requirements of paragraph (e)(1)(v) of this section.

(iii) For the purposes of paragraph (e)(1)(ii)(A) of this section, a covered entity receives satisfactory assurances from a party seeking protecting health information if the covered entity receives from such party a written statement and accompanying documentation demonstrating that:

(A) The party requesting such information has made a good faith attempt to provide written notice to the individual (or, if the individual's location is unknown, to mail a notice to the individual's last known address);

(B) The notice included sufficient information about the litigation or proceeding in which the protected health information is requested to permit the individual to raise an objection to the court or administrative tribunal; and

(C) The time for the individual to raise objections to the court or administrative tribunal has elapsed, and:

(*1*) No objections were filed; or

(*2*) All objections filed by the individual have been resolved by the court or the administrative tribunal and the disclosures being sought are consistent with such resolution.

(iv) For the purposes of paragraph (e)(1)(ii)(B) of this section, a covered entity receives satisfactory assurances from a party seeking protected health information, if the covered entity receives from such party a written statement and accompanying documentation demonstrating that:

(A) The parties to the dispute giving rise to the request for information have agreed to a qualified protective order and have presented it to the court or administrative tribunal with jurisdiction over the dispute; or

(B) The party seeking the protected health information has requested a qualified protective order from such court or administrative tribunal.

(v) For purposes of paragraph (e)(1) of this section, a qualified protective order means, with respect to protected health information requested under paragraph (e)(1)(ii) of this section, an order of a court or of an administrative tribunal or a stipulation by the parties to the litigation or administrative proceeding that:

    (A) Prohibits the parties from using or disclosing the protected health information for any purpose other than the litigation or proceeding for which such information was requested; and

    (B) Requires the return to the covered entity or destruction of the protected health information (including all copies made) at the end of the litigation or proceeding.

(vi) Notwithstanding paragraph (e)(1)(ii) of this section, a covered entity may disclose protected health information in response to lawful process described in paragraph (e)(1)(ii) of this section without receiving satisfactory assurance under paragraph (e)(1)(ii)(A) or (B) of this section, if the covered entity makes reasonable efforts to provide notice to the individual sufficient to meet the requirements of paragraph (e)(1)(iii) of this section or to seek a qualified protective order sufficient to meet the requirements of paragraph (e)(1)(iv) of this section.

(2) *Other uses and disclosures under this section.* The provisions of this paragraph do not supersede other provisions of this section that otherwise permit or restrict uses or disclosures of protected health information.

(f) *Standard: Disclosures for law enforcement purposes.* A covered entity may disclose protected health information for a law enforcement purpose to a law enforcement official if the conditions in paragraphs (f)(1) through (f)(6) of this section are met, as applicable.

(1) *Permitted disclosures: Pursuant to process and as otherwise required by law.* A covered entity may disclose protected health information:

    (i) As required by law including laws that require the reporting of certain types of wounds or other physical injuries, except for laws subject to paragraph (b)(1)(ii) or (c)(1)(i) of this section; or

    (ii) In compliance with and as limited by the relevant requirements of:

        (A) A court order or court-ordered warrant, or a subpoena or summons issued by a judicial officer;

        (B) A grand jury subpoena; or

        (C) An administrative request, including an administrative subpoena or summons, a civil or an authorized investigative demand, or similar process authorized under law, provided that:

            (*1*) The information sought is relevant and material to a legitimate law enforcement inquiry;

            (*2*) The request is specific and limited in scope to the extent reasonably practicable in light of the purpose for which the information is sought; and

            (*3*) De-identified information could not reasonably be used.

(2) *Permitted disclosures: Limited information for identification and location purposes.* Except for disclosures required by law as permitted by paragraph (f)(1) of this section, a covered entity may disclose protected health information in response to a law enforcement official's request for such information for the purpose of identifying or locating a suspect, fugitive, material witness, or missing person, provided that:

    (i) The covered entity may disclose only the following information:

        (A) Name and address;

        (B) Date and place of birth;

        (C) Social security number;

        (D) ABO blood type and rh factor;

        (E) Type of injury;

        (F) Date and time of treatment;

        (G) Date and time of death, if applicable; and

        (H) A description of distinguishing physical characteristics, including height, weight, gender, race, hair and eye color, presence or absence of facial hair (beard or moustache), scars, and tattoos.

    (ii) Except as permitted by paragraph (f)(2)(i) of this section, the covered entity may not disclose for the purposes of identification or location under paragraph (f)(2) of this section any protected health information related to the individual's DNA or DNA analysis, dental records, or typing, samples or analysis of body fluids or tissue.

(3) *Permitted disclosure: Victims of a crime.* Except for disclosures required by law as permitted by paragraph (f)(1) of this section, a covered entity may disclose protected health information in response to a law enforcement official's request for such information about an individual who is or is

suspected to be a victim of a crime, other than disclosures that are subject to paragraph (b) or (c) of this section, if:

  (i) The individual agrees to the disclosure; or

  (ii) The covered entity is unable to obtain the individual's agreement because of incapacity or other emergency circumstance, provided that:

  (A) The law enforcement official represents that such information is needed to determine whether a violation of law by a person other than the victim has occurred, and such information is not intended to be used against the victim;

  (B) The law enforcement official represents that immediate law enforcement activity that depends upon the disclosure would be materially and adversely affected by waiting until the individual is able to agree to the disclosure; and

  (C) The disclosure is in the best interests of the individual as determined by the covered entity, in the exercise of professional judgment.

(4) *Permitted disclosure: Decedents.* A covered entity may disclose protected health information about an individual who has died to a law enforcement official for the purpose of alerting law enforcement of the death of the individual if the covered entity has a suspicion that such death may have resulted from criminal conduct.

(5) *Permitted disclosure: Crime on premises.* A covered entity may disclose to a law enforcement official protected health information that the covered entity believes in good faith constitutes evidence of criminal conduct that occurred on the premises of the covered entity.

(6) *Permitted disclosure: Reporting crime in emergencies.* (i) A covered health care provider providing emergency health care in response to a medical emergency, other than such emergency on the premises of the covered health care provider, may disclose protected health information to a law enforcement official if such disclosure appears necessary to alert law enforcement to:

  (A) The commission and nature of a crime;

  (B) The location of such crime or of the victim(s) of such crime; and

  (C) The identity, description, and location of the perpetrator of such crime.

  (ii) If a covered health care provider believes that the medical emergency described in paragraph (f)(6)(i) of this section is the result of abuse, neglect, or domestic violence of the individual in need of emergency health care, paragraph

(f)(6)(i) of this section does not apply and any disclosure to a law enforcement official for law enforcement purposes is subject to paragraph (c) of this section.

(g) *Standard: Uses and disclosures about decedents —*(1) *Coroners and medical examiners.* A covered entity may disclose protected health information to a coroner or medical examiner for the purpose of identifying a deceased person, determining a cause of death, or other duties as authorized by law. A covered entity that also performs the duties of a coroner or medical examiner may use protected health information for the purposes described in this paragraph.

  (2) *Funeral directors.* A covered entity may disclose protected health information to funeral directors, consistent with applicable law, as necessary to carry out their duties with respect to the decedent. If necessary for funeral directors to carry out their duties, the covered entity may disclose the protected health information prior to, and in reasonable anticipation of, the individual's death.

(h) *Standard: Uses and disclosures for cadaveric organ, eye or tissue donation purposes.* A covered entity may use or disclose protected health information to organ procurement organizations or other entities engaged in the procurement, banking, or transplantation of cadaveric organs, eyes, or tissue for the purpose of facilitating organ, eye or tissue donation and transplantation.

(i) *Standard: Uses and disclosures for research purposes —*(1) *Permitted uses and disclosures.* A covered entity may use or disclose protected health information for research, regardless of the source of funding of the research, provided that:

  (i) *Board approval of a waiver of authorization.* The covered entity obtains documentation that an alteration to or waiver, in whole or in part, of the individual authorization required by §164.508 for use or disclosure of protected health information has been approved by either:

  (A) An Institutional Review Board (IRB), established in accordance with 7 CFR lc.107, 10 CFR 745.107, 14 CFR 1230.107, 15 CFR 27.107, 16 CFR 1028.107, 21 CFR 56.107, 22 CFR 225.107, 24 CFR 60.107, 28 CFR 46.107, 32 CFR 219.107, 34 CFR 97.107, 38 CFR 16.107, 40 CFR 26.107, 45 CFR 46.107, 45 CFR 690.107, or 49 CFR 11.107; or

  (B) A privacy board that:

  (*1*) Has members with varying backgrounds and appropriate professional competency as necessary to review the effect of the research protocol on the individual's privacy rights and related interests;

(2) Includes at least one member who is not affiliated with the covered entity, not affiliated with any entity conducting or sponsoring the research, and not related to any person who is affiliated with any of such entities; and

(3) Does not have any member participating in a review of any project in which the member has a conflict of interest.

(ii) *Reviews preparatory to research.* The covered entity obtains from the researcher representations that:

(A) Use or disclosure is sought solely to review protected health information as necessary to prepare a research protocol or for similar purposes preparatory to research;

(B) No protected health information is to be removed from the covered entity by the researcher in the course of the review; and

(C) The protected health information for which use or access is sought is necessary for the research purposes.

(iii) *Research on decedent's information.* The covered entity obtains from the researcher:

(A) Representation that the use or disclosure sought is solely for research on the protected health information of decedents;

(B) Documentation, at the request of the covered entity, of the death of such individuals; and

(C) Representation that the protected health information for which use or disclosure is sought is necessary for the research purposes.

(2) *Documentation of waiver approval.* For a use or disclosure to be permitted based on documentation of approval of an alteration or waiver, under paragraph (i)(1)(i) of this section, the documentation must include all of the following:

(i) *Identification and date of action.* A statement identifying the IRB or privacy board and the date on which the alteration or waiver of authorization was approved;

(ii) *Waiver criteria.* A statement that the IRB or privacy board has determined that the alteration or waiver, in whole or in part, of authorization satisfies the following criteria:

(A) The use or disclosure of protected health information involves no more than a minimal risk to the privacy of individuals,

based on, at least, the presence of the following elements;

(1) An adequate plan to protect the identifiers from improper use and disclosure;

(2) An adequate plan to destroy the identifiers at the earliest opportunity consistent with conduct of the research, unless there is a health or research justification for retaining the identifiers or such retention is otherwise required by law; and

(3) Adequate written assurances that the protected health information will not be reused or disclosed to any other person or entity, except as required by law, for authorized oversight of the research study, or for other research for which the use or disclosure of protected health information would be permitted by this subpart;

(B) The research could not practicably be conducted without the waiver or alteration; and

(C) The research could not practicably be conducted without access to and use of the protected health information.

(iii) *Protected health information needed.* A brief description of the protected health information for which use or access has been determined to be necessary by the IRB or privacy board has determined, pursuant to paragraph (i)(2)(ii)(C) of this section;

(iv) *Review and approval procedures.* A statement that the alteration or waiver of authorization has been reviewed and approved under either normal or expedited review procedures, as follows:

(A) An IRB must follow the requirements of the Common Rule, including the normal review procedures (7 CFR 1c.108(b), 10 CFR 745.108(b), 14 CFR 1230.108(b), 15 CFR 27.108(b), 16 CFR 1028.108(b), 21 CFR 56.108(b), 22 CFR 225.108(b), 24 CFR 60.108(b), 28 CFR 46.108(b), 32 CFR 219.108(b), 34 CFR 97.108(b), 38 CFR 16.108(b), 40 CFR 26.108(b), 45 CFR 46.108(b), 45 CFR 690.108(b), or 49 CFR 11.108(b)) or the expedited review procedures (7 CFR 1c.110, 10 CFR 745.110, 14 CFR 1230.110, 15 CFR 27.110, 16 CFR 1028.110, 21 CFR 56.110, 22 CFR 225.110, 24 CFR 60.110, 28 CFR 46.110, 32 CFR 219.110, 34 CFR 97.110, 38 CFR 16.110, 40 CFR 26.110, 45 CFR 46.110, 45 CFR 690.110, or 49 CFR 11.110);

(B) A privacy board must review the proposed research at convened meetings at which a majority of the privacy board members are present, including at least one member who satisfies the criterion stated in paragraph (i)(1)(i)(B)(2) of this section, and the alteration or waiver of authorization must be approved by the majority of the privacy board members present at the meeting, unless the privacy board elects to use an expedited review procedure in accordance with paragraph (i)(2)(iv)(C) of this section;

(C) A privacy board may use an expedited review procedure if the research involves no more than minimal risk to the privacy of the individuals who are the subject of the protected health information for which use or disclosure is being sought. If the privacy board elects to use an expedited review procedure, the review and approval of the alteration or waiver of authorization may be carried out by the chair of the privacy board, or by one or more members of the privacy board as designated by the chair; and

(v) *Required signature.* The documentation of the alteration or waiver of authorization must be signed by the chair or other member, as designated by the chair, of the IRB or the privacy board, as applicable.

(j) *Standard: Uses and disclosures to avert a serious threat to health or safety*—(1) *Permitted disclosures.* A covered entity may, consistent with applicable law and standards of ethical conduct, use or disclose protected health information, if the covered entity, in good faith, believes the use or disclosure:

  (i) (A) Is necessary to prevent or lessen a serious and imminent threat to the health or safety of a person or the public; and

  (B) Is to a person or persons reasonably able to prevent or lessen the threat, including the target of the threat; or

  (ii) Is necessary for law enforcement authorities to identify or apprehend an individual:

  (A) Because of a statement by an individual admitting participation in a violent crime that the covered entity reasonably believes may have caused serious physical harm to the victim; or

  (B) Where it appears from all the circumstances that the individual has escaped from a correctional institution or from lawful custody, as those terms are defined in §164.501.

(2) *Use or disclosure not permitted.* A use or disclosure pursuant to paragraph (j)(1)(ii)(A) of this section may not be made if the information described in paragraph (j)(1)(ii)(A) of this section is learned by the covered entity:

  (i) In the course of treatment to affect the propensity to commit the criminal conduct that is the basis for the disclosure under paragraph (j)(1)(ii)(A) of this section, or counseling or therapy; or

  (ii) Through a request by the individual to initiate or to be referred for the treatment, counseling, or therapy described in paragraph (j)(2)(i) of this section.

(3) *Limit on information that may be disclosed.* A disclosure made pursuant to paragraph (j)(1)(ii)(A) of this section shall contain only the statement described in paragraph (j)(1)(ii)(A) of this section and the protected health information described in paragraph (f)(2)(i) of this section.

(4) *Presumption of good faith belief.* A covered entity that uses or discloses protected health information pursuant to paragraph (j)(1) of this section is presumed to have acted in good faith with regard to a belief described in paragraph (j)(1)(i) or (ii) of this section, if the belief is based upon the covered entity's actual knowledge or in reliance on a credible representation by a person with apparent knowledge or authority.

(k) *Standard: Uses and disclosures for specialized government functions*—(1) *Military and veterans activities*—(i) *Armed Forces personnel.* A covered entity may use and disclose the protected health information of individuals who are Armed Forces personnel for activities deemed necessary by appropriate military command authorities to assure the proper execution of the military mission, if the appropriate military authority has published by notice in the Federal Register the following information:

  (A) Appropriate military command authorities; and

  (B) The purposes for which the protected health information may be used or disclosed.

  (ii) *Separation or discharge from military service.* A covered entity that is a component of the Departments of Defense or Transportation may disclose to the Department of Veterans Affairs (DVA) the protected health information of an individual who is a member of the Armed Forces upon the separation or discharge of the individual from military service for the purpose of a determination by DVA of the individual's eligibility for or entitlement to benefits under laws administered by the Secretary of Veterans Affairs.

(iii) *Veterans.* A covered entity that is a component of the Department of Veterans Affairs may use and disclose protected health information to components of the Department that determine eligibility for or entitlement to, or that provide, benefits under the laws administered by the Secretary of Veterans Affairs.

(iv) *Foreign military personnel.* A covered entity may use and disclose the protected health information of individuals who are foreign military personnel to their appropriate foreign military authority for the same purposes for which uses and disclosures are permitted for Armed Forces personnel under the notice published in the Federal Register pursuant to paragraph (k)(1)(i) of this section.

(2) *National security and intelligence activities.* A covered entity may disclose protected health information to authorized federal officials for the conduct of lawful intelligence, counter-intelligence, and other national security activities authorized by the National Security Act (50 U.S.C. 401, *et seq.*) and implementing authority (e.g., Executive Order 12333).

(3) *Protective services for the President and others.* A covered entity may disclose protected health information to authorized federal officials for the provision of protective services to the President or other persons authorized by 18 U.S.C. 3056, or to foreign heads of state or other persons authorized by 22 U.S.C. 2709(a)(3), or to for the conduct of investigations authorized by 18 U.S.C. 871 and 879.

(4) *Medical suitability determinations.* A covered entity that is a component of the Department of State may use protected health information to make medical suitability determinations and may disclose whether or not the individual was determined to be medically suitable to the officials in the Department of State who need access to such information for the following purposes:

(i) For the purpose of a required security clearance conducted pursuant to Executive Orders 10450 and 12698;

(ii) As necessary to determine worldwide availability or availability for mandatory service abroad under sections 101(a)(4) and 504 of the Foreign Service Act; or

(iii) For a family to accompany a Foreign Service member abroad, consistent with section 101(b)(5) and 904 of the Foreign Service Act.

(5) *Correctional institutions and other law enforcement custodial situations.* (i) *Permitted disclosures.* A covered entity may disclose to a correctional institution or a law enforcement official having lawful custody of an inmate or other individual protected health information about such inmate or individual,

if the correctional institution or such law enforcement official represents that such protected health information is necessary for:

(A) The provision of health care to such individuals;

(B) The health and safety of such individual or other inmates;

(C) The health and safety of the officers or employees of or others at the correctional institution;

(D) The health and safety of such individuals and officers or other persons responsible for the transporting of inmates or their transfer from one institution, facility, or setting to another;

(E) Law enforcement on the premises of the correctional institution; and

(F) The administration and maintenance of the safety, security, and good order of the correctional institution.

(ii) *Permitted uses.* A covered entity that is a correctional institution may use protected health information of individuals who are inmates for any purpose for which such protected health information may be disclosed.

(iii) *No application after release.* For the purposes of this provision, an individual is no longer an inmate when released on parole, probation, supervised release, or otherwise is no longer in lawful custody.

(6) *Covered entities that are government programs providing public benefits.* (i) A health plan that is a government program providing public benefits may disclose protected health information relating to eligibility for or enrollment in the health plan to another agency administering a government program providing public benefits if the sharing of eligibility or enrollment information among such government agencies or the maintenance of such information in a single or combined data system accessible to all such government agencies is required or expressly authorized by statute or regulation.

(ii) A covered entity that is a government agency administering a government program providing public benefits may disclose protected health information relating to the program to another covered entity that is a government agency administering a government program providing public benefits if the programs serve the same or similar populations and the disclosure of protected health information is necessary to coordinate the covered functions of such programs or to improve administration and management relating to the covered functions of such programs.

(l) *Standard: Disclosures for workers' compensation.* A covered entity may disclose protected health information as authorized by and to the extent necessary to comply with laws relating to workers' compensation or other similar programs, established by law, that provide benefits for work-related injuries or illness without regard to fault.

[65 FR 82802, Dec. 28, 2000, as amended at 67 FR 53270, Aug. 14, 2002]

§ 164.514 Other requirements relating to uses and disclosures of protected health information.

(a) *Standard: De-identification of protected health information.* Health information that does not identify an individual and with respect to which there is no reasonable basis to believe that the information can be used to identify an individual is not individually identifiable health information.

(b) *Implementation specifications: Requirements for de-identification of protected health information.* A covered entity may determine that health information is not individually identifiable health information only if:

(1) A person with appropriate knowledge of and experience with generally accepted statistical and scientific principles and methods for rendering information not individually identifiable:

  (i) Applying such principles and methods, determines that the risk is very small that the information could be used, alone or in combination with other reasonably available information, by an anticipated recipient to identify an individual who is a subject of the information; and

  (ii) Documents the methods and results of the analysis that justify such determination; or

(2) (i) The following identifiers of the individual or of relatives, employers, or household members of the individual, are removed:

  (A) Names;

  (B) All geographic subdivisions smaller than a State, including street address, city, county, precinct, zip code, and their equivalent geocodes, except for the initial three digits of a zip code if, according to the current publicly available data from the Bureau of the Census:

    (1) The geographic unit formed by combining all zip codes with the same three initial digits contains more than 20,000 people; and

    (2) The initial three digits of a zip code for all such geographic units containing 20,000 or fewer people is changed to 000.

  (C) All elements of dates (except year) for dates directly related to an individual, including birth date, admission date, discharge date, date of death; and all ages over 89 and all elements of dates (including year) indicative of such age, except that such ages and elements may be aggregated into a single category of age 90 or older;

  (D) Telephone numbers;

  (E) Fax numbers;

  (F) Electronic mail addresses;

  (G) Social security numbers;

  (H) Medical record numbers;

  (I) Health plan beneficiary numbers;

  (J) Account numbers;

  (K) Certificate/license numbers;

  (L) Vehicle identifiers and serial numbers, including license plate numbers;

  (M) Device identifiers and serial numbers;

  (N) Web Universal Resource Locators (URLs);

  (O) Internet Protocol (IP) address numbers;

  (P) Biometric identifiers, including finger and voice prints;

  (Q) Full face photographic images and any comparable images; and

  (R) Any other unique identifying number, characteristic, or code, except as permitted by paragraph (c) of this section; and

  (ii) The covered entity does not have actual knowledge that the information could be used alone or in combination with other information to identify an individual who is a subject of the information.

(c) *Implementation specifications: Re-identification.* A covered entity may assign a code or other means of record identification to allow information de-identified under this section to be re-identified by the covered entity, provided that:

(1) *Derivation.* The code or other means of record identification is not derived from or related to information about the individual and is not otherwise capable of being translated so as to identify the individual; and

(2) *Security.* The covered entity does not use or disclose the code or other means of record identification for any other purpose, and does not disclose the mechanism for re-identification.

(d) (1) *Standard: Minimum necessary requirements.* In order to comply with §164.502(b) and this section, a covered entity must meet the requirements of paragraphs (d)(2) through (d)(5) of this section with respect to a request for, or the use and disclosure of, protected health information.

(2) *Implementation specifications: Minimum necessary uses of protected health information.* (i) A covered entity must identify:

  (A) Those persons or classes of persons, as appropriate, in its workforce who need access to protected health information to carry out their duties; and

  (B) For each such person or class of persons, the category or categories of protected health information to which access is needed and any conditions appropriate to such access.

  (ii) A covered entity must make reasonable efforts to limit the access of such persons or classes identified in paragraph (d)(2)(i)(A) of this section to protected health information consistent with paragraph (d)(2)(i)(B) of this section.

(3) *Implementation specification: Minimum necessary disclosures of protected health information.* (i) For any type of disclosure that it makes on a routine and recurring basis, a covered entity must implement policies and procedures (which may be standard protocols) that limit the protected health information disclosed to the amount reasonably necessary to achieve the purpose of the disclosure.

  (ii) For all other disclosures, a covered entity must:

  (A) Develop criteria designed to limit the protected health information disclosed to the information reasonably necessary to accomplish the purpose for which disclosure is sought; and

  (B) Review requests for disclosure on an individual basis in accordance with such criteria.

  (iii) A covered entity may rely, if such reliance is reasonable under the circumstances, on a requested disclosure as the minimum necessary for the stated purpose when:

  (A) Making disclosures to public officials that are permitted under §164.512, if the public official represents that the information requested is the minimum necessary for the stated purpose(s);

  (B) The information is requested by another covered entity;

  (C) The information is requested by a professional who is a member of its workforce or is a business associate of the covered entity for the purpose of providing professional services to the covered entity, if the professional represents that the information requested is the minimum necessary for the stated purpose(s); or

  (D) Documentation or representations that comply with the applicable requirements of §164.512(i) have been provided by a person requesting the information for research purposes.

(4) *Implementation specifications: Minimum necessary requests for protected health information.* (i) A covered entity must limit any request for protected health information to that which is reasonably necessary to accomplish the purpose for which the request is made, when requesting such information from other covered entities.

  (ii) For a request that is made on a routine and recurring basis, a covered entity must implement policies and procedures (which may be standard protocols) that limit the protected health information requested to the amount reasonably necessary to accomplish the purpose for which the request is made.

  (iii) For all other requests, a covered entity must:

  (A) Develop criteria designed to limit the request for protected health information to the information reasonably necessary to accomplish the purpose for which the request is made; and

  (B) Review requests for disclosure on an individual basis in accordance with such criteria.

(5) *Implementation specification: Other content requirement.* For all uses, disclosures, or requests to which the requirements in paragraph (d) of this section apply, a covered entity may not use, disclose or request an entire medical record, except when the entire medical record is specifically justified as the amount that is reasonably necessary to accomplish the purpose of the use, disclosure, or request.

(e) (1) *Standard: Limited data set.* A covered entity may use or disclose a limited data set that meets the requirements of paragraphs (e)(2) and (e)(3) of this section, if the covered entity enters into a data use agreement with the limited data set recipient, in accordance with paragraph (e)(4) of this section.

(2) *Implementation specification: Limited data set:* A limited data set is protected health information that excludes the following direct identifiers of the individual or of relatives, employers, or household members of the individual:

  (i) Names;

  (ii) Postal address information, other than town or city, State, and zip code;

  (iii) Telephone numbers;

  (iv) Fax numbers;

  (v) Electronic mail addresses;

  (vi) Social security numbers;

  (vii) Medical record numbers;

(viii) Health plan beneficiary numbers;

(ix) Account numbers;

(x) Certificate/license numbers;

(xi) Vehicle identifiers and serial numbers, including license plate numbers;

(xii) Device identifiers and serial numbers;

(xiii) Web Universal Resource Locators (URLs);

(xiv) Internet Protocol (IP) address numbers;

(xv) Biometric identifiers, including finger and voice prints; and

(xvi) Full face photographic images and any comparable images.

(3) *Implementation specification: Permitted purposes for uses and disclosures.* (i) A covered entity may use or disclose a limited data set under paragraph (e)(1) of this section only for the purposes of research, public health, or health care operations.

(ii) A covered entity may use protected health information to create a limited data set that meets the requirements of paragraph (e)(2) of this section, or disclose protected health information only to a business associate for such purpose, whether or not the limited data set is to be used by the covered entity.

(4) *Implementation specifications: Data use agreement. —*
(i) *Agreement required.* A covered entity may use or disclose a limited data set under paragraph (e)(1) of this section only if the covered entity obtains satisfactory assurance, in the form of a data use agreement that meets the requirements of this section, that the limited data set recipient will only use or disclose the protected health information for limited purposes.

(ii) *Contents.* A data use agreement between the covered entity and the limited data set recipient must:

(A) Establish the permitted uses and disclosures of such information by the limited data set recipient, consistent with paragraph (e)(3) of this section. The data use agreement may not authorize the limited data set recipient to use or further disclose the information in a manner that would violate the requirements of this subpart, if done by the covered entity;

(B) Establish who is permitted to use or receive the limited data set; and

(C) Provide that the limited data set recipient will:

(*1*) Not use or further disclose the information other than as permitted by the data use agreement or as otherwise required by law;

(*2*) Use appropriate safeguards to prevent use or disclosure of the information other than as provided for by the data use agreement;

(*3*) Report to the covered entity any use or disclosure of the information not provided for by its data use agreement of which it becomes aware;

(*4*) Ensure that any agents, including a subcontractor, to whom it provides the limited data set agrees to the same restrictions and conditions that apply to the limited data set recipient with respect to such information; and

(*5*) Not identify the information or contact the individuals.

(iii) *Compliance.* (A) A covered entity is not in compliance with the standards in paragraph (e) of this section if the covered entity knew of a pattern of activity or practice of the limited data set recipient that constituted a material breach or violation of the data use agreement, unless the covered entity took reasonable steps to cure the breach or end the violation, as applicable, and, if such steps were unsuccessful:

(1) Discontinued disclosure of protected health information to the recipient; and

(2) Reported the problem to the Secretary.

(B) A covered entity that is a limited data set recipient and violates a data use agreement will be in noncompliance with the standards, implementation specifications, and requirements of paragraph (e) of this section.

(f) (1) *Standard: Uses and disclosures for fundraising.* A covered entity may use, or disclose to a business associate or to an institutionally related foundation, the following protected health information for the purpose of raising funds for its own benefit, without an authorization meeting the requirements of §164.508:

(i) Demographic information relating to an individual; and

(ii) Dates of health care provided to an individual.

(2) *Implementation specifications: Fundraising requirements.* (i) The covered entity may not use or disclose protected health information for fundraising purposes as otherwise permitted by paragraph (f)(1) of this section unless a statement required by §164.520(b)(1)(iii)(B) is included in the covered entity's notice;

(ii) The covered entity must include in any fund-raising materials it sends to an individual under this paragraph a description of how the individual may opt out of receiving any further fundraising communications.

(iii) The covered entity must make reasonable efforts to ensure that individuals who decide to opt out of receiving future fundraising communications are not sent such communications.

(g) *Standard: Uses and disclosures for underwriting and related purposes.* If a health plan receives protected heath information for the purpose of underwriting, premium rating, or other activities relating to the creation, renewal, or replacement of a contract of health insurance or health benefits, and if such health insurance or health benefits are not placed with the health plan, such health plan may not use or disclose such protected health information for any other purpose, except as may be required by law.

(h) (1) *Standard: Verification requirements.* Prior to any disclosure permitted by this subpart, a covered entity must:

(i) Except with respect to disclosures under §164.510, verify the identity of a person requesting protected health information and the authority of any such person to have access to protected health information under this subpart, if the identity or any such authority of such person is not known to the covered entity; and

(ii) Obtain any documentation, statements, or representations, whether oral or written, from the person requesting the protected health information when such documentation, statement, or representation is a condition of the disclosure under this subpart.

(2) *Implementation specifications: Verification.* (i) *Conditions on disclosures.* If a disclosure is conditioned by this subpart on particular documentation, statements, or representations from the person requesting the protected health information, a covered entity may rely, if such reliance is reasonable under the circumstances, on documentation, statements, or representations that, on their face, meet the applicable requirements.

(A) The conditions in §164.512(f)(1)(ii)(C) may be satisfied by the administrative subpoena or similar process or by a separate written statement that, on its face, demonstrates that the applicable requirements have been met.

(B) The documentation required by §164.512(i)(2) may be satisfied by one or more written statements, provided that

each is appropriately dated and signed in accordance with §164.512(i)(2)(i) and (v).

(ii) *Identity of public officials.* A covered entity may rely, if such reliance is reasonable under the circumstances, on any of the following to verify identity when the disclosure of protected health information is to a public official or a person acting on behalf of the public official:

(A) If the request is made in person, presentation of an agency identification badge, other official credentials, or other proof of government status;

(B) If the request is in writing, the request is on the appropriate government letterhead; or

(C) If the disclosure is to a person acting on behalf of a public official, a written statement on appropriate government letterhead that the person is acting under the government's authority or other evidence or documentation of agency, such as a contract for services, memorandum of understanding, or purchase order, that establishes that the person is acting on behalf of the public official.

(iii) *Authority of public officials.* A covered entity may rely, if such reliance is reasonable under the circumstances, on any of the following to verify authority when the disclosure of protected health information is to a public official or a person acting on behalf of the public official:

(A) A written statement of the legal authority under which the information is requested, or, if a written statement would be impracticable, an oral statement of such legal authority;

(B) If a request is made pursuant to legal process, warrant, subpoena, order, or other legal process issued by a grand jury or a judicial or administrative tribunal is presumed to constitute legal authority.

(iv) *Exercise of professional judgment.* The verification requirements of this paragraph are met if the covered entity relies on the exercise of professional judgment in making a use or disclosure in accordance with §164.510 or acts on a good faith belief in making a disclosure in accordance with §164.512(j).

§ 164.520 Notice of privacy practices for protected health information.

(a) *Standard: Notice of privacy practices—(1) Right to notice.* Except as provided by paragraph (a)(2) or (3) of this section, an individual has a right to adequate notice of the uses and disclosures of protected health information that may be made by the covered entity, and of the individual's rights and the covered entity's legal duties with respect to protected health information.

(2) *Exception for group health plans.* (i) An individual enrolled in a group health plan has a right to notice:

(A) From the group health plan, if, and to the extent that, such an individual does not receive health benefits under the group health plan through an insurance contract with a health insurance issuer or HMO; or

(B) From the health insurance issuer or HMO with respect to the group health plan through which such individuals receive their health benefits under the group health plan.

(ii) A group health plan that provides health benefits solely through an insurance contract with a health insurance issuer or HMO, and that creates or receives protected health information in addition to summary health information as defined in §164.504(a) or information on whether the individual is participating in the group health plan, or is enrolled in or has disenrolled from a health insurance issuer or HMO offered by the plan, must:

(A) Maintain a notice under this section; and

(B) Provide such notice upon request to any person. The provisions of paragraph (c)(1) of this section do not apply to such group health plan.

(iii) A group health plan that provides health benefits solely through an insurance contract with a health insurance issuer or HMO, and does not create or receive protected health information other than summary health information as defined in §164.504(a) or information on whether an individual is participating in the group health plan, or is enrolled in or has disenrolled from a health insurance issuer or HMO offered by the plan, is not required to maintain or provide a notice under this section.

(3) *Exception for inmates.* An inmate does not have a right to notice under this section, and the requirements of this section do not apply to a correctional institution that is a covered entity.

(b) *Implementation specifications: content of notice —(1) Required elements.* The covered entity must provide a notice that is written in plain language and that contains the elements required by this paragraph.

(i) *Header.* The notice must contain the following statement as a header or otherwise prominently displayed: "THIS NOTICE DESCRIBES HOW MEDICAL INFORMATION ABOUT YOU MAY BE USED AND DISCLOSED AND HOW YOU CAN GET ACCESS TO THIS INFORMATION. PLEASE REVIEW IT CAREFULLY."

(ii) *Uses and disclosures.* The notice must contain:

(A) A description, including at least one example, of the types of uses and disclosures that the covered entity is permitted by this subpart to make for each of the following purposes: treatment, payment, and health care operations.

(B) A description of each of the other purposes for which the covered entity is permitted or required by this subpart to use or disclose protected health information without the individual's written authorization.

(C) If a use or disclosure for any purpose described in paragraphs (b)(1)(ii)(A) or (B) of this section is prohibited or materially limited by other applicable law, the description of such use or disclosure must reflect the more stringent law as defined in §160.202 of this subchapter.

(D) For each purpose described in paragraph (b)(1)(ii)(A) or (B) of this section, the description must include sufficient detail to place the individual on notice of the uses and disclosures that are permitted or required by this subpart and other applicable law.

(E) A statement that other uses and disclosures will be made only with the individual's written authorization and that the individual may revoke such authorization as provided by §164.508(b)(5).

(iii) *Separate statements for certain uses or disclosures.* If the covered entity intends to engage in any of the following activities, the description required by paragraph (b)(1)(ii)(A) of this section must include a separate statement, as applicable, that:

(A) The covered entity may contact the individual to provide appointment reminders or information about treatment alternatives or other health-related benefits and services that may be of interest to the individual;

(B) The covered entity may contact the individual to raise funds for the covered entity; or

(C) A group health plan, or a health insurance issuer or HMO with respect to a group health plan, may disclose protected health information to the sponsor of the plan.

(iv) *Individual rights.* The notice must contain a statement of the individual's rights with respect to protected health information and a brief description of how the individual may exercise these rights, as follows:

(A) The right to request restrictions on certain uses and disclosures of protected health information as provided by §164.522(a), including a statement that the covered entity is not required to agree to a requested restriction;

(B) The right to receive confidential communications of protected health information as provided by §164.522(b), as applicable;

(C) The right to inspect and copy protected health information as provided by §164.524;

(D) The right to amend protected health information as provided by §164.526;

(E) The right to receive an accounting of disclosures of protected health information as provided by §164.528; and

(F) The right of an individual, including an individual who has agreed to receive the notice electronically in accordance with paragraph (c)(3) of this section, to obtain a paper copy of the notice from the covered entity upon request.

(v) *Covered entity's duties.* The notice must contain:

(A) A statement that the covered entity is required by law to maintain the privacy of protected health information and to provide individuals with notice of its legal duties and privacy practices with respect to protected health information;

(B) A statement that the covered entity is required to abide by the terms of the notice currently in effect; and

(C) For the covered entity to apply a change in a privacy practice that is described in the notice to protected health information that the covered entity created or received prior to issuing a revised notice, in accordance with §164.530(i)(2)(ii), a statement that it reserves the right to change the terms of its notice and to make the new notice provisions effective for all protected health information that it maintains. The statement must also describe how it will provide individuals with a revised notice.

(vi) *Complaints.* The notice must contain a statement that individuals may complain to the covered entity and to the Secretary if they believe their privacy rights have been violated, a brief description of how the individual may file a complaint with the covered entity, and a statement that the individual will not be retaliated against for filing a complaint.

(vii) *Contact.* The notice must contain the name, or title, and telephone number of a person or office to contact for further information as required by §164.530(a)(1)(ii).

(viii) *Effective date.* The notice must contain the date on which the notice is first in effect, which may not be earlier than the date on which the notice is printed or otherwise published.

(2) *Optional elements.* (i) In addition to the information required by paragraph (b)(1) of this section, if a covered entity elects to limit the uses or disclosures that it is permitted to make under this subpart, the covered entity may describe its more limited uses or disclosures in its notice, provided that the covered entity may not include in its notice a limitation affecting its right to make a use or disclosure that is required by law or permitted by §164.512(j)(1)(i).

(ii) For the covered entity to apply a change in its more limited uses and disclosures to protected health information created or received prior to issuing a revised notice, in accordance with §164.530(i)(2)(ii), the notice must include the statements required by paragraph (b)(1)(v)(C) of this section.

(3) *Revisions to the notice.* The covered entity must promptly revise and distribute its notice whenever there is a material change to the uses or disclosures, the individual's rights, the covered entity's legal duties, or other privacy practices stated in the notice. Except when required by law, a material change to any term of the notice may not be implemented prior to the effective date of the notice in which such material change is reflected.

(c) *Implementation specifications: Provision of notice.* A covered entity must make the notice required by this section available on request to any person and to individuals as specified in paragraphs (c)(1) through (c)(3) of this section, as applicable.

(1) *Specific requirements for health plans.* (i) A health plan must provide notice:

(A) No later than the compliance date for the health plan, to individuals then covered by the plan;

(B) Thereafter, at the time of enrollment, to individuals who are new enrollees; and

(C) Within 60 days of a material revision to the notice, to individuals then covered by the plan.

(ii) No less frequently than once every three years, the health plan must notify individuals then covered by the plan of the availability of the notice and how to obtain the notice.

(iii) The health plan satisfies the requirements of paragraph (c)(1) of this section if notice is provided to the named insured of a policy under which coverage is provided to the named insured and one or more dependents.

(iv) If a health plan has more than one notice, it satisfies the requirements of paragraph (c)(1) of this section by providing the notice that is relevant to the individual or other person requesting the notice.

(2) *Specific requirements for certain covered health care providers.* A covered health care provider that has a direct treatment relationship with an individual must:

(i) Provide the notice:

(A) No later than the date of the first service delivery, including service delivered electronically, to such individual after the compliance date for the covered health care provider; or

(B) In an emergency treatment situation, as soon as reasonably practicable after the emergency treatment situation.

(ii) Except in an emergency treatment situation, make a good faith effort to obtain a written acknowledgment of receipt of the notice provided in accordance with paragraph (c)(2)(i) of this section, and if not obtained, document its good faith efforts to obtain such acknowledgment and the reason why the acknowledgment was not obtained;

(iii) If the covered health care provider maintains a physical service delivery site:

(A) Have the notice available at the service delivery site for individuals to request to take with them; and

(B) Post the notice in a clear and prominent location where it is reasonable to expect individuals seeking service from the covered health care provider to be able to read the notice; and

(iv) Whenever the notice is revised, make the notice available upon request on or after the effective date of the revision and promptly comply with the requirements of paragraph (c)(2)(iii) of this section, if applicable.

(3) *Specific requirements for electronic notice.* (i) A covered entity that maintains a web site that provides information about the covered entity's customer services or benefits must prominently post its notice on the web site and make the notice available electronically through the web site.

(ii) A covered entity may provide the notice required by this section to an individual by e-mail, if the individual agrees to electronic notice and such agreement has not been withdrawn. If the covered entity knows that the e-mail transmission has failed, a paper copy of the notice must be provided to the individual. Provision of electronic notice by the covered entity will satisfy the provision requirements of paragraph (c) of this section when timely made in accordance with paragraph (c)(1) or (2) of this section.

(iii) For purposes of paragraph (c)(2)(i) of this section, if the first service delivery to an individual is delivered electronically, the covered health care provider must provide electronic notice automatically and contemporaneously in response to the individual's first request for service. The requirements in paragraph (c)(2)(ii) of this section apply to electronic notice.

(iv) The individual who is the recipient of electronic notice retains the right to obtain a paper copy of the notice from a covered entity upon request.

(d) *Implementation specifications: Joint notice by separate covered entities.* Covered entities that participate in organized health care arrangements may comply with this section by a joint notice, provided that:

(1) The covered entities participating in the organized health care arrangement agree to abide by the terms of the notice with respect to protected health information created or received by the covered entity as part of its participation in the organized health care arrangement;

(2) The joint notice meets the implementation specifications in paragraph (b) of this section, except that the statements required by this section may be altered to reflect the fact that the notice covers more than one covered entity; and

(i) Describes with reasonable specificity the covered entities, or class of entities, to which the joint notice applies;

(ii) Describes with reasonable specificity the service delivery sites, or classes of service delivery sites, to which the joint notice applies; and

(iii) If applicable, states that the covered entities participating in the organized health care arrangement will share protected health information with each other, as necessary to carry out treatment, payment, or health care operations relating to the organized health care arrangement.

(3) The covered entities included in the joint notice must provide the notice to individuals in accordance with the applicable implementation

specifications of paragraph (c) of this section. Provision of the joint notice to an individual by any one of the covered entities included in the joint notice will satisfy the provision requirement of paragraph (c) of this section with respect to all others covered by the joint notice.

(e) *Implementation specifications: Documentation.* A covered entity must document compliance with the notice requirements, as required by §164.530(j), by retaining copies of the notices issued by the covered entity and, if applicable, any written acknowledgments of receipt of the notice or documentation of good faith efforts to obtain such written acknowledgment, in accordance with paragraph (c)(2)(ii) of this section.

[65 FR 82802, Dec. 28, 2000, as amended at 67 FR 53271, Aug. 14, 2002]

§ 164.522 Rights to request privacy protection for protected health information.

(a) (1) *Standard: Right of an individual to request restriction of uses and disclosures.* (i) A covered entity must permit an individual to request that the covered entity restrict:

    (A) Uses or disclosures of protected health information about the individual to carry out treatment, payment, or health care operations; and

    (B) Disclosures permitted under §164.510(b).

  (ii) A covered entity is not required to agree to a restriction.

  (iii) A covered entity that agrees to a restriction under paragraph (a)(1)(i) of this section may not use or disclose protected health information in violation of such restriction, except that, if the individual who requested the restriction is in need of emergency treatment and the restricted protected health information is needed to provide the emergency treatment, the covered entity may use the restricted protected health information, or may disclose such information to a health care provider, to provide such treatment to the individual.

  (iv) If restricted protected health information is disclosed to a health care provider for emergency treatment under paragraph (a)(1)(iii) of this section, the covered entity must request that such health care provider not further use or disclose the information.

  (v) A restriction agreed to by a covered entity under paragraph (a) of this section, is not effective under this subpart to prevent uses or disclosures permitted or required under §§1 64.502(a)(2)(ii), 164.510(a) or 164.512.

(2) *Implementation specifications: Terminating a restriction.* A covered entity may terminate its agreement to a restriction, if:

  (i) The individual agrees to or requests the termination in writing;

  (ii) The individual orally agrees to the termination and the oral agreement is documented; or

  (iii) The covered entity informs the individual that it is terminating its agreement to a restriction, except that such termination is only effective with respect to protected health information created or received after it has so informed the individual.

(3) *Implementation specification: Documentation.* A covered entity that agrees to a restriction must document the restriction in accordance with §164.530(j).

(b) (1) *Standard: Confidential communications requirements.* (i) A covered health care provider must permit individuals to request and must accommodate reasonable requests by individuals to receive communications of protected health information from the covered health care provider by alternative means or at alternative locations.

  (ii) A health plan must permit individuals to request and must accommodate reasonable requests by individuals to receive communications of protected health information from the health plan by alternative means or at alternative locations, if the individual clearly states that the disclosure of all or part of that information could endanger the individual.

(2) *Implementation specifications: Conditions on providing confidential communications.* (i) A covered entity may require the individual to make a request for a confidential communication described in paragraph (b)(1) of this section in writing.

  (ii) A covered entity may condition the provision of a reasonable accommodation on:

    (A) When appropriate, information as to how payment, if any, will be handled; and

    (B) Specification of an alternative address or other method of contact.

  (iii) A covered health care provider may not require an explanation from the individual as to the basis for the request as a condition of providing communications on a confidential basis.

  (iv) A health plan may require that a request contain a statement that disclosure of all or part of the information to which the request pertains could endanger the individual.

§ 164.524 Access of individuals to protected health information.

(a) *Standard: Access to protected health information—*
   (1) *Right of access.* Except as otherwise provided in paragraph (a)(2) or (a)(3) of this section, an individual has a right of access to inspect and obtain a copy of protected health information about the individual in a designated record set, for as long as the protected health information is maintained in the designated record set, except for:

   (i) Psychotherapy notes;

   (ii) Information compiled in reasonable anticipation of, or for use in, a civil, criminal, or administrative action or proceeding; and

   (iii) Protected health information maintained by a covered entity that is:

   (A) Subject to the Clinical Laboratory Improvements Amendments of 1988, 42 U.S.C. 263a, to the extent the provision of access to the individual would be prohibited by law; or

   (B) Exempt from the Clinical Laboratory Improvements Amendments of 1988, pursuant to 42 CFR 493.3(a)(2).

   (2) *Unreviewable grounds for denial.* A covered entity may deny an individual access without providing the individual an opportunity for review, in the following circumstances.

   (i) The protected health information is excepted from the right of access by paragraph (a)(1) of this section.

   (ii) A covered entity that is a correctional institution or a covered health care provider acting under the direction of the correctional institution may deny, in whole or in part, an inmate's request to obtain a copy of protected health information, if obtaining such copy would jeopardize the health, safety, security, custody, or rehabilitation of the individual or of other inmates, or the safety of any officer, employee, or other person at the correctional institution or responsible for the transporting of the inmate.

   (iii) An individual's access to protected health information created or obtained by a covered health care provider in the course of research that includes treatment may be temporarily suspended for as long as the research is in progress, provided that the individual has agreed to the denial of access when consenting to participate in the research that includes treatment, and the covered health care provider has informed the individual that the right of access will be reinstated upon completion of the research.

   (iv) An individual's access to protected health information that is contained in records that are subject to the Privacy Act, 5 U.S.C. 552a, may be denied, if the denial of access under the Privacy Act would meet the requirements of that law.

   (v) An individual's access may be denied if the protected health information was obtained from someone other than a health care provider under a promise of confidentiality and the access requested would be reasonably likely to reveal the source of the information.

   (3) *Reviewable grounds for denial.* A covered entity may deny an individual access, provided that the individual is given a right to have such denials reviewed, as required by paragraph (a)(4) of this section, in the following circumstances:

   (i) A licensed health care professional has determined, in the exercise of professional judgment, that the access requested is reasonably likely to endanger the life or physical safety of the individual or another person;

   (ii) The protected health information makes reference to another person (unless such other person is a health care provider) and a licensed health care professional has determined, in the exercise of professional judgment, that the access requested is reasonably likely to cause substantial harm to such other person; or

   (iii) The request for access is made by the individual's personal representative and a licensed health care professional has determined, in the exercise of professional judgment, that the provision of access to such personal representative is reasonably likely to cause substantial harm to the individual or another person.

   (4) *Review of a denial of access.* If access is denied on a ground permitted under paragraph (a)(3) of this section, the individual has the right to have the denial reviewed by a licensed health care professional who is designated by the covered entity to act as a reviewing official and who did not participate in the original decision to deny. The covered entity must provide or deny access in accordance with the determination of the reviewing official under paragraph (d)(4) of this section.

(b) *Implementation specifications: Requests for access and timely action —*(1) *Individual's request for access.* The covered entity must permit an individual to request access to inspect or to obtain a copy of the protected health information about the individual that is maintained in a designated record set. The covered entity may require individuals to make requests for access in writing, provided that it informs individuals of such a requirement.

(2) *Timely action by the covered entity.* (i) Except as provided in paragraph (b)(2)(ii) of this section, the covered entity must act on a request for access no later than 30 days after receipt of the request as follows.

  (A) If the covered entity grants the request, in whole or in part, it must inform the individual of the acceptance of the request and provide the access requested, in accordance with paragraph (c) of this section.

  (B) If the covered entity denies the request, in whole or in part, it must provide the individual with a written denial, in accordance with paragraph (d) of this section.

  (ii) If the request for access is for protected health information that is not maintained or accessible to the covered entity on-site, the covered entity must take an action required by paragraph (b)(2)(i) of this section by no later than 60 days from the receipt of such a request.

  (iii) If the covered entity is unable to take an action required by paragraph (b)(2)(i)(A) or (B) of this section within the time required by paragraph (b)(2)(i) or (ii) of this section, as applicable, the covered entity may extend the time for such actions by no more than 30 days, provided that:

  (A) The covered entity, within the time limit set by paragraph (b)(2)(i) or (ii) of this section, as applicable, provides the individual with a written statement of the reasons for the delay and the date by which the covered entity will complete its action on the request; and

  (B) The covered entity may have only one such extension of time for action on a request for access.

(c) *Implementation specifications: Provision of access.* If the covered entity provides an individual with access, in whole or in part, to protected health information, the covered entity must comply with the following requirements.

  (1) *Providing the access requested.* The covered entity must provide the access requested by individuals, including inspection or obtaining a copy, or both, of the protected health information about them in designated record sets. If the same protected health information that is the subject of a request for access is maintained in more than one designated record set or at more than one location, the covered entity need only produce the protected health information once in response to a request for access.

  (2) *Form of access requested.* (i) The covered entity must provide the individual with access to the protected health information in the form or format requested by the individual, if it is readily producible in such form or format; or, if not, in a readable hard copy form or such other form or format as agreed to by the covered entity and the individual.

  (ii) The covered entity may provide the individual with a summary of the protected health information requested, in lieu of providing access to the protected health information or may provide an explanation of the protected health information to which access has been provided, if:

  (A) The individual agrees in advance to such a summary or explanation; and

  (B) The individual agrees in advance to the fees imposed, if any, by the covered entity for such summary or explanation.

(3) *Time and manner of access.* The covered entity must provide the access as requested by the individual in a timely manner as required by paragraph (b)(2) of this section, including arranging with the individual for a convenient time and place to inspect or obtain a copy of the protected health information, or mailing the copy of the protected health information at the individual's request. The covered entity may discuss the scope, format, and other aspects of the request for access with the individual as necessary to facilitate the timely provision of access.

(4) *Fees.* If the individual requests a copy of the protected health information or agrees to a summary or explanation of such information, the covered entity may impose a reasonable, cost-based fee, provided that the fee includes only the cost of:

  (i) Copying, including the cost of supplies for and labor of copying, the protected health information requested by the individual;

  (ii) Postage, when the individual has requested the copy, or the summary or explanation, be mailed; and

  (iii) Preparing an explanation or summary of the protected health information, if agreed to by the individual as required by paragraph (c)(2)(ii) of this section.

(d) *Implementation specifications: Denial of access.* If the covered entity denies access, in whole or in part, to protected health information, the covered entity must comply with the following requirements.

  (1) *Making other information accessible.* The covered entity must, to the extent possible, give the individual access to any other protected health information requested, after excluding the protected health information as to which the covered entity has a ground to deny access.

(2) *Denial.* The covered entity must provide a timely, written denial to the individual, in accordance with paragraph (b)(2) of this section. The denial must be in plain language and contain:

   (i) The basis for the denial;

   (ii) If applicable, a statement of the individual's review rights under paragraph (a)(4) of this section, including a description of how the individual may exercise such review rights; and

   (iii) A description of how the individual may complain to the covered entity pursuant to the complaint procedures in §164.530(d) or to the Secretary pursuant to the procedures in §160.306. The description must include the name, or title, and telephone number of the contact person or office designated in §164.530(a)(1)(ii).

(3) *Other responsibility.* If the covered entity does not maintain the protected health information that is the subject of the individual's request for access, and the covered entity knows where the requested information is maintained, the covered entity must inform the individual where to direct the request for access.

(4) Review of denial requested. If the individual has requested a review of a denial under paragraph (a)(4) of this section, the covered entity must designate a licensed health care professional, who was not directly involved in the denial to review the decision to deny access. The covered entity must promptly refer a request for review to such designated reviewing official. The designated reviewing official must determine, within a reasonable period of time, whether or not to deny the access requested based on the standards in paragraph (a)(3) of this section. The covered entity must promptly provide written notice to the individual of the determination of the designated reviewing official and take other action as required by this section to carry out the designated reviewing official's determination.

(e) *Implementation specification: Documentation.* A covered entity must document the following and retain the documentation as required by §164.530(j):

(1) The designated record sets that are subject to access by individuals; and

(2) The titles of the persons or offices responsible for receiving and processing requests for access by individuals.

§ 164.526 Amendment of protected health information.

(a) *Standard: Right to amend.* (1) *Right to amend.* An individual has the right to have a covered entity amend protected health information or a record about the individual in a designated record set for as long as the protected health information is maintained in the designated record set.

(2) *Denial of amendment.* A covered entity may deny an individual's request for amendment, if it determines that the protected health information or record that is the subject of the request:

   (i) Was not created by the covered entity, unless the individual provides a reasonable basis to believe that the originator of protected health information is no longer available to act on the requested amendment;

   (ii) Is not part of the designated record set;

   (iii) Would not be available for inspection under §164.524; or

   (iv) Is accurate and complete.

(b) *Implementation specifications: requests for amendment and timely action.* (1) *Individual's request for amendment.* The covered entity must permit an individual to request that the covered entity amend the protected health information maintained in the designated record set. The covered entity may require individuals to make requests for amendment in writing and to provide a reason to support a requested amendment, provided that it informs individuals in advance of such requirements.

(2) *Timely action by the covered entity.* (i) The covered entity must act on the individual's request for an amendment no later than 60 days after receipt of such a request, as follows.

   (A) If the covered entity grants the requested amendment, in whole or in part, it must take the actions required by paragraphs (c)(1) and (2) of this section.

   (B) If the covered entity denies the requested amendment, in whole or in part, it must provide the individual with a written denial, in accordance with paragraph (d)(1) of this section.

   (ii) If the covered entity is unable to act on the amendment within the time required by paragraph (b)(2)(i) of this section, the covered entity may extend the time for such action by no more than 30 days, provided that:

   (A) The covered entity, within the time limit set by paragraph (b)(2)(i) of this section, provides the individual with a written statement of the reasons for the delay and the date by which the covered entity will complete its action on the request; and

   (B) The covered entity may have only one such extension of time for action on a request for an amendment.

(c) *Implementation specifications: Accepting the amendment.* If the covered entity accepts the requested amendment, in whole or in part, the covered entity must comply with the following requirements.

  (1) *Making the amendment.* The covered entity must make the appropriate amendment to the protected health information or record that is the subject of the request for amendment by, at a minimum, identifying the records in the designated record set that are affected by the amendment and appending or otherwise providing a link to the location of the amendment.

  (2) *Informing the individual.* In accordance with paragraph (b) of this section, the covered entity must timely inform the individual that the amendment is accepted and obtain the individual's identification of and agreement to have the covered entity notify the relevant persons with which the amendment needs to be shared in accordance with paragraph (c)(3) of this section.

  (3) *Informing others.* The covered entity must make reasonable efforts to inform and provide the amendment within a reasonable time to:

    (i) Persons identified by the individual as having received protected health information about the individual and needing the amendment; and

    (ii) Persons, including business associates, that the covered entity knows have the protected health information that is the subject of the amendment and that may have relied, or could foreseeably rely, on such information to the detriment of the individual.

(d) *Implementation specifications: Denying the amendment.* If the covered entity denies the requested amendment, in whole or in part, the covered entity must comply with the following requirements.

  (1) *Denial.* The covered entity must provide the individual with a timely, written denial, in accordance with paragraph (b)(2) of this section. The denial must use plain language and contain:

    (i) The basis for the denial, in accordance with paragraph (a)(2) of this section;

    (ii) The individual's right to submit a written statement disagreeing with the denial and how the individual may file such a statement;

    (iii) A statement that, if the individual does not submit a statement of disagreement, the individual may request that the covered entity provide the individual's request for amendment and the denial with any future disclosures of the protected health information that is the subject of the amendment; and

    (iv) A description of how the individual may complain to the covered entity pursuant to the complaint procedures established in §164.530(d) or to the Secretary pursuant to the procedures established in §160.306. The description must include the name, or title, and telephone number of the contact person or office designated in §164.530(a)(1)(ii).

  (2) *Statement of disagreement.* The covered entity must permit the individual to submit to the covered entity a written statement disagreeing with the denial of all or part of a requested amendment and the basis of such disagreement. The covered entity may reasonably limit the length of a statement of disagreement.

  (3) *Rebuttal statement.* The covered entity may prepare a written rebuttal to the individual's statement of disagreement. Whenever such a rebuttal is prepared, the covered entity must provide a copy to the individual who submitted the statement of disagreement.

  (4) *Recordkeeping.* The covered entity must, as appropriate, identify the record or protected health information in the designated record set that is the subject of the disputed amendment and append or otherwise link the individual's request for an amendment, the covered entity's denial of the request, the individual's statement of disagreement, if any, and the covered entity's rebuttal, if any, to the designated record set.

  (5) *Future disclosures.* (i) If a statement of disagreement has been submitted by the individual, the covered entity must include the material appended in accordance with paragraph (d)(4) of this section, or, at the election of the covered entity, an accurate summary of any such information, with any subsequent disclosure of the protected health information to which the disagreement relates.

    (ii) If the individual has not submitted a written statement of disagreement, the covered entity must include the individual's request for amendment and its denial, or an accurate summary of such information, with any subsequent disclosure of the protected health information only if the individual has requested such action in accordance with paragraph (d)(1)(iii) of this section.

    (iii) When a subsequent disclosure described in paragraph (d)(5)(i) or (ii) of this section is made using a standard transaction under part 162 of this subchapter that does not permit the additional material to be included with the disclosure, the covered entity may separately transmit the material required by paragraph (d)(5)(i) or (ii) of this section, as applicable, to the recipient of the standard transaction.

(e) *Implementation specification: Actions on notices of amendment.* A covered entity that is informed by another covered entity of an amendment to an individual's protected health information, in accordance with paragraph (c)(3) of this section, must amend the protected health information in designated record sets as provided by paragraph (c)(1) of this section.

(f) *Implementation specification: Documentation.* A covered entity must document the titles of the persons or offices responsible for receiving and processing requests for amendments by individuals and retain the documentation as required by § 164.530(j).

§ 164.528 Accounting of disclosures of protected health information.

(a) *Standard: Right to an accounting of disclosures of protected health information.* (1) An individual has a right to receive an accounting of disclosures of protected health information made by a covered entity in the six years prior to the date on which the accounting is requested, except for disclosures:

   (i) To carry out treatment, payment and health care operations as provided in § 164.506;

   (ii) To individuals of protected health information about them as provided in § 164.502;

   (iii) Incident to a use or disclosure otherwise permitted or required by this subpart, as provided in § 164.502;

   (iv) Pursuant to an authorization as provided in § 164.508;

   (v) For the facility's directory or to persons involved in the individual's care or other notification purposes as provided in § 164.510;

   (vi) For national security or intelligence purposes as provided in § 164.512(k)(2);

   (vii) To correctional institutions or law enforcement officials as provided in § 164.512(k)(5);

   (viii) As part of a limited data set in accordance with § 164.514(e); or

   (ix) That occurred prior to the compliance date for the covered entity.

(2) (i) The covered entity must temporarily suspend an individual's right to receive an accounting of disclosures to a health oversight agency or law enforcement official, as provided in § 164.512(d) or (f), respectively, for the time specified by such agency or official, if such agency or official provides the covered entity with a written statement that such an accounting to the individual would be reasonably likely to impede the agency's activities and specifying the time for which such a suspension is required.

   (ii) If the agency or official statement in paragraph (a)(2)(i) of this section is made orally, the covered entity must:

   (A) Document the statement, including the identity of the agency or official making the statement;

   (B) Temporarily suspend the individual's right to an accounting of disclosures subject to the statement; and

   (C) Limit the temporary suspension to no longer than 30 days from the date of the oral statement, unless a written statement pursuant to paragraph (a)(2)(i) of this section is submitted during that time.

(3) An individual may request an accounting of disclosures for a period of time less than six years from the date of the request.

(b) *Implementation specifications: Content of the accounting.* The covered entity must provide the individual with a written accounting that meets the following requirements.

(1) Except as otherwise provided by paragraph (a) of this section, the accounting must include disclosures of protected health information that occurred during the six years (or such shorter time period at the request of the individual as provided in paragraph (a)(3) of this section) prior to the date of the request for an accounting, including disclosures to or by business associates of the covered entity.

(2) Except as otherwise provided by paragraphs (b)(3) or (b)(4) of this section, the accounting must include for each disclosure:

   (i) The date of the disclosure;

   (ii) The name of the entity or person who received the protected health information and, if known, the address of such entity or person;

   (iii) A brief description of the protected health information disclosed; and

   (iv) A brief statement of the purpose of the disclosure that reasonably informs the individual of the basis for the disclosure or, in lieu of such statement, a copy of a written request for a disclosure under §§ 164.502(a)(2)(ii) or 164.512, if any.

(3) If, during the period covered by the accounting, the covered entity has made multiple disclosures of protected health information to the same person or entity for a single purpose under §§ 164.502(a)(2)(ii) or 164.512, the accounting may, with respect to such multiple disclosures, provide:

   (i) The information required by paragraph (b)(2) of this section for the first disclosure during the accounting period;

(ii) The frequency, periodicity, or number of the disclosures made during the accounting period; and

(iii) The date of the last such disclosure during the accounting period.

(4) (i) If, during the period covered by the accounting, the covered entity has made disclosures of protected health information for a particular research purpose in accordance with §164.512(i) for 50 or more individuals, the accounting may, with respect to such disclosures for which the protected health information about the individual may have been included, provide:

(A) The name of the protocol or other research activity;

(B) A description, in plain language, of the research protocol or other research activity, including the purpose of the research and the criteria for selecting particular records;

(C) A brief description of the type of protected health information that was disclosed;

(D) The date or period of time during which such disclosures occurred, or may have occurred, including the date of the last such disclosure during the accounting period;

(E) The name, address, and telephone number of the entity that sponsored the research and of the researcher to whom the information was disclosed; and

(F) A statement that the protected health information of the individual may or may not have been disclosed for a particular protocol or other research activity.

(ii) If the covered entity provides an accounting for research disclosures, in accordance with paragraph (b)(4) of this section, and if it is reasonably likely that the protected health information of the individual was disclosed for such research protocol or activity, the covered entity shall, at the request of the individual, assist in contacting the entity that sponsored the research and the researcher.

(c) *Implementation specifications: Provision of the accounting.* (1) The covered entity must act on the individual's request for an accounting, no later than 60 days after receipt of such a request, as follows.

(i) The covered entity must provide the individual with the accounting requested; or

(ii) If the covered entity is unable to provide the accounting within the time required by paragraph (c)(1) of this section, the covered entity

may extend the time to provide the accounting by no more than 30 days, provided that:

(A) The covered entity, within the time limit set by paragraph (c)(1) of this section, provides the individual with a written statement of the reasons for the delay and the date by which the covered entity will provide the accounting; and

(B) The covered entity may have only one such extension of time for action on a request for an accounting.

(2) The covered entity must provide the first accounting to an individual in any 12 month period without charge. The covered entity may impose a reasonable, cost-based fee for each subsequent request for an accounting by the same individual within the 12 month period, provided that the covered entity informs the individual in advance of the fee and provides the individual with an opportunity to withdraw or modify the request for a subsequent accounting in order to avoid or reduce the fee.

(d) *Implementation specification: Documentation.* A covered entity must document the following and retain the documentation as required by §164.530(j):

(1) The information required to be included in an accounting under paragraph (b) of this section for disclosures of protected health information that are subject to an accounting under paragraph (a) of this section;

(2) The written accounting that is provided to the individual under this section; and

(3) The titles of the persons or offices responsible for receiving and processing requests for an accounting by individuals.

§ 164.530 Administrative requirements.

(a) (1) *Standard: Personnel designations.* (i) A covered entity must designate a privacy official who is responsible for the development and implementation of the policies and procedures of the entity.

(ii) A covered entity must designate a contact person or office who is responsible for receiving complaints under this section and who is able to provide further information about matters covered by the notice required by §164.520.

(2) *Implementation specification: Personnel designations.* A covered entity must document the personnel designations in paragraph (a)(1) of this section as required by paragraph (j) of this section.

(b) (1) *Standard: Training.* A covered entity must train all members of its workforce on the policies and procedures with respect to protected health information required by this subpart, as necessary and appropriate for the members of the workforce to carry out their function within the covered entity.

(2) *Implementation specifications: Training.* (i) A covered entity must provide training that meets the requirements of paragraph (b)(1) of this section, as follows:

    (A) To each member of the covered entity's workforce by no later than the compliance date for the covered entity;

    (B) Thereafter, to each new member of the workforce within a reasonable period of time after the person joins the covered entity's workforce; and

    (C) To each member of the covered entity's workforce whose functions are affected by a material change in the policies or procedures required by this subpart, within a reasonable period of time after the material change becomes effective in accordance with paragraph (i) of this section.

    (ii) A covered entity must document that the training as described in paragraph (b)(2)(i) of this section has been provided, as required by paragraph (j) of this section.

(c) (1) *Standard: Safeguards.* A covered entity must have in place appropriate administrative, technical, and physical safeguards to protect the privacy of protected health information.

    (2) (i) *Implementation specification: Safeguards.* A covered entity must reasonably safeguard protected health information from any intentional or unintentional use or disclosure that is in violation of the standards, implementation specifications or other requirements of this subpart.

    (ii) A covered entity must reasonably safeguard protected health information to limit incidental uses or disclosures made pursuant to an otherwise permitted or required use or disclosure.

(d) (1) *Standard: Complaints to the covered entity.* A covered entity must provide a process for individuals to make complaints concerning the covered entity's policies and procedures required by this subpart or its compliance with such policies and procedures or the requirements of this subpart.

    (2) *Implementation specification: Documentation of complaints.* As required by paragraph (j) of this section, a covered entity must document all complaints received, and their disposition, if any.

(e) (1) *Standard: Sanctions.* A covered entity must have and apply appropriate sanctions against members of its workforce who fail to comply with the privacy policies and procedures of the covered entity or the requirements of this subpart. This standard does not apply to a member of the covered entity's workforce with respect to actions that are covered by and that meet the conditions of §164.502(j) or paragraph (g)(2) of this section.

    (2) *Implementation specification: Documentation.* As required by paragraph (j) of this section, a covered entity must document the sanctions that are applied, if any.

(f) *Standard: Mitigation.* A covered entity must mitigate, to the extent practicable, any harmful effect that is known to the covered entity of a use or disclosure of protected health information in violation of its policies and procedures or the requirements of this subpart by the covered entity or its business associate.

(g) *Standard: Refraining from intimidating or retaliatory acts.* A covered entity—

    (1) May not intimidate, threaten, coerce, discriminate against, or take other retaliatory action against any individual for the exercise by the individual of any right established, or for participation in any process provided for by this subpart, including the filing of a complaint under this section; and

    (2) Must refrain from intimidation and retaliation as provided in §160.316 of this subchapter.

(h) *Standard: Waiver of rights.* A covered entity may not require individuals to waive their rights under §160.306 of this subchapter or this subpart as a condition of the provision of treatment, payment, enrollment in a health plan, or eligibility for benefits.

(i) (1) *Standard: Policies and procedures.* A covered entity must implement policies and procedures with respect to protected health information that are designed to comply with the standards, implementation specifications, or other requirements of this subpart. The policies and procedures must be reasonably designed, taking into account the size of and the type of activities that relate to protected health information undertaken by the covered entity, to ensure such compliance. This standard is not to be construed to permit or excuse an action that violates any other standard, implementation specification, or other requirement of this subpart.

    (2) *Standard: Changes to policies or procedures.* (i) A covered entity must change its policies and procedures as necessary and appropriate to comply with changes in the law, including the standards, requirements, and implementation specifications of this subpart;

    (ii) When a covered entity changes a privacy practice that is stated in the notice described in §164.520, and makes corresponding changes to its policies and procedures, it may make the changes effective for protected health information that it created or received prior to the effective date of the notice revision, if the covered entity has, in accordance with §164.520(b)(1)(v)(C), included in the notice a statement reserving its right to make such a change in its privacy practices; or

(iii) A covered entity may make any other changes to policies and procedures at any time, provided that the changes are documented and implemented in accordance with paragraph (i)(5) of this section.

(3) *Implementation specification: Changes in law.* Whenever there is a change in law that necessitates a change to the covered entity's policies or procedures, the covered entity must promptly document and implement the revised policy or procedure. If the change in law materially affects the content of the notice required by §164.520, the covered entity must promptly make the appropriate revisions to the notice in accordance with §164.520(b)(3). Nothing in this paragraph may be used by a covered entity to excuse a failure to comply with the law.

(4) *Implementation specifications: Changes to privacy practices stated in the notice.* (i) To implement a change as provided by paragraph (i)(2)(ii) of this section, a covered entity must:

(A) Ensure that the policy or procedure, as revised to reflect a change in the covered entity's privacy practice as stated in its notice, complies with the standards, requirements, and implementation specifications of this subpart;

(B) Document the policy or procedure, as revised, as required by paragraph (j) of this section; and

(C) Revise the notice as required by §164.520(b)(3) to state the changed practice and make the revised notice available as required by §164.520(c). The covered entity may not implement a change to a policy or procedure prior to the effective date of the revised notice.

(ii) If a covered entity has not reserved its right under §164.520(b)(1)(v)(C) to change a privacy practice that is stated in the notice, the covered entity is bound by the privacy practices as stated in the notice with respect to protected health information created or received while such notice is in effect. A covered entity may change a privacy practice that is stated in the notice, and the related policies and procedures, without having reserved the right to do so, provided that:

(A) Such change meets the implementation specifications in paragraphs (i)(4)(i)(A)–(C) of this section; and

(B) Such change is effective only with respect to protected health information created or received after the effective date of the notice.

(5) *Implementation specification: Changes to other policies or procedures.* A covered entity may change, at any time, a policy or procedure that does not materially affect the content of the notice required by §164.520, provided that:

(i) The policy or procedure, as revised, complies with the standards, requirements, and implementation specifications of this subpart; and

(ii) Prior to the effective date of the change, the policy or procedure, as revised, is documented as required by paragraph (j) of this section.

(j) (1) *Standard: Documentation.* A covered entity must:

(i) Maintain the policies and procedures provided for in paragraph (i) of this section in written or electronic form;

(ii) If a communication is required by this subpart to be in writing, maintain such writing, or an electronic copy, as documentation; and

(iii) If an action, activity, or designation is required by this subpart to be documented, maintain a written or electronic record of such action, activity, or designation.

(2) *Implementation specification: Retention period.* A covered entity must retain the documentation required by paragraph (j)(1) of this section for six years from the date of its creation or the date when it last was in effect, whichever is later.

(k) *Standard: Group health plans.* (1) A group health plan is not subject to the standards or implementation specifications in paragraphs (a) through (f) and (i) of this section, to the extent that:

(i) The group health plan provides health benefits solely through an insurance contract with a health insurance issuer or an HMO; and

(ii) The group health plan does not create or receive protected health information, except for:

(A) Summary health information as defined in §164.504(a); or

(B) Information on whether the individual is participating in the group health plan, or is enrolled in or has disenrolled from a health insurance issuer or HMO offered by the plan.

(2) A group health plan described in paragraph (k)(1) of this section is subject to the standard and implementation specification in paragraph (j) of this section only with respect to plan documents amended in accordance with §164.504(f).

§ 164.532 Transition provisions.

(a) *Standard: Effect of prior authorizations.* Notwithstanding §§ 164.508 and 164.512(i), a covered entity may use or disclose protected health information, consistent with paragraphs (b) and (c) of this section, pursuant to an authorization or other express legal permission obtained from an individual permitting the use or disclosure of protected health information, informed consent of the individual to participate in research, or a waiver of informed consent by an IRB.

(b) *Implementation specification: Effect of prior authorization for purposes other than research.* Notwithstanding any provisions in § 164.508, a covered entity may use or disclose protected health information that it created or received prior to the applicable compliance date of this subpart pursuant to an authorization or other express legal permission obtained from an individual prior to the applicable compliance date of this subpart, provided that the authorization or other express legal permission specifically permits such use or disclosure and there is no agreed-to restriction in accordance with § 164.522(a).

(c) *Implementation specification: Effect of prior permission for research.* Notwithstanding any provisions in §§ 164.508 and 164.512(i), a covered entity may, to the extent allowed by one of the following permissions, use or disclose, for research, protected health information that it created or received either before or after the applicable compliance date of this subpart, provided that there is no agreed-to restriction in accordance with § 164.522(a), and the covered entity has obtained, prior to the applicable compliance date, either:

  (1) An authorization or other express legal permission from an individual to use or disclose protected health information for the research;

  (2) The informed consent of the individual to participate in the research; or

  (3) A waiver, by an IRB, of informed consent for the research, in accordance with 7 CFR 1c.116(d), 10 CFR 745.116(d), 14 CFR 1230.116(d), 15 CFR 27.116(d), 16 CFR 1028.116(d), 21 CFR 50.24, 22 CFR 225.116(d), 24 CFR 60.116(d), 28 CFR 46.116(d), 32 CFR 219.116(d), 34 CFR 97.116(d), 38 CFR 16.116(d), 40 CFR 26.116(d), 45 CFR 46.116(d), 45 CFR 690.116(d), or 49 CFR 11.116(d), provided that a covered entity must obtain authorization in accordance with § 164.508 if, after the compliance date, informed consent is sought from an individual participating in the research.

(d) *Standard: Effect of prior contracts or other arrangements with business associates.* Notwithstanding any other provisions of this subpart, a covered entity, other than a small health plan, may disclose protected health information to a business associate and may allow a business associate to create, receive, or use protected health information on its behalf pursuant to a written contract or other written arrangement with such business associate that does not comply with §§ 164.502(e) and 164.504(e) consistent with the requirements, and only for such time, set forth in paragraph (e) of this section.

(e) *Implementation specification: Deemed compliance—*
  (1) *Qualification.* Notwithstanding other sections of this subpart, a covered entity, other than a small health plan, is deemed to be in compliance with the documentation and contract requirements of §§ 164.502(e) and 164.504(e), with respect to a particular business associate relationship, for the time period set forth in paragraph (e)(2) of this section, if:

  (i) Prior to October 15, 2002, such covered entity has entered into and is operating pursuant to a written contract or other written arrangement with a business associate for such business associate to perform functions or activities or provide services that make the entity a business associate; and

  (ii) The contract or other arrangement is not renewed or modified from October 15, 2002, until the compliance date set forth in § 164.534.

  (2) *Limited deemed compliance period.* A prior contract or other arrangement that meets the qualification requirements in paragraph (e) of this section, shall be deemed compliant until the earlier of:

  (i) The date such contract or other arrangement is renewed or modified on or after the compliance date set forth in § 164.534; or

  (ii) April 14, 2004.

  (3) *Covered entity responsibilities.* Nothing in this section shall alter the requirements of a covered entity to comply with part 160, subpart C of this subchapter and §§ 164.524, 164.526, 164.528, and 164.530(f) with respect to protected health information held by a business associate.

Glossary

Abortion Termination of a pregnancy before the viability of the fetus.

Abstracting The process of collecting, tabulating, aggregating, and summarizing selected data elements.

Abuse A pattern of practices or customs that is unsound or inconsistent with ethical business, fiscal, or health care practices or customs.

Acceptance process A step in the procurement activity where the buyer examines the goods received or the services contracted to determine whether they comply with the purchase order.

Access control The level of permission granted to a particular user in a database.

Account A separate recording for each asset and liability.

Accountant The business person who keeps, examines, and adjusts the financial records of an organization.

Accounting The system for recording, stating, or auditing business transactions.

Accreditation The process by which an external entity reviews an organization or program of study to determine if the organization or program meets certain predetermined standards.

Accrual accounting The recording of an activity at the time the activity occurs.

Active euthanasia The practice of actions that speed the process of dying; also called *positive euthanasia*.

Administrative bodies Executive branch agencies that operate to interpret law and to promulgate and enforce rules and regulations; found at the federal, state, and local levels.

Administrative data The basic identification and financial data routinely collected from every patient.

Administrative law The decisions and regulations issued by government agencies that are charged with interpreting statutory law.

Admission register A listing of all patients admitted to a particular health care facility, typically arranged in chronological order by date and time of admission.

Admission review A step in the utilization review process performed during admission to the facility as a means to determine whether the admission or procedure/treatment plan is medically necessary and appropriate for the setting.

Admissions coordinator A health care professional who directs the patient registration functions, setting guidelines for preregistration and registration of patients and managing the computerized registration process.

Advance directive Written instructions describing the kind of health care the patient wishes to have or not have in the event that she becomes incapacitated.

Affinity diagram A diagram that organizes information into a visual pattern to show the relationship between factors in a problem.

Agent In epidemiology, the factor that causes a disease.

Aggregate data collection The combining of specific data into larger groupings that can be used to describe a bigger concept. For example, disease rates (e.g. tuberculosis) in small areas are grouped together for a location (e.g., a state) but will not identify individual patients.

Allied health professional An individual, other than a physician, dentist, nurse, or physician assistant, who has graduated from an educational program in a science relating to health care and shares the responsibility (with clinicians) for the delivery of health care services to the patient.

Allografts Organ or tissue transplants using a donor's body part.

Ambulatory health care The care given to patients who are not confined to an institutional bed as inpatients at the time care is rendered.

American Health Information Management Association (AHIMA) The primary professional association for health information management professionals in the United States.

Analysis and results Steps in a research study that show the statistical methods of analysis employed in the study and any findings of statistical significance in the research.

Analytic epidemiology A type of epidemiology in which an investigative technique is used to determine a statistical correlation between a specific factor and a given disease.

ANOVA (or *F* test) A test performed when a need exists to compare more than two groups.

Appeal The action of asking a higher court to review the activities in a trial court to determine whether an error occurred.

Application program Software that performs tasks on behalf of the end user and are typically self-contained.

Application service provider An organization that—for a fee—provides customers with access to software applications located on servers away from the customer's site.

Applied research Research that is designed to answer a practical question.

Applied statistics The use of statistics and statistical theory in real-life situations.

Artificial insemination The act of planting sperm into a woman's body to facilitate conception.

ASC X12 An ANSI-accredited standards development organization that develops specifications for communication between software applications.

Assault A threat that does not involve physical contact.

Assent A minor's agreement to participate in research.

Asset Something of value that can be used to serve an organization's needs.

Assigning work The matching of an individual employee with specific work that needs to be performed.

At-will employment An employment arrangement that allows the employer to terminate the employee at any time and allows the employee to leave the employer at any time.

Auditors Accountants who perform inspections of an organization's financial affairs.

Audits The activities associated with the inspection of an organization's accounts, reports, and statements.

Audit trails The paths that clearly show the sequence of events leading to an entry in a given account.

Authentication The act or process of ensuring the entry in a record for both accuracy and authorship.

Authorship The method of identifying the health care provider who made an entry in a record.

Autografts Organ or tissue transplants using one's own body parts.

Autonomy An ethical concept referring to independence, self-determination, or freedom.

Autopsy rate The total number of autopsies (postmortem) performed on inpatient deaths for a period divided by the total number of inpatient deaths (including newborns, children, and adults).

Backup regime A portion of a disaster recovery plan that allows for copying on a regular basis the data stored on a computer or server so that they can be restored should the original data be destroyed.

Balance billing Any charges not paid by the private insurance company or a patient's employer become the responsibility of the patient.

Balance sheet A financial report that summarizes the true financial condition of an organization, showing its assets, liabilities, and the owners' equity in the organization at a specified point in time.

Bar graph A method used to present the frequency of data through the use of horizontal and vertical axes. Typically, the horizontal axis (*x*-axis) shows discrete categories, and the vertical axis (*y*-axis) shows the number or frequency.

Battery Physical contact that involves injury or offense.

Benchmarking The structured process of comparing outcomes with those of an acknowledged superior performer as a means of improving performance.

Beneficence An ethical concept referring to the qualities of kindness, mercy, and charity.

Best interests standard An ethical concept used when determining what is in the best interest of an individual in the event that the individual cannot make such a decision herself.

Bidirectional data flow The flow of data that begins in a linear arrangement but changes by rearranging the data so that it returns to the sender at some point and then continues toward the original linear path.

Bioethics The study of ethical issues that result from technologic and scientific advances, especially in biology and medicine.

Birth register A listing of those patients born at a particular health care facility, typically arranged in chronological order by date of birth.

Bit The basic unit of measure for computer storage; a single digit representing either 0 or 1.

Bivariate regression A form of regression analysis in which the focus is on two variables to provide an answer.

Blind study A variation of clinical trials wherein the participant is not informed about which kind of therapy she is receiving, absent what is required for informed consent, during the course of the clinical trial.

Block grants Designated amounts of funding provided by Congress to individual states that decide where and how to spend the monies provided.

Blue Cross/Blue Shield Association The single largest trade association of private health care insurers in the United States.

Board certified A specialty board of physicians has determined through rigorous examination that the specialist may limit her practice due to her advanced training and demonstration of competence.

Bond rating An indication of the likelihood that a bond issuer will repay both the principal and interest to the buyer.

Bookkeeper The businessperson who records entries in the financial records of an organization.

Bookkeeping The record-keeping aspect of accounting.

Bottom-up process A budget process that allows lower-level and middle-level managers the opportunity to contribute to development of priorities and objectives in the budget process.

Brainstorming An idea-generation method in which ideas are offered about a particular topic in an unrestrained manner by all members of a group within a short time period.

Breach of contract The failure of the parties to a contract to perform according to the contract's terms.

Budget An organization's revenue and expenditure plan.

Budget organization plan A financial tool that documents an organization's budgetary processes and procedures and generally contains three elements: organizational structure; duties and responsibilities; and operational processes.

Budgeting A step in the planning process involving all money matters, including the planning for, allocation of, requests for, accountings of, and control of financial resources.

Bylaws The framework used to identify the roles and responsibilities of the board and its members.

Byte A unit of measure for computer storage or memory size and for data transfer speed; a group of eight bits.

Cable modem A hardware device that works via cable television connections, allowing one to transmit and receive all data as digital signals.

Cancer registry A listing of patients who have been diagnosed with or received treatment for a form of cancer and certain benign conditions. Also includes the topography, morphology, and other information relevant to the disease. May include data on the patient's follow-up treatment and length of survival.

Capital Money that is invested in a business to help that business grow.

Capital expenditure budget A budget focusing on an organization's long-term projects.

Capitation A payment method using a fixed amount per member per month to a contracted provider for health care services, regardless of the quantity or nature of the services rendered.

Career development The planned efforts and activities employed to align an individual's career needs with an organization's workforce requirements.

Case-control study A retrospective observational study in which the focus is on the event to be studied and not the risk factor.

Case fatality rate The measurement of how deadly a disease is within a given population.

Case management The ongoing review of patient care in various health care settings related to assuring the medical necessity of the encounter and the appropriateness of the clinical services provided.

Case managers Also known as *utilization coordinators*; employees with responsibility for managing the review process and coordinating the patient's care with physicians and other members of the treatment team. These employees are often trained as nurses or health information management professionals.

Case mix The type and volume of patients a hospital treats.

Case mix management The manner in which an organization analyzes the case mix as it relates to reimbursement and the organization's financial health.

Cash accounting The recording of an activity only when cash is received and paid, regardless of when services were performed.

Cash budget A budget that focuses on the amount of cash flow in an organization on a weekly, monthly, or quarterly basis so that the organization knows how much money it will have on hand to cover the payments to be made during those time frames.

Cash flow statement A financial report that summarizes the cash inflows and outflows of an organization at a specified point in time.

CATCH Comprehensive Assessment for Tracking Community Health; a performance initiative in the public health context developed by the University of South Florida.

Categorical data A set of data in which the values belonging to the set can be sorted according to logical categories, wherein no category overlaps another category (e.g., sorting towels according to color).

Categorical imperative A fundamental principle of deontology in which a command derived from a principle does not allow exceptions; developed by philosopher Immanuel Kant.

Cause-and-effect diagram A diagram that identifies major categories of factors that influence an effect, and the subfactors within each major category; sometimes referred to as a *fishbone diagram*.

CD-ROM drive An optical storage medium that uses the same technology as music compact discs and stores vast amounts of information. The acronym stands for "compact disc read-only memory."

Census The number of inpatients present in a health care facility at any time.

Central processing unit A piece of hardware used in personal computers that is responsible for executing programs, performing calculations, and moving data between memory and long-term storage media.

Certificate of destruction A document that shows what data or records were destroyed, who destroyed those data or records, and the method used for that destruction.

Certificate-of-need program A state program that requires health care facilities to justify the need to purchase new equipment, buy or create buildings, and offer new services.

CHAMPVA Civilian Health and Medical Program of the Department of Veterans Affairs; A federal government program designed to finance and provide care for veterans of the armed services who are permanently and totally disabled, survivors of veterans who died from service-related conditions, and survivors of military personnel who died in the line of duty.

Change management A management theory that addresses large-scale change within an organization's operation or structure.

Chargemaster A tally or master listing developed by a health care provider of all the elements involved in providing the service to be billed.

Chief financial officer The businessperson who oversees an organization's finances.

Chiropractor A health care professional with specialized education and training who treats the body's structural and neurological systems.

Chi-square (χ^2) A predictive statistic that measures the relationship between two variables that are categorical (placing subjects into categories).

Civil law Law that does not include criminal law; primarily focuses on private rights and remedies.

Claim A statement submitted to a third-party payer seeking to be paid for the services rendered and/or supplies provided to the patient by the health care provider.

Claims examiner A professional who reviews health care claims for medical necessity and reasonableness of costs.

Classical management A management approach that focuses on the organization as a whole, rather than on individual functions, to improve performance.

Classification systems Groupings of similar items, such as diseases and procedures, that serve as a way to organize related entities for easy retrieval.

Clinical data The collected and maintained data that relate to the patient's course of treatment and care.

Clinical data repository The electronic storage of data and information from individual patient medical records.

Clinical information system A system that has as its central focus clinical data, not financial or billing information.

Clinical privileges The permission granted and the limits set by a hospital's governing board that allow the physician to treat patients at the hospital.

Clinical research Research performed in the real world where control over variables may be difficult.

Clinical research associate A health care professional who assists in the design, implementation, and monitoring of clinical research studies, including the design of data collection instruments and the preparation of reports concerning study findings.

Clinical terminology A recognized system of preferred clinical or medical terminology.

Clinical trials Investigations that assess the difference between two clinical populations with respect to the outcome of therapy or treatments using human beings as the subjects.

Clinical vocabulary A vocabulary that specializes in words or phrases of a clinical or medical nature.

Closed-panel arrangement A setup whereby physicians may only treat those patients who are members of an HMO plan.

Coaching The process of equipping people with the tools, knowledge, and opportunities they need to develop themselves and become more effective.

Codes of ethics Written lists of a profession's values and standards of conduct.

Coding The process by which a numeric code listed in a classification system is assigned to data found in the health record (e.g., diagnoses and procedures).

Coding compliance program The efforts made to establish effective internal controls that detect, correct, and prevent coding errors and promote adherence to the applicable local, state, and federal laws and regulations and the program requirements of federal, state, and private health plans.

Cohort study A prospective observational study that follows two or more groups in a population that are or are not exposed to the risk factor under investigation.

Cold feed The process of having one computer application (e.g., Admission, Discharge, and Transfer, or ADT system) directly deposit data elements into a specialized data collection system.

Common law Judicial decisions that interpret relevant constitutional provisions, federal or state statutes, regulations, and previous court decisions.

Common Procedural Terminology (CPT) A coding system developed by the American Medical Association for use in physician offices.

Common rule Regulations jointly promulgated by several federal departments and agencies that address protections for human subjects involved in research.

Communication The process of sharing meaning through the intentional or unintentional sending and receiving of messages.

Communities of Practice (CoP) A Web-based program that provides a virtual network for AHIMA members who share common interests.

Community mental health care A health care delivery system designed for mentally ill patients to receive the least restrictive alternative if each patient is able to control her behavior and cooperate with treatment plans.

Comparative justice An ethical concept that refers to balancing the competing interests of individuals and groups against one another, with no independent standard used to make the comparison.

Compensation The wages, salaries, incentives, and supplemental benefits provided to staff.

Complaint A written document that describes the jurisdiction of the court in which the lawsuit is filed, the grounds for the lawsuit, and the type of relief the plaintiff demands.

Completeness To be entire, or lacking in nothing.

Compliance The efforts to establish a culture that promotes prevention, detection, and resolution of instances of conduct that do not conform to applicable local, state, and federal laws and regulations.

Compliance program A program that ensures the use of effective internal controls that promote adherence to applicable local, state, and federal laws and regulations and the program requirements of federal, state, and private health plans.

Component state associations (CSA) Health information management associations located in every state, Washington, D.C., and Puerto Rico. The component state associations provide leadership, networking, and professional education opportunities at the state level for AHIMA members.

Computer room A separate room that holds computer equipment.

Computer virus A small computer program capable of copying itself from one computer to another; almost exclusively written to cause damage on the computers they infect.

Conclusion and discussion Steps in research study that attempt to integrate the results into other findings in the field and show whether support existed for the hypothesis listed in the first stage of the study.

Concurrency control The ability of a database to resolve the conflict between two simultaneous uses of the same portion of the same database.

Concurrent data collection Data can be gathered at the time they are entered through the use of modern interface and transmission standards.

Concurrent review A step in the utilization review process that involves assuring continued medical necessity and appropriateness of the care being delivered; also referred to as *continued stay review.*

Conduct problems Problems that relate to the employee's ability to comply with organizational rules governing employee behavior.

Confidentiality The obligation of the health care provider to maintain patient information in a manner that will not permit dissemination beyond the health care provider.

Conflict of interest Situations in which a professional's interests or commitments compromise his judgment, research report, or communications to research subjects, participants, patients, or clients; may be of a personal or financial nature or may involve competing loyalties.

Constitutional law Provisions found in constitutions; considered superior or supreme above laws that arise from other sources.

Consultation rate The number of patients receiving a consultation by a physician whose expertise is different from the patient's attending physician, divided by the total number of patients discharged.

Continuous data The values that lie within a certain range; examples include height, weight, temperature, length, and the time required to run a mile.

Continuous quality improvement The systematic, team-based approach to process and performance improvement.

Continuum of care The concept of matching an individual with the appropriate level and type of health, social, psychological, or medical care of service within an organization or across multiple organizations.

Contraception A means of family planning wherein efforts are used to prevent or interfere with conception or impregnation through voluntary or artificial means.

Contract dispute A written claim, demand, or assertion of a contracting party that includes a detailed statement of the legal and factual basis of the dispute and a proposal for resolution.

Control Within the research context, the investigator's ability to eliminate interfering and irrelevant influences so that only the variables may be manipulated and therefore measured.

Control chart A graph with statistically-generated upper and lower control limits used to measure key processes over time.

Controlled clinical trials Clinical trials that utilize randomization.

Controller The businessperson who assesses the organization's financing and manages its cash, credit, and inventories.

Controlling The process of ensuring that activities are accomplished as planned and correcting any significant deviations from the plan.

Core measurements Standardized sets of valid, reliable, and evidence-based measures.

Corporate negligence The failure of a hospital, entrusted with the task of providing accommodations necessary to carry out its purpose, to follow the established standard of conduct with which it should conform.

Correlation A mutual relation or interdependence between two or more things.

Cost accounting The day-to-day management of an organization's cash, credit, inventory, liabilities, and expenses; sometimes referred to as *managerial accounting*.

Cost allocation The activity of determining how to allocate overhead or indirect expenses to a given charge in order to obtain reimbursement for those overhead expenses.

Cost/benefit analysis The systematic method of assessing the economic desirability of alternatives based upon evaluating initial and ongoing expenses (costs) against an expected return (benefits).

Court order A ruling by a court that authorizes disclosure that would otherwise be prohibited by statute and regulation.

Court system The judicial branch of government; that governmental branch vested with the authority to adjudicate and resolve disputes of parties who cannot resolve their disputes themselves.

Coverage Those health care services previously identified as reimbursable under the insurance plan.

Covered entities Health plans, clearinghouses (e.g., claims data processors), and health care providers engaged in HIPAA transactions.

CPT Common Procedural Terminology; a coding system developed by the American Medical Association for use in physicians' offices.

Crackers Criminal hackers.

Credentialing process The process of obtaining written proof of qualifications, including diplomas conferred by educational programs; certification or registration conferred by professional groups; and legal licenses conferred by governmental agencies.

Credits Increases in assets and liabilities.

Criminal law Law that refers to conduct the government has declared injurious to the public order, with specific punishments identified for violations.

Criteria The standards upon which judgments can be made, or the expected level(s) of achievement.

Critical path The longest sequence in a PERT network.

Cross-sectional study Studies that examine the current rates of disease frequency against other factors; also called a *prevalence study*.

C-section rate The percentage of deliveries performed by Cesarean section as compared to all deliveries.

Daily inpatient census The number of patients present at the official census-taking time each day plus the number of patients who were admitted and discharged that same day.

Data Raw facts and figures.

Data aggregation studies Clinical research that involves the collection of data from large numbers of medical records without focusing on direct patient contact.

Data analyst A health information management professional who is responsible for analyzing records and data both quantitatively and qualitatively.

Database The structured storage or collection of data on multiple entities and their relationships, often arranged for ease and speed of retrieval.

Database management The ability to manage a database so as to create, modify, delete, and view given data as necessary.

Data dictionary The standardized definitions of each data element in a database.

Data element A single fact or measurement.

Data flow The movement of data through a system and to those in need of it.

Data mart A subset of a data warehouse, generally restricted to a single business function/process or group of related business functions/processes targeted toward a particular business group.

Data mining The process of finding unknown dependencies in large data sets using automated means.

Data quality The high grade, superiority, or excellence of data.

Data Safety Monitoring Board   A group, frequently distinct from an institutional review board (IRB), that provides information to the IRB concerning participant safety and study integrity.

Data Safety Monitoring Plan   Mechanisms used by study investigators to evaluate study data to ensure participant safety and study integrity, with information reported to the IRB.

Data set   A list of recommended data elements with uniform definitions.

Data standards   Uniform uses of common terms and methods for sharing data.

Data warehouses   Very large databases that store both historical and current information from a variety of sources and are optimized for fast query answering.

Death register   A listing of patients who died at a particular health care facility, typically arranged in chronological order by date of death; may be differentiated by age (e.g., fetal death registry).

Debits   Decreases in assets and liabilities.

Decision making   The act of reaching a conclusion; part of the directing function of management.

Deeming authority   Compliance with the requirements and standards of accrediting organizations may substitute for compliance with the federal government's Medicare Conditions of Participation for Hospitals as published by the Centers for Medicare and Medicaid Services.

Defamation   The wrongful injuring of another person's reputation.

Defendant   The person or organization that is sued by the plaintiff.

De-identified health information   Information that is stripped of individual identifiers.

De-identified patient data   Data that cannot be traced to a particular patient.

Delegating   To entrust another person with selected powers and functions, who then acts on behalf of the person making the request.

Delegating authority   To transfer some of a manager's decision-making authority to subordinates.

Delegation of authority   The establishment of limits upon the authority of individuals to act within an organization.

Demographic statistics   The study of human populations, focusing on the size of the populations and how they change over time.

Dentist   An individual with specialized education and training who is concerned with the teeth, oral cavity, and associated structures of the mouth.

Deontology   An ethical decision-making theory based on moral rules and unchanging principles that are derived from reason and can be applied universally; sometimes referred to as *formalism* or *duty orientation.*

Descriptive epidemiology   A type of epidemiology in which activities focus on investigating and describing the occurrence and distribution of disease in a population.

Descriptive research   Research that describes individuals, groups, or situations as a means to apply the acquired knowledge to future individuals, groups, or situations.

Descriptive statistics   The statistics used to characterize or summarize a given population.

Diagnosis-related groups (DRG)   A classification system that groups patients who are medically related by diagnosis, treatment, and length of stay, using the International Classification of Diseases, ninth revision, Clinical Modification codes.

Digital imaging system   A system by which paper documents are scanned on devices that work similar to a photocopier, allowing the image to be saved to an optical disc, a compact disc, or magnetic tape.

Disability   A physical or mental impairment that substantially limits one or more of the major life activities of an employee, a record of such an impairment, or being regarded as having such an impairment.

Disaster planning   A planning method that focuses on how to minimize the effect disruptions or destructions may have on organizations.

Disaster recovery plans   The blueprints used to resume immediate computer operations in the event of a problem.

Disbursements   Cash paid.

Discharge register   A listing of patients discharged from a particular health care facility, typically arranged in chronological order by date of discharge.

Discrete data Those data in which the specific values are distinct and separate, and points between the values are not considered valid. Two typical examples are the grades assigned to a course (A+, A, A−,B+, B, B−, etc.) and blood groups (O, A, B, AB).

Disease index A listing of diseases and conditions according to the classification system used by a health care facility or private provider.

Disk drive A hardware device that depends on reading and writing data from a rotating disk for its operation.

Disparagement The belittling or criticizing of the skills, knowledge, or qualifications of another professional.

Distribution A pattern with an upper limit and a lower limit and a clustering of scores around a middle measurement.

Distributive justice An ethical concept that refers to the fair distribution of burdens and benefits using an independent standard.

Diversity The myriad of differences between and among people in a defined setting.

Document and repository manager A professional who is responsible for ensuring long-term data integrity and access through the development of retention policies and procedures, determination of appropriate media for data and record storage, and maintenance of data control inventories.

Domain name The name given to a server or group of servers connected to the Internet; the wording following the @ symbol in an e-mail address.

Double-blind study A variation of clinical trials in which neither the patient nor the clinicians are aware of which participants have been assigned to receive the experimental intervention.

Double-effect principle A principle that recognizes that ethical choices may result in untoward outcomes; one may proceed with an ethical choice presenting a double effect if the untoward outcome is not the intended outcome but a secondary outcome, and is outweighed by the intended positive or neutral outcome.

DSL Digital subscriber line; a means of transmitting data as digital signals that requires the use of traditional telephone wiring; uses a higher frequency than is needed for voice transmissions.

DSM-IV Diagnostic and Statistical Manual of Mental Disorders, published by the American Psychiatric Association and used to classify mental health issues.

Durable power of attorney for health care A written document that allows a competent individual to name someone else to exercise health-related decisions on her behalf in the event that she becomes incapacitated or unable to make decisions; a form of advance directive.

Dysfunctional conflicts Conflicts that result in destructive behavior and prevent the organization from achieving its goals.

E-discovery A form of discovery that seeks information stored electronically.

Educational informatics A subset of the informatics discipline that applies technology to facilitate the learning process; sometimes referred to as *e-learning*.

Efficacy Within the research context, the benefits that accrue to the individual receiving care.

Efficiency Within the research context, the resources consumed by the treatment.

E-health consumers Individuals whose individually identifiable health information is collected, maintained, or displayed over the Internet.

E-health organizations Entities and organizations that collect and display individually identifiable health information over the Internet.

E-learning A subset of the informatics discipline that applies technology to facilitate the learning process; sometimes referred to as *educational informatics*.

Electronic data interchange (EDI) A method of electronic mail messaging conveyed between computers without manual intervention.

Electronic health (e-health) Health improvement and disease management techniques that use the Web and other interactive electronic communication tools.

Electronic health record (EHR) A record that resides in an electronic system specifically designed to support users by providing accessibility to complete and accurate data, alerts, reminders, clinical decision support systems, links to medical knowledge, and other aids.

Emergency room register A listing of patients treated at a particular health care facility's emergency room, typically arranged in chronological order.

Employee An individual hired by another, such as a business firm, to work for wages or salary.

Employer Those persons, businesses, or organizations that provide work, engage services or labor, and pay for the work performed.

Employment The process of providing work, engaging services or labor, and paying for the work performed.

Encoders Software tools that incorporate the text and logic of coding systems in an automated form. These programs operate by browsing the classification system to match the language contained in the patient health record.

Encryption The mechanism employed so that no third party can eavesdrop on communication.

Endemic Diseases that are habitually peculiar to a particular locality.

Enterprise master patient index A single listing or database, shared by multiple health care facilities, that contains information about the patients treated at the facilities.

Entrepreneur A person who conceives of a product or service idea, pursues opportunities for innovation, and starts an organization to provide the product or services.

Environment In epidemiology, the aggregate of the things, conditions, or influences that surround the host, (e.g., physical, biological, social, or economic).

Environmental analysis The process of assessing an organization's external environment, including an evaluation of national, political, economic, social, legal, and technological forces that may affect the organization.

Epidemics Diseases that affect many persons in a community, area, or region at the same time, arising from a common source and clearly in excess of normal expectancy.

Epidemiology The study of the cause and distribution of diseases.

EPO Exclusive provider organization; a form of managed care similar to a PPO except that the patient must stay within the provider network to receive care.

Eponyms Words based on the personal names of people, such as Addison's disease.

Ergonomics The design of products, processes, and systems to meet the requirements and capacities of those people who use them.

Essential job functions Those functions and duties that are required for a particular job; the core functions and duties of the job.

Ethical acts Actions that can be judged as proper or acceptable behavior based on some standard of right and wrong.

Ethical challenges Situations in which no clear-cut "right" answer exists, and an individual is required to make a choice between two or more equally unfavorable alternatives or between a neutral alternative and a tempting but unfavorable alternative.

Ethical concepts Abstract ideas or thoughts dealing with ethics that help to serve as part of the values that undergird decision making.

Ethical theories Systematic statements or plans of principles used to deal with ethical dilemmas.

Ethics The study of moral choices that conform to professional standards of conduct.

Ethics committees Groups formed within an organization to establish new and evaluate existing ethics codes and corporate policies, and to address ethical issues that arise in the workplace.

Etiquette The principles of how human beings relate to one another under certain circumstances.

Eugenics The effort to improve the human species through control of hereditary factors in mating; a breeding practice aimed at producing superior offspring.

Euthanasia The act or practice of causing death painlessly, with the aim to end suffering.

Executive orders Orders issued by the chief executive at either the federal or state level; used to interpret or implement a provision of a constitution or law.

Expense budget A budget that focuses on the costs of an organization.

Expenses Amount paid.

Experimental epidemiology A type of epidemiology in which an investigative technique is used to determine the cause of disease using controlled experiments.

Experimental research Research that uses variables, control, and randomization in an experiment.

Explanation of benefits A statement sent to both the health care provider and the patient explaining what amounts the third-party payer has paid associated with the claim submitted by the health care provider.

Explicit knowledge The knowledge that can be recorded, archived, codified, or embedded into products.

Extensible markup language (XML) A programming language that works with raw data, allowing it to be treated in a similar fashion.

Extranet An intranet system that allows selected external users limited access to private networks.

Failure to warn The doctrine describing a psychotherapist's failure to take steps to protect an innocent third party from a dangerous patient; sometimes referred to as *failure /to protect.*

False imprisonment The unlawful restraint of an individual's personal liberty, or unlawful restraining or confining of an individual.

Family planning The behavior associated with controlling the size of one's family or spacing the births within that family.

Fee for service A payment method in which a fee is paid for each service rendered.

Fidelity An ethical concept referring to faithfulness, loyalty, and devotion to one's obligations or duties.

Finance The science of money, credit, and banking. In the business world, this term refers to raising, managing, and making money for the organization.

Financial accounting The periodic assessment of an organization's financial health on a monthly, quarterly, or annual basis.

Financial Accounting Standards Board (FASB) The governing body of the accounting profession.

Financial management The efficient and effective use of financial resources to achieve the organization's mission.

Firewall Hardware or software that sits at the perimeter of a network or single computer and permits or denies access to the network or single computer; monitors all traffic from the Internet.

Five "why"s An idea-generation method in which the root cause(s) of a problem are discovered by asking the question "why" at least five times in a given discussion.

Floppy disk A removable flexible disk made of plastic and coated with a magnetic oxide layer.

Flowchart A diagram, often using standard geometric symbols, that shows steps in a sequence of operations.

Force field analysis A tool used to prioritize ideas, applicable to identifying and visualizing the relationships of significant influencing forces.

Forecasting A financial projection of how an organization is likely to perform in the future.

Forms control The actions that focus on the management of forms already designed, including how those forms will be amended or changed over time.

Forms design The actions that focus on determining the purpose, use, and users of a form and the data elements contained within it.

Fraction A part of an entire whole.

Fraud The intentional deception of another to that person's detriment.

Frequency polygon A method used to present data, showing how a single variable is used; presented in line rather than bar form.

Fringe benefits Services and programs offered to employees that supplement wages and salaries.

Full-time employee An employee who works 30 hours per week or more.

Functional conflicts Conflicts of a constructive nature that support the goals of the organization.

Functional limitation A physical or mental limitation of a major life activity caused by a disability.

Gantt chart A graphic representation of the time relationships in a project.

General ledger The complete set of accounts established and maintained by an organization.

Generalists Physicians who conduct a wide or unlimited practice, to include comprehensive care of an individual or family.

Generally accepted accounting principles The official rule book of accounting represented by thousands of pages of rules and guidelines.

Gene therapy Involves genetically altering organisms for various purposes; sometimes referred to as *genetic engineering.*

Genetic screening A laboratory test wherein a person's genetic makeup is tested to reveal a predisposition to certain diseases or other abnormalities; a form of prenatal testing.

Goals The statements of the process by which the future will be reached. Goals specify a course of action in support of objectives.

Graphical user interface A method of displaying text and graphics on a computer screen.

Grievance A complaint regarding policies and procedures of an organization or a protest of treatment thought or perceived to be unjust by an employee.

Groupers Software programs that use branching logic to arrive at the most accurate diagnosis-related group.

Hackers Persons who gain unauthorized access to computer systems and networks.

Hard drive A magnetic storage device that stores individual data on the surface of a rapidly rotating metal disk that is coated with a film of magnetizable material.

Hardware The physical electronic components of a computer system.

HCPCS Healthcare Common Procedure Coding System; an expanded version of CPT that includes codes for nonphysician services.

Health care fraud and abuse The false misrepresentation or intentional deception of fact that is a departure from reasonable use and could result in unauthorized payment.

Health care informatics A discipline that focuses on studying both the structure and general properties of information, and the design and implementation of technology to use and communicate that information. This discipline concentrates on how to use technology to facilitate acquiring, processing, interpreting, using, and communicating health care data.

Health information The meaningful data relating to the health of an individual that is created or received by a health care provider, health plan, public health authority, employer, life insurer, school or university, or health care clearinghouse.

Health information administrator A professional who focuses on managing computer-based or paper-based record systems and ensuring compliance with external and internal standards relating to health records and information.

Health information department That area of an organization responsible for managing appropriate use of and access to patient-specific health information.

Health information department director A professional, who may be a Registered Health Information Administrator

(RHIA) or a Registered Health Information Technician (RHIT), responsible for the administrative functions of the health information department.

Health information management The body of knowledge required and the practice of managing a health record and the data contained within it, all in compliance with regulatory, accrediting, quality, and ethical standards, and with the goal to facilitate health care delivery and decision making for multiple purposes across diverse organizations, settings, and disciplines.

Health information technician A professional who focuses on completeness, accuracy, and proper entry of health care data, using computer applications to improve patient care and control health care costs.

Health insurance specialist A professional who reviews health care claims for medical necessity and reasonableness of costs.

Health Level Seven (HL7) An ANSI-accredited standards development organization that develops specifications to allow different health care software applications within an organization to communicate with one another.

Health record An ordered set of documents (in the paper context) or a collection of data (in the electronic context) that contains a complete and accurate description of a patient's history, condition, diagnostic and therapeutic treatment, and results of treatment.

Health record content The characteristics essential to constitute an adequate health record.

Health savings accounts A means of allowing individuals who buy high-deductible insurance coverage to save money for out-of-pocket costs in tax-free accounts. These insurance plans typically have lower monthly premiums than would be standard in the industry but may require patients to pay large amounts of money before the insurance plan covers any cost.

Health services manager A professional who coordinates the delivery of health care, whether on a departmental or organization-wide basis.

Health system A network of organizations that concentrates on delivering a single type of service (e.g., acute care hospitals) over a geographic region.

HEDIS Health plan employer data and information set; a set of performance measures for health plans.

Heterografts Tissue or organ transplants that involve placing animal tissue, cells, or organs into human bodies.

Histogram A method used to present frequency of data using horizontal and vertical axes, wherein the vertical axis contains continuous intervals for categories.

HMO Health maintenance organization; a form of managed care. A prepaid, organized system for providing comprehensive health care services within a geographic area to all persons under contract; emphasizes preventive medicine.

Home health agency An organization that provides nursing and other professional and technical services to patients at their places of residence.

Homografts A transplant of tissue or organ using a donor's body part.

Hospice care The health care provided to manage symptoms for patients considered terminally ill, with a life expectancy of less than six months if their disease follows its normal course.

Hospital A health care organization that has a governing body, an organized medical and professional staff, and inpatient facilities; provides medical, nursing, and related services for ill and injured patients 24 hours per day, seven days per week.

Host In epidemiology, the living being upon whom the agent acts, such as the human being.

Hostile work environment A form of sexual harassment in which the presence of unwelcome sexual conduct in the work environment is sufficiently pervasive or severe to alter the terms or conditions of employment.

Human Genome Project An enterprise designed to map the genes found in human DNA and determine the sequences of the chemical base pairs that make up human DNA.

Humanistic management A management approach that focuses on social relationships in the workplace as a means to increase efficiency and productivity.

Human subject A living individual from whom an investigator conducting research obtains data, materials (organs, tissues, or fluids), or identifiable private information.

Hypertext markup language (HTML) A programming language that allows the display of information in a similar format on different operating systems and system hardware.

Hypothesis A tentative assertion assumed by the researcher until the assumption is tested.

ICD International Classification of Diseases; a classification system developed by the World Health Organization.

ICD-9-CM International Classification of Diseases, ninth revision, Clinically Modified.

ICD-10 International Classification of Diseases, 10th revision.

Identity theft The knowing transfer or use, without lawful authority, of the identity of another person with the intent to commit, aid, or abet any unlawful activity that constitutes a violation of federal, state, or local law.

Impaired colleagues Those colleagues who can no longer function appropriately in the workplace due to abuse of substances such as alcohol or drugs.

Incentives The additional compensation an employee receives beyond the base salary or wage.

Incidence The relative frequency of an event.

Incidence rates The proportion of newly reported cases of a disease for a particular time period divided by the total population at risk during the same period.

Incident report The documentation of an adverse incident, describing the time, date, and place of occurrence, the incident itself, the condition of the subject of the incident, statements or observations of witnesses, and any responsive action taken by the health care provider or organization.

Income statement A financial report that summarizes revenue and expenses of an organization at a specified point in time, noting profits and extraordinary gains and losses.

Independent contractor An individual who agrees to perform certain work according to her own means, manner, and methods of performance.

Index Something that serves as a pointer, indicator, or guide to facilitate reference; a tool for finding specific information.

Inferential statistics Statistics used to reach conclusions based upon data from a sample, wherein the patterns in data are modeled so that randomness and uncertainty in observations are addressed.

Inflation The persistent rise in the average level of prices.

Informatics A discipline that focuses on studying both the structure and general properties of information and the design and implementation of technology to use and communicate that information.

Information Organized and classified data put into context; so-called "meaningful" data.

Information brokering The business of buying and selling information as a commodity.

Information security policies Those policies that define the framework around which an information security program is managed.

Information system A set of connecting and communicating computers, devices, and software that supports the delivery of patient care and the day-to-day business of health care.

Information systems life cycle The succession of stages of an information system.

Informed consent The communication of definite knowledge of an event or fact to the patient so that she may voluntarily agree to or forgo treatment.

Inpatient service day The services received by one patient during one 24-hour period.

Institutional animal care and use committees A group formally designated by an institution to safeguard the rights and welfare of animals used in research.

Institutional review board (IRB) A group formally designated by an institution to safeguard the rights and welfare of human subjects by reviewing, approving, and monitoring medical research.

Insured The person holding the policy or receiving the care under a private health care insurance process.

Insurer The insurance company that agrees to pay the health care provider's charges for the treatment rendered to the insured, up to previously specified limits.

Integrated delivery system A network of organizations that provide coordinated health care services.

Integrity controls The ability of a database management system to check all entered data against specified constraints or rules and determine whether there is an inconsistency.

Intentional tort Those civil wrongs committed by persons with the intent to do something wrong.

Interactive voice recognition A computer application that allows a person to use a telephone to gain access by voice alone to information in a computer.

Interface The hardware or software necessary to connect the components of an information system together or to connect one information system to another.

Internal analysis The process of assessing an organization's internal environment in order to gain an understanding of the organization's functions and to develop a factual portrait of the organization.

Internal controls The accounting procedures, precautions, and forms established to prevent and minimize errors and fraud.

International health agencies Governmental and nongovernmental entities that transcend national borders to perform public work in health care.

Internet A worldwide network of smaller networks.

Internet protocol A communication technology that controls all traffic on the Internet.

Internet protocol address A unique number assigned to each host computer connected to the Internet so as to distinguish the computers from one another.

Internet service provider A company that provides Internet services and sells access to the Internet.

Interval data A data set that is both ordered and constant but contains no natural zero as a point of reference.

Intranet A private network that is accessible only within an organization.

Invasion of privacy The dissemination of information about another person's private, personal matters.

In vitro fertilization The fertilization of human gametes outside the human body in a test tube or other artificial environment.

Involuntary commitments Admissions to a health care facility that occur against a patient's will.

IPA Independent practice association; a form of managed care; a community-based group of independent practitioners who contract to provide care for prepaid, enrolled individuals.

Integrated Services Digital Network (ISDN) A public digital data network intended to supplant traditional telephone systems.

Job The tasks and responsibilities that are the regular assignment of an individual.

Job analysis To determine the content of a job.

Job description A written statement summarizing what an employee does, how it is done, and why it is done.

Job enrichment A method of making a job more meaningful and rewarding that entails modifying the job itself by introducing into it additional motivating factors that meet an employee's higher-order needs.

Job evaluation Compares tasks within jobs to one another and provides a basis for grading or ranking jobs.

Job satisfaction A feeling derived from those things that keep an employee from actively seeking other employment.

Journal A book or document in which each transaction is entered in chronological order; a running log of activity during a given time period.

Jurisdiction The authority of a court and its judicial officers to hear and decide a case.

Justice An ethical concept referring to the obligation to be fair to all people.

Keyboard A hardware device used to enter numbers, characters, and commands into a computer.

Knowledge The understanding and use, often in the forms of mental models, scripts, and schemata, of a range of information.

Knowledge management A management theory that focuses on the strategies, policies, actions, and tools involved in creating an environment that facilitates the creation, transfer, and sharing of knowledge within an organization.

Knowledge management system A mechanism or process that captures information, uses and refines that information to assist understanding, and transfers or shares that information with others.

Labor analytics The activity and business of determining whether a work area has enough staff, too many staff, or are working under a staffing shortage.

Laboratory research Research performed in the laboratory setting under tight control.

Laptop computer A computer that, because of its small size, can be conveniently balanced on a person's knees.

Law A body of rules of action or conduct prescribed by a controlling authority that has binding legal force.

Leadership An ability to inspire and influence others to accomplish planned objectives.

Leading The management function that involves motivating employees, directing others, resolving conflicts, and selecting effective communication channels.

Leased employees Individuals employed by a service firm who are assigned to work at a business or organization; sometimes referred to as *temporary employees.*

Length of stay The number of calendar days from the day of patient admission to the day of discharge.

Liability A debt or obligation owed by an organization.

Licensing The action of a governmental entity to confer a right to practice an occupation or provide a service. Licensing controls the number of individuals who are permitted to practice an occupation or provide a service, and licenses are generally granted to individuals who present proof of specified educational requirements and pass an examination administered by an appropriate state board.

Limited data set A form of data in which direct identifiers have been removed, but other data such as city, state, zip codes, dates of service, birth, and death remain.

Line graph A method that uses lines to represent data in numerical form.

Literature review A review of research that has already been performed on a topic that is the focus of a research study.

Living will A document, executed while a patient is competent, that provides direction as to medical care the patient should receive in the event that she is incapacitated or unable to make personal decisions; a form of advance directive.

Local area network A type of network that connects computers located in the same office or firm, or found in the same or closely adjacent areas or buildings.

Long-term care facility An institution that offers health care to patients who are not in an acute episode of illness and need continuous nursing service in an inpatient setting.

Mainframe A computer containing a powerful central processing unit that controls the activity of a "dummy" monitor.

Maintenance factors Those things within a job that help people who are performing at acceptable levels to remain doing so.

Major diagnostic category The first level of a decision tree to reach a diagnosis-related group, generally based on an organ or system.

Malpractice Professional misconduct that can include both intentional and nonintentional torts.

Managed care Health plans that integrate fully the financial and delivery aspects of health care.

Management The process of activities for creating objectives and for teaming with people to meet those objectives through efficient and effective use of resources. Generally includes planning, organizing, directing, controlling, and leading.

Management by objectives An approach to operational planning in which performance objectives are jointly planned by managers and employees with periodic review of progress and rewards based on this progress.

Managerial accounting The day-to-day management of an organization's cash, credit, inventory, liabilities, and expenses.

Master budget The combination of all budgets into one large blueprint for the organization's financial plan.

Master patient index A listing or database of all the patients treated by a health care facility, typically arranged according to an identification process.

Mathematical statistics The theoretical basis of statistics.

Mean An arithmetic average.

Median The middle score in a distribution when the scores are arranged in order of magnitude.

Medicaid Formally known as the Medical Assistance Program, a program designed to provide financing for health care of poor or impoverished persons.

Medical abandonment The unilateral severing, by the physician, of the physician-patient relationship without giving the patient reasonable notice at a time when there is a necessity for continuing care.

Medical language The words, their pronunciation, and the methods of combining them that have been established by long usage and are understood by the medical profession.

Medical library science A discipline with a focus on published data and how it is catalogued, abstracted, and retrieved by groups and individuals.

Medical necessity The principle requiring health care providers to make reasonable efforts to limit the treatments and services rendered the patient to those that are necessary to accomplish the intended purpose of care.

Medical office manager A health care professional who coordinates the activities of a health care provider's office,

including the health information, personnel, finance, insurance, and risk management functions.

Medical record See *health record.*

Medical staff Those physicians with extensive training in various disciplines who have received permission from a hospital's governing board to provide clinical services at the hospital.

Medical staff coordinator A member of the hospital's administrative staff who coordinates all efforts related to procuring written documentation of a physician's qualifications to provide clinical services.

Medical transcription The act of transcribing prerecorded dictation to create medical reports, correspondence, and other administrative material.

Medicare Formally known as the Health Insurance Act for the Aged, a program designed to provide financing for health care to all persons over age 65, regardless of financial need.

Meeting A purposeful coming together of people or things.

Mental health The ability to cope with and adapt to the recurrent stresses of everyday life.

Mental illness The inability of one to cope effectively with the recurrent stresses of everyday life.

Mental imaging An idea-generation method in which a group visualizes a detailed picture of an ideal situation, identifying both the key relationships and obstacles that will need to be addressed in order to influence eventual success.

Mentoring The act of advising another through an established formal relationship.

Metadata Unseen information in common text files, which can indicate when a document was created or revised and can contain edits, notes, or other private data.

Methods The procedures and processes employed. Within the research context, they may include, but are not limited to, identifying the research population, the recruitment strategies, and the informed consent process if human beings are involved; the location and time window for the research; the administration/types of treatment; and assessments of effectiveness and safety.

Method used A step in research design that identifies the research population, the recruitment strategies, and the informed consent process if human beings are involved; the location and time window for the research; the administration/types of treatment; and assessments of effectiveness and safety.

Metropolitan area network Large computer networks that connect an array of computers across a campus or city, often employing wireless infrastructure or optical fiber connections to link between sites.

Minimum data set An agreed-upon and accepted set of terms and uniform definitions constituting a core of data.

Minimum necessary standard The principle requiring health care providers to make reasonable efforts to limit the patient-specific health information disclosed to the least amount necessary to accomplish the intended purpose of the use, disclosure, or request.

Minimum risk The probability and magnitude of harm or discomfort anticipated in the research are not greater in and of themselves than those ordinarily encountered in daily life or during the performance of routine physical/psychological examinations or tests.

Mission statement The documentation of the purpose of an organization.

Mobile A computer hardware object that can be carried or wheeled from place to place.

Mode A score that happens with the greatest frequency.

Modem A hardware device that lets a computer transfer information over a telephone line.

Monitor A piece of hardware that displays the output of a computer.

Morals The principles or fundamental standards of "right" conduct that an individual internalizes.

Morbidity Diseases of human beings.

Morbidity rates The ratio of sick to well persons in the community.

Mortality Deaths.

Mortality rates The rate of death in a given population or community.

Motivation The need or drive that stimulates a person to some action or behavior.

Motivators Those things that cause people to do more than just get by.

Mouse A piece of hardware; a small hand control with buttons that control the position of the cursor on the monitor screen.

Multidirectional data flow The flow of data that may begin as: (1) bidirectional but then changes to rearrange the data by sending it to multiple locations; or (2) by sending the data to multiple locations before the course of the data flow ends.

Multivariate regression A form of regression analysis in which the focus is on numerous variables to provide an answer.

Multivoting A tool for prioritizing ideas; determined by allowing each group member to vote for items she believes have the highest priority.

Natality Births.

Negligence The failure to do something (or to refrain from doing something) that a reasonable, prudent person would do (or would refrain from doing) in a similar situation.

Negotiation The process of conferring, discussing, or bargaining to reach an agreement.

Network A collection of computers connected together by way of cables or wireless links so that they can exchange data with one another.

Nomenclature A systematic listing of proper names for concepts, items, actions, and other aspects of a particular area of interest or knowledge.

Nominal data A data set that classifies values but does not require a logical ordering of those values.

Nominal group technique A tool for prioritizing ideas wherein a list of ideas is labeled alphabetically and each group member prioritizes the list by writing a number beside each lettered idea.

Nonessential job functions Those functions and duties that are desirable but not required for a particular job.

Nonintentional tort Those civil wrongs committed by persons who lack the intent to do something wrong.

Nonmaleficence An ethical concept referring to the prohibition against doing harm; operates through the obligation to prevent evil or harm.

Nosocomial infection rate The number of hospital-based infections divided by the total number of discharges (including deaths).

Null hypothesis A mathematical concept in which there is no difference in the variables; will always be 0.

Number index A listing of all the identification numbers assigned to patients at a health care facility or provider practice setting, typically arranged with accompanying patient name.

Nurse An individual with specialized education and training who provides services essential to the promotion, maintenance, and restoration of health and well-being and the prevention of illness.

Objectives Broad statements that define the future, whether of the organization or the department.

Object query language An extension of structured query language that can be used with object-oriented databases.

Observational studies Investigations based on observation rather than experimentation.

Occupancy rate The percentage of use of available beds or bassinets on a specific day or for a specific time period.

Occupational health A medical subspecialty focused on anticipating, evaluating, and controlling the environmental factors arising in or from the workplace that result in injury, illness, and impairment, or otherwise affect the well-being of the workforce.

Online analytical processing Data analysis program used to access data housed in a data warehouse.

Operating room register A listing of patients who have undergone operations at a particular health care facility.

Operating system The software that controls how the computer works.

Operational planning A planning method concerned with creating short-term plans that specify the details of how the strategic plans, goals, and objectives will be implemented.

Optimizing programs Software programs that seek the highest-paying diagnosis-related group based on the codes assigned and in compliance with prevailing regulations.

Optometrist A health care professional who diagnoses and provides selective eye treatment.

Ordinal data A data set that is ordered, though the differences between the values are not important.

Ordinances Laws that arise from the actions of municipal bodies such as boards of alderman or city councils.

Organizational chart A document, whether paper-based or electronic, that maps how positions within a department or organization are tied together along the principal lines of authority.

Organizational design The planning and fitting together of the people and activities involved in doing the work of an organization.

Organizational structure The manner in which work and responsibilities are divided within the organization.

Organizing To determine what tasks should be done, who shall do them, the reporting structure, and at what level decisions will be made.

Organ transplantation A form of surgery wherein one body part (tissue or organ) is transferred from one site to another or from one individual to another.

Orientation A program designed to help acclimate new employees to an organization and allow them to make a productive beginning on the job.

ORYX Initiative A performance improvement initiative of the Joint Commission (formerly the Joint Commission on Accreditation of Healthcare Organizations) used to examine a health care organization's internal performance over time and to compare the organization's performance with that of others.

Outcomes The changes, whether positive or negative, that can be attributed to the task at hand.

Outsourcing The delegation of non-care operations from the internal production of a business to an external entity that specializes in an operation. Some outsourcing is performed offshore, typically overseas.

Owners' equity The ownership capital base of a business.

Pandemics Epidemics that spread quickly over a wide geographic area.

Pareto chart A bar graph used to identify and separate major and minor problems.

Pareto principle A theory of wealth distribution in which the wealth in any country is held by a few, while the majority of its citizens struggle for the remaining dollars. This is commonly known as the 80/20 Rule.

Participatory management A management approach involving the use of expectations and information within an organization as a way to motivate people to work.

Part-time employee An employee who works less than 30 hours per week.

Passive euthanasia The practice in which no heroic measures are taken to preserve life, thereby causing death; also called *negative euthanasia*.

Paternalism An ethical model under which the health care professional acted in the role of a father to his children, deciding what was best for the patient's welfare without first being required to consult with the patient.

Patient rights Recognition that the patient is entitled to determine for herself the extent to which she will receive or forgo care and treatment.

Pearson product-moment correlation A regression analysis formula used to determine whether a relationship exists between two variables when both variables are numbers (either interval or ratio data).

Percentage A specified amount in every hundred.

Performance evaluation A formal opportunity to review and evaluate an employee on a periodic basis.

Performance improvement A clinical function focused on how to improve patient care.

Performance problems Those problems that impact or relate directly to the employee's ability to carry out critical job duties and meet required job standards.

Perinatal ethics The ethical questions and concerns involved with or occurring during the period closely surrounding birth.

Peripheral A form of computer hardware that is added to a host computer to expand its capabilities; peripherals are generally considered optional in nature.

Permission The level of access given by the operating system to a person or group of persons.

Personal computer A computer that contains a central processing unit, frequently located at an employee workstation.

Personal digital assistant A computer that by its size can conveniently be held in one hand while standing.

Personal health record (PHR) A collection of important health data for a patient that is actively maintained and updated; may be kept by the patient or on behalf of a person for whom another has responsibility.

Personal power The power that rests on the positive regard that others accord an individual.

PERT Program Evaluation and Review Technique; a planning tool used to track activities according to a time sequence, thereby showing the interdependence of activities.

PHI Protected health information; individually identifiable health information that has been electronically maintained or transmitted by a covered entity, as well as such information when it takes any other form.

Philanthropic foundations Organizations designed to distribute donated funds in an effort to better humankind.

Phishing The act of requesting personal information using a false e-mail address; generally used as a way to commit identity theft or fraud.

Physical layout A model of space in actual miniaturized detail of the physical environment at issue.

Physician An individual authorized to practice medicine who has graduated from a college of medicine or osteopathy and is licensed by the appropriate board.

Physician assistant An individual with specialized education and practical training who provides patient services under the direction and supervision of a physician or surgeon responsible for her performance.

Physician index A listing of all the patients a given physician has treated at a health care facility, indexed by physician name or code number.

Pie chart A method used to present the frequency of data through the use of a circle drawn and divided into sections that correspond to the frequency in each category.

Placebos Medically inert substances that are used as a control in testing the effectiveness of another medicated substance; in clinical trials, something that resembles treatment that ensures that the participant does not know she is in a control group.

Plaintiff The person or organization that initiates a lawsuit.

Planning Those activities that outline what needs to be done and how to accomplish that effort.

Podiatrist A health care professional with specialized education and training who is concerned with diagnosing, treating, and preventing abnormal foot conditions.

Policy A decision-making guide that establishes the parameters for taking action and meeting objectives.

Population An entire group with a common observable characteristic.

POS Point-of-service plan; a form of managed care. A health plan that allows the patient to choose the type of provider from which she will receive care at or near the point in time when she will receive the care.

Position summary A portion of a job description that identifies the job's purpose, describes how it contributes to accomplishing the overall objectives of the organization, and distinguishes the job from others in the organization.

Positional power The power that rests on the authority inherent in the job status, title, or rank.

PPO Preferred provider organization; a form of managed care; a network of participating hospitals, physicians, medical groups, and other providers who contract with a sponsor, such as an insurance company or employer, to provide services to those enrolled in the PPO.

Preadmission review A step in the utilization review process that is performed prior to admission to the facility and operates to determine if the admission and procedure/treatment plan are medically necessary and appropriate for the setting.

Preemption A legal doctrine stating that certain matters are of such a national, as opposed to local, nature that federal laws preempt, or take precedence over, state and local laws.

Premium A specific amount or fee prepaid to an insurer on a regular basis (e.g., monthly).

Prenatal surgery Surgery upon the fetus prior to birth.

Prenatal testing Those tests performed after conception but before birth that are designed to detect fetal abnormalities.

Pretrial conference A meeting between the parties and the trial judge to discuss the status and issues of a case.

Prevalence rates The proportion of known cases of a disease for a particular time period divided by the total population for the same period.

Primary care The care provided by the health care professional at the initial point of contact and in the coordination of all aspects of the patient's health care.

Primary data Those data obtained from an original source, such as the patient record or a daily census report.

Primary prevention A focus of epidemiology in which healthy population groups are examined and actions are suggested to prevent members of the healthy population group from developing a given disease.

Printers Hardware devices that reproduce on paper the text and image found on the computer.

Privacy The right to be left alone; the right to control personal information.

Privacy officer Privacy officer identified pursuant to the Health Insurance Portability and Accountability Act (HIPAA) with the responsibility for developing and implementing requisite privacy policies and procedures, receiving complaints, and disseminating information about an entity's privacy practices.

Privacy Rule A rule issued pursuant to the Health Insurance Portability and Accountability Act (HIPAA) establishing the concept of protected health information at the federal level.

Private health care insurance A means of financing health care wherein the insured prepays a specific amount to an insurer on a regular basis in exchange for the insurer's agreement to pay the health care provider's charges for the treatment rendered to the insured, up to previously specified limits.

Private law Law that refers to conflicts between private parties.

Procedure The series of interrelated steps that are documented and used to give standardization to routing tasks or structured problems.

Procedure index A listing of operations and procedures according to the classification system used by the health care facility or private provider.

Process capability analysis A statistical tool used to examine the steps in a process, measure the time spent on each step, and identify bottlenecks.

Process capability ratio diagram A model of each step (component) of a process that demonstrates how much time is spent on each component.

Process improvement The efforts to implement changes to business processes as a means to improve performance.

Procurement The activities involved in the purchasing of goods and the contracting for services.

Productivity The ability to produce work outcomes in a timely manner.

Professional association A body of people with specialized learning who exert mental, rather than manual, labor and organize for a common purpose or object.

Professional Standards Review Organizations (PSRO) Groups tasked with monitoring the appropriateness and quality of outcomes.

Programming language A created language used to write application and utility programs.

Project management A subset of management involving temporary endeavors undertaken to produce a definite product or service.

Prospective Looking forward.

Prospective payment system A payment method that establishes rates, prices, or budgets for future reimbursement before the health care provider delivers services or incurs costs.

Public health A health care discipline dealing with the community at large, focused on protecting and improving community health via organized community effort and preventive delivery of medical, social, and sanitary services.

Public health informatics A subset of the informatics discipline that applies technology to public health practice, research, and learning.

Public health surveillance statistics Statistics that focus on the illnesses, conditions, and diseases of human beings.

Public law Law that refers to conflicts between the government and private parties or between two or more branches of government.

Purchase order A document that formalizes the purchase transaction between a buyer and supplier/vendor.

Pure research Research that is abstract and general, seeking to generate knowledge for knowledge's sake.

Qualifications The necessary skills, education, experience, and licensure required for a position.

Qualitative analysis An analysis activity that concentrates on the record and not the quality of the medical care rendered to the patient. Focus is on ensuring that the requirements of statutory provisions, administrative regulations, accrediting standards, professional guidelines, and institutional standards are met.

Qualitative form Statistical analysis expressed with regard to quality.

Qualitative research The methodology that relies upon generating descriptive theory using data gleaned from an investigation.

Quality assurance Those actions taken to establish, protect, promote, and improve the quality of health care.

Quality assurance coordinator A health care professional who measures and assesses the quality of clinical and patient-care services and offers recommendations for improvement.

Quality improvement A model that involves choosing a problem or process to study, collecting data to measure the problem or process, assessing the data, and developing a method of improvement.

Quality management The concept that every aspect of health care quality may be subject to managerial oversight.

Quantitative analysis An analysis activity that concentrates on what forms or data should be present in, but are missing from, the health record. Focus is on assembling and analyzing the record for accuracy and completeness.

Quantitative form Statistical analysis expressed with regard to quantity.

Quantitative research The methodology that relies upon testing theories to establish facts, show causal explanations and relationships between variables, and make predictions.

Quaternary care The most complex level of medical and surgical care available. Quaternary care facilities are often affiliated with universities and research institutions.

Quid pro quo Literally, "this for that"; a form of sexual harassment.

Randomization Within the research context, every subject in a research population is given an equal chance of either being selected for the study sample (referred to as *random selection*) or being assigned to the experimental group or the control group (referred to as *random assignment*).

Rate A special kind of ratio in which the two quantities being compared are of different units or kinds.

Rate formulae The number of times something happens divided by the number of times it could have happened.

Ratio A quantity that signifies the amount of one quantity relative to another.

Reasonable accommodation Any change to the work environment or the manner in which things are customarily done that enables a qualified person with a disability to have equal employment opportunities.

Receipts Cash received.

Recognition programs An established program that provides formal acknowledgment and approval of an employee's efforts and accomplishments.

Record retention policies The general principles that determine the length of time medical records must be maintained by the health care provider.

Record retention schedule A document that details what data will be retained, the retention period, and the manner in which the data will be stored.

Records management system System that operates to control data, and the records housing those data, from the time of creation, collection, or receipt until destruction. The three main components of such as system are: data storage, retention, and destruction.

Recruitment The process of finding employees for an organization.

Registration The action of a nongovernmental entity, such as a professional association, to recognize those individuals who meet specified standards such as education and experience. This recognition is typically given after an individual successfully completes an examination given by the nongovernmental entity. Certification is issued, and the individual receives specific credentials.

Registry A collection of records in which regular entry is made of particulars or details of a kind that are considered important enough to be exactly or formally recorded; always a formal collection, often an official collection.

Regression analysis A statistical tool that is used to investigate relationships among variables by modeling the relationships and determining their magnitude. In other words, regression analysis is a tool that uses statistical techniques to identify correlations among variables that are not otherwise obvious.

Regular employee One who has a continuing relationship with an employer; sometimes referred to as a *common law employee*.

Regulations The prescribed courses of action that arise from law, principle, or custom.

Rehabilitation care facility An institution offering health care services to patients who need to restore the functional abilities, assume complete activities of daily living (ADLs), or engage in an occupation.

Reimbursement methodologies The theories and practices utilized to pay for the services provided by health care professionals.

Relative risk ratios An estimate of how much the risk of acquiring a disease increases as a result of an individual's exposure to a known risk factor or a particular causal agent.

Release of information The process of granting health care providers and institutions the authority to disclose patient-specific health information to persons not otherwise authorized by law.

Releases Upgrades to software application that provide routine maintenance, patches, or fixes to existing functionality.

Reliability The repeatability of a measurement.

Request for information (RFI) A formal document that seeks product information and is often used as a tool to prescreen vendors.

Request for proposal (RFP) A formal document that indicates an organization's intent to procure products or services based upon specifications and provisions included in the document, and the guidelines to be used by those who wish to bid for the contract.

Request for quotation (RFQ) A formal document that seeks from a group of vendors pricing information for specific products or services.

Requirements Those things considered necessary, obligatory, or demanded as a condition.

Research The careful, diligent, and exhaustive search designed to discover new facts and relationships; revise accepted conclusions, theories, or laws in light of newly discovered facts and relationships; gain solutions to problems; or discover specific answers to specific questions, all in a reliable, objective, and organized way.

Research methodology The manner employed in which problems are solved through careful, diligent, and exhaustive searches.

Res ipsa loquitur A Latin phrase meaning "the thing speaks for itself"; applies to situations in which the defendant had exclusive control over the thing that caused harm to the patient and the harm itself could only have occurred through negligence.

Resource-based relative value scale (RBRVS) A diagnosis-related-group-type system adopted by Medicare for reimbursement of physician services.

Respondeat superior The liability of a superior for the acts of a subordinate or servant acting within the scope of her authority; sometimes referred to as *vicarious liability*.

Retention The ability of an organization to retain employees.

Retrospective Looking backward.

Retrospective data collection The process of converting the paper record into a computerized abstract of the same; performed after the patient is discharged.

Return on investment The process of evaluating an investment by comparing the magnitude and timing of expected gains against investment costs.

Revenue Income received.

Revenue cycle management The efficient and effective use of administrative and clinical functions to capture, manage, and collect revenue related to the delivery of patient services.

Reward programs An established program that provides formal compensation in return for an employee's service or merit.

Rights Just claims or entitlements, whether based on law, ethics, or morality, that others are obliged to respect.

Risk The estimate of probability of loss from a given event upon the operational or financial performance of an organization.

Risk assessment A method used to measure an organization's level of preparedness to prevent and recover from a disaster.

Risk factors The factors that are associated with, or increase the risk of, acquiring a disease.

Risk management A nonclinical function focused on how to reduce medical, financial, and legal risk to an organization.

Risk manager A professional who acts to reduce medical, financial, and legal risk to an organization through investigation, analysis, and recommendations for corrective action.

Root-cause analysis An activity designed to identify the cause of an event.

Rounding The process of reducing the number of significant digits in a number.

Rules The principles established by authorities that prescribe or direct certain action or forbearance from action.

Safeguarding of assets The careful control of valuable assets so that those persons lacking authority cannot gain access to them.

Salaries A rate of pay given on a weekly, monthly, or yearly schedule.

Sales budget A budget that focuses on the projected sales of products or services.

Sample A subset or small part of a population.

Scanners A hardware component that converts printed pages or graphic images into a file, which can be stored in a computer and retrieved by an end user.

Scientific management A management approach that measures the efficiency and productivity of an operation using scientific means.

Scientific method The process of discovery by systematic investigation.

Secondary care The care provided by a specialist, often at the request of the primary care physician.

Secondary data Data derived from primary data.

Secondary prevention A focus of epidemiology that identifies, through screening techniques, those people who are in the preclinical and clinical stages of a disease and applies intervention techniques early in the disease progression process.

Security The means to regulate access to, and ensure preservation of, data.

Security Rule A rule issued pursuant to the Health Insurance Portability and Accountability Act (HIPAA) specifying the use of integrity controls, encryption technology, management techniques, access controls, workforce security standards, and training requirements relating to the transmission of electronic protected health information.

Selection The process an organization engages in to choose who will work for it.

Sentinel event An unexpected occurrence that invokes death or serious physical or psychological injury, or risk thereof.

Separation The process of ending employment.

Separation of duties The effort to separate different parts of the same transaction among different individuals and departments so that no one person may control an entire transaction from start to finish.

Separation of powers The doctrine of division of power between the branches of government and the system of checks and balances that supports that division.

Serial numbering system An ordered number arrangement used to assign patients in chronological order as they are admitted or readmitted to the same health care facility.

Serial-unit numbering system A modified version of the serial numbering system, wherein a new number is assigned to the same patient regardless of the number of times the patient is admitted or registered at the same health care facility; the number assigned from the prior admission or registration is updated to reflect the most recently assigned number.

Serious health condition Any injury, illness, impairment, or physical or mental condition that requires inpatient care at a hospital, hospice, or residential medical care facility, or continuing treatment by a health care provider.

Servers Computers that provide shared services to other computers on a network.

Signal An object used to convey data.

Simple regression A form of regression analysis that focuses on only one variable to provide an answer.

SNDO Standard Classified Nomenclature of Disease, published by the American Medical Association, used for classifying diagnostic terminology in order of localization (site) and etiology (cause).

SNOMED Systematized Nomenclature of Medicine, published by the American College of Pathologists; a comprehensive nomenclature with multiple axes that is compatible with computer applications.

SNOP Systematized Nomenclature of Pathology, published by the American College of Pathologists, used for classifying pathological specimens.

Social and behavioral research Studies that focus on research dealing with human attitudes, beliefs, and behaviors.

Software The programs that tell a computer what to do and how to do it.

Source document Paperwork that evidences the terms and conditions of a transaction.

Specialists Physicians who limit their practices to a particular branch of medicine or surgery.

Specifications The features required of a product or service, often taking the form of quality, price, quantity, service, delivery, or performance.

Staffing The process of assigning workers to all positions in an organization.

Standard deviation The square root of a variance.

Standard generalized markup language A separate programming language that served as the basis for extensible markup language.

Standards Criteria established as a basis for comparing matters such as quantity, quality, value, or weight. Within a computer context, the technical specifications or other precise criteria to be used consistently as rules, guidelines, or other definitions of characteristics in order to ensure that materials, products, processes, or services are fit for their purposes.

Statistical literacy The ability to determine whether a conclusion or study is credible based on the results of statistical findings.

Statistically significant A result that is unlikely to have occurred by chance, wherein the test condition being examined has no effect.

Statistics The mathematics of the collection, organization, and interpretation of numerical data, especially the analysis of population characteristics by inference from sampling.

Statistics budget A budget that focuses on the volume and type of health care services provided in the past and compares it to an estimate of future needs for health care services.

Statute of limitations The time period established by law in which a person can bring a legal action for an injury or breach of contract.

Statutory employee One who has been designated by specific laws as subject to the tax withholding requirements imposed upon employers but might not otherwise be considered an employee.

Statutory law Laws created by the legislative branches of the federal and state governments.

Stem cell research The careful, systematic study and investigation of a special kind of cell not committed to conduct a specific function, which has the capability to renew itself and differentiate into specialized cells.

Sterilization The actions taken to make an individual incapable of reproducing, whether by removing the reproductive organs or by preventing them from functioning effectively.

Strategic planning The process of determining the long-term vision and goals of an enterprise and how to fulfill them.

Structured query language A language used by nonprogrammers to retrieve information contained in relational databases.

Study rationale A step in research design that demonstrates why a certain study should be performed.

Subpoena A command issued by a court or other authorized official to appear or present certain documents and other things.

Subpoena duces tecum A subcategory of subpoena that commands one to produce books, documents, and other physical things.

Substantially equal A concept applied in sex discrimination cases to describe jobs that are performed under similar working conditions and require equal skill, effort, and responsibility.

Supervision The process by which an individual directs others to perform work on time using available resources (money, materials, and manpower) and in a manner that meets or exceeds performance standards.

Supplemental benefits Services and programs offered to employees beyond the base salary or wage.

Surgical assistant A physician assistant who helps the surgeon during operative procedures.

Surrogate mother One who agrees to bear a child conceived through artificial means and to relinquish it upon its birth to others for rearing.

Survey A collection of facts, figures, or opinions taken from individuals or groups who are the objects of an investigation.

SWOT technique A form of analysis used to identify strengths, weaknesses, opportunities, and threats an organization may have in relation to the competitive marketplace.

Tacit knowledge Personal knowledge, or knowledge that is known by an individual but is difficult to convey to others.

Team A group of people working together in a coordinated effort.

Team building The process by which a selected group of people are organized and developed so that each team member's actions work interdependently toward a common objective.

Telecommuting Any arrangement in which an employee regularly performs officially assigned duties at home or other work sites geographically convenient to the residence of the employee.

Telehealth The use of electronic communications and information technologies to provide or support clinical care at a distance.

Telemedicine The use of electronic communications and information technologies to provide or support clinical care at a distance.

Terminology A systematic listing of proper names for concepts, items, actions, and other aspects of a particular area of interest or knowledge.

Tertiary care The specialized medical and surgical care provided for complex or unusual medical problems; the care provided at health care facilities possessing advanced technologies and specialized intensive care units.

Tertiary prevention A focus of epidemiology that concentrates on limiting the level of disability and increasing the probability of rehabilitation for persons in an advanced stage of disease or disability.

Theory X A participatory management theory that holds that the average employee dislikes work, possesses relatively little ambition, wishes to avoid responsibility, prefers to be directed by others, and wants security above everything else.

Theory Y A participatory management theory that holds that work may be a source of employee satisfaction and that employees, under proper conditions, will not only accept but seek responsibility.

Theory Z A participatory management theory that holds that the responsibilities sought by employees and over which they are capable of self-control are culturally related.

Third-party administrators Independent organizations that possess expertise in all or a portion of the claims process that administer health insurance plans on behalf of companies.

Third-party payers Organizations or entities willing to pay for health care services rendered to the patient by the health care provider, according to preexisting arrangement using set criteria.

Timeliness Within the context of the health record, the entry of data at a suitable time period, such as contemporaneously or as soon as possible after care is rendered.

Top-down process The budget process wherein upper-level management or a budget committee communicate to lower-level and middle-level managers the priorities and objectives for the budget year and distribute the final budget.

Total quality management A customer-focused management philosophy that challenges an organization to exceed customer expectations while still maintaining a cost-competitive market position.

Tracer methodology A means of tracing the delivery of the patient's care through the health record and interviews with members of the health care team (and often the patient); employed by the Joint Commission (formerly the Joint Commission on Accreditation of Healthcare Organizations).

Training Those experiences designed to further the learning of behaviors that contribute to the organization's goals.

Treasurer The businessperson who oversees the organization's assets and financial planning.

Trend chart A graphical presentation of data that shows patterns or shifts according to time.

Trial A hearing or determination by a court of the issues existing between the parties to a lawsuit.

TRICARE A federal government program related to the financing and provision of care for active-duty members of the armed services, and retired members of the military and their dependents, who receive care at nonmilitary treatment facilities.

T-test A measurement of the observed beta $[T = \beta - b^\wedge / s]$ where the observed data (T) equals beta (β) minus the null hypothesis ($b^\wedge$), divided by the standard deviation (s).

Tumor registrar A health care professional who identifies, collects, and maintains information about tumors, including cancer, that are diagnosed and treated by an organization.

Type I error A type of error that occurs when a sample point falls outside the upper or lower control limits, though there is no special cause to explain it.

Type II error A type of error that indicates that a special cause exists, but the sampling isn't sensitive enough to discover it, so it remains unnoticed (and unresolved).

Unbundling To bill for a package of health care procedures on an individual basis rather than on a combined basis.

Undue hardship An instance when a specific accommodation requested by the employee causes significant difficulty or expense to the employer.

Unemployment insurance A program designed to provide regular income to those who have lost a job.

Unidirectional data flow The flow of data in a linear arrangement, crossing from one person to another without interruption.

Unified Medical Language System (UMLS) A project of the National Library of Medicine with the goal of enabling computer systems to understand medical meaning, thereby allowing health professionals and researchers to retrieve and integrate electronic biomedical information from various sources.

Unit numbering system An ordered number arrangement used to assign patients numbers upon admission or registration to a health care facility; the same number follows the patient throughout any subsequent admissions or registrations.

Univariate regression A form of regression analysis that focuses on only one variable to provide an answer.

Upcoding The practice of selecting a code and submitting a bill for a higher level of reimbursement than actually rendered in order to receive a higher reimbursement.

Usual, customary, and reasonable costs A method used to determine health care payments that combines the provider's usual charge for a given procedure or service, the amount customarily charged for the same procedure or service by other providers in the area, and the reasonable costs of a procedure or service following medical review of the case.

Utilitarianism An ethical theory that proposes that everyone, including persons, organizations, and society in general, should make choices that promote the greatest balance of good over harm for everyone.

Utilization coordinators Also known as *case managers*; employees with responsibility for managing the review process and coordinating the patient's care with physicians and other members of the treatment team. These employees are often trained as nurses or health information management professionals.

Utilization management The combination of planned functions directed to patients in a health care facility or setting that includes the prudent use of resources, appropriate treatment management, and early comprehensive discharge planning for continuation of care.

Utilization review The clinical review of the appropriateness of admission and planned use of resources, which can be and often is initiated prior to admission and conducted at specific time frames as defined in an organization's utilization review plan. The review involves the process of comparing preestablished criteria against the health care provided to the patient to determine whether that care is necessary.

Utilization review coordinator A professional who compares preestablished criteria to the health care provided to the patient to determine whether that care is necessary; the coordinator communicates those results using narrative and graphical reports.

Utility program Software that performs simple operations on files created by other programs; typically used to automate frequently required tasks.

Validity The accuracy of a measurement.

Value-added concept The unique contribution of an activity is measured by the difference between the original component materials and the finished work product.

Values The concepts that give meaning to an individual's life and serve as the framework for decision making.

Variables Those things that may vary or change and therefore can be manipulated or measured.

Variances Inconsistencies between two numbers or statements.

Vector In epidemiology, an agent capable of transmitting a pathogen from one organism to another organism.

Veracity An ethical concept involving habitual truthfulness and honesty.

Versions Upgrades to software applications that provide new functionality.

Virtual private network A wide-area network that connects private subscribers together using the public Internet as the transport medium while ensuring through encryption technology that the private subscribers' traffic is not readable by the Internet at large.

Virus scan The process of searching a hard drive or network data stream to detect the presence of computer viruses.

Vision statement An idealized goal that proposes a new future for an organization.

Vital statistics Data on human events, such as statistics related to births, deaths, fetal deaths, marriages, divorces, and induced terminations of pregnancy (abortion).

Vocabulary A list of words or phrases, with their meanings, that have been accepted by a discipline, group, or organization to express, organize, and index the concepts and phenomena of interest.

Voice recognition technology A computer application that uses voice patterns to allow a computer to record and automatically translate voice into written language in real time.

Voluntary health agencies Nongovernmental organizations created to perform public work in health care through private means.

Wages An hourly rate of pay.

Waste The squandering of resources or use of resources without gain or advantage.

Whistle-blowers Individuals—typically current or former employees of a health care provider or organization—who have learned of fraud and abuse and wish to expose the activity.

Wide-area network A network that connects computers that are geographically separated, typically by cities, counties, or continents.

Wireless A computer object equipped with a special card that enables it to broadcast and receive radio or cellular signals that reach a network via access points.

Wisdom The ability to judge matters soundly, especially as they relate to life, conduct, and practical affairs.

Withdrawing treatment The decision of the patient, her family, or legal guardian to discontinue activities or remove forms of patient care.

Withholding treatment The decision of the patient, her family, or legal guardian to refrain from giving permission for treatment or care.

Work distribution chart Records the work activities performed, the time it takes to perform the work, the individual performing the work, and the amount of time each individual spends on each activity.

Workers' compensation A program designed to replace income and provide medical expenses to employees who suffer work-related injuries, illnesses, or death.

Work motivation Those things that stimulate an employee to exceed basic performance expectations.

Workplace barrier A workplace obstacle, whether physical or procedural, that prevents an employee from performing the duties of the job, whether those duties are considered essential or marginal.

Work simplification A method used to find easier and better ways of doing work.

World Wide Web A set of technology standards that enables the publishing of multimedia documents to be read by anyone with access to the Internet.

Xenografts Transplants that involve animal tissue, cells, or organs placed into human bodies.

Index

Note: Abbreviated names are listed at as spelled out; a comprehensive list of abbreviations can be found in Appendix A (pages 363–369)

A

Abbreviations, health information management (HIM), 363–69
ABC codes. *See* Alternative billing codes
Abortion, 88–89
Abstracting, 116–17
Abuse and fraud, 58–59, 66–70, 96, 133, 361
Acceptance process, 343
Access, 60–64, 96
    control, 173, 323
Account, 335
Accountant, 333
Accounting, 334–39
Accreditation
    educational requirements, 29–33
    by Joint Commission (JC), 47–48
    by National Committee for Quality Assurance, 147
    medical staff, 21–22
    origins, 7, 141
    research organizations, 237
    Web resources, 371
Accredited Standards Committee (ASC), 174
Accrual accounting, 337. *See also* Accounting
Active euthanasia, 92
Adler, Alfred, 12
Administration and administrative simplification, HIPAA, 49, 56–58, 393–99
Administrative bodies, 49–52
Administrative data, 101–2
Administrative law, 46
Admission register, 117
Admission reviews, 161
Admissions coordinators, 37
Adoption, 87
Advance directives, 64–65, 91
Affinity diagrams, 148, 273–74
Age discrimination, 295
Age Discrimination in Employment Act (ADEA), 292, 295
Agency for Healthcare Research and Quality (AHRQ), 10, 50, 145

Agent, 242
Aggregate data collection, 196
AIDS/HIV
    confidentiality, 66, 90
    reporting requirements, 117
    research, 225
Allied health professional, 19
Allografts, 90
Alternative Billing Codes (ABC codes), 135
Ambulatory health care, 16–17
American Association of Medical Record Librarians (AAMRL), 28
American Association on Mental Retardation (AAMR), 135
American College of Surgeons (ACS), 6–7, 14, 28
American Dental Association, 48, 135
American Health Information Management Association (AHIMA), 9, 14, 28–32, 34–35, 48, 81, 83, 96, 113, 129, 133–34
American Hospital Association (AHA), 6, 14, 84–85, 129, 132–33
American Lung Association, 14
American Medical Association (AMA), 5, 14, 28, 126–27
American Medical Record Association (AMRA), 28
American National Standards Institute (ANSI), 173–74
American Osteopathic Association (AOA), 7, 14, 47, 81–83
American Psychiatric Association (APA), 12, 134
American Red Cross, 14
American Veterinary Health Information Management Association (AVHIMA), 38
Americans with Disabilities Act (ADA), 260, 292–93, 295–96
Analysis, regression, 203–9
Analysis methods, 175–76
Analytic epidemiology, 243
Animal research, 236–37
ANOVA test, 208

Anti-kickback statutes, 67
Appeal, 49
Application of classification systems, 128–32
Application program, 317
Application service providers (ASPs), 322
Applications, technology, 325–29
Applied research, 224
Applied statistics, 190
Artificial insemination, 88
Assault, 54
Assent, 235
Assets, 337, 339
Assigning work, 262–63
Associations, professional, 14, 48, 373–74
At-will employment, 292
Audit trails, 336
Auditors, 336
Audits, 336–37
Authentication, 103, 321, 328
Authorship, 103, 328
Autografts, 90
Autonomy, 76–77
Autopsy rate, 199

B

Background checks, 285–86
Backup regime, 322
Balance billing, 356
Balance sheet, 337–38
Baldridge Award, 143–44
Bar graph, 149, 201
Barriers, workplace, 296
Barton, Clara, 14
Basic Nomina Anatomica, 126
Battery, 54
Beginning of life issues, 87–89
Behaviors, problem, 301–2
Belmont Report, 232
Benchmarking, 131, 148, 153, 157, 276
Beneficence, 77–78
Bentham, Jeremy, 80
Best interest standard, 78

Bidirectional data flow, 107, 109
Bioethics, 86–93, 371
Birth register, 117
Bit, 317
Bivariate regression, 203
Blind studies, 227
Block grants, 12
Blue Cross/Blue Shield, 7, 351
Board certified, 19
Bond rating, 334
Bookkeeper/bookkeeping, 333, 335
Bottom-up process, 340
Brainstorming, 148, 272
Breach of contract, 54
Budget organization plan, 339
Budgets, 252, 334–35, 339–42
Bush, George W., 146
Business associates, 56
Bylaws, 18, 21
Byte, 317

C

Cable modem, 320
Cancer registry, 36, 117
Capital expenditure budget, 341
Capital, 334
Capitation, 8, 358–59
Career development, 303
Careers, HIM, 33–39
Case-control study, 228
Case fatality rates, 199
Case management, 160
Case managers, 160
Case mix, 135, 209, 357
Case mix management, 136
Cash accounting, 337
Cash budget, 341
Cash flow statement, 337, 340
Categorical data, 200
Categorical imperative, 80
Causality, epidemiology, 244
Cause-and-effect diagram, 148, 274
CD-ROM device/drive, 314–15
Census, 190
Center for Medicare and Medicaid Services
    (CMS), 10, 47–48, 49, 50, 57, 69,
    128–29, 130, 134, 143, 153–54, 160,
    163, 350, 361
Centers for Disease Control and Prevention
    (CDC), 10, 36, 50, 117, 175, 179, 190–91
Central processing units (CPUs), 314–15
Certificate of destruction (COD), 113–14
Certificate-of-need program, 357
Certification. See Accreditation
Certified Coding Associate (CCA), 30
Certified Coding Specialist (CCS), 30–31
Change management, 270
Charge description master (CDM)
    coordinators, 37
Chargemaster, 356
Chi-square, 208–9
Chief executive officer, 18, 20
Chief financial officer (CFO), 18, 333
Chief information officer (CIO), 18, 313
Chiropractor, 19
Circular organizational charts, 257–58
Civil law, 46
Civil lawsuit procedures, 52–53

Civil Rights Act (Title VII), 292–95, 307
Civilian Health and Medical Program of the
    Department of Veterans Affairs
    (CHAMPVA), 350
Claims, 352
Claims examiners, 37
Classical management, 268
Classification systems, 123–38
    application of, 128–32
    defined, 128
    emerging issues, 135–36
    HIM transformation, 132–33
    historical view, 128–32
    languages, 125–28
    nomenclature, 125–28
    other systems, 133–35
    vocabularies, 126–28
    Web resources, 137
Clinical data, 101–2
    repository, 175
    representation, 136
    specialist, 223
Clinical information system, 327
Clinical privileges, 21
Clinical research, 224
    associates, 37
Clinical terminology, 126
Clinical trials, 226–27
Clinical vocabulary, 126
Closed-panel arrangement, 354
Coaching, 304
Codes of ethics, 81–84, 371–72
Coding, 96, 128, 133–34, 136, 372
Coding compliance program, 133
Codman, A. E., 141
Cohort studies, 227
Cold feed, 197
Commission on Accreditation for
    Health Informatics and
    Information Management
    Education (CAHIIM), 28
Committee review, research, 235–36
Common law, 46
Common rule, 233
Communication, 268
Communication technologies, 319–21
Communities of practice (CoP), 29
Community mental health care, 12
Comparative justice, 78
Compensation, 286, 290, 298–99
Competencies, AHIMA, 31–32
Complaint, 52
Completeness, 48–49, 103
Compliance, 21, 45, 106, 133
Compliance programs, 69, 133, 163, 361
Component state associations (CSAs), 29
Comprehensive Assessment for Tracking
    Community Health (CATCH), 158
Computer room, 315
Computer viruses, 321–22
Computerized physician order entry
    (CPOE), 325
Computers, 314–17
Conceptualization, 196
Concurrency control, 173
Concurrent data collection, 197
Concurrent reviews, 161
Conduct problems, 302

Confidentiality, 59–60, 79, 84. See also
    specific topics
    data flow, 108
    employee orientation, 290
    HIV/AIDS, 89
    mental health and, 66
    research, 234, 237
    risk management, 158
    security, 322, 324
    substance abuse and, 66
    telecommuting, 307
Conflict of interest, 93, 95–96, 234
Conflict resolution, 267–68
Constitutional law, 46
Consultation rate, 199
Consulting health setting, 38
Consumer Assessment of Healthcare Plans
    Survey (CAHPS), 145
Consumer Credit Protection Act, 293
Consumer culture, 8, 84
Continuing education research, 237
Continuous data, 200
Continuous quality improvement, 142
Continuum of care, 15–16
Contraception, 88
Contract dispute, 343–44
Control charts, 149, 151, 211–12
Controlled clinical trials, 227
Controllers, 333
Controlling, management, 262–65
Controls
    cost, 84
    data, 109–10, 173
    management, 264
    research, 225
Core measurements, 153
Corporate culture, 93
Corporate integrity agreement, 69
Corporate negligence, 55
Correct Coding Initiative (CCI), 69, 361
Correctional facility setting, 37–38
Correlation, 203–4
Cost accounting, 335
Cost allocation, 357
Cost-benefit analysis, 80, 334
Cost controls, 8, 84
Court orders, 65
Court system, 49–53
Coverage, 351
Covered entities, 56
Crackers, 322
Credentialing. See Accreditation
Credits, 339
Criminal law, 46
Criteria, 157
Critical path, 255
Crosby, Phillip, 143
Cross-sectional studies, 227
C-section rate, 199
Current Dental Terminology (CDT), 135
Current Procedural Terminology (CPT),
    127–30, 133, 197, 358

D

Daily inpatient census, 198
Data, content and structures, 99–121.
    See also Research
    access to, 60–64

collection and maintenance, 102–3
control of, 109–10
data handling, 110–15
destruction of, 112–13, 115
exchange, 181–83
flow of, 101–9
form design and control, 109–10
indices, 115–17
integrity, 116
presentation of, 148–52, 199–203
quality of, 141–56
registries, 117–19
research, 105
retention of, 49, 110–15
Sedona Guidelines for handling, 114–15
storage of, 110–12
types of, 101–4
users/uses of, 104–9
Web resources, 120, 375
Data, defined, 101, 169, 275
Data aggregation studies, 226
Data analysts, 35
Data dictionary, 170
Data element, 176
Data Elements for Emergency Department Systems (DEEDS), 179
Data mapping, 136, 170
Data mart, 176
Data mining, 176
Data model, 171
Data Safety Monitoring Board (DSMB), 234
Data Safety Monitoring Plan (DSMP), 234
Data sets, 176–81, 191
Data standards, 126, 127, 173–75
Data warehouses, 158, 175–76
Database, defined, 169–70
Database management, 167–85
    controls, 173
    data exchange, 181–83
    data processing, 169–70
    data sets, 176–81
    data standards, 173–75
    database design, 171–73
    defined, 170
    development of, 170–71
    retrieval and analysis methods, 175–76
    Web resources, 184–85
De-identified data, 60, 117, 233
De Morbis Artificam Diatriba, 13
Death, 10–11, 17, 91–93, 239, 243
Death register, 117
Debits, 339
Decision making, 85–87, 261–62
Deeming authority, 47
Defamation, 54
Defendant, 52
Deficit Reduction Act (2005), 68–69
De-identified health information, 60, 180–81, 233, 236
Delegating authority, 259, 336
Delegating work, 262–63
Deming, W. Edwards, 143, 269
Demographic statistics, 191
Demotion, 302
Dentist, 19
Deontology, 80–81
Department of Veterans Affairs (VA), 47, 163

Descriptive epidemiology, 243
Descriptive research, 224
Descriptive statistics, 190
Design, research, 229–30
Destruction of data, 112–13, 115
Diagnosis-related groups (DRGs)
    defined, 130, 357
    discharge data, 177
    fraud and abuse prevention, 68–69
    origins, 8
    patient status code, 163
    regression analysis, 209
    reimbursement, 130–31
    typical structure for, 131
Diagnostic and Statistical Manual of Mental Disorders (DSM-IV), 134
Digital imaging, 327
Digital imaging system, 111
Digital subscriber lines (DSL), 320
Direct patient care settings, 37–39
Directing, principles of management, 261–63
Disability, 295
Disability discrimination, 295–96
Disaster planning, 112, 252–54
Disaster recovery plans, 252–53, 322
Disbursements, 337
Discharge planning, 161
Discharge register, 117
Discharge status, 161–62
Discipline, employment, 302–3
Disclosure, health care data, 61–63
Discovery, 52–53
Discrete data, 199–200
Discrimination, employment, 292–97
Disease index, 116
Diseases of the Mind, 11
Disk drives, 314
Disparagement, 94
Distribution, 208
Distributive justice, 78–79
Diversity, 292–97, 307–8
Dix, Dorothea, 12
Do Not Resuscitate (DNR) orders, 92
Document and repository manager, 35
Domain name, 320
Donabedian, Avedis, 143
Double-blind studies, 227
Double effect principle, 78
DRGs. See Diagnosis-related groups (DRGs)
Drucker, Peter, 269
DSM-IV (Diagnostic and Statistical Manual of Mental Disorders), 134
Durable power of attorney for health care, 64–65, 92
Dysfunctional conflicts, 267

E

E-codes, ICD-9-CM, 130
E-discovery, 53
E-health, 325–26, 372
E-HIM, 30, 34, 197
E-learning, 325
E-prescribing, 325
Ebers Papyrus, 4
Education, 5–6, 19, 29–33, 105
Educational informatics, 325
Efficacy, 226

Efficiency, 226
80/20 Rule, 214
Electronic data interchange (EDI), 174
Electronic health record (EHR), 9, 36, 104, 110, 146, 159, 327–29. See also specific topics
    advantages of, 104
    data abstraction and, 197
    data exchange, 360
    digital imaging systems and, 111–12
    discovery issues, 50
    forms design and, 110
    health information management and, 29–30
    informed consent and, 65
    job descriptions and, 300
    nomenclatures and vocabularies, 127
    record storage and destruction, 113
Emergency room register, 117
Emerging issues/trends, 135–36, 237–38
Employee Eligibility Verification (I-9) form, 286–89
Employee Retirement Income Security Act (ERISA), 293, 298
Employment, 283–308. See also Human resource management; Management
    career development, 303–4
    coaching, 304
    compensation, 286, 299
    data use, 106
    defined, 283, 299
    developing others, 303–4
    discipline and grievance, 302
    employee rights, 292–99
    entrance interviews, 290
    ethics, 94–95
    exit interviews, 291
    grievances, 302–3
    health record data uses, 106
    job qualifications, 295–97, 300
    mentoring, 304
    organizational charts, 256–58
    orientation and training, 286–90
    performance evaluations, 300–301
    problem behaviors, 301–2
    recruitment, 284
    reference checks, 284–85
    retention, 290–91
    selection, 284–86
    separation, 291
    supervision, 93–95, 299–307
    supervisor evaluations, 301
    team building, 304–5
    telecommuting, 305–7
    workplace protections, 297–98
Encoders, 132
Encryption, 321
Endemic, 243
Enterprise master patient index, 116
Enterprise risk management (ERM), 159
Entity-relationship (ER) model, 171–72
Environment, 242
Environmental analysis, 250
Epidemics, 240
Epidemiologists, 238
Epidemiology, 191, 238–44. See also specific topics
    analytic, 243
    causal relationships, 243–44

Epidemiology (*continued*)
descriptive, 243
disease prevention and progression, 240–41
experimental, 243–44
notification process and, 191
Eponyms, 125
Equal Employment Opportunity Commission (EEOC), 296, 307
Equal Employment Opportunity (EEO) Act, 293
Equal Pay Act (EPA), 292, 298
Ergonomics, 260–61
Essential job functions, 300
Ethical acts, 75
Ethical concepts, 76
Ethics and ethical standards, 73–98
bioethics, 86–93, 371
challenges, 93–97
codes of ethics, 81–84, 133–34, 371–72
coding, 133–34
decision making, 81–87
defined, 75, 93
employment, 94–95
general, 93–94
health care and HIM, 95–97
health maintenance organizations and, 79
impaired colleagues, 93
informed consent and, 79–80
models of, 76–81
prospective payment systems and, 79
research, 232, 238
supervision, 94–95
theories, 80–81
Web resources, 98
Ethics committees, 82, 84
Etiquette, 75
Eugenics, 12, 89–90
Euthanasia, 92
Evaluation
defined, 130
job evaluation, 259
performance, 300–301
research into, 229
Exclusive provider organization (EPO), 354–55
Executive orders, 46
Exit interviews, 291
Expedited review, research, 235–36
Expense budget, 341
Expenses, 337
Experimental epidemiology, 243
Experimental research, 224
Explanation of benefits (EOB), 352
Explicit knowledge, 275
Extensible markup language (XML), 317
External forces, and the law, 45–49
Extranet, 321

F

Failure to warn, 55
Fair Credit Reporting Act (FCRA), 285, 292
Fair Labor Standards Act (FLSA), 292, 298
False Claims Act (FCA), 67–69
False imprisonment, 54–55
Family and Medical Leave Act (FMLA), 292, 294, 298

Family planning, 87–88
Federal efforts. *See* Government efforts
Federal Employees Compensation Act (FECA), 299, 351
Federal Employer's Liability Act, 293
Federal Labor Standards Act (FLSA), 298
Federal Register, 47, 293
Fee-for-service (FFS), 8, 355–57
Fidelity, 78
Finance, 333
Financial accounting, 337–39
Financial Accounting Standards Board (FASB), 337
Financial management, 331–46
accounting, 335–39
budgets, 339–42
defined, 335
overview, 333–35
procurement, 342–45
Web resources, 346, 372
Firewall, 321
Flash drives, 314–15
Flexner, Abraham, 6, 229
Floppy disks, 314
Flow of data, 101–9
Flowcharts, 260–61, 273–74
Food & Drug Administration, 10, 47, 226
FOCUS PDCA, 143–44
Force field analysis, 273
Forecasting, 342
Forms, design and control, 109–10
Foundation of Research and Education in Health Information Management (FORE), 15, 29
Fractions, 193–94
Fraud and abuse, 9, 58–59, 66–70, 133, 296, 361
Frequency polygon, 203
Freud, Sigmund, 12
Fringe benefits, 7
Full-time employees, 283
Functional conflicts, 267
Functional limitation, 296

G

Gantt, Henry, 254, 268
Gantt charts, 148, 254, 271
Gene therapy, 91
General ledger, 335
Generalists, 19
Generally accepted accounting principles (GAAP), 337
Genetic research, 238
Genetic screening, 89
Goals, 251
Governing body, hospitals, 17–18, 20
Government efforts. *See also specific topics*
community mental health care, 12–13
data exchange, 181–83
employment laws, 292–93
government entity roles, 46–47
health record data uses, 105–6
licensing of physicians, 6
payers, 349–51
public health, 10, 145–46
quality health care, 145–46, 155–56
Web resources, 372–73

Graphical user interface (GUI), 171
Grievance, 302–3
Groupers, 132

H

Hackers, 322
Handwritten data, legibility, 143
Hard drives, 314
Hardware, computer, 314–16
Hawthorne studies, 269
Hazards, workplace, 13
Healthcare Cost and Utilization Project (HCUP), 145
Health care data. *See* Data, content and structures
Health care delivery system, 1–24
health care professionals, 18–20
historical development, 3–14
international health agencies, 15
medical staff, 20–22
philanthropic foundations, 15
professional associations, 14
variety and settings, 15–18
voluntary health agencies, 14–15
Web resources, 24
Health care facilities, 6, 13–14
Health Care Financing Administration (HCFA), 143
Health care fraud and abuse, 58–59, 66–70, 96, 133, 361
Healthcare Fraud and Abuse Control Program, 59
Health care informatics, 32–33, 324–25
Health Care Informatics Standards Board (HISB), 173–74
Healthcare Integrity and Protections Data Bank (HIPDB), 59
Health care information systems, 313
Health information, 27–33. *See also* Health information management (HIM)
Health information administrator, 31
Health information department, 35
Health information department director, 35
Health information management (HIM), 25–41. *See also specific topics*
abbreviations, 363–69
accreditation, 29–33
as allied health profession, 20
careers, 33–39
committees, 21
credentials, 28–29
defined, 27
educational requirements, 29–33
epidemiology and, 239
ethical challenges, 95–97
functional knowledge, 30
health information, 27–33
historical development of the profession, 27–29
legal issues, 55–66, 391–92
performance improvement, 156–58
productivity, 209–14
regional health information organizations and, 183
risk management, 158–59
statistics, 209–14
transformation, 132–33
Web resources, 41, 309

Health information technician, 20, 31
Health insurance, 7, 351
Health Insurance Portability and
    Accountability Act (HIPAA)
    administration, 49, 56–58, 393–99
    business associates, 56
    careers, 33
    complaint process, 58
    court orders and, 65–66
    covered entities, 56
    credentials, 31
    data sets, 180–81
    data standards, 174–75, 180–81
    de-identified data, 60, 180–81, 233
    disaster recovery plan, 254
    electronic exchange of data, 360
    employees, 299
    fraud and abuse, 9, 58–59, 66–70, 133,
        298, 361
    law enforcement and, 64
    as legal force, 56–59
    mandatory disclosure, 61–62
    personal health record (PHR), 106
    outsourcing use and, 36
    patient rights, 57, 60, 84–85
    preemption, 58
    privacy, 381–89, 399–443
    Privacy Officer, 36, 57–61
    Privacy Rule, 57–61, 63, 66, 84, 180–81,
        233, 299, 323–24, 377–84
    record access, 106
    record destruction, 113
    record storage, 112
    record retention, 113
    regional health information
        organizations, 183
    research regulations, 233
    revenue cycle time, 360–61
    risk management, 158
    role of, 47
    safe harbor provision, 233
    security, 399–443
    Security Officer, 34, 36, 57, 324
    Security Rule, 9, 36, 57, 113, 158,
        322–24
    security standards, 322–24
    subpoenas and, 65–66
    unique identifiers, 116
    valid release form, 62
Health insurance specialists, 37
Health Level Seven (HL7), 174–75
Health maintenance organizations (HMOs),
    8, 79, 353–54
Health Plan Employer Data and
    Information Set (HEDIS), 147, 179–80,
    354
Health protections, workplace, 297–98
Health records. See also Data, content and
    structures abbreviations used, 103
    accreditation standards, 102
    administrative data in, 101–2, 107
    clinical data in, 101–2, 107
    content of, 48
    defined, 27, 101
    destruction of, 110, 112–15
    electronic health record (EHR), 9, 36,
        104, 146, 159, 327–29
    ownership of, 61

personal health record (PHR), 106–7, 156
    purposes of, 101, 105–6
    right of access to, 60–61
    retention of, 49, 112–13
    standardization of, 28–29
    storage of, 110–11
    types of, 103
    users of, 104–6, 111
    Web resources, 120, 375
Health savings accounts (HSAs), 8
Health service managers, 37
Health statistics, 187–219
    central tendency, 194
    data collection, 195–97
    data presentation, 199–203
    data transformation, 187–88
    defined, 192
    descriptive, 190
    ethics and, 96
    epidemiology and, 191
    formulae, 198–99
    fractions, 193–94
    health information management (HIM),
        209–14
    literacy in, 192–209
    percentage, 192–93
    ratios, 193
    regression analysis, 203–9
    standard deviation, 194–95
    t-test, 195–96
    types of, 190–92
    vital, 190–91
    Web resources, 218–19
Health system, defined, 355
Healthcare Common Procedure Coding
    System (HCPCS), 134, 358
Healthcare Facilities Accreditation Program
    (HFAP), 7
Herzberg, Frederick, 266
Heterografts, 90
Hierarchy of needs, Maslow's, 265–66
Hill-Burton Act, 7
HIM. See Health information management
    (HIM)
HIPAA. See Health Insurance Portability
    and Accountability Act (HIPAA)
Hippocrates, 4
Hippocratic Oath, 5, 59, 77
Histograms, 149–50, 203
Historical view
    classification systems, 128–32
    data quality, 141–47
    database management development,
        170–71
    early history, 3–4
    epidemiology, 240
    health information management
        profession, 27–29
    management theories, 268–69
    mental health, 10–13
    occupational health, 13–14
    philanthropic foundations, 15
    public health, 9–10
    research, 224, 232–33, 240
    U.S. health care, 4–5
    voluntary health agencies, 14–15
HIV/AIDS, 90
    confidentiality, 66, 90

reporting requirements, 117
    research involving, 225
HMO Act, 353
Home health agency, 17
Home Health Care report, 155
Home health setting, 38
Homografts, 90
Hospice care, 17
Hospital Compare report, 154–56
Hospital Quality Alliance (HQA), 154
Hospitals, 5–7, 17–18, 20–21
Hospital Survey and Construction Act (Hill-
    Burton), 7
Host, 242
Hostile work environment, 294
Hours of employment, 298–99
Human Genome Project (HGP), 91
Human resource management, 281–309. See
    also Employment; Management
    defined, 283
    employee rights, 292–99
    impaired colleagues, 93
    staffing, 284–91
    supervision, 94–95, 299–307
    Web resources, 309
    workforce diversity, 307–8
Human subjects, research, 231–35
Humanistic management, 269
Hypertext markup language (HTML), 317
Hypothesis, 230

I

I-9 form, Employee Eligibility Verification,
    286–89
Identifier numbers, database, 180
Identity theft, 63–64
Immigration Reform and Control Act
    (IRCA), 292, 295
Impaired colleagues, 93–94
In vitro fertilization, 88
Incentives, 286
Incidence, 227
Incidence rates, 199–200, 228
Incident reports, 110
Income statement, 337, 339
Identity theft, 63–64
Independent contractor, 284
Independent practice associations (IPA), 8
Index, 115, 197
Indian Health Service (IHS), 47, 351
Indices, 115–17, 197
Inferential statistics, 190
Infertility treatments, 87
Inflation, 352
Influencing factors, ethical decisions, 81–86
Informatics, 32–33, 324–25. See also specific
    topics
    health statistics and, 192
Information, 62, 169, 275
Information brokering, 326
Information systems and technology, 311–30
    applications and trends, 325–29
    communication, 319–21
    communication technologies, 319–21
    computers, 314–17
    in early U.S., 5
    electronic health records, 327–29
    ethical decision making, 85

Information systems and technology (*continued*)
    information systems, 174, 313–24
    IT life cycle, 317–19
    ONCHIT, 9
    quality improvement, 145–46
    research, 237–38
    security, 321–24
    Web resources, 330
Informed consent, 64–65, 234. *See also specific topics*
    autonomy, 77
    ethics and, 79–80
Inpatient service day, 198
Inpatient settings (hospitals), 5–7, 17–18, 20–21
Institutional animal care and use committees (IACUC), 236–37
Institutional review boards (IRBs), 230–38. *See also specific topics*
    accreditation of, 237
    continuing education, 237–38
    exempt review, 236
    expedited review, 235–36
Insurance, 7, 299, 351
Insured, 351
Insurer, 351
Integrated delivery system (IDS), 354–55
Integrated health record, 103
Integrated Services Digital Networks (ISDNs), 320
Integrity control, 173
Intentional torts, 54–55
Interactive voice recognition (IVR), 327
Interface, 174
Internal analysis, 250
Internal controls, 335–36
International Classification
    of Diseases (ICD), 128–30, 135, 137, 197
    of Functioning, Disability and Health (ICF), 135
    of Injuries, Disabilities, and Handicaps (ICIDH), 135
International health agencies, 15
International Standards Organization (ISO), 173
Internet, 319–20
Internet protocol (IP) address, 320
Internet service provider (ISP), 320
Interoperability, 181
Interval data, 201
Interviews, employee, 285, 291
Intranet, 321
Invasion of privacy, 54
Involuntary commitments, 55
Ishikawa, Kaoru, 270

J

Job, 258. *See also* Employment
Job analysis, 258
Job description, 259, 300
Job enrichment, 266–67
Job evaluation, 259
Job satisfaction, 266
Joint Commission (JC), 7, 9, 47–48, 102, 143, 157–60, 180, 354

Joint Commission on Accreditation of Healthcare Organizations (JCAHO), 7, 142. *See also* Joint Commission (JC)
Joint Commission on Accreditation of Hospitals (JCAH), 141–42
Joint Commission on Mental Illness and Health (JCMIH), 12
Journal, 335
Judicial process, 65–66
Jung, Carl, 12
Juran, Joseph M., 143, 269
Jurisdiction, 49
Jury System Improvement Act, 293
Justice, 78–79

K

Kaizen teams, 143
Kant, Immanuel, 80
Keyboards, 314–15
Knowledge, 275
Knowledge management, 275–76
Knowledge management system (KMS), 276

L

Labor analytics, 210
Laboratory research, 224
Languages, 125–28
Laptop computers, 316
Law, defined, 45, 75. *See also* Legal issues
Leadership, 265
Leading, 265–68
Leased employees, 283
Left-to-right organizational charts, 257–58
Legal issues, 43–72
    access to health care data, 60–64
    civil procedures, 52–53
    court system in, 49–53
    employment application, 293–99
    ethical decision making, 85–87
    and ethical practice, 75–76
    external forces, 45–49
    fraud and abuse, 66–70
    health information management (HIM), 55–66, 391–92
    health record data, 105
    HIPAA, 56–59
    identity theft, 63–64
    informed consent, 64–65
    judicial process, 65–66
    liability, 53–55
    privacy and confidentiality, 59–60, 79
    Web resources, 71
Legibility of handwritten data, 143
Length of stay (LOS), 198
Lexicon, 127
Liability, 53–55, 339
Licensing, 6, 48
Life, quality of, 90, 92
Limited data set, 180, 233
Line graphs, 149, 151, 201
Links, 321
Literature review, 230
Living wage laws, 293
Living will, 65, 92
Local area network (LAN), 319
Local data exchange efforts, 182–83
Local efforts. *See* Government efforts

Logical Observation Identifiers Names and Codes (LOINC), 127
Long-term care facility, 18

M

MacEachern, Malcolm, 28
Mainframe computers, 315
Maintenance factor, 266
Major diagnostic category (MDC), 130
Malcolm Baldridge National Quality Award, 143–44
Malpractice, 55
Managed care, 8, 33, 352
Managed care organizations, 14, 352–55
Management, 247–79. *See also* Employment; Quality care management
    controlling, 263–65
    defined, 130, 249
    directing, 261–63
    historical overview, 268–69
    leading, 265–68
    organizing, 255–61
    planning, 249–55
    principles of, 249–68
    of revenue cycles, 359–61
    supervisory, 94–95, 300–307
    theories of, 268–77
    Web resources, 289, 374
Management by objectives (MBOs), 251
Managerial accounting, 335–37
Manuscripts, research publication, 230–31
Martin, Franklin, 28
Maslow, Abraham, 265–66
Master budget, 341
Master patient index (MPI), 115–16, 176
Mathematical statistics, 190
Mayo, Elton, 269
McGregor, Douglas, 269
Mean, 194
Median, 194
Medicaid
    eligibility, 350
    fraud and abuse control, 59, 67, 268
    healthcare for poor, 7–8
Medical abandonment, 54
Medical Expenditure Panel Survey (MEPS), 145
Medicare Integrity Program, 59
Medical language, 125
Medical library science, 32
Medical necessity, 351
Medical office managers, 37
Medical records. *See* Health records
Medical records committes, 21
Medical specialists, 19
Medical staff, 20–22
    bylaws, rules, and regulations, 21
    clinical privileges, 21–22
    credentialing process, 22
    medical record committees, 21
    organization, 20–21
Medical staff coordinators, 22, 37
Medical Subject Headings (MeSH), 127
Medical transcription, 35–36
Medicare, 156
    eligibility, 350
    fraud and abuse control, 66–68

health care for elders, 7–8
   prospective payment system in, 33
   reimbursement rule, 326
MEDLARS and MEDLINE, 127
Medicare Prescription Drug Improvement and Modernization Act, 154
Medicare Provider Analysis and Review (MEDPAR), 156
Meeting management, 276–77
Mental health, 10–13
Mental illness, 6, 10–13, 66
Mental imaging, 272
Mentoring, 304
Metadata, 53
Metathesaurus, 127
Methodology, research, 224–29
Methods, 230
Metropolitan area network (MAN), 319
Military Selective Service Act, 293
Mill, John Stuart, 80
Minimum data set, 176
Minimum Data Set for Long-Term Care (MDS), 177
Minimum necessary standard, 62
Minimum risk, 233
Mission statements, 250–51
Mobile objects, 316
Mode, 194
Modem, 320
Monitoring employee conduct, 95
Monitors, 314–15
Morals, 75
Morbidity, 191
Morbidity rates, 198
Mortality, 190
Mortality rates, 199, 243
Motivation, 265–66
Motivators, 266
Mouse, 314–15
Multidirectional data flow, 107–9
Multivariate regression, 203
Multivoting, 272–73
Myers, Grace Whiting, 28

N

Narrative style procedure, 260
Natality, 190
National Academy of Sciences, 146–47
National Association for Healthcare Quality (NAHQ), 147
National Association for Quality Assurance Professionals (NAQAP), 147
National Center for Health Statistics (NCHS), 128, 190–91
National Committee for Quality Assurance (NCQA), 48, 147, 179, 237, 354
National Committee on Vital and Health Statistics (NCVHS), 175–76, 179
National Drug Codes (NDC), 135
National Electronic Disease Surveillance System (NEDSS), 175
National Health Information Infrastructure (NHII), 175
National Institute of Mental Health (NIMH), 12
National Institutes of Health (NIH), 50, 237
National Labor Relations Act, 292

National Labor Relations Board (NLRB), 50–51, 298
National origin discrimination, 294–95
National Practitioner Data Bank, 22, 59, 177–79
National Vital Statistics System (NVSS), 190–91
Natural language processing encoding systems, 132
Negligence, 55
Negotiation, 267
Network, 319
Nomenclature, 125–28
Nominal data, 200
Nominal group technique, 148, 273
Nonessential job functions, 300
Nongovernment payers, 351–55
Nongovernmental entities, 47–48
Nonintentional torts, 54–55
Nonmaleficence, 77–78, 89–90
Nontraditional career settings, 37–39
Nosocomial infection rate, 199
Nosologists, 132
Notice of Privacy Practices, 60, 107, 382–89
Null hypothesis, 195
Number index, 116
Nurses, 19–20
Nursing Home Compare report, 153–54

O

Object-oriented/relational database model, 170
Object query language (OQL), 171
Objectives, 251
Observational studies, 227–28
Occupancy rate, 199
Occupational health, 13–14
Occupational Safety and Health Administration (OSHA), 13, 50, 260, 293, 297
Office of Inspector General (OIG), 68, 163, 361
Office of Managed Care (OMC), 253
Office of the National Coordinator for Health Information Technology (ONCHIT), 9
Older Workers Benefit Protection Act (OWBPA), 295
Online analytical processing (OLAP), 176
Operating room register, 117
Operating system, 317
Operational planning, 252
Operationalization, 196
Optimizing programs, 132
Optometrist, 19
Ordinal data, 201
Ordinances, 46
Organ transplantation, 90–91
Organizational charts, 17, 46, 50–51, 256–58
Organizational design, 255
Organizational structures, 255–56
Organizing, in management, 255–61
Orientation, employment, 286–90
ORYX Initiative, 157–58, 180
OSCAR database, 154
Others, development of, 303–4

Outcome Assessment and Information Set (OASIS), 177, 179
Outcomes, 105, 131, 153, 197
Outcomes research, 228–29
Outsourcing, 9, 36
Owner's equity, 339
Ownership, health care data, 61–63

P

Pandemics, 240
Pareto charts, 148–49, 274
Pareto principle, 214
Part-time employees, 283
Participatory management, 269, 304
Passive euthanasia, 92
Paternalism, 84, 88
Patient rights, and ethics, 60–61, 84–85
Patient Self-Determination Act (PSDA), 65, 85, 92
Payment Error and Prevention Program (PEPP), 361
Payment methodologies, 355–59
PDSA and PDCA, 143–44, 153, 272
Pearson product-moment correlation, 205
Percentages, 192
Performance
   evaluations, 300–301
   improvement, 143, 156–59
   monitoring, 265
   organizing work, 260
   problems, 301, 302
   standards, 264–65, 301
Perinatal ethics, 89
Peripherals, 314
Permanent medical data, 102
Permission, 321
Personal computers (PC), 314
Personal digital assistants (PDAs), 38, 316
Personal health record (PHR), 106–7, 156
Personal power, 265
Philanthropic foundations, 15
Physical layout, 260
Physician assistant (PA), 19
Physicians
   defined, 18–19
   index of, 117
   medical staff organization, 20–21
   quality improvement, 157–58
   self-referral, 67
Pie charts, 149–50, 201, 203
Placebos, 79, 227
Plaintiffs, 52
Plan-Do-Check-Act. *See* PDCA and PDSA
Plan-Do-Study-Act. *See* PDCA and PDSA
Planning, management, 249–55
Podiatrists, 19
Point-of-service plan (POS), 354–55
Policy, defined, 252
Population, 190, 241
Portals, 321
Position summary, 300
Positional power, 265
Post-acute transfer (PACT) policy, 161, 163
Power of attorney for health care, 64
Preadmission review, 161
Preemption, 58

Preferred provider organization (PPO), 8, 354–55
Premiums, 351
Prenatal testing/surgery, 89
Pretrial conference, 53
Prevalence rates, 198–99
Prevention of disease, epidemiology, 240
Primary care, 16
Primary care provider (PCP), 353
Primary data, 115
Primary prevention, 241
Printers, 314–15
Privacy, 59–60, 79. *See also specific topics*
    employee, 299
Privacy Act, 47, 285, 292
Privacy Officer, HIPAA, 36, 57–61
Privacy Rule, HIPAA, 57–61, 63, 66, 84, 180–81, 299, 323–24, 377–84
Private health insurance, 351
Private law, 45–46
Privileges, medical staff, 21–22
Problem behaviors, 301–2
Problem-oriented health record, 103
Procedure, 252
Procedure index, 116
Process capability analysis, 213–14
Process capability ratio diagram, 214
Process improvement, 143, 272–73
Procurement, 342–45. *See also specific topics*
    information technology example, 318
    transcription example, 203
Productivity, 209–14
Professional associations, 14, 48, 373–74
Professional Standards Review Organizations (PSROs), 33, 160
Professionals, health care, 18–20
Program Evaluation and Review Technique (PERT), 148, 254–55, 271
Programming language, 317
Progressive discipline, 302
Project management (PM), 270–71. *See also specific topics*
    information systems life cycle, 317–19
Proposal request, 344–45
Prospective payment system (PPS), 8, 33, 68, 130, 132, 160, 357–58
Prospective studies, 227
Protected health information (PHI), 9, 56–57, 196. *See also specific topics*
    access, 60–61
    accounting and disclosures of, 60, 389
    amendments, 84, 383, 386, 389
    defamation, 54
    de-identified data, 60, 180–181, 233
    disclosure to business associates, 56, 385, 387
    individual access to, 63, 84, 389
    minimum necessary concept, 62
    Notice of Privacy Practices, 60, 107, 382–89
    patient rights, 57, 84
    right of access to, 63, 84, 384
    use and disclosure, 61, 84, 383–84, 386
Provisional staff privileges, 21
Proxy, 64
Psychiatry, 12

Public health
    data uses, 105
    defined, 9
    disease registries, 117–19
    historical development, 9–10
    informatics, 325
    institutional review boards (IRBs), 232
    surveillance statistics, 191
Public law, 46
Publication, research, 230–31
Punishment, ethical behavior, 94–95
Purchase order, 343
Pure research, 224

Q

Qualifications, 300
Qualitative analysis, 104, 198
Qualitative form, 230
Qualitative research, 225–26
Quality, defined, 141
Quality assurance, 33, 37, 142
Quality assurance coordinators, 37
Quality care management, 139–66
    Baldridge Award, 143–45
    data quality, 141–56
    federal efforts, 145–46
    historical view, 141–47
    performance improvement, 156–59
    private efforts, 146–47
    quality improvement organizations, 142, 160
    quality indicator reports, 153–56
    risk management, 158–59
    Six Sigma methodology, 144–45
    timeline, 142
    tools for assessment, 147–56
    utilization management, 159–64
    Web resources, 165, 374
Quality circles, 143
Quality health care, 141
Quality improvement, 153
Quality improvement organizations, 142, 160
Quality management, 142
Quality of life, 90, 92
Quality of patient care, 105
Quantitative analysis, 104, 198, 226
Quantitative form, 230
Quantitative research, 225–26
Quantity of work, 264–65
Quaternary care, 16
Qui tam actions, 67
Quid pro quo, 294

R

Racial discrimination, 294–95
Randomization, 225, 227
Rate formulae, 198
Rates, 193
Ratios, 193
Reasonable accommodation, 296
Receipts, 337
Recognition programs, 290
Record retention policies, 49, 112, 113, 343
Record retention schedules, 112, 113

Records management system, 110. *See also* Health records
Recruitment, 284
Reference check, 284–85
Regional health information organization (RHIO), 39, 181–82
Registered Health Information Administrator (RHIA), 25, 28–29, 35. *See also specific topics*
Registered Health Information Technician (RHIT), 28–29, 35–36. *See also specific topics*
Registration, 20
Registries, 115
    adoption information registries, 118
    admission register, 117
    Alzheimer registries, 118
    birth defects registries, 118
    birth register, 117
    cancer register, 117, 118
    cardiac registries, 118
    congenital anomaly register, 118
    congenital malformations registries, 118
    death register, 117
    discharge register, 117
    emergency room register, 117
    immunization registries, 118
    implant registries, 118
    inpatient discharge database, 118
    insulin-dependent diabetes mellitus (IDDM) registries, 118
    National Exposure Registry, 118
    National Registry of Cardiopulmonary Resuscitation, 118
    National Registry of Myocardial Infarction, 118
    National Trauma Data Bank, 119
    operating room register, 117
    organ donor registry, 119
    rare disease registries, 119
    Surveillance, Epidemiology, and End Results Program, 119
    United States Eye Injury Registry, 119
    vital records, 119
Regression analysis, 203–9. *See also specific topics*
    causation and correlation, 203–4
    models, 205–9
Regular employee, 283
Regulation. *See* Compliance; Health Insurance Portability and Accountability Act (HIPAA)
Rehabilitation care facility, 18
Reimbursement methodologies, 347–62
    capitation, 358–59
    coding systems and, 129, 134
    defined, 349
    fee for service, 355–57
    government payers, 349–51
    managed care organizations, 352–55
    nongovernment payers, 351–52
    payment methodologies, 355–59
    prospective payment systems (PPS), 357–58
    resource-based relative value systems (RBRVS), 358
    revenue cycle management, 359–61
    third-party payers, 105, 349–55
    Web resources, 362, 372

Relational database model, 170
Relative risk ratio, 241
Release of information, 62
Releases, 319
Reliability, 196, 231
Religious discrimination, 294–95
Request for information (RFI), 344
Request for proposal (RFP), 344–45
Request for quotation (RFQ), 344
Requirements, 45
Res ipsa loquitur, 55
Research, 221–46. *See also specific topics*
    animals, 236–37
    Belmont Report, 232
    clinical trials, 226–27
    conflicts of interest, 234–35
    defined, 223
    design of, 229–30
    epidemiology, 238–44
    genetic, 238
    historical overview, 224
    informed consent, 234
    institutional review boards,
      231–38
    journals, 238–39
    methodology, 224–29
    outcomes, 228–29
    pioneers, 224
    principles of, 223–29
    publication process, 230–31
    qualitative, 225, 226
    quantitative, 225–26
    risk/benefit analysis, 233–34
    social and behavioral, 228
    study process, 229–31
    Web resources, 245
Research and support analyst, 223, 237
Resource-Based Relative Value Scale
    (RBRVS), 134, 358
Respondeat superior, 55
Retention
    of data, 49, 110–15
    of employees, 290–91
Retrieval and analysis methods, 175–76
Retrospective data collection, 197
Retrospective studies, 227
Return on investment analysis, 334
Revenue, 337
Revenue cycle management, 359–61
Review, 161–64, 233–37
Reward programs, 290
Rewards, ethical behavior, 95–96
Rights
    defined, 79
    employee, 292–93
    patient, 84–85
Risk
    assessment of, 252–53
    defined, 158, 241
    of disease, epidemiology, 241–42
    management of, 158–59
Risk factor, 241
Risk managers, 37
Roe v. Wade, 89
Role application, 48–49
Role modeling ethical behavior, 94–95
Root-cause analysis, 159
Rounding, 192

Rules, 21, 45
Rush, Benjamin, 11–12

S

Safety
    asset safeguards, 336
    telecommuting, 261, 306–7
    workplace, 297–98
Salary, 286
Sales budget, 341
Sample, 190
Scanners, 314–15
Scatter diagrams, 149–50, 152, 206–7
Scientific management, 268
Scientific method, 224
Secondary care, 16
Secondary data, 115
Secondary prevention, 241
Security, information technology, 321–24
Security Officer, HIPAA, 36, 57, 324
Security Rule, HIPAA, 9, 36, 57, 113, 158,
    322–24
Sedona Guidelines for data handling, 114–15
Selection, employment, 284–86
Selection tests, 285
Semantic Network, 127
Semantic object (SO) model, 171–72
Sentinel event, 159
Separation
    of duties, 336
    employment, 291
    of powers, 47
Serial numbering system, 111
Serial-unit numbering system, 111
Serious health condition, 294
Servers, 316
Service, fee for, 355–57
Settings, health care, 15–17, 37
72-Hour Rule, 68–69
Sex discrimination, 293–94
Sexual harassment, 294
Sexual relations, with patients, 95
Shewhart, Walter, 269
Signals, 275
Simple regression, 203
Six Sigma Improvement Methodology,
    144–45
SOAP notes, 103
Social and behavioral research (SBR), 228
Social Security Act (1965), 7
Software, computer, 314, 316–17
Source document, 336
Source-oriented health record, 103
Specialists, 19
Specifications, 343
Staffing, 284–91
Standard Classified Nomenclature of
    Disease (SNDO), 126–27
Standard deviation, 194–95
Standard generalized markup language, 317
Standards. *See also* Ethics and ethical
    standards; Health Insurance
    Portability and Accountability Act
    (HIPAA)
    defined, 45, 317
    for patient care and health records, 28–29
    types of work, 264–65

Stark laws, 67
State efforts. *See* Government efforts
Statistically significant, 195
Statistical literacy, 192–209
Statistics budget, 341
Statistics, 189. *See also* Health statistics
Statute of limitations, 112
Statutory employee, 284
Statutory law, 46
Stem cell research, 91
Sterilization, 89
Storage of data, 110–12
Strategic planning, management, 249–51
Structured query language (SQL), 171
Study rationale, 230
Subjects, research, 231–35
Subpoena, 65
Subpoena *duces tecum,* 65
Substance abuse, 93, 96
Substantially equal, 294
Supervision, defined, 93–95, 299. *See also*
    Employment
Supplemental benefits, 286
Surgical assistant (SA), 19
Surrogate mother, 88
Survey, 228
SWOT techniques, 250, 256
Systematized Nomenclature of Medicine
    (SNOMED), 126–27, 133
Systematized Nomenclature of Pathology
    (SNOP), 126–27, 133

T

T-test, 195–96
Tacit knowledge, 275
Tax Equity and Fiscal Responsibility Act
    (TEFRA), 8, 130, 160, 353
Taxonomies, 128
Team building, 304–5
Teams, 143, 305
Technology. *See* Information systems
    and technology
Telecenters, 306
Telecommuting, 261, 305–7
Telehealth, 326
Telemedicine, 326
Terminology, 126
Tertiary care, 16
Tertiary prevention, 241
Theories, management, 269–77
Theory X/Theory Y/Theory Z, 269, 304
Third-party administrators, 352
Third-party payers, 105, 349–55
Threats, disaster planning, 252–54
Timeliness, 103
Tissue transplantation, 90–91
Title VII, Civil Rights Act, 292–95, 307
Tools, 147–56
Top-down organizational charts, 257
Top-down process, 340
Torts, 54–55
Total quality management (TQM), 142,
    269–70
Traceability, 171
Tracer methodology, 9
Traditional career settings, 35–37
Training, employment, 286–90

Translation of Research into Practice (TRIP), 145
Treasurers, 333
Treatment, withdrawing or withholding, 92–93
Trend chart, 213
Trials, 49
TRICARE (military program), 350
Tumor registrar, 36
Two-factor theory, Herzberg's, 266
Type I/Type II errors, 212

U

UB-04 claim forms, 162–63
Unbundling, 67, 356
Undue hardship, 296
Unemployment insurance, 299
Unidirectional data flow, 107–8
Unified Medical Language System (UMLS), 127
Uniform Ambulatory Care Data Set (UACDS), 179
Uniform Health-care Information Act, 57
Uniform Hospital Discharge Data Set (UHDDS), 177–78
Uniformed Services Employment and Reemployment Rights Act, 293
Unions, 298
Unit numbering system, 111
United Nations Children's Fund (UNICEF), 15
United Network for Organ Sharing, 90, 117
Univariate regression, 203
Upcoding, 67, 133
U.S. Department of Health, Education and Welfare (DHEW), 7
U.S. Department of Health and Human Services (DHHS), 9–10, 49–51, 56–59, 66, 68–69, 102, 145, 174, 181, 232
U.S. Department of Justice, 51, 66
U.S. Department of Labor, 13, 50, 297
U.S. Food and Drug Administration (FDA), 10, 47
U.S. National Health Survey on Morbidity, 241
U.S. Public Health Service, 232
U.S. Supreme Court, 49, 89
Users/uses of data, 104–9

Usual, customary, and reasonable costs (UCR), 356–57
Utilitarianism, 80
Utility programs, 317
Utilization coordinators, 160
Utilization management, 159–64. *See also specific topics*
DRGs and, 131–132
review process 161–164
Utilization review, 33, 37, 160–64
Utilization review coordinators, 37

V

V-codes, ICD-9-CM, 130
Validity, 196, 231
Value-added concept, 33
Value systems, resource-based relative, 358
Values, 76
Variable medical data, 102
Variables, 225
Variances, 342
Vector, 242
Veracity, in medical research, 79–80
Versions, 319
Veterans Administration, 47, 163
Veterinary settings, 38
Vietnam-Era Veterans Readjustment Assistance Act (VEVRAA), 292
Virtual private network (VPN), 319
Virus scan, 321
Vision statement, 250
Vital statistics, 190
Vocabularies, 125–28
Voice recognition technology (VRT), 326–27
Voluntary health agencies, 14–15

W

Wages, 286
Waste, 66
Web resources, 371–79
accreditation, 371
in alphabetical order, 376–79
associations, 373–74
bioethics, 371
classification systems, 137

codes of ethics, 371–72
coding, 372
data content and structures, 120, 375
database management, 184–85
e-health, 372
ethics, 98
financial management, 346, 372
government efforts, 372–73
health care delivery system, 24
health information management (HIM), 41, 309
health records, 120, 375
health statistics, 218–19
information systems and technology, 330
legal issues, 71
management, 289, 374
quality care management, 165, 374
reimbursement methodologies, 362, 372
research, 245
Weed, Lawrence, 103
Whistle-blowers, 67
Wide area network (WAN), 319
Wireless objects, 316
Wisdom, 275
Withdrawing/withholding treatment, 92–93
Work distribution chart, 260
Work environment, organizing, 260–61
Work motivation, 266
Work simplification, 262–63
Worker Adjustment and Retraining Notification (WARN), 293
Workers' compensation, 299, 307, 351
Workforce diversity, 307–8
Workgroup for Electronic Data Interchange (WEDI), 173–74
Workplace barriers, 296
Workplace hazards, 13
World Health Organization (WHO), 15, 128, 232
World wide web, 320

X

Xenografts, 90
XML (extensible markup language), 317